Crime and Justice

Crime and Justice
A Review of Research

Edited by Michael Tonry

VOLUME 37

The University of Chicago Press, Chicago and London

The University of Chicago Press, Chicago 60637
The University of Chicago Press, Ltd., London

Printed in the United States of America

ISSN: 0192-3234

ISBN: 0-226-80875-0

LCN: 80-642217

The paper used in this publication meets the minimum requirements of American National Standard for Information Sciences—Permanence of Paper for Printed Library Materials, ANSI Z39.48-1984. ♾

Contents

Preface

The United States since 1973 has been engaged in what is sometimes referred to as an experiment in mass incarceration. When it began, American imprisonment rates were not much higher than those of most other Western countries and were lower than some. In 2007, the American imprisonment rate of 760 per 100,000 residents was the highest in the world, nearly eight times higher than that of all western European countries combined (95 per 100,000 residents) or that of Canada or Australia, and 10 times higher than the rates in Scandinavia.

Partly by coincidence, but also probably because American penal policies cry out for explanation and evaluation, seven of the nine essays in this volume concern punishment policies and their effects. Tapio Lappi-Seppälä shows that a country's punishment policies result not from crime trends or public opinion but from the deliberate policy choices of governments, and these in turn are related to income distribution, social welfare spending, and citizens' trust in one another and in government. American imprisonment patterns and policies are as they are because policy makers chose to make them that way. Essays by James Unnever and his colleagues and by Matthew Melewski and me explore whether and how American race relations influenced policy makers' choices. A second essay of mine demonstrates that recent American crime control policies cannot be justified on grounds that they could reasonably have been expected to have substantial deterrent effects. Essays by Joseph Murray and David Farrington and by Todd Clear demonstrate the detrimental effects of imprisonment on prisoners' children and on the communities from which prisoners come and to which they mostly return. Joan Petersilia documents the effects of recent punishment policies on California prisons. Taken together, these essays do not tell a happy or ennobling story.

The other two essays might be characterized as examinations of how successfully economists (Shawn Bushway and Peter Reuter) and criminologists (David Weisburd and Alex Piquero) explain crime, criminality, and the operations of the criminal justice system. Both are important analyses that point the way to improving the quality and usefulness of criminological research.

Crime and Justice volumes require lots of work by lots of people. To a person, the authors in this volume (at least seemingly) cheerfully endured a lengthy process of initial drafts, readers' reports, editorial comment letters, more drafts, and source and cite checks, and all this before the essays were delivered to Chicago for professional editing. The writers know better than anyone else that this volume would not exist save for the extraordinary care and professionalism of Adepeju Solarin and Su Smallen in shepherding the essays to completion and the volume to publication. I am grateful to them all.

Crime and Justice volumes have multiple aims. One is to provide accessible, easy-to-read introductions to their subjects. A second is to provide comprehensive, up-to-date, and authoritative overviews of the subjects they address. A third is to provide comprehensive bibliographies of classic and contemporary specialized literatures, so that people new to a subject can quickly identify the important foundation sources and make a running start at turning themselves into experts. Those are not small ambitions. Whether they have been achieved, readers will decide for themselves.

Michael Tonry
Deer Isle, Maine, July 2008

Michael Tonry and Matthew Melewski

The Malign Effects of Drug and Crime Control Policies on Black Americans

ABSTRACT

The disproportionate presence of blacks in American prisons, jails, and Death Rows, and the principal reasons for it—higher rates of commission of violent crimes and racially disparate effects of drug policies and sentencing laws governing violent and drug crimes—are well known. Since the late 1980s, black involvement in violent crime has declined substantially, but racial disproportions have not. Blacks are six to seven times more likely than whites to be in prison. Nearly a third of young black men are under criminal justice system control. A third of black boys born in 2001 are predicted to spend some time in prison. The simplest explanation for these patterns is that drug and sentencing policies that contribute to disparities have not been significantly changed in decades. The question then is, why not? The answer is that the white majority does not empathize with poor black people who wind up in prison. That in turn is because recent punishment policies have replaced the urban ghetto, Jim Crow laws, and slavery as a mechanism for maintaining white dominance over blacks in the United States.

Seen from outside the United States, and, we expect, as it will be seen by future generations of Americans, four aspects of contemporary crime control policies stand out: the world's highest imprisonment rate, the Western world's only use of capital punishment, the Western world's most severe punishments short of death, and the effects of those policies on black Americans. Gross racial disparities in impris-

Michael Tonry is Sonosky Professor of Law and Public Policy, University of Minnesota Law School, and senior fellow, Netherlands Institute for the Study of Crime and Law Enforcement. Matthew Melewski is a 2008 graduate of the University of Minnesota Law School. They are grateful to Alfred Blumstein, Richard Frase, Marc Mauer, Myron Orfield, and Kevin Reitz for helpful comments on earlier drafts.

0192-3234/2008/0037-0009$10.00

onment and entanglement in the criminal justice system result partly from racial differences in offending, but preponderantly from adoption and continuation of drug and crime control policies that affect black Americans much more severely than whites. Much of the harm being done to disadvantaged black Americans and their loved ones in the name of crime control was, and is, avoidable.

The litany of ways crime control policies disproportionately affect black Americans by now is so familiar as to be unsurprising. Blacks constituted 12.8 percent of the general population in 2005 but nearly half of prison inmates and 42 percent of Death Row residents. Imprisonment rates for black men were nearly seven times higher than for white men. About a third of young black men aged 20–29 were in prison or jail or on probation or parole on an average day in 2005. The Bureau of Justice Statistics (BJS) estimated in 2003 that 32 percent of black men born in 2001 will spend some part of their lives in a state or federal prison. That is a substantial underestimate of the likelihood that black men will spend time behind bars; it does not take account of jail confinement, which is much more common than time in prison (Bonczar 2003; BJS 2007, tables 6.33.2005, 6.17.2006, 6.80.2007).

What is surprising is not that these things are true, but that they are well known, have long been well known, and have changed little in recent decades. Few people except academics and liberal law reformers—seemingly almost no policy makers—much notice or care. The racial disparities caused by the federal 100-to-one law that punishes crack cocaine offenses much more severely than powder cocaine offenses were foreseeable when the law was passed (Tonry 1995, pp. 4–6) and were irrefutably documented long ago (McDonald and Carlson 1993). The law remains in effect, successively endorsed by the Reagan, Bush I, Clinton, and Bush II administrations.[1]

To take another example, the Congressional Black Caucus, during consideration of federal crime legislation in 1994, fought hard for a Racial Justice Act that would allow statistics on racial disparities in

[1] The U.S. Sentencing Commission repeatedly urged the Congress to repeal or diminish the crack/powder sentencing differential (e.g., U.S. Sentencing Commission 1995). Attorney General Janet Reno initially endorsed the commission's 1995 proposal to eliminate the 100-to-one differential, and, backtracking, she and "drug czar" General Barry McCaffrey later called for it to be reduced to 10-to-one, but to no avail (Tonry 2004, chap. 1). In 2007, the commission proposed amendment of guideline provisions that made federal sentencing even tougher than the mandatory minimum law required. The Congress through inaction allowed the amendments to take effect. The statute itself, which does the main damage, continued in effect early in 2008, unchanged.

capital punishment to be introduced in death penalty cases. David Baldus and his colleagues, using Georgia data on 2,000 cases from the 1970s, had convincingly shown that the racial characteristics of murder defendants and victims were powerfully associated with whether capital punishment is imposed (Baldus, Woodworth, and Pulaski 1990). Twenty-two percent of black killers of white victims were sentenced to death compared with 3 percent of white killers of blacks (prosecutors sought death in 70 percent of black-on-white killings and 19 percent of white-on-black). The U.S. Supreme Court in *McCleskey v. Kemp* (481 U.S. 279 [1987]) decided that such evidence was irrelevant in deciding claims about racial discrimination. Even though the court "assumed the study is statistically valid" (n. 8), it ruled that a defendant alleging discrimination had to prove that the prosecutor in that particular case had acted in a biased way. This is almost impossible to do; bigoted officials seldom admit to acting in bigoted ways.

For a time, it appeared likely that President Clinton would support the caucus. In the end, he did not. Instead he signed the Violent Crime Control and Law Enforcement Act of 1994, which created more than 50 new federal capital offenses; the caucus's proposed provision had been dropped (Gest 2001, pp. 230–35). For a few years in the 1990s, the caucus continued to support federal legislation attempting to reduce racial disparities in death penalty cases, but the issue gradually died down. The proportion of blacks on Death Row was about the same in 2007 as it had been in 1994.

A third example: Daniel Patrick Moynihan in 1965 urged a controversial welfare policy of benign neglect toward poor black Americans, arguing that they needed mostly to be let alone to get on with their lives. American crime control policies in the early twenty-first century do the opposite of that. They diminish the life chances of black men (Western 2006; Provine 2007) and undermine the social fabric of many poor black communities (Clear 2007).

Since at least 1980, American crime control policies have undermined achievement of full unbiased participation of black Americans in the nation's social, economic, and political life. Modern wars on crime and drugs, which date from the early 1970s, shortly after the first serious federal antidiscrimination laws were enacted, could not more effectively have kept black Americans "in their place" had they been designed with that aim in mind.

The following list of social, vocational, educational, and economic differences between blacks and whites is drawn from the 2007 *Statistical Abstract of the United States*:

- 33.3 percent of black children lived in households below the poverty line in 2004, compared with 14.2 percent of white children;
- the mortality rate for black infants in 2003 was 14 per 1,000 live births, compared with 5.7 per 1,000 for whites;
- per capita income for black Americans was $16,035 in 2004, compared with $25,203 for whites;
- 10 percent of adult blacks were unemployed and 35.8 percent were not in the labor force in 2005, compared with 4.4 and 33.7 percent of whites;
- 17.6 percent of blacks 25 and older had college degrees in 2005, compared with 28 percent of whites; and
- 48.1 percent of blacks owned their own homes in 2005, compared with 72.7 percent of whites (U.S. Department of Commerce 2006, tables 107, 214, 575, 685, 693, 954).

Those differences have been at least exacerbated by, and are probably substantially attributable to, the nearly seven-to-one racial difference in imprisonment rates that has been typical for the past quarter century, the staggering difference in black and white men's lifetime chances of going to prison, and the entanglement of a large minority of young black men in their 20s in the justice system at a time of life when other young men are building careers and conventional lives (Western 2006). Accumulating bodies of research show that going to prison reduces employment prospects and average and lifetime earnings (Fagan and Freeman 1999; Raphael, Holzer, and Stoll 2006) and reduces the later well-being of prisoners' children (Murray and Farrington, in this volume). A different literature shows that disadvantaged communities are damaged, not helped, when large numbers of their residents are sent to prison. Low levels of imprisonment at least arguably may prevent crime through deterrence, incapacitation, and removal of antisocial role models; high levels cause crime rates to increase and neighborhoods to deteriorate (Clear 2007; in this volume).

If incarceration rates for jail and prison together had remained at 1970 levels (around 130 per 100,000) or at 1980 levels (around 200), American crime control policies would have bitten much less deeply into black American communities. American crime rates reached their all-time high in 1981, so the 1980 comparison is probably the better one. Less than a third of black Americans in prison in 2008 would be there had 1980 rates continued. Many fewer black men would have suffered the pains of imprisonment, resulting stigma, and reduced employment prospects. There would have been many fewer broken black families, fewer negative role models for black boys, and more marriageable black men. There would have been less deterioration in poor black communities because tipping points would not have been reached. At a time when civil rights and welfare policies aimed at improving opportunities and living standards for black Americans, drug and crime policies worsened them.

Scholars have long paid attention to interactions among race, crime, and criminal justice (e.g., Du Bois [1899] 1988; Myrdal 1944). The modern literature dates from Alfred Blumstein's at the time courageous 1982 article showing that a principal reason why so many more blacks than whites were in prison was that they were much more often arrested for the kinds of crimes that typically resulted in prison sentences.[2] The more serious the crime, the more fully offending patterns appeared to explain racial disparities in imprisonment.[3] That conclusion was tested in lots of ways—for example, by comparing racial patterns in victims' identifications of assailants with racial patterns in arrests and by comparing arrests and victims' reports to prison admissions—but held up at least through the mid-1990s (Langan 1985; Tonry 1995, chaps. 2, 3).

Substantial literatures have continued to accumulate on racial pat-

[2] "Courageous" because at the time racial issues were so sensitive that few scholars, black or white, could write about racial differences in offending without being accused of racism, blaming the victims of racial discrimination, or perpetuating racially harmful stereotypes. William Julius Wilson, a black American who is among the most distinguished and influential sociologists of his generation, wrote a landmark book, *The Declining Significance of Race*, in which he argued that poor blacks' main problem was not racism and discrimination per se but the deindustrialization of the American economy and the loss of semi- and unskilled industrial jobs in American cities (Wilson 1978). In the preface to his next major book, *The Truly Disadvantaged*, he observed that critics "either labeled me a neoconservative or directly or indirectly tried to associate *The Declining Significance of Race* with the neoconservative movement. . . . I am a social democrat and probably to the left politically of the overwhelming majority of these critics" (1987, p. viii).

[3] Conversely, the less serious the offense, the less offending differences appeared to explain disparities. For drug offenses, arrests are simply artifacts of police tactics and cannot sensibly be used as behavioral measures. Blumstein's article was controversial at the time but in retrospect is easily consonant with research on sentencing outcomes, which generally shows few racial differences in the probability of imprisonment for the most serious offenses. The space for bias, unconscious stereotyping and attribution, and other nonoffense factors to affect outcomes increases as prison sentences become less likely (Spohn 2000).

terns in arrests (with particular emphasis on profiling) and on racial differences in sentencing. The arrest literature shows that blacks in most places are more likely than whites to be stopped by the police, regardless of whether rates for pedestrian stops are calculated according to neighborhood population or according to transient population, and for traffic stops regardless of whether rates are calculated according to general population or to drivers of automobiles vulnerable to being stopped. Once stopped, blacks (and Hispanics) are more likely than whites to be searched, to be arrested, and to have force used against them. Percentages of stops resulting in seizures of contraband, however, tend to be lower for blacks than for whites, suggesting that police are likelier to stop blacks for less valid, often pretextual, reasons (e.g., Engel and Calnon 2004, pp. 77–81).[4]

The sentencing literature documents relatively small racial differences. Black defendants, all else being equal, are slightly more likely than whites to be sentenced to confinement but, among those incarcerated, not to receive longer sentences (Spohn 2000, 2002). Blacks are less likely than whites to be diverted to nonincarcerative punishments and more likely in guidelines states to receive sentences at the tops rather than the bottoms of sentencing guidelines ranges (Tonry 1996, chap. 2). Individual studies present divergent findings, often showing disparities by race and ethnicity for men but not for women (or to different extents), for Hispanics but not for blacks, and for young offenders but not for older ones (or in each case vice versa) (e.g., Walker, Spohn, and DeLone 2006; Harrington and Spohn 2007, pp. 40–45).

In this essay we examine the empirical issues that Michael canvassed nearly 15 years ago in *Malign Neglect* (Tonry 1995) to see to what extent black/white differences in victimization, offending, drug use, arrest, sentencing, imprisonment, and capital punishment have changed. They have changed very little.

Section I surveys case processing data on arrest through capital punishment and discusses recent survey data on racial differences in drug use and trafficking. Although conscious bias and stereotyping probably explain some portion of racial disparities, and unconscious stereotyping surely does, the principal drivers of disparities in imprisonment continue to be racial differences in commission of "imprisonable" offenses

[4] Table 1 in Engel and Calnon (2004) summarizes data from 16 studies, of which 10 report higher hit rates for whites. Engel and Calnon's own study, based on National Crime Victimization Survey (NCVS) data, finds substantially higher white hit rates.

and the foreseeable disparate effects on blacks and whites of police tactics in the war on drugs and sentencing policies for violent and drug offenses.

Section II explains the patterns the preceding sections document. Because much racial disparity is attributable to the effects of policies that could have been foreseen to affect black offenders disproportionately severely and are now widely recognized to have that effect, the fundamental questions are how that could have happened and why it has been allowed to continue to happen. The answer is that political and ideological exigencies of the last quarter century have conduced to the adoption of crime control policies of unprecedented severity, the primary burdens of which have been borne by disadvantaged blacks (and, increasingly, Hispanics). The history of American race relations has produced political and social sensibilities that made white majorities comparatively insensitive to the suffering of disadvantaged blacks.

Section III proposes ways that avoidable disparities can be reduced.

I. Racial Differences in Criminal Justice System Case Processing

Here is what was known in the mid-1990s about racial disparities in the criminal justice system (Tonry 1995, chap. 2). For a century before the 1960s black people had been more likely to be held in prison than whites. Racial disparities began to rise in the 1960s and then shot up to all-time highs in the 1980s: blacks by then were half of American prisoners, though only 12 percent of the U.S. population, and had an imprisonment rate seven times higher than the white rate. Part of the reason for this was that blacks were sometimes treated more harshly than whites for reasons of bias or unconscious stereotyping. A larger part of the explanation, however, was that blacks were more likely than whites to be arrested for the "imprisonable" offenses of robbery, rape, aggravated assault, and homicide. Victimization data on victims' descriptions of assailants and police data on victim and offender characteristics in homicide cases suggested that the racial offending patterns shown in arrest data for serious crimes were not far off from reality. Critically, however, there had been no significant shifts in racial patterns in arrests for a quarter century, and involvement in serious violent crime could not explain why black imprisonment rates had risen so rapidly since the late 1960s. A principal driver of the increase was imprisonment for drug crimes (Blumstein and Beck 1999), and policy makers knew or should have known that the enemy foot soldiers in the war on drugs would be young, disadvantaged, inner-city members of minority groups (Tonry 1995).

Little in that paragraph would need to be changed to describe conditions in 2007 rather than in 1993–94. Racial differences in commission of serious violent crimes continue to be an important contributor to imprisonment disparities, but the absolute overrepresentation of blacks among arrestees has declined significantly. Imprisonment rates, however, were much higher in 2007 than in 1993, and with their increase the lifetime probability of imprisonment for black men and the percentage of young black men under justice system control both increased substantially. The black fractions of the prison, jail, and Death Row populations have changed little. Nor has the difference in black imprisonment rates compared to white rates changed significantly. Policies authorizing or requiring harsh punishments for drug offenses continue to be one major contributor to racial disparities. Another is staggering increases in severity of sentences for violent crime: if 40–50 percent of people arrested for violent crimes are black, then black Americans are foreseeably bearing the burdens of increased harshness.

A. Incarceration Rates

Figure 1 shows black and white percentages of state and federal prisoners from 1950 to 2006. Blacks were about a third of prisoners in 1960 and under 40 percent in 1970. The black percentage rose continuously to the mid-40s around 1980, rising slowly thereafter until the early 1990s and plateauing at about 50. For most years between 1991 and 2002, in absolute numbers there were more black than white prisoners. The black percentage has since declined slightly.

Calculation of trend data has been complicated by a BJS decision beginning in the late 1990s to report separate figures for blacks, whites, and Hispanics. In earlier years, Hispanics were included within racial categories and sometimes also reported separately. The BJS change had the effect of reducing "black" imprisonment rates. In our view, skin color and "racial" identity have been more salient social characteristics in recent decades in the United States than the Hispanic/non-Hispanic difference has been. Insofar as racial bias, stereotypes, and attributions have influenced officials' decisions, appearance is much more likely than a Hispanic surname or ancestry to have influenced decisions. Ac-

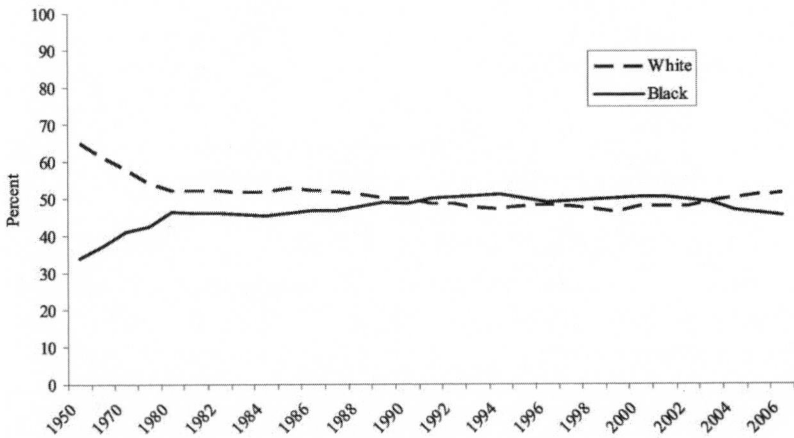

FIG. 1.—Percentage of state and federal prisoners, by race, 1950–2006. Sources: For 1950–80: Cahalan (1986); for 1980–2006: BJS, "Prisoners," various years. Until the late 1990s, race was broken down into three categories for all statistics: white, black, and other. In recent years, BJS added Hispanic as a racial category to various statistics, thus complicating linear representations of the data. In 1999, BJS added Hispanic as a racial category to combined state and federal prison statistics (skipping 1998 in the process). BJS also revised some data in later years, occasionally creating three different data points for a single year. In 2004, BJS added the category of "two or more races," further complicating the data. We have adopted the approach taken in Tonry (2005). The Hispanic category has been removed and redistributed for every year since 1999. This redistribution was made by examining the years 1990 and 1995, for which BJS has supplied data both with and without a separate Hispanic category. Approximately one-fourth of Hispanics were formerly counted as black in those years, and three-quarters were counted as white. For all years, the most recent published BJS data were used, except for 1990 and 1995. For those years, the older data without the Hispanic separation were used. The category of "two or more races" has been redistributed evenly between blacks and whites.

cordingly, in figure 1 (and other figures) we adjusted BJS prison population data to take account of the estimated black/white fractions among Hispanics.[5]

The jail story is much the same, as figure 2 shows. About a third of

[5] The method for redistributing Hispanics was determined by examining 1990 and 1995 data in which the BJS reported black/white figures including Hispanics and also reported Hispanics separately. For 1995, e.g., 17.6 percent of prisoners were classified as Hispanic. Excluding Hispanics, 45.7 percent of prisoners were black and 33.5 percent were white. Including Hispanics, 49.9 percent were black and 47.7 percent were white. Simple math shows that approximately one-fourth of Hispanics were counted as black and three-fourths as white (Tonry 2005, p. 1255, n. 99).

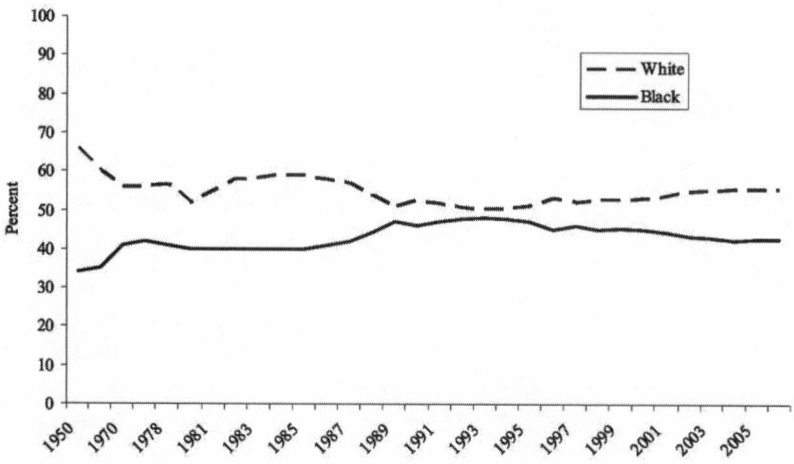

FIG. 2.—Percentage of local jail inmates, by race, 1950–2006. Sources: For 1950–83: Cahalan (1986); BJS (1984, 1990); for 1983–89: BJS, "Jail Inmates," various years; for 1990–95: Gilliard and Beck (1996); for 1996–2006: BJS, "Prison and Jail Inmates at Midyear," various years. BJS began using a separate Hispanics category much earlier in reporting jail data than in reporting prisoner data. For every year starting in 1990 the Hispanic category has been removed and redistributed, estimating that one-fourth of Hispanics were previously counted as black and three-quarters were counted as white.

jail inmates were black in 1950 and about 40 percent in 1970, a level around which the black percentage oscillated until the late 1980s. For a decade after that, coinciding with the most aggressive years of the war on drugs, blacks were 45–48 percent of inmates, after which the percentage declined somewhat. BJS data for the years 1990–2006 have been adjusted to distribute Hispanics between blacks and whites.

Because the preceding two figures are expressed in black/white percentages, they do not reflect the true magnitude of racial differences in imprisonment rates. It would be natural for someone new to the subject to compare the black percentage of the general population (12–13 percent) to the black percentages of the combined jail and prison populations (48–50 percent) and conclude that blacks are four times more likely to be confined than should be expected. The true difference in recent years has typically been about seven times. The reason is that whites are underrepresented in prison compared with their presence in the population and blacks are overrepresented. In 2006, for example, the total imprisonment rate for black men for jail

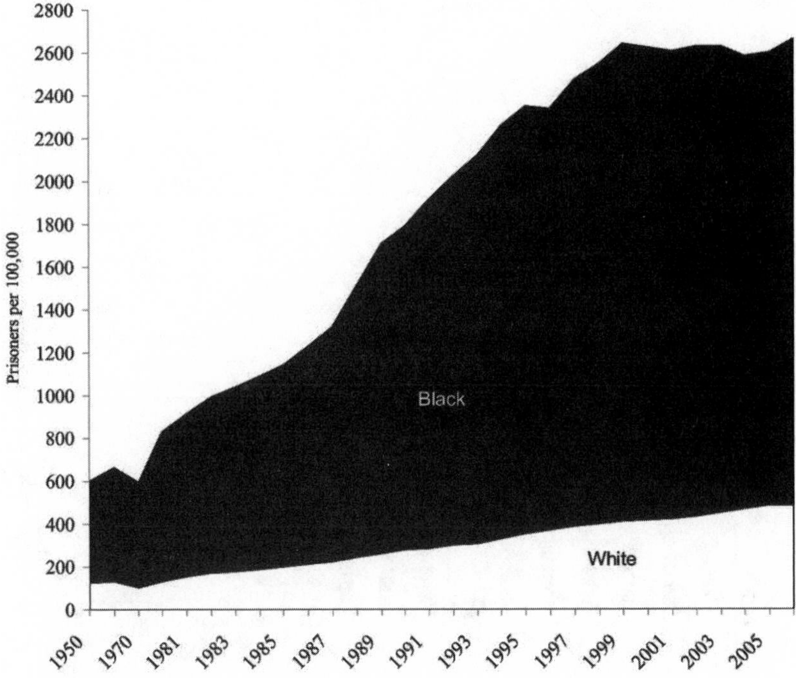

FIG. 3.—Incarceration in state and federal prisons and local jails per 100,000, by race, 1950–2006. Sources: BJS (1984, 1990; "Jail Inmates," various years; "Prisoners," various years; "Prison and Jail Inmates at Midyear," various years); Cahalan (1986); Gilliard and Beck (1996). The BJS occasionally publishes the number of prisoners in state and federal prisons and local jails, by race, as a ratio of the races' respective general populations (what we might call the total imprisonment rate). The publications are sporadic and interspersed with the ratio only for state prisons, only for state and federal prisons, only for local jails, or (most commonly) only for males. This graph is based on data used in figs. 1 and 2, then compared with population statistics provided by the Census Bureau.

and prison combined was 4,789 per 100,000 residents and the white rate was 737 per 100,000 (the corresponding rates for black and white women were 358 and 94) (Sabol, Minton, and Harrison 2007, table 14).[6]

Figure 3 shows aggregate black/white incarceration rates for jails and federal and state prisons from 1950 to 2006. Black rates dwarf those of whites. The increase in the black rate between 1980 and 2006 (1,834

[6] These numbers understate the rates since, per current BJS practice, Hispanic blacks and whites are excluded.

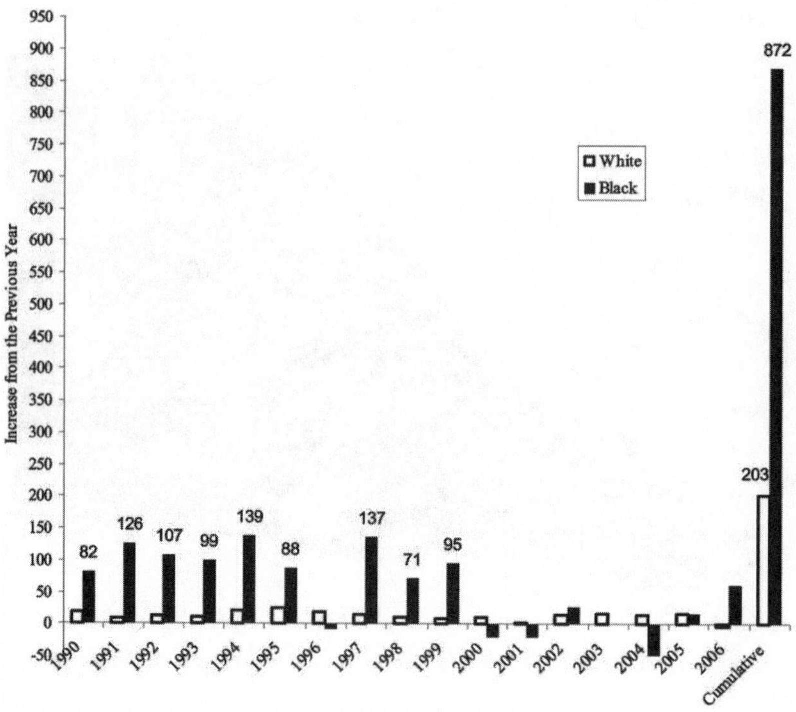

FIG. 4.—Increases in the total imprisonment rate per 100,000, by race, 1990–2006. Sources: Same as fig. 3.

per 100,000) was 3.8 times the total white rate (483 per 100,000) in 2006. The magnitude of racial differences in combined incarceration rates can be illustrated in another way. By 2006, the white rate (483), after 33 years of increases beginning in 1973, failed to reach the black rate in 1950 (598).

The racial difference in aggregate imprisonment rates is huge, as figure 3 shows. The extent to which increased imprisonment over recent decades has destabilized America's black population can be shown in another way. The nearly seven-to-one difference in imprisonment rates continued nearly unchanged for a quarter century. That means that the incremental increase for blacks each year, on average, has been seven times higher than the increase for whites. Figure 4 shows this. It depicts year-to-year increases in total imprisonment rates for blacks and whites from 1990 to 2006 and, following 2006, the cumulative

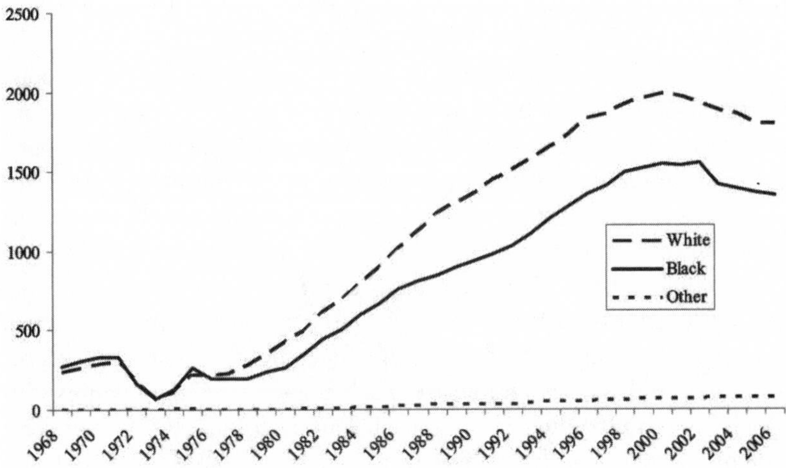

FIG. 5.—Prisoners under sentence of death, by race, 1968–2006. Source: Snell (2007)

increases. In 9 of the 17 years shown, the increase in black imprisonment rates exceeded 70 per 100,000. In four of those years, the increase exceeded 100 per 100,000. Those 1-year increases exceed the total imprisonment rates of Canada and most European countries.[7] Over 17 years, the black rate increased by 872 per 100,000 and the white rate by 203, a difference approaching 500 percent.

Racial disparities on Death Row parallel those for imprisonment generally. Figure 5 shows absolute numbers of blacks and whites on Death Row. The black fraction has not changed significantly for 25 years, despite a steep decline in homicide rates and despite, as we show below, a significant decline in the percentages of blacks arrested for homicide.

The disproportionate presence of blacks in American prisons and jails has not changed substantially since 1980. The important question is why.

[7] In 2005, the imprisonment rates for the Scandinavian countries ranged between 70 and 85 per 100,000 population. The rates for France, Germany, Belgium, and Austria were under 100 per 100,000. The Canadian rate was just above 100 per 100,000 (Walmsley 2007).

B. Racial Differences in Criminality as Explanations for Imprisonment Rates

Twenty-five years ago possible explanations for why the prison population was nearly half black were contentious and hotly disputed. Suspicions that criminal justice officials were racially biased and labored under the influence of racial stereotypes detrimental to blacks were widespread (e.g., American Friends Service Committee 1971). Within a decade, however, a consensus view emerged that, though bias and stereotyping existed, they were not the primary drivers of racial disparities in imprisonment. For serious violent crimes, a primary driver was racial differences in offending. Blacks committed homicides, rapes, robberies, and serious assaults at much higher rates than whites did. Much violent offending is intraracial. Failure to take black offenders' violent crimes seriously in effect would constitute indifference to black victims' violent victimization, and few people would want to do that. Racial disparities preponderantly based on offending differences were difficult to challenge on normative grounds.

There were two important caveats to the explanation that differences in racial offending explain differences in imprisonment. First, it applied mostly to serious violent offenses; for less serious offenses, offending explained much less of imprisonment disparities. For the most serious crimes, the crime itself appeared to be the primary factor explaining sentencing decisions, leaving comparatively little room for bias or stereotyping to operate. Less serious crimes allowed more room for discretionary decision making and the crime explained less. Second, for some crimes, arrest differences have no necessary link to offending differences; drug arrests are the most important example. Police can arrest street-level inner-city drug dealers almost at will, meaning that arrests are more a measure of police than of criminal activity. Disparities in arrests for drug offenses are the result of police policy choices.

The preceding paragraphs summarize analyses catalyzed by a landmark article by Alfred Blumstein (1982) that compared racial differences in arrests to racial differences in imprisonment, by offense and overall. It prompted additional more refined analyses by others (e.g., Langan 1985; Tonry 1995). The basic conclusion held up and was broadly confirmed by research on sentencing disparities that generally concluded that there are few racial differences in sentence lengths for offenders sent to prison (presumably mostly for more serious offenses and more chronic offenders); disparities are much more likely concerning the in/out decision (typically often concerning less serious offenses and offenders) (Blumstein et al. 1983; Spohn 2000; Harrington and Spohn 2007).

In this subsection, we summarize Blumstein's analysis, replicate the analysis for the year 2004, and consider other sources of data that might confirm or refute conclusions reached.

1. *Blumstein's Original Analysis.* Blumstein compared racial percentages among arrestees for particular offense categories to racial percentages among state prisoners sentenced following convictions for those offenses. Lots of questions can be raised as to whether arrests are a valid measure of offending (e.g., they might be systematically biased or erratically incomplete), whether jail inmates should have been taken into account, and whether they should be compared with racial patterns in prison admissions rather than in prison populations.[8] We return to some of those questions below. First we present Blumstein's analysis.

Table 1 sets out Blumstein's original analysis and adds one additional column of information. Columns 1 and 2 show black/white percentages among people serving prison sentences in 1979 for 11 offense categories and overall. Columns 3 and 4 show black/white percentages of people aged 18 and up arrested in 1979 for those offense categories and overall. Column 6, which was not in Blumstein's analysis, compares the black percentages in the preceding columns and shows, for example, that black arrests for homicide account for all but 1.3 percent of the black percentage among people imprisoned for homicide. The unexplained variations among people imprisoned for robbery and aggravated assault are larger, but still small. For lesser assaults, auto theft, and burglary, the unexplained variation ranges from 16.6 to 29.8 percent, with the largest unexplained variation being for drug crime (36.7 percent).

Blumstein used a different analysis. Results are shown in column 5. He compared black imprisonment relative to arrests to white imprisonment relative to arrests. Whites were relatively underrepresented in prison compared with their presence among arrestees (e.g., 47.7 percent of homicide prisoners but 48.5 percent of homicide arrestees; 57.7

[8] Blumstein (1982) identifies others. Use of aggregate national data, e.g., could camouflage stark differences between states (some of which might be very discriminatory, but this would pass unrecognized) and overlook offsetting racial biases (e.g., punishing blacks with white victims very harshly while punishing crimes involving black victims leniently or not at all).

TABLE 1

Comparison of Crime-Specific Percentage of Blacks in State Prison and in Arrests, 1979

	Prisoners		Arrests		% Black Prisoners Unexplained by Arrest	
Crime	White (1)	Black (2)	White (3)	Black (4)	Between Races (5)	Within Race (6)
Murder and nonnegligent manslaughter	47.7	52.3	48.4	51.6	2.8	1.3
Forcible rape	43.7	56.3	51.3	48.7	26.3	13.5
Robbery	38.8	61.2	42.9	57.1	15.6	6.7
Aggravated assault	57.7	42.3	59.0	41.0	5.2	3.1
Other violent	53.1	46.9	60.9	39.1	27.3	16.6
Burglary	57.7	42.3	67.1	32.9	33.1	22.2
Larceny/auto theft	50.7	49.3	65.4	34.6	45.6	29.8
Other property	64.4	35.6	65.4	34.6	4.3	2.8
Drugs	60.5	39.5	75.0	25.0	48.9	36.7
Public order	61.4	38.6	69.3	30.7	29.5	20.5
Other	71.7	28.3	66.3	33.7	−28.7	−19.1
Total	50.9	49.14	56.6	43.45	20.5	11.6

SOURCE.—Blumstein (1982).

percent of burglary prisoners but 67.1 percent of burglary arrestees). He thus compared blacks' presence in prison given an arrest for a particular offense to whites' presence. Between-race calculations (col. 5) produce higher rates of unexplained variation than do within-race calculations (col. 6) (20.5 percent overall compared with 11.6), but the results using either calculation were inconsistent with the hypothesis that racial bias and stereotyping explained the largest part of disparities in imprisonment rates for serious crimes.

Two primary objections to Blumstein's analysis are that arrests may themselves be a biased basis for comparison and that prison population data reflect a combination of prison admission rates with sentence lengths. Patrick Langan (1985) explored these objections. His aim was to get behind arrests by looking at data on assailants identified by victims and, to avoid the confounding interaction effects of prison admission rates and average sentence lengths, by looking at prison admission rates alone. He compared data from the NCVS for 1973, 1979, and 1982 on victims' characterizations of their assailants' race with racially disaggregated data on prison admissions. Because victimization

TABLE 2

Comparison of Crime-Specific Percentage of Blacks in State Prison and in Arrests, 2004

	Prisoners		Arrests		% Black Prisoners Unexplained by Arrest	
Crime	White (1)	Black (2)	White (3)	Black (4)	Between Races (5)	Within Race (6)
Murder and nonnegligent manslaughter	48.9	51.1	52.0	48.0	11.6	6.0
Forcible rape	61.7	38.3	67.7	32.3	23.2	15.7
Robbery	37.6	62.4	49.0	51.0	37.2	18.2
Assault	53.3	46.7	73.5	26.5	58.8	43.2
Burglary	59.1	40.9	72.6	27.4	45.5	33.0
Larceny/theft	58.8	42.2	71.1	28.9	44.3	31.5
Motor vehicle theft	63.3	36.7	67.4	32.6	16.7	11.2
Drugs	45.5	54.5	66.2	33.8	57.4	38.0
Violent crime	52.1	47.9	63.9	36.1	38.4	24.6
Property crime	60.3	39.7	71.1	28.9	38.3	27.3
Total	53.2	46.8	65.0	35.0	38.9	25.3

SOURCES.—Federal Bureau of Investigation (2005); BJS (2006).

NOTE.—Changes in BJS and FBI offense classifications since 1979 required that we estimate some numbers. We believe that we have closely approximated Blumstein's original calculations.

data do not include homicide and rape numbers in victimization data are too small to permit meaningful analyses, he looked at robbery, aggravated assault, and three property crimes. For robbery, his findings paralleled Blumstein's: victims' reports on offenders' race and prison admission data by race were nearly identical. Like Blumstein, Langan concluded that about 80 percent of racial disparity was explainable by reference to offending patterns and, overall, that "test results generally support the differential involvement [in crime] hypothesis" (p. 678).

2. *Replication Using 2004 Data.* We replicated Blumstein's analysis using arrest and prison population data for 2004. Table 2 shows the results. A much smaller part of racial disparities in imprisonment can be explained by arrest patterns in 2004 than Blumstein found for 1979. In Blumstein's between-race comparisons, arrests explained all but 2.8 percent of imprisonment disparities in homicide imprisonment; 11.6 percent remained unexplained in 2004. For robbery in 1979, 15.6 percent of imprisonment disparities went unexplained; in 2004, 37.2 per-

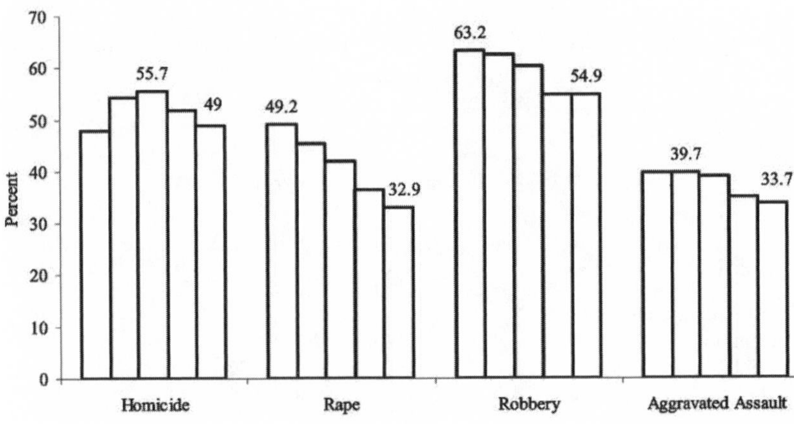

FIG. 6.—Black percentages among Uniform Crime Report violent index arrestees, 1982–2006 (5-year averages). Source: Federal Bureau of Investigation, *Crime in the United States*, various years.

cent. Overall, Blumstein's 1979 analysis left 20.5 percent of imprisonment disparities unexplained. He replicated the analysis using 1991 data and concluded that unexplained disparities had increased to 25 percent (Blumstein 1993). Our 2004 analysis left 38.9 percent unexplained. Had Blumstein in his 1982 article found unexplained disparities as large as we find for 2004, surely his conclusion would have been the opposite of what it was: such large unexplained variation creates a strong presumption of racial bias.

In trying to understand why the results are so different for 2004, we looked at racial trends in arrest patterns. Perhaps black percentages among arrestees for serious crimes rose rapidly after 1979, with black percentages in 2004 being anomalously low. As figure 6 shows, however, the opposite is true. Black Americans' involvement in violence is declining. The figure shows black percentages, averaged over 5-year periods, among people arrested for homicide, forcible rape, robbery, and aggravated assault. Although black Americans continue to be overrepresented among arrestees, the degree of overrepresentation has been falling for a quarter century. Fifty-six percent of homicide arrestees in 1992–96 were black; 49 percent were in 2002–6. In 1982–86, 49 percent of rape arrestees were black; 33 percent were in 2002–6. The declines are almost as steep for robbery and aggravated assault. That's

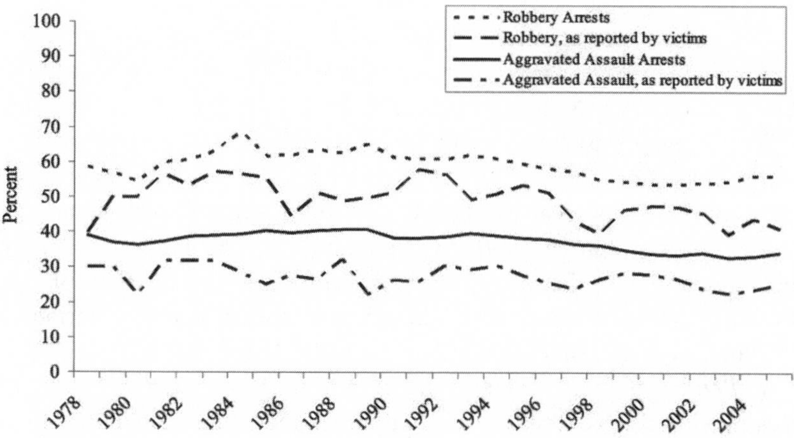

FIG. 7.—Percentage of blacks among lone offenders as perceived by victims and percentage of black arrests, 1978–2005. Sources: BJS, *Sourcebook of Criminal Justice Statistics* (http://www.albany.edu/sourcebook/), various years; Federal Bureau of Investigation, *Crime in the United States*, various years.

good news: black involvement in serious violent crime has been declining.

Perhaps, we thought, the explanation is to be found in changes in arrest data that operated to underreport black violence. To check this, using NCVS data we compared arrest percentages with robbery and aggravated assault victims' characterizations of the racial characteristics of their assailants. Figure 7 shows the result: no significant change in a quarter century. Black percentages among arrestees for both offenses have consistently tracked victims' characterizations but been higher. The reason is at least in part that many robberies and assaults involve more than one assailant, and the NCVS data pertain to crimes involving lone offenders.

So why are so many blacks in prison compared with whites? That question can be answered at (at least) two levels. The first, which we discuss in the remaining portion of this section, is mechanical: what are the mechanisms that put more blacks in prison than their population or crime participation percentages appear to justify? The second, which we discuss in Section II, is more difficult: what is it about American society and cultural norms that allowed those mechanisms to exist and allows them to persist?

C. What Are the Direct Causes of Racial Disparities in Imprisonment?

There are four plausible explanations for why there are so many more black prisoners than offending patterns suggest there should be. First, invidious bias and conscious stereotypes ("Many young black men are dangerous, so I must treat this young black man harshly") may cause police, prosecutors, and judges to treat black defendants more severely than they treat whites. Second, subtler forms of subconscious stereotyping and attribution may be operating. Third, disparities may be worsened by police practices that disproportionately affect blacks. Fourth, disparities may be worsened by sentencing policies relating to violent and drug crimes.

1. *Bias and Conscious Stereotyping.* We have the least to say about this hypothesis. No doubt some Americans, including some public officials, are racists and are biased against blacks. Larger numbers are no doubt affected by conscious stereotypes about blacks. Still more engage in "statistical discrimination," the attribution of traits that characterize groups to individual members of groups. This is one central issue in analyses of racial profiling. If many young black men in particular neighborhoods, who adopt particular styles of dress, are involved in gang activities or drug dealing, police seeing a young man in that neighborhood who fits that pattern may believe it likely that he is a gang member or drug dealer and stop him, even if the individualized basis for a stop that the law requires does not exist. To a police officer, this may seem an obvious and sensible thing to do. To a civil libertarian, such a stop is an obvious and intolerable instance of crude racial stereotyping. Efforts to establish from police stop data whether "yields" or "hit rates" for blacks and whites stopped by the police are higher or lower effectively assume that this form of statistical stereotyping could be acceptable: if blacks are stopped at twice the rate of whites but contraband is found in the same or a higher percentage of cases, that implicitly demonstrates that police are not acting in an invidious way but have valid reasons more often to be suspicious of blacks.

The effects of bias and stereotyping are likely to be different at police and sentencing stages. Research on profiling generally concludes that police do stop blacks disproportionately often on the streets and on the highway, generally do not achieve higher hit rates for blacks than for whites (e.g., Engel and Calnon 2004), but usually make more arrests. Inevitably this means that police practices lead to higher levels of black arrests, and therefore convictions and prisoners, than would otherwise exist. These practices are particularly likely to worsen racial disparities for drug and firearms offenses since those are the two kinds of illegal contraband police stops are most likely to yield. We discuss this further below in relation to drug policy.

On the basis of personal interactions over decades with judges in many American jurisdictions, we do not believe that invidious racial bias and gross stereotypes are likely substantially to affect sentencing decisions. This is a subject judges worry about and discuss often among themselves and with others. Sentencing research showing that there are few racial differences in sentence lengths is consistent with our belief (e.g., Spohn 2000, 2002). Sentencing research showing that there are often in/out differences is not necessarily strongly inconsistent with it. Black defendants, especially young ones, often have more extensive criminal records than whites, and judges take criminal records into account when deciding which defendants "deserve another chance." Similarly, black defendants on average have less stable home lives, less conventional employment records, and fewer educational attainments than whites, and judges take such things into account in deciding which defendants are more likely to succeed in community sentences and programs and which are more likely to reoffend.[9]

2. *Unconscious Stereotyping and Attribution.* In some ways it is surprising that the literature on sentencing disparities shows comparatively few differences in outcomes on the basis of race. Recent research on "colorism" and the significance of Afrocentric features in stereotyping offenders shows that stereotypes are deeply embedded in American culture and affect both white and black people (the fullest examination of this literature can be found in Blank, Dabaddy, and Citro [2004]). Analysts of "Afrocentric feature bias" posit that certain stereotypically African American facial features influence decision makers' (and research subjects') judgments about individual offenders. Although the number of studies is small, their implications are disturbing. One study found that people with more Afrocentric features appeared more "criminal" to observers and that the more Afrocentric features

[9] Our point in the text is not that the practices described in this and the preceding sentence are necessarily unobjectionable, but that many judges engage in them in good faith. Argument can be made that black defendants acquire more extensive criminal records at younger ages than whites because police are more likely to arrest them, and accordingly that the criminal record at least in part is more a product of police than of criminal activity, and in fairness should not be held against black defendants. Similarly, objections have long been made to taking account of social factors (household stability, employment, education) in sentencing, precisely because they are correlated with race.

an individual possessed, the more "criminal" he appeared (Eberhardt et al. 2004). In other studies, Afrocentric features were associated with longer prison sentences and increased frequency of capital sentencing (Blair, Judd, and Fallman 2004; Eberhardt et al. 2006).[10]

The study of Afrocentric feature bias emerged from research on "colorism," discrimination within racial groups on the basis of gradations in skin color (Jones 2000). Many studies have shown that people associate lighter skin tones among blacks with positive characteristics and darker skin tones with negative characteristics (e.g., Maddox and Gray 2002), but no published work has investigated colorism in criminal justice settings.

Several recent studies have tried to assess the significance of Afrocentric feature bias. Blair et al. (2002) found that individuals with more Afrocentric features were judged by college undergraduates to have stereotypical African American traits. Blair, Chapleau, and Judd (2005) showed that research subjects believed that individuals with more Afrocentric features were likely more often than others to behave aggressively.

Eberhardt et al. (2004) asked 182 police officers to examine photographs of male students and employees at Stanford University. Half were shown white faces and half were shown black faces. One-third of the officers were asked to rate the stereotypicality of each face on a scale, that is, how stereotypical each face was of members of the person's race. Another third, told that some of the faces might be of criminals, were asked to indicate whether the person "looked criminal." The last third were asked to rate attractiveness on a scale. Each officer completed only one of the three measures.

More black than white faces were thought to look criminal. Black faces rated above the median for stereotypicality were judged as criminal significantly more than were black faces rated below the median. The opposite was found for white faces. The authors concluded that the police officers thought that black faces looked more criminal and that "the more black, the more criminal" (Eberhardt et al. 2004, p. 889).

Blair, Judd, and Chapleau (2004) analyzed the Afrocentric features

[10] Another explanation is that many biases people harbor are not consciously accessible. The Implicit Association Test, which has been used to assess implicit attitudes toward different groups, has shown a significant implicit preference for whites among all races and ethnicities (Greenwald and Krieger 2006).

of inmates in the Florida Department of Corrections database. They asked undergraduates to rate the faces of a randomly selected sample of 216 inmates, 100 black and 116 white, in terms of the "degree to which each face had features that are typical of African Americans" (p. 676). After they controlled for race and criminal history, Afrocentric features were a significant predictor of sentence length. Within each race, more Afrocentric features were associated with longer sentences.[11]

Pizzi, Blair, and Judd (2005, p. 351) argued that judges and prosecutors have adapted to differences between racial groups but have not been sensitized to sentencing differences on the basis of Afrocentric features: "Racial stereotyping in sentencing decisions still persists. But it is not a function of the racial category of the individual; instead, there seems to be an equally pernicious and less controllable process at work. Racial stereotyping in sentencing still occurs based on the facial appearance of the offender. Be they White or African American, those offenders who possess stronger Afrocentric features receive harsher sentences for the same crimes."

Eberhardt et al. (2006, p. 383), using a database of death-eligible cases in Philadelphia, "examined the extent to which perceived stereotypicality of Black defendants influenced jurors' death-sentencing decisions in cases with both White and Black victims." Stanford undergraduates were shown pictures of 44 defendants, presented randomly and edited for uniformity, and asked to rate the stereotypicality of each black defendant's appearance. With stereotypicality as the only independent variable, 24.4 percent of black defendants rated below the median for stereotypicality received a death sentence, compared with 57.5 percent of black defendants rated above the median.

3. *Drug Policy.* American drug policies are a primary aggravator of racial disparities in imprisonment. Blumstein's 1982 analysis of 1979 prison population showed that arrest patterns for drug offenses explained the smallest percentage of racial disproportionality in imprisonment (48.9 percent unexplained) of any offense category at a time when 5.7 percent of prisoners (about 16,000 total) had been convicted of drug crimes (see table 1). Our analysis of 2004 data again showed

[11] Blair, Judd, and Fallman (2004, p. 677) note, however, that this does not necessarily imply explicit bias: "this form of stereotyping appears to occur without people's awareness and outside their immediate control."

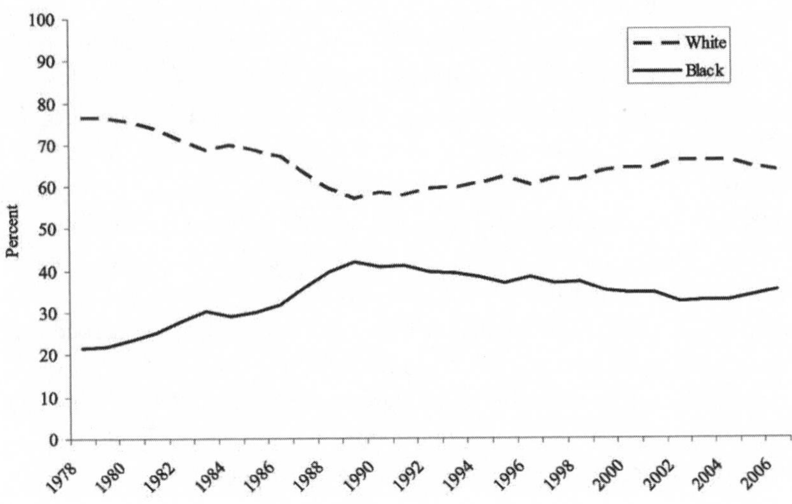

FIG. 8.—Total arrests for drug offenses, by race, 1978–2006. Sources: BJS, *Sourcebook of Criminal Justice Statistics* (http://www.albany.edu/sourcebook/), various years; Federal Bureau of Investigation, *Crime in the United States*, various years.

that drug arrests explained the smallest percentages of prison disproportionality (57.4 percent unexplained; see table 2).[12]

Figures 8 and 9 show why the black imprisonment rate for drug crimes is so high. Figure 8 shows black and white percentages among people arrested for drug crimes between 1978 and 2006. As recently as 1978, approximately 80 percent of adult drug arrestees were white. By 1989, the black share among all arrestees exceeded 40 percent, and in the years since it has fluctuated between 32 and 40 percent. How does it happen that 13 percent of the population make up 40 percent of drug arrestees?

The answer is that blacks are much more likely than whites to be arrested for drug crimes. Figure 9 shows total arrest rates of blacks and whites from 1978 to 2006. The white rate since 1978 has been approximately one-fourth the black one. Why are blacks so much more often arrested for drug crimes?

The answer is not, as table 3 shows, that blacks use drugs at much

[12] For assaults, 58.8 percent of disproportionality went unexplained, no doubt partly because assaults in 2004 were not limited to aggravated assaults as in Blumstein's (1982) data but included a substantial preponderance of less serious events.

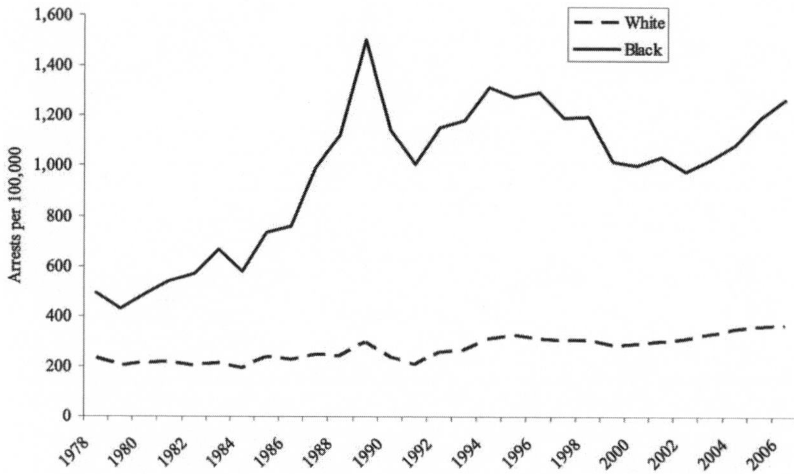

FIG. 9.—Total arrest rate for drug offenses, by race, 1978–2006. Sources: BJS, *Sourcebook of Criminal Justice Statistics* (http://www.albany.edu/sourcebook/), various years.

higher rates than whites do. National Institute of Drug Abuse surveys have tracked self-reported drug use since the 1970s. The table shows percentages of blacks and whites who reported using alcohol, any other drugs, and four categories of illicit substances ever, in the last year, and in the last month. In 2005 and 2006, larger percentages of whites reported using alcohol, cocaine (including crack), and hallucinogens, and the differences are large. Larger percentages of whites than blacks report having ever used marijuana, and slightly higher percentages of blacks report using marijuana recently. Only for crack (considered alone) do blacks report significantly higher use levels than whites, but the absolute levels are low. One conclusion is clear: the reason so many more blacks than whites are arrested or imprisoned for drug crimes is not that they use drugs much more extensively than whites do.

Another plausible reason why blacks might more often be arrested for drug crimes than are whites is that they are much more extensively involved in drug trafficking. National Institute of Drug Abuse (NIDA) surveys based on representative samples of the U.S. population indicate that this is not true.[13] Figure 10 shows self-reported drug selling by

[13] In recent years, reports of the National Survey on Drug Use and Health have identified the author as the Office of Applied Studies, Substance Abuse and Mental Health

TABLE 3
Percentage of Drug Use, by Race, 2005–6

	2005		2006	
Drug	White	Black	White	Black
Alcohol:				
Ever used	86.9	75.2	86.9	75.4
Within last year	70.5	55.5	70.4	55.1
Within last month	56.5	40.8	55.8	40.0
All illicit drugs:*				
Ever used	48.9	44.7	49.0	42.9
Within last year	14.5	16.0	14.8	16.4
Within last month	8.1	9.7	8.5	9.8
Marijuana:				
Ever used	43.7	39.0	43.9	37.6
Within last year	10.6	12.3	10.7	12.4
Within last month	6.1	7.6	6.4	7.4
Cocaine:†				
Ever used	15.5	9.8	16.3	9.1
Within last year	2.4	2.0	2.5	2.1
Within last month	1.0	1.1	.9	1.3
Crack:				
Ever used	3.2	4.9	3.3	5.3
Within last year	.5	1.2	.5	1.3
Within last month	.2	.8	.2	.8
Hallucinogens:				
Ever used	16.3	6.5	17.0	6.6
Within last year	1.8	.8	1.7	1.4
Within last month	.5	.2	.4	.5

SOURCE.—Office of Applied Studies, *National Survey on Drug Use and Health*, various years.

* Illicit drugs include marijuana/hashish, cocaine (including crack), heroin, hallucinogens, inhalants, or prescription-type psychotherapeutics used nonmedically.

† Includes crack cocaine.

12–17-year-old blacks and whites for the years 2001–6. Three to four percent of both groups reported selling drugs at least once in the preceding year, and 1 percent reported selling drugs at least 10 or more times during the preceding year. The black and white rates for most measures are nearly identical; on average for the entire period and for most years, white rates are slightly higher than black rates.

Representative national surveys undercount transient and homeless

Services Administration, which is how we refer to data from the survey in source notes. Predecessor surveys were published by the NIDA. Because most readers will be more familiar with that attribution, we refer to NIDA when discussing survey data in the text.

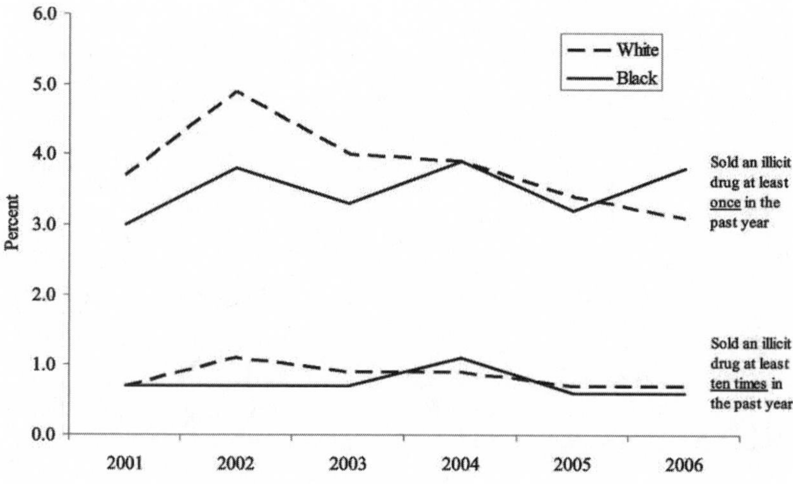

FIG. 10.—Illicit drug sales among youths aged 12–17, by race, 2001–6. Source: Office of Applied Studies, *National Survey on Drug Use and Health*, various years.

populations and do not count institutionalized populations (in prisons, jails, or mental institutions) at all. The effect is that measures that distinguish black and white rates may undercount black rates because relatively more blacks than whites have no permanent address and are confined in institutions. These problems, however, are much less significant for 12–17-year-olds, most of whom live with a parent or caretaker and few of whom are confined in institutions. However, even if these sampling problems to some degree affect the data in figure 10, they are unlikely to change significantly the drug trafficking patterns shown; for example, increasing black rates by 25 percent would not materially alter the black/white comparisons. It would make the black rates slightly higher than the white rates rather than slightly lower.

The reason why so many more blacks than whites are arrested and imprisoned for drug crimes is well known and long recognized. They are much easier to arrest. Much white drug dealing occurs behind closed doors and in private. Much black drug dealing occurs in public or semipublic, on the streets and in open-air drug markets. And much black drug dealing occurs between strangers. Figures 11 and 12 present NIDA self-report data for the total population for 2001–6 on locations and sources of subjects' most recent marijuana purchases. As figure 12 shows, in each year, 87–88 percent of whites made their purchases from

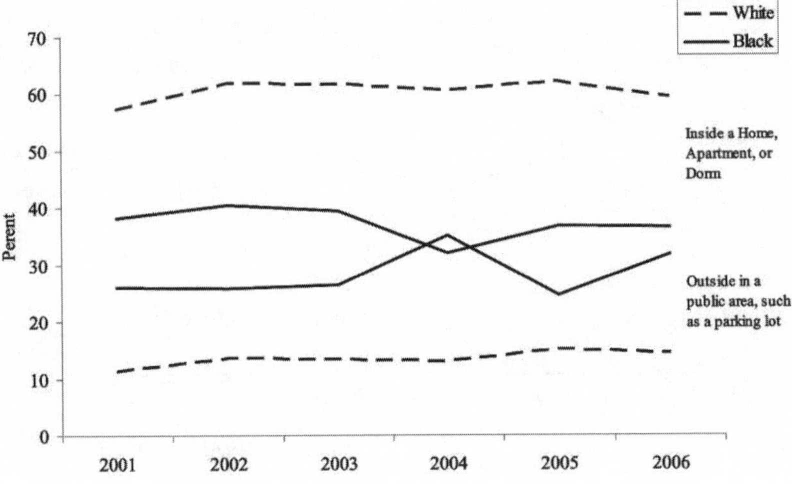

FIG. 11.—Location of last purchase of marijuana, by race, 2001–6. Source: Office of Applied Studies, *National Survey on Drug Use and Health*, various years. Categories do not account for 100 percent of purchases because the following response categories were excluded: inside a public building, such as a store or restaurant; inside a school building; outside on school property; and some other place.

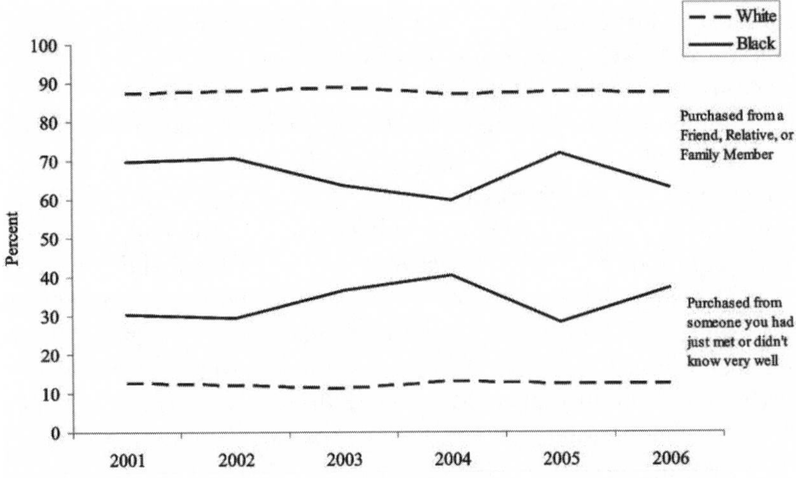

FIG. 12.—Source of last purchase of marijuana, by race, 2001–6. Source: Office of Applied Studies, *National Survey on Drug Use and Health*, various years.

friends, relatives, and family members. By contrast, blacks purchased marijuana from people they had just met or did not know well 30–40 percent of the time.

Figure 11 presents data on where marijuana is purchased. Depending on the year, 57–62 percent of purchases by whites occurred inside a home, apartment, or dorm, and only 11–14 percent outdoors in public spaces such as parking lots. For black purchasers, the pattern was starkly different. Forty percent or less of purchases occurred in private indoor spaces; 26–35 percent were made outdoors in public spaces.

Undercover drug agents can penetrate black urban drug markets relatively easily and make arrests almost at will. Most white drug dealing, by contrast, occurs within existing social networks in which people know one another, and in private. Undercover agents have to invest much more time in establishing their bona fides; the arrest yield from a fixed amount of time or effort is much lower when pursuing white than when pursuing black sellers.

In other words, black arrest rates are so much higher than white rates because police choose as a strategic matter to invest more energy and effort in arresting blacks. So many more blacks than whites are in prison because police officials have adopted practices, and policy makers have enacted laws, that foreseeably treat black offenders much more harshly than white ones.

4. *Sentencing Policies for Violent and Drug Crimes.* Sentencing policies for drug crimes and violent crimes have been a major driver of racial disparities in imprisonment since the mid-1970s. Until the early 1980s, the tougher laws mainly established mandatory minimum sentences for violent and gun crimes, but the minimums were usually 1 or 2 years or at most 5 (Shane-DuBow, Brown, and Olsen 1985). Beginning in the mid-1980s and continuing through the mid-1990s, epitomized by the federal 100-to-one law governing cocaine sentencing and California's three-strikes law that required sentences ranging from 25 years to life for third felonies, sentences for drugs, guns, and violence were made incomparably harsher.

Black Americans have borne the brunt of this tougher sentencing. For drug crimes, as we have already shown, police arrest policies produce arrest rates for blacks that are far out of proportion to blacks' drug use or involvement in drug trafficking. For understandable reasons of social disadvantage and limited life chances, blacks engage more

TABLE 4

New Commitments to State Prisons, by Race, 2003

	All	Black*	White*	Hispanic†
Violence, of which	28.2%	27.7%	26.1%	34.9%
Homicide	2.9	2.9	2.5	3.5
Robbery	7.6	**10.4**	**4.7**	**8.3**
Property	27.9	24.2	32.8	22.2
Drugs	30.7	**37.5**	**25.5**	**30.6**
Public order, of which	12.7	10.2	15	11.8
Guns	3.3	**4.2**	**2.1**	**3.7**
All	100	100	100	100

SOURCE.—BJS, National Corrections Reporting Program—2003 (fi6ncrp0304.csv), table 4.

* Includes persons of Hispanic origin.

† Includes persons of all races.

often in gun crimes and serious violent crimes. Laws that increase sentences for such crimes inevitably exacerbate racial disparities.

Table 4, for example, shows new state prison commitments by conviction offense and race for 2003, the most recent year for which data are available from the BJS National Corrections Reporting Program. Among whites, 53.7 percent were committed for violent, drug, or gun crimes, compared with 69.4 percent of black offenders (in both cases including Hispanic same-race offenders). The racial skew is even greater when the focus is narrowed to robbery, drugs, and guns (52.1 percent of black prisoners, 32.3 percent of whites). Among black prisoners, 37.5 percent were committed for drug crimes; among white prisoners, 25.5 percent were.

There have long been good reasons to believe that longer sentences for drug crimes have no effect on levels of drug use, drug prices, or drug trafficking (e.g., Wilson 1990; Dills, Miron, and Summers 2008; MacCoun and Martin, forthcoming). And there are good reasons to doubt that increasing penalties for particular violent or drug crimes from 3 years to 5, 5 years to 10, or 10 years to 20 has any discernible effects on crime rates (e.g., Doob and Webster 2003; Dills, Miron, and Summers 2008; Tonry, in this volume). Those things being true, to increase penalties for crimes with which blacks are charged, for whatever reason, is to increase racial disparities in prison for no good reason or for a not well-justified one.

5. *In Sum.* Black Americans suffer from imprisonment rates six to seven times higher than those of whites primarily for two reasons.

Police arrest policies for drugs target a type of drug trafficking (street-level transactions in inner-city areas) in which blacks are disproportionately involved. American sentencing laws and policies specify punishments that are both absolutely and relatively severe for violent, drug, and gun crimes for which blacks are more likely than whites to be arrested and prosecuted. Conscious bias and stereotyping, and unconscious stereotyping and attribution, no doubt play some roles in causing disparities, but smaller ones.

II. Making Sense of Racial Disparities

A primary aim of this essay was to see how patterns of racial disparity have changed since the mid-1990s. We learned three important things that provided one bit of good news and two of terrible news. The good news is that patterns of racial involvement in serious crime as shown in arrest data have changed. The percentages of people arrested for aggravated assault, robbery, rape, and homicide who are black have been declining and in 2006 were much lower than in 1985. One might hope, and expect, that racial disparities in imprisonment would have fallen commensurately.

The two bits of terrible news: The first is that blacks continue to make up about half of the prison population[14] and about the same percentage of Death Row inmates as in the 1980s. The chance that a black American is in prison in 2007 remains six to seven times higher than the chance that a white American is in prison. The declining involvement of blacks in serious violent crime has had no effect on racial disparities in prison.

The second is that insensitivity to the interests of black Americans continues to characterize American crime policies. Racial disparities in imprisonment continue to be generated by policy choices that were known, or should have been known, disproportionately to affect disadvantaged black Americans. In no significant respect have American drug policies changed since the 1980s—the federal 100-to-one rule is

[14] BJS (2007) data for midyear 2006 show that black men constituted 41 percent of male jail and prison inmates. The true figure in a country in which skin color matters much more than ethnicity is 46–48 percent (because a few years ago the BJS stopped counting black Hispanics as black and thereby reduced the black percentage by 10–12 percent; a quarter to a third of imprisoned Hispanics, who made up 21 percent of male inmates, are dark skinned). Forty-seven percent is to be sure less than 50 and is the result of the rapid increase in imprisonment of Hispanic people in recent years. There were more non-Hispanic blacks than non-Hispanic whites imprisoned in 2007.

the symbol of that—and they continue grossly disproportionately to ensnare young blacks and, increasingly, young Hispanics.[15] And American policies toughening penalties for violent crime have had the same effect. If the conditions of life faced by disadvantaged minority youths make them disproportionately likely to be involved in violent crime, then policies making punishments for violent crime enormously harsher will disproportionately affect them, and they have.

Loïc Wacquant's work provides insight into how that happened.[16] For a decade now, he has been writing articles on race and crime control policy. His basic argument is that American cultural practices and legal institutions have operated to maintain patterns of racial dominance and hierarchy for two centuries. Until the Civil War, slavery assured white domination. Within 30 years after the war, the practices and legal forms of discrimination known as "Jim Crow" laws restored white domination of blacks. In the "Great Migration" in the 1910s and 1920s, millions of blacks moved from the South to the North to escape Jim Crow; the big city ghettos, housing discrimination, and other forms of discrimination kept blacks in their subordinate place (Lieberson 1980). And when deindustrialization and the flight of jobs to the suburbs left disadvantaged blacks marooned in the urban ghettos, the modern wars on drugs and crime took over (Wacquant 2002*a*, 2002*b*).

Wacquant's writing is passionate and controversial, but it is time more people paid attention to it. The civil rights movement has borne fruit in the forms of increased economic and social integration of blacks in American society. The progress made is remarkable in light of the justice system experiences of black Americans.

Wacquant's argument is a functionalist one, about what criminal justice policies and practices do, rather than a political one about what

[15] The U.S. Sentencing Commission (2007) revisions to its crack and cocaine guidelines merely nibble at the edges of the disparities caused by the 100-to-one statute: "The sentencing commission's striking move on Tuesday, meant to address the wildly disproportionate punishments for crack and powder cocaine, will have only a minor impact. Unless Congress acts, many thousands of defendants will continue to face vastly different sentences for possessing and selling different types of the same thing" (Liptak 2007, p. A21).

[16] We do not here discuss features of American politics that made racial insensitivity more explicable in the last 30 years: the political ascendancy of the right wing of the Republican Party, embodying the contemporary resurgence of what Richard Hofstadter (1965) called the "paranoid streak in American politics," and the influence on it of fundamentalist Protestants. If crime and drugs are matters of good and evil, and criminals and drug users are evil, then there is little reason to expect sympathy or empathy toward them from the holders of those views (especially if the criminals and drug users are black and different). See Tonry (2008).

those practices and policies are intended to do. Thought of that way, thinking of what the machinery of the criminal justice system produces, it is hard not to see that it produces devastatingly reduced life chances for black Americans. If its aims were to reduce disadvantaged black men's chances of earning a decent living, or being successfully married and a good father, or being socialized into prosocial values, it is hard to see how the criminal justice system could do those things better (Western 2006). There has to be a reason why the criminal justice system treats American blacks so badly, why its foreseeable disparate impacts on blacks and whites are disregarded, and Wacquant's analysis provides a better explanation than any other that has been offered.

Wacquant's passion sometimes makes it easy for critics to dismiss his arguments as polemics. He is, however, no longer alone in suggesting that American criminal justice practices operate to keep poor blacks in their places. Here is what Douglas Massey, author (with Nancy Denton) of *American Apartheid* (1993), a widely praised and decidedly nonpolemical account of housing discrimination, had to say in *Categorically Unequal*, his 2007 book on social stratification:

> Whether whites care to admit it or not, they have a selfish interest in maintaining the categorical mechanisms that perpetuate racial stratification. As a result, when pushed by the federal government to end overt discriminatory practices, they are likely to innovate new and more subtle ways to maintain their privileged position in society. If one discriminatory mechanism proves impossible to sustain, whites have an incentive to develop alternatives that may be associated only indirectly with race and are therefore not in obvious violation of civil rights law. The specific mechanisms by which racial stratification occurs can thus be expected to evolve over time. (P. 54)

> [The] new emphasis on retribution and punishment was achieved . . . through the deliberate racialization of crime and violence in public consciousness by political entrepreneurs. (P. 94)

> As discrimination moved underground, new mechanisms for exclusion were built into the criminal justice system for Afro Americans. (P. 251)

And, to complete this span of the political spectrum, here is what Glenn C. Loury, a conservative black economist and the author of *The*

Anatomy of Racial Inequality (2002), had to say in introducing his 2007 Tanner Lectures at Stanford:

> We have embraced what criminologist Michael Tonry calls a policy of "malign neglect," and in doing so we, as a society, have stumbled more or less wittingly into a God-awful cul de sac. I will claim that the connection of this apparatus to the history of racial degradation and subordination in our country (lynching, minstrelsy, segregation, ghetto-ization) is virtually self-evident, and that the racial subtext of our law and order political discourse over the last three decades has been palpable. (Loury 2007, p. 9; references omitted)

There are also psychological explanations for racial disparities' persistence. System justification theory posits "a general human tendency to support and defend the social status quo, broadly defined" (Blasi and Jost 2006, p. 1123). People, regardless of their situation, try to rationalize the injustices and inequities they see (Chen and Tyler 2002). Stereotypes (such as that the rich are smart and the poor are lazy) are often employed to demonstrate that all members of the system deserve their status. Concerning the criminal justice system, about which concern about racial disparities in imprisonment might be expected, comfort can be found in racial stereotypes, such as that black Americans are especially criminal, so of course many of them are in prison.

The incentive to rationalize is clear. People who believe in a just system experience, by and large, more positive emotions than people who blame the system. For example, poor people who blame themselves for their own poverty are happier and more satisfied with life in general (Blasi and Jost 2006, p. 1141). By rationalizing the inequities one sees in American sentencing, one finds mental comfort.

A considerable literature on racial differences in attitudes toward and opinions about crime control policy shows that whites have substantially harsher attitudes concerning punishment and greater confidence in the justice system and its practitioners than do blacks (e.g., Unnever, Cullen, and Lero-Jonson, in this volume). Lawrence Bobo and Devon Johnson, concluding an extensive analysis of black/white differences in attitudes toward capital punishment and laws punishing crack cocaine traffickers (mostly black) much more harshly than powder cocaine traffickers (mostly white), observe that

> The most consistent predictor of criminal justice policy attitudes

> is, in fact, a form of racial prejudice. While white racial resentment does not ever explain a large share of the variation in any of the attitudes we have measured, it is the most consistently influential of the variables outside of race classification itself. This pattern has at least two implications. It further buttresses the concern that some of the major elements of public support for punitive criminal justice policies are heavily tinged with racial animus and thus quite likely to be resistant to change based on suasion and information-based appeals. What is more, this pattern reinforces the claim . . . that one major function of the criminal justice system is the regulation and control of marginalized social groups such as African Americans. (2004, pp. 171–72)

There are no easy paths out of the racial dead end in which American crime policy finds itself. The damage has been done to living black Americans: lives have been blighted, life chances have been reduced, and communities have been undermined. Even radical changes in American crime policies can change none of that.

III. How Can We Do Better?

Nonetheless, things can be done. One approach, radical decarceration, is corrective. Three others, elimination of bias and stereotyping, abandonment of policies and laws that do unnecessary damage, and creation of devices making their later replication of such policies and laws less likely, are preventative.

A. Radical Decarceration

Efforts to eliminate bias and stereotyping in official decision making are being made throughout the United States and should continue to be made. Unfortunately, such efforts, even if completely successful, can have only modest effects. The primary drivers of racial disparities are drug and sentencing policies. Table 5 illustrates why elimination of bias and disparities will not significantly lessen the damage racial disparities do. The top row shows black and white imprisonment rates in 2006.[17] The second row shows what would happen if black rates were decreased by 10 percent, which is a high estimate of the degree to which

[17] The black/white ratio is not higher than 5.5 : 1 because the table uses BJS data that exclude Hispanics of either race and because it contains combined data on men and women. The disparity ratio for women in 2006 (3.8 : 1) was significantly lower than that for men (6.3 : 1) (Sabol, Minton, and Harrison 2007, table 14).

TABLE 5

Disparity in Incarceration Rates, by Race

	Black	White	Ratio
	A. Disparity Reduced 10%		
Imprisonment rate, 2006	2,661	483	5.5 : 1
10% less disparity	2,395	483	5.0 : 1
Reduction in prison per 100,000	266	0	
	B. Use of Imprisonment Halved		
Imprisonment rate, 2006	2,661	483	5.5 : 1
Imprisonment halved	1,330	241	5.5 : 1
Reduction in prison per 100,000	1,330	241	
	C. Return to 1980 Imprisonment Rates		
Imprisonment rate, 1980	827	134	6.2 : 1
Reduction in prison per 100,000	1,834	349	

SOURCE.—Office of Applied Studies, *National Survey on Drug Use and Health*, various years.

bias and stereotyping enhance disparities, while white rates were left unchanged. The black imprisonment rate would fall from approximately 2,661 per 100,000 to 2,395 and the ratio of black-to-white imprisonment rates would fall from 5.5 : 1 to 5.0 : 1.

If instead, as the fifth row shows, the prison population were cut by half across the board, the ratio of imprisonment rates would remain the same but the black imprisonment rate would fall from 2,661 to 1,330. Or if, as the penultimate row shows, imprisonment rates were cut to 1980 levels, the black imprisonment rate would be 827 per 100,000.

The differing implications of these different approaches are enormous. The U.S. Census estimates that 38.34 million U.S. residents in 2006 were black. If the imprisonment rate were halved, the black rate would fall from 26,613 per million to 13,306. That means that over 500,000 fewer black Americans would be in prison or jail. Returning to the 1980s imprisonment rate would mean 702,400 fewer black Americans behind bars. By contrast, eliminating all effects of bias and stereotyping would free at most 101,900 black Americans.

Of course, every effort should be made to eliminate bias and stereotyping. Their diminution will reduce racial disparities and the absolute size of the bite prisons take out of the black population. In absolute terms, though, that will only nibble at the problem. Only radical decarceration can make a big difference. To attempt to limit damage done to people now entangled in the arms of the criminal justice system, devices need to be created for reducing the lengths of current prison sentences and releasing hundreds of thousands of people from prison. New systems of parole, pardon, and commutation will need to be developed, as well as programs of social welfare and support to ease peoples' transitions back into the free community.

B. Abandonment of Disparity-Causing Policies

To limit damage to disadvantaged young people not yet ensnared, legislatures will need to repeal laws authorizing capital punishment and creating mandatory minimum sentences, sentences of life without the possibility of parole, and truth-in-sentencing laws. Most such laws were adopted primarily for symbolic or expressive purposes rather than with any basis for believing that they would significantly affect crime rates and patterns, and they do great and disproportionate harm to black Americans.

American jurisdictions will need to establish principled new systems of sentencing guidelines coupled with mechanisms for shortening unduly, disparately, or disproportionately long prison sentences. New guidelines will need to call for proportionate sentences for most crimes measured mostly in weeks and months, as in most other Western countries, and in years only for the most serious crimes.

These may seem millenarian proposals. They are not. They would do little more than return American crime control and punishment policies to the mainstream of Western developed countries. Every other Western country manages to get by without capital punishment, life without the possibility of parole, and prison sentences measured primarily in years and decades.

Alfred Blumstein (1993) years ago showed that American practitioners and policy makers can respond quickly to racial disparity problems. He observed that from 1965 to 1969, white and nonwhite arrest rates for young offenders were indistinguishable; that from 1970 to 1980 white rates exceeded nonwhite rates; and that thereafter by 1989 nonwhite rates nearly tripled and white rates halved, leaving nonwhite rates nearly four times higher. Figure 13 tells the story. Here is what Blumstein surmises happened:

> The decline [in white arrest rates] after the 1974 peak was undoubtedly a consequence of the general trend toward decriminali-

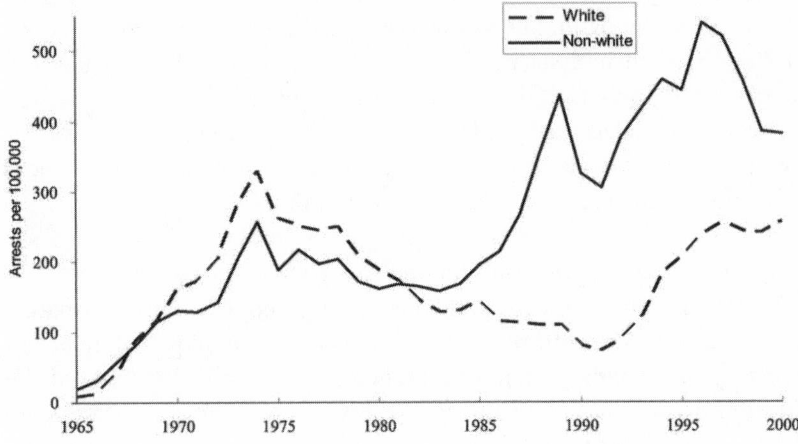

FIG. 13.—Juvenile arrest rate for drug offenses, by race, 1965–2000. Sources: Blumstein (1993); Blumstein and Wallman (2006).

> zation of marijuana in the United States. A major factor contributing to that decriminalization was probably a realization that the arrestees were much too often the children of individuals, usually white, in positions of power and influence. These parents certainly did not want the consequences of a drug arrest to be visited on their children, and so they used their leverage to achieve a significant degree of decriminalization. Following the peak, arrest rates for both racial groups declined, and continued to decline for whites. On the other hand, for non-whites, the decline leveled out in the early 1980s and then began to accelerate at a rate of between twenty and twenty-five percent per year, until the peak in 1989. This clearly reflects the fact that drug enforcement is a result of policy choices. (P. 758)

It is not completely cynical to wonder why soaring arrest rates for nonwhite kids in the 1980s did not provoke the kinds of reactions that Blumstein attributes to soaring arrest rates of white kids in the 1970s, and a comparable policy adjustment. Racially differentiated effects of American drug and sentencing policies have been starkly evident for a quarter century.

C. Race and Ethnicity Impact Statements

American governments have long used prophylactic measures to guard against unwanted effects of governmental decisions. To protect the public purse, legislatures in many states require that legislative proposals be accompanied by or trigger fiscal impact statements. Federal and state laws routinely require the preparation of environmental impact statements before building and other permits may be issued. It is a small step to require that proposals for policy and statutory changes relating to drug and crime control policies carry with them or trigger race and ethnicity impact statements. Projected new laws or policies likely disproportionately to affect members of minority groups adversely should be made subject to strong presumptions against their adoption.

If racially disparate effects of public policies are a problem, and in most policy realms that proposition is self-evident, policy makers in this realm also should be required to declare and justify disparate effects. The second edition of the *Model Penal Code* (American Law Institute 2007) provides that such statements be required, and a literature on the subject is beginning to develop (Tonry 2004, pp. 221–26; Mauer 2007).

D. Are Meaningful Changes Possible?

We realize that our proposals for radical reduction in America's prison population, repeal of repressive legislation, and requirement of race and ethnicity impact statements may strike some readers as fanciful. If racial disparities and the damage they have unarguably done to millions of individual black Americans and their families, and to black Americans as a group, are pressing social problems, then radical measures are called for.

There are pessimistic and optimistic ways to contemplate the future. The pessimistic one is to recall Loïc Wacquant's functionalist analysis of racial hierarchy in American history and the succession of mechanisms by which white domination has been maintained. If slavery was succeeded by Jim Crow, which was succeeded by the racially segregated northern ghettoes, which was succeeded by mass imprisonment, it is hard not to wonder what will substitute for mass imprisonment, or whether mass imprisonment will endure for the reasons Wacquant sketched.

The optimistic one focuses on the good things the civil rights movement accomplished. Sixty years ago, nearly all black Americans were second-class citizens; nearly all were victims of discriminatory practices, norms, and laws. That is no longer true. Today it is primarily disadvantaged black Americans who suffer, seemingly for the accident of their births. Perhaps as the normative developments that underlay the civil rights movement wrestle with the functionalist developments that Wacquant described, a time will come when our proposals do not look fanciful. They are simple proposals that aim to redress profound social injustices. Seen that way, they are not radical at all.

REFERENCES

American Friends Service Committee. 1971. *Struggle for Justice*. New York: Hill and Wang.

American Law Institute. 2007. *Model Penal Code: Sentencing*. 2nd ed. Tentative draft no. 1 (April 9). Philadelphia: American Law Institute.

Baldus, David C., George G. Woodworth, and Charles A. Pulaski Jr. 1990. *Equal Justice and the Death Penalty: A Legal and Empirical Analysis*. Boston: Northeastern University Press.

BJS (Bureau of Justice Statistics). 1984. "The 1983 Jail Census." Washington, DC: U.S. Department of Justice, Bureau of Justice Statistics.

———. 1990. "Profile of Jail inmates 1978." Washington, DC: U.S. Department of Justice, Bureau of Justice Statistics.

———. 2006. "Prisoners in 2004." Washington, DC: U.S. Department of Justice, Bureau of Justice Statistics.

———. 2007. "Prison and Jail Inmates at Midyear 2006." Washington, DC: U.S. Department of Justice, Bureau of Justice Statistics.

Blair, Irene V., Kristine M. Chapleau, and Charles M. Judd. 2005. "The Use of Afrocentric Features as Cues for Judgment in the Presence of Diagnostic Information." *European Journal of Social Psychology* 35:59–68.

Blair, Irene V., Charles M. Judd, and Kristine M. Chapleau. 2004. "The Influence of Afrocentric Facial Features in Criminal Sentencing." *Psychological Science* 15(10):674–79.

Blair, Irene V., Charles M. Judd, and Jennifer L. Fallman. 2004. "The Automaticity of Race and Afrocentric Facial Features in Social Judgments." *Journal of Personality and Social Psychology* 87(6):763–78.

Blair, Irene V., Charles M. Judd, Melody S. Sadler, and Christopher Jenkins. 2002. "The Role of Afrocentric Features in Person Perception: Judging by Features and Categories." *Journal of Personality and Social Psychology* 83(1): 5–25.

Blank, Rebecca M., Marilyn Dabaddy, and Constance F. Citro, eds. 2004. *Measuring Racial Discrimination*. Washington, DC: National Academy Press.

Blasi, Gary, and John T. Jost. 2006. "System Justification Theory and Research: Implications for Law, Legal Advocacy, and Social Justice." *California Law Review* 94:1119–68.

Blumstein, Alfred. 1982. "On Racial Disproportionality of the United States' Prison Populations." *Journal of Criminal Law and Criminology* 73:1259–81.

———. 1993. "Racial Disproportionality of U.S. Prison Populations Revisited." *University of Colorado Law Review* 64:743–60.

Blumstein, Alfred, and Allen Beck. 1999. "Population Growth in U.S. Prisons, 1980–1996." In *Prisons*, edited by Michael Tonry and Joan Petersilia. Vol. 26 of *Crime and Justice: A Review of Research*, edited by Michael Tonry. Chicago: University of Chicago Press.

Blumstein, Alfred, Jacqueline Cohen, Susan Martin, and Michael Tonry, eds. 1983. *Research on Sentencing: The Search for Reform*. Washington, DC: National Academy Press.

Blumstein, Alfred, and Joel Wallman. 2006. "The Crime Drop and Beyond." *Annual Review of Laws and Social Sciences* 2:125–46.

Bobo, Lawrence, and Devon Johnson. 2004. "A Taste for Punishment: Black and White Americans' Views on the Death Penalty and the War on Drugs." *Du Bois Review* 1:151–80

Bonczar, Thomas P. 2003. "Prevalence of Imprisonment in the U.S. Population, 1974–2001." Washington, DC: U.S. Department of Justice, Bureau of Justice Statistics.

Cahalan, Margaret W. 1986. *Historical Correction Statistics in the United States, 1850–1984*. Washington, DC: U.S. Department of Justice, Bureau of Justice Statistics.

Chen, Emmeline S., and Tom R. Tyler. 2002. "Cloaking Power: Legitimizing Myths and the Psychology of the Advantaged." In *The Use and Abuse of Power: Multiple Perspectives on the Causes of Corruption*, edited by Annette Y. Lee-Chai and John A. Bargh. New York: Psychology Press, Taylor and Francis.

Clear, Todd. 2007. *Imprisoning Communities: How Mass Incarceration Makes Disadvantaged Neighborhoods Worse*. New York: Oxford University Press.

———. In this volume. "Communities with High Incarceration Rates."

Dills, Angela K., Jeffrey A. Miron, and Garrett Summers. 2008. "What Do Economists Know about Crime?" Working Paper no. 13759. Cambridge, MA: National Bureau of Economic Research.

Doob, Anthony, and Cheryl Webster. 2003. "Sentence Severity and Crime: Accepting the Null Hypothesis." In *Crime and Justice: A Review of Research*, vol. 30, edited by Michael Tonry. Chicago: University of Chicago Press.

Du Bois, W. E. B. 1988. "The Negro Criminal." In *The Economics of Race and Crime*, edited by Samuel L. Myers and Margaret C. Simms. New Brunswick, NJ: Transaction Books. (Originally published 1899.)

Eberhardt, Jennifer L., Paul G. Davies, Valerie J. Purdie-Vaughns, and Sheri Lynn Johnson. 2006. "Looking Deathworthy: Perceived Stereotypicality of Black Defendants Predicts Capital-Sentencing Outcomes." *Psychological Science* 17(5):383–86.

Eberhardt, Jennifer L., Phillip Atiba Goff, Valerie J. Purdie, and Paul G. Davies. 2004. "Seeing Black: Race, Crime and Visual Processing." *Journal of Personality and Social Psychology* 87(6):876–93.

Engel, Robin Shepard, and Jennifer M. Calnon. 2004. "Examining the Influence of Drivers' Characteristics during Traffic Stops with Police: Results from a National Survey." *Justice Quarterly* 21(1):49–90.

Fagan, Jeffrey, and Richard B. Freeman. 1999. "Crime and Work." In *Crime and Justice: A Review of Research*, vol. 25, edited by Michael Tonry. Chicago: University of Chicago Press.

Federal Bureau of Investigation. 2005. *Crime in the United States, 2004*. Washington, DC: U.S. Department of Justice.

Gest, Ted. 2001. *Crime and Politics: Big Government's Erratic Campaign for Law and Order*. New York: Oxford University Press.

Gilliard, Darrell K., and Allen J. Beck. 1996. *Prison and Jail Inmates, 1995*. Washington, DC: U.S. Department of Justice, Bureau of Justice Statistics.

Greenwald, Anthony, and Linda Hamilton Krieger. 2006. "Implicit Bias: Scientific Foundations." *California Law Review* 94:945–67.

Harrington, Michael P., and Cassia Spohn. 2007. "Defining Sentence Type: Further Evidence against Use of the Total Incarceration Variable." *Journal of Research in Crime and Delinquency* 44(1):36–63.

Hofstadter, Richard. 1965. *The Paranoid Style in American Politics and Other Essays*. Chicago: University of Chicago Press.

Jones, Trina. 2000. "Shades of Brown: The Law of Skin Color." *Duke Law Journal* 49:1487–1557.

Langan, Patrick. 1985. "Racism on Trial: New Evidence to Explain the Racial Composition of Prisons in the United States." *Journal of Criminal Law and Criminology* 76:666–83.

Lieberson, Stanley. 1980. *A Piece of the Pie—Blacks and White Immigrants since 1980*. Berkeley and Los Angeles: University of California Press.

Liptak, Adam. 2007. "Whittling Away, but Leaving a Gap." *New York Times* (November 17), p. A21.

Loury, Glenn C. 2002. *The Anatomy of Racial Inequality*. Cambridge, MA: Harvard University Press.

———. 2007. "Racial Stigma, Mass Incarceration and American Values." Tanner Lectures in Human Values delivered at Stanford University, April 4 and 5. http://www.econ.brown.edu/fac/Glenn_Loury/louryhomepage/.

MacCoun, Robert, and Karin D. Martin. Forthcoming. "Drug Abuse." In *Handbook on Crime and Punishment*, edited by Michael Tonry. New York: Oxford University Press.

Maddox, Keith B., and Stephanie A. Gray. 2002. "Cognitive Representations of Black Americans: Reexploring the Role of Skin Tone." *Personality and Social Psychology Bulletin* 28:250–59.

Massey, Douglas S. 2007. *Categorically Unequal*. New York: Russell Sage Foundation.

Massey, Douglas S., and Nancy Denton. 1993. *American Apartheid: Segregation and the Making of the Underclass*. Cambridge, MA: Harvard University Press.

Mauer, Marc. 2007. "Racial Impact Statements as a Means of Reducing Unwarranted Sentencing Disparities." *Ohio State Journal of Criminal Law* 5: 19–46.

McDonald, Douglas C., and Kenneth C. Carlson. 1993. *Sentencing in the Federal Courts: Does Race Matter?* Washington DC: U.S. Department of Justice, Bureau of Justice Statistics.

Moynihan, Daniel Patrick. 1965. *The Negro Family: The Case for National Action*. Washington, DC: U.S. Department of Labor, Office of Policy Planning and Research.

Murray, Joseph, and David P. Farrington. In this volume. "Effects of Parental Imprisonment in Children."

Myrdal, Gunnar. 1944. *An American Dilemma—the Negro Problem and Modern Democracy*. New York: Harper and Row.

Pizzi, William T., Irene V. Blair, and Charles M. Judd. 2005. "Discrimination in Sentencing on the Basis of Afrocentric Features." *Michigan Journal of Race and Law* 10:327–53.

Provine, Doris Marie. 2007. *Unequal under Law: Race in the War on Drugs*. Chicago: University of Chicago Press.

Raphael, Steven, Harry Holzer, and Michael Stoll. 2006. "How Do Crime and Incarceration Affect the Employment Prospects of Less Educated Black Men?" In *Black Males Left Behind*, edited by Ronald Mincy. Washington, DC: Urban Institute.

Sabol, William J., Todd D. Minton, and Paige M. Harrison. 2007. "Prison and Jail Inmates at Midyear 2006." Washington, DC: U.S. Department of Justice, Bureau of Justice Statistics.

Shane-Dubow, Sandra, Alice P. Brown, and Erik P. Olsen. 1985. *Sentencing Reform in the United States: History, Content and Effect*. Washington, DC: U.S. Government Printing Office.

Snell, Tracy L. 2007. "Capital Punishment, 2006." Washington, DC: U.S. Department of Justice, Bureau of Justice Statistics.

Spohn, Cassia. 2000. "Thirty Years of Sentencing Reform: The Quest for a Racially Neutral Sentencing Process." In *Criminal Justice 2000*, vol. 3, edited by the U.S. National Institute of Justice. Washington, DC: U.S. Department of Justice, National Institute of Justice.

———. 2002. *How Do Judges Decide? The Search for Fairness and Justice in Punishment*. Thousand Oaks, CA: Sage.

Tonry, Michael. 1995. *Malign Neglect: Race, Crime, and Punishment in America*. New York: Oxford University Press.

———. 1996. *Sentencing Matters*. New York: Oxford University Press.

———. 2004. *Thinking about Crime: Sense and Sensibility in American Penal Culture*. New York: Oxford University Press.

———. 2005. "Obsolescence and Immanence in Penal Theory and Policy." *Columbia Law Review* 105:1233–75.

———. 2008. "Crime and Human Rights—How Political Paranoia, Religious Fundamentalism, and Constitutional Obsolescence Combined to Devastate Black America." *Criminology* 46(1):1–34.

———. In this volume. "Learning from the Limits of Deterrence Research."

Unnever, James D., Francis T. Cullen, and Cheryl N. Lero-Jonson. In this volume. "Race, Racism, and Support for Capital Punishment."

U.S. Department of Commerce. 2006. *Statistical Abstract of the United States: 2007*. Washington, DC: U.S. Government Printing Office.

U.S. Sentencing Commission. 1995. *1995 Special Report to the Congress: Cocaine and Federal Sentencing Policy*. Washington, DC: U.S. Sentencing Commission.

———. 2007. *Cocaine and Federal Sentencing Policy*. Washington, DC: U.S. Sentencing Commission.

Wacquant, Loïc. 2002*a*. "Deadly Symbiosis: Rethinking Race and Imprisonment in Twenty-first-Century America." *Boston Review* (April/May).

———. 2002*b*. "From Slavery to Mass Incarceration." *New Left Review* 13(January–February):41–60.

Walker, Samuel, Cassia Spohn, and Miriam DeLone. 2006. *The Color of Justice: Race, Ethnicity, and Crime in America*. 4th ed. Belmont, CA: Wadsworth.

Walmsley, Roy. 2007. *World Prison Population List*. 7th ed. London: International Centre for Prison Studies.

Western, Bruce. 2006. *Punishment and Inequality in America*. New York: Russell Sage Foundation.

Wilson, James Q. 1990. "Drugs and Crime." In *Drugs and Crime*, edited by Michael Tonry and James Q. Wilson. Vol. 13 of *Crime and Justice: A Review of Research*, edited by Michael Tonry and Norval Morris. Chicago: University of Chicago Press.

Wilson, William Julius. 1978. *The Declining Significance of Race: Blacks and American Institutions*. Chicago: University of Chicago Press.

———. 1987. *The Truly Disadvantaged: The Inner City, the Underclass, and Public Policy*. Chicago: University of Chicago Press.

James D. Unnever, Francis T. Cullen, and Cheryl Lero Jonson

Race, Racism, and Support for Capital Punishment

ABSTRACT

There is a clear racial divide in support for the death penalty, with whites favoring and blacks opposing this sanction. This divide has persisted for decades and remains statistically and substantively significant even when controls are introduced for the known correlates of death penalty attitudes. A meaningful portion of this chasm is explained, however, by racism, with whites who manifest animus to blacks being more likely to embrace the lethal punishment of offenders. This relationship likely exists cross-nationally. Data from Great Britain, France, Spain, and Japan show that animosity to racial or ethnic minorities predicts support for capital punishment in these nations. In the United States, the greater support for capital punishment among whites, particularly those who harbor racial or ethnic resentments, undermines the legitimacy of the state and its use of the ultimate penalty. Consistent with conflict theory, white support of the death penalty is likely based on the perceived "social threat" posed by racial, ethnic, and immigrant groups. African American opposition to the death penalty is perhaps best explained by a historically rooted fear of state power, which is captured by the concept of the "state threat" hypothesis.

In the past half century, the United States experienced a dramatic transformation in race relations. The civil rights movement helped to usher in myriad political, social, and economic gains for minorities. These advances transformed the racial landscape, breaking down caste-like barriers and opening up diverse opportunities for inclusion and

James D. Unnever is associate professor of criminology at the University of South Florida–Sarasota. Francis T. Cullen is Distinguished Research Professor of Criminal Justice, and Cheryl Lero Jonson is a PhD student in criminal justice, both at the University of Cincinnati. We are grateful to Lydia Saad of the Gallup Organization for her generous assistance.

0192-3234/2008/0037-0001$10.00

social mobility (Thernstrom and Thernstrom 1997). This social convergence—the lives of blacks and whites becoming more alike—has potentially diminished race-specific views on everyday challenges and public policy. It is perhaps not surprising to learn that African Americans and whites embrace similar aspirations to pursue the American dream and move into the middle class (Wolfe 1998).

Other commentators paint a bleaker portrait. In many ways, contends Hacker (2003, book cover), the United States remains "two nations, black and white, separate, hostile, unequal." Race divides; it has the capacity to define issues and split America, seemingly at any moment. "For all the complexities of today's identity quarrels," observes Gitlin (1995, p. 228), "race is the origin or at least the template for most of them, and the concept of 'race,' the way most people use it, usually means the most profound either/or: black or white." As he continues, "History is stamped on the skin, a remark or a flash of anger away. The present is always rekindling the flammable past" (p. 229).

By Hacker's (2003, p. 252) account, "a huge racial chasm remains"—a cleavage that has concrete consequences. This divide between African Americans and whites is perhaps most strikingly illustrated by the prevailing degree of de facto racial segregation in housing—so much so that Massey and Denton (1993) refer to the nation's residential racial separation as "American apartheid." Even with some decline in the isolation of blacks from whites since 1990, the degree of segregation "remains extreme" in many metropolitan areas (Charles 2003, p. 172). Recent figures from the U.S. census confirm that "racial disparities in income, education and home ownership persist and, by some measurements, are growing" (Ohlemacher 2006, p. A1). Thus, as of 2005, three-fourths of whites owned their homes, compared to 46 percent of blacks; African Americans' household income was 60 percent of whites', a difference of $19,683; and, while 30 percent of whites held college degrees, only 17 percent of African Americans did (Ohlemacher 2006). Blacks are three times more likely than whites to live below the poverty line (24 percent vs. 8 percent) and almost twice as likely to lack health insurance (20 percent vs. 11 percent; Ulick 2005, p. 46).

Although disquieting, these global statistics mask the extent to which different types of race-based disadvantaged are concentrated in innercity neighborhoods, creating an underclass of the "truly disadvantaged" (Wilson 1987; Small and Newman 2001). These "savage inequalities," to borrow Kozol's (1991) phrase, were revealed by the differential impact of Hurricane Katrina within New Orleans. In the city's minority neighborhoods, where poverty rates doubled the national average, the capacity to escape and endure the aftermath of the hurricane was tragically circumscribed. The nation learned that in matters of race, New Orleans was "one city, two worlds" (Ulick 2005, p. 47).

These racial inequalities are reproduced within the realm of crime and criminal justice (Sampson and Lauritsen 1997). Studies show that racial inequality and related concentrated disadvantage are strong predictors of community differences in crime rates (Sampson, Raudenbush, and Earls 1997; Pratt and Cullen 2005; Peterson, Krivo, and Browning 2006). Compared with whites, African Americans have higher rates of criminal victimization and arrests (Catalano 2005; Federal Bureau of Investigation 2005; see also Barak, Leighton, and Flavin 2007). This racial disparity is especially pronounced for violent offenses. Although blacks constitute approximately 12 percent of the population, the number of black arrests for murder and nonnegligent manslaughter in 2004 was only slightly lower than the figure for whites (4,760 vs. 4,935), and it was higher within America's cities (3,530 vs. 2,913; Federal Bureau of Investigation 2005, pp. 298, 309). Most troubling, based on 2000 data, Fox and Zawitz (2003, p. 2) estimate that "blacks were 6 times more likely to be homicide victims and 7 times more likely than whites to commit homicides." African Americans also are differentially involved in the criminal justice system. There is an ongoing debate over whether this disparity is mainly due to blacks' greater involvement in crime or also due to discrimination in decision making by criminal justice officials (compare Thernstrom and Thernstrom 1997 to Tonry 1995; Miller 1996; Barak, Leighton, and Flavin 2007; see also Mitchell 2005). Regardless, it appears that in many cities, contact with the justice system is a common experience for African American males (Tonry 1995; Miller 1996; Mauer 1999). In 2005, it was reported that on any given day, 11.9 percent of black males between the ages of 20 and 39 were in prison or jail—an incarceration rate "5 to 7 times greater than those for white males in the same age groups" (Harrison and Beck 2006, p. 10). The Bureau of Justice Statistics (2006) further estimates that based on current rates of first incarceration for males, 32 percent of blacks will enter state or federal prison during their lifetime; the comparable figure is 17 percent for Hispanics and 5.9 percent for whites (see also Bonczar and Beck 1997).

In light of these seemingly intractable social and criminal justice disparities—all to the disadvantage of blacks—African Americans and whites might be expected to approach social issues, in this case crime control, with very different orientations. Tonry (2004) has recently introduced the term "sensibilities" to describe how people at a moment in history think about crime. These worldviews are "social and collective rather than idiosyncratic and individual" (p. 70). They do not fully determine how someone will think but compose a coherent cultural reality that shapes how a person is likely to interpret and evaluate events that transpire. Here, the key question is whether African Americans and whites have different sensibilities about the punishment of crime.

This potential racial divide in sensibilities in thinking about crime is important: it has clear implications for the legitimacy accorded to the criminal justice system. To the extent that blacks and whites hold different views on the fairness of the justice system, these feelings can surface and create racial conflict. In the O. J. Simpson case, for example, one poll found that "85 percent of blacks agreed with the verdict, while only 34 percent of the whites did" (Thernstrom and Thernstrom 1997, p. 516).

Kinder and Sanders (1996) provide a useful framework for understanding where, on policy issues, the racial divide in public opinion will be wide or narrow, differentiating among the domains of "race policy," "implicit racial issues," and general social issues. They note that concerning areas of "race policy"—especially "equal opportunity, federal assistance [for African Americans], and affirmative action"—the "differences between blacks and whites are extraordinary" (p. 27). For example, a 2003 poll of 1,201 adults in the United States conducted by the Pew Research Center found a gap of 32 percentage points in support for racial preferences between whites and nonwhites and a difference of 33 percentage points in the belief that programs to increase the number of minorities in college is a "good thing." Similarly, Kinder and Sanders (1996, p. 29) note that "blacks and whites also differ sharply over . . . 'implicit' or 'covert' racial policies. Such issues do not explicitly mention race but may be widely understood to have a racial implication" (e.g., support for food stamps or welfare). A recent example is the response to Hurricane Katrina. A 2005 survey of 1,252 respondents revealed that 79 percent of African Americans agreed that the federal government should spend whatever is necessary to rebuild and restore people in their homes in Hurricane Katrina's aftermath;

only 33 percent of whites endorsed this expenditure, a gap of 46 percentage points. The racial gap widened when the respondents were queried as to whether the federal government's response would have been faster if the victims had been whites; 84 percent of African Americans agreed, as opposed to just 20 percent of whites, a divide of 64 percentage points (Dawson, Lacewell, and Cohen 2006). However, on general policy issues, racial differences tend to be small and inconsistent, with "blacks and whites taking on roughly the same position" (Kinder and Sanders 1996, p. 29). For instance, "black Americans are noticeably more liberal on gay rights, but somewhat more conservative on school prayer" (p. 29).

Notably, a review of the existing literature suggests that there are three prominent points at which African American and white sensibilities differ and create a racial divide in thinking about crime and its punishment: perceptions of injustice, police behavior, and capital punishment. Consistent with Kinder and Sanders's (1996) perspective, each of these domains involves policies that are either explicitly or implicitly racial. An example of where the racial divide is not extensive is in citizens' ratings of the relative seriousness of different types of crimes and on the relative severity of the sentences they should receive (Jacoby and Cullen 1998). The racial implications in this domain are not clear, and attitudes converge.

The first area of racial divide is the extent to which people perceive that the criminal justice system is marked by injustice. Compared with whites, African Americans are more likely to believe that they are treated inequitably by criminal justice officials and by the courts at sentencing. Indeed, even with a range of factors controlled, race is a robust predictor of perceptions of injustice (see, e.g., Hagan and Albonetti 1982; Henderson et al. 1997; Wortley, Hagan, and Macmillan 1997; Roberts and Stalans 2000; Hagan, Shedd, and Payne 2005; Buckler, Unnever, and Cullen, forthcoming). These attitudes, moreover, are found across age and class position (Hagan and Albonetti 1982; Henderson et al. 1997; Weitzer and Tuch 1999; Brooks and Jeon-Slaughter 2001; Engel 2005; Hagan, Shedd, and Payne 2005).

Second, African Americans tend to have less confidence in or positive attitudes toward the police than do whites (see, e.g., Webb and Marshall 1995; Cao, Frank, and Cullen 1996; Hurst, Frank, and Browning 2000; Reisig and Parks 2000; cf. Frank et al. 1996). They are more likely to report that bias and racial profiling shape law enforcement's discretionary decision making (Weitzer 2000; Weitzer and Tuch 2002, 2005; Engel 2005; see also Barak, Leighton, and Flavin 2007). For example, African Americans perceive that they are disproportionately "hassled"—stopped without cause—by police officers (Browning et al. 1994; Engel 2005; Reitzel and Piquero 2006). African Americans also are less likely to endorse police use of force, including deadly force, against offenders (Cullen et al. 1996; Halim and Stiles 2001; Wilson and Dunham 2001).

The third area—and the focus of this essay—is the death penalty, which is often claimed to reflect both criminal injustice and differential application of force. It is instructive that there are strong racial differences in public support for capital punishment. Two hard facts characterize the death penalty. First, the United States is the only Western industrialized nation that executes convicted murderers, and, second, race is integrally implicated in the application of the death penalty within the nation. At year-end 2005, 36 states and the federal prison system held 3,254 prisoners under a sentence of death. Despite comprising only 12 percent of the population, blacks accounted for 42 percent of those under a capital sentence. This figure has been virtually unchanged since 1994, when it was 41 percent (Bonczar and Snell 2005). Again, commentators debate the reason for this disparity—differential involvement in capital crimes versus inequitable application of the death penalty (especially for African Americans who murder white victims; compare, e.g., Thernstrom and Thernstrom 1997 with Ogletree 2002; Radelet and Borg 2000). But the inescapable reality is that public policy debates on capital punishment cannot avoid this racial disparity.

In this context, it is perhaps not surprising that African Americans and whites have quite divergent sensibilities about capital punishment, with blacks decidedly less likely to support it (Barkan and Cohn 1994; Soss, Langbein, and Metelko 2003; Bobo and Johnson 2004; Baker, Lambert, and Jenkins 2005; Cochran and Chamlin 2006; Unnever and Cullen 2007*a*). This racial divide is often masked when references are made to national polling data—such as that reported by the General Social Survey (GSS) and Gallup polls—showing that upwards of 70 percent of Americans who are surveyed express support for executing convicted murderers. As Igo (2007, p. 19) illuminates in *The Averaged American*, opinion polls historically have captured the sentiments of the typical respondent, with the "aggregating technologies, by their very nature, [placing] new cultural emphasis on the center point, the scientifically derived mean and median." But there is a cost to reporting what this representative citizen believes. "Proclamations about 'Americans' could not be made without suppressing the voices and experiences of some," observes Igo (p. 18). The pollsters' "suppositions about who constituted the public meant that some Americans—African Americans, immigrants, and poor people, among others—were systematically excluded from their statistics, and that the nation surveyed was always a partial one" (pp. 18–19).

This socially constructed reality that the American public supports capital punishment is consequential. Politicians and public law enforcement personnel often ignore African Americans' voices—blacks' opposition to capital punishment—and justify their own support for the death penalty by noting that they are simply responding to public opinion. Consider, for example, the remarks by then-governor George Pataki as he announced his success in having the state of New York reinstate capital punishment. "September 1, 1995, marked the end of a long fight for justice in New York and the beginning of a new era in our state that promises safer communities, fewer victims of crime, and renewed personal freedom." Continuing on, he noted that for "22 consecutive years, my predecessors had ignored the urgent calls for justice from our citizens—their repeated and pressing demands for the death penalty in New York State. Even after the legislature passed a reinstatement of the capital punishment law, it was vetoed for 18 years in a row" (Pataki 1997). Similarly, on his relatively well-known pro–death penalty Web site, an Indiana prosecuting attorney observed that "along with almost three-fourths of the American public, I believe in capital punishment. I believe that there are some defendants who have earned the ultimate punishment our society has to offer by committing murder with aggravating circumstances present" (Stewart 2007). Echoing these sentiments, in 2000, Texas Governor George W. Bush asserted that "the reason I support the death penalty is because it saves lives. That's why I support it, and the people of my state support it too" (quoted in *On the Issues* 2000).

As Gottschalk (2006) documents, capital punishment was not a highly contentious political issue until the 1970s. Public opinion initially emerged as relevant when the Supreme Court began to assess whether executions violated society's "evolving standards of decency" (p. 219). However, as Gottschalk shows, the salience of public opinion in the death penalty debate was dramatically heightened in the immediate aftermath of the U.S. Supreme Court's *Furman v. Georgia* decision (408 U.S. 228 [1972]), which vacated over 600 death sentences. In arguing against this decision, the dissenting jurists asserted that the American public still supported capital punishment. As Gottschalk (2006, pp. 218–19) notes:

> This was a dramatic reframing of the issue of capital punishment that had wider political repercussions. It essentially legitimized public sentiment as the main political terrain on which the death penalty would be contested . . . over the coming decades. It contributed to a collapse between the state and society in the making of penal policy not experienced elsewhere. This helped to legitimate a Roman Coliseum view of how to make penal policy. If the Romans wanted Christians thrown to the lions, so be it. . . . Even though Furman was a muddled decision, it was pivotal in steering the debate in this direction because the fiercest opponents and proponents did agree on one thing: public sentiment was critical.

Importantly, scholars have raised some disconcerting issues related to politicians and the courts basing their justification for supporting capital punishment on American public opinion. Again, this focus on the "average American" (Igo 2007) obscures black voices: whereas the majority of whites support the death penalty, the majority of African Americans oppose state executions. Scholars also question the degree to which racial animus shapes public opinion. Indeed, some scholars even question whether the base support for capital punishment resides among whites who harbor racial resentments (Barkan and Cohn 1994; Soss, Langbein, and Metelko 2003; Unnever and Cullen 2007*a*).

In this context, Section I explores the extent to which African Americans and whites differ in their support for the death penalty and documents a clear, long-standing racial divide in attitudes. Section II examines two theses that might account for this racial divide. One suggests that race is of declining significance; its effects will disappear—are spurious—once other correlates of death penalty attitudes are controlled. The second thesis contends that certain subgroups of African Americans who socially converge with whites (e.g., hold conservative political values) will have opinions that mirror their white counterparts. There is little support for either of these propositions. To a degree, it appears that being an African American is, to use Hughes's (1945) classic concept, a "master status" that shapes sensibilities about the death penalty. As Hughes (1945, p. 357) observes, "Membership in the Negro race . . . may be called a master status-determining trait. It tends to overpower, in most crucial situations, any other characteristic that might run counter to it" (see also Becker 1963). In the current case, the thesis is that for African Americans, their racial status trumps other social statuses in shaping their views toward the death penalty.

Section III then probes whether racism or animus toward African Americans helps to explain why whites are more likely to support the death penalty. The analysis reveals that, to a disquieting extent, negative sentiment about African Americans is a robust predictor of support for the death penalty. Let us hasten to caution that any discussion of "racism" is fraught with difficulty. As Goldhagen (2007) recently commented about anti-Semitism, the construct covers accusations from "Jews are cheap" to the eliminationist ideology that justified the Holocaust (see also Goldhagen 1997). Racism is a similarly expansive construct that might be expressed in various ways, ranging from offensive and ill-informed stereotypes to hate. In the capital punishment research, diverse measures have been used to capture animus toward blacks. Individual studies can be challenged for employing limited measures (often constructed from items available in secondary data sets) that assess only a slice of the complex construct of "racism." The field awaits a study that unpacks racism into its components and tests each dimension's effects systematically. Even so, taken together, the extant studies reach remarkably consistent results: negative views toward African Americans—what scholars in this area have termed "racism" or "racial animus"—predict a range of political attitudes, including greater support for capital punishment.

Section IV considers whether the findings on the effects of racism in the United States are a matter of American exceptionalism or portend a broad trend found in other advanced Western-style democracies. The case that the findings are idiosyncratic to the United States rests on the country's unique racial history and enduring racial problem. Increasingly, however, Western nations are addressing the issue of immigration and the presence of ethnic and racial minorities. The literature on the topic is limited, but extant data sets do allow us to investigate whether racial or ethnic animus affects death penalty attitudes globally. As we show, such animus is a strong predictor of support for capital punishment in every nation analyzed.

Section V concludes by suggesting two hypotheses to account for the impact of race and racism on death penalty attitudes. First, we propose that African Americans' wariness about capital punishment is based on a historically rooted view of the state as posing a threat to their well-being. Second, we propose that white racial animosity is associated with support for capital punishment because minorities, including African Americans, are perceived to pose a "social threat." Finally, we raise the possibility that the hidden cost of the continued execution of offenders is that it exacerbates racial conflict and reduces the legitimacy of the state.

I. The Racial Divide in Support for Capital Punishment

The GSS is a personal interview survey of U.S. households that is conducted almost annually by the National Opinion Research Center (NORC). James A. Davis, Tom W. Smith, and Peter V. Marsden are the principal investigators. The first survey took place in 1972, and since then more than 38,000 respondents have answered over 3,260 different questions. Notably, previous researchers have used the GSS to show that African Americans are less likely than whites to support capital punishment (Combs and Comer 1982; Cochran and Chamlin 2006). Also using the GSS, we extend their analysis to assess the racial divide in public opinion across a 30-year time span. Figure 1 shows the level of support for the death penalty by whites and African Americans from 1974 to 2004.

Across this entire period, African Americans are substantively less likely than whites to support the death penalty; there is a clear and persistent racial divide in public opinion. As seen in figure 1, in 1974, 69.8 percent of whites and 39.9 percent of African Americans supported the death penalty—a gap of 29.9 percentage points. In 2004, 72.5 percent of whites and 41.7 percent of African Americans supported capital punishment—a gap of 30.8 percentage points. Thus, over a 30-year period, the divide between whites and African Americans in their opinions about the death penalty has remained virtually the same.

On average, these data indicate that 77.5 percent of whites over the years supported the death penalty compared with 49.3 percent of African Americans. Therefore, these data suggest that whereas a strong

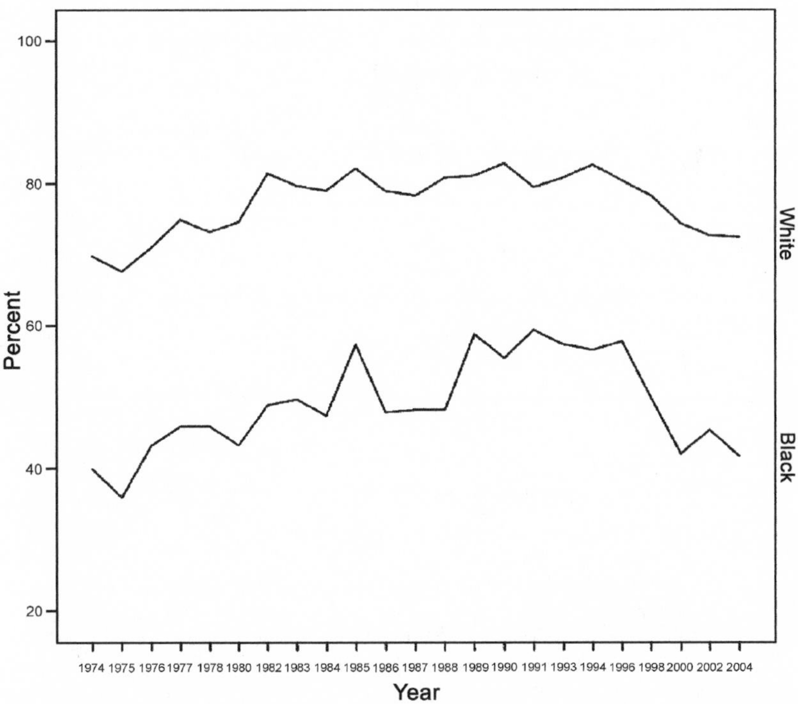

FIG. 1.—Percent in support of capital punishment by race, 1974–2004. Source: General Social Surveys, Cumulative File, 1972–2004 (Davis, Smith, and Marsden 2005). Response is to the question "Do you favor or oppose the death penalty for persons convicted of murder?"

majority of whites support capital punishment, African Americans' opposition to this sanction is extensive (50.7 percent).

A similar portrait of the racial divide is provided by data compiled through the Gallup Poll. As can be seen from table 1, over the past two decades, white support for capital punishment has consistently equaled or exceeded 70 percent, whereas African American support has typically hovered around 50 percent. During the current decade, it is notable that black endorsement of the death penalty has declined markedly, from over 50 percent in the 1990s to a mean of 42.0 percent in the 2000s. Across all years represented in table 1, the average percentage supporting the death penalty has been 71.8 percent for whites and 44.2 percent for African Americans, a difference of 27.6 percentage points.

TABLE 1

Percent Support for Capital Punishment by Race: Gallup Polls, 1972–2006

Year	White	African American
1972*	57	27
1978	64	41
1981	70	42
1985*	77	52
1986–88*	78	52
1991–94*	80	56
1995–99	77	52
2000*	70	38
2001*	71	38
2002*	75	50
2003*	74	41
2004–5*	70	42
2006*	70	43

SOURCES.—Personal communication from Lydia Saad (May 1, 2007); see also Saad (2007).

NOTE.—Question asked in the Gallup Poll: "Are you in favor of the death penalty for a person convicted of murder?" The polling data are averaged because either more than one poll was undertaken within a given year or small samples required using polls conducted across years or both.

* Averaged score for a given year or across years.

Harris Poll data are consistent with the results from the GSS and Gallup surveys (Taylor 2004). The respondents were asked, "Do you believe in capital punishment, that is, the death penalty, or are you opposed to it?" The percentages of whites and blacks supporting capital punishment were as follows: 1999, 77 percent versus 39 percent; 2000, 71 percent versus 36 percent; 2001, 73 percent versus 46 percent; and 2003, 74 percent versus 40 percent. Across these four years, the gap between whites and African Americans is 33.5 percentage points (73.8 percent vs. 40.3 percent).

Clearly, a racial divide in American public opinion about capital punishment exists and is enduring. These results also qualify any claims that the "American public" strongly embraces the use of the death penalty. In reality, the data show that this ostensible social reality is generated mainly by the responses of whites and is not applicable to the "African American public." This failure to disaggregate opinion polls—the long-standing tendency to focus exclusively on what Igo

(2007) calls the "averaged American"—inadvertently privileges or treats as normative a white as opposed to an Afrocentric view of the world.

Scholars recognize that the wording of the death penalty question alters the level of support expressed by the respondents (Roberts and Hough 2005). Cullen, Fisher, and Applegate (2000) discuss this phenomenon. They note that support for capital punishment declines considerably when respondents are offered the choice between executing convicted murderers or sentencing them to life without the possibility of parole. For example, in a study of Tennessee residents, Moon et al. (2000) report that 76 percent of the respondents favored the death penalty for adults. By contrast, when they were offered the alternative of life without the possibility of parole, 45 percent preferred this option to the death penalty (see also Vogel and Vogel 2003).

The methodological concern is whether the racial divide holds when the question format changes from asking whether people support the death penalty for convicted offenders (yes or no) to whether they support the death penalty versus life imprisonment without the possibility of parole. Unnever and Cullen (2005) show that a racial divide persists even when respondents are asked, first, whether they support the death penalty or, second, whether they support the death penalty when life imprisonment without the possibility of parole is an alternative. Using data from a 2003 Gallup poll, these researchers constructed a dichotomous measure (1 = favors the death penalty; 0 = life imprisonment without the possibility of parole). The data set also contained a more traditional yes-no measure of support for capital punishment. In a multivariate model controlling for a range of attitudinal predictors, Unnever and Cullen showed that regardless of which question was asked, African Americans were statistically and substantively less likely to support the death penalty (a two-tailed test of significance where $p < .05$).

Another consideration is whether the racial divide is affected by the use of a Likert scale to investigate the extent to which the respondents support the death penalty (strongly disagree to strongly agree) as opposed to a dichotomous yes-no response set. Unnever and Cullen (2007*a*) analyzed the 2000 National Election Study (NES), which included a measure that assessed the degree to which individuals support the death penalty. The respondents included in this national poll were first asked the following question: "Do you favor or oppose the death penalty for persons convicted of murder?" Two responses were offered: "favor" or "oppose." They were then asked either "Do you favor the death penalty for persons convicted of murder strongly or not strongly?" or "Do you oppose the death penalty for persons convicted of murder strongly or not strongly?" The responses to these questions were used to construct a Likert scale that assessed the level of support for capital punishment. In the multivariate analysis of this measure, race was again found to be one of the most substantive predictors of support for capital punishment ($\beta = .13, p < .001$), with whites expressing greater levels of support than African Americans. In conjunction with the findings noted above, this study shows that there is a racial divide regardless of how public opinion about capital punishment is measured.

II. Social Convergence as an Explanation of the Racial Divide

In the early 1970s, researchers put forth the argument that the United States was becoming a great "melting pot" and that through "assimilation" there would be a convergence of public opinion across a spectrum of public policy issues including the death penalty (Glenn 1974–75). The assimilation, or social convergence, hypothesis thus suggests that racial differences in attitudes toward capital punishment occur only because African Americans and whites differ in their structural locations, political worldview, or religious beliefs (Unnever and Cullen 2007*b*). The assimilation, or social convergence, perspective therefore suggests that African Americans and whites who are similarly situated will have the same opinions about the death penalty. Below, we consider two versions of this explanation.

A. The Declining Significance of Race Hypothesis

This hypothesis suggests that although racial differences in death penalty attitudes appear, they are not due to race, per se, but to variables associated both with African American status and with level of support for capital punishment (e.g., disadvantaged structural location, liberal political attitudes, and mistrust in government; see Cochran and Chamlin 2006; Unnever and Cullen 2007*b*). When these variables are controlled, the impact of race on capital punishment opinions should decrease markedly, even to the point of being fully spurious. Therefore, this hypothesis suggests that race is not a master status that organizes sensibilities about punishment. To address this thesis, we focus on two questions: First, can other factors account for the racial divide in public opinion about the death penalty? Second, if they cannot, then how much of the gap between African American and white public opinion about capital punishment do they explain?

1. *Do Other Factors Account for the Racial Divide?* The answer to this question is no; the racial divide in public opinion about capital punishment remains, regardless of what correlates are included in the analysis. For example, Stack (2003) analyzed the 1985 and 1990 GSS and regressed (using logistic regression) support for the death penalty on 21 correlates (including, e.g., gender, age, marital status, region, political orientation, and authoritarianism). Even with these variables in his multivariate analysis, he found that race was a substantive predictor of support for capital punishment (odds ratio = 3.95). African Americans were significantly less likely to support the death penalty than whites (Wald $\chi^2 = 29.36$).

In a more recent study, Cochran and Chamlin (2006) set out to examine systematically whether racial differences in other social domains (e.g., structural locations, attitudes, experience with crime, and criminal justice) could account for the racial divide in public support for capital punishment. They investigated the cumulative GSS (from 1972 to 1996). They also undertook a supplementary analysis of data drawn from two surveys, conducted in 1999 ($n = 636$) and in 2000 ($n = 697$), of adults randomly called to jury service in Hillsborough County (Tampa), Florida.

Cochran and Chamlin (2006) report that an analysis of their first Tampa-based survey showed that 69.7 percent of the white respondents supported capital punishment, compared with 51.0 percent of the black respondents. This difference was statistically significant ($p < .05$), and the odds of death penalty support were substantially greater for whites than for blacks (odds ratio = 0.464). They also found a racial gap when analyzing the data from their second Tampa-based survey. This time they found that 86.4 percent of the whites supported capital punishment, compared with 64.4 percent of the black respondents. There were significant differences in the level of death penalty support ($p < .05$), and the odds of blacks supporting capital punishment were less than a third the odds of whites (odds ratio = 0.279). Notably, when controlling for a roster of variables, their analysis of the cumulative GSS reproduced a significant racial gap ($p < .05$) in public support for the death penalty.

Thus, Cochran and Chamlin (2006, p. 97) conclude that racial differences in death penalty support were not the result of "differences in socioeconomic status achievements, subcultural orientations, political persuasion, religion, right-to-life views, attitudes support for social welfare, views on distributive justice, perceptions about criminal justice, fear of crime, victimization experience, media exposure, punitiveness, nor attribution styles." Clearly, race is of enduring, not declining, significance in shaping views toward the execution of offenders.

2. *How Much Do the Correlates Narrow the Racial Divide?* To address this issue, we turn to Unnever and Cullen's (2007*a*) analysis of data from the cumulative GSS, conducted by the NORC. Their sample comprised the years 1974, 1976, 1977, 1980, 1982, 1984, 1987–91, 1993, 1994, 1996, 1998, 2000, and 2002 and included 13,823 respondents, of whom 1,915 were African American.

Initially, using binary logistic regression, Unnever and Cullen examined whether race directly affected support for the death penalty, while controlling for age, gender, education, central city residence, church attendance, and fear of walking alone at night. After these factors were controlled, African Americans were significantly less likely than whites to support capital punishment ($p < .001$). They next examined the degree to which other factors—born and currently living in the South, affiliation with a Christian fundamentalist denomination, confidence in the government, and having a conservative political orientation—mediated the effect of race on support for capital punishment. The influence of race decreased after including these other correlates, but only 10 percent of the effect of the race coefficient on support for the death penalty was mediated or accounted for by the other variables in the model. Notably, after controlling for their entire array of correlates, they still found that African Americans were significantly less likely than whites to support capital punishment ($p < .001$). In short, the extant research indicates that African Americans are less likely to support the death penalty, everything else being equal, and that other plausible attitudinal predictors decrease the racial divide in support for capital punishment only marginally.

B. The Subgroup Hypothesis

Scholars have examined the social convergence hypothesis from a second angle. The social convergence hypothesis posits that the effects of assimilation should be equal across race, with these ameliorating factors bringing African Americans and whites closer together. Unnever and Cullen (2007*b*) have investigated this possibility (for a description of this study, see above). They examined whether factors that should bridge the racial divide in support for capital punishment equally affect African Americans and whites. They tested whether the effects of income, being a southerner, having confidence in the government, having a conservative political orientation, and belonging to a Christian fundamentalist denomination on public support for the death penalty varied across race. This was assessed by entering interaction terms into the equation (e.g., race × income).

This analysis allows for an assessment of whether there are specific subgroups of African Americans whose views coincide with those of white respondents. We might expect that African Americans who are affluent, from the South, have confidence in the government, are conservative, and are religious fundamentalists would be more likely to support the death penalty. Thus, it is reasonable to assume, for example, that whites and African Americans who identified themselves as very politically conservative would equally support capital punishment

Unnever and Cullen (2007*b*) found that the five factors noted above each increased support for capital punishment among whites to some degree. They report that the predicted probability of whites with the highest income level supporting capital punishment was .814, and the predicted probability for whites with the least amount of income was .638, a difference of 17.6 percent, everything else being equal. The predicted probability of native southern whites supporting capital punishment was .801, and the predicted probability for nonnative southerners was .779, a difference of 2.2 percent, while controlling for the other covariates. The predicted probability of supporting the death penalty for whites with a great deal of confidence in government officials was .784, and the predicted probability for whites with hardly any confidence was .787, a difference of .003 percent. The predicted probability of extremely conservative whites supporting capital punishment was .928, and the predicted probability for extremely liberal whites was .674, a difference of 25.4 percent. The predicted probability of white fundamentalists supporting capital punishment was .805, and the predicted probability for white nonfundamentalists was .779, a difference of 2.6 percent.

The impact among African Americans, however, was more complex. For blacks in the sample, income and confidence in the government did increase death penalty support. But the effects were limited, with the level of support for capital punishment for African Americans who are affluent and who trust the government remaining far below that of whites with similar views (a gap of about 20 percentage points). Further, the influence of being a political conservative had little impact on African American death penalty attitudes (in contrast to its substantive impact on white sentiments), and embracing fundamentalist religious beliefs actually increased the racial divide in support for the death penalty (see Britt 1998). Similarly, the predicted probability of native southern African Americans supporting the death penalty was .515, and the predicted probability for nonnative southern blacks was .585. Thus, being a native southern African American decreased support for capital punishment by 7 percentage points.

C. Summary: Race as a Master Status

Taken together, these results suggest that the racial divide in support for capital punishment is not spurious or limited to a specific segment of the African American community. Instead, race appears to be a master status (Hughes 1945), a social location that distinctly shapes how African Americans think about the death penalty. Ambivalence about, if not outright opposition to, the death penalty appears integral to African American sensibilities about crime and its punishment. What might explain this reluctance by African Americans to embrace the state's use of lethal sanction against those convicted of murder?

Contemporary factors do not fully account for African Americans' disproportionate opposition to the death penalty. Even when a range of factors are controlled—including indicators of social and economic disadvantage—a racial divide persists. Further, racial differences in support for capital punishment are long-standing and not due to recent social or political events. These findings lead us to conclude that African Americans' views on capital punishment are cultural and deeply rooted. Compared with whites, African Americans have a different cultural sensibility concerning the death penalty. We return to this issue in the final section of this essay.

III. Racism and Support for the Death Penalty

Americans with negative attitudes toward African Americans—views described in the literature interchangeably as "racism" or as "racial animus"—tend to interpret crime-related policies through a racial lens (Cohn, Barkan, and Halteman 1991; Young 1992; Barkan and Cohn

1994; Borg 1997; Arthur 1998; Johnson 2001; Sears and Henry 2003; Soss, Langbein, and Metelko 2003; Bobo and Johnson 2004; Chiricos, Welch, and Gertz 2004; Young 2004; Barkan and Cohn 2005). This interest in racism shifts the focus from the social convergence of African Americans with the dominant social order to how whites' views on race might contribute to the racial divide in support for capital punishment. In this section, we explore whether the animus toward African Americans among whites enhances their support for capital punishment.

A. The Changing Face of American Racism

On a broad level, Feagin and Sikes (1994, p. 3) define racism as both "the prejudices and discriminatory actions of particular white bigots" and the "institutionalized discrimination and . . . the recurring ways in which white people dominate black people in almost every major area of this society." A key component of racism is thus negative beliefs about and feelings toward African Americans. Within the public opinion area, scholars explicitly employ the term "racism" to describe white sentiments toward blacks, and they suggest that racism still shapes American public policy opinion, including opinion about capital punishment, in the twenty-first century. Consistent with usage in this scholarly domain, we use the terms "racism" or "racial animus" in our discussions of this literature.

In using the concept of racism, it is important to be judicious since this term is not only difficult to define precisely but, when applied, also pregnant with social stigma. In this regard, some scholars have suggested that the concept of racism—especially "symbolic racism" (discussed below)—may be used inappropriately to describe white attitudes about race that are based on conservative principles, such as individualism and strict equal opportunity, rather than on antipathy to minorities (for discussions, see Bobo, Kluegel, and Smith [1997] and Sears et al. [2000]). Thus, opposition to welfare or affirmative action may be principled—"everyone should be treated equally regardless of race"—and not a sign of racial animus or resentment; saying that "blacks are more violent" may be a rough, practical estimate of racial disparities in crime and not an expression of antipathy. Further, it is possible that these underlying conservative beliefs produce views toward both blacks and capital punishment, thus rendering spurious any apparent association between racial attitudes and crime policy attitudes.

Two considerations, however, undermine these arguments. First, the multivariate analyses demonstrating the impact of measures of racism or racial animus on support for capital punishment control for a wide range of variables, including political and religious conservatism (see also Sears et al. 2000, p. 18). In these studies, conservatism tends to have statistically significant effects, but racial animus remains a robust predictor of death penalty attitudes. Second, studies using diverse measures of racism—a number of which are composed of items clearly tapping into antipathy toward African Americans and not conservative principles—reach the same conclusion: negative feelings toward blacks increase punitive sentiments, including embrace of the death penalty. The consensus of the social science literature is that racism—whether expressed through prejudice, stereotypes, negative affect, or resentment—remains a source of Americans' views toward crime control and a range of public policies (Kinder and Sanders 1996; Tuch and Martin 1997; Hurwitz and Peffley 1998; Sears, Sidanius, and Bobo 2000).

In any event, it is important to note that contemporary racism has experienced an important transformation that has led to much controversy over how best to capture its essence. Historically, white racism manifested itself through Jim Crow racism. "Jim Crow" racism, or "old racism," is built on derogations of African Americans as genetically and socially inferior. These negative stereotypes referred to African Americans as being unintelligent, lazy, and untrustworthy. This belief system was linked to the collateral notion that "blacks were supposed to 'stay in their place,' separate and subordinate to whites, especially in public" and to legal practices that enforced discrimination (Sears et al. 2000, p. 9).

Scholars have noted that this traditional form of racism and its impact on public opinion have declined over time (Kinder and Sanders 1996). The scholarly challenge is to describe what has emerged in its place—a set of attitudes that is more subtle and less obviously racist (Sears et al. 2000). Most often, researchers refer to this new, or "modern," form of racism as "symbolic racism," as "racial resentments," or as African Americans being "culturally deficient" (Bobo and Kluegel 1993; Kinder and Sanders 1996; Bonilla-Silva 1997; Sears et al. 1997; Virtanen and Huddy 1998; Sears et al. 2000; Feagin and O'Brien 2003; Sears and Henry 2003).

The literature on symbolic racism or racial resentment argues that individuals who currently harbor racial animus no longer believe African Americans are genetically inferior to whites or talk about them in these terms. Thus, their racism is not manifested in coarse negative stereotypes portraying African Americans as biologically deficient. While such thinking declines,

> the socialization of negative affect and stereotypes about blacks continues, leaving a reservoir of racial antipathy decoupled from racialist beliefs. . . . Blacks are perceived by many whites to violate such cherished American values as the work ethic, self-reliance, impulse control, and obedience to authority. The new racism is said to derive from a coalescing of negative racial affect with the perceived violation of such traditional values. Finally, the content of the new racism includes the beliefs that discrimination no longer poses a major barrier to the advancement of blacks, that blacks should try harder to make it on their own, that they are demanding too much, and that they are often given special treatment by government and other elites. (Sears et al. 2000, p. 17; see also Kinder and Sanders 1996)

This perspective thus emphasizes that symbolic racism is a mixture of "individualistic interpretation of social problems" (by itself not racist) with "antiblack feeling" (Sears, Henry, and Kosterman 2000, p. 108). This emergent set of beliefs leads to the view that whites are not responsible for existing racial barriers and inequality and that if there is a group that deserves government assistance, it is white males (Hogan, Chiricos, and Gertz 2005). In short, there is racial resentment (Kinder 1986; Kinder and Sanders 1996). As Chiricos, Hogan, and Gertz (1997, p. 124) state, "Today, much racial anger and fear among whites are directed toward the 'gains' that African-Americans have made in the workplace as a result of affirmative action, and resonate the economic insecurities of a changing 'global economy.'" They add that any relationship that is found between white racial animus and support for more punitive crime control policies, such as the death penalty, may reflect an "angry White male phenomenon" (Hogan, Chiricos, and Gertz 2005, p. 405). They argue that this phenomenon reflects a belief among "angry White males" (p. 395) that there is an "undeserving poor" (p. 392)—consisting of welfare recipients, recent immigrants, beneficiaries of affirmative action, and criminals. Hogan and his colleagues conclude that "angry White males" express their economic insecurity and animus toward the "undeserving poor" through a "vocabulary of punitive motive" that results in their endorsement of harsh crime control policies (2005, p. 405).

The focus on this "new racism" should not obscure the fact that even if in decline, prejudice against African Americans has hardly vanished. Sniderman, Piazza, and Harvey (1998, pp. 26–27) note that "prejudice consists in attributions (1) about groups or members of groups, by virtue of their membership in the group, that are (2) disparaging and hostile, (3) false, or at least without warrant, and (4) consistently made." In this regard, Peffley and Hurwitz show that racial stereotypes continue to be prevalent. Thus, in a survey of 1,841 respondents, they found that "a substantial proportion of whites" agreed that "most blacks are lazy (31 percent), not determined to succeed (22 percent), aggressive (50 percent), and lacking in discipline (60 percent)" (1998, pp. 62–63). They conclude, "A sizable number of whites—as many as one in two—openly endorses frankly negative characterizations of 'most' blacks" (p. 63). They also demonstrate that these negative stereotypes clearly shape views toward welfare and crime.

The literature on support for capital punishment has not ignored the question of whether whites who harbor racial resentments and negative views toward African Americans are especially likely to endorse the execution of convicted murderers. Below we review this literature.

B. *Racism and Support for the Death Penalty*

Studies based on data collected by various polling organizations and using various measures of racial prejudice report that racial animosity is one of the most robust and consistent predictors of support for the death penalty (Barkan and Cohn 1994; Borg 1997; Soss, Langbein, and Metelko 2003; Bobo and Johnson 2004; see also Elberhardt et al. 2006). Barkan and Cohn (1994), using the 1990 GSS, created two measures of racial prejudice. Their "Antipathy to Blacks" scale was constructed using two items that asked respondents to indicate the degree to which they favored or opposed "living in a neighborhood where half your neighbors were Blacks" and "having a close relative or family member marry a Black person" (p. 203). Their "racial stereotyping" scale was constructed using six items that asked respondents to indicate on seven-point scales the degree to which they thought African Americans were lazy, unintelligent, wanting to live off of welfare, unpatriotic, violent, and poor. The alpha reliability coefficient for the antipathy to blacks scale was .67, and for the racial stereotype scale, it was .69. Using logistic regression and one-tailed tests of significance, Barkan and Cohn (1994, p. 206) found that "White people are both prejudiced against Blacks and more likely to favor capital punishment."

Also employing data from the GSS (1974–94), Arthur (1998) investigated the effects of racial attitudes on death penalty attitudes. His analysis consistently showed that racial animus increased punitiveness. For example, capital punishment was significantly related to such beliefs as whites "having the right to keep blacks out of their neighborhoods if they want to," whites being able to exclude blacks from their social clubs, blacks "not having the motivation or will power to pull themselves out of poverty," and blacks getting "more attention from the government than they deserve" (pp. 138–39).

Similarly, employing the 1992 American NES, Soss, Langbein, and Metelko (2003) created a racial prejudice scale. They constructed the scale to capture both the cognitive and affective components of anti-black racial attitudes. It was based on three measures of group stereotyping and one measure of group-based antipathy. The stereotype items assessed the difference between how white respondents rated black as opposed to white people on the traits of intelligence, laziness, and propensity toward violence. Their affective measure was a standard feeling thermometer score indicating how "warm" or "cool" white respondents feel toward African Americans. A factor analysis of these four variables produced a single-factor solution, suggesting that, as a group, they measure a coherent underlying construct. Using ordered logistic regression and two-tailed tests of significance, Soss, Langbein, and Metelko (2003) found that the most robust predictor of whites' support for the death penalty was their level of racial prejudice.

Bobo and Johnson (2004) engaged this topic by analyzing the 2001 Race, Crime, and Public Opinion Study. They created a "racial resentment" scale by averaging responses to the following six items: (1) "Irish, Italian, Jewish and many other minorities overcame prejudice and worked their way up. Blacks should do the same without any special favors." (2) "Over the past few years, Blacks have gotten less than they deserve." (3) "Government officials usually pay less attention to a request or complaint from a Black person than from a White person." (4) "Most Blacks who receive money from welfare programs could get along without it if they tried." (5) "It's really a matter of some people not trying hard enough; if Blacks would only try harder, they could be just as well off as Whites." And (6) "generations of slavery and discrimination have created conditions that make it difficult for Blacks to work their way out of the lower class" (Bobo and Johnson 2004, p. 158). Using ordinary least squares (OLS) regression and two-tailed tests of significance, they report that their racial resentment scale was a significant predictor of support for capital punishment.

Finally, Unnever and Cullen (2007*a*, p. 1301) attempted systematically to analyze the relationship between racial animus and support for the death penalty. Using the 2000 NES, they constructed a scale that measured negative racial stereotypes, or Jim Crow racism. The scale was based on the following three items: (1) "Where would you rate blacks on a scale of 1 to 7 (where 1 indicates hard working, 7 means lazy, and 4 indicates most blacks are not closer to one end or the other)?" (2) "Where would you rate blacks on a scale of 1 to 7 (where 1 indicates intelligent, 7 means unintelligent, and 4 indicates most blacks are not closer to one end or the other)?" And (3) "where would you rate blacks on a scale of 1 to 7? (1 indicates trustworthy, 7 is untrustworthy, and 4 indicates most blacks are not closer to one end or the other)." They also developed a scale that measured racial resentment, or symbolic racism. This scale was based on four items: (1) "Irish, Italians, Jewish and many other minorities overcame prejudice and worked their way up. Blacks should do the same without any special favors." (2) "Over the past few years, blacks have gotten less than they deserve." (3) "It's really a matter of some people not trying hard enough; if blacks would only try harder, they could be just as well off as whites." And (4) "generations of slavery and discrimination have created conditions that make it difficult for blacks to work their way out of the lower class" (p. 1300).

Using OLS regression, Unnever and Cullen (2007*a*) assessed the degree to which the American public supported the death penalty on both of these scales simultaneously. The analysis contained a variety of other correlates, including, for example, political conservatism. They found that Jim Crow racism failed to achieve statistical significance as a predictor of public support for the death penalty, while controlling for symbolic racism ($\beta = .00$, $p > .05$, two-tailed test of significance). However, their results indicated that their measure of symbolic racism positively predicted the degree to which Americans supported capital punishment. Indeed, symbolic racism was the most robust predictor of the strength of support for the death penalty, while controlling for other correlates ($\beta = .20$, $p < .001$, two-tailed test of significance).

Using the 2002 GSS, Unnever, Cullen, and Fisher (2005, p. 12) examined the relationship between support for the death penalty and racial and ethnic animus. First, they constructed a measure of racial and ethnic intolerance and assessed whether it predicted support for the death penalty. Their measure was based on three questions: (1) "In general, how warm or cool do you feel towards African Americans?" (2) "In general, how warm or cool do you feel towards Asian Americans?" And (3) "in general, how warm or cool do you feel towards Hispanics?" These items range from one ("very warm") to nine ("very cool"). They combined these three measures into a scale ($\alpha = .92$) and regressed support for the death penalty on it while controlling for other correlates. They also disaggregated their race and ethnic animus scale into its three components and regressed each on support for capital punishment. Unnever, Cullen, and Fisher (2005) reported that Americans who held both racial and ethnic animus (the combined scale) were significantly more likely to support the death penalty. However, they also found that each measure, as a separate factor, significantly predicted the embrace of capital punishment. This suggests that not only racial animus but also ethnic animus is a source of death penalty attitudes.

C. *White Racism and the Racial Divide*

Thus far, our review of the research has generated two reliable findings. First, race is one of the most consistent and robust predictors of support for the death penalty. Whites are significantly more likely than African Americans to support capital punishment. This finding holds true even after controlling for other correlates of support for the death penalty. There is a racial divide in support for the death penalty. Second, racial animus is one of the most consistent and robust predictors of support for the death penalty. Whites who harbor racial animus toward African Americans, particularly those who endorse the new form of racism—that is, who are symbolic racists—are significantly more likely to support capital punishment.

We now turn to an intriguing research question: Can "white racism" account for the racial divide in public support for the death penalty? In their study using 2000 NES data (described above), Unnever and Cullen (2007*a*) attempted to address this issue. Their research investigated whether the divide between African Americans and whites in their support for capital punishment results from the undue influence of white racism. They tested this hypothesis in two ways. First, they empirically assessed whether the direct effect of race on support for the death penalty would be reduced to zero if a measure of white racism was included in the regression equation. Second, they eliminated individuals who they identified as white racists from their analysis and then examined the gap between African Americans and whites in their opinions about capital punishment. Together, these analyses examined whether whites and African Americans who were not racists share similar opinions about the death penalty.

Unnever and Cullen (2007*a*) started by constructing a measure of white racism. They reasoned that the issue of white racism should be seen from the perspective of African Americans. They therefore created an Afrocentric definition of white racism. Their measure defined "white racists" as those individuals who scored above the African American mean on the symbolic racist scale (the scale items were presented above). Stated simply, Unnever and Cullen considered individuals as racists if they viewed African Americans with more racial animosity than the average African American had toward his or her own race.

Unnever and Cullen report that the most robust predictor of the degree to which Americans supported the death penalty was their measure of white racism. That is, they found that the more the respondents believed that African Americans were "irresponsible" or were "culturally deficient" (Feagin and O'Brien 2003), the more likely they were to support executing convicted murderers, while controlling for other factors. They also found that a substantial percentage of the racial divide results from the undue influence of white racism: one-third of the effect of the race coefficient on support of the death penalty was attributable to those individuals who possessed more racial animosity than the average African American. In addition, after deleting individuals who scored above the African American mean on the symbolic racism scale, they found that only a slim majority of nonracist whites—54 percent—supported the death penalty and that the difference between blacks and whites had narrowed to a 10-percentage-point gap.

Notably, Unnever and Cullen (2007*a*) explored two alternative measures of white racism and how they affected support for the death penalty. These two alternatives measures were constructed similarly to their Afrocentric measure of white racism, but they altered the baseline for assessing those with racial animus. For the first of these two alternative measures, they substituted the population mean on symbolic racism for the African American mean, and for the second measure they used the white mean on the symbolic racism scale. Thus, these measures had different baselines (African American, population, and white means on the symbolic racism scale) and assessed the degree to which the respondents expressed racial animus. Including the population mean measure of white racism in the OLS regression equation reduced the racial divide in support for the death penalty by 25 percent. Including the white mean baseline measure of white racism reduced the racial divide by 30 percent. Thus, depending on how white racism was measured, they concluded that from 25 to 39 percent of the racial divide in the degree to which Americans supported capital punishment can be accounted for by the undue influence of white racism.

In sum, the research by Unnever and Cullen (2007*a*) reached four conclusions. First, white racism significantly predicted support for the death penalty. Second, white racism significantly contributed to creating a racial divide in public opinion about capital punishment. Third, the influence of white racism accounted for approximately a third of the racial divide in public support for the death penalty. Fourth, even so, the racial divide in support for capital punishment persisted after the effect of white racism was controlled. Accordingly, future research should continue to probe why this divide appears intractable and how the collective histories of African Americans (and perhaps whites) shape their sensibilities about the state's use of lethal punishment.

D. *Are the Effects of Racism Specific to Capital Punishment?*

Racial thinking—holding negative views of African Americans—is also implicated in support for more generally harsher criminal justice sanctions (for a review, see Cohn and Barkan [2004]). Multivariate studies using different measures of racial prejudice and of punitiveness reach the same conclusion: white respondents who manifest racial animus are more likely to support punitive crime control policies (see, e.g., Cohn, Barkan, and Halteman 1991; Johnson 2001, 2008; Unnever, Cullen, and Jones 2008). There also is evidence that racial prejudice is related to whites' support for spending more money to fight crime (Barkan and Cohn 2005) and for police use of force (Barkan and Cohn 1998). Further, research shows that "racial typification of crime"—seeing crime disproportionately as a "black problem"—is a firm predictor of support for punitive measures (Chiricos, Welch, and Gertz 2004; Welch 2004; see also Barkan and Cohn 2005; Hurwitz and Peffley

2005). Taken together, this body of studies reveals that the effects of racism are not specific to capital punishment but are general in fostering the embrace of harsh criminal justice responses to crime.

IV. Racial Animus and Support for Capital Punishment: A Cross-National Perspective

Given the contentious history of race relations in the United States, it is perhaps unsurprising that racial animus shapes attitudes about the death penalty and other crime-related policies. However, is this a case of American exceptionalism? Is the United States unique in the degree to which racism is integral to sensibilities about crime control? Or do racial or ethnic animosities also influence the opinions of citizens in other nations?

Two factors suggest that the salience of race or ethnicity is rising in other Western industrial democracies. First, as Tonry (1997, p. 11) observes, "racial disparities in America's justice system are paralleled by comparable minority group disparities in other countries." Second, the place of racial and ethnic minorities in Western nations has emerged as an important issue. "Race relations and political controversies about immigrants," notes Tonry (1997, p. 2), "are high on the political and policy agendas of many countries." Racial or ethnic animosity, moreover, is at the heart of this concern. A higher crime rate among some minority groups, continues Tonry, "all too often fosters negative stereotypes of minority groups and both discrimination and xenophobia directed at them." This situation has likely been exacerbated in the post-9/11 era (Keaten and Benczenleitner 2006).

Pettigrew (1998) documents the growth in Europe of prejudice, discrimination, and violence against immigrants, whether drawn from former colonies, guest workers, or refugees and asylum seekers. European nations are not characterized by a melting pot ideology but rather often resist granting immigrants citizenship and a sense of belonging. Relevant to our concerns, Pettigrew presents data on out-group prejudice from seven European samples in four nations polled in the Eurobarometer Survey 30 conducted in 1988. The nations included Great Britain, France, the Netherlands, and West Germany. Importantly, the survey instrument contained questions on both "blatant" and "subtle" forms of prejudice. Similar to Jim Crow racism, blatant prejudice "is the traditional form; it is hot, close, and direct. . . . It involve[s] open rejection of minorities based on presumed biological differences" (Pettigrew 1998, p. 83). In contrast, and much like symbolic racism or racial resentment, subtle racism "is the modern form; it is cool, distant, and indirect." It involves the "perceived threat of the minority to traditional values, the exaggeration of cultural differences with the minority, and the absence of positive feelings toward them" (p. 83). An example of an item measuring subtle prejudice would be "West Indians living here should not push themselves where they are not wanted" (for items in the prejudice scales, see Meertens and Pettigrew [1997]).

Pettigrew (1998) shows that both forms of prejudice exist across nations and are positively interrelated (r = .48 to .70). Notably, consistent with research in the United States, he reports that subtle prejudice is more extensive than blatant prejudice. This racial or ethnic animus is not simply predicted by political conservatism but also is more prevalent among less educated, older Europeans, those who only have friends from their own ethnic group, and those who believe that their group is threatened by minorities (1998, pp. 84–85). Further, prejudice is found across nations to predict policies toward immigration.

In short, Pettigrew (1998) demonstrates that animus toward minorities is prevalent in Europe and has policy implications. However, exploring how race or ethnicity and racism might influence public opinion on crime control is hampered by the relatively small non-U.S. literature on the subject. Surveys in other nations frequently do not ask the race of the respondent (Tonry 1997). Even so, by exploring available data sets, we were able to examine how racial or ethnic animus affects support for the death penalty in four nations: Great Britain, France, Spain, and Japan. In each case, data sets were available that measured support for the death penalty and contained questions that assessed the degree to which the respondents expressed racial or ethnic animus. More specifically, these surveys investigated the level of animus respondents had toward immigrants or "foreigners"—groups identified by Tonry (1997) and others (Hogan, Chiricos, and Gertz 2005) as ones that are susceptible to "typifications" associating them with crime and analogous behaviors.

Admittedly, the analysis to be presented must be viewed with a grain of salt. In particular, the measures of racial or ethnic animus are limited, and thus the complex nature of racism is not fully assessed (see Pettigrew 1998). Even so, these assessments of racial or ethnic animus employ items that assess negative views toward minorities. These items tend to capture subtle racism or racial resentment. Further, the consistency of the findings across national borders suggests that such animus is intimately implicated in support for capital punishment. At the very least, the findings set forth a provocative and troubling thesis that future research can profitably examine with more refined measures.

Even in countries that do not have the death penalty (all but Japan), a substantial portion of each nation's populace supports its use. More instructive for our purpose, the analysis revealed that, as in the United States, racial or ethnic animus is a robust predictor of punitiveness in the samples from each of the four nations.

A. Great Britain

The issue of racial disparities and whether racial animosities predict more punitive attitudes in general has not received the same attention in Great Britain as in the United States. Some research, however, examines racial disparities in attitudes toward the police and courts (see, e.g., Jefferson and Walker 1993; Clancy et al. 2001; Allen et al. 2006). In general, these studies show that whites and blacks (Afro-Caribbeans) do not significantly differ in their attitudes and that Asians (people from the Indian subcontinent) are the least likely to report negative attitudes (e.g., some groups are treated unfairly by the justice system). As Hough and Roberts (2004, p. 3) observe, "Findings from the British Crime Survey . . . show that in England and Wales, black and minority ethnic groups express higher levels of confidence than white groups in most aspects of the criminal justice system. . . . This suggests that minority perceptions of justice are more positive in England and Wales than in the U.S." Even so, to our knowledge, existing research has not examined whether race and racism predict greater support for capital punishment among people residing in Great Britain.

1. *Support for the Death Penalty.* The death penalty has been abolished in member states of the European Union (Hood 2001). To become a member, a country must end its use of capital punishment. (For a complete listing of the countries and when they abolished the death penalty, visit http://web.amnesty.org/pages/deathpenalty-countries-eng.) Despite these sweeping changes, Zimring (2003) and others (Steiker 2002) note that the abolition of capital punishment occurred even though the majority of Europeans expressed support for the death penalty. The levels of support in some countries rivaled those reported

within the United States. In Great Britain, the last person executed was in 1964. The nation completely repealed the last remnants of its death penalty statutes in 1998 (for piracy, treason, and military offenses; Hood 2001).

We analyzed the 1997 British General Election Cross-Section Survey (Heath et al. 1997). This survey included a question that asks whether "Britain should bring back the death penalty." The death penalty question included five responses ranging from (one) "strongly disagree" to (five) "strongly agree." Twenty-two percent strongly agreed, 26 percent agreed, 15 percent were not sure either way, 19 percent disagreed, and 17 percent strongly disagreed that the death penalty should be reinstated. Thus, these data indicate that in 1997, 33 years after the last person was executed in England, nearly half of Britons (48 percent) expressed support for reinstating the death penalty, whereas only 36 percent disagreed.

2. *Are There Racial Differences in Support for the Death Penalty?* Unlike France, Spain, and Japan, the polls in Great Britain that we analyzed included questions that asked the respondents to self-report their race. Indeed, the 1997 British General Election Cross-Section Survey had a complementary survey—the British General Election Study, 1997: Ethnic Minority Survey (Heath and Saggar 1997)—which oversampled minority groups. We merged these two data sets and, after deleting the 106 individuals who had answered both surveys, had a combined sample of 4,214 respondents.

We used this merged data set to consider whether there is a racial divide in support for the death penalty in Great Britain. A cross-tabulation of the data found that 22 percent of whites, compared to 15 percent of blacks, expressed "strong support" for capital punishment, whereas 17 percent of whites "strongly disagreed," in comparison to 30 percent of blacks. We also regressed support for reinstating the death penalty on race after controlling for the respondents' age, gender, and level of education. We found that whites were significantly more likely to endorse reinstating capital punishment than blacks. Thus, as in the United States, Great Britain has a racial divide in support for the death penalty.

3. *Do Racial or Ethnic Resentments Predict Greater Support for the Death Penalty?* Following the same procedure used by U.S. researchers (see, e.g., Soss, Langbein, and Metelko 2003), we deleted the ethnic and racial minorities (blacks) in the 1997 British General Election Cross-

TABLE 2

Racial or Ethnic Animus and Public Support for the Death Penalty

Variable	Great Britain	France	Spain	Japan
Age	−.03	−.02	.03	−.02
Male	.07*	−.00	−.02	.25*
Education	−.22*	−.17*	−.13*	−.03
Racial or ethnic animus	.30*	.46*	.13*	.09*
R^2	.17	.30	.04	.07
N	3,335	3,754	863	2,399
% support	48.7	55.6	47.2	58.9

SOURCES.—The 1997 British General Election Cross-Section Survey (Heath et al. 1997), the 1995 French Election Study (Lewis-Beck, Mayer, and Boy 1995), the Center for Research on Social Reality [Spain] Survey, November 1992: Social Ethics (CIRES 1992), and the 2001 Japanese General Social Survey (Tanioka et al. 2001).

NOTE.—The results for Great Britain, France, and Spain are standardized ordinary least squares regression coefficients. The analysis for Great Britain includes whites only. The dependent variable for Spain is a scale that sums across six measures assessing support for the death penalty. The percentage of support for the death penalty in Spain is for murderers in general. The analysis for Japan is based on a binary variable (1 = support; 0 = does not support and does not know), and the results are standardized logistic regression coefficients. The percentage of support for the death penalty for Great Britain, France, and Spain includes those who agree and those who strongly agree, and the percentage of support in Japan is for those who agree with capital punishment.

* $p < .001$.

Section Survey. This procedure allowed us to assess whether whites in Great Britain who harbor racial resentments were more likely to support reinstating capital punishment.

The 1997 British General Election Cross-Section Survey included a measure that allowed us to assess the level of white racial or ethnic resentment: "Immigration by black people and Asians has been . . . ." The responses ranged from (one) "very good for Britain" to (five) "very bad for Britain." Thirty-eight percent of the respondents stated that the immigration of blacks and Asians has been either "fairly bad" (26 percent) or "very bad" for Britain (12 percent). We regressed support for reinstating the death penalty on this measure, while controlling for the respondent's age, gender, and education level. Table 2 reports the results from this analysis. It shows that white racial or ethnic resentment significantly predicts greater support for reinstating capital punishment, while controlling for the demographic characteristics of the respondents. Indeed, an examination of the standardized regression coefficients indicates that it has the largest association with support for reinstating the death penalty.

In a supplementary analysis, we created another measure of white racial or ethnic resentment. This measure was constructed from a range of responses to the question of whether equal opportunities for ethnic minorities have (one) "not gone far enough" or (five) "gone much too far." Similarly to the results presented in table 2, we found that white Britons were significantly more likely to support reinstating the death penalty if they also believed that the extension of equal opportunities to ethnic minorities had gone too far. Its standardized regression coefficient was the largest in the equation.

In sum, these data indicate that whites were more likely than blacks to support reinstating capital punishment in Great Britain. The results further show that whites who express racial or ethnic resentments were significantly more likely to endorse reinstating the death penalty. These findings closely parallel those found in the United States.

B. France

As noted above, the data from France, Spain, and Japan did not include any measures that specifically asked the respondents to self-report their race or ethnicity. Consequently, for these three countries our analyses focused on whether racial or ethnic animus predicts greater support for the death penalty. We could not locate any existing research that investigated whether individuals in France who harbor racial resentments were more likely to support the death penalty.

1. *Support for the Death Penalty.* We analyzed the 1995 French Election Study (Lewis-Beck et al. 1995). The last execution in France took place in 1977. France completely abolished capital punishment in 1981 (Hood 2001).

The French Election Study included a question that parallels the one asked in Great Britain. Thus, the respondents were asked whether "the death penalty should be reinstated." The responses ranged from (one) "strongly disagree" to (four) "strongly agree." The data show that 32 percent strongly agreed, 25 percent agreed, 13 percent disagreed, and 30 percent strongly disagreed that capital punishment should be reinstated. Thus, these results indicate that the majority of the French population, 57 percent, supported the reinstatement of the death penalty.

2. *Do Racial or Ethnic Resentments Predict Greater Support for the Death Penalty?* The French Election Study included a question that assessed the level of animus the French have toward immigrants. This question asked whether "there are too many immigrants in France." Responses

ranged from (one) "strongly disagree" to (four) "strongly agree." The vast majority of the French, 75 percent, stated that they either agree or strongly agree that France has too many immigrants.

We regressed the capital punishment question on the racial or ethnic animus measure while controlling for the respondent's age, gender, and level of education. The results are reported in table 2. The analysis reveals that those who stated that there were too many immigrants were significantly and substantively more likely to express support for reinstating capital punishment. Indeed, while controlling for the demographic characteristics of the respondents, the standardized regression coefficient for the racial or ethnic animus question was .46 (p = .000). We also replicated the analysis with another measure of racial or ethnic animus taken from the French Election Study—"It is only fair for Muslims living in France to have mosques to practice their religion." Again, individuals who disagreed with this statement were significantly more likely to support the reinstatement of the death penalty ($\beta = .20$, $p = .000$). In sum, similar to the results we reported for Great Britain, the French were more likely to endorse reinstating the death penalty if they harbored racial or ethnic resentments.

C. *Spain*

We were not able to find any existing analyses of public opinion data that examined whether racial or ethnic animus predicted greater support for the death penalty (or punitiveness, in general) in Spain. However, we were able to locate a data set that allowed us to investigate this question. We analyzed the Center for Research on Social Reality [Spain] Survey, November 1992: Social Ethics (CIRES 1992). The sample included persons living in Spain aged 18 and over. Notably, the last execution carried out in Spain occurred in 1975. Spain completely abolished its use of the death penalty for all crimes in 1995 (Hood 2001).

1. *Support for the Death Penalty.* The survey included six questions that examined the level of support for the death penalty across different circumstances. These questions asked respondents whether they supported capital punishment for murder in general, the murder of a public official, the murder of a minor, a terrorist act that kills civilians, the murder of someone who was kidnapped, and drug traffickers. The responses to each of these queries ranged from (one) "strongly disagree" to (five) "strongly agree." A frequency analysis of the data showed that

13 percent strongly agreed, 34 percent agreed, 4 percent were indifferent, 31 percent disagreed, and 17 percent strongly disagreed with supporting the execution of murderers in general. Thus, the distribution of support for the death penalty was essentially bimodal, with 48 percent in disagreement and 47 percent in agreement.

2. *Do Racial or Ethnic Resentments Predict Greater Support for the Death Penalty?* We created a scale that summed across the responses to the six conditions under which the respondent could support the death penalty (α = .97). The Social Reality [Spain] Survey also included a question that assessed the level of animus the respondents have toward immigrants. The translated version of this question is "In many places in Europe, and even in Spain, there seem to be problems with cohabitation between native populations and immigrants. How do you think this problem could be solved?" Three responses were offered: (1) "creating neighborhoods exclusively for the immigrants" (7 percent), (2) "allowing into neighborhoods only those immigrants who are good citizens" (25 percent), and (3) "allowing everyone to freely chose their place of residence" (68 percent).

We regressed our death penalty scale on the racial or ethnic animus question while controlling for the respondent's age, gender, and level of education and report the results in table 2. The results show that Spaniards who harbored racial or ethnic animus were significantly more likely to support the death penalty. Thus, the results indicate that individuals living in Spain who believed that immigrants should live in segregated neighborhoods were significantly more likely to support the death penalty. Again, these findings coincide with those reported by respondents in Great Britain and France.

D. Japan

Japan and the United States are the only two industrialized Western-style democracies that use the death penalty. Japan hangs convicted murderers. There were 142 persons on death row in Japan as of July 2004 (Johnson 2006).

1. *Support for the Death Penalty.* Johnson (2006) argues that one reason Japan retains the death penalty and refuses to sign international treaties prohibiting its use is because elites are bolstered by the majority of Japanese "passively" supporting capital punishment. Johnson (2006, p. 270) observes, however, that "if there is any country where Marshall's hypothesis accurately describes the shallow roots

of pro–death penalty opinion, and if there is any place where exposure to more of the 'presently available information' could undermine support for capital punishment, it may be Japan, for nowhere else does the state kill so secretly." It is noteworthy that the majority of Japanese support the death penalty despite their cultural emphasis on the reintegration of the offender (Hamilton et al. 1988).

We could not locate any studies of Japanese public opinion that address whether racial or ethnic animus predicts greater support for the death penalty. However, we were able to locate a data set that allowed us to investigate this question. We analyzed the 2001 Japanese General Social Survey (JGSS; Tanioka et al. 2001), a two-stage stratified random nationwide survey of men and women aged 18 and over. The JGSS included a question that measured support for capital punishment: "Do you agree or disagree with the death penalty?" Three responses were "agree," "disagree," and "don't know." The data show that 59 percent of Japanese support capital punishment, 11 percent disagreed, and 30 percent responded that they do not know. The latter category exceeds the percentages usually found among U.S. residents.

2. *Do Racial or Ethnic Resentments Predict Greater Support for the Death Penalty?* The 2001 JGSS also included a measure of racial or ethnic animus: "Are you for or against an increase in the number of foreigners in your community?" Two response categories were offered, "agree" and "disagree." Sixty-two percent of the respondents reported that they were against an increase in the number of foreigners in their community.

We created a binary measure of support for the death penalty (1 = support; 0 = oppose) and regressed it on the measure of racial or ethnic animus while controlling for the respondents' age, gender, and level of education. These results are presented in table 2. The results show that the Japanese respondents were significantly more likely to support capital punishment if they expressed animus toward foreigners.

E. Summary of Cross-National Results

In sum, this cross-national research is consistent with the data from the United States. There is a racial divide in public support for bringing back the death penalty in Great Britain; whites were significantly more likely than blacks to support reinstating capital punishment. In addition, consistent with findings of studies conducted in the United

States, those living in England and residents of France, Spain, and Japan who harbor racial or ethnic resentments were significantly and robustly more likely to support capital punishment. Taken together, these findings indicate that public opinion about crime is inextricably related to racial or ethnic animus. People in the United States and in Western countries are more likely to support capital punishment if they express racial and ethnic animus.

V. State Threat and Social Threat

Western governments are not well-oiled machines but messy enterprises in which competing interests vie to have their views of reality enshrined in social policy and law. Even so, these nations' commonweal also depends on the state maintaining legitimacy. This is particularly important in the area of criminal justice, where the state imposes its power on its citizens. And no sanction is more open to debate than capital punishment—the so-called ultimate penalty. The death penalty is of enormous symbolic importance since its use occasions an ongoing public conversation over the capacity of the state to act in a just way.

The core findings of the existing literature on race, racism, and capital punishment are disquieting. First, there is a long-standing, durable racial divide in the public's opinions about the death penalty; African Americans are significantly less likely than whites to support executing convicted murderers. Second, although not eliminating the racial divide, a substantively important percentage of the difference between African Americans and whites in their opinions about the death penalty arises from racial resentments among whites. The base of support for capital punishment thus resides among whites who harbor racial resentments toward African Americans. This finding, however, is not a matter of American exceptionalism. In samples drawn from four other Western industrial nations, racial or ethnic animus was a robust predictor of support for the death penalty.

Taken together, these results suggest that race (or ethnicity) and racial animosity are key reasons why people support or oppose capital punishment. In a democracy, however, there is ostensibly no rational legal reason why these factors should shape policy toward the death penalty. They are antidemocratic considerations and potential sources of social and political conflict (Cohn and Barkan 2004). They also call the very legitimacy of capital punishment into question.

A. The Racial Divide: State Threat Hypothesis

The racial divide not only exists but also defies easy explanation. Thus, it might seem at first glance that race is a proxy for a series of other factors—such as class disadvantage or liberal political attitudes—that, once controlled, would wipe out any race effect on death penalty attitudes. Or we might expect that picking out subgroups of African Americans—such as those who are more conservative, affluent, or religious—might reveal attitudinal convergence. But the opposite is the case. Instead, it appears that African Americans as a group have a different sensibility about capital punishment than whites. They simply think differently about it.

We offer one possible explanation for the racial divide that can help account for its long-standing nature and seeming intractability. In America, the state is perceived by African Americans not as neutral but rather as an institution that has traditionally protected the interests of the majority group and undermined their interests. More important, the criminal justice system is seen as unjust and potentially as an instrument of oppression (Hagan and Albonetti 1982; Henderson et al. 1997). In short, the state is a potential threat to African Americans (Oshinsky 1996; Ogletree 2002; see also Wacquant 2001).

In this context, the death penalty takes on special significance. It is the ultimate weapon of state criminal justice power. It is also an instrument of social control that has arisen out of a racially specific history of the use of white violence to oppress African Americans (Oshinsky 1996; Ogletree 2002). Over time, blacks have had reason to see the ruling class's use of lethal force as a means to exert power over them. This unique experience has fostered wariness among African Americans about the state's power to take life (Unnever and Cullen 2007*b*).

Southern whites historically used diverse techniques to control African Americans (Tolnay, Beck, and Massey 1992). Before the Civil War, slaveholders were the primary agents of social control. Although slaveholders arbitrarily and harshly punished slaves, lethal violence was rarely used. But with the passage of the Thirteenth Amendment to the U.S. Constitution ending slavery, the social control of African Americans was transferred officially to local criminal justice systems and unofficially to vigilante mobs (Tolnay, Beck, and Massey 1992; Oshinsky 1996; Zimring 2003; Garland 2005). One of the more disquieting aspects of this transfer of social control was the epidemic of lynchings that occurred in the South in the late 1800s and early 1900s. During this period, 73 percent of all lynching victims were African American (1,748 African American men, women, and children were lynched by white men), and over 95 percent of those were tortured and killed in former slave states (Tolnay, Deane, and Beck 1996; Clarke 1998). Tolnay, Deane, and Beck (1996) argue that the function of racially motivated lynchings was to perpetuate white supremacy, especially the economic dominance of whites.

Clarke (1998, p. 276) argues that public lynchings had a pernicious consequence for southern black culture; they created a subculture of fear that "informed the actions of every black man, woman and child throughout the South." Tolnay, Deane, and Beck (1996) add that young African American men learned early in their lives that at any moment they could be the next target of a lynching mob. According to Clarke (1998), this fear was not attenuated by the eventual decline of lynchings by the 1920s. Rather, he contends that the number of lynchings decreased because they were supplanted by a more palatable form of violence—state executions. Southern white leaders acknowledged that capital punishment could serve the same function as lynchings—the control and intimidation of African Americans. Indeed, court-ordered executions were considered by both white and black southerners as legal lynchings (Oshinsky 1996; Ogletree 2002).

Among other factors, lynchings that terrorized African Americans contributed to the decision of many blacks to migrate out of the South. Tolnay and Beck's (1992) research indicates that southern African Americans were more likely to leave areas where mob violence was greatest. It is likely that African Americans fleeing the fear of being lynched in the South disseminated a deep-seated dislike for capital punishment among blacks throughout the United States. Thus, a potential unintended consequence of the Great Migration was the cultural transmission of the history of southern lynchings among African Americans.

Unnever and Cullen (2007*b*) conclude that African American opposition to the death penalty is potentially grounded in their collective history of experiencing the discriminatory violence of state-condoned executions. Ogletree (2002, p. 15), calling the death penalty the "black man's burden," has linked African Americans' experience with lynching to contemporary capital punishment. He observes (2002, p. 23),

> Given the many similarities between the illegal but often officially sanctioned practice of lynching, and the current imposition of the death penalty, it seems at times that the only difference between lynching and capital punishment is the gloss of legality and procedural regularity that the latter enjoys. In this regard, application of the death penalty may be fairer than the vigilante justice that characterized the Jim Crow era, but not by much.
>
> In fact, a number of scholars and activists have referred to America's history of lynching and Jim Crow as the appropriate point of reference for an understanding of the dynamics of our current legal system. Reverend Jackson used the title "Legal Lynching" for his book on the death penalty; and Professor Emma Coleman Jordan has hypothesized that "lynching [is] a contemporary civic metaphor for the black experience within the American legal system."

B. White Racism: The Social Threat Hypothesis

In short, one possibility is that African Americans are more likely to oppose capital punishment because of an ingrained fear of lethal state power, which they see as disproportionately applied to blacks. The control of the state—especially law enforcement and criminal justice institutions—by whites, who are often perceived as racially biased, exacerbates this view of the state as a threat to blacks. However, there is still the finding that feelings of racial and ethnic animus drives up white support for the death penalty. These animosities appear to have general effects, increasing white punitiveness generally and fostering support for capital punishment cross-nationally—indeed, even in countries where the death penalty has been abolished. Why is this?

Conflict theory has suggested a compelling hypothesis: racial and ethnic minorities pose a social threat to majority group members. Conflict theory further argues that governments respond to the threats posed by the "undeserving poor" in three ways. First, they criminalize behaviors that disproportionately occur among these groups (e.g., crack cocaine vs. powder cocaine; see Tonry 1997; Beckett and Sasson 2000). Second, law enforcement targets these groups—for example, the war on street drugs—resulting in more arrests and prosecutions. Third, governments pass more punitive crime control measures, such as three-strikes-and-you're-out laws; they then ratchet up the severity of punishments for crimes that the threatening groups disproportionately commit through mandatory prison sentences for violent crimes, truth-in-sentencing laws, and the death penalty. And, of course, governments have available to them the specter of the death penalty. They can reinstate the death penalty, as New York did in 1995, they can pass new legislation that will expedite the "machinery of death" resulting in more people being executed more quickly, and they can expand its scope (Foucault 1979; *Callins v. Collins*, 510 U.S. 1141 [1994]; Unnever and Cullen 2005).

However, these arguments have been challenged. Perhaps, the most salient of these criticisms is that minority groups—especially those that are truly disadvantaged and live in urban segregated communities characterized by a culture of hypermasculinity (Anderson 1999)—are hardly a threat to political and economic elites. That most crime is apolitical, intraclass, and intraracial belies the argument that the "undeserving poor" (immigrants, welfare recipients, and street criminals) have a class consciousness that will compel them to organize and seriously challenge existing political, economic, and social institutions.

We consider this criticism to have serious traction; however, we do not believe that the "baby should be thrown out with the bath water." Rather, the literature clearly indicates that whites more than African Americans support punitive crime control policies and, more specifically, that a specific segment of whites—those who harbor racial and ethnic animus—are particularly vocal in their punitive attitudes. Thus, we pose a more grounded version of conflict theory, one that incorporates the findings presented in this essay.

The "undeserving poor" do pose a threat but not to corporate and political elites. These disparate groups of unassimilated immigrants, welfare recipients, and criminals instead pose a symbolic threat to individuals who are serious stakeholders in the existing normative order. (In the context of the United States, commentators refer to this segment as "angry young White males" [Hogan, Chiricos, and Gertz 2005].) However, we do not assume that the normative order is one characterized by norms and values that are equally shared by all. Certainly, the persistence of the racial divide in support for the death penalty excludes this possibility. Instead, the data indicate that the normative order in Western-style democracies includes within it groups of individuals that harbor racial and ethnic animosities. The segments of the population that harbor racial and ethnic sentiments associate crime with the "undeserving poor." The end result of this typification process is that racists righteously believe that criminals and their kind deserve to be punished to the fullest extent of the law.

Together, these findings suggest that the "undeserving poor," perhaps best characterized by a member of a minority group who purposefully eschews proffered benefits and instead attempts to profit from crime, pose a threat to those who do not like them and are closer to them economically and socially than are elites who live in cloistered gated communities. Thus, the threat the "undeserving poor" symbolically represents may be more salient to those who are truly offended by their presence and behavior—those who harbor racial and ethnic resentments. In addition, this group becomes the vehicle through which this threat is articulated to the political elite. As a result, political elites posture as "law and order" candidates to appease this threat as it is expressed through the racial and ethnic biased lens of those who are racists. The end result is that elites enact policies advocated by this vocal minority as a way to cement their positions of political power. Racist sentiments become institutionalized and more minorities become disenchanted. The racial gap persists and perhaps widens with no end in sight.

C. The Hidden Cost of Capital Punishment

In assessing how groups differ in society—whether by race, class, or gender—there is the risk of exaggerating the differences that are detected. In the current analysis, we would be remiss if we did not note that many African Americans support the death penalty and many white Americans do not. Still, there remains a substantively important, deeply entrenched divide between blacks and whites (Cochran and Chamlin 2006; Unnever and Cullen 2007*a*, 2007*b*). It is disquieting that an important source of white support for capital punishment is rooted in symbolic racism or racial animus.

Beyond moral and crime control considerations, there are debates over the financial costs of the death penalty, which outstrip those incurred by a life sentence in prison (Radelet and Borg 2000). But our findings also point to another outcome, one deserving of future research: capital punishment may carry with it the hidden cost of exacerbating racial divisions and conflict. In a democratic society, it should be a concern that the state's most lethal sanction is the occasion for racial disagreements. The United States remains "two nations." African Americans and whites clearly have different sensibilities about the death penalty.

For African Americans, we suspect that the ready use of capital punishment is simply more evidence that the state is unsympathetic to the experience of being black in the United States. In a criminal justice system that African Americans see as fundamentally unjust (Hagan and Albonetti 1982; Henderson et al. 1997), the risk that the death penalty is applied inequitably and sometimes mistakenly seems to make no difference to the white majority or to the state. The voices of blacks are not heard or are dismissed as unjustified complaints. On issues of injustice—whether with regard to criminal justice or broader social issues—white Americans more often see political institutions as operating equitably and see injustice as an episodic rather than as an institutionalized practice (Bobo 2001; Weitzer and Tuch 2005). To make matters worse, the strongest advocates of capital punishment among whites are those who like African Americans the least. The notion that the death penalty is inextricably linked to racial hostility is thus not an imaginary social construction by blacks but appears to be an empirical reality. The legitimacy of capital punishment, the state, and the national ideology of equality is called into question.

REFERENCES

Allen, Jonathon, Suzanne Edmonds, Alison Patterson, and Dominic Smith. 2006. *Policing and the Criminal Justice System—Public Confidence and Perceptions: 2004/05 British Crime Survey*. Home Office Statistical Bulletin 7/06. London: Home Office.

Anderson, Elijah. 1999. *Code of the Street: Decency, Violence, and the Moral Life of the Inner City*. New York: Norton.

Arthur, John A. 1998. "Racial Attitudes and Opinions about Capital Punishment: Preliminary Findings." *International Journal of Comparative and Applied Criminal Justice* 22(2):131–44.

Baker, David N., Eric G. Lambert, and Morris Jenkins. 2005. "Racial Differences in Death Penalty Support and Opposition: A Preliminary Study of White and Black College Students." *Journal of Black Studies* 35(4):201–24.

Barak, Gregg, Paul Leighton, and Jeanne Flavin. 2007. *Class, Race, Gender, and Crime: The Social Realities of Justice in America*. Lanham, MD: Rowman & Littlefield.

Barkan, Steven E., and Steven F. Cohn. 1994. "Racial Prejudice and Support for the Death Penalty by Whites." *Journal of Research in Crime and Delinquency* 31(2):202–9.

———. 1998. "Racial Prejudice and Support by Whites for Police Use of Force: A Research Note." *Justice Quarterly* 15(4):743–53.

———. 2005. "Why Whites Favor Spending More Money to Fight Crime: The Role of Racial Prejudice." *Social Problems* 52(2):300–14.

Becker, Howard S. 1963. *Outsiders: Studies in the Sociology of Deviance*. New York: Free Press.

Beckett, Katherine, and Theodore Sasson. 2000. *The Politics of Injustice: Crime and Punishment in America*. Thousand Oaks, CA: Pine Forge.

Bobo, Lawrence D. 2001. "Racial Attitudes and Relations at the Close of the Twentieth Century." In *America Becoming: Racial Trends and Their Consequences*, edited by Neil J. Smelser, William Julius Wilson, and Faith Mitchell. Washington, DC: National Academy Press.

Bobo, Lawrence D., and Devon Johnson. 2004. "A Taste for Punishment: Black and White Americans' Views on the Death Penalty and the War on Drugs." *Du Bois Review: Social Science Research on Race* 1(1):151–81.

Bobo, Lawrence D., and James R. Kluegel. 1993. "Opposition to Race-Targeting: Self-Interest, Stratification Ideology, or Racial Attitudes?" *American Sociological Review* 58(4):443–64.

Bobo, Lawrence D., James R. Kluegel, and Ryan Smith. 1997. "Laissez-Faire Racism: The Crystallization of a Kinder, Gentler, Antiblack Ideology." In *Racial Attitudes in the 1990s: Continuity and Change*, edited by Steven A. Tuch and Jack K. Martin. Westport, CT: Praeger.

Bonczar, Thomas P., and Allen J. Beck. 1997. *Lifetime Likelihood of Going to State or Federal Prison*. Washington, DC: U.S. Department of Justice, Bureau of Justice Statistics.

Bonczar, Thomas P., and Tracy L. Snell. 2005. *Capital Punishment, 2004*. Washington, DC: U.S. Department of Justice, Bureau of Justice Statistics.

Bonilla-Silva, Eduardo. 1997. "Rethinking Racism: Toward a Structural Interpretation." *American Sociological Review* 62(3):465–80.

Borg, Marian J. 1997. "The Southern Subculture of Punitiveness? Regional Variation in Support for Capital Punishment." *Journal of Research in Crime and Delinquency* 34(1):25–45.

Britt, Chester L. 1998. "Race, Religion, and Support for the Death Penalty: A Research Note." *Justice Quarterly* 15(1):175–91.

Brooks, Richard R. W., and Haekyung Jeon-Slaughter. 2001. "Race, Income, and Perceptions of the U.S. Court System." *Behavioral Sciences and the Law* 19(2):249–64.

Browning, Sandra Lee, Francis T. Cullen, Liqun Cao, Reneé Kopache, and Thomas J. Stevenson. 1994. "Race and Getting Hassled by the Police: A Research Note." *Police Studies* 17(1):1–11.

Buckler, Kevin, James D. Unnever, and Francis T. Cullen. Forthcoming. "Perceptions of Injustice Revisited: A Test of Hagan et al.'s Comparative Conflict Theory." *Journal of Crime and Justice*.

Bureau of Justice Statistics. 2006. *Criminal Offenders Statistics*. http://www.ojp.usdoj.gov/bjs/crimoff.htm#lifetime.

Cao, Liqun, James Frank, and Francis T. Cullen. 1996. "Race, Community Context, and Confidence in the Police." *American Journal of Police* 15(1):3–22.

Catalano, Shannan M. 2005. *Criminal Victimization, 2004*. Washington, DC: U.S. Department of Justice, Bureau of Justice Statistics.

Charles, Camille Zubrinsky. 2003. "The Dynamics of Racial Segregation." In *Annual Review of Sociology*, vol. 29, edited by Karen S. Cook and John Hagan. Palo Alto, CA: Annual Reviews.

Chiricos, Ted, Michael Hogan, and Marc Gertz. 1997. "Racial Composition of Neighborhood and Fear of Crime." *Criminology* 35(1):107–32.

Chiricos, Ted, Kelly Welch, and Marc Gertz. 2004. "Racial Typification of Crime and Support for Punitive Measures." *Criminology* 42(2):359–89.

CIRES (Centro de Investigaciones Sobre la Realidad Social). 1992. Center for Research on Social Reality [Spain] Survey, November 1992: Social Ethics. Computer file. Madrid: Anàlisis Sociòlógicos Económicos y Politicos. Distributed by Inter-university Consortium for Political and Social Research, Ann Arbor, MI.

Clancy, Anna, Mike Hough, Rebecca Aust, and Chris Kershaw. 2001. *Crime, Policing, and Justice: The Experience of Ethnic Minorities—Findings from the 2000 British Crime Survey*. Home Office Research Study no. 223. London: Home Office.

Clarke, James W. 1998. "Without Fear or Shame: Lynching, Capital Punishment, and the Subculture of Violence in the American South." *British Journal of Political Science* 28(2):269–89.

Cochran, John K., and Mitchell B. Chamlin. 2006. "The Enduring Racial Divide in Death Penalty Support." *Journal of Criminal Justice* 34(1):85–99.

Cohn, Steven F., and Steven E. Barkan. 2004. "Racial Prejudice and Public Attitudes about the Punishment of Criminals." In *For the Common Good: A Critical Examination of Law and Social Control*, edited by R. Robin Miller and Sandra Lee Browning. Durham, NC: Carolina Academic Press.

Cohn, Steven F., Steven E. Barkan, and William A. Halteman. 1991. "Punitive Attitudes toward Criminals: Racial Consensus or Racial Conflicts?" *Social Problems* 38(2):287–96.

Combs, Michael W., and John C. Comer. 1982. "Race and Capital Punishment: A Longitudinal Analysis." *Phylon* 43(4):350–59.

Cullen, Francis T., Liqun Cao, James Frank, Robert H. Langworthy, Sandra Lee Browning, Reneé Kopache, and Thomas J. Stevenson. 1996. "'Stop or I'll Shoot': Racial Differences in Support for Police Use of Deadly Force." *American Behavioral Scientist* 39(4):449–60.

Cullen, Francis T., Bonnie S. Fisher, and Brandon K. Applegate. 2000. "Public Opinion about Punishment and Corrections." In *Crime and Justice: A Review of Research*, vol. 27, edited by Michael Tonry. Chicago: University of Chicago Press.

Davis, James A., Tom W. Smith, and Peter V. Marsden. 2005. General Social Surveys, 1972–2004. ICPSR04295-v1. Cumulative computer file. Chicago: National Opinion Research Center. Distributed by Roper Center for Public Opinion Research, University of Connecticut, Storrs, CT, and Inter-university Consortium for Political and Social Research, Ann Arbor, MI.

Dawson, Michael, Melissa H. Lacewell, and Cathy Cohen. 2006. "2005 Racial

Attitudes and the Katrina Disaster Study." Initial report from the University of Chicago Center for the Study of Race Politics and Culture. http://www-news.uchicago.edu/releases/06/images/katrina_report.doc.

Elberhardt, Jennifer L., Paul G. Davies, Valerie J. Purdie-Vaughns, and Sheri Lynn Johnson. 2006. "Looking Deathworthy: Perceived Stereotypicality of Black Defendants Predicts Capital Sentencing Outcomes." *Psychological Science* 17(5):383–86.

Engel, Robin Shepard. 2005. "Citizens' Perceptions of Distributive and Procedural Injustice during Traffic Stops with Police." *Journal of Research in Crime and Delinquency* 42(4):445–81.

Feagin, Joe R., and Eileen O'Brien. 2003. *White Men on Race: Power Privilege and the Shaping of Cultural Consciousness*. New York: Beacon.

Feagin, Joe R., and Melvin P. Sikes. 1994. *Living with Racism: The Black Middle-Class Experience*. Boston: Beacon.

Federal Bureau of Investigation. 2005. *Crime in the United States, 2004: Uniform Crime Reports*. Washington, DC: U.S. Government Printing Office.

Foucault, Michel. 1979. *Discipline and Punish: The Birth of the Prison*. New York: Vintage.

Fox, James Alan, and Marianne W. Zawitz. 2003. *Homicide Trends in the United States: 2000 Update*. Washington, DC: U.S. Department of Justice, Bureau of Justice Statistics.

Frank, James, Steven Brandl, Francis T. Cullen, and Amy Stichman. 1996. "Reassessing the Impact of Race on Citizens' Attitudes toward the Police." *Justice Quarterly* 13(2):321–34.

Garland, David. 2005. "Penal Excess and Surplus Meaning: Public Torture Lynchings in Twentieth-Century America." *Law and Society Review* 39(4): 793–833.

Gitlin, Todd. 1995. *The Twilight of Common Dreams: Why America Is Wracked by Culture Wars*. New York: Metropolitan.

Glenn, Norval D. 1974–75. "Recent Trends in White-Nonwhite Attitudinal Differences." *Public Opinion Quarterly* 38(4):596–604.

Goldhagen, Daniel Jonah. 1997. *Hitler's Willing Executioners: Ordinary Germans and the Holocaust*. New York: Vintage.

———. 2007. "The Globalization of Anti-Semitism." Bea and Henry Winkler Lecture presented at the University of Cincinnati, April 18.

Gottschalk, Marie. 2006. *The Prison and the Gallows: The Politics of Mass Incarceration in America*. New York: Cambridge University Press.

Hacker, Andrew. 2003. *Two Nations: Black and White, Separate, Hostile, Unequal*. Rev. ed. New York: Scribner.

Hagan, John, and Celesta Albonetti. 1982. "Race, Class, and the Perception of Criminal Injustice in America." *American Journal of Sociology* 88(2):329–55.

Hagan, John, Carla Shedd, and Monique R. Payne. 2005. "Race, Ethnicity, and Youth Perceptions of Criminal Injustice." *American Sociological Review* 70(3):381–407.

Halim, Shaheen, and Beverly L. Stiles. 2001. "Differential Support for Police Use of Force, the Death Penalty, and Perceived Harshness of the Courts:

Effects of Race, Gender, and Region." *Criminal Justice and Behavior* 28(1): 3–23.

Hamilton, V. Lee, Joseph Sanders, Yoko Hosoi, Zensuke Ishimura, Nozomu Matsubara, Haruo Nishimura, Nobuho Tomita, and Kazuhiko Tokoro. 1988. "Punishment and the Individual in the United States and Japan." *Law and Society Review* 22(2):301–28.

Harrison, Paige M., and Allen J. Beck. 2006. *Prison and Jail Inmates at Midyear 2005*. Washington, DC: U.S. Department of Justice, Bureau of Justice Statistics.

Heath, A., R. Jowell, J. K. Curtice, and P. Norris. 1997. British General Election Cross-Section Survey, 1997. 2nd ICPSR version. Computer file. London: Social and Community Planning Research. Distributed by The Data Archive, Colchester, and Inter-university Consortium for Political and Social Research, Ann Arbor, MI.

Heath, A., and S. Saggar. 1997. British General Election Survey: Ethnic Minority Survey, 1997. 2nd ICPSR version. Computer file. London: Social and Community Planning Research. Distributed by The Data Archive, Colchester, and Inter-university Consortium for Political and Social Research, Ann Arbor, MI.

Henderson, Martha L., Francis T. Cullen, Liqun Cao, Sandra Lee Browning, and Reneé Kopache. 1997. "The Impact of Race on Perceptions of Criminal Injustice." *Journal of Criminal Justice* 25(6):447–62.

Hogan, Michael J., Ted Chiricos, and Marc Gertz. 2005. "Economic Insecurity, Blame, and Punitive Attitudes." *Justice Quarterly* 22(3):392–412.

Hood, Roger. 2001. "Capital Punishment: A Global Perspective." *Punishment and Society* 3(3):331–54.

Hough, Mike, and Julian V. Roberts. 2004. *Confidence in Justice: An International Review*. Home Office Research Study no. 243. London: Home Office.

Hughes, Everett Cherrington. 1945. "Dilemmas and Contradictions of Status." *American Journal of Sociology* 50(5):353–59.

Hurst, Yolander G., James Frank, and Sandra Lee Browning. 2000. "The Attitudes of Juveniles toward the Police: A Comparison of Black and White Youth." *Policing* 23(1):37–53.

Hurwitz, Jon, and Mark Peffley, eds. 1998. *Perception and Prejudice: Race and Politics in the United States*. New Haven, CT: Yale University Press.

———. 2005. "Playing the Race Card in the Post–Willie Horton Era: The Impact of Racialized Code Words on Support for Punitive Crime Policy." *Public Opinion Quarterly* 69(1):99–112.

Igo, Sarah E. 2007. *The Averaged American: Surveys, Citizens, and the Making of a Mass Public*. Cambridge, MA: Harvard University Press.

Jacoby, Joseph E., and Francis T. Cullen. 1998. "The Structure of Punishment Norms: Applying the Rossi-Berk Model." *Journal of Criminal Law and Criminology* 89(1):245–312.

Jefferson, Tony, and Monica A. Walker. 1993. "Attitudes to the Police of Ethnic Minorities in a Provincial City." *British Journal of Criminology* 33(2): 251–66.

Johnson, David T. 2006. "Where the State Kills in Secret: Capital Punishment in Japan." *Punishment and Society* 8(3):251–85.

Johnson, Devon. 2001. "Punitive Attitudes on Crime: Economic Insecurity, Racial Prejudice, or Both?" *Sociological Focus* 34(1):33–54.

———. 2008. "Racial Prejudice, Perceived Injustice, and the Black-White Gap in Punitive Attitudes." *Journal of Criminal Justice* 36(2):198–206.

Keaten, Jamey, and Palma Benczenleitner. 2006. "European Minorities Torn between Worlds." *Washington Post*, November 25. http://www.washingtonpost.com/wp-dyn/content/article/2006/11/25/AR2006112500301.html.

Kinder, Donald R. 1986. "The Continuing American Dilemma: White Resistance to Racial Change 40 Years after Myrdal." *Journal of Social Issues* 42(2): 151–71.

Kinder, Donald R., and Lynn M. Sanders. 1996. *Divided by Color: Racial Politics and Democratic Ideals*. Chicago: University of Chicago Press.

Kozol, Jonathan. 1991. *Savage Inequalities: Children in America's Schools*. New York: Crown.

Lewis-Beck, Michael S., et al. 1995. French National Election Study, 1995. ICPSR version. Computer file. Iowa City: University of Iowa, Department of Political Science; Paris: Centre d'Etude de la Vie Politique Francaise. Distributed by Inter-university Consortium for Political and Social Research, Ann Arbor, MI.

Massey, Douglas S., and Nancy A. Denton. 1993. *American Apartheid: Segregation and the Making of the Underclass*. Cambridge, MA: Harvard University Press.

Mauer, Marc. 1999. *Race to Incarcerate*. New York: New Press.

Meertens, Roel W., and Thomas F. Pettigrew. 1997. "Is Subtle Prejudice Really Prejudice?" *Public Opinion Quarterly* 61(1):54–71.

Miller, Jerome G. 1996. *Search and Destroy: African-American Males in the Criminal Justice System*. New York: Cambridge University Press.

Mitchell, Ojmarrh. 2005. "A Meta-analysis of Race and Sentencing Research: Explaining the Inconsistencies." *Journal of Quantitative Criminology* 21(4): 439–66.

Moon, Melissa M., John Paul Wright, Francis T. Cullen, and Jennifer Pealer. 2000. "Putting Kids to Death: Specifying Public Support for Juvenile Capital Punishment." *Justice Quarterly* 17(4):663–84.

Ogletree, Charles J.; Jr. 2002. "Black Man's Burden: Race and the Death Penalty in America." *Oregon Law Review* 81(1):15–38.

Ohlemacher, Stephen. 2006. "Census Shows Racial Inequalities Persist in Pay, Schooling, Homes." *Cincinnati Enquirer*, November 14, pp. A1, A9.

On the Issues. 2000. George W. Bush quote on the death penalty. *On the Issues*. http://www.ontheissues.org/George_W__Bush.htm.

Oshinsky, David M. 1996. *"Worse Than Slavery": Parchman Farm and the Ordeal of Jim Crow Justice*. New York: Simon & Schuster.

Pataki, George. 1997. "Death Penalty Is a Deterrent: Capital Punishment Gives Killers Good Cause to Fear Arrest and Conviction." *USA Today*, March. http://findarticles.com/p/articles/mi_m1272/is_n2622_v125/ai_19217186.

Peffley, Mark, and Jon Hurwitz. 1998. "Whites' Stereotypes of Blacks: Sources and Consequences." In *Perception and Prejudice: Race and Politics in the United States*, edited by Jon Hurwitz and Mark Peffley. New Haven, CT: Yale University Press.

Peterson, Ruth D., Lauren J. Krivo, and Christopher R. Browning. 2006. "Segregation and Race/Ethnic Inequality in Crime: New Directions." In *Taking Stock: The Status of Criminological Theory—Advances of Criminological Theory*, vol. 15, edited by Francis T. Cullen, John Paul Wright, and Kristie R. Blevins. New Brunswick, NJ: Transaction.

Pettigrew, Thomas F. 1998. "Reactions toward the New Minorities of Western Europe." In *Annual Review of Sociology*, vol. 24, edited by John Hagan and Karen S. Cook. Palo Alto, CA: Annual Reviews.

Pratt, Travis C., and Francis T. Cullen. 2005. "Assessing Macro-Level Predictors and Theories of Crime: A Meta-analysis." In *Crime and Justice: A Review of Research*, vol. 32, edited by Michael Tonry. Chicago: University of Chicago Press.

Radelet, Michael L., and Marian J. Borg. 2000. "The Changing Nature of Death Penalty Debates." In *Annual Review of Sociology*, vol. 26, edited by Karen S. Cook and John Hagan. Palo Alto, CA: Annual Reviews.

Reisig, Michael D., and Roger B. Parks. 2000. "Experience, Quality of Life, and Neighborhood Context: A Hierarchical Analysis of Satisfaction with Police." *Justice Quarterly* 17(3):607–30.

Reitzel, John, and Alex R. Piquero. 2006. "Does It Exist? Studying Citizens' Attitudes of Racial Profiling." *Police Quarterly* 9(2):161–83.

Roberts, Julian V., and Mike Hough. 2005. *Understanding Public Attitudes to Criminal Justice*. New York: Open University Press.

Roberts, Julian V., and Loretta J. Stalans. 2000. *Public Opinion, Crime, and Criminal Justice*. Boulder, CO: Westview.

Saad, Lydia. 2007. "Racial Disagreement over Death Penalty Has Varied Historically." *Gallup News Service*, July 30. http://www.galluppoll.com.

Sampson, Robert J., and Janet L. Lauritsen. 1997. "Racial and Ethnic Disparities in Crime and Criminal Justice in the United States." In *Ethnicity, Crime, and Immigration*, edited by Michael Tonry. Vol. 21 of *Crime and Justice: A Review of Research*, edited by Michael Tonry. Chicago: University of Chicago Press.

Sampson, Robert J., Stephen W. Raudenbush, and Felton Earls. 1997. "Neighborhoods and Violent Crime: A Multilevel Study of Collective Efficacy." *Science* 277(August 15):916–24.

Sears, David O., and P. J. Henry. 2003. "The Origins of Symbolic Racism." *Journal of Personality and Social Psychology* 85(2):259–75.

Sears, David O., P. J. Henry, and Rick Kosterman. 2000. "Egalitarian Values and Contemporary Racial Politics." In *Racialized Politics: The Debate about Racism in America*, edited by David O. Sears, Jim Sidanius, and Lawrence Bobo. Chicago: University of Chicago Press.

Sears, David O., John J. Hetts, Jim Sidanius, and Lawrence Bobo. 2000. "Race in American Politics: Framing the Debates." In *Racialized Politics: The Debate about Racism in America*, edited by David O. Sears, Jim Sidanius, and Lawrence Bobo. Chicago: University of Chicago Press.

Sears, David O., Jim Sidanius, and Lawrence Bobo, eds. 2000. *Racialized Politics: The Debate about Racism in America*. Chicago: University of Chicago Press.

Sears, David O., Colette Van Laar, Mary Carrillo, and Rick Kosterman. 1997. "Is It Really Racism? The Origins of White Americans' Opposition to Race-Targeted Policies." *Public Opinion Quarterly* 61(1):16–53.

Small, Mario Luis, and Katherine Newman. 2001. "Urban Poverty after *The Truly Disadvantaged*: The Rediscovery of the Family, the Neighborhood, and Culture." In *Annual Review of Sociology*, vol. 27, edited by Karen S. Cook and John Hagan. Palo Alto, CA: Annual Reviews.

Sniderman, Paul M., Thomas Piazza, and Hosea Harvey. 1998. "Prejudice and Politics: An Intellectual Biography of a Research Project." In *Perception and Prejudice: Race and Politics in the United States*, edited by Jon Hurwitz and Mark Peffley. New Haven, CT: Yale University Press.

Soss, Joe, Laura Langbein, and Alan R. Metelko. 2003. "Why Do White Americans Support the Death Penalty?" *Journal of Politics* 65(2):397–421.

Stack, Steven. 2003. "Authoritarianism and Support for the Death Penalty: A Multivariate Analysis." *Sociological Focus* 36(4):333–52.

Steiker, Carol. 2002. "Capital Punishment and American Exceptionalism." *Oregon Law Review* 81(1):97–130.

Stewart, Steven D. 2007. "A Message from the Prosecuting Attorney." Office of the Clark County Prosecuting Attorney. http://www.clarkprosecutor.org/html/death/death.htm.

Tanioka, Ichiro, Noriko Iwai, Michio Nitta, and Hiroki Sato. 2001. Japanese General Social Survey, 2000. ICPSR version. Computer file. Osaka: Osaka University of Commerce, Office of Japanese General Social Surveys. Distributed by Inter-university Consortium for Political and Social Research, Ann Arbor, MI.

Taylor, Humphrey. 2004. "More than Two-thirds of Americans Continue to Support the Death Penalty." Harris Interactive. http://www.harrisinteractive.com/harris_poll/index.asp?PID=431.

Thernstrom, Stephen, and Abigail Thernstrom. 1997. *America in Black and White: One Nation, Indivisible—Race in Modern America*. New York: Simon & Schuster.

Tolnay, Stewart E., and E. M. Beck. 1992. "Racial Violence and Black Migration in the American South, 1910 to 1930." *American Sociological Review* 57(1):103–16.

Tolnay, Stewart E., E. M. Beck, and James L. Massey. 1992. "Black Competition and White Vengeance: Legal Execution of Blacks as Social Control in the Cotton South, 1890 to 1929." *Social Science Quarterly* 73(3):627–44.

Tolnay, Stewart E., Glenn Deane, and E. M. Beck. 1996. "Vicarious Violence: Spatial Effects on Southern Lynchings, 1890–1910." *American Journal of Sociology* 102(3):788–815.

Tonry, Michael. 1995. *Malign Neglect: Race, Crime, and Punishment in America*. New York: Oxford University Press.

———. 1997. "Ethnicity, Crime, and Immigration." In *Ethnicity, Crime, and Immigration*, edited by Michael Tonry. Vol. 21 of *Crime and Justice: A Review of Research*, edited by Michael Tonry. Chicago: University of Chicago Press.

———. 2004. *Thinking about Crime: Sense and Sensibility in American Penal Culture*. New York: Oxford University Press.

Tuch, Steven A., and Jack K. Martin, eds. 1997. *Racial Attitudes in the 1990s: Continuity and Change*. Westport, CT: Praeger.

Ulick, Josh. 2005. "Portrait of the Poor." *Newsweek*, September 19, pp. 46–47.

Unnever, James D., and Francis T. Cullen. 2005. "Executing the Innocent and Support for Capital Punishment: Implications for Public Policy." *Criminology and Public Policy* 4(1):3–37.

———. 2007*a*. "The Racial Divide in Support for the Death Penalty: Does White Racism Matter?" *Social Forces* 85(3):1281–1301.

———. 2007*b*. "Reassessing the Racial Divide in Support for Capital Punishment: The Continuing Significance of Race." *Journal of Research in Crime and Delinquency* 44(1):1–35.

Unnever, James D., Francis T. Cullen, and Bonnie S. Fisher. 2005. "Empathy and Support for Capital Punishment." *Journal of Crime and Justice* 24(1): 1–34.

Unnever, James D., Francis T. Cullen, and James D. Jones. 2008. "Public Support for Attacking the 'Root Causes' of Crime: The Impact of Egalitarian and Racial Beliefs." *Sociological Focus* 41(1):1–33.

Virtanen, Simo V., and Leonie Huddy. 1998. "Old-Fashioned Racism and New Forms of Racial Prejudice." *Journal of Politics* 60(2):311–32.

Vogel, Brenda L., and Ronald E. Vogel. 2003. "The Age of Death: Appraising Public Opinion of Juvenile Capital Punishment." *Journal of Criminal Justice* 31(2):169–83.

Wacquant, Loïc. 2001. "Deadly Symbiosis: When Ghetto and Prison Meet and Mesh." *Punishment and Society* 3(1):95–134.

Webb, Vincent J., and Chris E. Marshall. 1995. "The Relative Importance of Race and Ethnicity on Citizen Attitudes toward the Police." *American Journal of Police* 14(2):45–64.

Weitzer, Ronald. 2000. "Racialized Policing: Residents' Perceptions in Three Neighborhoods." *Law and Society Review* 34(1):129–55.

Weitzer, Ronald, and Steven A. Tuch. 1999. "Race, Class, and Perceptions of Discrimination by the Police." *Crime and Delinquency* 45(4):494–507.

———. 2002. "Perceptions of Racial Profiling: Race, Class, and Personal Experience." *Criminology* 40(2):435–56.

———. 2005. "Racially Biased Policing: Determinants of Citizen Perceptions." *Social Forces* 83(3):1009–30.

Welch, Kelly A. 2004. "Punitive Attitudes and the Racial Typification of Crime." PhD dissertation, School of Criminology and Criminal Justice, Florida State University.

Wilson, George, and Roger Dunham. 2001. "Race, Class, and Attitudes toward

Crime Control: The Views of the African American Middle Class." *Criminal Justice and Behavior* 28(3):259–78.

Wilson, William Julius. 1987. *The Truly Disadvantaged: The Inner City, the Underclass, and Public Policy*. Chicago: University of Chicago Press.

Wolfe, Alan. 1998. *One Nation, after All: What Middle-Class Americans Really Think about God, Country, Family, Racism, Welfare, Immigration, Homosexuality, Work, the Right, the Left, and Each Other*. New York: Viking Penguin.

Wortley, Scot, John Hagan, and Ross Macmillan. 1997. "Just Des(s)erts? The Racial Polarization of Perceptions of Criminal Injustice." *Law and Society Review* 31(4):637–76.

Young, Robert L. 1992. "Religious Orientation, Race, and Support for the Death Penalty." *Journal for the Scientific Study of Religion* 31(1):76–87.

———. 2004. "Guilty until Proven Innocent: Conviction Orientation, Racial Attitudes, and Support for Capital Punishment." *Deviant Behavior* 25(2): 151–67.

Zimring, Franklin E. 2003. *The Contradictions of American Capital Punishment*. New York: Oxford University Press.

Todd R. Clear

The Effects of High Imprisonment Rates on Communities

ABSTRACT

When large numbers of parent-aged adults, especially men, cycle through stays in prison and jail at very high rates, communities are negatively affected in myriad ways, including damage to social networks, social relationships, and long-term life chances. These effects impair children, family functioning, mental and physical health, labor markets, and economic and political infrastructures. There are considerable methodological challenges in trying to link the consequences of concentrated incarceration to reduced public safety. Findings from studies are mixed. Yet, as empirical evidence grows of the negative collateral consequences of concentrated incarceration, the likelihood that concentrated incarceration is criminogenic in its effects on those communities becomes stronger. No well-established or proven strategy exists for combating the effects of concentrated incarceration on communities. Most current debates about penal policy are essentially oblivious to the problem. Solutions must flow from changes in the nation's penal philosophy and its sentencing laws.

At no other time or place in world history has there been as long and as large a sustained growth of incarceration as a social policy as has happened in the United States between 1972 and the present. What we do today is often described as "mass incarceration." From 200,000 prisoners in 1972, the prison population has increased to over 1.5 million (over 2.3 million behind bars when jail populations are included). This has been produced not by higher crime rates but by increased rates of sentencing to prison and increased lengths of stay (Raphael and Stoll 2007). This has been especially true with regard to the en-

Todd R. Clear is professor of criminal justice, John Jay College, City University of New York.

0192-3234/2008/0037-0004$10.00

forcement of drug laws, which provide a nearly elastic supply of potential arrests and prison sentences (Fagan 2004).

There are strong indications that such growth will continue for another decade, whatever happens to crime rates (Austin, Naro, and Fabelo 2007). During a period when prisons grew each year without stopping, no other social fact matched the same pattern, not crime, the economy, wartime, age cohorts, or anything else we are accustomed to thinking about as an aspect of crime. What has been the consequence of this unprecedented, generation-long commitment to prison growth?

In this essay, I consider the effects of the growing number of people who go to prison on the communities these prisoners come from. This is not the usual way we consider the impact of incarceration. Usually we think of incarceration as an intervention into the life of a person who has been convicted of a crime. We ask such questions as the following: Was the person deterred from further crime? Were programs provided that ameliorate the troubles that led to the criminal involvement in the first place, problems such as wrongful thinking or inadequate education and skills? Did imprisonment embitter an already ambivalent attitude toward society and its rules, provoking worse adjustment after release?

What we know about the way that prison affects those who go there is, surprisingly, much less than we ought to know. (For a review on this matter, see Gendreau and Cullen [1999] and Smith, Goggin, and Gendreau [2002].) More than 600,000 people are sent to prison in the United States each year; worldwide the figure is a few times that number. With numbers so large, we can assume that people's responses to being imprisoned run the gamut of human experience. As a group, some will appear to have been "turned around," and others—perhaps the larger proportion—will have been cast deeper into the life of crime. If prison is meant to convey a message to those who go there, a few get it; many do not. About one-third of those who go to prison once come back again; of those who go to prison a second time, four-fifths will return repeatedly (Hughes, Wilson, and Beck 2001). Regarding imprisonment as an educational device, we can offer two conclusions. First, its lessons for individuals range widely, from reformative to the exact opposite. Second, as a device to promote law-abiding behavior by those who go there, the results are dim.

The individual-level effects of incarceration on those who go to prison ripple outward. Imprisonment is also an intervention into the lives of people who may never go there themselves. There are three levels of such effects. Imprisonment affects the children of people who are locked up and their families; it affects community infrastructure—the relations among people in communities and the capacity of a community to be a good place to live, work, and raise children—and it affects how safe a community is to live in. One essay in the current volume reviews the way incarcerating people affects their loved ones, especially their children (Murray and Farrington, in this volume). The purpose of my essay is to explore what we know about the unintended consequences of imprisonment for communities, especially community quality of life, but also public safety.

The most commonly expected community-level consequence of incarceration is crime control through deterrence and incapacitation. There is a substantial body of literature on this topic, including three recent review essays (Spelman 2000*a*, 2000*b*; Stemen 2007). Estimates of the crime-prevention effects of incarceration vary, from very sizable impacts on the order of a 9 percent drop in crime for every 10 percent increase in the rate of incarceration (see, e.g., Marvell and Moody 1997) to much smaller ones on the order of a 0.05 percent crime drop for that same level of increase (see also Western 2006) to none at all (Kovandzic and Vieraitis 2006). Three main conclusions can be drawn from this literature.

First, the range of estimates does not tend to converge on a single reliable statistic (compare Western [2006] to Spelman [2000*b*]). Second, a host of impediments, both of method and of logic, confront any attempt to estimate the true crime-prevention effects of incarceration, and even seemingly strong designs are subject to fundamental concerns (see Webster, Doob, and Zimring's [2006] critique of Kessler and Levitt [1999]). Third, more recent studies using more complete data sets and more reliable methods tend to produce smaller overall estimates of the crime-reduction effects of prison growth (Sweeten and Apel, forthcoming). At least one study suggests why, concluding that the past decade's massive growth in imprisonment has diluted the ability to prevent crime through incapacitation (Liedka, Piehl, and Useem 2006).

There are good reasons to doubt the size of the crime-prevention impact of imprisonment. These stem from the massive natural experiment in imprisonment for crime control now under way in the United States. Prison populations have grown every year since 1973—we have a generation of increasing imprisonment. The external validity challenge to a strong prison-reduces-crime argument is illustrated in figure 1, which shows the pattern of crime rates and the prison population between 1931 and 2005. Crime rates started growing in the 1960s and roughly doubled from 1960 to 1970, a period when prison populations were in slight decline (going from a rate of about 120 per 100,000 in 1960 to about 100 per 100,000 in 1970). Since 1973, imprisonment rates have grown monotonically upward. Crime rates have been anything but monotonic. They more than doubled in the 1970s, peaking in 1981, and then dropped nearly one-sixth until the mid-1980s. They rose again to a peak in the early 1990s, declining almost one-third from that peak. Incarceration rates grew steeply in the 1980s and began to decelerate in the late 1990s, growing much more slowly since about 2000. Today, the crime rate is about what it was in 1970, when the prison expansion started. So whatever the true impact of imprisonment is, it cannot be simply linear and additive for the last 30 years.

There are easy explanations for the disconnect between incarceration growth and crime rates, though (again) we cannot say precisely how they work. We know that some crime is replaced. That is, when a person is locked up for a given crime, he is incapacitated from committing more crime during his prison stay, but others replace him and commit at least some of those crimes anyway. This is most obviously true for drug sales, which continue with little interruption. It appears also to be true for much of the crime committed by young men in groups, including predatory street crime (Felson 2003). Locking up some who are actively criminal may destabilize criminal networks in ways that provoke more violence rather than less (Blumstein and Beck 1999). The larger number of people cycling through the prison system may itself be a problem if going to prison increases the chances of criminal behavior, as some have suggested (see Gendreau and Cullen 1999).

In general, then, the crime-reduction effects of imprisonment are unlikely to be very large. What about the other effects of incarceration on communities?

This essay examines studies of the effects of incarceration on communities where it occurs at high levels of concentration. Here is what the literature shows.

Incarceration is concentrated in communities of disadvantage, especially communities of color. Because residential housing is segregated and incarceration is concentrated among poor black men, incarceration is

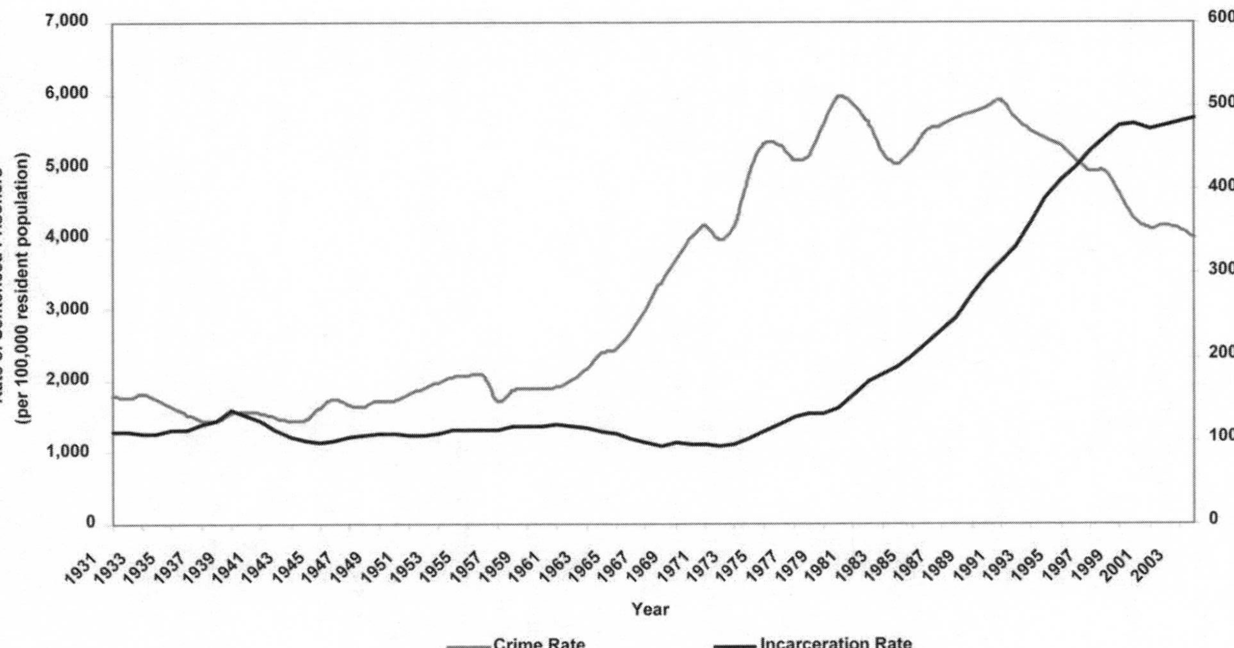

FIG. 1.—Improvement rate per 100,000 population, sentenced state and federal prisoners, and crime rate per 100,000 population, 1931–2005. Source: Austin et al. 2007.

a particularly dominant characteristic of a small number of urban, impoverished neighborhoods. In those places, parent-aged adults, especially men, cycle through stays in prison and jail at astounding rates.

Those communities are negatively affected by this concentration of incarceration in myriad ways. Penal system cycling for young adults affects social networks, social relationships, and long-term life prospects; subsequently, communities where incarceration is concentrated suffer damage at the hands of the penal system. These destructive effects are felt in the lives of children, as well as in family functioning, mental and physical health, labor markets, and the economic and political infrastructures of these places.

The negative effects of high rates of concentrated incarceration probably decrease public safety. There are considerable methodological challenges in trying to link the consequences of concentrated incarceration to reduced public safety, and the findings from current studies are mixed. Yet, as empirical evidence of the negative collateral consequences of incarceration grows, the case that concentrated incarceration has become criminogenic in its effects on involved communities has become stronger.

No well-established or proven strategy exists for combating the effects of concentrated incarceration on communities. Most current debates about penal policy are oblivious to the problem of concentrated incarceration. Any solutions to this problem must flow from changes in penal philosophy and in sentencing laws.

This essay has three sections. Section I describes the nature of concentrated incarceration and shows how it might affect communities through its effects on social networks and informal social control. Section II summarizes studies of the effects of incarceration on children, families, and the fabric of community life. It closes by considering the ways in which incarceration may affect public safety in communities; this includes a discussion of the methodological considerations in modeling these effects. Section III proposes policy and research agendas suggested by these results.

I. The Concentration of Incarceration in Communities

Incarceration is not an equal opportunity activity. It concentrates in four important ways. Men are almost 15 times more likely to end up in prison than are women, blacks are almost seven times more likely to go there than are whites, and people who fail to finish high school are three times more likely to spend time behind prison bars than are high school graduates. Prison is also for younger adults: 69 percent of the confined are under age 40. These differential odds of incarceration are additive. Western has estimated that almost six in 10 black males who do not finish high school go to prison during their lifetimes. (For all of the above, see Harrison and Beck [2006] and Western [2006, p. 27].)

These four layers of concentration—race, age, gender, and human capital—come together to produce the fifth and crucial sphere of concentrated incarceration: place. The extreme racial and socioeconomic segregation of housing in the United States means that the odds of incarceration add up in some places to reach stunning levels. Lynch and Sabol (2004*a*) estimated that, in some of the poorest neighborhoods in Cleveland and Baltimore, almost one out of every five males aged 18–44 was behind bars on any given day. It is important to know that this daily count of neighborhood residents behind bars masks a more substantial flow in and out. One-fifth may be locked up on any given day, but from one day to the next, as different men go in and out of the prison, a different set of men get their turn behind bars. In some areas of Brooklyn, one of every three youth aged 16–24 living in the neighborhood is removed and sent to prison or jail each year (Cadora 2007). For many who are removed, the stay is brief, but added up across numerous years, incarceration in these neighborhoods is nearly ubiquitous. Figure 2 is a map of the neighborhood incarceration rates of Brooklyn, showing how incarceration concentrates in a handful of neighborhoods.

When Dina Rose and I interviewed about 125 people in two very poor neighborhoods in Tallahassee, we learned that every family in our sample was touched by prison—all reported a family member in prison within the past 5 years, and whatever the effects of incarceration are on those imprisoned, effects were felt by everyone in our sample. If nearly every family in a high-incarceration neighborhood is touched by imprisonment, what fingerprints, exactly, does that touch leave behind?

Three recent ethnographies give us a picture of these dynamics. Donald Braman (2004) spent 2 years studying families from poor, high-incarceration areas of Washington, DC. He provides detailed descriptions of how incarceration affected 12 families. From their stories, he

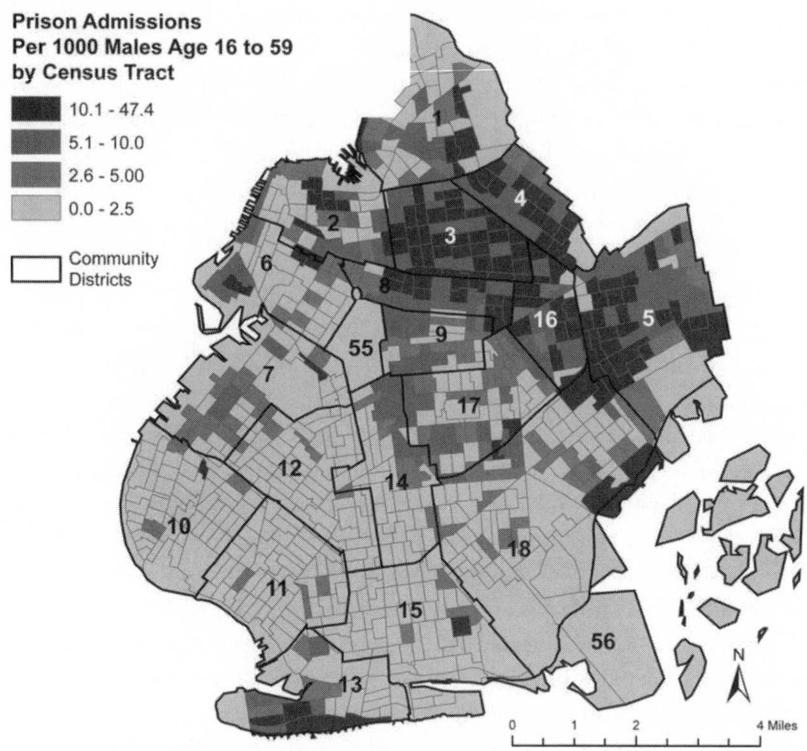

FIG. 2.—Prison admissions per 1,000 males aged 16–59 by census tract. Map provided by Charles Swartz, Justice Mapping, Inc., New York, June 12, 2007.

documents how incarceration breaks families apart, strains their economic resources, weakens parental involvement with children, and leads to emotional and social isolation. He shows the ways that having a male family member go to prison interferes with employment prospects for those who remain behind, and he concludes that, on balance, the consequences of incarceration borne by families are a net negative.

Adrian Nicole LeBlanc (2004), a journalist, spent 10 years documenting the lives of women in an extended Latina family in the South Bronx region of New York City. She showed how cycles of stays in both prison and jail become crucial events in the lives of young mothers as they struggle with the ways in which incarceration affects relationships, especially those with children. Her descriptions of how criminal justice and welfare interact to dominate the lives of these young mothers show how incarceration becomes a thread in the fabric of community life there.

Johnna Christian (2004) studied some families living in the Queens borough of New York who had men in upstate prisons. She traveled with the families as they made the daylong trek from Columbus Circle in New York City to upstate prisons, visiting loved ones. She documented the fiscal and emotional costs these families bear to maintain ties to their family members in prison, and she describes the influence of incarceration as a force in one Queens neighborhood.

The perspectives taken in each of these studies are a bit different, but what they report is broadly consistent. The effects of family members' incarceration are not straightforward. Most of the men who ended up behind bars engaged in behavior that created strains on the family. When they were arrested and ended up cycling through prison or jail, some of that strain was lessened. But, at the same time, a new set of strains came along. Families struggled financially to deal with court costs and later the need to provide support for people who were locked up. Parenting with someone behind bars is an emotional and practical strain. A host of destabilizing consequences—housing changes, school maladaptations, welfare problems, and strains on relationships—follow the person's trip to the prison. Each researcher concludes that incarceration effects are a net negative for the families they studied. As Braman puts it, "Incarceration forcibly restructures household composition and kin relations" (2004, p. 10).

There are sound theoretical reasons to expect the ripple effects of high levels of incarceration to be both substantial and problematic (Rose and Clear 1998). We know that social networks are the building blocks of human and social capital. That is, the relationships people develop and maintain define the limits of the support they may engender to help them accomplish their aims and deal with life problems as they arise. Incarceration affects social networks by removing one of the members of a poor family's network. About three-quarters of minority men who go to prison are fathers (Western 2006, p. 137). But almost always the person is also a child and a sibling of others.

The work done by social networks is crucial to quality of life, forming the basis for social support, providing access to goods and services, and structuring the limits of a person's lifelong long-term opportunities and short-term problem solving. So-called "strong" ties, those that are reciprocated in ways that do not create relationships outside the network, are good for intimate support but not for building social capital. "Weak" ties, those that create bridges to other networks, are useful for expanding one's horizons and may offer access to assistance from people who are not in one's network but who are connected through that (weak) bond (for a classic discussion on this matter, see Granovetter [1993]). Studies of social networks in impoverished places find that these are dominated by strong ties (Dominguez and Watkins 2003) and that a substantial portion of ties that provide social support are ties to government services (Bursik and Grasmick 1993).

When a loved one goes to prison, a strong tie is threatened for the person who remains behind. That person can either invest personal capital in maintaining that tie or learn how to live without it. People use both strategies. When the tie is broken, there is a need to replace it with another intimate tie. A replacement loved one is needed. In poor places where many men either are locked up or are poor prospects for relationships because of their criminal histories, women looking for "good" male partners are at a distinct numerical disadvantage. (I return to this issue in the next section.) For those who try to sustain the tie, there are considerable costs in time, money, and emotional investment. But, in general, in places where strong ties dominate social networks and government social services are the main source of social support, removing a strong tie has little impact on the size or shape of a social network (Rengifo and Waring 2005).

Yet, there are opportunity costs borne by social networks in places with high incarceration rates. The ordinary role played by young men in social networks is "entrepreneurial." They are supposed to be entering the labor market meeting new people (and bringing back those weak ties to their own networks), thereby expanding the productive capacity of all the networks of which they are a part. Young men bridge their personal networks to those of others, thereby expanding access to social capital for all their ties. Men in prison cannot perform that function in the free world; they can only link their networks to the prison world.

Social networks are also the foundation for informal social control. Hunter (1985) identified two types of informal social control: parochial and private. Both are a product of social networks. Parochial controls are provided by contacts with neighbors and other local adults whose living circumstances put them in a child's life. Private controls are provided by intimates, especially family members. The capacity of these informal social controls is an aspect of the size and nature of social networks that place parochial and private ties in the youth's life.

Social networks are not necessarily always insulators against crime. In poor neighborhoods, social ties may promote social capital in ways that increase criminal activity (Browning, Feinberg, and Dietz 2004). People who are actively engaged in crime use their exchange relations to promote their criminal activity just as they do other activities. So while social networks are the building blocks of informal social control, they can also strengthen the capacity for crime. Imprisonment does not alter by much the social networks of a person's nonincarcerated strong ties, and to the degree that incarceration increases that person's ties to others who are criminally active, it may promote greater crime as well (Rengifo 2007).

Social control theories also emphasize the normative aspect of community safety. Sampson, Raudenbush, and Earls (1997, p. 918) proposed that communities are made safe when people share a normative expectation that these researchers call "collective efficacy," or the degree of "social cohesion among neighbors combined with their willingness to intervene on behalf of the common good." Bursik and Grasmick (1993) developed an extension of social disorganization theory in which they showed how community-level processes can bolster informal social control and thereby reduce crime. In both instances, incarceration can play a role, because, when intimates are removed to prison, people often respond by isolating themselves in ways that undermine norms of cooperation and mutual support. Similarly, Tyler and his colleagues (e.g., Tyler and Fagan 2005) have developed a series of arguments regarding the role of "legitimacy" in reducing crime. When the law is seen as fair, they find, there is a greater tendency to comply with it. So in communities where many people are removed for incarceration, to the degree that these removals are seen as unfair, the rule of law is weakened.

Thus, there are several theoretical mechanisms through which incarceration might affect communities, especially community safety. To these community-level normative perspectives can be added the raw effects of mathematics: having a large number of people who have been to prison as residents bodes poorly for a community's general level of crime. For example, if going to prison reduces a person's ability to get and to keep a job, even by a small factor, then neighborhoods where many people have been to prison are also neighborhoods where those

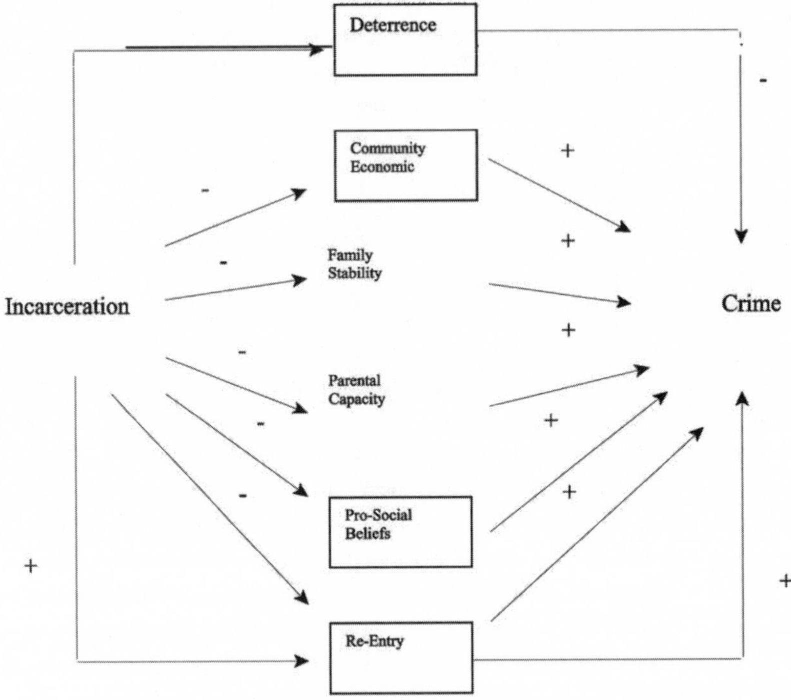

FIG. 3.—Model of interactions between crime, incarceration, and individual, familial, and environmental factors. Source: Clear (2007).

people have trouble in the job market. The implications include higher unemployment and lower incomes.

There are substantial problems in modeling the community-level effects of incarceration. These are illustrated by the relationship between incarceration and crime, shown as a simple conceptual model in figure 3 (Clear 2007, p. 150). The figure shows that incarceration tends to reduce crime through incapacitation and deterrence but that it also tends to increase crime through destabilization of families and by undermining other sources of informal social control. Thus, incarceration both increases and decreases crime. This figure oversimplifies that pattern, because crime also has effects on families, the economy, and other sources of informal social control. There are also likely to be interactions among these forces that are not included in the conceptual model.

This bidirectional causation and mutual causality make it exceedingly difficult to sort out exactly what causes what and by how much. Some researchers attempt to model directly the effects of incarceration on some aspect of interpersonal or community dynamic. Others seek to infer effects on communities by adding up effects on individuals, such as is done in studies of labor market participation after incarceration and studies of legal legitimacy.

In each of these cases, questions persist about the reliability of precise estimates. Causal bidirectionality creates modeling challenges. That so many network- and community-level forces exert pressure in multiple directions, both receiving the effects of incarceration and producing changes in rates of incarceration, means that there is a spatial overdetermination of effects. The kinds of data now available do not allow modeling of all the recursive paths over time, with all the necessary controls and interactions, in order to sustain an unassailable claim that incarceration has this specific weight in producing this specific outcome. Yet, as we travel through the host of studies bearing on the ways in which incarceration effects are felt through the range of human patterns in families, communities, and the polity, at some point the limitations of design begin to become less important than the sheer logical power of consistently problematic outcomes realized in domain after domain. What emerges is a tightly coupled system of effects, many small; but when these are aggregated, they make up an overwhelming dynamic of which incarceration is a significant part. In the search for a more finely tuned understanding of exactly what causes what and by how much, it is important not to lose sight of the bigger picture. When communities suffer these ill effects, children are more likely to become delinquent (Rucker 2007) and incarceration, at high levels, can become a self-sustaining system. In another context, I referred to this system of effects as "death by a thousand little cuts" (Clear 2007, p. 93).

II. The Effects of Incarceration on Communities

Two general kinds of studies examine the effects of incarceration on communities. Some studies attempt to establish ways in which incarceration directly causes some sort of community-level outcome. Studies of public health, labor market participation, and children are often of this type. Other studies examine how incarceration contributes logically to community-level problems, for example, institutional infrastructure. It is not crucial to bear this distinction in mind, because of the way incarceration is embedded in a system of mutual effects. However, the limits in methodologies are sometimes important, particularly when the outcome of interest is public safety.

A. Children and Families

The family is the basic building block of informal social control. Families are the main institution by which children are socialized, and the family is the core source of social support upon which people feel free to draw. Yet families are changing in America, especially poor families. Some changes for American poor people have been devastating: divorce rates are one-third higher and births to unmarried mothers have doubled, as has the rate of households headed by single mothers (see Western, Lopoo, and McLanahan 2004). Incarceration is a key ingredient in these changes, affecting, as it does, children, marriage, parenting, and interpersonal relationships.

1. *Children.* Estimates of the number of children with a parent in prison run as high as 2.3 million, or almost 3 percent of the under-age-18 population (Martone 2005). Rucker (2007) has estimated that 20 percent of black children had a father with an incarceration history, with 33 percent of black children whose fathers who did not graduate from high school having one. These children are affected by having a parent behind bars, both directly and indirectly through the ways incarceration affects their life chances.

Several recent studies examine how incarceration affects children (for a review, see Murray [2005]). A recent systematic review of controlled studies of how incarceration affects children (Murray and Farrington, in this volume) finds strong evidence that incarceration exacerbates certain problems of growing up. They describe a dozen studies showing that parental incarceration is a risk factor for later delinquency and conclude that having a parent incarcerated makes the child three to four times more likely to develop a record for juvenile delinquency. The five studies they review about mental health suggest that having an incarcerated parent makes a child two and a half times more likely to develop a serious mental disorder. Studies also suggest a link between parental incarceration and school failure, underemployment, and illegal drug use.

These studies do not necessarily demonstrate that incarceration causes these problematic child outcomes. Indeed, the evidence that

Murray and Farrington provide from controlled experiments on this issue is mixed, with some studies indicating that preexisting risks may account for at least some of the consequences of parental incarceration. Nonetheless, there is no question that children whose parents go to prison have, on average, worse life outcomes in a variety of ways, ranging from mental health and social functioning to deviant behavior and crime.

2. *Families and Marriage.* Incarceration policy has been a contributor to the deterioration of poor American families. As many as 700,000 families have a loved one behind bars on any given day (Lynch and Sabol 2004*b*, p. 283). Almost three of five African American high school dropouts will spend some time in prison (Pettit and Western 2004), and two-fifths are fathers who were living with their children before they entered prison (Western, Pattillo, and Weiman 2004). One-fourth of juveniles convicted of crime have children (Nurse 2004). Phillips et al. (2006, p. 103) point out that "there is evidence . . . that the arrest of parents disrupts marital relationships, separates children and parents, and may contribute to the permanent legal dissolution of these relationships. It may also contribute to the establishment of grandparent-headed households and, upon parents' return home from prison, to three-generation households."

Poor neighborhoods in which there is a large ratio of adult women to men are places where female-headed, single-parent families are common. Incarceration is one of several dynamics that remove black males from their neighborhoods, producing this ratio (Darity and Myers 1994). In a county-level analysis for 1980 and 1990, Sabol and Lynch (2003) found that removals to and returns from prison increased the rate of female-headed households in the county. Analyzing the National Longitudinal Survey of Youth, Harvard economist Adam Thomas (2005) found that going to prison substantially reduces the likelihood of being married. The effects hold across all racial and ethnic groups, but they are strongest for black males over 23 years old, whose likelihood of getting married drops by 50 percent following incarceration. Previously incarcerated men who do become involved with women are more likely to cohabit without marriage. Western's (2006) analysis estimates that going to prison cuts the rate of marriage within a year of the birth of a child by at least one-half and about doubles the chance of separating in that same year (Thomas 2005, figs. 6.8, 6.9). It is not surprising that Lynch and Sabol (2004*b*, p. 283) estimate that 66 percent of the ever-married prison population are currently divorced, compared to a rate of 17 percent for nonimprisoned adults. Phillips et al.'s (2006) longitudinal study of poor, rural children in North Carolina found that having a parent get arrested leads to family breakup and family economic strain, both of which are risk factors for later delinquency.

3. *Parenting.* While they are locked up, many men maintain contact with their children; about half receive mail, phone calls, or both, and one-fifth receive visits (Mumola 2000, cited in Western, Pattillo, and Weiman 2004, table 1.5). But the rate at which mothers dissolve their relationships with their children's father during the latter's imprisonment is very high, even for fathers who were active in their children's lives prior to being arrested—only 20–25 percent of prisoners are visited in prison by their children (Western, Pattillo, and Weiman 2004, pp. 10–11). Nonetheless, some fathers who have had little contact with their children before imprisonment renew those bonds during incarceration. Edin, Nelson, and Paranal (2004, p. 57) show that "incarceration often means that fathers miss out on . . . key events that serve to build parental bonds and to signal . . . that they intend to support their children both financially and emotionally. . . . The father's absence at these crucial moments . . . can weaken his commitment to the child years later, and the child's own commitment to his or her father."

4. *Family Functioning.* Lynch and Sabol (2004*b*) have estimated that between one-fourth and one-half of all prisoners disrupt a family when they are removed for incarceration. Murray (2005) lists a dozen studies of ways that the incarceration of a male parent or spouse (or partner) affects the functioning of the family unit left behind. The most prominent effect is economic—spouses and partners report various forms of financial hardship, sometimes extreme, that result from the loss of income after the male partner's incarceration. This "loss of income is compounded by additional expenses of prison visits, mail, telephone calls . . . and sending money to [the person] imprisoned" (Murray 2005, p. 445). Because most families of prisoners start with limited financial prospects, even a small financial detriment can be devastating.

After the male's imprisonment, the family responds in a variety of ways. Families often move, leading to disruptions that may include the arrival of replacement males in the family and reduced time for maternal parenting owing to secondary employment (Edin, Nelson, and

Paranal 2004). Moves may also result in more crowded living conditions (especially when the prisoner's family moves in with relatives) and changes in educational districts, which may produce disruptions in schooling.

There are also relationship problems. Female partners who find a male replacement for the man who has gone to prison often face the psychological strains that accompany the arrival of a new male in the household. Prisoners' spouses and partners report strains in relationships with other family members and neighbors. Carlson and Cervera (1992) showed that women often have to rely on family and friends to fill the hole left by the incarcerated husband, providing money, companionship, and babysitting, and generally straining those ties. Strains in relationships with children are also reported, resulting from emotional and functional difficulties that spouses and partners encounter when a male partner goes to prison (Nurse 2004).

5. *Intimate (Sexual) Relations.* The incarceration of large numbers of parent-aged males restricts the number of male partners available in the neighborhood. This means that mothers find more competition for intimate partners who can serve as parents for their children. In the context of more competition for male support, mothers may feel reluctant to end relationships that are unsuitable for children. Likewise, men living with advantageous gender ratios may feel less incentive to remain committed in their parenting partnerships.

Citing these dynamics, epidemiologists James Thomas and Elizabeth Torrone (2006) investigated the role of high rates of incarceration on sexual behavior in poor neighborhoods. Analyzing North Carolina counties and communities, they found that incarceration rates in one year predicted later increases in rates of gonorrhea, syphilis, and chlamydia among women. They also found that a doubling of incarceration rates increased the incidence of childbirth by teenage women by 71.61 births per 100,000 teenage women. They conclude that "high rates of incarceration can have the unintended consequence of destabilizing communities and contributing to adverse health outcomes" (Thomas and Torrone 2006, p. 1). This latter finding is notable because, for mothers, teenage births are more likely to lead to lower wages, underemployment, reliance upon welfare, and single parenthood; for children of mothers who have their first child at a very early age, there is an increased likelihood of arrest for delinquency and violent crime (Pogarsky, Lizotte, and Thornberry 2003).

Incarceration, which distorts local sex ratios, also seems to explain at least part of the higher rate of HIV among African American men and women. Johnson and Raphael (2005, p. 3) analyzed data on AIDS infection rates provided by the U.S. Centers for Disease Control and Prevention from 1982 to 2001 and found "very strong effects of male incarceration rates on both male and female AIDS infection rates [and] . . . the higher incarceration rates among black males over this period explain a large share of the racial disparity in AIDS between black women and women of other racial and ethnic groups."

B. Community Institutions and Infrastructure

Impoverished places are poor because people there do not make much money, from work or otherwise. They are also places, disconnected from mainstream political life, where negative attitudes toward formal social institutions are common. Incarceration exacerbates these problems.

1. *The Economics of Community Life.* People who get into trouble with the law are characterized by poor work records before they get arrested. Only 42 percent of mothers and 55 percent of fathers who are incarcerated were working full time at the time of their arrest; 32 percent of mothers and 18 percent of fathers were unemployed and not even looking for work (Uggen, Wakefield, and Western 2005).

Going to prison further deteriorates these already weak employment prospects. While during their initial period of release from incarceration both men and women are slightly more likely to be employed than before imprisonment, these short-term effects rapidly wear off as their participation in the labor market diminishes over time (see LaLonde and George [2003]; Cho and LaLonde [2005] for women; Western, Kling, and Weiman [2001] for men). Jeffrey Grogger (1995) demonstrates that merely being arrested has a short-term negative impact on earnings, while Richard Freeman (1992) shows that suffering a conviction and imprisonment has a permanent impact on earning potential. Jeffrey Kling (1999) finds small effects on the earnings of people convicted of federal crimes, mostly concentrated among those convicted of white-collar crimes. Western (2006, fig. 5.1) estimates that going to prison reduces annual earnings by about one-third among people sent to state prison, and he argues that "incarceration carries not just an economic penalty on the labor market; it also confines ex-prisoners to bad jobs that are characterized by high turnover and little chance of moving up the ladder" (p. 128).

Not only does this mean that these neighborhoods have large concentrations of residents who are less engaged in the job market and earn diminished income, but men who are "stuck in low-wage or unstable jobs [find] that their opportunities for marriage will be limited . . . [and] the stigma of incarceration makes single mothers reluctant to marry or live with the fathers of their children" (Uggen, Wakefield, and Western 2005, p. 221), with the result that both work and marriage prospects are degraded (Huebner 2005).

2. *The Production of Local Labor Markets.* The economic prospects of people who live in poor communities are linked. Family members earning money contribute to the welfare of their families, and this is true even when some of those earnings are from criminal activity such as drug sales. Edin and Lein's (1997) study of poor mothers found that up to 91 percent of them reported that they had received money from members in their networks; 55 percent had received cash from their families, 32 percent from their boyfriends, and 41 percent from their child's father. Incarceration removes from the neighborhood many of the men who had provided support to these women. The concentration of formerly incarcerated men in poor neighborhoods may also damage the labor market prospects of others in the community. Roberts (2004, p. 1294) points out that "the spatial concentration of incarceration . . . impedes access to jobs for youth in those communities because it decreases the pool of men who can serve as their mentors and their links to the working world . . . generating employment discrimination against entire neighborhoods." Sabol and Lynch (2003) have shown that, as county-level incarceration rates grow, so do unemployment rates for blacks who live in those counties.

Ethnographies (Sullivan 1989; Venkatesh 1997, 2006) show how, in impoverished neighborhoods, a work-aged male generates economic activity that translates into purchases at the local deli, child support, and similar expenditures. This economic value is generated in a variety of endeavors, including off-the-books work, intermittent illicit drug trade, theft, welfare, and part-time employment. Many, if not most, of those who engage in crime also have legal employment, so their removal from the neighborhood removes a worker from the local legal economy (Fagan and Freeman 1999). In large numbers, incarceration raids supplies of local human capital and leaves a gap in employable residents. Even families that reap the individual benefit of newly available employment suffer the indirect costs of depleted neighborhood economic strength. One estimate (Holzer 2007) holds that increases in incarceration since 1980 have reduced young black male labor force activity by 3–5 percent.

3. *Attitudes toward Authority and the State.* Peter St. Jean (2006) has gathered extensive crime and community data on the neighborhoods of Buffalo (New York), including interviews of "old heads" in poor, primarily black areas. He concludes that "preexisting socio-economic and other conditions [combine with] law enforcement factors—profiling, discrimination, different responses to crime committed by blacks and Hispanics as opposed to whites—to produce a pervasive sense of cynicism" (p. 7). Crutchfield (2005) investigated the effects of concentrated levels of young men in reentry on the attitudes of neighbors who had not been to prison. He found that in "neighborhoods with relatively large concentrations of former prisoners and, by extension . . . communities with more churning of people into and out of the prison system . . . [the negative attitude] in those places that we ordinarily attribute to economic disadvantage is due in part to sentencing patterns and correctional policies" (p. 2). Tyler and Fagan (2005) show that people in New York City neighborhoods where incarceration rates are highest tend to view the police as unfair and disrespectful: this corrodes their views of the legitimacy of policing and broader governmental authority and, in turn, signals their withdrawal from social regulation and political life.

4. *Voting.* More than 5.3 million people in the United States are estimated to have been prohibited from voting as a consequence of their criminal records (Uggen and Manza 2006). These disenfranchised Americans tend to concentrate in poor neighborhoods, so that mass incarceration "translates the denial of individual felons' voting rights into disenfranchisement of entire communities" (Roberts 2004, p. 1292). A study of voter disenfranchisement patterns in Atlanta (King and Mauer 2004, p. 15) found that predominantly black areas have a voter disenfranchisement rate three to four times higher than the rates in predominantly white areas. The disenfranchisement effect "contributes to a vicious cycle . . . that further disadvantages low-income communities of color . . . [and] a diminished impact on public policy." People with felony arrests who may legally vote are 18 percent less likely to vote than those who have not been arrested; people in prison

who are allowed to vote are 27 percent less likely to do so than their nonincarcerated counterparts (Uggen and Manza 2005). Jeffrey Fagan (2006) and his colleagues found that, while poor neighborhoods had very low rates of voter participation in elections, the nonparticipation was not directly affected by the rate of incarceration. They showed that voter registration and participation rates were lower in neighborhoods with high rates of incarceration, especially in neighborhoods where enforcement of drug laws was the primary engine fueling the incarceration rate.

5. *Collective Action.* Lynch and Sabol (2004*b*, p. 157) investigated how incarceration affected community-level variables, including collective efficacy, in Baltimore neighborhoods. They found that "incarceration reduces community solidarity and attachment to communities" and weakens "the social processes on which social controls depend."

C. *Public Safety*

The concept of "coercive mobility" was developed by Rose and Clear (1998) to refer to two particular ways by which high rates of incarceration can increase crime in impoverished places. First, removal of young residents for imprisonment is a mobility process that affects crime (Shaw and McKay 1942). It changes the density and spread of what Bursik and Grasmick (1993) have called secondary relational networks. This reduces the capacity of those networks to link to resources outside the neighborhood and to bring them to bear on problems of people in the neighborhood. This weakens attachment to the neighborhood and ties to neighbors and thereby erodes the collective efficacy that Sampson and others have argued serves as a foundation for informal social control. The social stresses identified by Weatherburn and Lind (2001) are increased by incarceration-induced parental disruptions that lead to changes in the home and increased stresses on the home. Since these occur in the context of low social supports in highly economically stressed communities, parental incarceration generates the parental dysfunctions that lead to delinquency. In short, high rates of removal of parent-aged residents from poor communities set off a series of effects that destabilize the capacities of those communities to provide informal social control.

The second effect occurs with reentry into the community of those who were incarcerated. This is a much more straightforward effect.

Poor communities that absorb large numbers of people returning from prison have higher crime rates, not just because these people commit the crimes but also because they are needy residents who tie up the limited interpersonal and social resources of their families and networks, weakening the ability of the families and networks to perform other functions of informal social control and to import resources from outside the neighborhood—a problem Bursik and Grasmick (1993) have discussed. The coercive mobility thesis posits a tipping point at which the most deleterious effects of coercive mobility take effect after a large number of people are caught up in the removal and return cycle.

1. *Testing the Coercive Mobility Hypothesis.* The coercive mobility hypothesis has been tested by several researchers, with mixed results. In the first attempt, Clear et al. (2003) modeled the effect of 1995 incarceration rates on 1996 crime rates in Tallahassee neighborhoods, controlling for neighborhood-level measures of social disorganization (concentrated disadvantage), reentry rates in 1996, and violent crime in 1995. Using a quadratic for neighborhood incarceration rates, they tested for a nonlinear (tipping point) effect. They argue that this is a good test of the coercive mobility hypothesis because it models the effects of incarceration rates in one year on crime in a later year, controlling for previous levels of crime and neighborhood characteristics.

These results suggest that there are two different effects of neighborhoods' incarceration experiences on their rates of crime. One is linear: the number of people returning to prison has a direct and positive impact on crime, so that with each additional person reentering a neighborhood, the neighborhood's crime rate can be expected to increase. The second effect is curvilinear: "Increasing admissions to prison in one year has a negligible effect on crime at low levels, a negative effect on crime the following year when the rate is relatively low, but, after a certain concentration of residents is removed from the community through incarceration, the effect of additional admissions is to increase, not decrease, crime" (Clear et al. 2003, p. 55). This finding tends to confirm the coercive mobility hypothesis.

The Tallahassee coercive mobility model has been replicated in six locations. The first replication occurred in Tallahassee itself (Waring, Scully, and Clear 2005), where data from additional years were added to the original sample, allowing for analysis of effects of concentrated incarceration across a 9-year period, 1994–2002. Coercive mobility models equivalent to those originally published in 2002 were estimated. The results were virtually identical to those reported in the earlier paper (Clear et al. 2003). When these results are disaggregated for type of crime, there is curvilinearity for burglary, drug crime, and auto theft but not for robbery (Waring, Scully, and Clear 2005).

There have been five additional studies in other locations. Renauer and his colleagues (2006) employed the Tallahassee coercive mobility model on neighborhoods in Portland (Oregon), testing the effects of prison sentence removals in 2000 on crime in the following year. They found that, while coercive mobility variables were not significantly predictive of property crime (although the correlations were generally in the right direction), they were predictive of violent crime in the same curvilinear way as occurred in Tallahassee.

In Columbus (Ohio), a similar direct replication was attempted (Powell et al. 2004). The curves for violent crime are similar to those found in Tallahassee. For property crime, it is at the middle level that concentrated incarceration tended to lead to an increase in crime, and this effect was quite pronounced. Levels of crime began dropping at the highest levels of incarceration.

In Chicago, Susan George and her colleagues (George, LaLonde, and Schuble 2005) tested the effect of female incarceration in 1999 on drug crime in 2000. Studying female incarceration is an important extension of the Rose-Clear coercive mobility hypothesis. While the aggregate number of women who go through the incarceration process is much smaller than the aggregate number of men (about one-tenth), George and her colleagues found that drug crime is associated with incarceration of women in the same pattern elicited between total incarceration and total crime in Tallahassee.

In Cleveland and Baltimore (Bhati, Lynch, and Sabol 2005), coercive mobility models were substantially similar to those in the original Tallahassee analysis. When Bhati and his colleagues analyzed the data using an instrument, the findings changed, a result that is discussed more below.

Taken together, these results lend credence to, though only partial support for, the coercive mobility thesis as modeled by Clear et al. (2003). However, problems of sample size, control variables, and extreme cases make assessments of statistical significance problematic.

Two recent studies give additional credibility to the tipping point idea. Fagan and his colleagues (Fagan, West, and Holland 2003, p. 23) investigated the effects of incarceration on crime rates at the neighborhood level in New York City, from 1985 to 1996, and found that "over time, incarceration creates more incarceration in a spiraling dynamic." In a neighborhood study not involving incarceration, Robert J. Kane (2006) investigated the effect of "arrest rigor" (arrests for violent crime per officer) on rates of burglary and robbery in New York City precincts. He reports that "the study found a curvilinear relationship between arrests per officer and subsequent burglary and robbery rates; as arrests per officer increased, robbery and burglary decreased to a point; but when a threshold of arrest vigor was reached, robbery and burglary began to increase" (p. 208). Because arrest rates are so closely linked to incarceration rates, these results are consistent with the predictions of the coercive mobility hypothesis.

2. *Estimation Problems.* The general theme of this analysis is to propose that incarceration "causes" various social problems when it is concentrated in poor communities and, through them, causes crime. There are two substantial problems in applying a causal framework to these data: simultaneity and endogeneity.

Simultaneity is the idea that crime rates "cause" incarceration rates, while at the same time incarceration rates "cause" crime rates. The conceptual problem is that, while the theory posits that incarceration causes crime, it is far more straightforward to assume that crime causes incarceration—which could fully explain a positive correlation between incarceration and crime, even after statistical controls. The usual solution to this problem is to use time-ordered data to model the reciprocal effect, known as a nonrecursive path model.

Endogeneity arises when the relationship being displayed is spurious, because both crime and incarceration are caused by a third (unmodeled) variable. It is plausible, for example, that both crime and incarceration result from external processes, such as concentrated disadvantage and economic marginality. The usual way to address this problem is to include more variables in the study as statistical controls, making sure that the causal relationship between incarceration and crime is not eliminated when other factors are taken into account. Another option, one favored by economists, is to employ an exogenous variable as an instrument. Instrumentation is used to eliminate the correlation between crime and incarceration that is a result of the way crime "causes" incarceration, leaving only the part that results from the way incarceration causes crime.

3. *A Competition of Models.* Bhati and his colleagues (Bhati, Lynch, and Sabol 2005; see also Lynch and Sabol 2004*b*) approach the simultaneity and endogeneity problems by instrumentation. They employ drug arrests as an instrumental variable. Drug arrests are useful, they argue, because the number of drug arrests is directly related to the number of people going to prison, but drug arrests are elastic in the sense that there is a nearly inexhaustible supply of potential arrestees and so there need not be any relationship between crime and the rate of drug arrests. To further cleanse the simultaneity problem, they "take the residual of the regression of the change in drug arrest rates between 1987 and 1992 on the change in index crime rate over the same period and then regress the change in the prison admission rate on this residual. The instrument satisfies the conceptual and empirical requisites of an instrument: it was correlated with the incarceration rate and independent of the crime rate" (Lynch and Sabol 2004*b*, p. 150).

Lynch and Sabol's resulting analysis not only fails to confirm the results from the coercive mobility models described above but finds evidence of the opposite effect. When the instrument is added to their model, the sign for the relationship between incarceration and crime changes, with higher incarceration rates now predicting lower crime rates. (As indicated earlier, they also find that incarceration has negative impacts on some underlying processes of informal social control.) They conclude that their work provides "some support for both those who argue that high levels of incarceration undermine the ability of neighborhoods to perform their social functions and for those who allege that incarceration is beneficial for communities" (Lynch and Sabol 2004*b*, p. 158).

The results of instrumented models pose a profound challenge to the coercive mobility hypothesis. Yet the choice of an instrument is crucial. By using drug arrests, Lynch and Sabol have a plausible candidate but one that is potentially contaminated because the "discretionary portion" of the supply of potential arrests is linked to the very neighborhoods that have high rates of incarceration. In Chicago (George, LaLonde, and Schuble 2005), drug crime rates are associated with incarceration rates for women in exactly the manner predicted by the coercive mobility hypothesis. It is not clear whether using this variable as an instrument will elucidate the relationship or tend to eliminate the effects of how the coercive mobility process works in these neighborhoods. If the latter is the case, then the very places of interest—high-incarceration places—are controlled out of the model.

4. *Alternate Dependent Variables.* An ingenious way to avoid problems inherent in trying to model the relationship between adult incarcerations and adult crime is to incorporate a dependent variable that is clean of the simultaneity problems of adult crime. This would occur, for example, if one were to model the effect of adult incarcerations on juvenile crime. It can be argued that high rates of adult incarcerations, concentrated in the poorest communities, would lead to weakened supervision by parental or adult supervisory figures and that this would translate into more juvenile crime. But there is no plausible reason to think that increases in juvenile delinquency rates would increase the chances of adult incarceration in a given neighborhood.

This strategy has been used by Ralph Taylor and his colleagues (Taylor et al. 2006). They analyze the effects of adult arrest rates in Philadelphia police districts on later rates of serious juvenile delinquency between 1994 and 2004. Two of their findings are important. First, they find the familiar pattern, as have others who modeled coercive mobility directly, that higher rates of adult incarceration predict higher rates of lawbreaking in later periods. Second, they find that the effects of adult arrest rates on juvenile delinquency become more intensely associated with the neighborhood itself if more time is allowed to pass between the period of adult arrest and the rate of delinquency.

5. *Incarceration and Crime.* Every study to date that examines the effects of high rates of incarceration finds evidence of various problems for individuals and institutions. Studies find as well that incarceration has deleterious effects on community-level informal social control. The few studies that attempt to assess directly the effects of high rates of incarceration at the community level provide findings that are dependent on the modeling strategy selected. To date, there is no definitive answer to the question. What is to be made of this?

Despite the absence of a single, definitive study, it is hard to see how incarceration cannot be implicated as a problem for poor communities. There are simply too many studies that point to the problem for the hypothesized connection to be ignored. Incarceration is, after all, an intervention that is directed at the poorest communities, and it has the aim of imposing long-term negative consequences on the people who experience it. Most of those who are incarcerated return to those communities. There is good evidence that high rates of incarceration destabilize families, increase rates of delinquency, increase rates of teenage births, foster alienation of youth from prosocial norms, damage frail social networks, and weaken labor markets. It is a stretch of logic to think that concentrated incarceration could contribute to all of these problems, each of which tends to weaken informal social control, but somehow not erode the very public safety that depends upon informal social control. We cannot be sure that this is the case, but neither can we ignore the substantial probability.

There is, after all, a great deal at stake. The consequences of being wrong do not fall equally in both directions. If we approach incarceration as a problem that needs to be confronted, we will look for imaginative solutions that will have as their aim the reduction of a host of community problems stemming from mass confinement of community residents. If we are successful, we will strengthen families, reduce delinquency, decrease health problems, and establish a basis for a more vibrant labor market. If the coercive mobility thesis turns out to have been wrong, we will not, in the end, have reduced crime. As a package, this seems like a net improvement on the current situation in these impoverished places.

Alternatively, we might choose not to address the problems of incarceration in poor communities because we think it has not been sufficiently demonstrated that incarceration damages public safety. What if we are wrong? Then we will unwittingly contribute not only to the damage wreaked by mass imprisonment but also to the victimization resulting from crime rates that are kept high by it. Given these stakes, there is a clear moral requirement that we do something about mass incarceration of people from impoverished places.

III. What to Do: Research and Policy Implications

It seems that, at the very least, incarceration in impoverished places joins forces with an array of other problems to make things worse. There are ways in which incarceration also helps, but on balance there is good reason to think that, operating at very high levels, incarceration is more part of the problem than part of the solution. A tightly bound, mutually reinforcing set of interacting forces plays out in these places. Incarceration is one of them, breaking up families, subverting parental roles, weakening social control ties, further eroding an already attenuated labor market, and undermining confidence in the legal order. In these places, incarceration is one of the processes that maintains the criminal behavior of the current generation and helps produce the next generation of delinquents. But it is not known exactly how—and to what degree—incarceration is a cause of these problems or a result of them, or both.

A. Research Needs

The research agenda should focus on clarifying the nature of the link between incarceration and problematic outcomes in impoverished places. Longitudinal studies of a large sample of neighborhoods will help sort out the modeling problems, and the use of multiple outcome measures will offer a view inside the black box, to see how incarceration rates produce changes that relate to public safety. Since imprisonment almost certainly has both positive and negative effects in these neighborhoods, extensive sorts of data are needed to sort out the nature of the cause and effect relationships. Patterns of incarceration over lengthy periods—decades, at a minimum—will allow for more sensitive modeling of the reciprocal effects of incarceration rates on crime. If these data can be linked to family and social network data, hypotheses can be tested about precisely how the incarceration of a person in the network affects network- and family-level outcomes. It would be good, as well, to have individual-level data about the people being removed and returned, including especially their criminal history, to see if the effects are mediated by different kinds of arrest patterns and different types of people being incarcerated.

A more elaborate theoretical foundation will vastly improve the chances of addressing the modeling problem. The Rose-Clear "coercive mobility" framework is useful as a start, but ethnographic work has suggested that a specification that includes informal social control measures, social network measures, and family and personal health measures will provide a sounder test of how incarceration works when concentrated at the community level.

B. Policy Needs

The policy agenda is more challenging than the research agenda because the studies cited here turn contemporary crime policy on its head. Today, imprisonment is so naturally seen as the prime solution to any problem of social control that to lay out its role as an engine of crime shakes crime strategy at its core. Strategic adjustments will not be enough; rather, a basic rethinking of crime policy is necessary.

To be sure, the problem does not apply everywhere but concentrates in a subset of troubled neighborhoods, affecting a concentrated residential population. This is good news and bad news. The good news is that some solutions need not be systemwide. Community-specific projects can do some good. The bad news is that the fix, whatever it is, cannot be an intensified version of contemporary criminal justice thinking. Adjustments in crime policy that take account of the effects in these very poor places will be forced to challenge the premises of crime policy everywhere. We cannot arrest our way out of this problem—strategies of wholesale arrest are themselves a part of the problem. Just as clearly, however, we cannot ignore criminal behavior, somehow accepting that we have already exceeded the quota of arrests that serve the long-term public safety interests of these places.

The conundrum in these hard-hit places is not only that the justice system lacks the tools for the problem but that the three most commonly discussed policy ideas are essentially irrelevant. In today's policy environment, energetic discussions are devoted to debates between advocates for rehabilitation and proponents of punishment. There is a new industry of proposals for reentry programs, some emphasizing toughness, others emphasizing support. And the often weak voice of those who call for "alternatives to incarceration" also claims to address the problem of overincarceration.

None of these ideas can help much. The problem of mass incarceration is entirely produced by the simple mathematics of two pressure points—how many people enter prison and how long they stay there. Rehabilitation programs, reentry programs, and alternatives to incarceration do not have a track record that suggests big effects on these two pressure points. Even when they are successful, they work at the margins, reducing reentry to the prison system by a few percentage points, no more. All fail to address length of stay in any meaningful way. When these strategies fail—and they often do—they add to the numbers at each pressure point. Rehabilitation programs, reentry programs, and alternatives to incarceration are good ideas in their own right, and they deserve support, but they will not deal with the problem of high incarceration rates in impoverished places.

If the problem of mass incarceration is the large number of people who go into prison and how long they stay there, then the solution is for fewer to go in and for shorter stays. In other words, the solution is not programmatic; it is legislative. We need sentencing reform. There is no getting around this.

This is not the place to outline a systematic strategy for sentencing reform. It is sufficient here to call attention to the general outlines of just what such a strategy will involve. To work, a strategy will incorporate three areas of sentencing reform: doing away with prison penalties for ordinary drug crimes, eliminating mandatory minimum sentences for other felonies, and abolishing technical revocations of probation and parole. It will also roll back time served. One recent study concludes that these changes would reduce the prison population to about the level it had in the mid-1980s (Austin et al. 2007).

Most important of all, we have to adopt a new emphasis for the work of the justice system. As Donald Braman has said, "The question . . . is not merely how to punish and deter offenders, but how to encourage and strengthen the bonds that make families possible, give life to community, and ultimately determine the character of our society as a whole" (2004, p. 224).

This cannot be done without adopting a new philosophy of justice. We have recently completed a third of a century in which the dominant paradigm—a grand social experiment, if you will—has been a punitive form of retributive justice (Frost and Clear, forthcoming). It is time to declare that experiment a failure and to put an end to it. Until the well-being of those communities that are hit hard by both crime and justice is put at the forefront, the problems described in this essay will get worse.

REFERENCES

Austin, James, Todd Clear, Troy Duster, David F. Greenberg, John Irwin, Candace McCoy, Alan Mobley, Barbara Owen, and Joshua Page. 2007. *Unlocking America: Why and How to Reduce America's Prison Population.* Santa Monica, CA: JFA Institute.

Austin, James, Wendy Naro, and Tony Fabelo. 2007. *The 2006 National Prison Population Forecast.* Report of the JFA Institute. Philadelphia: Pew Charitable Trust.

Bhati, Avi, James Lynch, and William Sabol. 2005. "Baltimore and Cleveland: Incarceration and Crime at the Neighborhood Level." Paper presented at the meetings of the American Society of Criminology, Toronto, November 18.

Blumstein, Alfred, and Allen Beck. 1999. "Population Growth in U.S. Prisons, 1980–1996." In *Prisons*, edited by Michael Tonry and Joan Petersilia. Vol. 26 of *Crime and Justice: An Annual Review of Research*, edited by Michael Tonry. Chicago: University of Chicago Press.

Braman, Donald. 2004. *Doing Time on the Outside: Incarceration and Family Life in America*. Ann Arbor: University of Michigan Press.

Browning, Christopher R., Seth L. Feinberg, and Robert D. Dietz. 2004. "The Paradox of Social Organization: Networks, Collective Efficacy, and Violent Crime in Urban Neighborhoods." *Social Forces* 83(2):505–34.

Bursik, Robert J., Jr., and Harold G. Grasmick. 1993. *Neighborhoods and Crime: The Dimensions of Effective Community Control*. New York: Lexington.

Cadora, Eric. 2007. "Structural Racism and Neighborhood Incarceration." Paper presented at the Aspen Roundtable on Mass Incarceration, Aspen, CO, June 3.

Carlson, Bonnie, and Neil Cervera. 1992. *Inmates and Their Wives*. Westport, CT: Greenwood.

Cho, Rosa, and Robert LaLonde. 2005. "The Impact of Incarceration in State Prison on the Employment Prospects of Women." IZA Discussion Paper no. 1792, October. http://www.ssrn.com/abstract=826456.

Christian, Johnna R. 2004. "Exploring the Effects of Incarceration on Communities." PhD diss., School of Criminal Justice, University at Albany.

Clear, Todd R. 2007. *Imprisoning Communities: How Mass Incarceration Makes Disadvantaged Places Worse*. New York: Oxford University Press.

Clear, Todd R., Dina R. Rose, Elin Waring, and Kristen Scully. 2003. "Coercive Mobility and Crime: A Preliminary Examination of Concentrated Incarceration and Social Disorganization." *Justice Quarterly* 20(1):33–64.

Crutchfield, Robert D. 2005. "Neighborhoods, Collective Efficacy, and Inmate Release: A Summary of Preliminary Analyses." Unpublished manuscript. Seattle: Department of Sociology, University of Washington.

Darity, William A., and Samuel L. Myers Jr. 1994. *The Black Underclass: Critical Essays on Race and Unwantedness*. New York: Garland.

Dominguez, Silvia, and Celeste Watkins. 2003. "Creating Networks for Survival and Mobility: Social Capital among African-American and Latin-American Low-Income Mothers." *Social Problems* 50(1):111–35.

Edin, Kathryn, and Laura Lein. 1997. "Work, Welfare, and Single Mothers' Economic Survival Strategies." *American Sociological Review* 62(2):253–66.

Edin, Kathryn, Timothy Nelson, and Rechelle Paranal. 2004. "Fatherhood and Incarceration as Potential Turning Points in the Criminal Careers of Unskilled Men." In *Imprisoning America: The Social Effects of Mass Incarceration*, edited by Mary Pattillo, David Weiman, and Bruce Western. New York: Russell Sage.

Fagan, Jeffrey. 2004. "Crime, Law, and the Community Dynamics of Incarceration in New York City." In *The Future of Imprisonment in the 21st Century*, edited by Michael Tonry. New York: Oxford University Press.

———. 2006. "Incarceration and Voting." Unpublished memorandum. New York: Project on Concentrated Incarceration, Open Society Institute.

Fagan, Jeffrey, and Richard B. Freeman. 1999. "Crime and Work." In *Crime and Justice: A Review of Research*, vol. 25, edited by Michael Tonry. Chicago: University of Chicago Press.

Fagan, Jeffrey, Valerie West, and Jan Holland. 2003. "Reciprocal Effects of Crime and Incarceration in New York City Neighborhoods." Unpublished manuscript. New York: Center for Violence Research and Prevention, Columbia University.

Felson, Marcus. 2003. "The Process of Co-offending." In *Theory for Practice in Situational Crime Prevention*, edited by Margaret J. Smith and Derek B. Cornish. *Crime Prevention Studies*, vol. 16. Monsey, NY: Criminal Justice Press.

Freeman, Richard B. 1992. "Crime and Unemployment of Disadvantaged Youth." In *Drugs, Crime and Social Isolation: Barriers to Urban Opportunity*, edited by Adele Harrell and George Peterson. Washington, DC: Urban Institute.

Frost, Natasha, and Todd R. Clear. Forthcoming. "The Great Punishment Experiment." *Studies in Law, Politics, and Society.*

Gendreau, Paul, Claire Groggin, and Francis T. Cullen. 1999. "The Effects of Prison Sentences on Recidivism." Report prepared for the Solicitor General Canada, cat. no. J42-87/199E. Ottawa: Public Works and Services of Canada.

George, Susan, Robert LaLonde, and Todd Schuble. 2005. "Socio-economic Indicators, Criminal Activity, and the Concentration of Female Ex-Prisoners in Chicago Neighborhoods." Unpublished manuscript. Chicago: University of Chicago.

Granovetter, Mark. 1993. "The Strength of Weak Ties." *American Journal of Sociology* 78(6):1360–80.

Grogger, Jeffrey. 1995. "The Effect of Arrests on the Employment and Earnings of Young Men." *Quarterly Journal of Economics* 110(1):51–71.

Harrison, Paige M., and Allen J. Beck. 2006. "Prison and Jail Inmates at Midyear 2005." In *Bureau of Justice Statistics Bulletin.* Washington, DC: U.S. Government Printing Office.

Holzer, Harry J. 2007. "Collateral Costs: The Effects of Incarceration on Employment and Earnings among Young Men." Paper presented to the Russell Sage Incarceration Policy Working Group, Russell Sage Foundation, New York, May 3.

Huebner, Beth M. 2005. "The Effect of Incarceration on Marriage and Work in the Life Course." *Justice Quarterly* 22(3):281–301.

Hughes, Timothy A., Doris James Wilson, and Allen J. Beck. 2001. *Trends in State Parole, 1990–2000.* Washington, DC: Bureau of Justice Statistics.

Hunter, Albert J. 1985. "Private, Parochial and Public Social Orders: The Problem of Crime and Incivility in Urban Communities." In *The Challenge of Social Control: Citizenship and Institution Building in Modern Society*, edited by Gerald D. Suttles and Mayer N. Zald. Norwood, NJ: Aldex.

Johnson, Rucker C. 2007. "Intergenerational Risks of Criminal Involvement and Incarceration." Paper presented to the Russell Sage Incarceration Policy Working Group, Russell Sage Foundation, New York, May 3.

Johnson, Rucker C., and Steven Raphael. 2005. "The Effects of Male Incarceration on Dynamics of AIDS Infection Rates among African-American Women and Men." Unpublished manuscript. Berkeley: Goldman School of Public Policy, University of California.

Kane, Robert J. 2006. "On the Limits of Social Control: Structural Deterrence and the Policing of Suppressible Crimes." *Justice Quarterly* 23(2):186–213.

Kessler, Daniel, and Steven D. Levitt. 1999. "Using Sentence Enhancements to Distinguish between Deterrence and Incapacitation." *Journal of Law and Economics* 42(1):343–63.

King, Ryan S., and Marc Mauer. 2004. *The Vanishing Black Electorate: Felony Disenfranchisement in Atlanta, Georgia*. Washington, DC: Sentencing Project.

Kling, Jeffrey. 1999. "The Effect of Prison Sentence Length on Subsequent Employment and Earnings of Criminal Defendants." Discussion Paper on Economics no. 208. Princeton, NJ: Woodrow Wilson School, Princeton University.

Kovandzic, Tomislav, and Lynne M. Vieraitis. 2006. "The Effect of County-Level Prison Population Growth on Crime Rates." *Criminology and Public Policy* 5(2):101–32.

LaLonde, Robert, and Susan George. 2003. "Incarcerated Mothers: The Project on Female Prisoners and Their Children." Unpublished manuscript. New York: Open Society Institute.

LeBlanc, Adrian Nicole. 2004. *Random Family: Love, Drugs, Trouble, and Coming of Age in the Bronx*. New York: Scribner.

Liedka, Raymond V., Anne Morrison Piehl, and Bert Useem. 2006. "The Crime Control Effects of Incarceration: Does Scale Matter?" *Criminology and Public Policy* 5(2):245–76.

Lynch, James P., and William J. Sabol. 2004*a*. "Assessing the Effects of Mass Incarceration on Informal Social Control in Communities." *Criminology and Public Policy* 3(2):267–94.

———. 2004*b*. "Effects of Incarceration on Informal Social Control in Communities." In *Imprisoning America: The Social Effects of Mass Incarceration*, edited by Mary Pattillo, David Weiman, and Bruce Western. New York: Russell Sage.

Martone, Cynthia. 2005. *Loving through Bars: Children with Parents in Prison*. Santa Monica, CA: Santa Monica Press.

Marvell, Thomas B., and Carlisle E. Moody. 1997. "The Impact of Prison Growth on Homicide." *Homicide Studies* 1(3):205–33.

Mumola, Christopher. 2000. "Incarcerated Parents and Their Children." Washington, DC: Bureau of Justice Statistics, U.S. Department of Justice.

Murray, Joseph. 2005. "The Effects of Imprisonment on the Families and Children of Prisoners." In *The Effects of Imprisonment*, edited by Allison Liebling and Shadd Maruna. Cullompton, Devon, UK: Willan.

Murray, Joseph, and David P. Farrington. In this volume. "Effects of Parental Imprisonment on Children."

Nurse, Anne M. 2004. "Returning to Strangers: Newly Paroled Young Fathers and Their Children." In *Imprisoning America: The Social Effects of Mass Incarceration*, edited by Mary Pattillo, David Weiman, and Bruce Western. New York: Russell Sage.

Pettit, Becky, and Bruce Western. 2004. "Mass Imprisonment and the Life Course: Race and Class Inequality in U.S. Incarceration." *American Sociological Review* 69(2):151–69.

Phillips, Susan D., Alaatin Erkanli, Gordon P. Keeler, E. Jane Costello, and Adrian Angold. 2006. "Disentangling the Risks: Parent Criminal Justice Involvement and Child's Exposure to Family Risks." *Criminology and Public Policy* 5(4):101–206.

Pogarsky, Greg, Alan J. Lizotte, and Terence P. Thornberry. 2003. "The Delinquency of Children Born to Young Mothers: Results from the Rochester Youth Development Study." *Criminology* 41(4):1249–86.

powell, john a., Ruth D. Peterson, Lauren J. Krivo, Paul E. Bellair, and Kecia Johnson. 2004. "The Impact of Mass Incarceration on Columbus, Ohio." Unpublished manuscript. Columbus: Ohio State University.

Raphael, Steve, and Michael A. Stoll. 2007. "Why Are So Many Americans in Prison?" Paper presented to the Russell Sage Incarceration Policy Working Group, Russell Sage Foundation, New York, May 3.

Renauer, Brian C., Wm. Scott Cunningham, Bill Feyerherm, Tom O'Connor, and Paul Bellatty. 2006. "Tipping the Scales of Justice: The Effect of Overincarceration on Neighborhood Violence." *Criminal Justice Policy Review* 17(3): 362–79.

Rengifo, Andres. 2007. "Neighborhood Effects and Informal Social Control: Examining the Role of Social Networks on the South Bronx." PhD dissertation, Program in Criminal Justice, Graduate School of the City University of New York.

Rengifo, Andres, and Elin Waring. 2005. "A Network Perspective on the Impact of Incarceration on Communities." Paper presented to the annual meetings of the American Society of Criminology, Toronto, November 17.

Roberts, Dorothy. 2004. "The Social and Moral Cost of Mass Incarceration in African American Communities." *Stanford Law Review* 56(5):1271–1305.

Rose, Dina R., and Todd R. Clear. 1998. "Incarceration, Social Capital and Crime: Examining the Unintended Consequences of Incarceration." *Criminology* 36(3):441–79.

Sabol, William J., and James P. Lynch. 2003. "Assessing the Longer-Run Effects of Incarceration: Impact on Families and Employment." In *Crime Control and Social Justice: The Delicate Balance*, edited by Darnell Hawkins, Samuel Myers Jr., and Randolph Stine. Westport, CT: Greenwood.

Sampson, Robert J., Stephen W. Raudenbush, and Felton Earls. 1997. "Neighborhoods and Violent Crime: A Multilevel Study of Collective Efficacy." *Science* 277(August):918–24.

Shaw, Clifford R., and Henry D. McKay. 1942. *Juvenile Delinquency and Urban Areas*. Chicago: University of Chicago Press.

Smith, Paula, Claire Goggin, and Paul Gendreau. 2002. *The Effects of Prison*

Sentences and Intermediate Sanctions on Recidivism: General Effects and Individual Differences. Ottawa: Public Works and Government Services of Canada.

Spelman, William. 2000*a*. "The Limited Importance of Prison Expansion." In *The Crime Drop in America*, edited by Alfred Blumstein and Joel Walman. New York: Cambridge University Press.

———. 2000*b*. "What Recent Studies Do (and Don't) Tell Us about Imprisonment and Crime." In *Crime and Justice: A Review of Research*, vol. 27, edited by Michael Tonry. Chicago: University of Chicago Press.

Stemen, Don. 2007. *Reconsidering Incarceration: New Directions for Reducing Crime*. New York: Vera Institute of Justice.

St. Jean, Peter. 2006. "The Buffalo Neighborhoods Project." Unpublished manuscript. Buffalo: University of Buffalo, State University of New York.

Sullivan, Mercer L. 1989. *Getting Paid: Youth, Crime and Work in the Inner City*. Ithaca, NY: Cornell University Press.

Sweeten, Gary, and Robert Apel. Forthcoming. "Incapacitation: Revisiting an Old Question with a New Method and New Data." *Journal of Quantitative Criminology*.

Taylor, Ralph, John Goldkamp, Phil Harris, Peter Jones, Maria Garcia, and Eric McCord. 2006. "Community Justice Impacts over Time: Adult Arrest Rates, Male Serious Delinquency Prevalence, Rates within and between Philadelphia Communities." Paper presented at the Eastern Sociological Society meetings, Boston, February.

Thomas, Adam. 2005. "The Old Ball and Chain: Unlocking the Correlation between Incarceration and Marriage." Unpublished manuscript. Cambridge, MA: John F. Kennedy School, Harvard University.

Thomas, James C., and Elizabeth Torrone. 2006. "Incarceration as Forced Migration: Effects on Selected Community Health Outcomes." *American Journal of Public Health* 96(10):1–5.

Tyler, Tom R., and Jeffrey Fagan. 2005. "Legitimacy and Cooperation: Why Do People Help the Police Fight Crime in Their Communities?" Columbia Public Law Research Paper no. 06-99. http://www.ssrn.com/ abstract.

Uggen, Christopher, and Jeff Manza. 2005. "Lost Voices: The Civic and Political Views of Disenfranchised Felons." In *Imprisoning America: The Social Effects of Mass Incarceration*, edited by Mary Pattillo, David Weiman, and Bruce Western. New York: Russell Sage.

———. 2006. *Locked Out: Felon Disenfranchisement and American Democracy*. New York: Oxford University Press.

Uggen, Christopher, Sara Wakefield, and Bruce Western. 2005. "Work and Family Perspectives on Reentry." In *Prisoner Reentry and Crime in America*, edited by Jeremy Travis and Christy Visher. New York: Cambridge University Press.

Venkatesh, Sudhir Alladi. 1997. "The Social Organization of Street Gang Activity in an Urban Ghetto." *American Journal of Sociology* 103(1):82–111.

———. 2006. *Off the Books: The Underground Economy of the Urban Poor*. Cambridge, MA: Harvard University Press.

Waring, Elin, Kristen Scully, and Todd R. Clear. 2005. "Coercive Mobility in an Eight-Year Tallahassee Sample: A Follow-Up of the Original Tallahassee Coercive Mobility Study." Paper presented to the Consortium to Study Concentrated Incarceration in Poor Communities, a project of the Open Society Institute, New York, April 20.

Weatherburn, Don, and Bronwyn Lind. 2001. *Delinquency-Prone Communities*. New York: Cambridge University Press.

Webster, Cheryl Marie, Anthony N. Doob, and Franklin E. Zimring. 2006. "Proposition 8 and Crime Rates in California: The Case of the Disappearing Deterrent." *Criminology and Public Policy* 5(3):1501–28.

Western, Bruce. 2006. *Punishment and Inequality in America*. New York: Russell Sage.

Western, Bruce, Jeffrey Kling, and David Weiman. 2001. "The Labor Market Consequences of Incarceration." *Crime and Delinquency* 47(3):410–38.

Western, Bruce, Leonard M. Lopoo, and Sara McLanahan. 2004. "Incarceration and the Bonds between Parents in Fragile Families." In *Imprisoning America: The Social Effects of Mass Incarceration*, edited by Mary Pattillo, David Weiman, and Bruce Western. New York: Russell Sage.

Western, Bruce, Mary Pattillo, and David Weiman. 2004. In *Imprisoning America: The Social Effects of Mass Incarceration*, edited by Mary Pattillo, David Weiman, and Bruce Western. New York: Russell Sage.

Joseph Murray and David P. Farrington

The Effects of Parental Imprisonment on Children

ABSTRACT

The number of children experiencing parental imprisonment is increasing in Western industrialized countries. Parental imprisonment is a risk factor for child antisocial behavior, offending, mental health problems, drug abuse, school failure, and unemployment. However, very little is known about whether parental imprisonment causes these problems. Parental imprisonment might cause adverse child outcomes because of the trauma of parent-child separation, stigma, or social and economic strain. Children may have worse reactions to parental imprisonment if their mother is imprisoned or if parents are imprisoned for longer periods of time or in more punitive social contexts. Children should be protected from harmful effects of parental imprisonment by using family-friendly prison practices, financial assistance, parenting programs, and sentences that are less stigmatizing for offenders and their families.

Children of prisoners have been called the "forgotten victims" of crime (Matthews 1983), the "orphans of justice" (Shaw 1992*a*), the "hidden victims of imprisonment" (Cunningham and Baker 2003), "the Cinderella of penology" (Shaw 1987, p. 3), and the "unseen victims of the prison boom" (Petersilia 2005, p. 34). Given the strong evidence that crime runs in families (Farrington, Barnes, and Lambert 1996; Farrington et al. 2001), the long interest in "broken homes" and crime (Bowlby 1946; McCord, McCord, and Thurber 1962; Juby and Farrington 2001), and the large increase in rates of imprisonment in West-

Joseph Murray is a British Academy Postdoctoral Fellow at the Institute of Criminology and research fellow, Darwin College, University of Cambridge. David P. Farrington is professor of psychological criminology at the Institute of Criminology, University of Cambridge. We thank Terrie Moffitt, Friedrich Lösel, Christopher Wildeman, Martin Killias, Christopher Mumola, Marc Mauer, Holly Foster, and Michael Tonry for helpful comments, and Henara Costa for help producing the essay.

0192-3234/2008/0037-0002$10.00

ern industrialized countries, especially in the United States and the United Kingdom (Walmsley 2005), it is surprising that researchers and policy makers have largely neglected to consider the effects of parental imprisonment on children. As Shaw (1987) pointed out over 20 years ago, if we do not attend to the effects of imprisonment on children, we run the risk of punishing innocent victims, neglecting a seriously at-risk group, and possibly causing crime in the next generation.

Tonry and Petersilia (1999) argued that there are six kinds of collateral effects of imprisonment that should be studied: effects on prisoners while confined in prison, effects on prisoners' relationships and employment after release, effects on their physical and mental health, effects on exprisoners' criminal behavior, effects on prisoners' spouses or partners and their children, and effects of imprisonment on the larger community. Although only the first kind of collateral effect has a sizable literature, research is emerging on the collateral effects of imprisonment on employment (Fagan and Freeman 1999; Western, Kling, and Weiman 2001; Western 2002) and on the social fabric of communities (Clear, Rose, and Ryder 2001; Rose and Clear 2003; Lynch and Sabol 2004; Clear 2007). In some cases, research on the effects of imprisonment on prisoners has led to policy change. For example, awareness of increasing suicide rates in prisons generated large-scale research projects on this topic and implementation of improved suicide prevention strategies (Liebling 1999). The effects of imprisonment on children deserve similar research attention and large-scale programs to support this vulnerable population.

In volume 26 of *Crime and Justice*, Hagan and Dinovitzer (1999) reviewed theories about why imprisonment might harm families and communities and summarized some of the empirical research on these topics. They argued that the effects of parental imprisonment on children "may be the least understood and most consequential implication of the high reliance on incarceration in America" (Hagan and Dinovitzer 1999, p. 122). This essay builds upon their work by thoroughly evaluating the empirical evidence on the effects of parental imprisonment on children. In this essay, we investigate four key questions: Is parental imprisonment associated with adverse outcomes for children? Does parental imprisonment cause adverse outcomes for children? Why might parental imprisonment cause adverse outcomes for children? Why do some children have poor outcomes following parental imprisonment while others do not?

Unfortunately, there is little high-quality evidence on these topics, reflecting a lack of academic and public interest in the plight of prisoners' children (by contrast, see the extensive research on children of divorce; Amato and Keith 1991; Rodgers and Pryor 1998; Emery 1999). Where possible, we review evidence from large-scale longitudinal surveys. To provide further evidence of this type we present new results from the Cambridge Study in Delinquent Development. Where large-scale surveys are lacking, we review results from smaller-scale exploratory studies of prisoners' children and propose hypotheses that should be tested in future research.

We conclude that parental imprisonment is a strong risk factor (and possible cause) for a range of adverse outcomes for children, including antisocial behavior, offending, mental health problems, drug abuse, school failure, and unemployment. Parental imprisonment might cause these outcomes through several processes: the trauma of parent-child separation, children being made aware of their parent's criminality, family poverty caused by the imprisonment, strained parenting by remaining caregivers, stigma, and stresses involved in maintaining contact with the imprisoned parent. However, there is little empirical evidence on the importance of these mechanisms.

Children may be more affected by parental imprisonment if their mother is imprisoned, if parents are imprisoned more frequently or for longer periods of time, and if parents are imprisoned in more punitive conditions. Children may be protected from harmful effects of parental imprisonment by having stable caregiving arrangements, by their families receiving social and economic support, and by living in places with more sympathetic public attitudes toward crime and punishment. Programs that might prevent adverse outcomes for children of prisoners include provision of financial assistance, social support, parenting programs, improved prison visiting procedures, and alternative forms of punishment such as community service and day fines. Large-scale research projects are needed to advance knowledge about the effects of parental imprisonment on children.

This essay is organized as follows: Section I defines key terms; estimates the number of children with imprisoned parents in the United States, England, and Wales; and describes criteria for inclusion of studies in this review. Sections II, III, and IV examine the associations between parental imprisonment and child antisocial behavior, mental health problems, and other adverse outcomes, respectively. Section V examines whether parental imprisonment is a cause of adverse outcomes for children, and Section VI examines theories about why parental imprisonment might cause adverse outcomes for children. Section VII examines moderating factors that might influence the relationship between parental imprisonment and child outcomes. Section VIII offers policy and research recommendations.

I. Introduction

Before examining the effects of parental imprisonment on children, we define parental imprisonment and child outcomes, summarize what is known about the numbers of children experiencing parental imprisonment in the United States and in England and Wales, and describe how we selected studies for examination.

We use the term *parental imprisonment* to refer to custodial confinement of a parent in jails or prisons (state or federal in the United States) or open or closed prisons (local or training in the United Kingdom). We are primarily concerned with the environmental effects of parental imprisonment on children. Therefore, we focus on parental imprisonment occurring during childhood (as opposed to parental imprisonment occurring before children's births). We discuss the effects of different types of imprisonment, for example, maternal versus paternal imprisonment, in Section VII.

We examine child outcomes that occur during parental imprisonment and also later in life. We review three types of adverse outcomes that may follow parental imprisonment: antisocial and delinquent behavior, mental health problems, and other adverse outcomes (alcohol and drug abuse, school failure, and unemployment). Antisocial behavior refers to a wide variety of behaviors that violate societal norms and laws (Rutter, Giller, and Hagell 1998). The main mental health outcomes investigated are anxiety and depression, but we also consider the effects of parental imprisonment on neurosis (general emotional distress) and low self-esteem.

A. Size of the Problem

With unprecedented numbers of people being sent to prison in Western industrialized countries, such as the United States and the United Kingdom, it is likely that unprecedented numbers of children are experiencing parental imprisonment. The number of children experiencing parental imprisonment can be counted in two ways. The first is to count how many children have a parent in prison at one point in time, which is called the *point prevalence*. This reflects the daily prison population. The second is to count how many children have a parent imprisoned at some stage during a period of time, which is called the *cumulative prevalence*. This reflects the population of prison receptions. We review here what is known about the point prevalence and cumulative prevalence of children experiencing parental imprisonment in the United States and in England and Wales.[1]

1. *Point Prevalence.* In the United States, national inmate surveys have been conducted every 5 years since 1974, providing information about the number of children with a parent in prison at particular times (Johnson and Waldfogel 2004). In an important study, Mumola (2000) used data from the 1997 Survey of Inmates in State and Federal Correctional Facilities to calculate the number of children of prisoners in the United States at the end of 1999. He estimated that there were 1.5 million children with an imprisoned parent (2.1 percent of the nation's children under age 18), over half a million more than in 1991. Between 1991 and 1999, the number of children with a mother in prison nearly doubled (up 98 percent), while the number of children with a father in prison grew by 58 percent. Nevertheless, in 1999, the vast majority (92 percent) of children with an imprisoned parent had a father in prison. Parental imprisonment disproportionately affected ethnic minorities. Black children (7.0 percent) were nearly nine times more likely than white children (0.8 percent) to have a parent in a state or federal prison. Hispanic children (2.6 percent) were three times more likely than white children to have a parent in prison.

In England and Wales, the last National Prison Survey was conducted in 1991. It showed that 32 percent of male prisoners and 47 percent of female prisoners had dependent children living with them before coming to prison (Dodd and Hunter 1992), although data were not collected on the numbers of children. We are not aware of up-to-date estimates of the point prevalence of children with imprisoned parents in England and Wales. However, we estimate that roughly 88,000

[1] For data on other jurisdictions, see Cunningham and Baker (2004) on Canada; Quilty et al. (2004) on Australia; and the European Action Research Committee on the Children of Imprisoned Parents (1996) on seven other European countries.

children under age 18 (0.8 percent of the population) had a parent in prison in England and Wales in midyear 2006.[2]

2. *Cumulative Prevalence.* The number of children experiencing parental imprisonment may be underestimated because very little is known about the occurrence of parental imprisonment over time. We are not aware of any evidence-based statistics on the cumulative prevalence of children experiencing parental imprisonment in the United States. In England and Wales, it is often stated that between 125,000 and 150,000 children experience parental imprisonment each year (Ramsden 1998, p. 12; Home Secretary, Lord Chancellor, and Attorney General 2002, p. 85; Social Exclusion Unit 2002, p. 111; H. M. Treasury 2003, p. 43). However, only two small-scale surveys provide relevant evidence. Twenty years ago, Shaw (1987) estimated that 100,000 children experienced paternal imprisonment each year in England and Wales, based on a survey of 415 men arriving at Leicester prison. Recently, Murray (2007) estimated that approximately 127,000 (95 percent confidence interval equals 103,000–151,000) children under age 18 experience parental imprisonment each year in England and Wales, based on a survey of 150 men arriving at Bedford prison and data from a Home Office survey of imprisoned women (Caddle and Crisp 1997). The proportion of children who experience parental imprisonment at some stage between their birth and their eighteenth birthday is not known.

In summary, the number of children experiencing parental imprisonment is increasing, especially in the United States. Large-scale surveys should be conducted to estimate accurately the point prevalence and cumulative prevalence of children experiencing parental imprisonment, to ensure that there are adequate services to support them.

B. *Criteria for Including Studies in This Review*

The main aim of this essay is to investigate the possible causal effects of parental imprisonment on children. A first step toward investigating this is to establish whether parental imprisonment is associated with child outcomes. If there is no association, it is unlikely that parental imprisonment causes child outcomes. Therefore, we first review evidence on the associations between parental imprisonment and child

[2] This is based on the number of children under age 18 in England and Wales midyear 2006 (Office of National Statistics 2007), the number of prisoners in England and Wales in June 2006 (Home Office 2007), and estimates that imprisoned men have, on average, 1.15 children (Murray 2007) and imprisoned women have, on average, 1.36 children (2,168 children/1,599 women; Caddle and Crisp 1997).

outcomes. To test for an association, rates of the outcome must be compared between children of prisoners and a suitable control group.

To make this comparison, three things are required. First, there must be a control group. The study must include children of prisoners and at least one group of children without imprisoned parents (preferably drawn from the general population of the same age as the children of prisoners). Second, the study must use a consistent measure of the child outcome. The same measure should be used for children of prisoners and controls. Third, effect sizes must be reported, or enough numerical information to calculate effect sizes, and, ideally, significance levels.

These requirements were set as minimum criteria for including studies in the first sections of this review. Ideally, further criteria might have been used to include only studies with high methodological quality. Additional criteria might have included the use of well-validated measures (to increase construct validity), appropriate statistical tests (to increase statistical conclusion validity), a quasi-experimental design (to increase internal validity), or appropriate sampling strategies (to increase external validity; Shadish, Cook, and Campbell 2002; Farrington 2003*b*). However, because setting additional selection criteria would have excluded nearly all studies of prisoners' children from our analysis, we did not do this. Instead, we discuss the methodological limitations of existing studies and requirements for improved future research.

We cannot claim to have conducted an exhaustive systematic review of studies of prisoners' children, which would have required searching all major abstracting systems and thousands of references. However, we did search key books and articles (e.g., Shaw 1992*b*; Gabel and Johnston 1995; Johnston 1995; Hagan and Dinovitzer 1999; Travis and Waul 2003*b*; Pattillo, Weiman, and Western 2004) and electronic databases, including PsychInfo, Criminal Justice Abstracts, and Web of Science (using the keywords prison, incarceration, jail, mother, father, parent, and child), and we examined over 150 full-text articles on parental imprisonment to identify studies relevant to this review.

Sometimes a study used more than one measure of a child outcome. For example, arrest records and conviction records might both have been used to assess criminal behavior. In general, we only report results for one measure of a child outcome in each study. We chose measures that were taken a long time after parental imprisonment in preference to measures taken soon after parental imprisonment, in order to examine more serious, long-lasting effects of parental imprisonment. We chose clinical measures (e.g., of depression) over subclinical measures (e.g., of dysthymia), because they are more valid. In order to increase sensitivity of measurement, we chose more general measures of outcomes (e.g., arrests for any crime) over more specific measures (e.g., arrests for violent crimes). We chose measures with higher response rates over measures with lower response rates, because results based on higher response rates are more generalizable.

Because we only review studies that include control groups, standard measures, and numeric information, several important qualitative studies of children of prisoners are excluded from Sections II–V (e.g., Zalba 1964; Sack, Seidler, and Thomas 1976; Baunach 1985; Skinner and Swartz 1989; Kampfner 1995; Boswell and Wedge 2002; Braman 2004; Bernstein 2005). These studies are important because they provide qualitative accounts of how some children experience parental imprisonment and suggest possible mechanisms by which parental imprisonment might affect children. We use these studies to inform our discussion of mediators and moderators in Sections VI and VII.

II. Effects on Child Antisocial Behavior

It is frequently claimed that children of prisoners are five to six times more likely than their peers to be convicted or imprisoned (Jacobs 1995, p. 3; Moses 1995, p. 3; Hagan and Dinovitzer 1999, pp. 146–47; Simmons 2000, p. 6; Springer, Lynch, and Rubin 2000, p. 431; Van Wormer and Bartollas 2000, p. 60; Petersilia 2003, p. 8). However, after attempting to trace the sources of these claims, we did not find evidence to support them. In this section, we review evidence on the strength of association between parental imprisonment and child antisocial behavior. From the results of several prospective longitudinal studies we conclude that children of prisoners have about three times the risk for antisocial behavior compared to their peers.

A. Review of 11 Prior Studies

Eleven prior studies of the antisocial behavior of prisoners' children included control groups, standard measures, and numeric information for calculating an effect size. We summarize these studies in the text below and in table 1. We categorize the studies into three groups. The first group (general population studies) used samples drawn from general populations of children. In most cases these studies used a prospective longitudinal design. These studies provide the best evidence on the association between parental imprisonment and child outcomes. The second group (studies with matched control groups) used control groups who were at risk for reasons other than parental imprisonment (e.g., children separated from parents because of parental divorce). Most of these studies used cross-sectional designs (in which child outcomes were assessed while parents were in prison) or retrospective designs (in which parental imprisonment was measured retrospectively at the time of outcome assessment). These studies may underestimate the association between parental imprisonment and child outcomes, because control groups were at risk for other reasons. However, they can be useful for evaluating causal hypotheses about the effects of parental imprisonment on children (see Sec. V). The third group (clinic and court-based studies), which used retrospective designs, recruited children of prisoners and controls at clinics or courts. Findings from these studies are the most difficult to interpret, because children at clinics and courts are likely to have higher rates of problem behavior than other children. Although we note the limitations of these studies for the present purposes, this does not necessarily imply that the original study designs were weak, as sometimes they were conducted with other aims.

For each study we calculated a standardized effect size (the odds ratio [OR]) to summarize the strength of the association between parental imprisonment and child antisocial behavior. Odds ratios are interpretable as the increase in the odds of an outcome associated with parental imprisonment.[3] Conventionally, an odds ratio of 2.0 or greater is considered to indicate a strong relationship between a risk factor and an outcome (Cohen 1996).

[3] Odds ratios are calculated from 2 × 2 contingency tables using the following formula:

	No Outcome	Outcome
Nonrisk category	*a*	*b*
Risk category	*c*	*d*

$$\mathrm{OR} = \frac{\text{odds of outcome in risk category}}{\text{odds of outcome in nonrisk category}} = \frac{d/c}{b/a} = (a \times d)/(b \times c).$$

TABLE 1

Previous Studies of Parental Imprisonment and Child Antisocial Behavior

Study	Study Design	Imprisoned Parents	Children (Age at Outcome)	Controls Matched	Outcome Measure	Effect Size: OR (95% CI)
Huebner and Gustafson (2007), United States	General population: prospective	Mothers (any imprisonment 1979–2000)	E = 31 C = 1,666 (aged 18–24)	Mother's age	Convicted between 1994 and 2000 (self-report)	3.1* (1.4, 7.1)[a]
Murray, Janson, and Farrington (2007), Stockholm, Sweden	General population: prospective	Primarily fathers (any imprisonment, child aged 0–19)	E = 283 C = 14,589 (aged 30)	Child age, city of residence	Offended 19–30 (official records)	2.4* (1.9, 3.2)
Bor, McGee, and Fagan (2004), Australia	General population: prospective	Mothers' current partners (any imprisonment, up to child age 5)	E = 265 C = 4,591 (aged 14)	Child age	Delinquency (mother rating)	1.3*[,b]
Kandel et al. (1988), Denmark	General population: retrospective	Fathers (imprisoned at any time)	E = 92 C = 513 (aged 35)	Child age[c]	Jailed plus one additional offense (official records)	8.5* (5.0, 14.6)[a]
Moerk (1973), probably United States	Matched control: retrospective	Fathers (imprisoned for at least one month after birth of child)	E = 24 C = 24 (aged 11–20)	Father absence (divorce), SES, ethnicity, age at separation, age at study	Behavior problems (mother rating)	.8 (.3, 2.7)[d]
Stanton (1980), California, United States	Matched control: cross-sectional	Mothers (in county jails)	E = 22 C = 18 (aged 4–18)	Maternal criminality (probation)	Poor behavior in school (teacher rating)	3.5 (.9, 14.1)[a]

Study	Design	Parental imprisonment	Sample	Comparison	Outcome	OR (95% CI)
	Matched control: prospective	Mothers (in county jails)	E = 24 C = 17 (aged 4–18)	Maternal criminality (probation)	Trouble with police/ school /neighbors (mother rating)	2.3 (.6, 9.3)[a]
Trice and Brewster (2004), Virginia, United States	Matched control: cross-sectional	Mothers (in state prisons)	E = 47 C = 41 (aged 13–20)	Controls were best friends of prisoners' children	Arrested (guardian report)	3.0* (1.1, 8.7)[d]
Dannerbeck (2005), Missouri, United States	Court-based: retrospective	Mothers and fathers (ever imprisoned)	E = 346 C = 766 (age not known)	Both groups were "adjudicated youths"	Prior referral to court (self-report and official records)	2.2* (1.6, 3.0)[a]
Gabel and Shindledecker (1993), New York, United States	Clinic-based: retrospective	Mothers and fathers (ever imprisoned)	E = 11 C = 20 (aged 6–12)	Both groups attended day hospital	Externalizing problems (teacher rating) Delinquency (teacher rating)	2.3 (.6, 8.9)[e] 3.3 (.8, 13.0)[e]
Bryant and Rivard (1995), South Carolina, United States	Clinic-based: retrospective	Mothers and fathers (no details)	E = 66 C = 114 (aged 5–17)	Both groups were clients of social services and clinics for emotional disturbance	Offended (official records)	1.9* (1.0, 3.5)[d]
Phillips et al. (2002), Arkansas and Texas, United States	Clinic-based: retrospective	Mothers and fathers (ever in any jail/prison)	E = 98 C = 146 (aged 11–18)	Both groups attended mental health clinics	Conduct disorder (clinical diagnosis)	1.9* (1.1, 3.2)[d]

NOTE.—E = children of prisoners; C = controls; OR = odds ratios; 95 percent CI = 95 percent confidence interval around odds ratios; SES = socioeconomic status.

[a] Our calculation of odds ratios from contingency tables.

[b] Our calculation of odds ratios from r.

[c] Fathers of controls had no criminal record.

[d] Our calculations of numbers in E and C groups and odds ratios.

[e] Our calculation of odds ratios from means and standard deviations.

* $p < .05$.

1. *General Population Studies.* Huebner and Gustafson (2007) compared rates of adult offending behavior of 31 children whose mothers had been imprisoned and 1,666 children whose mothers had not been imprisoned, in the National Longitudinal Survey of Youth (United States). This survey is a nationally representative, prospective longitudinal study of males and females who were aged 14–22 in 1979 (Center for Human Resource Research 2006). Mothers in this survey were disproportionately young, economically disadvantaged, and of minority race. Maternal imprisonment was measured in annual interviews with the mothers from 1979 to 1994 and in biannual interviews from 1996 to 2000. This measure is likely to exclude occasions of short-term imprisonment (under 3 months) and occasions of imprisonment occurring between interviews (Huebner and Gustafson 2007). In 2000, children of the mothers were between 18 and 24 years old. Adult convictions of the children were measured using self-reports between 1994 and 2000. No adult conviction occurred before maternal imprisonment.

In Huebner and Gustafson's study, 26 percent of children with imprisoned mothers were convicted as an adult, compared with 10 percent of controls. This translates into an effect size (odds ratio) that is large (3.1) and statistically significant (95 percent confidence interval [CI] = 1.4–7.1). The main limitation of this study is that paternal imprisonment was not measured. Another limitation is that some child participants were too young (under age 18) to have been at risk when adult convictions were measured.

Murray, Janson, and Farrington (2007) compared rates of adult criminal behavior of 283 children whose parents were imprisoned and 14,589 children without imprisoned parents in Project Metropolitan (Sweden). This study is a prospective longitudinal survey of 15,117 children born in 1953 and living in Stockholm in 1963 (Janson 2000; Hodgins and Janson 2002, chaps. 2 and 3). Parental imprisonment (from the children's births until they were age 19) was measured using the criminal records of the children's parents (in nearly all cases the father). Child criminal behavior between ages 19 and 30 was measured using criminal records. Of prisoners' children, 25 percent offended as adults, compared with 12 percent of controls (OR = 2.4; CI = 1.9–3.2). The main limitation of this study is that maternal imprisonment was only measured for a small number of cases.

Bor, McGee, and Fagan (2004) compared delinquency rates of 265 children of imprisoned parents and 4,591 controls in the Mater University Study of Pregnancy (Australia). This study is a prospective longitudinal survey of 8,458 women who were pregnant in Australia in 1981 (Najman et al. 2005). When the children were age 5, their mothers were asked about any occasion on which their partner had been imprisoned. Therefore, parental imprisonment in this study might refer to imprisonment before the child was born and does not necessarily refer to imprisonment of the child's biological parent. Child delinquency was measured using the delinquency scale of the Child Behavior Checklist (Achenbach 1991*a*), which mothers completed when the children were age 14. Bor and colleagues (2004) reported a significant correlation ($r = .08, p < .01$) between parental imprisonment and child delinquency in adolescence. This translates into a small odds ratio of 1.3 (see the appendix for calculations). No other statistics were available to calculate a confidence interval. The study has three limitations for present purposes. First, parental imprisonment may not refer to the children's parents. Second, the interview measure of parental imprisonment may be unreliable (on the discrepancy between maternal and paternal reports of paternal imprisonment, see Bendheim-Thoman Center for Research on Child Wellbeing [2002]). Third, parental imprisonment may refer to imprisonment before children's births. Therefore, the study did not necessarily measure environmental exposure of children to parental imprisonment.

Kandel and her colleagues (1988) compared criminal outcomes of 92 children whose fathers had been imprisoned and 513 children whose fathers had no criminal record. The children were born between 1936 and 1938 in Denmark and were studied in 1972. Paternal imprisonment was measured using official records and presumably refers to any imprisonment up to 1972 (although this was not stated in the study report). Child criminal behavior was measured using official records and referred to having at least one jail sentence plus an additional offense up to 1972. Of children whose fathers were imprisoned, 39 percent were imprisoned themselves, compared to 7 percent of controls. This translates into a large (8.5) and significant (CI = 5.0–14.6) odds ratio, showing a strong positive association between paternal imprisonment and children's own imprisonment. However, because the control group consisted of fathers with no criminal record, this may overestimate the association between paternal imprisonment and child criminal outcomes. Two additional limitations of this study are that the children were not studied prospectively and the measure of paternal imprisonment was not well defined.

2. *Studies with Matched Control Groups.* Moerk (1973) compared 24 boys who experienced father absence because of paternal imprisonment with 24 boys who experienced father absence because of parental divorce (probably in the United States). Children of prisoners and controls were matched on social class, ethnicity, age at the time of separation, and age at the time of the study. No information was reported about how paternal imprisonment (or divorce) was measured or about how children were sampled for the study. Participants were assessed for "behavioral changes" in interviews with their mothers and coded "affected" or "not affected." The behavioral outcome might only refer to antisocial behaviors, but it could also refer to other problem behaviors. No details were reported. Of boys from prisoners' homes, 58 percent were rated as having behavior problems compared with 63 percent of boys from divorced homes (OR = 0.8; CI = 0.3–2.7).[4] However, children of divorce are likely to be at increased risk compared to the general population of children of that age. Therefore, using children of divorce as a comparison group is likely to underestimate the zero-order association between parental imprisonment and child behavior problems. The study has three other limitations for present purposes. The number of children studied was small, the study lacked reliable measures of parental imprisonment and child behaviors, and there was clear evidence of "fishing" in the analyses: 45 tests of statistical significance were conducted without correcting for multiple tests.

In what is considered a classic study, Stanton (1980) compared children of 54 jailed mothers and children of 21 mothers on probation (United States). The mothers had a total of 166 children, aged 4–18 years old. The children in the study had been living with their mother before her arrest. Data on the children were collected from children's mothers, children's outside caregivers, and children's teachers during the mother's imprisonment. Of 22 children with jailed mothers, 50 percent were rated by teachers as showing poor or below-average school behavior, compared to 22 percent of 18 controls (OR = 3.5; CI = 0.9–14.1). However, there are three problems with this first stage of Stanton's study. First, the response rate of teachers was low. Second, teachers

[4] The table of results presented "means and frequencies" (Moerk 1973, pp. 308–9). We assume that the results for behavioral variables referred to frequencies.

might have known if children had mothers in jail, which might have influenced their ratings of child behavior. Third, children of jailed mothers were more likely than children of probation mothers (12 percent vs. 6 percent) to be absent from school (sometimes because of behavioral problems), and this might have biased the results.

Stanton also reinterviewed the mothers 1 month after their release from jail. At that time, the mothers reported on whether their children had been in trouble with the police, the school, or neighbors (although the reference period was not specified). Of 24 children of jailed mothers, 42 percent had been in trouble, compared to 24 percent of 17 children with mothers on probation (OR = 2.3; CI = 0.6–9.3). Overall, the study has four limitations for assessing the zero-order association between maternal imprisonment and child antisocial outcomes. First, using children of probation mothers as a comparison group is likely to underestimate the association between maternal imprisonment and child antisocial outcomes. Second, the number of children studied was small, and attrition was high. Third, the study used unreliable outcome measures. Fourth, four of the probation mothers in the study had previously been imprisoned, confounding the comparison between their children and the children of jailed mothers.

Trice and Brewster (2004) compared 47 adolescents whose mothers were imprisoned and 41 of the adolescents' "best friends" (United States). Children of imprisoned mothers were identified by distributing questionnaires to women in prison. Imprisoned mothers gave children's caregivers a questionnaire to fill in. Children's caregivers then gave a similar questionnaire to the parents of the child's same-sex best friend. Caregivers reported whether the student had been arrested during the previous year. Of children with imprisoned mothers, 34 percent were arrested, compared to 15 percent of their best friends (OR = 3.0; CI = 1.1–8.7). However, the children's best friends are not likely to be representative of the general population, and co-offending may have biased these results. For present purposes, there are three other limitations of this study. First, whether children in the control group had experienced parental imprisonment was not known. Second, outcomes were not measured reliably. Third, the outcome measure referred to arrests over the previous year, and it is possible that this reference period included some time before mothers were imprisoned. Therefore, the causal direction of effects is ambiguous.

3. *Studies of Children at Courts and Clinics.* Dannerbeck (2005) used

court records to compare 346 delinquent youths who had a history of parental imprisonment and 766 delinquent youths without a history of parental imprisonment (United States). Parental imprisonment was measured by criminal justice officials asking youths, "Have either of your parents ever been incarcerated in jail or prison?" Therefore, parental imprisonment did not necessarily occur during the youth's lifetime. A delinquent outcome of "prior referrals to juvenile authorities" was self-reported by youths and verified using court records. Of youths with a history of parental imprisonment, 84 percent had a prior referral, compared to 70 percent of controls (OR = 2.2; CI = 1.6–3.0). Although the sample size was large in this study, the fact that both the control group and the children of prisoners were recruited from courts makes it difficult to interpret the results. Additionally, there are three other limitations of the study for present purposes. First, the measure of parental imprisonment was self-reported by youths to criminal justice officials and may be unreliable. Second, parental imprisonment referred to any time in the past, possibly before children were born. Third, the outcome referred to events (prior delinquency referrals) that might have occurred before parental imprisonment.

Gabel and Shindledecker (1993) compared behavioral ratings of 11 children in a day hospital who had a history of parental imprisonment and 20 children in that setting who had no history of parental imprisonment (United States). Parental imprisonment "at any time in the past" was measured on the basis of interviews with children's caregivers and through "available charts" (Gabel and Shindledecker 1993, p. 657). Teachers reported child "total externalizing problems" and "delinquency" on the Achenbach Teacher Report Form (Achenbach 1991*b*), sometime between enrollment in the hospital and 1 month later.[5] Outcome scores were reported separately for 10 girls and 21 boys. Because of the small numbers, we pooled the scores of girls and boys. We calculated odds ratios for the associations between parental imprisonment and child outcomes for all children in the study (from the standardized mean differences; see the appendix). The odds ratio between parental imprisonment and child externalizing problems was large (2.3) but not significant (CI = 0.6–8.9). The odds ratio between parental imprisonment and child delinquency was also large (3.3) but not significant (CI = 0.8–13.0). Because samples were recruited at a hospital,

[5] "Externalizing problems" refer to aggressive, antisocial, and delinquent behaviors.

it is not known if the results are representative of the general population of children. The study has two other limitations for present purposes. The number of children in the study was small, and parents may have been imprisoned only before children were born.

Bryant and Rivard (1995) examined Department of Juvenile Justice records of 180 youths who were clients of social services and clinics for emotionally disturbed children (United States). They reported the relationship between parental imprisonment and youth offending. Parental imprisonment was determined from records of the two agencies where participants were clients. Details were not reported, but we assume that parental imprisonment referred to imprisonment at any time, even before children's births. Sixty-six youths had a history of parental imprisonment. The authors reported that the proportion of youths who had imprisoned parents depended on whether youths had a record of minor offending (60 percent), a record of major offending (36 percent), or no record of offending (31 percent). For present purposes, we calculated the odds ratio for youth offending (major or minor) according to whether youths' parents had been imprisoned or not. This odds ratio was quite large (1.9) and just statistically significant (CI = 1.0–3.5). As children of prisoners and controls were clients of social services and clinics for emotional disturbance, this casts doubt on the generalizability of the results. An additional limitation of the study for present purposes is that details were not given about the measurement of parental imprisonment, which might have referred to imprisonment before the children's births.

In a sample of 258 adolescents receiving routine mental health services, Phillips and her colleagues (2002) compared 98 adolescents whose mother, father, or stepparent had ever been imprisoned with 146 controls (United States). Parental imprisonment was derived from one self-report item on a questionnaire given to youths' adult caregivers. Conduct disorder was measured within one week of intake to the mental health services (baseline), using the Diagnostic Interview Schedule for Children (Shaffer et al. 2000).[6] Of adolescents with a history of parental imprisonment, 40 percent were diagnosed with conduct disorder, compared with 26 percent of controls (OR = 1.9; CI = 1.1–3.2). For present purposes, this study has two limitations.

[6] Although follow-up measures were also taken 6 months later, only results obtained at baseline are reviewed here, because follow-up results might have been influenced by the treatment received at the clinics.

The clinic sample is unlikely to be representative of the general population, and parental imprisonment might have occurred before the children's births.

B. New Findings from the Cambridge Study in Delinquent Development

Recently, we analyzed data collected on males in the Cambridge Study in Delinquent Development (the Cambridge Study) to assess the association between parental imprisonment and child antisocial-delinquent outcomes through the life course (Murray and Farrington 2005). The Cambridge Study is a prospective longitudinal study of 411 boys who were born in 1953 and were living in a working-class area of South London at ages 8–9 (for overviews of the study, see Farrington 1995, 2003*a*; Farrington et al. 2006). For the purposes of this essay, several new analyses were conducted using Cambridge Study data (see the appendix for details).

Antisocial-delinquent outcomes were compared between 23 boys who were separated because of parental imprisonment (between birth and age 10) and four control groups: boys with no history of parental imprisonment or separation from a parent by age 10, boys separated because of hospitalization or death, boys separated for other reasons (principally because of parental conflict), and boys whose parents were imprisoned only before the boy's birth. Parental imprisonment was measured using conviction records of the boys' biological mothers and fathers and social workers' records regarding imprisonment of parents on remand (for over 1 month). Antisocial-delinquent outcomes were assessed between ages 14 and 50, using self-reports of the study males, parents' reports, teachers' reports, and criminal records of the study males. We summarize here the results of comparing boys separated because of parental imprisonment and boys with no history of parental imprisonment or separation. This comparison may overestimate the zero-order association between parental imprisonment and child antisocial outcomes, because boys separated from parents for other reasons are not included in the comparison. In Sections V and VI we discuss other comparisons to consider the possible causal effects of parental imprisonment on children.

Parental imprisonment during childhood was a strong predictor of antisocial-delinquent outcomes through the life course (table 2). For example, of boys separated because of parental imprisonment, 65 percent were convicted between ages 19 and 32, compared with 21 percent of boys with no history of parental imprisonment or separation

TABLE 2

Cambridge Study Results on Parental Imprisonment and Child Antisocial Behavior

	History of Parental Imprisonment					Odds Ratios Comparing Prison (E) and:			
Sons' Outcomes (Age)	No Prison (A): No Separation (n = 227)	No Prison (B): Separated[a] (n = 77)	No Prison (C): Separated[b] (n = 61)	Prison (D): Pre-birth (n = 17)	Prison (E): 0–10 (n = 23)	No Prison (A)	No Prison (B)	No Prison (C)	No Prison (D)
Antisocial personality (14)	15.9%	15.6%	32.8%	11.8%	60.9%	8.3*	8.4*	3.2*	11.7*
Antisocial personality (18)	17.1%	15.7%	23.3%	46.7%	71.4%	12.2*	13.4*	8.2*	2.9
Antisocial personality (32)	19.1%	16.4%	29.6%	40.0%	71.4%	10.6*	12.7*	5.9*	3.8
Antisocial personality (48)	19.4%	16.7%	29.4%	21.4%	52.2%	4.5*	5.5*	2.6	4.0
Self-reported violence (18)	18.0%	15.7%	25.0%	20.0%	42.9%	3.4*	4.0*	2.3	3.0
Self-reported delinquency (18)	24.0%	18.6%	20.0%	40.0%	52.4%	3.5*	4.8*	4.4*	1.7
Self-reported delinquency (32)	18.7%	17.8%	25.9%	40.0%	52.4%	4.8*	5.1*	3.1*	1.7
Convicted (10–18)	21.4%	20.3%	27.9%	58.8%	65.2%	6.9*	7.4*	4.9*	1.3
Convicted (19–32)	21.2%	23.0%	34.4%	43.8%	65.2%	7.0*	6.3*	3.6*	2.4
Convicted (33–50)	9.3%	13.7%	23.7%	21.4%	26.1%	3.4*	2.2	1.1	1.3
Imprisoned by 40	8.1%	9.2%	11.5%	6.3%	30.4%	4.9	4.3*	3.4*	6.6
Weighted mean odds ratios						**5.7***	**6.0***	**3.4***	**3.1***

SOURCE.—Adapted from Murray and Farrington (2005).

NOTE.—Summary results for the weighted mean odds ratios in boldface.

[a] Parent-son separation within first 10 years of son's life because of death or hospitalization.

[b] Parent-son separation within first 10 years of son's life for reasons other than death, hospitalization, or imprisonment.

* $p < .05$.

(OR = 7.0; CI = 2.8–17.5). An average (weighted mean) odds ratio was calculated for the 11 antisocial-delinquent outcomes, measured up to age 50 (see the appendix for these calculations). In comparing boys separated because of parental imprisonment and boys with no history of parental imprisonment or separation, the average odds ratio was large (5.7) and significant (CI = 4.3–7.6). The main limitation of the Cambridge Study for assessing the association between parental imprisonment and child antisocial behavior is the small number of boys with imprisoned parents in the study.

C. *Conclusion*

Only four prior studies used general population samples to assess the association between parental imprisonment and child antisocial behavior (Kandel et al. 1988; Bor, McGee, and Fagan 2004; Huebner and Gustafson 2007; Murray, Janson, and Farrington 2007). In all four studies, parental imprisonment was positively associated with child antisocial-delinquent outcomes. In the Cambridge Study, parental imprisonment predicted official and self-report measures of offending and was very strongly related with measures of antisocial personality, even up to age 48. We calculated the average association between parental imprisonment and child antisocial-delinquent behavior across all five of these studies. The average odds ratio was 3.4, showing that parental imprisonment (compared with no history of parental imprisonment) approximately trebles the risk for antisocial-delinquent behavior of children.[7]

III. Effects on Child Mental Health

Philbrick (1996, p. 12) claimed that up to 30 percent of prisoners' children experience mental health problems during childhood and adolescence, compared to about 10 percent of the general population. However, no evidence was cited to support this claim. In this section, we review evidence on the association between parental imprisonment and child mental health problems.

[7] We calculated the geometric mean of the five odds ratios (using the average odds ratio from the Cambridge Study: 5.7). Because the confidence interval for one study (Bor, McGee, and Fagan 2004) was unknown, we were unable to calculate a confidence interval for the geometric mean. We note that the samples and measures used in these studies were different and therefore that this average result may be unreliable.

A. Review of Five Prior Studies

Five studies of mental health outcomes among children of prisoners included control groups, standard measures, and numeric information that made it possible to calculate an effect size. We summarize these studies in the text below and in table 3 (all but one of these studies also appear in table 1). Only one study (Friedman and Esselstyn 1965) used a general population sample to examine the association between parental imprisonment and child mental health. The limitations of the other studies are similar to the limitations noted in Section II, and we do not repeat them here.

1. *General Population Study.* Friedman and Esselstyn (1965) compared the "self-concept" of 90 boys whose fathers were imprisoned and 154 controls (in two control groups; United States). The two control groups were randomly selected for the study (presumably using school registers, although the research report does not make this clear). None of the controls had a father who had been imprisoned, according to school principals and administrators. Teachers rated the boys' self-concept on the Pupil Adjustment Inventory (University of Pennsylvania 1957). Of prisoners' children, 45 percent had below-average self-concept compared to 29 percent and 14 percent of the two control groups. Comparing children of prisoners and the two control groups combined yielded an odds ratio of 2.5 (CI = 1.4–4.3), showing a significant positive association between paternal imprisonment and a child's poor self-concept. However, for present purposes, this study is limited for three reasons: maternal imprisonment was not taken into account, official records were not used to verify the status of children in the control group, and the meaning of "self-concept" is not clear.

2. *Studies with Matched Control Groups.* Moerk (1973, reviewed above) compared rates of neurosis of 24 boys of imprisoned fathers and 24 boys separated from their father because of divorce. Neurosis was measured using the Tennessee Self Concept Scale (Fitts 1965). Children of prisoners scored, on average, 84.8 on the neurosis scale, compared to 80.4 for controls. This small difference was not significant (at the .05 level). No further statistics were reported (such as standard deviations, t-values, or exact p-values). Therefore, it was not possible to derive an effect size for the association between parental imprisonment and child neurosis.

Stanton (1980, reviewed above) compared rates of low self-esteem

TABLE 3

Previous Studies of Parental Imprisonment and Child Mental Health

Study	Study Design	Imprisoned Parents	Children (Age at Outcome)	Controls Matched?	Outcome Measure	Effect Size: OR (95% CI)
Friedman and Esselstyn (1965), Santa Clara, United States	General population: cross-sectional	Fathers (in Elmwood rehabilitation center at least six months)	E = 90 C = 154 (kindergarten to seventh grade)	School registers	Self-concept (teacher rating)	2.5* (1.4, 4.3)[a]
Moerk (1973), probably United States	Matched control: retrospective	Fathers (imprisoned for at least one month after birth of child)	E = 24 C = 24 (aged 11–20)	Father absence (divorce), SES, ethnicity, age at separation, age at study	Neurosis (self-report)	Mean E = 84.8; mean C = 80.4
Stanton (1980), California, United States	Matched control: cross-sectional	Mothers (in county jails)	E = 22 C = 18 (aged 4–18)	Maternal criminality (probation)	Low self-esteem (teacher/counselor ratings)	5.1* (1.2, 20.5)[b]
Gabel and Shindledecker (1993), New York, United States	Clinic-based: retrospective	Mothers and fathers (ever imprisoned)	E = 11 C = 20 (aged 6–12)	Both groups attended day hospital	Internalizing problems (teacher rating)	.6 (.1, 2.2)[c]

Phillips et al. (2002), Arkansas and Texas, United States	Clinic-based: retrospective	Mothers and fathers (ever in any jail/prison)	E = 99 C = 137 (aged 11–18)	Both groups attended mental health services	Major depressive disorder (clinical diagnosis)	.3* (.1, .7)[a]
			E = 94 C = 135 (aged 11–18)		Generalized anxiety disorder (clinical diagnosis)	.6 (.2, 1.7)[a]
			E = 104 C = 148 (aged 11–18)		Separation-anxiety disorder (clinical diagnosis)	1.2 (.7, 2.0)[a]

NOTE.—E = children of prisoners; C = controls; OR = odds ratios; 95 percent CI = 95 percent confidence interval around odds ratios; SES = socioeconomic status.

[a] Our calculations of numbers in E and C groups and odds ratios.

[b] Our calculation of odds ratios from contingency tables.

[c] Our calculation of odds ratios from means and standard deviations.

* $p < .05$.

of 22 children with jailed mothers and 18 children of mothers on probation. Low self-esteem was rated by teachers or counselors. For teachers, the Coopersmith Behavior Rating Form (Coopersmith 1967) was used. Of children with jailed mothers, 59 percent were rated as having low self-esteem, compared to 22 percent of children whose mothers were on probation (OR = 5.1; CI = 1.2–20.5).

3. *Studies of Children at Clinics.* Gabel and Shindledecker (1993, reviewed above) compared internalizing problems of 11 children of prisoners and 20 controls at a hospital clinic.[8] Internalizing problems were measured using the Achenbach Teacher Report Form (Achenbach 1991*b*). Combining the mean internalizing scores for boys and girls, we calculated an odds ratio for the association between parental imprisonment and child internalizing problems. This odds ratio was 0.6 (CI = 0.1–2.2), reflecting an inverse (but statistically insignificant) relationship.

Phillips and her colleagues (2002, reviewed above) compared depression and anxiety of adolescents whose parents had ever been imprisoned and controls. Both groups were receiving mental health services. Child depression and anxiety were measured using the Diagnostic Interview Schedule for Children (Shaffer et al. 2000). Children of prisoners were significantly less likely to have major depression (9 percent) than controls (23 percent; OR = 0.3; CI = 0.1–0.7). Children of prisoners were also less likely to have generalized anxiety disorders (6 percent) than controls (10 percent; OR = 0.6; CI = 0.2–1.7), but the difference was not statistically significant. Children of prisoners had similar rates of separation anxiety disorder (28 percent) to controls (25 percent; OR = 1.2; CI = 0.7–2.0).

B. *New Findings from the Cambridge Study in Delinquent Development*

Recently, we analyzed data from the Cambridge Study to assess the association between parental imprisonment and child mental health problems (Murray and Farrington 2008). We compared mental health outcomes of 23 children separated because of parental imprisonment (between birth and age 10) and four control groups. We summarize here the results of comparing boys separated because of parental im-

[8] "Internalizing problems" refer to "a core disturbance in intropunitive emotions and moods (e.g., sorrow, guilt, fear, and worry)" (Zahn-Waxler, Klimes-Dougan, and Slattery 2000, p. 443).

prisonment and boys with no history of parental imprisonment or separation.

Neuroticism during adolescence (at ages 14 and 16) was measured using two self-report personality questionnaires (the New Junior Maudsley Inventory [Furneaux and Gibson 1966] and the Eysenck Personality Questionnaire [Eysenck and Eysenck 1964]). Anxiety-depression during adulthood (at ages 32 and 48) was measured using the self-report General Health Questionnaire (Goldberg and Williams 1988). For this essay, we calculated odds ratios for the association between parental imprisonment and child mental health problems (for results using continuous outcome measures, see Murray and Farrington [2008]).

Parental imprisonment during childhood was a strong risk factor for boys' mental health problems in the Cambridge Study (table 4). For example, of boys separated because of parental imprisonment, 36 percent had high levels of anxiety-depression at age 48, compared to 15 percent of boys with no history of parental imprisonment or separation (OR = 3.2; CI = 1.2–8.4). Parental imprisonment predicted mental health problems through the life course with an average odds ratio of 2.5 (CI = 1.6–4.0).

C. Conclusions

Only one prior study (Friedman and Esselstyn 1965) and the Cambridge Study used general population samples to investigate the association between parental imprisonment and child mental health outcomes. In both studies, odds ratios for mental health problems were 2.5. We conclude that parental imprisonment is probably associated with at least double the risk for mental health problems of children.

IV. Effects on Child Drinking, Drugs, Education, and Employment

Previous reviews of the effects of parental imprisonment on children have focused on child antisocial behavior and mental health problems. Here, we review evidence on the association between parental imprisonment and other adverse outcomes for children: drinking and drug abuse, school failure, and unemployment.

TABLE 4

Cambridge Study Results on Parental Imprisonment and Child Mental Health

Sons' Outcomes (Age)	History of Parental Imprisonment					Odds Ratios Comparing Prison (E) and:			
	No Prison (A): No Separation (n = 227)	No Prison (B): Separated:[a] (n = 77)	No Prison (C): Separated:[b] (n = 61)	Prison (D): Pre-birth (n = 17)	Prison (E): 0–10 (n = 23)	No Prison (A)	No Prison (B)	No Prison (C)	No Prison (D)
Neuroticism (14)	24.0%	21.3%	23.0%	31.3%	47.8%	2.9*	3.4*	3.1*	2.0
Neuroticism (16)	25.9%	20.8%	24.6%	41.2%	43.5%	2.2	2.9*	2.4	1.1
Anxiety-depression (32)	23.4%	16.4%	29.6%	26.7%	38.1%	2.0	3.1*	1.5	1.7
Anxiety-depression (48)	15.1%	14.5%	17.0%	14.3%	36.4%	3.2*	3.4*	2.8	3.4
Weighted mean odds ratios						**2.5***	**3.2***	**2.3***	**1.8**

SOURCE.—Adapted from Murray and Farrington (2008).

NOTE.—Summary results for the weighted mean odds ratios in boldface.

[a] Parent-son separation within first 10 years of son's life because of death or hospitalization.

[b] Parent-son separation within first 10 years of son's life for reasons other than death, hospitalization, or imprisonment.

* $p < .05$.

A. Review of Three Prior Studies

Only three prior studies of drinking and drug abuse, education, and employment of prisoners' children included control groups, standard measures, and numeric information for calculating an effect size. These studies are summarized in the text below and in table 5 (all three studies also appear in tables 1 and 3). None of these studies used a general population sample of children.

1. *Studies with Matched Control Groups.* Stanton (1980, reviewed above) compared the academic performance of 23 children of jailed mothers and 18 children of probation mothers. Academic performance was measured using school records, showing the child's rank within his or her class. Of children of jailed mothers, 70 percent had below-average academic performance, compared with 17 percent of children whose mothers were on probation (OR = 11.4; CI = 2.5–52.5). This was a very large effect size.

Trice and Brewster (2004, reviewed above) compared rates of failure and dropping out of school of 47 children of incarcerated mothers and 41 of these children's best friends. Academic failure was measured by receiving a failing grade on a school report card in the previous year. Academic failure and dropping out of school were measured using caregivers' reports. Children of prisoners were significantly more likely (45 percent) than controls (20 percent) to have failed academically (OR = 3.3; CI = 1.3–8.7). Prisoners' children were also significantly more likely (36 percent) than controls (7 percent) to have dropped out of school (OR = 7.2; CI = 1.9–26.8).

2. *Study of Children at a Clinic.* Phillips and her colleagues (2002, reviewed above) compared rates of alcohol and drug abuse dependency of children of prisoners and controls receiving mental health services. Substance abuse was measured using the Diagnostic Interview Schedule for Children (Shaffer et al. 2000). At the time of intake into mental health services, 16 percent of prisoners' children abused or were dependent on alcohol, compared to 12 percent of controls (OR = 1.3; CI = 0.6–2.7). Of prisoners' children, 20 percent abused or were dependent on marijuana, compared with 13 percent of controls (OR = 1.6; CI = 0.8–3.3). Of prisoners' children, 1 percent abused or were dependent on other substances, compared to 6 percent of controls (OR = 0.2; CI = 0.0–1.3).

TABLE 5

Previous Studies of Parental Imprisonment and Child Alcohol, Drugs, and Education

Study	Study Design	Imprisoned Parents	Children (Age at Outcome)	Controls Matched?	Outcome Measure	Effect Size: OR (95% CI)
Stanton (1980), California, United States	Matched control: cross-sectional	Mothers (in county jails)	E = 23 C = 18 (aged 4–18)	Maternal criminality (probation)	Poor academic performance (academic records)	11.4* (2.5, 52.5)[a]
Trice and Brewster (2004), Virginia, United States	Matched control: cross-sectional	Mothers (in state prisons)	E = 47 C = 41 (aged 13–20)	Controls were best friends of prisoners' children	Failing classes (guardian report)	3.3* (1.3, 8.7)[b]
					Dropped out of school (guardian report)	7.2* (1.9, 26.8)[b]
Phillips et al. (2002), Arkansas and Texas, United States	Matched control: retrospective	Mothers and fathers (ever in any prison/jail)	E = 103 C = 148 (aged 11–18)	Both groups attended mental health clinics	Alcohol problem (clinical diagnosis)	1.3 (.6, 2.7)[b]
			E = 102 C = 147 (aged 11–18)		Marijuana problem (clinical diagnosis)	1.6 (.8, 3.3)[b]
			E = 100 C = 148 (aged 11–18)		Other substance problem (clinical diagnosis)	.2 (.0, 1.3)[b]

NOTE.—E = children of prisoners; C = controls; OR = odds ratios; 95 percent CI = 95 percent confidence interval around odds ratios.

[a] Our calculation of odds ratios from contingency tables.

[b] Our calculations of numbers in E and C groups and odds ratios.

* $p < .05$.

B. New Results from the Cambridge Study in Delinquent Development

For this essay, we analyzed the relationships between parental imprisonment and 12 drinking, drug, education, and employment outcomes, and two summary measures of "poor life success" in the Cambridge Study. Average odds ratios were not calculated because of the heterogeneity of the outcomes. However, poor life success referred to a combined score for poor accommodation history, poor cohabitation history, poor employment history, alcohol use, drug use, anxiety-depression, and offending behavior. (For details of these measures, see the appendix.) We compared 23 boys who were separated because of parental imprisonment (between birth and age 10) and four control groups on each outcome (table 6). We summarize here the comparison of boys separated because of parental imprisonment and boys with no history of parental imprisonment or separation.

Parental imprisonment during childhood significantly predicted poor life success in adulthood. For example, of boys separated because of parental imprisonment, 35 percent were rated as having poor life success at age 48, compared to 9 percent of boys with no history of parental imprisonment or separation (OR = 5.1; CI = 1.9–13.6). With respect to individual outcome measures, parental imprisonment strongly predicted poor educational outcomes at ages 14 (OR = 8.1 and 10.3) and 18 (OR = 3.9) and unemployment at ages 18 (OR = 13.0) and 32 (OR = 3.1). There was also a strong relationship between parental imprisonment and drug use at ages 32 (OR = 3.7) and 48 (OR = 3.6). However, parental imprisonment did not significantly predict drinking problems at any age.

C. Conclusions

Few studies have investigated the relationship between parental imprisonment and child drinking, drug, education, and employment outcomes. Previous studies are based on unrepresentative samples, and results should be treated with caution. Nevertheless, in previous studies and in the Cambridge Study, parental imprisonment strongly predicted school failure. Results from the Cambridge Study also suggested that parental imprisonment was a risk factor for drug abuse and unemployment. However, parental imprisonment was not consistently associated with drinking problems.

TABLE 6

Cambridge Study Results on Parental Imprisonment and Child Alcohol, Drugs, Education, and Employment

Sons' Outcomes (Age)	History of Parental Imprisonment					Odds Ratios Comparing Prison (E) and:			
	No Prison (A): No Separation (n = 227)	No Prison (B): Separated:[a] (n = 77)	No Prison (C): Separated:[b] (n = 61)	Prison (D): Pre-birth (n = 17)	Prison (E): 0–10 (n = 23)	No Prison (A)	No Prison (B)	No Prison (C)	No Prison (D)
Binge drinking (18)	20.8%	18.6%	16.7%	20.0%	38.1%	2.3	2.7*	3.1*	2.5
Drinking problem (32)	35.6%	37.0%	35.2%	60.0%	57.1%	2.4	2.3	2.5	.9
Drinking problem (48)	24.4%	11.1%	17.6%	28.6%	30.4%	1.4	3.5*	2.0	1.1
Drug use (18)	30.9%	22.9%	36.7%	26.7%	47.6%	2.0	3.1*	1.6	2.5
Drug use (32)	19.7%	9.6%	25.9%	6.7%	47.6%	3.7*	8.6*	2.6	12.7*
Drug use (48)	17.4%	13.9%	17.6%	.0%	43.5%	3.6*	4.8*	3.6*	10.8*[c]
School failure (14)	21.1%	29.0%	32.8%	18.8%	68.4%	8.1*	5.3*	4.4*	9.4*
Truant (14)	21.6%	26.0%	34.4%	35.3%	73.9%	10.3*	8.1*	5.4*	5.2*
No exams (18)	45.2%	50.7%	56.7%	66.7%	76.2%	3.9*	3.1*	2.4	1.6
Unemployed (18)	19.8%	7.2%	27.3%	33.3%	76.2%	13.0*	41.0*	8.5*	6.4
Unemployed (32)	19.7%	20.5%	27.8%	26.7%	42.9%	3.1*	2.9*	2.0	2.1
Unemployed (48)	6.1%	6.3%	20.9%	8.3%	13.6%	2.4	2.4	.6	1.7
Poor life success (32)	20.1%	19.2%	35.2%	26.7%	52.4%	4.4*	4.6*	2.0	3.0
Poor life success (48)	9.5%	6.9%	17.6%	7.1%	34.8%	5.1*	7.1*	2.5	6.9

[a] Parent-son separation within first 10 years of son's life because of death or hospitalization.

[b] Parent-son separation within first 10 years of son's life for reasons other than death, hospitalization, or imprisonment.

[c] For prison pre-birth, the zero was replaced by one to calculate the odds ratio.

* $p < .05$.

V. Does Parental Imprisonment Have a Causal Effect?

Parental imprisonment is a strong predictor of adverse outcomes for children throughout their lives. However, that does not imply that parental imprisonment has a causal effect on children. Instead of being a cause, parental imprisonment might predict adverse child outcomes because it is associated with preexisting disadvantages that themselves cause adverse child outcomes. As one female prisoner in the study by Healey, Foley, and Walsh (2000, p. 23) stated, "the damage was done before I came to prison." This idea corresponds to the "selection perspective" that Hagan and Dinovitzer (1999) theorized might explain adverse outcomes among children of prisoners. In particular, parental criminality, parental mental illness, and other environmental risks before parental imprisonment might cause child behavior problems, rather than parental imprisonment itself. We discuss how these preexisting disadvantages might explain the link between parental imprisonment and adverse child outcomes. We then review the available evidence on whether parental imprisonment causes adverse outcomes for children.

A. Does the Relationship Reflect the Intergenerational Transmission of Criminality?

Prisoners tend to be highly criminal, and parental criminality might explain the link between parental imprisonment and adverse child outcomes. Parental criminal convictions, regardless of the sentences that follow them, are a strong predictor of children's own criminal behavior, as has been shown in a number of classic studies in criminology (Glueck and Glueck 1950; McCord, McCord, and Zola 1959; Robins, West, and Herjanic 1975; Smith 1991; Farrington, Barnes, and Lambert 1996; Fergusson, Horwood, and Nagin 2000; Farrington et al. 2001). In their meta-analysis, Lipsey and Derzon (1998) concluded that, on average, having antisocial parents predicted serious and violent offending with an odds ratio of 5.0. Therefore, the association between parental imprisonment and child antisocial behavior might merely reflect the effects of parental criminality and parental antisocial behavior on children.

Farrington and his colleagues (2001) suggested six explanations for the intergenerational transmission of criminality: intergenerational exposure to risk (e.g., parents and children might be trapped in a cycle of poverty); assortative mating—children with two antisocial parents are even more likely to be antisocial than those with only one; imitation and teaching of crime; criminal parents tend to live in bad neighborhoods and use poor child-rearing methods; official (police and court) bias; and genetic mechanisms.

Crowe (1974) investigated the genetic risk associated with maternal imprisonment by comparing adopted children according to whether or not their biological mothers were imprisoned. Of 37 adopted children of prisoners, 19 percent were convicted as adults, compared with 3 percent of 37 controls (OR = 8.4; CI = 1.0–72.2). Of 46 adopted children of prisoners, 13 percent had an antisocial personality disorder in adulthood compared with 2 percent of 46 controls (who had a "probable antisocial personality disorder"; OR = 6.8; CI = 0.8–58.5). These findings suggest that children of prisoners may be at risk for antisocial outcomes partly because of genetic mechanisms.

In summary, antisocial outcomes for children of prisoners might be a consequence of the effects of parental criminality and antisocial tendencies on children. Antisocial tendencies might be transmitted to children of prisoners via mechanisms of poor parenting, imitation of behavior, social labeling, residing in bad neighborhoods, or through genes.

B. Does the Relationship Reflect the Intergenerational Transmission of Mental Health Problems?

Prisoners are also much more likely to have mental health problems than the general population. Therefore, the association between parental imprisonment and child mental health problems might merely reflect the effects of parental mental illness on children. In a national study of psychiatric morbidity among prisoners in England and Wales, Singleton and her colleagues (1998) found rates of depression of 33 percent and 51 percent among male and female prisoners, respectively, compared with 8 percent and 11 percent in the general population (see also Butler et al. [2006] for data from Australia; James and Glaze [2006] for data from the United States).

More than 20 studies report an association between parental mental illness and childhood anxiety (see the review by Klein and Pine [2002, pp. 497–99]), and children of depressed parents have about three times the risk of developing major depression themselves compared to children of nondepressed parents (Weissman et al. 1997; Weissman et al. 2006). Intergenerational continuities in mental illness might partly be explained by genetic effects and partly by environmental adversities associated with parental mental illness, such as maladaptive parenting, marital dysfunction, and stress (Garber 2000; Zahn-Waxler et al. 2000).

In Crowe's (1974) adoption study, of 46 children of imprisoned mothers, 9 percent had a history of depression, compared with 7 percent of 46 controls (OR = 1.4; CI = 0.3–6.5). This result suggests that maternal imprisonment might not be associated with genetic risk for depression. However, the confidence interval was wide, and the results did not disprove the genetic hypothesis. In summary, children of prisoners may be at increased risk for mental health problems because parental mental illness has an environmental or genetic risk for children.

C. Does the Relationship Reflect Other Adversities Correlated with Parental Imprisonment?

Parental imprisonment is associated with many other social adversities that might put children at risk (Travis and Waul 2003*a*). Reviewing research from England and Wales, the Social Exclusion Unit (2002) reported that 27 percent of prisoners were taken into care in childhood, compared to 2 percent of the general population; 81 percent of prisoners were unmarried prior to imprisonment, compared to 39 percent of the general population; 52 percent of male prisoners and 71 percent of female prisoners had no educational qualifications, compared to 15 percent of the general population; 67 percent of prisoners were unemployed prior to imprisonment, compared to 5 percent of the general population; and 72 percent of prisoners were on benefits prior to imprisonment, compared to 14 percent of working-age people in the general population (see Dodd and Hunter [1992] for most of the original data; for relevant statistics from the United States, see Harlow [2003]; Mumola and Karberg [2006]).[9]

Three general population studies also show that children of prisoners are exposed to more social and economic disadvantage than their peers. Murray and Farrington (2005) calculated the number of childhood risk factors for antisocial-delinquent behavior among boys in the Cambridge Study. The risk factors examined were high daring, low IQ, and low junior school attainment of the boy, poor parental supervision, poor parenting attitudes of mothers and fathers, poor parental

[9] The general population referred to by the Social Exclusion Unit is not always matched on age with the comparatively young prison population. Therefore, the differences between prisoners and the general population may be overestimated, e.g., for rates of unemployment or marriage.

relations, neuroticism of mothers and fathers, low family income, low family social class, and large family size. Boys who had been separated from a parent because of parental imprisonment had, on average, significantly more (5.4) risk factors at age 10 than boys who had no history of parental imprisonment or separation (2.3).

Using data from the Great Smoky Mountains Study, which is a prospective longitudinal survey of over 1,400 children in North Carolina, Phillips and her colleagues (2006) found that parental imprisonment was associated with economic strain and instability in children's care and living arrangements. Huebner and Gustafson (2007) concluded that maternal imprisonment was associated with poor parental supervision in the National Longitudinal Survey of Youth, although it was not significantly associated with poor home environment (indexed by child responsibilities at home, child discipline, and time spent together by family members). However, none of these studies demonstrated the time-ordering of childhood disadvantage and parental imprisonment. Hence, parental imprisonment might have caused an increase in these childhood risk factors.

Children of prisoners might experience high levels of social and economic disadvantage even before their parents are imprisoned. For example, in a cross-sectional study of 56 family members visiting prisons, Arditti, Lambert-Shute, and Joest (2003) found that, before the imprisonment, 39 percent of families had been living on incomes under $15,000 per year. The poverty level in the United States for a family of four at that time was $18,100. In summary, parental imprisonment might be associated with negative child outcomes because children of prisoners are disproportionately exposed to preexisting social disadvantage, not because parental imprisonment has a causal effect.

D. *Conclusions from Empirical Studies*

In this section, we review studies that have tried to disentangle the causal impact of parental imprisonment on children from the effects of preexisting disadvantage. The best way to test whether something has a causal effect is to conduct an experiment. For example, an experiment in Switzerland randomly assigned offenders who were sentenced to short prison terms and who volunteered for the study either to serve their sentence in prison (as usual) or to perform a community service (Killias, Aebi, and Ribeaud 2000*a*, 2000*b*). To date, no similar experiment has included child outcomes and tested whether parental imprisonment causes problems for children. We review quasi-experimental studies that used statistical controls or matched control groups to estimate the causal effects of parental imprisonment on children. However, these methods are weaker for drawing causal inferences than randomized experiments (Shadish, Cook, and Campbell 2002). Therefore, causal conclusions must be very tentative. Ideally, quasi-experimental studies should control for child adjustment prior to parental imprisonment, but no study has done this to date.

1. *General Population Studies.* Using data from the National Longitudinal Survey of Youth, Huebner and Gustafson (2007) compared the adult criminal outcomes of 30 children whose mothers were imprisoned and 1,666 controls, statistically controlling for child characteristics and background risks. The factors that were controlled for were child demographics, child delinquency in adolescence, maternal demographics, maternal smoking during pregnancy, maternal delinquency, maternal absence for reasons other than imprisonment, parental supervision, home environment, and peer pressure. After controlling for these background factors, maternal imprisonment still significantly predicted adult convictions, with an adjusted odds ratio of 3.0. Maternal imprisonment also independently predicted whether the child spent time on probation as an adult, with an adjusted odds ratio of 4.0. These results are consistent with the idea that parental imprisonment has a causal effect on children. It is possible that the effects of maternal imprisonment on adult criminal behavior were underestimated in this study, because adolescent delinquency was controlled for and adolescent delinquency might be an intervening link between maternal imprisonment and adult criminal behavior.

In the Cambridge Study, we investigated whether separation because of parental imprisonment predicted adverse child outcomes after controlling for background risks (Murray and Farrington 2005, 2008). First, we compared boys separated because of parental imprisonment (from birth to age 10) and boys whose parents were imprisoned only before the boy's birth. The logic of this comparison is that boys whose parents were imprisoned only before the boy's birth were not directly exposed to parental imprisonment, but they should have similar levels of background risk as boys separated because of parental imprisonment. In this comparison, separation because of parental imprisonment predicted higher rates of antisocial behavior, mental health problems, and other adverse outcomes than parental imprisonment before the boy's birth (see comparison E/D in tables 2, 4, and 6). Comparing the two groups on 11 antisocial-delinquent outcomes, the average odds ratio was large (3.1) and significant (CI = 1.7–5.4). Comparing the two groups on four mental health outcomes, the average odds ratio was quite large (1.8) and nearly significant (CI = 0.9–3.6). Comparing the two groups on poor life success at ages 32 and 48, odds ratios were large (3.0 and 6.9, respectively) but not significant (CI = 0.7–12.6 and 0.8–63.0, respectively). These results are consistent with the idea that exposure to parental imprisonment has a causal effect on children.

Second, in the Cambridge Study we investigated whether parental imprisonment predicted boys' antisocial and mental health outcomes after statistically controlling for other childhood risk factors, such as low IQ, parental criminality, family poverty, and poor parenting. Although the effects of parental imprisonment were reduced after controlling for other childhood risks, parental imprisonment still significantly predicted antisocial and mental health problems through the life course (Murray and Farrington 2005, 2008). Third, we combined both approaches (using boys whose parents were imprisoned only before the boy's birth as the control group and statistically controlling for background risks). In these analyses, we still found that separation because of parental imprisonment predicted antisocial and mental health problems through the life course (Murray and Farrington 2005, 2008).

Using data from Project Metropolitan, we used the same methods as in the Cambridge Study to investigate the independent effects of parental imprisonment on children (Murray, Janson, and Farrington 2007). In Project Metropolitan, parental imprisonment after the child's birth (up to age 19) did not predict significantly higher rates of criminal behavior than parental imprisonment occurring before the child's birth. Also, parental imprisonment in childhood did not predict children's criminal behavior after statistically controlling for levels of parental criminality. These findings suggested that parental imprisonment did not cause children's offending in Project Metropolitan; rather, parental criminality explained the association between the two.

Using data from the Mater University Study of Pregnancy, Bor and his colleagues (2004) tested whether parental imprisonment predicted adolescent antisocial behavior, statistically controlling for a range of other maternal and family characteristics. The other maternal and family factors controlled were teenage mother, single parent at birth, family income, changes in marital status, marital conflict, and parental arrest. After controlling for these factors, parental imprisonment did not significantly predict adolescent antisocial behavior (effect sizes were not reported).

2. *Study with a Matched-Control Group.* In Stanton's study (1980), a case-control design (Schlesselman 1982) was used to try to disentangle the effects of parental imprisonment from background risks. The children of 54 jailed mothers were compared with the children of 21 mothers on probation. The logic of this comparison was that children of jail and probation mothers should have similar levels of background adversity, and so differences in child outcomes might be attributed to the differences in criminal justice sanctioning of their mothers. As we described earlier, compared to mothers on probation, there were large effects of maternal imprisonment on teachers' ratings of child problem behavior (OR = 3.5; CI = 0.9–14.1), child poor self-concept (OR = 4.6; CI = 1.1–18.2), and child academic performance (OR = 11.4; CI = 2.5–52.5). These results are consistent with a causal effect of parental imprisonment on children.

However, the jailed mothers differed from probation mothers in their previous criminal convictions and employment and education histories, which might have acted as confounding factors. Significantly more jailed mothers in the study had prior adult arrests than probation mothers (59 percent vs. 29 percent). Therefore, the association between maternal imprisonment and adverse child outcomes might be explained by differences in mothers' criminal and social histories, rather than maternal imprisonment itself. Another limitation of this study was that some of the mothers in the probation group had previously been to jail, confounding the comparison between their children and the children of jailed mothers.

3. *Studies of Children at Courts and Clinics.* Two court and clinic studies also investigated whether parental imprisonment predicted child delinquency independent of background risks (Bryant and Rivard 1995; Dannerbeck 2005). However, given the unrepresentativeness of these samples, we only briefly report the findings here. Bryant and Rivard (1995) found that parental imprisonment significantly predicted minor offending (OR = 5.2; CI = 1.9–13.7), even after controlling for other risk factors (including single mother, parental substance abuse, marital disharmony, sibling imprisonment, and several measures of the youth's problem behaviors). However, parental imprisonment did not predict major offending after controlling for these background risks

(OR = 1.2; CI = 0.5–3.0). Dannerbeck (2005) also did not find a significant association between parental imprisonment and youths' prior court referrals, after controlling for background factors of parental mental illness and substance abuse, inadequate parenting, child abuse, out of home placement, and age of the youth at the first referral to court. However, both studies used measures of antisocial behavior as control variables (alcohol and substance abuse in Bryant and Rivard's study and age of first court referral in Dannerbeck's study). As these behaviors may overlap with the delinquent outcomes (Farrington 1991), controlling for them might have underestimated the effects of parental imprisonment on child delinquency.

In summary, there is no experimental evidence on which to draw firm conclusions about the causal effects of parental imprisonment on children. Five quasi-experimental studies used reasonably representative samples of prisoners' children and controls to estimate the effects of parental imprisonment on children, independent of background risks. Three found an independent effect of parental imprisonment on child antisocial behavior (Stanton 1980; Murray and Farrington 2005; Huebner and Gustafson 2007), while two did not find an independent effect (Bor, McGee, and Fagan 2004; Murray, Janson, and Farrington 2007). Only two studies examined the effects of parental imprisonment on child mental health, drug use, school failure or unemployment, using suitable controls (Stanton 1980; Murray and Farrington 2008; tables 4 and 6). Both studies suggested some independent effect of parental imprisonment on these outcomes. In conclusion, parental imprisonment might cause child antisocial behavior, mental health problems, drug use, school failure, and unemployment, but more rigorous tests of this hypothesis are required.

VI. Mediating Factors and Theories

In this section, we review theories about why parental imprisonment might cause adverse outcomes for children. *Mediators* refer to the mechanisms through which parental imprisonment might harm children (Baron and Kenny 1986; Murray 2005), which are reviewed in this section. Different criminological theories suggest different mediating mechanisms. It is critical to test for mediating mechanisms in carefully designed empirical studies (Rutter 2003). Mediators should be investigated by testing whether, when the postulated mediator is

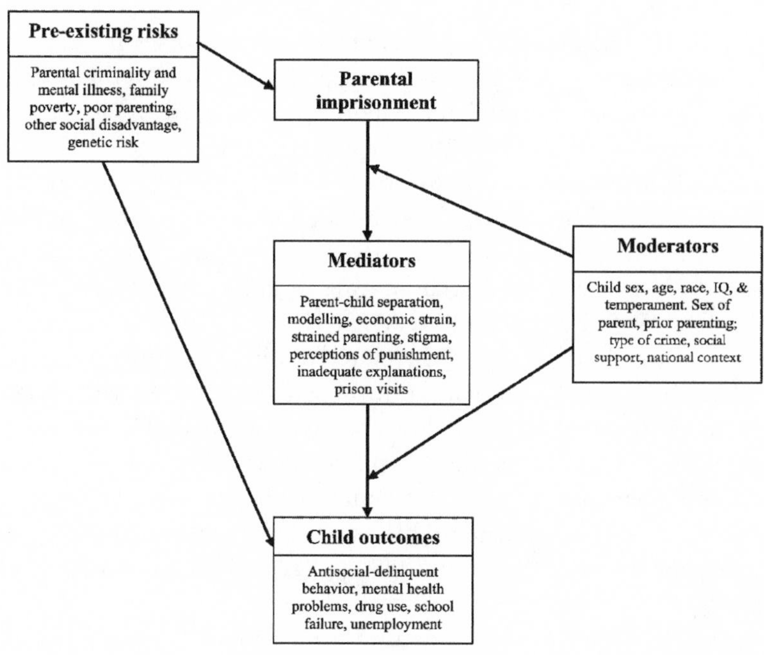

FIG. 1.—Parental imprisonment and child outcomes (conceptual model). Source: adapted from Murray (2005).

controlled for, the association between parental imprisonment and the child outcome is reduced (Baron and Kenny 1986; see also Kraemer, Lowe, and Kupfer 2005).

Figure 1 shows possible mediators, *pre-existing risks*, and *moderators* of the relationship between parental imprisonment and child outcomes. Preexisting risks refer to the disadvantages that exist before parental imprisonment and might account for child outcomes after parental imprisonment, as reviewed in Section V. Moderators refer to factors that alter how parental imprisonment affects children (Baron and Kenny 1986; Murray 2005), which are reviewed in Section VII.

The studies we review in this section and in Section VII have different methodological qualities. Some studies are small scale and cross-sectional. Other studies are large scale and longitudinal. We give greater weight to findings derived from large-scale longitudinal surveys.

A. Trauma Theories

Parental imprisonment might cause adverse outcomes for children because of the trauma of parent-child separation. The idea that parent-child separation is harmful for children is suggested by attachment theory (Bowlby 1969, 1973, 1980) and social bonding theory (Hirschi 1969), which we refer to as *trauma theories*. Consistent with trauma theories, small-scale studies often report that children show sadness and miss their imprisoned parent (Sack, Seidler, and Thomas 1976; Sack 1977; Fritsch and Burkhead 1981; Skinner and Swartz 1989; Kampfner 1995; Boswell and Wedge 2002; Poehlmann 2005). In a recent cross-sectional study of 54 children with imprisoned mothers, Poehlmann (2005) found that most (63 percent) children had insecure attachment feelings toward their imprisoned mothers. Recent legislation in the United States (the Adoption and Safe Families Act) makes it more difficult for prisoners to reunite with their children after release, which may exacerbate problems caused by separation during parental imprisonment (Petersilia 2003, pp. 126–27; Bernstein 2005, pp. 148–49).

One prediction that can be derived from trauma theories is that the longer the time that parents are imprisoned and the more often that parents are imprisoned, the more likely it is that children have adverse outcomes. Consistent with this hypothesis, in the Cambridge Study, boys were significantly more likely to be chronic offenders in adulthood if their parents were imprisoned for longer than 2 months than if their parents were imprisoned for less than 2 months (35 percent vs. 7 percent; Murray, Janson, and Farrington 2007). In Project Metropolitan, there was also a dose-response relationship between the number of times parents were imprisoned and the number of times children offended as adults (Murray, Janson, and Farrington 2007). However, these differences may reflect the fact that longer-sentence prisoners and parents who were imprisoned more frequently were more antisocial than other prisoners.

Separation because of parental imprisonment might be a particularly harmful form of separation for children because it is often unexpected, sometimes violent at the time of arrest, and often unexplained, and because children are severely restricted in their contact with imprisoned parents (Shaw 1987; Bernstein 2005; Poehlmann 2005). If separation because of parental imprisonment is particularly harmful for children, children of prisoners should have worse outcomes than children separated from parents for other reasons. Consistent with this, in the Cambridge Study, boys separated because of parental imprisonment had higher rates of antisocial behavior, mental health problems, and poor life success than boys separated from parents for other reasons, even after other risk factors were controlled for (see tables 2, 4, and 6 and Murray and Farrington [2005, 2008]). Moerk (1973) did not find such differences in his small-scale retrospective study. However, in the National Longitudinal Survey of Youth, the effects of maternal imprisonment on adult criminal outcomes were also larger than the effects of maternal absence for other reasons (Huebner and Gustafson 2007).

In summary, the evidence to date is generally consistent with the idea that traumatic separation because of parental imprisonment is harmful for children. However, it is difficult to isolate the effects of separation from the effects of other adversities that often follow parental imprisonment (e.g., loss of family income and stigma). These effects have not been successfully disentangled to date. Therefore, it is not possible to state conclusively that traumatic separation is an important cause of adverse child outcomes following parental imprisonment.

B. Modeling and Social Learning Theories

According to social learning theories (e.g., Matsueda 1988), parental imprisonment might cause child antisocial behavior because children become more likely to imitate their parent's antisocial behavior following parental imprisonment. This may be because children are made more aware of their parent's criminality when their parent is imprisoned. For example, Sack (1977) reported that, in his small-scale clinical study, some of the boys with fathers in prison imitated their father's crime. However, there have been no rigorous tests of whether parental imprisonment makes children more aware of their parent's criminality and whether this awareness mediates the relationship between parental imprisonment and child antisocial behavior.

C. Strain Theories

Hagan and Dinovitzer (1999) hypothesized that the loss of economic and social capital following parental imprisonment might cause adverse outcomes for children and labeled this idea "the strain perspective." We review evidence on whether economic strain and strained childcare might cause adverse outcomes for children after parental imprisonment.

1. *Economic Strain.* Parental imprisonment might cause adverse outcomes for children because it causes economic strain (lowered family income), which is consistently associated with child antisocial behavior. In the meta-analysis by Lipsey and Derzon (1998), low family social class was one of the two strongest family predictors of serious and violent delinquency in young adulthood. In the Cambridge Study, family poverty measured at age 10 was one of the six most important independent predictors of later offending (Farrington 2003*a*). Both in the Cambridge Study (Murray and Farrington 2005) and in the Great Smoky Mountains Study (Phillips et al. 2006), children of prisoners experienced higher rates of economic strain than other children. However, neither study established if economic strain increased from before to after parental imprisonment.

Parental imprisonment might cause an increase in economic strain in the short term because imprisoned parents cannot contribute to family income (Travis and Waul 2003*a*) and because families often have to pay for prison visits, letters, telephone calls (especially if prisoners call collect, as in the United States), and sending money to imprisoned relatives. In a cross-sectional study of 56 families of prisoners, Arditti and her colleagues (2003) found that family poverty significantly increased after the imprisonment of a family member, according to retrospective reports. Other small-scale studies also report that families experience economic difficulties following the imprisonment of a relative (Morris 1965; Ferraro et al. 1983; Richards et al. 1994; McEvoy et al. 1999). In the long term, imprisonment may also cause unemployment and fewer educational opportunities among exprisoners, which may expose children to further economic strain. In summary, although several studies report that economic strain is common among families of prisoners, they have not demonstrated that this mediates the effects of parental imprisonment on children.

2. *Strained Child Care.* Children's caregivers often experience considerable distress during parental imprisonment (see Murray [2005] for a review), and children often have unstable care arrangements after parental imprisonment (Phillips et al. 2006). Therefore, parental imprisonment might decrease the quality of parental care and supervision that children receive, and this might cause their behavior problems (Eddy and Reid 2003).

In the Cambridge Study, boys separated because of parental imprisonment were more likely than those without imprisoned parents to be poorly supervised and to have fathers with cruel, passive, or neglecting attitudes, or who used harsh or erratic discipline, when boys were age 10 (Murray and Farrington 2005). These parenting variables were also independent predictors of boys' delinquent development in the Cambridge Study (Farrington 2003*a*). In the Great Smoky Mountains Study, parental arrest or imprisonment was associated with the use of harsh discipline by parents, overprotective or intrusive parenting, and child abuse (sexual and physical; Phillips et al. 2006). In the National Longitudinal Survey of Youth, maternal imprisonment was associated with poor parental supervision (Huebner and Gustafson 2007). Thus, three large-scale longitudinal studies show that children of prisoners are exposed to higher than average levels of potentially harmful parenting practices. However, none of the projects tested whether parental imprisonment caused an increase in those parenting risks over preexisting levels.

Based on a cross-sectional study of 118 Israeli inmates and their wives, Lowenstein (1986) suggested that children were more affected by strained caregiving during paternal imprisonment than by separation from their fathers (see also Mackintosh, Myers, and Kennon 2006). However, this hypothesis was not adequately tested in Lowenstein's study, which did not include a control group or any formal test of mediation. In summary, it is plausible that parental imprisonment causes strained parenting and that this in turn causes adverse outcomes for children. However, this mediation model has not been tested effectively thus far.

D. *Stigma and Labeling Theories*

Parental imprisonment might cause children to experience stigma, bullying, and teasing, which might increase their antisocial behavior and mental health problems (Zalba 1964; Sack, Seidler, and Thomas 1976; Sack 1977; Boswell and Wedge 2002; Braman and Wood 2003). In interviews with 127 caregivers of children with imprisoned fathers, Boswell and Wedge found that some children "got verbal abuse from other children. . . . The pressure was so great that the children didn't want to go to school" (child's caregiver, quoted in Boswell and Wedge [2002, p. 67]). The problem may be exacerbated in the United States, where criminal records are publicly available and widely accessed (Petersilia 2003, pp. 107–12). As Myers and her colleagues (1999, p. 20) argue, stigma "may be fueled by the politics of [being] 'tough on crime.'" It is also possible that there is official bias against children of prisoners, making them more likely than other children to be prosecuted or convicted for their crimes. These stigma and labeling theories correspond to what Hagan and Dinovitzer (1999) called the "stigmatization perspective."

There have been no systematic studies of whether social stigma mediates the relationship between parental imprisonment and adverse outcomes for children. However, some evidence regarding official bias comes from the Cambridge Study. If children of prisoners are more likely to be prosecuted or convicted than their peers because of official bias, there should be stronger effects of parental imprisonment on official measures of offending (convictions) than on self-report measures of offending (which are not influenced by police or court bias). However, parental imprisonment had similar effects on convictions and self-reported offending behavior in the Cambridge Study (see table 2), suggesting that official bias did not account for the high rate of offending among children of prisoners.

E. Other Mediating Factors

Parental imprisonment might affect children in more subtle ways than are suggested by the traditional criminological theories reviewed above. Although the empirical evidence is sparse, we consider three other mediating factors here that might link parental imprisonment and child outcomes.

1. *Perceptions of Punishment.* Parental imprisonment might change children's perceptions of punishment and the consequences of wrongdoing, which might in turn influence their behavior. Two opposite predictions might be made about this. According to social learning theories, behavior can be influenced by observing what happens to other people, as well as by actual experiences of rewards and punishments (Bandura 1969). Following this line of thought, experiencing parental imprisonment might make children estimate a higher probability of punishment following rule breaking and therefore make them less likely to offend. Rational choice theories of offending would also predict this, because parental imprisonment would increase the perceived costs of offending. However, if children believe that their parent's punishment is unfair (see, e.g., Brown et al. 2002), they may develop a hostile attitude toward authority figures and be more likely to offend themselves (on which see Sherman's defiance theory [1993]). At pres-

ent, there is no empirical evidence that makes it possible to assess these competing predictions.

2. *Inadequate Explanations.* What children are told about their parent's absence might also mediate the effects of parental imprisonment on children. Several studies show that children are often told lies or nothing at all about their father's imprisonment, although children may be more likely to be told the truth about their mother's imprisonment (Caddle and Crisp 1997). In Sack and Seidler's (1978) study in the United States, and in Shaw's (1987, 1992*a*) study in England, approximately one-third of children were lied to about the whereabouts of their imprisoned father, one-third were told a fudged truth, and one-third were told the whole truth.[10] When no information is available to children about parental absence, children tend to blame themselves, possibly increasing the risk of adverse reactions (Hinshaw 2005; see also Boss 2007).

Researchers and support groups for prisoners' families commonly argue that children are better off knowing the truth about their parent's imprisonment, rather than experiencing confusion and deceit, and some children themselves have stated this preference (Boswell and Wedge 2002). However, we are aware of only one cross-sectional study that compared child outcomes according to what they were told about their parent's imprisonment. Poehlmann found that children who were given "emotionally open and developmentally appropriate" (Poehlmann 2005, p. 685) information were more likely to have secure attachment feelings toward their caregivers than children who were given less appropriate or no information. However, there was no association between being given open and appropriate explanations and children's attachment feelings for their mothers, and other child outcomes were not investigated. The effects of what children are told about their parent's imprisonment should be investigated in longitudinal studies.

3. *Prison Visits.* In the context of parent-child separation caused by divorce, good quality parent-child contact can help reduce child distress following separation (Amato and Gilbreth 1999; Dunn 2004). However, active parenting is extremely difficult to achieve in the prison context. Moreover, prison visits can involve the strains of long distance travel, stressful prison search procedures, a lack of physical contact during visits, and the difficulty of leaving parents at the end of a visit (McDermott and King 1992; Peart and Asquith 1992; Boswell and

[10] See McEvoy et al. (1999) for different estimates among families of politically motivated prisoners in Northern Ireland.

Wedge 2002; Brown et al. 2002). There might also be adverse "contagion effects" on children as a result of visiting prisons. For example, participating in "Scared Straight" prison visiting programs appears to cause an increase in delinquency for at-risk children (Petrosino, Turpin-Petrosino, and Buehler 2003). Accordingly, prison visits might either relieve strain for children or cause them more difficulties.

Some small-scale studies report that prison visits can be confusing and upsetting for children and that visiting imprisoned parents is associated with worse outcomes for children (Fritsch and Burkhead 1981; Richards et al. 1994; Poehlmann 2005). However, other small-scale studies suggest that children prefer to maintain contact with their imprisoned parent (Sack and Seidler 1978; Boswell and Wedge 2002; Brown et al. 2002) and that visiting imprisoned parents might reduce child disruptive and anxious behaviors and encourage better parent-child relations (Sack and Seidler 1978; Stanton 1980). In a study of 47 children of imprisoned mothers, Trice and Brewster (2004) reported that children were significantly less likely to be out of school and suspended if they had more frequent contact with their imprisoned mothers, by letter, phone, or visits. To date, no large-scale study has tested the effects of parent-child contact on children during parental imprisonment.

Future research should investigate the effects of different types of parent-child contact during parental imprisonment, using longitudinal designs, and controlling for background factors such as the quality of the parent-child relationship before the imprisonment.

F. Conclusions

There is little high-quality evidence on why parental imprisonment might cause adverse outcomes for children. Future studies should investigate whether mechanisms that are theoretically plausible, such as traumatic separation, economic strain, social stigma, and strained parenting, mediate the effects of parental imprisonment on children. Quasi-experimental analyses in longitudinal surveys are needed, following children before, during, and after parental imprisonment.

VII. Moderating Factors

Children might react to parental imprisonment in different ways, depending on their individual characteristics, family environments, and wider social factors. Factors that influence how children react to parental imprisonment are called moderators (Baron and Kenny 1986; Murray 2005). Identifying moderators can help explain why some children have adverse outcomes after parental imprisonment while others lead normal lives. Moderators should be identified by testing for statistical interactions between parental imprisonment and potential moderators in predicting child outcomes (Baron and Kenny 1986; Kraemer, Lowe, and Kupfer 2005). Very few studies have tested for statistical interactions in this way. In this section, we review evidence on possible moderators of the effects of parental imprisonment on children, giving greater weight to findings that are based on large-scale studies with tests of statistical interactions.

A. Maternal versus Paternal Imprisonment

Researchers commonly suggest that imprisonment of a mother is more damaging for children than imprisonment of a father (Fishman 1983; Koban 1983; Richards et al. 1994; Hagan and Dinovitzer 1999, p. 143). In relation to other types of parent-child separation, separation from a mother does seem to be more harmful for children than separation from a father (Juby and Farrington 2001). Maternal imprisonment might be more harmful than paternal imprisonment for several reasons. First, children are more likely to live with their mother before her imprisonment (Koban 1983; Mumola 2000), and, because of prior care arrangements, children might have stronger attachment relations with their mother. Second, when mothers are imprisoned, children are less likely to be placed with their other parent and are more likely to be placed in foster care (Koban 1983; Mumola 2000). Third, because there are fewer women's facilities, it is likely that imprisoned mothers are held further away from home, making it harder for children to visit (Koban 1983; Hagan and Coleman 2001). However, Mumola (2000) found that mothers and fathers in state facilities were equally likely to report at least monthly visits from their children, and imprisoned mothers had more regular contact with their children by telephone and mail. Also, maternal imprisonment is usually shorter than paternal imprisonment, which may help children to cope better with maternal imprisonment.

The hypothesis that maternal imprisonment is more harmful than paternal imprisonment should be tested by examining whether the association between parental imprisonment and child problem behavior is significantly stronger when mothers are imprisoned than when fathers are imprisoned. We are not aware of any study that has done this. Small-scale studies report mixed findings on the different effects of maternal and paternal imprisonment. In a comparison of 65 children of imprisoned mothers and 59 children of imprisoned fathers, Richards and his colleagues (1994) found worse effects for children of imprisoned mothers. However, Sack and colleagues (1976) reported more aggressive problems for children of imprisoned fathers. Fritsch and Burkhead (1981) concluded that children of imprisoned mothers were more likely to show withdrawn behavior, while children of imprisoned fathers were more likely to show discipline problems.

One problem with these studies is that differences in child outcomes following maternal and paternal imprisonment might be explained by different levels of other risk factors experienced by children of imprisoned mothers and fathers. For example, Johnson and Waldfogel (2004) calculated that imprisoned mothers had more risk factors for child behavior problems (3.4) than imprisoned fathers (2.7), using data on 2,047 imprisoned mothers and 6,870 imprisoned fathers in the 1997 Survey of Inmates in State and Federal Correctional Facilities.[11] In summary, although it is plausible that maternal imprisonment is more harmful than paternal imprisonment for children, conclusive evidence is lacking.

Some infants live with their mothers in prison in mother and baby units. This may reduce the trauma of separation for children, but it might also mean living in an environment that is detrimental to child development (Jiménez 2002; Eloff and Moen 2003). Catan (1992) compared the development of 74 babies living with their mothers in prison and 33 controls, who were living outside with relatives or social services. Babies in prison generally made similar developmental progress (in locomotor, social, linguistic, fine-motor coordination, and cognitive development) to the control group in the study (and also similar to the general population of contemporary British babies). However, babies who spent longer than average in prison showed a slight decline in locomotive and cognitive development over a 4-month period. Further investigation of the effects of mother and baby units is needed.

B. *Child Age*

Theoretically, children might react to parental imprisonment differently at different developmental stages. Johnston (1995) suggested that

[11] The nine risk factors examined were unmarried, low education, substance abuse, mental or emotional problems, low socioeconomic status, history of prior imprisonment, history of physical or sexual abuse experienced by the parent, parent ever lived in foster care as a child, and parent's own parent had ever been imprisoned.

parental crime, arrest, and imprisonment are likely to disrupt children's attachment relations in infancy, cause developmental regression and poor self-concept in early to middle childhood, and cause antisocial behavior and delinquency during adolescence (see also Myers et al. 1999). Johnston hypothesized that the long-term effects of parental crime, arrest, and imprisonment may be most harmful for children between ages 2–6, because they "cannot process or adjust to trauma without assistance" (Johnston 1995, p. 74). In research on children's reactions to parental divorce, the evidence is inconsistent. According to the meta-analysis by Wells and Rankin (1991, p. 87) there is no clear evidence that the effects of broken homes differ according to the age of children at the time of the separation.

Using data from Project Metropolitan, Murray and colleagues (2007) compared the effects of parental imprisonment according to the age of the children at the time of parental imprisonment (birth to age 6 vs. ages 7–19). The effects of parental imprisonment during both age periods were very similar (odds ratios for child offending in adulthood were 2.4 for the younger children and 2.6 for the older children, not significantly different).

In Poehlmann's (2005) study of children aged 2–7 with imprisoned mothers, younger children had less secure attachment feelings toward their imprisoned mothers than older children. Based on clinical observations of children with imprisoned fathers, Sack (1977) suggested that boys aged 6–12 were the most likely to become aggressive in reaction to their father's imprisonment. Neither study included a control group without imprisoned parents and therefore could not test for statistical interactions. In summary, although there are theoretical reasons why children may react differently to parental imprisonment at different developmental stages, there is little evidence relevant to this hypothesis.

C. *Child Sex*

The fact that antisocial behavior is generally more prevalent among boys, and anxiety and depression are generally more prevalent among girls, suggests that males and females might react differently to life events such as parental imprisonment. Hence, child sex may moderate the effects of parental imprisonment on children. However, research on other risk factors suggests that this is unlikely to be the case. In the most comprehensive investigation of the causes of sex differences in antisocial behavior to date, Moffitt and her colleagues (2001) found that boys and girls were similarly affected by risk factors such as parental criminality, harsh discipline, and maternal mental illness in the Dunedin Longitudinal Study, which is a large-scale prospective longitudinal study of 1,037 children in New Zealand.

Comparing the effects of parental imprisonment on 7,277 girls and 7,595 boys in Project Metropolitan, Murray and colleagues (2007) found that parental imprisonment in childhood was a strong predictor of adult criminal behavior for both males and females, but the effects were slightly stronger for females. The odds ratio for female chronic offending was significantly larger than the odds ratio for male chronic offending (5.5 vs. 3.0). However, Murray and his colleagues were unable to test why the effects were stronger for girls or to rule out the hypothesis that this finding was the result of there being fewer female offenders in the cohort than male offenders (and hence female offenders being more extreme).

Small-scale studies show mixed results on sex differences in children's reactions to parental imprisonment. Gabel and Shindledecker (1993) and Sack (1977) both reported that boys had worse antisocial reactions, but Friedman and Esselstyn (1965) found worse effects for girls. More large-scale longitudinal studies are needed to test whether there is an interaction between parental imprisonment and child sex in predicting child outcomes.

D. Child Social Class

It is unclear how social class might affect the relationship between parental imprisonment and delinquency. The greater resources of middle- and upper-class families might protect children from some consequences of parental imprisonment, but parental imprisonment might also carry more social stigma for these families (Lowenstein 1986). In Project Metropolitan, the effects of parental imprisonment were not significantly different for working-class children compared with middle- or upper-class children (Murray, Janson, and Farrington 2007). For example, odds ratios for crime in adulthood were 2.1 for working-class children and 2.3 for middle- to upper-class children (not significantly different). In a small-scale cross-sectional study, Anderson (1966) also reported that the families of prisoners experienced similar levels of "crisis," regardless of their social class.

E. *Child Race*

Race or ethnicity might moderate the effects of parental imprisonment on children, although there have been no large-scale studies of this issue. Exploratory studies suggest that black families can experience racism from police and prison staff (Light 1994) and that black children with imprisoned parents are particularly vulnerable to racism from peers (Amira 1992). In a cross-sectional survey, Baunach (1985) conducted a rare comparison of children of imprisoned mothers according to the race of the mothers. She reported that children's problems (as reported by their mothers) did not differ significantly according to whether their mothers were black or white. In a cross-sectional study of 93 black prisoners and their wives, Schneller (1976) found difficulties that were similar to difficulties reported for white families in other studies (e.g., economic strain, loneliness, depression, and problems of "nerves" or "emotions").

In the United States, parental imprisonment is more prevalent among African Americans (49 percent of parents in state prisons and 44 percent of parents in federal prisons were black in 1997; Mumola 2000). It is of high importance to investigate whether parental imprisonment has different effects on children according to their race and ethnicity.

F. *Other Possible Moderators*

As well as the demographic variables considered above, many other child, family, and wider social factors might moderate the effects of parental imprisonment on children. We review some potentially important ones here.

1. *Genetics.* There might be gene-environment interactions in the effects of parental imprisonment on children. One example of a gene-environment interaction in developmental psychopathology concerns the effects of child abuse on children. In the Dunedin Longitudinal Study, Caspi and his colleagues (2002) showed that a gene for MAOA (the neurotransmitter metabolizing enzyme, monoamine oxidase) expression protected children from antisocial outcomes following abuse, and this finding has been replicated in several other studies (Kim-Cohen et al. 2006). It is possible that genetic factors also moderate the effects of parental imprisonment on children, but no study has tested this to date.

2. *Individual Resilience Factors.* "Resiliency" research suggests that children can be protected from adversity by having an above-average

IQ, an easy temperament, secure parental attachment, and positive peer relations (Garmezy and Rutter 1983; Rutter 1990; Masten et al. 1999; Luthar 2003). In their follow-up of Danish men born in the 1930s, Kandel and her colleagues (1988) compared 50 offspring of imprisoned fathers and 48 controls on IQ scores and criminal records up to 1972. They found a significant interaction between paternal imprisonment, offspring IQ (at the time of follow-up), and offspring criminality. Among the offspring of imprisoned fathers, higher IQ scores were associated with a lower probability of offending, but this was not the case among children whose fathers were not imprisoned. This interaction remained significant after statistically controlling for the number of years of education and social class of the offspring. This suggested a buffering effect of high IQ for children of imprisoned fathers.

There are no other studies that have tested interactions between parental imprisonment and potential resilience factors in predicting child outcomes. However, three recent studies suggest that child hopefulness and social support is associated with fewer mental health problems for children of prisoners (Hagen, Myers, and Mackintosh 2005) and that stable and affectionate caregiving is associated with fewer mental health problems and more secure attachment toward caregivers (Poehlmann 2005; Mackintosh, Myers, and Kennon 2006). Further research is required to test possible resilience mechanisms for children of prisoners.

3. *Parent-Child Relationships before Imprisonment.* Parent-child relationships and parenting practices prior to imprisonment are also likely to influence how children react to the event. Parental imprisonment is likely to be more disruptive for children who were more attached and positively involved with their parent prior to imprisonment (Fritsch and Burkhead 1981). In some cases, where children have experienced abusive relationships, children might even benefit from parental imprisonment. A recent large-scale study in England and Wales suggests that, on average, children who spend more time living with their antisocial fathers have worse conduct problems than children who are separated from their antisocial fathers (Jaffee et al. 2003). However, there are no empirical tests of how parenting characteristics prior to parental imprisonment influence children's reactions to the event.

4. *Type of Crime.* Children's reactions to parental imprisonment might also vary according to the type of crime committed by their parent. One would expect that more stigmatized offenses, such as sex of-

fenses, would exacerbate the effects of parental imprisonment on children (see, e.g., Lowenstein 1986), but this has not been systematically investigated.

5. *Neighborhood Context.* Over 30 years ago, Schwartz and Weintraub (1974) hypothesized that, in neighborhoods with high imprisonment rates, children can be more open about their situation and feel less social stigma. Possibly, because prison populations have grown so dramatically in recent decades, and imprisonment is such a common event in some communities (Clear, Rose, and Ryder 2001; Pettit and Western 2004), the stigma of imprisonment may have been reduced (Nagin 1998, p. 22). However, stigma might be especially high in neighborhoods with high imprisonment rates, because many victims of crime also live in those neighborhoods (Braman 2004). Clear and colleagues (2001) argue that imprisonment causes stigma for exoffenders, their families, and communities, even where imprisonment rates are high, but large-scale studies of this topic are lacking.

6. *Cross-National Differences.* There might also be cross-national differences in the effects of parental imprisonment on children. For example, in the International Self-Reported Delinquency Study (Junger-Tas, Marshall, and Ribeaud 2003) across 11 European countries, father absence (for various reasons) was more strongly associated with serious delinquency for boys in Anglo-Saxon countries than in northwest European countries. Comparing the effects of disrupted families in England and Switzerland, Haas and her colleagues (2004) found that separation from a mother in England predicted court convictions more strongly than it did in Switzerland.

We compared as closely as possible the effects of parental imprisonment on child offending in England (in the Cambridge Study) and in Sweden (in Project Metropolitan; Murray, Janson, and Farrington 2007). Children were born in the same year in the two studies (1953), and both cohorts lived in capital cities (London and Stockholm). Additionally, we matched the samples as closely as possible on sex (male), class (working class), age at the time of parental imprisonment (birth to 19), and age at the time of the outcome (19–30). The results showed that parental imprisonment predicted offending behavior in England independent of parental criminality, but it did not in Sweden. We speculated that, unlike in England, Swedish children may have been protected from adverse effects of parental imprisonment by more family-friendly prison policies, a welfare-oriented juvenile justice system, an extended social welfare system, a less diverse population, and more sympathetic public attitudes toward crime and punishment. The results might also be explained by Swedish prisoners being more similar to the general population than in England because of the high prevalence of drunk drivers in Swedish prisons. As Bronfenbrenner (1979, p. 7) argued, child development may be "enhanced by the adoption of public policies and practices that create additional settings and societal roles conducive to family life." There have been no other cross-national studies of the effects of parental imprisonment on children, and these results require replication.

G. *Conclusions*

There is little convincing evidence on moderators of the effects of parental imprisonment on children. The limited evidence to date suggests that children may have worse reactions if their mother is imprisoned, if parents are imprisoned for longer periods of time, and if parents are held in more punitive penal contexts. Children might be protected from harmful effects of parental imprisonment by higher levels of intelligence, hopefulness, and social support, and by living in a country with liberal prison policies and strong welfare provision. Future studies need to use appropriate tests of statistical interactions to investigate these possibilities more rigorously.

VIII. Conclusion

In this section we summarize findings on the effects of parental imprisonment on children and consider their implications for policy, practice, and future research.

A. *What Are the Effects of Parental Imprisonment on Children?*

Compared with other risk factors in criminology, parental imprisonment has received little research attention. Yet, it certainly is a risk factor, and its effects appear to be relatively strong, with multiple adverse outcomes. In their meta-analysis of other risk factors, Lipsey and Derzon (1998) found that odds ratios for serious and violent delinquency were 2.4 for low child IQ, 5.0 for antisocial parents, 1.7 for abusive parents, 2.0 for broken homes, 3.0 for poor parent-child relations, and 5.4 for low family socioeconomic status. The present review shows that parental imprisonment roughly trebles the risk for child antisocial behavior. In the Cambridge Study, parental imprisonment predicted antisocial-delinquent behavior through the life course with an average odds ratio of 5.7 and predicted violence with an odds ratio of 3.4. Odds ratios for poor mental health, drug use, school failure, and unemployment were all 2.0 or larger in the Cambridge Study. Thus, parental imprisonment is a relatively strong predictor of multiple adverse outcomes for children. Parental imprisonment might cause adverse outcomes for children via mechanisms of traumatic separation, economic and social strain, and stigma, but stronger tests of causation and mediation are required to draw firm conclusions.

It is possible that parental imprisonment is more harmful for children if their mother is imprisoned, if children have little social support, or if they live in punitive social contexts. Further research is required on how the effects of parental imprisonment differ according to individual and family attributes and social context. As prison populations grow and change over time, the effects of parental imprisonment on children might also change. For example, the rates of imprisonment of women, ethnic minorities, and drug and violent offenders have been increasing faster than for other populations in the United States in recent decades (Blumstein and Beck 1999; Harrison and Beck 2006).

Parental imprisonment differs from many classic risk factors in criminology because it is determined not only by individuals' behavior but also, critically, by state actions. It is important to prevent harmful effects of state actions on children. In the following section we offer policy recommendations to reduce harmful effects of parental imprisonment on children.

B. Implications for Policy and Practice

The main policy issue raised by this review is that imprisoning parents might harm children and contribute to the intergenerational transmission of offending. The UN Convention on the Rights of the Child states that children should be protected from any form of discrimination or punishment based on their parents' status or activities and that the best interests of the child should be the primary consideration in actions concerning children by courts of law (Articles 2 and 3, UN General Assembly 1989).

An obvious option for preventing harmful effects of parental imprisonment is to imprison fewer parents. This could be achieved by increasing the use of alternative forms of punishment, such as probation, intensive supervision, house arrest, electronic monitoring, community service, and day fines. Sentencing reforms could be introduced with a presumption against the use of imprisonment (in favor of intermediate sentences; Tonry 1998), and guidelines could be introduced to reduce sentence lengths and increase the use of parole and prison amnesties (Tonry 2003; Scottish Consortium on Crime and Criminal Justice 2005). Given that women tend to be imprisoned for more minor offenses than men, and the possibility that maternal imprisonment might be more harmful for children, these reforms may be particularly urgent for women. However, the obstacles to such criminal justice reforms are complex (Tonry 1996, chap. 4) and often political (Tonry 2004). While such reforms are being pursued, it is important also to implement programs that reduce harmful effects of parental imprisonment when it does occur.

Depending on why children of prisoners are at risk, different interventions will be needed to protect them. Programs for children of prisoners should be developed based on what is known about the causes of their outcomes. Based on four key theories about why parental imprisonment might cause adverse outcomes for children (reviewed in Sec. VI), we propose a range of interventions that might prevent harmful effects of parental imprisonment on children (see also Murray and Farrington 2006).

1. *Trauma Theories.* Based on trauma theories, the harmful effects of parental imprisonment on children might be prevented using four strategies. Children could be provided with stable care arrangements during parental imprisonment, ideally with families or friends (Trice and Brewster 2004; Bernstein 2005). Children's caregivers could be given professional advice about how to provide honest and clear explanations about parental absence to children (Poehlmann 2005). Counseling and therapeutic services could be offered to children of prisoners to help them cope psychologically with the separation (Sack, Seidler, and Thomas 1976; Hames and Pedreira 2003). Children's opportunities to maintain good-quality contact with their imprisoned parent could be increased, in particular by providing child-friendly visiting arrangements in prisons (Council of Europe 1997; Trice and Brewster 2004; Bernstein 2005). However, it is important to investigate under what conditions children might benefit from contact with their imprisoned parent.

2. *Strained Caregiving.* Based on theories about strained caregiving,

four well-tested parenting programs might be used to prevent adverse outcomes for children of prisoners (Eddy and Reid 2003). Nurse home-visiting programs could be used to support mothers in high-risk circumstances and improve prenatal care and maternal health (Olds et al. 1998). Parent-management training programs could be used that enhance parenting skills and parents' handling of child misbehavior (Webster-Stratton 1998; Sanders et al. 2000; Scott et al. 2001). Multisystemic therapy could be used to target parent-child interactions as well as wider social problems of youth (Henggeler et al. 1998). And multidimensional treatment foster care could be used to provide therapeutic care for youngsters removed from their homes and to encourage reintegration and support of children with their natural family (Chamberlain and Reid 1998; on parenting programs in prisons, see Loper and Tuerk [2006]).

3. *Economic Strain.* Based on theories of economic strain, three modes of financial support might be provided to families of prisoners to alleviate children's difficulties. Emergency funds could be given to help families of prisoners overcome the immediate financial difficulties after the imprisonment (Council of Europe 1997). Free transport or financial assistance to families could be provided for prison visits, and the costs of telephone calls between prison and home could be reduced or eliminated (Bernstein 2005). Prisoners could be provided with more paid jobs while in custody, and work schemes that employ former prisoners could be increased (Council of Europe 1997; Clear, Rose, and Ryder 2001; Petersilia 2003, pp. 195–98).

4. *Stigma.* Based on theories of stigma, three policies might be considered to reduce the stigma experienced by children of prisoners, as well as by prisoners themselves. The public identification of offenders could be prohibited, not only before conviction but also afterward (Walker 1980; Petersilia 2003, pp. 215–16). Offenders could be diverted away from courts to restorative justice conferences, which emphasize reconciliation between offenders, victims, family members, friends, and the community (Braithwaite and Mugford 1994; Braithwaite 1999; Sherman et al. 2005; Sherman and Strang 2007). More community services could be used that emphasize the positive contributions that exoffenders can make to the community (Clear, Rose, and Ryder 2001; Maruna and LeBel 2002, p. 167).

The effectiveness of these programs should be carefully evaluated using systematic reviews and in demonstration projects using randomized controlled trials. Programs that are found to improve child outcomes following parental imprisonment should be implemented on a large scale.

C. Research Implications

Hagan and Dinovitzer (1999, p. 152) rightly argued that "the implication of not having better and more systematic research on the collateral effects of imprisonment is that we are making penal policy in a less than fully, indeed poorly, informed fashion," and they laid out a useful framework for future research. We describe key research needs on the effects of parental imprisonment on children in this section (see also Murray 2005; Murray and Farrington 2006; Murray 2007).

First, there is a need for replication studies that test how strongly parental imprisonment and adverse child outcomes are associated. These studies should be conducted using prospective longitudinal designs, with representative samples, suitable control groups, and reliable and valid measures of key constructs. Other child outcomes that were not reviewed in this essay, because of a lack of evidence, should also be studied; for example, gang membership, physical illness, and mortality.

Second, there is a great need for more research on the causal effects of parental imprisonment on children. A key problem is to disentangle the causal effects of imprisonment from the effects of preexisting disadvantage. Randomized experiments that might rigorously investigate this issue are ethically and practically possible (see, e.g., Killias, Aebi, and Ribeaud 2000*a*, 2000*b*). If child outcomes are measured in experiments that randomly assign convicted parents to prison (the usual treatment) or other (e.g., community) sentences, the causal effects of parental imprisonment on children could be estimated with greater validity than has been possible to date. Quasi-experimental designs (Shadish, Cook, and Campbell 2002) investigating within-individual change over time and analytic techniques such as propensity scores (Rosenbaum and Rubin 1983) should also be used to estimate the causal effects of parental imprisonment on children.

Third, there is a need for better research on the mechanisms linking parental imprisonment and child outcomes. Theory and qualitative research suggest many possible pathways, but we still lack systematic tests of these mechanisms. Longitudinal research should measure child adjustment and hypothesized mechanisms before, during, and after parental imprisonment. Tests should be conducted to see whether the mechanisms increase following parental imprisonment and whether they mediate the effects of parental imprisonment on children.

Fourth, factors that alter the impact of parental imprisonment on children (moderators) need to be investigated. These can be examined in longitudinal studies that include enough children of prisoners and controls to test for interaction effects between parental imprisonment and variables, such as the sex of the child, the sex of the imprisoned parent, and levels of social support, in predicting the child outcome.

Fifth, there is a need to know about effective intervention programs to reduce the undesirable effects of parental imprisonment. Knowledge could be drawn from other areas of child development (e.g., research on reducing the effects of parental mental illness and the effects of parental divorce on children). Qualitative and quantitative research should be used to investigate additional support needs of prisoners' families, and systematic evaluation of intervention programs should be conducted to test how effectively they reduce adverse outcomes among children of prisoners (see the systematic review of experimental evaluations of parenting programs in prisons by Dowling and Gardner [2005]).

Sixth, there is a need for regular surveys, including imprisoned men and women, and longitudinal follow-up of prison receptions, to monitor accurately the number of children who experience parental imprisonment.

It is clear from the research reviewed here that the children of prisoners are an extremely high-risk group, and the best scientific methods should be used to test whether and how parental imprisonment affects them. The time is ripe for funding agencies and researchers to collaborate in implementing an ambitious research agenda to advance knowledge about the effects of parental imprisonment on children. We hope that our essay will encourage this goal to be achieved sooner rather than later.

APPENDIX

A. Methods to Calculate Odds Ratios from Other Statistics

Where research reports provided means and standard deviations for children of prisoners and controls, we calculated odds ratios using the following three steps:

1. The pooled standard deviation (s_{pooled}) was calculated using the following formula:

$$s_{\text{pooled}} = \sqrt{\frac{(n_1 - 1)s_1^2 + (n_2 - 1)s_2^2}{n_1 + n_2 - 2}}$$

(Lipsey and Wilson 2001, p. 173), where n_1 = the number in group 1, n_2 = the number in group 2, s_1 = the standard deviation for group 1, and s_2 = the standard deviation for group 2.

2. The standardized mean difference (ES_{sm}) was calculated using the following formula:

$$ES_{sm} = \frac{M_1 - M_2}{s_{\text{pooled}}}$$

(Lipsey and Wilson 2001, p. 198), where M_1 = the mean of group 1, and M_2 = the mean of group 2.

3. The odds ratio (OR) was calculated from the standardized mean difference (ES_{sm}) using the following formula:

$$\text{OR} = \exp^{(\pi ES_{sm}/\sqrt{3})}$$

(Lipsey and Wilson 2001, p. 198).

Where research reports provided a correlation coefficient (Pearson's r) for the association between parental imprisonment and child outcomes, an odds ratio was calculated by first estimating the standardized mean difference (ES_{sm}), using the following formula:

$$ES_{sm} = \frac{2r}{\sqrt{1 - r^2}}.$$

Then the odds ratio was calculated using the equation in step 3, above.

B. New Analyses of Data from the Cambridge Study in Delinquent Development

1. Antisocial-Delinquent Outcomes. Previous results on the association between parental imprisonment and boys' antisocial-delinquent outcomes can be found in Murray and Farrington (2005). For this essay, we analyzed the relationship between parental imprisonment and four new antisocial-delinquent outcomes: antisocial personality at age 48 and three conviction variables (convicted between ages 10 and 18, convicted between ages 19 and 32, and convicted between ages 33 and 50). The new measure of antisocial personality at age 48 was similar to the measure at age 32 and comprised 11 items (referring to the previous 5 years): convicted, self-reported delinquency, involved in fights, taken drugs, heavy drinking, poor relations with female partner, ever divorced or separated, unemployed for over 10 months, antiestablishment, impulsive, and tattooed.

Weighted mean odds ratios were calculated for outcomes in the Cambridge Study using the following three steps:

1. A weight (w_{LOR}) was calculated for the natural logarithm of each odds ratio (LOR), using the following formula:

$$w_{\mathrm{LOR}} = 1/se^2_{\mathrm{LOR}}$$

(Lipsey and Wilson 2001, p. 54), where se_{LOR} = the standard error of the LOR.

2. The weighted mean LOR ($\overline{ES}$) was calculated using the following formula:

$$\overline{ES} = \frac{\Sigma\,(w_i \mathrm{LOR}_i)}{\Sigma\, w_i}$$

(Lipsey and Wilson 2001, p. 114), where LOR_i = the natural logarithm of each odds ratio, and w_i = the weight of each LOR.

3. The weighted mean odds ratio was calculated as the exponent of $\overline{ES}$.

2. Mental Health Outcomes. Previous results on parental imprisonment and boys' mental health outcomes in the Cambridge Study can be found in Murray and Farrington (2008). Previous results were mostly presented using continuous outcome variables. For this essay, we used dichotomized mental health outcome variables for consistency with the antisocial outcomes. Outcome scales (of neuroticism at ages 14 and 16, and anxiety-depression at ages 32 and 48) were dichotomized into the worst quarter versus the remainder. Weighted mean odds ratios were calculated for all four mental health outcomes, using the same formulas as above.

3. Drinking, Drugs, Education, and Employment Outcomes. For this essay, we analyzed three new drinking outcomes, three new drug outcomes, three new education outcomes, three new employment outcomes, and one new summary measure of poor life success (at age 48). All of these outcomes, apart from education outcomes and the combined life-success scores, were based on self-reports of the study males. As far as possible, having a problem present was defined as being in the worst quarter in the sample.

Binge drinking at age 18 referred to having drunk over 13 units of alcohol in one evening during the previous month. Drinking problems at ages 32 and 48 referred to combined measures of drunk driving, heavy drinking, binge drinking, and a high CAGE alcoholism score (Mayfield, McLoed, and Hall 1974). Drugs at age 18 referred to ever having taken an illicit drug. Drugs at ages 32 and 48 referred to the use of cannabis or other drugs during the previous 5 years. School failure at age 14 referred to low class position according to school records. Truant at age 14 referred to being truant according to the boy's teacher. No exams at age 18 referred to no school examinations having been taken or passed. Unemployed at age 18 referred to having been unemployed for over 5 weeks in the previous year. Unemployed at age 32 referred to having been unemployed for over 5 months in the previous 5 years. Unemployed at age 48 referred to having been unemployed for over 10 months in the previous 5 years. Poor life success at age 48 was a combined scale, based on accommodation history, cohabitation history, employment history, involvement in fights, alcohol use, drug use, self-reported offending, anxiety-depression, and convictions over the previous 5 years (Farrington et al. 2006).

REFERENCES

Achenbach, Thomas M. 1991*a*. *Manual for the Child Behavior Checklist/4–18 and 1991 Profile*. Burlington: University of Vermont.

———. 1991*b*. *Manual for the Teacher Report Form and 1991 Profile*. Burlington: University of Vermont.

Amato, Paul R., and Joan G. Gilbreth. 1999. "Nonresident Fathers and Children's Well-Being: A Meta-analysis." *Journal of Marriage and the Family* 61: 557–73.

Amato, Paul R., and Bruce Keith. 1991. "Parental Divorce and Adult Well-Being: A Meta-analysis." *Journal of Marriage and the Family* 53:43–58.

Amira, Ya'el. 1992. "We Are Not the Problem: Black Children and Their Families within the Criminal Justice System." In *Prisoners' Children: What Are the Issues?* edited by Roger Shaw. London: Routledge.

Anderson, Nancy N. 1966. *Prisoners' Families: A Study of Family Crisis*. Minneapolis: University of Minnesota.

Arditti, Joyce A., Jennifer Lambert-Shute, and Karen Joest. 2003. "Saturday Morning at the Jail: Implications of Incarceration for Families and Children." *Family Relations* 52:195–204.

Bandura, Albert. 1969. *Principles of Behavior Modification*. New York: Holt.

Baron, Reuben M., and David A. Kenny. 1986. "The Moderator-Mediator Variable Distinction in Social Psychological Research: Conceptual, Strategic, and Statistical Considerations." *Journal of Personality and Social Psychology* 51: 1173–82.

Baunach, Phyllis J. 1985. *Mothers in Prison*. New Brunswick, NJ: Transaction Books.

Bendheim-Thoman Center for Research on Child Wellbeing. 2002. *Incarceration and the Bonds among Parents*. Fragile Families Research Brief no. 12. Princeton, NJ: Princeton University.

Bernstein, Nell. 2005. *All Alone in the World: Children of the Incarcerated*. New York: New Press.

Blumstein, Alfred, and Allen J. Beck. 1999. "Population Growth in U.S. Prisons, 1980–1996." In *Prisons*, edited by Michael Tonry and Joan Petersilia. Vol. 26 of *Crime and Justice: A Review of Research*, edited by Michael Tonry. Chicago: University of Chicago Press.

Bor, William, Tara R. McGee, and Abigail A. Fagan. 2004. "Early Risk Factors for Adolescent Antisocial Behaviour: An Australian Longitudinal Study." *Australian and New Zealand Journal of Psychiatry* 38:365–72.

Boss, Pauline. 2007. "Ambiguous Loss Theory: Challenges for Scholars and Practitioners." *Family Relations* 56:105–11.

Boswell, Gwyneth, and Peter Wedge. 2002. *Imprisoned Fathers and Their Children*. London: Jessica Kingsley.

Bowlby, John. 1946. *Forty-four Juvenile Thieves: Their Characters and Home-Life*. London: Balliere, Tindall & Cox.

———. 1969. *Attachment and Loss*. Vol. 1, *Attachment*. London: Hogarth Press and the Institute of Psycho-Analysis.

———. 1973. *Attachment and Loss*. Vol. 2, *Separation, Anxiety and Anger*. London: Hogarth Press and the Institute of Psycho-Analysis.

———. 1980. *Attachment and Loss*. Vol. 3, *Loss, Sadness and Depression*. London: Hogarth Press and the Institute of Psycho-Analysis.

Braithwaite, John. 1999. "Restorative Justice: Assessing Optimistic and Pessimistic Accounts." In *Crime and Justice: A Review of Research*, vol. 25, edited by Michael Tonry. Chicago: University of Chicago Press.

Braithwaite, John, and Stephen Mugford. 1994. "Conditions of Successful Reintegration Ceremonies: Dealing with Juvenile Offenders." *British Journal of Criminology* 34:139–71.

Braman, Donald. 2004. *Doing Time on the Outside: Incarceration and Family Life in Urban America*. Ann Arbor: University of Michigan Press.

Braman, Donald, and Jenifer Wood. 2003. "From One Generation to the Next: How Criminal Sanctions Are Reshaping Family Life in Urban America." In *Prisoners Once Removed: The Impact of Incarceration and Reentry on Children, Families, and Communities*, edited by Jeremy Travis and Michelle Waul. Washington, DC: Urban Institute.

Bronfenbrenner, Urie. 1979. *The Ecology of Human Development*. Cambridge, MA: Harvard University Press.

Brown, Kelli, Liz Dibb, Felicity Shenton, and Nicola Elson. 2002. *No-One's Ever Asked Me: Young People with a Prisoner in the Family*. London: Federation of Prisoners' Families Support Groups (now called Action for Prisoners' Families).

Bryant, Elizabeth S., and Jeanne C. Rivard. 1995. "Correlates of Major and Minor Offending among Youth with Severe Emotional Disturbance." *Journal of Emotional and Behavioral Disorders* 3:76–84.

Butler, Tony, Gavin Andrews, Stephen Allnutt, Chika Sakashita, Nadine E. Smith, and John Basson. 2006. "Mental Disorders in Australian Prisoners: A Comparison with a Community Sample." *Australian and New Zealand Journal of Psychiatry* 40:272–76.

Caddle, Diane, and Debbie Crisp. 1997. *Imprisoned Women and Mothers*. Research Study no. 162. London: Home Office.

Caspi, Avshalom, Joseph McClay, Terrie E. Moffitt, Jonathan Mill, Judy Martin, Ian W. Craig, Alan Taylor, and Richie Poulton. 2002. "Role of Genotype in the Cycle of Violence in Maltreated Children." *Science* 297:851–54.

Catan, Liza. 1992. "Infants with Mothers in Prison." In *Prisoners' Children: What Are the Issues?* edited by Roger Shaw. London: Routledge.

Center for Human Resource Research. 2006. *NLSY79 User's Guide*. Columbus: Ohio State University.

Chamberlain, Patricia, and John B. Reid. 1998. "Comparison of Two Community Alternatives to Incarceration for Chronic Juvenile Offenders." *Journal of Consulting and Clinical Psychology* 66:624–33.

Clear, Todd R. 2007. *Imprisoning Communities: How Mass Incarceration Makes Disadvantaged Neighborhoods Worse*. New York: Oxford University Press.

Clear, Todd R., Dina R. Rose, and Judith A. Ryder. 2001. "Incarceration and the Community: The Problem of Removing and Returning Offenders." *Crime and Delinquency* 47:335–51.

Cohen, Patricia. 1996. "Childhood Risks for Young Adult Symptoms of Personality Disorder: Method and Substance." *Multivariate Behavioral Research* 31:121–48.

Coopersmith, Stanley. 1967. *The Antecedents of Self-Esteem*. San Francisco: W. H. Freeman.

Council of Europe. 1997. *Recommendation 1340 (1997) on the Social and Family Effects of Detention*. Strasbourg, France: Parliamentary Assembly, Council of Europe.

Crowe, Raymond R. 1974. "An Adoption Study of Antisocial Personality." *Archives of General Psychiatry* 31:785–91.

Cunningham, Alison, and Linda Baker. 2003. *Waiting for Mommy: Giving a Voice to the Hidden Victims of Imprisonment*. London, Canada: Centre for Children and Families in the Justice System.

———. 2004. *Invisible Victims: The Children of Women in Prison*. Centre for Children and Families in the Justice System. Available from http://www.voicesforchildren.ca/report-Dec2004-1.htm (downloaded October 2006).

Dannerbeck, Anne M. 2005. "Differences in Parenting Attributes, Experiences, and Behaviors of Delinquent Youth with and without a Parental History of Incarceration." *Youth Violence and Juvenile Justice* 3:199–213.

Dodd, Tricia, and Paul Hunter. 1992. *The National Prison Survey 1991*. London: H. M. Stationery Office.

Dowling, Samantha, and Frances Gardner. 2005. *Parenting Programmes for Improving the Parenting Skills and Outcomes for Incarcerated Parents and Their Children (Protocol)*. Cochrane database of Systematic Reviews (issue 4). Available from http://www.mrw.interscience.wiley.com/cochrane/clsysrev/articles/CD005557/frame.html (downloaded March 2007).

Dunn, Judy. 2004. "Annotation: Children's Relationships with Their Nonresident Fathers." *Journal of Child Psychology and Psychiatry* 45:659–71.

Eddy, J. Mark, and John B. Reid. 2003. "The Adolescent Children of Incarcerated Parents." In *Prisoners Once Removed: The Impact of Incarceration and Reentry on Children, Families and Communities*, edited by Jeremy Travis and Michelle Waul. Washington, DC: Urban Institute.

Eloff, Irma, and M. Moen. 2003. "An Analysis of Mother-Child Interaction Patterns in Prison." *Early Child Development and Care* 173:711–20.

Emery, Robert E. 1999. *Marriage, Divorce, and Children's Adjustment*. 2nd ed. Thousand Oaks, CA: Sage.

European Action Research Committee on the Children of Imprisoned Parents. 1996. *Children of Imprisoned Parents: Family Ties and Separation*. Montrouge, France: Fédération des Relais Enfants-Parents.

Eysenck, Hans J., and Sybil B. G. Eysenck. 1964. *Manual of the Eysenck Personality Inventory*. London: University of London Press.

Fagan, Jeffrey, and Richard B. Freeman. 1999. "Crime and Work." In *Crime and Justice: A Review of Research*, vol. 25, edited by Michael Tonry. Chicago: University of Chicago Press.

Farrington, David P. 1991. "Antisocial Personality from Childhood to Adulthood." *Psychologist* 4:389–94.

———. 1995. "The Development of Offending and Antisocial Behaviour from Childhood: Key Findings from the Cambridge Study in Delinquent Development." *Journal of Child Psychology and Psychiatry* 36:929–64.

———. 2003*a*. "Key Results from the First Forty Years of the Cambridge Study in Delinquent Development." In *Taking Stock of Delinquency: An Overview of Findings from Contemporary Longitudinal Studies*, edited by Terence P. Thornberry and Marvin D. Krohn. New York: Kluwer Academic/ Plenum.

———. 2003*b*. "Methodological Quality Standards for Evaluation Research." *Annals of the American Academy of Political and Social Science* 587:49–68.

Farrington, David P., Geoffrey C. Barnes, and Sandra Lambert. 1996. "The Concentration of Offending in Families." *Legal and Criminological Psychology* 1:47–63.

Farrington, David P., Jeremy W. Coid, Louise Harnett, Darrick Jolliffe, Nadine Soteriou, Richard Turner, and Donald J. West. 2006. *Criminal Careers up to Age 50 and Life Success up to Age 48: New Findings from the Cambridge Study in Delinquent Development*. Research Study no. 299. London: Home Office.

Farrington, David P., Darrick Jolliffe, Rolf Loeber, Magda Stouthamer-Loeber, and Larry M. Kalb. 2001. "The Concentration of Offenders in Families, and Family Criminality in the Prediction of Boys' Delinquency." *Journal of Adolescence* 24:579–96.

Fergusson, David M., L. John Horwood, and Daniel S. Nagin. 2000. "Offending Trajectories in a New Zealand Birth Cohort." *Criminology* 38: 525–51.

Ferraro, Kathleen J., John M. Johnson, Stephen R. Jorgensen, and F. G. Bolton Jr. 1983. "Problems of Prisoners' Families: The Hidden Costs of Imprisonment." *Journal of Family Issues* 4:575–91.

Fishman, Susan H. 1983. "The Impact of Incarceration on Children of Offenders." *Journal of Children in Contemporary Society* 15:89–99.

Fitts, William H. 1965. *Tennessee Self Concept Scale Manual*. Nashville: Counselor Records and Tests.

Friedman, Sidney, and T. Conway Esselstyn. 1965. "The Adjustment of Children of Jail Inmates." *Federal Probation* 29:55–59.

Fritsch, Travis A., and John D. Burkhead. 1981. "Behavioral Reactions of Children to Parental Absence Due to Imprisonment." *Family Relations* 30:83–88.

Furneaux, W. Desmond, and Hamilton B. Gibson. 1966. *The New Junior Maudsley Inventory Manual*. London: University of London Press.

Gabel, Katherine, and Denise Johnston, eds. 1995. *Children of Incarcerated Parents*. New York: Lexington Books.

Gabel, Stewart, and Richard Shindledecker. 1993. "Characteristics of Children Whose Parents Have Been Incarcerated." *Hospital and Community Psychiatry* 44:656–60.

Garber, Judy. 2000. "Development and Depression." In *Handbook of Developmental Psychopathology*, edited by Arnold J. Sameroff, Michael Lewis, and Suzanne M. Miller. New York: Kluwer Academic/ Plenum.

Garmezy, Norman, and Michael Rutter, eds. 1983. *Stress, Coping, and Development in Children*. New York: McGraw-Hill.

Glueck, Sheldon, and Eleanor Glueck. 1950. *Unraveling Juvenile Delinquency*. Cambridge, MA: Harvard University Press.

Goldberg, David P., and Paul Williams. 1988. *A User's Guide to the General Health Questionnaire*. Windsor, England: NFER-Nelson.

H. M. Treasury. 2003. *Every Child Matters*. CM 5860. Norwich: H. M. Stationery Office.

Haas, Henriette, David P. Farrington, Martin Killias, and Ghazala Sattar. 2004. "The Impact of Different Family Configurations on Delinquency." *British Journal of Criminology* 44:520–32.

Hagan, John, and Juleigh P. Coleman. 2001. "Returning Captives of the American War on Drugs: Issues of Community and Family Reentry." *Crime and Delinquency* 47:352–67.

Hagan, John, and Ronit Dinovitzer. 1999. "Collateral Consequences of Imprisonment for Children, Communities and Prisoners." In *Prisons*, edited by Michael Tonry and Joan Petersilia. Vol. 26 of *Crime and Justice: A Review of Research*, edited by Michael Tonry. Chicago: University of Chicago Press.

Hagen, Kristine A., Barbara J. Myers, and Virginia H. Mackintosh. 2005. "Hope, Social Support, and Behavioral Problems in At-Risk Children." *American Journal of Orthopsychiatry* 75:211–19.

Hames, Carolyn C., and Debra Pedreira. 2003. "Children with Parents in Prison: Disenfranchised Grievers Who Benefit from Bibliotherapy." *Illness, Crisis and Loss* 11:377–86.

Harlow, Caroline W. 2003. *Education and Correctional Populations*. Special Report. Washington, DC: Bureau of Justice Statistics.

Harrison, Paige M., and Allen J. Beck. 2006. *Prison and Jail Inmates at Midyear 2005*. Bulletin. Washington, DC: Bureau of Justice Statistics.

Healey, Karen, Denise Foley, and Karyn Walsh. 2000. *Parents in Prison and Their Families: Everyone's Business and No-One's Concern*. Brisbane, Queensland: Catholic Prison Ministry.

Henggeler, Scott W., Sonja K. Schoenwald, Charles M. Borduin, Melisa D. Rowland, and Phillippe B. Cunningham. 1998. *Multisystemic Treatment of Antisocial Behavior in Children and Adolescents*. New York: Guilford.

Hinshaw, Stephen P. 2005. "The Stigmatization of Mental Illness in Children and Parents: Developmental Issues, Family Concerns, and Research Needs." *Journal of Child Psychology and Psychiatry* 46:714–34.

Hirschi, Travis. 1969. *Causes of Delinquency*. Berkeley: University of California Press.

Hodgins, Sheilagh, and Carl-Gunnar Janson. 2002. *Criminality and Violence among the Mentally Disordered: The Stockholm Metropolitan Project*. Cambridge: Cambridge University Press.

Home Office. 2007. *Population in Custody Monthly Tables: June 2006 England and Wales*. London: Home Office. Available from http://www.homeoffice.gov.uk/ (downloaded November 2007).

Home Secretary, Lord Chancellor, and Attorney General. 2002. *Justice for All*. CM 5563. Norwich: H. M. Stationery Office.

Huebner, Beth M., and Regan Gustafson. 2007. "The Effect of Maternal Incarceration on Adult Offspring Involvement in the Criminal Justice System." *Journal of Criminal Justice* 35:283–96.

Jacobs, Ann L. 1995. "Protecting Children and Preserving Families: A Cooperative Strategy for Nurturing Children of Incarcerated Parents." Paper presented at the Family to Family Initiative Conference (Annie E. Casey Foundation), Baltimore, October.

Jaffee, Sara R., Terrie E. Moffitt, Avshalom Caspi, and Alan Taylor. 2003. "Life with (or without) Father: The Benefits of Living with Two Biological Parents Depend on the Father's Antisocial Behavior." *Child Development* 74:109–26.

James, Doris J., and Lauren E. Glaze. 2006. *Mental Health Problems of Prison and Jail Inmates*. Special Report. Washington, DC: Bureau of Justice Statistics.

Janson, Carl-Gunnar. 2000. "Project Metropolitan." In *Seven Swedish Longitudinal Studies in the Behavioral Sciences*, edited by Carl-Gunnar Janson. Stockholm: Forskningsradsnamuden.

Jiménez, Jesús M. 2002. "Children and Mothers in Prison: Family and School Developmental Settings in Spanish Penitentiary Centres." *Infancia y Aprendizaje* 25:183–94.

Johnson, Elizabeth I., and Jane Waldfogel. 2004. "Children of Incarcerated Parents: Multiple Risks and Children's Living Arrangements." In *Imprisoning America: The Social Effects of Mass Incarceration*, edited by Mary Pattillo, David Weiman, and Bruce Western. New York: Russell Sage.

Johnston, Denise. 1995. "Effects of Parental Incarceration." In *Children of Incarcerated Parents*, edited by Katherine Gabel and Denise Johnston. New York: Lexington Books.

Juby, Heather, and David P. Farrington. 2001. "Disentangling the Link between Disrupted Families and Delinquency." *British Journal of Criminology* 41:22–40.

Junger-Tas, Josine, Ineke H. Marshall, and Denis Ribeaud. 2003. *Delinquency in an International Perspective: The International Self-Reported Delinquency Study (ISRD)*. The Hague: Kugler/Monsey.

Kampfner, Christina J. 1995. "Post-traumatic Stress Reactions in Children of Imprisoned Mothers." In *Children of Incarcerated Parents*, edited by Katherine Gabel and Denise Johnston. New York: Lexington Books.

Kandel, Elizabeth, Sarnoff A. Mednick, Lis Kirkegaard-Sorensen, Barry Hutchings, Joachim Knop, Raben Rosenberg, and Fini Schulsinger. 1988. "IQ as a Protective Factor for Subjects at High Risk for Antisocial Behavior." *Journal of Consulting and Clinical Psychology* 56:224–26.

Killias, Martin, Marcelo F. Aebi, and Denis Ribeaud. 2000*a*. "Does Community Service Rehabilitate Better than Short-Term Imprisonment? Results of a Controlled Experiment." *Howard Journal* 39:40–57.

———. 2000*b*. "Learning through Controlled Experiments: Community Service and Heroin Prescription in Switzerland." *Crime and Delinquency* 46: 233–51.

Kim-Cohen, Julia, Avshalom Caspi, Alan Taylor, Brenda Williams, Rhiannon Newcombe, Ian W. Craig, and Terrie E. Moffitt. 2006. "MAOA, Maltreatment, and Gene-Environment Interaction Predicting Children's Mental Health: New Evidence and a Meta-analysis." *Molecular Psychiatry* 11:903–13.

Klein, Rachel G., and Daniel S. Pine. 2002. "Anxiety Disorders." In *Child and Adolescent Psychiatry*, edited by Michael Rutter and Alan Taylor. Malden, MA: Blackwell.

Koban, Linda A. 1983. "Parents in Prison: A Comparative Analysis of the Effects of Incarceration on the Families of Men and Women." *Research in Law, Deviance and Social Control* 5:171–83.

Kraemer, Helena C., Karen K. Lowe, and David J. Kupfer. 2005. *To Your Health: How to Understand What Research Tells Us about Risk*. New York: Oxford University Press.

Liebling, Alison. 1999. "Prison Suicide and Prisoner Coping." In *Prisons*, edited by Michael Tonry and Joan Petersilia. Vol. 26 of *Crime and Justice: A Review of Research*, edited by Michael Tonry. Chicago: University of Chicago Press.

Light, Roy. 1994. *Black and Asian Prisoners' Families*. Bristol, England: Bristol Centre for Criminal Justice.

Lipsey, Mark W., and James H. Derzon. 1998. "Predictors of Violent or Serious Delinquency in Adolescence and Early Adulthood: A Synthesis of Longitudinal Research." In *Serious and Violent Juvenile Offenders*, edited by David P. Farrington and Rolf Loeber. Thousand Oaks, CA: Sage.

Lipsey, Mark W., and David B. Wilson. 2001. *Practical Meta-analysis*. Thousand Oaks, CA: Sage.

Loper, Ann B., and Elena H. Tuerk. 2006. "Parenting Programs for Incarcerated Parents: Current Research and Future Directions." *Criminal Justice Policy Review* 17:407–27.

Lowenstein, Ariela. 1986. "Temporary Single Parenthood—the Case of Prisoners' Families." *Family Relations* 35:79–85.

Luthar, Suniya S., ed. 2003. *Resilience and Vulnerability: Adaptation in the Context of Childhood Adversities*. Cambridge: Cambridge University Press.

Lynch, James P., and William J. Sabol. 2004. "Effects of Incarceration on Informal Social Control in Communities." In *Imprisoning America: The Social Effects of Mass Incarceration*, edited by Mary Pattillo, David Weiman, and Bruce Western. New York: Russell Sage.

Mackintosh, Virginia H., Barbara J. Myers, and Suzanne S. Kennon. 2006. "Children of Incarcerated Mothers and Their Caregivers: Factors Affecting the Quality of Their Relationship." *Journal of Child and Family Studies* 15: 581–96.

Maruna, Shadd, and Thomas P. LeBel. 2002. "Revisiting Ex-Prisoner Reentry: A Buzzword in Search of a Narrative." In *Reform and Punishment: The Future of Sentencing*, edited by Sue Rex and Michael Tonry. Cullompton, England: Willan.

Masten, Ann S., Jon J. Hubbard, Scott D. Gest, Auke Tellegen, Norman Garmezy, and Marylouise Ramirez. 1999. "Competence in the Context of Adversity: Pathways to Resilience and Maladaption from Childhood to Late Adolescence." *Development and Psychopathology* 11:143–69.

Matsueda, Ross L. 1988. "The Current State of Differential Association Theory." *Crime and Delinquency* 34:277–306.

Matthews, Jill. 1983. *Forgotten Victims: How Prison Affects the Family*. London: National Association for the Care and Resettlement of Offenders.

Mayfield, Demmie, Gail McLoed, and Patricia Hall. 1974. "The CAGE Questionnaire: Validation of a New Alcoholism Screening Instrument." *American Journal of Psychiatry* 131:1121–23.

McCord, Joan, William McCord, and E. Thurber. 1962. "Some Effects of Paternal Absence on Male Children." *Journal of Abnormal Social Psychology* 64:361–69.

McCord, William, Joan McCord, and Irving K. Zola. 1959. *Origins of Crime: A New Evaluation of the Cambridge-Somerville Youth Study*. New York: Columbia University Press.

McDermott, Kathleen, and Roy D. King. 1992. "Prison Rule 102: Stand by Your Man." In *Prisoners' Children: What Are the Issues?* edited by Roger Shaw. London: Routledge.

McEvoy, Kieron, David O'Mahony, Carol Horner, and Olwen Lyner. 1999. "The Home Front: The Families of Politically Motivated Prisoners in Northern Ireland." *British Journal of Criminology* 39:175–97.

Moerk, Ernst L. 1973. "Like Father Like Son: Imprisonment of Fathers and the Psychological Adjustment of Sons." *Journal of Youth and Adolescence* 2: 303–12.

Moffitt, Terrie E., Avshalom Caspi, Michael Rutter, and Phil A. Silva. 2001. *Sex Differences in Antisocial Behaviour: Conduct Disorder, Delinquency, and Violence in the Dunedin Longitudinal Study*. Cambridge: Cambridge University Press.

Morris, Pauline. 1965. *Prisoners and Their Families*. Woking, England: Unwin Brothers.

Moses, Marilyn C. 1995. *Keeping Incarcerated Mothers and Their Daughters Together: Girl Scouts beyond Bars*. Washington, DC: National Institute of Justice (Program Focus).

Mumola, Christopher J. 2000. *Incarcerated Parents and Their Children*. Special Report. Washington, DC: Bureau of Justice Statistics.

Mumola, Christopher J., and Jennifer C. Karberg. 2006. *Drug Use and Dependence, State and Federal Prisoners, 2004*. Special Report. Washington, DC: Bureau of Justice Statistics.

Murray, Joseph. 2005. "The Effects of Imprisonment on Families and Children of Prisoners." In *The Effects of Imprisonment*, edited by Alison Liebling and Shadd Maruna. Cullompton, England: Willan.

———. 2007. "The Cycle of Punishment: Social Exclusion of Prisoners and Their Children." *Criminology and Criminal Justice* 7:55–81.

Murray, Joseph, and David P. Farrington. 2005. "Parental Imprisonment: Effects on Boys' Antisocial Behaviour and Delinquency through the Life-Course." *Journal of Child Psychology and Psychiatry* 46:1269–78.

———. 2006. "Evidence-Based Programs for Children of Prisoners." *Criminology and Public Policy* 5:721–36.

———. 2008. "Parental Imprisonment: Long-Lasting Effects on Boys' Internalizing Problems through the Life Course." *Development and Psychopathology* 20(1):273–90.

Murray, Joseph, Carl-Gunnar Janson, and David P. Farrington. 2007. "Crime in Adult Offspring of Prisoners: A Cross-National Comparison of Two Longitudinal Samples." *Criminal Justice and Behavior* 34:133–49.

Myers, Barbara J., Tina M. Smarsh, Kristine Amlund-Hagen, and Suzanne Kennon. 1999. "Children of Incarcerated Mothers." *Journal of Child and Family Studies* 8:11–25.

Nagin, Daniel S. 1998. "Criminal Deterrence Research at the Outset of the Twenty-first Century." In *Crime and Justice: A Review of Research*, vol. 23, edited by Michael Tonry. Chicago: University of Chicago Press.

Najman, Jake M., William Bor, Michael O'Callaghan, Gail M. Williams, Rosemary Aird, and Greg Shuttlewood. 2005. "Cohort Profile: The Mater–University of Queensland Study of Pregnancy (MUSP)." *International Journal of Epidemiology* 34:992–97.

Office of National Statistics. 2007. *England and Wales: Estimated Resident Population by Single Year of Age and Sex; Mid-2006 Population Estimates.* Office of National Statistics. Available from http://www.statistics.gov.uk/ (downloaded November 2007).

Olds, David L., Charles R. Henderson, Robert Cole, John Eckenrode, Harriet Kitzman, Dennis Luckey, Lisa Pettitt, Kimberley Sidora, Pamela Morris, and Jane Powers. 1998. "Long-Term Effects of Nurse Home Visitation on Children's Criminal and Antisocial Behavior: 15-Year Follow-up of a Randomized Controlled Trial." *Journal of the American Medical Association* 280: 1238–44.

Pattillo, Mary, David Weiman, and Bruce Western, eds. 2004. *Imprisoning America: The Social Effects of Mass Incarceration.* New York: Russell Sage.

Peart, Kate, and Stewart Asquith. 1992. *Scottish Prisoners and Their Families: The Impact of Imprisonment on Family Relationships.* Glasgow: Centre for the Study of the Child and Society, University of Glasgow.

Petersilia, Joan. 2003. *When Prisoners Come Home: Parole and Prisoner Reentry.* Oxford: Oxford University Press.

———. 2005. "From Cell to Society: Who Is Returning Home?" In *Prisoner Reentry and Crime in America*, edited by Jeremy Travis and Christy Visher. Cambridge: Cambridge University Press.

Petrosino, Anthony, Carolyn Turpin-Petrosino, and John Buehler. 2003. "Scared Straight and Other Juvenile Awareness Programs for Preventing Juvenile Delinquency: A Systematic Review of the Randomized Experimental Evidence." *Annals of the American Academy of Political and Social Science* 589:41–62.

Pettit, Becky, and Bruce Western. 2004. "Mass Imprisonment and the Life Course: Race and Class Inequality in US Incarceration." *American Sociological Review* 69:151–69.

Philbrick, David. 1996. "Child and Adolescent Mental Health and the Prisoner's Child." Paper presented at the NEPACS conference, the Child and the Prison, Grey College, Durham, England, September 28.

Phillips, Susan D., Barbara J. Burns, H. Ryan Wagner, Teresa L. Kramer, and James M. Robbins. 2002. "Parental Incarceration among Adolescents Receiving Mental Health Services." *Journal of Child and Family Studies* 11: 385–99.

Phillips, Susan D., Alaattin Erkanli, Gordon P. Keeler, E. Jane Costello, and Adrian Angold. 2006. "Disentangling the Risks: Parent Criminal Justice Involvement and Children's Exposure to Family Risks." *Criminology and Public Policy* 5:677–703.

Poehlmann, Julie. 2005. "Representations of Attachment Relationships in Children of Incarcerated Mothers." *Child Development* 76:679–96.

Quilty, Simon, Michael H. Levy, Kirsten Howard, Alex Barratt, and Tony Butler. 2004. "Children of Prisoners: A Growing Public Health Problem." *Australian and New Zealand Journal of Public Health* 28:339–43.

Ramsden, Sally. 1998. *Working with the Children of Prisoners: A Resource for Teachers*. London: Save the Children.

Richards, Martin, Brenda McWilliams, Lucy Allcock, Jill Enterkin, Patricia Owens, and Jane Woodrow. 1994. *The Family Ties of English Prisoners: The Results of the Cambridge Project on Imprisonment and Family Ties*. Cambridge: Centre for Family Research, University of Cambridge.

Robins, Lee N., Patricia A. West, and Barbara L. Herjanic. 1975. "Arrests and Delinquency in Two Generations: A Study of Black Urban Families and Their Children." *Journal of Child Psychology and Psychiatry* 16:125–40.

Rodgers, Bryan, and Jan Pryor. 1998. *Divorce and Separation: The Outcomes for Children*. York, England: Joseph Rowntree Foundation.

Rose, Dina R., and Todd R. Clear. 2003. "Incarceration, Reentry, and Social Capital: Social Networks in the Balance." In *Prisoners Once Removed: The Impact of Incarceration and Reentry on Children, Families, and Communities*, edited by Jeremy Travis and Michelle Waul. Washington, DC: Urban Institute.

Rosenbaum, Paul R., and Donald B. Rubin. 1983. "The Central Role of the Propensity Score in Observational Studies for Causal Effects." *Biometrika* 70:41–55.

Rutter, Michael. 1990. "Psychosocial Resilience and Protective Mechanisms." In *Risk and Protective Factors in the Development of Psychopathology*, edited by Jon E. Rolf, Ann S. Masten, Dante Cicchetti, Keith H. Nüchterlein, and Sheldon Weintraub. Cambridge: Cambridge University Press.

———. 2003. "Crucial Paths from Risk Indicator to Causal Mechanism." In *Causes of Conduct Disorder and Juvenile Delinquency*, edited by Benjamin B. Lahey, Terrie E. Moffitt, and Avshalom Caspi. New York: Guilford.

Rutter, Michael, Henri Giller, and Ann Hagell. 1998. *Antisocial Behavior by Young People*. Cambridge: Cambridge University Press.

Sack, William H. 1977. "Children of Imprisoned Fathers." *Psychiatry* 40: 163–74.

Sack, William H., and Jack Seidler. 1978. "Should Children Visit Their Parents in Prison?" *Law and Human Behavior* 2:261–66.

Sack, William H., Jack Seidler, and Susan Thomas. 1976. "The Children of Imprisoned Parents: A Psychosocial Exploration." *American Journal of Orthopsychiatry* 46:618–28.

Sanders, Matthew R., Carol Markie-Dadds, Lucy A. Tully, and William Bor. 2000. "The Triple P-Positive Parenting Program: A Comparison of Enhanced, Standard and Self-Directed Behavioral Family Intervention for Parents of Children with Early Onset Conduct Problems." *Journal of Consulting and Clinical Psychology* 68:624–40.

Schlesselman, James J. 1982. *Case-Control Studies: Design, Conduct, Analysis*. New York: Oxford University Press.

Schneller, Donald P. 1976. *The Prisoner's Family: A Study of the Effects of Imprisonment on the Families of Prisoners*. San Francisco: R and E Research Associates.

Schwartz, Mary C., and Judith F. Weintraub. 1974. "The Prisoner's Wife: A Study in Crisis." *Federal Probation* 38:20–27.

Scott, Stephen, Quentin Spender, Moira Doolan, Brian Jacobs, and Helen Aspland. 2001. "Multicentre Controlled Trial of Parenting Groups for Childhood Antisocial Behaviour in Clinical Practice." *British Medical Journal* 323: 1–7.

Scottish Consortium on Crime and Criminal Justice. 2005. *Reducing the Prison Population: Penal Policy and Social Choices*. Edinburgh: Scottish Consortium on Crime and Criminal Justice.

Shadish, William R., Thomas D. Cook, and Donald T. Campbell. 2002. *Experimental and Quasi-Experimental Designs for Generalized Causal Inference*. Boston: Houghton Mifflin.

Shaffer, David, Prudence Fisher, Christopher P. Lucas, Mina K. Dulcan, and Mary E. Schwab-Stone. 2000. "NIMH Diagnostic Interview Schedule for Children, Version IV (NIMH DISC-IV): Description, Differences from Previous Versions, and Reliability of Some Common Diagnoses." *Journal of the American Academy of Child and Adolescent Psychiatry* 39:28–38.

Shaw, Roger. 1987. *Children of Imprisoned Fathers*. Bungay, England: Richard Clay.

———. 1992*a*. "Imprisoned Fathers and the Orphans of Justice." In *Prisoners' Children: What Are the Issues?* edited by Roger Shaw. London: Routledge.

———, ed. 1992*b*. *Prisoners' Children: What Are the Issues?* London: Routledge.

Sherman, Lawrence W. 1993. "Defiance, Deterrence and Irrelevance: A Theory of the Criminal Sanction." *Journal of Research in Crime and Delinquency* 30:445–73.

Sherman, Lawrence W., and Heather Strang. 2007. *Restorative Justice: The Evidence*. London: Smith Institute.

Sherman, Lawrence W., Heather Strang, Caroline Angel, Daniel Woods,

Geoffrey C. Barnes, Sarah Bennett, and Nova Inkpen. 2005. "Effects of Face-to-Face Restorative Justice on Victims of Crime in Four Randomized, Controlled Trials." *Journal of Experimental Criminology* 1:367–95.

Simmons, Charlene W. 2000. *Children of Incarcerated Parents*. Sacramento: California Research Bureau.

Singleton, Nicola, Howard Meltzer, Rebecca Gatward, Jeremy Coid, and Derek Deasy. 1998. *Psychiatric Morbidity among Prisoners in England and Wales*. London: H. M. Stationery Office.

Skinner, Donald, and Leslie Swartz. 1989. "The Consequences for Preschool Children of a Parent's Detention: A Preliminary South African Clinical Study of Caregivers' Reports." *Journal of Child Psychology and Psychiatry* 30: 243–59.

Smith, W. Randall. 1991. *Social Structure, Family Structure, Child Rearing, and Delinquency: Another Look*. Project Metropolitan Research Report no. 33. Stockholm: Department of Sociology, University of Stockholm.

Social Exclusion Unit. 2002. *Reducing Re-offending by Ex-Prisoners*. London: Social Exclusion Unit.

Springer, David W., Courtney Lynch, and Allen Rubin. 2000. "Effects of a Solution-Focused Mutual Aid Group for Hispanic Children of Incarcerated Parents." *Child and Adolescent Social Work Journal* 17:431–42.

Stanton, Ann M. 1980. *When Mothers Go to Jail*. Lexington, MA: Lexington Books.

Tonry, Michael. 1996. *Sentencing Matters*. New York: Oxford University Press.

———. 1998. "Intermediate Sanctions in Sentencing Guidelines." In *Crime and Justice: A Review of Research*, vol. 23, edited by Michael Tonry. Chicago: University of Chicago Press.

———. 2003. "Reducing the Prison Population." In *Confronting Crime: Crime Control Policy under New Labour*, edited by Michael Tonry. Cullompton, England: Willan.

———. 2004. *Punishment and Politics: Evidence and Evaluation in the Making of English Crime Control Policy*. Cullompton, England: Willan.

Tonry, Michael, and Joan Petersilia. 1999. "American Prisons." In *Prisons*, edited by Michael Tonry and Joan Petersilia. Vol. 26 of *Crime and Justice: A Review of Research*, edited by Michael Tonry. Chicago: University of Chicago Press.

Travis, Jeremy, and Michelle Waul. 2003*a*. "Prisoners Once Removed: The Children and Families of Prisoners." In *Prisoners Once Removed: The Impact of Incarceration and Reentry on Children, Families, and Communities*, edited by Jeremy Travis and Michelle Waul. Washington, DC: Urban Institute.

———. 2003*b*. *Prisoners Once Removed: The Impact of Incarceration and Reentry on Children, Families, and Communities*. Washington, DC: Urban Institute.

Trice, Ashton D., and Joanne Brewster. 2004. "The Effects of Maternal Incarceration on Adolescent Children." *Journal of Police and Criminal Psychology* 19:27–35.

UN General Assembly. 1989. *The Convention on the Rights of the Child*. New York: United Nations.

University of Pennsylvania. 1957. *Pupil Adjustment Inventory Rater's Manual.* Boston: Houghton Mifflin.

Van Wormer, Katherine S., and Clemens Bartollas. 2000. *Women and the Criminal Justice System.* Needham Heights, MA: Allyn & Bacon.

Walker, Nigel. 1980. *Punishment, Danger and Stigma: The Morality of Criminal Justice.* Oxford: Blackwell.

Walmsley, Roy. 2005. *World Prison Population List.* 6th ed. London: International Centre for Prison Studies, Kings College London.

Webster-Stratton, Carolyn. 1998. "Preventing Conduct Problems in Head Start Children: Strengthening Parenting Competencies." *Journal of Consulting and Clinical Psychology* 66:715–30.

Weissman, Myrna M., Virginia Warner, Priya Wickramaratne, Donna Moreau, and Mark Olfson. 1997. "Offspring of Depressed Parents: 10 Years Later." *Archives of General Psychiatry* 54:932–40.

Weissman, Myrna M., Priya Wickramaratne, Yoko Nomura, Virginia Warner, Daniel Pilowsky, and Helen Verdeli. 2006. "Offspring of Depressed Parents: 20 Years Later." *American Journal of Psychiatry* 163:1001–8.

Wells, L. Edward, and Joseph H. Rankin. 1991. "Families and Delinquency: A Meta-Analysis of the Impact of Broken Homes." *Social Problems* 38:71–93.

Western, Bruce. 2002. "The Impact of Incarceration on Wage Mobility and Inequality." *American Sociological Review* 67:526–46.

Western, Bruce, Jeffrey R. Kling, and David F. Weiman. 2001. "The Labor Market Consequences of Incarceration." *Crime and Delinquency* 47:410–27.

Zahn-Waxler, Carolyn, Bonnie Klimes-Dougan, and Marcia J. Slattery. 2000. "Internalizing Problems of Childhood and Adolescence: Prospects, Pitfalls, and Progress in Understanding the Development of Anxiety and Depression." *Development and Psychopathology* 12:433–66.

Zalba, Serapio R. 1964. *Women Prisoners and Their Families.* Los Angeles: Delmar.

Joan Petersilia

California's Correctional Paradox of Excess and Deprivation

ABSTRACT

Rapidly expanding prison populations in California have brought a host of management challenges. One in seven state prisoners is housed there. California spends more than $9 billion a year on its correctional system, yet 66 percent of released inmates return to prison within 3 years. Prison assaults, homicide, and suicides are more common in California than nationally, fueled by a growing number of gang-affiliated prisoners and inmates serving long "three strikes" sentences. Few improvements have occurred despite a much-touted reform effort beginning 2003. Some blame the politically potent prison guards union, because guards' high salaries leave little funding for inmate programs. Others blame California's determinate sentencing law, which makes parole release automatic. California needs to reverse its 3-decade-old determinate sentencing law, establish a sentencing commission, implement evidence-based rehabilitation programs, adopt a parole violation decision matrix, invest in intermediate sanctions, and work collaboratively with communities on reentry programs.

The unprecedented expansion of the U.S. prison population is well known. The combined federal and state imprisonment rate hovered around 110 per 100,000 from 1926 to 1973, with little variation (Blumstein and Beck 1999). However, it has since grown steadily to 491 per 100,000 at year-end 2005, five times higher than in 1973. When jail inmates are added, the overall rate is 738 per 100,000 residents (Walmsley 2007). More than 2.3 million people are now incarcerated,

Joan Petersilia is professor of criminology, law, and society in the School of Social Ecology, University of California, Irvine. Thanks to Todd Clear, Roxanne Lieb, Kevin Reitz, and Michael Tonry, and for their comments on an earlier draft of this essay.

0192-3234/2008/0037-0003$10.00

and the buildup continues.[1] At year-end 2005, one in every 136 U.S. residents was incarcerated in state or federal prison or a local level, the highest rate in U.S. history and in the world (Walmsley 2007). Some see this as a "great experiment in social control," for it encompasses the greatest expansion of government control over individual citizens ever undertaken by a democratic state (Clear, Cole, and Reisig 2006, p. 5). Others say that Americans live in an era of "mass incarceration" or "mass imprisonment" (Garland 2001; Mauer and Chesney-Lind 2002).

Scholars have sought to explain why this happened late in the twentieth century, noting the importance of American politics and culture (Garland 2001; Tonry 2004). Others have studied the effects of expanded imprisonment on racial minorities, labor markets, political participation, community well-being, and family formation (Mauer and Chesney-Lind 2002; Clear et al. 2003; Braman 2004; Pattillo, Weiman and Western 2004; Clear 2007). Researchers have also studied the effects of incarceration on crime rates (Blumstein and Wallman 2000; Spelman 2000; Levitt 2004), the psychological adjustment of those incarcerated (Haney 2006), and prisoner reintegration (Petersilia 2003; Travis 2005). These studies document the significant collateral costs of increased imprisonment and raise questions as to whether resulting reductions in crime are commensurate with the negative consequences.

Less studied but critically important is the effect of the buildup on state prison systems and on prison management. The war on drugs, mandatory sentencing, and the institutionalization of the mentally ill have dramatically changed the demographic and offense composition of the prison population. Prisons are increasingly filled with minority inmates, particularly blacks and Latinos. Prison gangs have emerged with new power and influence, challenging the ability of prison administrators to control the prison environment. Some contend that staff and inmate assaults are common and that there is a pervasive culture of fear and violence in many U.S. prisons (Gibbons and Katzenbach 2006). Budgets have not kept pace with population growth, causing overcrowding and reductions in prison work and education programs. Prison guard unions—their ranks swelling due to expanded hiring—exert growing influence. These aspects of America's prisons

[1] The Department of Justice recently released figures showing that the nation's prison and jail population grew by 2.7 percent (58,463) in 2005, 33 years of successive annual increases of inmates (Harrison and Beck 2006).

are a critical part of the untold mass incarceration story since they powerfully affect costs, effectiveness, and public safety.

State prison systems contain 87 percent of all U.S. prisoners. At year-end 2005, there were 1.5 million state and federal prisoners, and the federal system held just 12 percent (Harrison and Beck 2006). Four states, California, Texas, New York, and Florida, account for 39 percent of all state prisoners (Harrison and Beck 2006).

California's 171,800 prisoners as of March 2007 constitute the largest prison population of any state (California Department of Corrections and Rehabilitation 2007). One in seven (13.5 percent) state prisoners is incarcerated in California. Texas used to house more prisoners than California but its prison population began to stabilize in 2004 and now stands at 153,849 (Fabelo 2007), while California's increases continue. Between 1980 and 2007, California's population increased over sevenfold, from 23,264 to 171,800, compared with a fourfold increase nationally. And despite a 2003 vow by California governor Arnold Schwarzenegger to reduce the prison population, it continues to surge, recent projections predicting 191,000 prisoners in 2010 (California Department of Corrections and Rehabilitation 2006*a*).

California's distinctive correctional history and national influence also make its experience instructive. California was the nation's premier corrections system from the 1940s through the 1960s. Daniel Glaser (1995) described how good ideas were routinely introduced and rigorously evaluated, with the best of them being exported nationally and internationally. Wardens wrote books, including the groundbreaking 1952 study *Prisoners Are People* by Kenyon Scudder (1952), and held advanced degrees in social work (Pomfret 2006). The department at one time had 80 researchers on staff and developed the nation's first inmate classification system, the first recidivism prediction scoring system, and an array of model prison and parole programs, including today's well-regarded therapeutic communities for treating drug abusers (Glaser 1995). John Conrad, who worked in the California system between 1947 and 1967, observed, "It is hard to recapture the excitement of those days. It was an exhilarating experience to engage in an enterprise in which all participants are convinced that they are leading the world to great improvements in rehabilitation programs. We knew that was the case; we could see the improvements and their effects, and we heard the acclaim from travelers who came from all over the world to see for themselves" (quoted in Glaser 1995, p. 40). California was the model of good correctional management and inmate programming, and its practices profoundly influenced American corrections for over 30 years.

California's political mood and optimism regarding corrections changed dramatically in the 1970s. Tough law-and-order rhetoric by elected officials led to mandatory sentences for a host of crimes, and more people faced prison terms. In 1976, California became the second state after Maine to abolish indeterminate sentencing, which had explicitly embraced rehabilitation as a correctional goal and tied a prisoner's release date to his or her rehabilitative progress. California adopted the Uniform Determinate Sentencing Law, which abolished discretionary parole for most inmates and declared that the goal of imprisonment was punishment and not rehabilitation (Messinger and Johnson 1978). By 2002, 16 states had followed California's example, adopting determinate sentencing and abolishing discretionary parole for most inmates (Petersilia 1999). In 1994, Californians passed Proposition 184, the nation's toughest three strikes law mandating 25-years-to-life sentences for most felony offenders with two previous serious convictions. In the following decade, 26 states and the federal government passed three strikes statutes of their own, but none was as severe or had nearly as much effect on the prison population (Zimring, Hawkins, and Kamin 2003).[2]

California is a bellwether state when it comes to crime policy. Any examination of the effects of America's prison buildup would be incomplete without a detailed examination of its effects in California, including how prison expansion has influenced inmate characteristics, budgets and staff, inmate classification levels, gang proliferation, treatment and work programs, parole services, and recidivism.

Answering these and other related questions leads me to conclude that California's prison system can best be described as a "paradox of

[2] Under Proposition 184, California's three strikes law, if a defendant is convicted of a felony and has one, two, or more prior convictions that qualify as "strikes," the defendant will be sentenced for the current offense under the three strikes law. Although prior strikes most commonly are serious or violent felonies, the current conviction can be for any felony. The defendant's sentence is increased depending on how many prior "strikes" he or she has. If the defendant has one prior conviction, the normal term under the determinate sentencing law is doubled. If the defendant has two or more prior convictions, the defendant is to be sentenced to an indeterminate term of 25 years to life. The court does have some discretion under the three strikes law. The court may, in the interests of justice, dismiss prior strike convictions (*People v. Superior Court*, 113 CA.4th 497 [1996]). See http://www.lhc.ca.gov/lhcdir/sentencing/WeinsteinJune06.pdf (accessed November 2, 2006).

excess and deprivation."[3] Corrections expenditures are among the highest in the nation—per inmate, per staff, and as a share of the overall state budget. Yet a federal court is threatening to take over the entire prison system, in response to claims that conditions there violate the constitutional rights of prisoners. Nearly 50 percent of all prisoners released in 2006 sat idle—meaning they did not participate in any work assignment or rehabilitation programs—for the entire time they were in prison (California Expert Panel 2007). They return to communities unprepared for reentry, and two-thirds are returned to prison within 3 years, nearly twice the average national rate. No other state spends more on its corrections system and gets back less.

California's prison system is in crisis. It has deteriorated from being one of the best systems in the country to being dysfunctional. For 3 decades, California legislators and the voters have radically transformed the penal system by enacting hundreds of new sentencing laws, building 22 new prisons, and dismantling most rehabilitation programs. Even inmates willing to participate in rehabilitation programs are often deterred from doing so because gang leaders discourage them from cooperating with the authorities. High recidivism rates threaten public safety and add significantly to severe overcrowding. The prison system now houses nearly twice as many prisoners as it was designed to hold, and prisoners sleep in makeshift classrooms, gyms, and recreation areas. Prison growth is being driven by increases in new admissions and by parolees who commit new crimes or violate the terms of their release and are re-incarcerated. The courts have intervened. Nearly all aspects of prison and parole operations are now governed by consent decrees based on federal and state court litigation. Current population projections indicate the situation will only worsen.

There are no simple or inexpensive fixes. A four-point plan, however, would fundamentally alter the state's sentencing, prison, and parole release policies. The overarching goal is to realign correctional resources with offender risk and focus on enhancing offenders' chances for successful reentry. The first step is vital: creating a sentencing commission to document current practices and their effects and to insulate elected officials from pressures to respond automatically to high-visibility crimes by enacting more punitive laws. Sentencing commissions can prescribe longer terms for the most violent offenders and direct

[3] This term is borrowed from Enthoven and Kronick (1989).

low-risk inmates to effective intermediate sanctions, reducing prison crowding without new prison building.

Second, California must implement evidence-based rehabilitation programs. Well-run, well-targeted educational and vocational programs, substance abuse treatment, cognitive behavioral therapies, and reentry partnerships can reduce recidivism by 5–30 percent. Success translates into fewer returns to prison and therefore less crowding. Third, parole managers should develop and implement a structured parole violation decision-making system that takes account of the severity of the violation and the offender's risk level when determining what to do. Use of a structured decision-making tool will permit prison beds to be reserved for the most serious offenders. Resources otherwise spent on prison cells could be spent on intensive community-based intermediate sanctions.

Finally, perhaps most importantly, we must recognize that all prisoner reentry is local. Nearly all prisoners eventually return home to families, neighborhoods, and communities. We must invest in community partnerships that help offenders make the transition from formal social-control agencies (e.g., law enforcement, parole) to informal ones (e.g., loved ones, peers, employers).

None of these recommendations can work in isolation. They must be implemented as part of a comprehensive package. If California finds the political will to implement them successfully, its penal system may once again return to prominence, and many more prisoners will return home to live crime-free lives.

Here is how this essay is organized. Section I provides an overview of California's adult corrections system, considering whether the size of the prison population results from particularly high levels of crime or a particularly heavy-handed use of prison sentences relative to other states. Section II describes the management of California prisons, discussing the prison classification process, inmate security levels, staff-to-inmate ratios, and the growth and power of the California Correctional Peace Officers Association (CCPOA). Section III reviews evidence from California and the nation on inmate escapes, suicides, homicides, and assaults and summarizes what is known about prison gangs in California. Section IV describes California prison rehabilitation programs and the extent to which inmates needing specific programs get them in prison. California's program participation rates are compared with that of the nation and other large states. Section V describes the prison population in terms of demographic characteristics, prior criminal record, and conviction crimes, including how these characteristics have changed over time and how California prisoners compare to prisoners nationwide. Section VI describes prison release and parole supervision and discusses parole caseload size and supervision requirements. Section VII discusses California's recidivism rates, variously defined, and compares them with those of other large states. This section elaborates on California's unique system for handling administrative or technical violations. Section VIII offers conclusions and recommendations.

I. Understanding California's Booming Prisons

"California is different," Californians often say, with a population that puts unique demands on its correctional system. While this is true in some ways, California uses prisons much as the rest of the country does. Recognizing the similarities clarifies some of the ways in which the state most significantly differs from the rest of the country.

With 35.9 million residents, California is the nation's most populous state (U.S. Census Bureau 2006). Texas, next most populous, has 22.9 million residents. Any discussion of the size of California's prison population must take account of the size of its resident population.

The Bureau of Justice Statistics (BJS) reports that California's incarceration rate is not especially high by U.S. standards. The rate (state prisoners with a sentence of more than 1 year per 100,000 residents) is only slightly above the national average. As figure 1 shows, 456 per 100,000 California residents were in prison in 2004 on any one day (about one-half of 1 percent, or one of every 219 Californians) compared to the U.S. average of 432 per 100,000 population (one of every 231 U.S. residents).[4] Put another way, California has 12.2 percent of the resident population, and 12.9 percent of the state prison population.[5]

[4] Since Californians are 12.9 percent of the total U.S. prison population, they may disproportionately skew the average U.S. incarceration rate of 432 per 100,000. The rate was recomputed without California, and the U.S. prison incarceration rate dropped to 3.4 per 100,000, making California's prison incarceration rate still close to the national average.

[5] In 2006, California had an estimated 35,871,648 residents compared to 22,851,820 in Texas. U.S. Census estimates for 2004 were used to estimate the incarceration rates in fig. 1 since comparable state prison populations could be obtained for that year. State prison populations are from Harrison and Beck (2005).

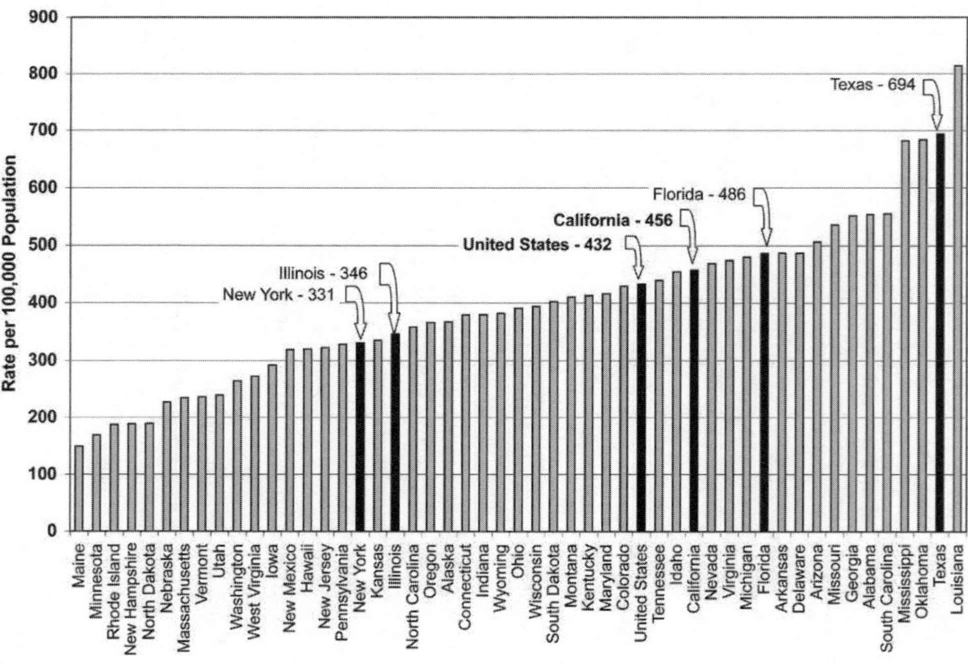

FIG. 1.—Prison incarceration rate by state, 2004. Source: Harrison and Beck (2005, table 4). http://www.ojp.usdoj.gov/bjs/pub/pdf/p04.pdf. The incarceration rate is defined as prisoners with a sentence of more than 1 year per 100,000 total residents.

However, these national comparisons should not make Californians complacent. Several other large states—for example, New York, Illinois, Ohio, Pennsylvania—have lower percentages of their populations in prison and have lower crime rates.[6] Moreover, the total U.S. incarceration rate (combining jails and prisons) is 738 per 100,000 of the national population, four times the world average of 166 per 100,000 (Walmsley 2007). In 2006, 9.25 million people were held in jails and prisons throughout the world, and 2.19 million of them (23 percent) were held in the United States. The United States has less than 5 percent of the world's population but nearly one-fourth of its incarcerated people (Hartney 2006). These are 1-day counts; the lifetime probability of serving a prison sentence in the United States is much higher. The Bureau of Justice Statistics estimates that one in every 37 U.S. adults will serve time in a state or federal prison during his or her lifetime, and the rates are much higher for certain age and racial groups, particularly black males in their twenties (Bonczar 2003).

The probability of being sentenced to prison after a felony conviction in California is also comparable to the national average (40 percent), and for some crimes—such as drug possession or aggravated assault—the chances convicted offenders will be sentenced to prison are below average (see table 1). However, California's postconviction probability of imprisonment for larceny (46 percent) is much higher than elsewhere (excluding California, 34 percent).

Data from the National Judicial Reporting Program suggest that the lengths of prison term initially imposed upon conviction in California are similar to those imposed in other states having determinate sentencing systems and that California inmates serve initial prison terms that do not differ significantly in length from national averages (Petersilia 2006). The average prison sentence imposed in California is currently 48 months, and the average time served is 25 months (California Department of Corrections and Rehabilitation 2006*b*). These figures suggest that California's prison population is not attributable to especially heavy-handed imposition of prison sentences. The National Judicial Reporting Program data set, however, does not contain

[6] The relationship between incarceration and crime is complex. Scholars have estimated that perhaps one-quarter of the drop in crime during the 1990s can be attributed to increased incarceration, whereas other factors such as variations in the composition of the population, the economy, changes in drug markets, strength of law enforcement, and community responses to crime were more significant (Levitt 2004; Steman 2007).

TABLE 1

Sentenced to Prison after Felony Conviction, California versus the Nation (in Percent)

Most Serious Conviction Crime	California	Nationwide	Nationwide (without California)
Murder	97	91	90
Sexual assault	52	59	60
Robbery	70	70	71
Aggravated assault	39	41	42
Other violent	42	42	41
Burglary	41	47	48
Larceny	46	36	34
Fraud	27	31	32
Drug possession	23	34	37
Drug trafficking	46	42	42
Weapons offense	43	45	45
Other offense	42	34	34
Total	40	40	40

SOURCE.—Reanalysis of *National Judicial Reporting Program* (NJRP) 2002 data, Bureau of Justice Statistics.

very detailed information on crimes and offenders' backgrounds, so it is impossible to control statistically for all relevant variables.

California's crime rate is also not particularly high. It is about 2 percent lower than the national average (California Office of the Attorney General 2006). California residents report 4,004 index crimes per 100,000 residents—slightly below the national average of 4,063.[7] Florida and Texas have much higher crime rates, as do many smaller states (Federal Bureau of Investigation 2006).[8]

The correctional system includes much more than prisons, of course. But even when taking account of individuals on probation, parole, and in jail, California's comparatively moderate and mainstream use of prison supervision is apparent. As figure 2 shows, 725,085 people, 2.78 percent of Californians over age 18, were under some form of adult correctional control at year-end 2004. The national average is 3.1 percent (Lin and Jannetta 2006). Lin and Jannetta compared California's

[7] Total index crime rate derived by adding violent and property index crime rates. Index crimes are murder, rape, robbery, aggravated assault, burglary, larceny, and motor vehicle theft (*Crime in the United States 2005*, Federal Bureau of Investigation, http://www.fbi.gov/ucr/05cius/, accessed April 2007).

[8] Since police and community reporting practices vary considerably, aggregate UCR crime rates across states obscure many important differences (for a complete discussion, see Ruth and Reitz [2003]).

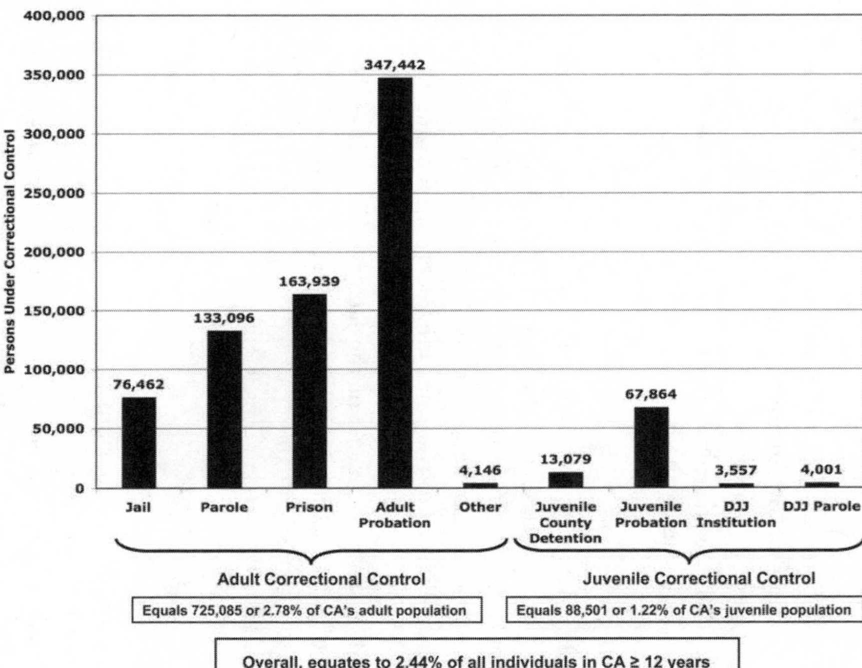

FIG. 2.—Californians under correctional control in 2004. Source: Lin and Jannetta (2006)

rates with those nationally and concluded that "with the exception of parole supervision, California's adult correctional control rates are not unusually high relative to those in other states" (2006, p. 1).

California's prison population thus does not come from particularly high levels of crime or particularly heavy-handed use of correctional sanctions. The state's numbers are mostly a function of its high population. As the most populous state in the country—with more than 50 percent more people than its closest rival, Texas—California produces high numbers of prisoners by enforcing the law and locking up residents at rates that, by American standards, are ordinary. One can argue that "American standards" are more punitive than necessary, and I have made that case elsewhere (Petersilia 2003), but California does not stand out in terms of the commonly used indexes.

II. Managing California's Prisons

California's system is similar to those of other states in the percentage of total population in prison on any one day, the probability of being sentenced to prison upon conviction, and the lengths of sentences imposed and initially served. But once offenders step foot inside a California prison, their experiences differ significantly from those of inmates in other states. In terms of the facilities that house them, the probability of participating in useful rehabilitation programs, the influence of prison gangs, and the characteristics of correctional officers who control their day-to-day lives, California prisoners live in a much different environment than do prisoners elsewhere.

A. Reception, Custody, and Security

Inmates come to prison from a variety of backgrounds and with diverse familiarity with the prison system. Some are hardened and violent offenders. Others are nonviolent and new to prisons. Sixty-one percent of offenders coming to prison in a given year are parolees who have had their parole terms revoked by parole authorities after having previously served time behind bars. The other 39 percent come as a result of new convictions, and these people are not as sophisticated as revoked parolees at navigating the serious currents behind prison bars. The first job of prison administrators is to sort inmates into housing assignments that will, to the greatest extent possible, reduce escapes and minimize the dangers inherent in the prison environment.

Inmate classification is their primary tool. This little known process affects not only facility and cell assignments but also sets the tone for every aspect of an inmate's highly regulated existence: from the safety of an inmate's day-to-day environment to the amount of cell space he or she will have, to opportunities to participate in educational programs and employment. This is because an inmate's classification score heavily influences in what prison the inmate will serve time. Depending on the facility to which an inmate is assigned, the chances for participating in education, work, and rehabilitation programs, associating with other inmates, and maintaining family connections will range from fairly significant to virtually nonexistent.

Classification starts in one of six reception centers. During the course of a 60-day stay, incoming prisoners are evaluated, their case summaries are prepared, classification scores are computed, and they are assigned to one of 33 prisons or 40 camps. Camps, which are used for low-level offenders, are minimum-security facilities located in wilderness areas. They house about 4,500 prisoners (about 3 percent of the total), who are typically trained as firefighters. Prisons range from minimum-security facilities with open, dormitory-style housing to highly fortified Secure Housing Units (SHUs) used to confine high-risk prisoners.

During classification each prisoner is given a medical exam, a mental health and developmental disabilities assessment, and educational tests. The resulting classification score and other case factors are used to determine the facility or camp to which a prisoner will be transferred. Inmates' classification scores are recalculated at least yearly depending on their behavior and programming.

California's reception centers use an objective classification instrument, based on research conducted by former UCLA sociologist Richard Berk, that was adopted in March 2003.[9] A lower score indicates that a prisoner has lower security and custody needs than a prisoner with a higher score. Four levels of security have been established, with higher numbers indicating higher security levels. California has several prisons to house inmates from each level.

Sometimes it is said that California cannot implement treatment and work programs that exist in other states because its prison population

[9] Berk's classification research was the result of a court order in *Wilson v. Deukmejian* (Super. Ct. Cal Sep. 13, 1983), which held that California's classification factors were not tied closely enough to likely inmate behavior. See Berk and de Leeuw (1999).

is higher risk and cannot "program" as easily as prisoners in other states.

California's population does not, however, appear to be higher risk than the populations of comparable states, at least on the basis of prison classification levels reported to the American Correctional Association in 2004 (American Correctional Association 2005). One in four (24 percent) California prisoners is classified "close/maximum," which is the case for about 40 percent of prisoners in Florida and New York. Twenty-one percent of California's prisoners—28,000—are classified minimum risk, which is similar to or higher than the percentages in other large state prison systems, with the notable exception of Texas, where 58 percent of the total prison population is classified as minimum risk. We cannot be sure that these states are using the same factors to determine prisoner risk levels, but a recent review of prison classification and risk assessments suggests that states use similar factors (e.g., age, gender, gang membership, history of violence; Austin 2003).

An inmate's classification score is often not the determining factor in housing assignments. Instead, inmates' personal characteristics or their conviction offenses often lead to "administrative placements" determined by department policy. For example, sex offenders are typically kept in higher-security facilities because, were they to escape, however unlikely, it could be a public relations disaster.

Administrators can override the classification score. The most common adjustment is called a "population override" and occurs when no bed is available in the kind of facility that would normally be used for an inmate with a given score. Under those circumstances, the classification staff representative has total discretion over prisoner placement. This override has become increasingly common as California prisons filled beyond their designed capacities. Moving inmates to areas not designed to hold them has produced adverse consequences for the facilities and the inmates.[10]

Richard Berk reported that such administrative decisions, rather than classification scores, determined about 25 percent of California's prison placements in 2005, and he believes that many of these "population overrides" result in higher-security placements.[11] There are significant

[10] California prisons were operating at 200 percent of design capacity in July 2007. A group of experienced California prison wardens told the Corrections Independent Review Panel in 2004 that the capacity of the state's prisons to support full inmate programming in a safe and secure environment is 111,309 inmates, or 145 percent of design capacity.

[11] Personal email to author, Richard Berk, on September 15, 2005.

ramifications of assignments to more heavily fortified facilities: violence rates are higher, the housing cost per prisoner is higher, and a lower level of programming is available to inmates. In other words, the pressures of overcrowding frequently lead to housing assignments that are more expensive and dangerous than is necessary and less likely to encourage rehabilitation. Moreover, although most prisoners would prefer to be in a prison located near family and friends—and maintaining family ties increases parole success (Bobbitt and Nelson 2004)—population overrides often send inmates to facilities hundreds of miles from family members, severely limiting opportunities for weekend visits.

Prison classification affects not only where inmates serve time but what programs they can participate in. Prisoners in a maximum-security prison or unit spend a good part of the day in their cell, are strictly regulated in their movement, and are surrounded by a secure perimeter with extensive gun coverage. In a minimum-security conservation camp, prisoners spend a large part of the day out of their dorm and have few restrictions on movement within an unfenced security or work area. These variations in level of movement translate into tremendous differences in their ability to participate in rehabilitation and work programs.

A housing assignment that prevents an inmate from working will also extend his or her sentence and contribute to overcrowding, because most prisoners can reduce the lengths of their terms by staying out of trouble and working. Work assignments are broadly defined to include education and vocational training as well as more traditional work that supports the prison's operation, such as gardening, maintenance, or food service. Most prisoners earn "day-for-day" credit, which gives them 1 day off their sentence for each day they have a work assignment. Prisoners on a waiting list for an assignment earn 1 day off for every 2 days they are unassigned. Thus, an inmate who is placed in a facility with minimal programming as a result of a population override is cut off from a basic mechanism for demonstrating rehabilitation and shortening his time in prison. Assigning inmates to appropriate prisons works to their advantage by allowing them to earn time back through labor and good conduct. Such assignments also benefit the state by producing ex-inmates who have taken steps toward rehabilitation and saving the state money through shorter sentences.

B. The Cost of Imprisonment

The California prison system is incredibly expensive. At the beginning of the building boom in the early 1980s, adult corrections accounted for about 3 percent of California's General Fund expenditures at a cost of about $1 billion per year (Little Hoover Commission 2007). By 2006, the budget for adult corrections had increased to $9.15 billion and consumed 9 percent of the state's entire budget. As shown in figure 3, California has continuously shifted resources toward prisons and away from other areas. Between 1984 and 2006, overall state expenditures increased 294 percent but expenditures for adult corrections increased 1,094 percent. Expenditures for social services increased 182 percent; health services, 371 percent; and mental health services, 241 percent.

The average annual cost of housing a California prisoner in 2006 was $34,150 (35 percent higher than the national average of $24,397). The cost for each adult parolee was $4,067. The cost for each juvenile in state corrections was $71,700 (California Department of Corrections and Rehabilitation 2006*b*; Petersilia 2006).[12] The Department of Finance reports that the 2007 per capita costs will increase again: $43,149 for prisons, $4,930 for parole, and $216,081 for juveniles, and $12,804 for juvenile parole (California Department of Finance 2007).

Why are the costs so high? The extra money does not go to rehabilitation programs, as the 2006–7 budget indicates that less than 5 percent of expenditures is for programming (California Legislative Analyst's Office 2007). Most of the increases are either health care expenditures resulting from federal court orders or salary increases for correctional officers. Judges over the past 12 years have taken control over vast segments of California's prison system, ordering fixes that have already cost taxpayers more than $1 billion and will cost nearly $8 billion more over the next 5 years (Furillo 2007).[13] Medical, mental health, and dental care, juvenile incarceration practices, treatment of physically and developmentally disabled inmates, and due process for

[12] Overall expenditures for California's youth corrections system have declined primarily because the population has declined. Since 1984, the number of youth incarcerated in the state system has declined from over 10,000 to a 2006 average daily population of 2,647. The incarcerated youth population is projected to drop to 1,993 in 2007. A number of reasons explain the decline, including subsidies for counties to retain less serious youth at the local level, new laws that transfer serious youth to adult courts and prisons, and a decline in the number of youth arrested.

[13] For a description of the major lawsuits affecting the California corrections system, see Prison Law Office, http://www.prisonlaw.com, accessed May 21, 2007.

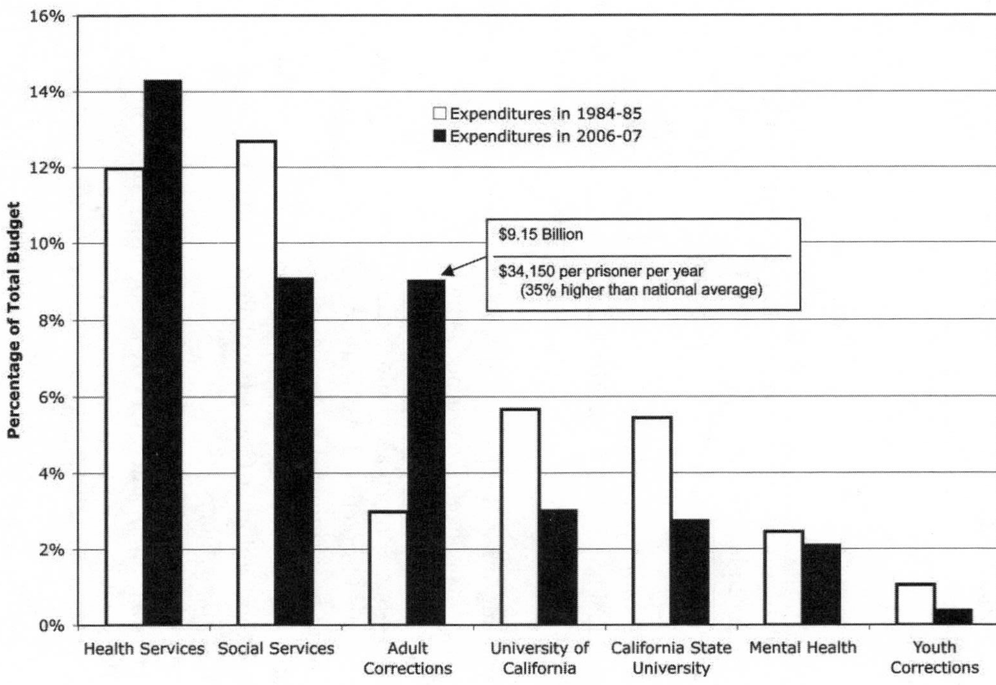

FIG. 3.—Expenditures for California adult corrections compared to other vital state services. Source: Little Hoover Commission (2007)

parolees have all been found to be unconstitutional. The annual per capita costs for California prison health care were about $2,500 per inmate in 1997 but reached $9,330 by 2006 (California Legislative Analyst's Office 2007).

California's spending on prison staff salaries and benefits have also outpaced inflation and other state employees' salary increases. The issue cannot be understood without considering the role of the correctional officers' union.

C. The California Correctional Peace Officers Association

As California's prison population grew, so did its workforce. The California Department of Corrections and Rehabilitation (CDCR)—which runs juvenile and adult prisons and parole—in 2006 needed nearly 55,000 employees, with 46,759 employed in youth or adult institutions, 3,126 in parole, and 4,513 in administration; 33,350 of the total staff are sworn peace officers (California Department of Corrections and Rehabilitation 2006*b*). Together, they represent 16 percent of California's employee pool, making corrections the largest civil employer.

The spending on staff salaries and benefits accounts for 70 percent of the corrections budget. That is not as high as in some other states—New York, for example, spends 77 percent of its corrections budget on staff salaries—but California's is above the national average of 65 percent (American Correctional Association 2005). Staff salaries, therefore, ought to be scrutinized as a cause of California's unusually high per-inmate costs. Discussion of personnel costs inevitably implicates the role of the California Correctional Peace Officers Association in lobbying for its members.

Correctional officers are unionized in California and in 28 other states (Petersilia 2006). But CCPOA is not just another union. Over the past 20 years, it has emerged as one of the state's most powerful unions and has used its lobbying and political activities to influence elections and legislation. When crime began to rise in the 1970s and politicians began advocating more punitive policies, California built more prisons—22 since 1984—that had to be staffed. Between 1980 and 2005, CCPOA membership soared from 5,000 to over 33,000. The formula is simple: more prisoners lead to more prisons; more prisons require more guards; more guards means more dues-paying members and fund-raising capability; and fund-raising, of course, translates into political influence. Throughout the late 1980s and 1990s, CCPOA-sponsored legislation was successful more than 80 percent of the time (Institute of Governmental Studies 2005). CCPOA made large contributions to the 1994 campaign for the three strikes initiative and is credited with helping the proposition pass with over 70 percent of the vote. Since 1994, California courts have sent more than 80,000 second strikers and 7,500 third strikers to state prison (Petersilia 2006).

The political power of CCPOA is likely to increase as CDCR has promised to accelerate its efforts to fill an overall 20 percent staff vacancy rate. As these ranks grow, so too will CCPOA membership and the union's financial leverage; today's membership dues generate about $23 million a year. Thirty-five percent of that money—$8 million per year—goes to lobbying (Macallair 2002). With projected increases in staff hiring, CCPOA will be collecting well over $25 million a year for many years to come.

CCPOA focuses primarily on officer safety and security. The union has negotiated better working conditions, staff training, and safety equipment, including the right to carry weapons. But CCPOA's most visible success has been its ability to win favorable pay and benefit packages for members—exactly what a good union is supposed to do. As of July 2006, the average California correctional officer earned $73,248 a year.[14] The average salary of a California correctional officer is more than the average salary of an assistant professor with a PhD at the University of California, which in 2006 was $60,000 per year (University of California 2006). With overtime, it is not uncommon for California correctional officers—who are required only to have a high school diploma or a GED—to earn over $100,000 a year. A *Los Angeles Times* investigation found that 6,000 correctional officers earned more than $100,000 in 2006, with hundreds earning more than legislators and other state officials (Morain 2006).

CCPOA retirement benefits are also far better than those of most other state employees. The CCPOA formula as of January 1, 2006, used a multiplication factor of 3.0 at age 50 (the minimum retirement age): the number of years union members have worked for the state multiplied by three is the percentage of salary they will get at retirement. Correctional officers who retire at age 50 after 20 years on the

[14] Agreement between State of California and California Correctional Peace Officers Association (CCPOA Agreement), July 1, 2001, through July 2, 2006, http://www.dpa.ca.gov/collbarg/contract/BU06Contract2001-2006.pdf (accessed April 2006).

job will receive 60 percent of their monthly salary during retirement (20 × 3.0). The maximum retirement benefits are 90 percent, which means that after working for 30 years, correctional officers get 90 percent of their monthly salary in retirement benefits for life. Since 90 percent is the maximum one can earn in retirement, working past 30 years is basically working for free. Previous contracts used 2.5 as the multiplier, but recent negotiations increased it to 3.0.[15]

State legislators have claimed that this is a different kind of retirement system than other state employees have. However, California Highway Patrol (CHP) employees receive the same benefit. Compared with the retirement system of California teachers, however, there is a large disparity. Teachers receive a pension calculated as 2.5 percent of their salaries per year of employment at age 63.[16]

California correctional officers receive greater financial benefits than many other state employees and most correctional officers nationwide, but they work in extremely difficult conditions. CCPOA's motto, displayed prominently on its Web site and all of its literature, is that correctional officers "walk the Toughest Beat in the State." There is some evidence to support this claim. California's inmate-to-staff ratio is 6.46 inmates per correctional officer, compared to a national average of 4.47. California assigns twice as many inmates to a given officer as New York does and also assigns more than other large states like Florida, Texas, and Illinois. Only Alabama, Oklahoma, and Nevada have higher inmate-to-staff ratios (Bureau of Justice Statistics 2000).

Numbers like this give the officers' union a strong basis to claim that California prisons are "understaffed," and they frequently make that claim. CDCR is currently between 2,000 and 4,000 correctional officers short, depending on whose numbers are used. Because new officers were not hired and trained in 2004–5, existing officers were required to work overtime, which in turn inflated their salaries. CPPOA members often say they would rather earn their regular salaries and not be forced to work so much overtime. They believe they get blamed by the media and the legislature for earning such high salaries, which are caused by the administration's failure to hire the

[15] Agreement between State of California and California Correctional Peace Officers Association, July 1, 2001, through July 2, 2006, at 10.02(D). See http://www.dpa.ca.gov/collbarg/contract/bumenu.shtm.

[16] Agreement between the State of California and Bargaining Unit 3, Professional Educators and Librarians, Jan. 31, 2002–July 2, 2003, at 101. See http://www.dpa.ca.gov/collbarg/contract/bumenu.shtm.

required staff. The union has for several years been urging the CDCR to reopen its training academy, hire new recruits, and reduce officer overtime charges. But the state cannot afford to hire more officers because of their high salaries and pensions. This is another example of excess leading to deprivation: the highest guard salaries in the nation have produced a catch-22: the state can no longer afford to hire and train new personnel, resulting in one of the highest inmate-to-staff ratios in the nation.

Although the CCPOA is often criticized in the press, and there are ample reasons to be concerned about its power, it is also true that California's unusually good treatment of its correctional officers benefits the state. In 2004, for example, only 1,000 of California's 33,500 sworn peace officers left the CDCR, an annual turnover rate of 3.6 percent. This is very low for public service generally and quite unusual in correctional settings, where staff burnout is typically a significant problem. California may have the lowest turnover rate of any state corrections department. In many states, by contrast, turnover rates hover around 20 percent. In Texas, the annual turnover in 2004 was 21 percent, in Kentucky it was 32 percent, in Florida it was 13 percent, and in Illinois it was 8 percent (American Correctional Association 2005). The administrative, training, and transactional implications of these low turnover rates are significant. California may recoup some of the money spent on relatively high wages by avoiding other personnel expenses. Better staff retention and greater professionalization may also influence the conditions within California prisons, such as escapes, suicide attempts, and incidents of gang violence and assaults.

III. Escapes, Suicides, Homicides, Assaults, and Prison Gangs

The most fundamental goal of a prison administrator is to operate a secure prison where staff and inmates are relatively safe from assaults or other violent acts. A secure prison is one in which inmates do not escape and are unable to get into prohibited areas. California's overcrowding, combined with staff vacancies, racial tensions, and a scarcity of work and treatment programs, has created a volatile situation. In his 2007 State of the State Address, Governor Schwarzenegger said, "Our prison system is a powder keg. It poses a danger to the prisoners, a danger to the officers, and a danger to the well-being of the public.

We have thousands of prisoners housed in gymnasiums. . . . That is a danger and that is a disgrace" (Schwarzenegger 2007). If harsher prison conditions increase the propensity to recidivate, and there is evidence that they do (Chen and Shapiro 2004), the potential for prisons to decrease crime in the long run is severely diminished.

A. Escapes

California has one of the lowest prison escape rates in the nation. In recent years its escape rate has declined while those of many other states have increased (Culp 2005). In 2004, the California prison escape rate (per 100 average daily population) was 0.01 percent, or 16 inmates out of the approximately 165,000 housed that year (California Department of Corrections and Rehabilitation 2006*a*). Only one escape was from a secure facility; the rest occurred through "walkaways" by work crews. The state's escape rate has remained at 0.01 percent for each of the last 5 years, having declined significantly since 1986, when there were 70 escapes in a population of 59,000. In Florida, by contrast, the escape rate rose from 0.04 percent in 2003 to 0.11 percent 1 year later (Florida Department of Corrections 2005).

While California's low escape rate may be related to the quality of its correctional staff, escapes are also a function of facility construction and inmate mobility. Most prisons are relatively new—22 of the 33 facilities have been built since 1980—and incorporate advances in correctional construction and security technology. In addition, however, California inmates may be on lockdown more than inmates in other states and have less mobility and therefore less opportunity to participate in programs. These restrictive living conditions make escapes unlikely.

B. Prison Suicide, Homicide, and Assaults

Suicide and homicide rates have declined significantly in U.S. state prisons since the 1980s. The Bureau of Justice Statistics reports that the suicide rate in state prisons dropped from 34 per 100,000 inmates in 1980 to 14 per 100,000 in 2002 (the latest data available). Homicide rates dropped even more, from 54 per 100,000 inmates in 1980 to eight in 1990 and four in 2002 (Mumola 2005). California's prison suicide and homicide rates have also declined substantially since the 1980s, although its suicide rate increased in 2005.

In the 20 years between 1965 and 1985, 16 correctional officers were killed by inmates. By contrast, over the next 20 years two correctional officers were killed. Judging by these numbers, California prisons appear to have become safer for both inmates and correctional officers. To some extent, this may be attributed to CCPOA's strong emphasis on the safety of its members.

Nonetheless, California has higher rates of both prison suicide and homicide than the United States as a whole, and its homicide rate is higher than the rates of other large states. There were 87 homicides in U.S. prisons in 2001–2 (the latest year for which national figures are available), and 21 of them, or 24 percent, took place in California. During the same period there were 337 prison suicides, with 15 percent of the total in California. California's prison homicide rate, at seven per 100,000 inmates, is more than twice that of Texas and more than three times higher than in New York, Illinois, and Florida.

California's prison suicide rate, at 16 per 100,000 inmates, is higher than the national average (Mumola 2005). The highest suicide rates nationwide were among violent offenders—more than twice as high as for nonviolent offenders, and violent offenders were the victims of 61 percent of all state prison homicides. Suicide rates also increased with inmate age. Inmates ages 18–24 were the least likely to commit suicide (38 suicides per 100,000 inmates). This rate increased 24 percent for inmates ages 25–34 (47), and 39 percent for inmates ages 35–44 (53). The oldest inmates, ages 55 or older, had the highest suicide rate (58 per 100,000). Most state prison suicides (65 percent) took place after the inmate's first year of confinement, and 33 percent took place after the inmate had served at least 5 years in prison (Mumola 2005). These data suggest that as the inmate population ages, and lengths of terms increase, suicide and homicide rates are likely to increase. Since both these factors characterize California's prison population, they may account for California's higher-than-average numbers and also for the recent increase in prisoner suicides.

The California Legislative Analyst's Office (2005*b*) compared California's prison assault numbers with those of other large states and found that California reported considerably more violence behind bars—nearly twice the number of assaults as Texas and almost three times the number of assaults as the federal prison system, although both these systems had roughly the same number of inmates as California. Many factors may explain California's troublingly high numbers: they may be a function of varying definitions from system to system of what constitutes an assault, they may be related to differences in characteristics of those incarcerated in California (recall that 78 percent of Texas inmates are classified minimum risk), and they may be a product of running prisons at 200 percent of capacity. Nonetheless, such high rates are a cause for serious concern.

Sumner and Matsuda (2006) recently analyzed all officially recorded reports of adult inmate violence in California prisons between 1975 and 2004 in which an inmate was the aggressor. During this 29-year period, most Crime Incident Reports (837s) reflected inmate-on-inmate nonsexual violence (79 percent), and 16 percent reflected inmate-on-staff nonsexual violence. The incidents of inmate-on-inmate violence rose slowly from 1975 to 1990 and then increased dramatically starting in 1993 until they peaked in 2000 and began to decline. Since 2003, such incidents have again been increasing. Official reports of inmate-on-staff violence do not reveal the same dramatic increase but did increase slightly over this period.

Increased inmate-on-inmate violence is probably caused in part by prison population increases. Thus, figure 4 shows the growth both in the inmate population and officially reported inmate-on-inmate violence in adult prisons. Although both have increased, the growth in violence is greater for some years. Notably, between 1989 and 1992, the number of inmates issued 837s for inmate-on-inmate violence decreased slightly although the population was increasing.

It is not clear what explains these numbers. Prison managers attribute the upward trend to increased gang activity. One official noted that "prison gang members and associates are responsible for the largest percentage of violence in our institutions."[17] Gangs are widespread in California and clearly contribute to the prison assault rate.

C. *Sexual Assault and Prison Rape*

Prison rape and sexual assault are problems with immense consequences for inmates and officials. They represent an administrative challenge and a public health and human rights issue. The topic received little policy or research attention until the U.S. Congress passed the Prison Rape Elimination Act (PREA) of 2003 (P.L. 108–79, 42 USC § 15601). PREA authorized funding for state-level programs and accompanying research.

[17] "A Necessary Evil?" *Los Angeles Times Magazine*, October 19, 2003, p. 12, quoting Steve Moore in an article on the then-new Pelican Bay maximum security prison.

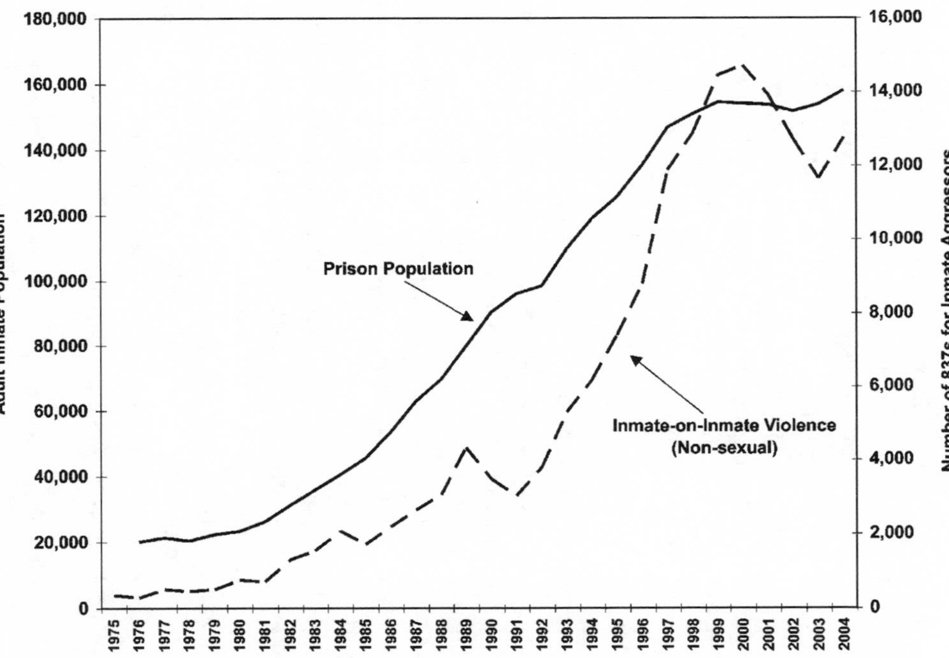

FIG. 4.—California prison population and crime incident reports (837s) for inmate-on-inmate violence, 1975–2004

The PREA funding permitted researchers in 2006 to implement a rigorous study of sexual assault and rape in California correctional facilities. The study combined official record data and interviews (Jenness et al. 2007). The interviews were designed to obtain accounts of victimization experienced by inmates during their incarceration history in California correctional facilities (i.e., juvenile hall, jail, prison).[18]

Inmates were asked, "Have you ever had to do sexual things against your will with other inmates while incarcerated?" and "Just to be sure, have any of the following things ever happened to you with other inmates while incarcerated: groping or fondling, kissing, genital contact, oral sex, or penetration against your will?" Inmates who responded "yes" were classified as having experienced sexual assault or engaging in sexual activity against their will. Inmates were also asked, "Well, what about sexual things [with other inmates while incarcerated] that were perhaps not against your will, but you would have rather not done?"

Slightly more than 4 percent of the randomly selected inmates reported experiencing sexual assault while in a California correctional facility, and 1.3 percent of inmates reported engaging in sexual acts that they did not define as being against their will but nonetheless would rather not have done. In sharp contrast, 59 percent of the transgender inmates reported experiencing sexual assault while in a California correctional facility, and 48 percent reported engaging in sexual acts that, from their point of view, were not against their will, but nonetheless they would rather not have done. Using two different measures of rape—one that relies on the inmates' own assessment of incidents and one that relies on a definition of rape as "oral or anal penetration by force or threat of force"—2 or 3 percent of randomly sampled inmates described at least one occurrence of rape, as did 41 or 50 percent of transgender sample inmates.[19] The researchers used

[18] Face-to-face interviews were conducted with 322 randomly selected prisoners and 39 purposively sampled transgender prisoners. Official data were also collected for each study participant, including race/ethnicity, mental health status, gang membership, custody level, sex offender registration, and commitment offense. The sampling and informed consent procedures yielded a response rate of over 85 percent, and subsequent analyses revealed that the randomly selected participants were statistically similar to the general California inmate population in most major respects. The UCI research findings address prevalence, victim characteristics, incidence characteristics, and the nature of the lived experience of sexual assault.

[19] The lower estimates derive from the inmates' assessment of rape and the higher estimates derive from the definition of rape used by the research team.

accepted statistical procedures to extrapolate an estimate of the prevalence of prison assault and rape for the total California prison population.

The Jenness et al. results show that transgender inmates have dramatically higher rates of sexual assault and rape. Not one Asian inmate or inmate between the ages of 18 and 25 reported being sexually assaulted, but at least one inmate in every other demographic category did report being sexually assaulted. However, inmates with different characteristics did not report sexual assault with the same frequency. Inferential statistical models show that inmates with mental health problems, nonheterosexual inmates (i.e., gay, bisexual, and other), and black inmates are especially vulnerable to sexual assault.

The Jenness et al. study does not permit a comparison of sexual assault and rape rates between California and other states. A report from the Bureau of Justice Statistics, however, shows that levels of reported sexual violence are lower in California prisons than in other large states, including Florida, Ohio, and Texas (Beck and Harrison 2006). One explanation offered is that the strong gang presence inside California prisons reduces the incidence of prison rape, since sexual violation of an inmate of a different gang is cause for gang retaliation. Whether this is true is unknown, but the influence of prison gangs in all aspects of daily life in the prisons is incontestable.

D. *Prison Gangs*

California is often cited as the birthplace of America's most notorious prison gangs. It holds the largest group of gang-affiliated prisoners (Carlson 2001). The influence of these groups on prison violence is widely recognized by state officials. For example, in a recent Supreme Court case, *Johnson v. California* (543 U.S. 499 [2005]), which challenged the policy of placing new inmates only with cellmates of the same race to avoid gang violence, officials described a "violent and murderous" gang culture. Research confirms what practitioners believe: in a comprehensive study of prison gangs, Gaes and his colleagues found that gang affiliation increases the likelihood of violence and other forms of prison misconduct, even after controlling for individual inmate characteristics associated with a violent predisposition (Gaes 2001).

A prison cannot function properly if its staff cannot maintain sufficient control over the inmates. Gangs are in effect unauthorized prisoner associations and thus represent competing sources of authority. As the number of prison-gang members grows, the balance of power shifts from management to the gangs and administrators lose leverage they need to achieve safety and correctional goals. Moreover, as gang power grows, the gangs become more credible sources of authority and protection, which further increases pressures on new inmates to join. The situation is cyclical and toxic. As gangs gain power, prisoners perceive the prison as being less safe and administrators in less control, causing more of them to join gangs for protection. As more inmates join the gang, the gang becomes more powerful, thus creating even more prison instability, which in turn leads to more recruits.

California officially recognizes seven prison gangs, although only six were thought to be operating in 2006: the Mexican Mafia, La Nuestra Familia, the Aryan Brotherhood, the Nazi Low Riders, the Northern Structure, and the Black Guerilla Family. California also identifies disruptive groups, which are typically street gangs and include Public Enemy Number One (PEN1), the Crips, Sureños, Norteños, and the Northern Ryders. Although both prison gangs and disruptive groups threaten prison security, prison gangs are the greater threat. Almost without exception, prison gangs form along racial and ethnic lines and are less concerned with physical territory than street gangs are.[20] The Mexican Mafia and Nuestra Familia are predominately Latino, African Americans join the Black Guerilla Family, and whites make up the Aryan Brotherhood and Nazi Low Riders.

It is unknown—and probably unknowable—how many California inmates are members or affiliates of gangs. Estimates vary widely. The power of prison gangs is achieved through secrecy, and gangs often target informants for assassination. In addition, gang members go to great lengths to hide their affiliations from authorities, because once verified as gang members they will be placed in administrative segregation, which makes it more difficult to continue their criminal activities within and outside the prison.

Prison gang experts assert that over one-third of California's inmates were being "tracked" for prison gang activity (Carlson 2001). In 2002, the state corrections director testified that there were probably

[20] Historically, street gangs and prison gangs were also distinguished by their internal structure and leadership, with prison gangs being organized into more complex hierarchies with rank differentiation among members and powerful, criminally sophisticated leaders. Yet experts believe that these differences are no longer true, and that street gangs have become as sophisticated and dangerous as prison gangs (Fleisher and Rison 2000).

40,000–60,000 gang members of all types in California prisons.[21] A spokesman for the CDCR told me that as of December 2005 there were 3,400 validated gang members or associates and an additional 4,400 validated or associate members of street gangs or disruptive groups. In addition, there were about 2,150 inactive members of the prison gangs, and about 100 for the disruptive groups. These estimates suggest there are about 10,000 officially identified gang members in prison, or about 6 percent of all prisoners.

Everyone agrees that most prison gang members remain undetected and are increasing in numbers, leading to serious problems that are likely to become increasingly more intractable. The huge growth in the prison population in recent decades has provided a steady stream of new recruits to the prison gangs, which experts say has produced increased turmoil and violence and a serious deterioration in the quality of life inside prisons.

IV. Program Needs versus Treatment Received

The vast majority of California prisoners do not receive the rehabilitation they need. Like prisoners in other states, they have problems with substance abuse, lack of education, and inadequate job skills. In some respects, California prisoners have even more severe deficiencies than their counterparts elsewhere. Despite these critical needs, California provides fewer rehabilitation programs than do comparable states, so the prison experience often fails to give inmates the tools they need for successful reintegration.

Nearly all U.S. prisons operate treatment and work programs. Ninety-seven percent of all confinement facilities have inmate counseling programs, 90 percent have drug and alcohol counseling, 80 percent have secondary education programs, and 54 percent have vocational training programs (Bureau of Justice Statistics 2003). California, too, has a variety of prison programs, and a number are promising (Werth and Sumner 2006). But the state's prison population has expanded so rapidly that prison administrators have been unable to meet the expanding demand for these programs.

California is not alone in this. Lynch and Sabol (2001) compared

[21] Testimony before Senate Select Committee on Security Housing Units in California Prisons, September 15, 2003. See http://www.prisons.org/SHU%20Hearing%201.pdf, accessed April 2006.

national prison program participation rates during the past decade and found that approximately a third of inmates about to be released in 1997 participated in vocational (27 percent) or educational (35 percent) programs—down from 31 percent and 43 percent, respectively, in 1991. Once-vibrant California programs were also pared back in response to political pressure and the belief that they were ineffective.

This drop in participation is worrisome because California prisoners have acute needs. Reanalysis of the Bureau of Justice Statistics' 1997 *Survey of Inmates in State and Federal Correctional Facilities* conducted by University of California, Irvine, researchers suggests problem areas. Compared to their counterparts in New York, Texas, and the United States overall, California prisoners were more likely to report a high need for alcohol- and substance-abuse programs—factors that are related to recidivism (Gendreau, Little, and Goggin 1996). For example, 56 percent of California prisoners had a "high need" for drug treatment programs (fig. 5). High need meant that they reported major drug-related issues across several areas, including using drugs frequently, being under the influence when committing crimes, using different types of drugs, struggling with treatment programs, and getting into trouble at work, at home, or with the police because of their drug use. In New York, by contrast, 43 percent of inmates self-reported having high needs for this type of programming. The national average is 49 percent.

Compared to other states, California serves a smaller percentage of its inmates with serious needs for rehabilitative programs, and its failures are particularly acute in areas in which they are most needed. Thus, the percentage of needy inmates who receive drug treatment is far lower than in comparable states. Prisoners with a serious need for drug counseling were over three times more likely to get counseling if they were serving time in New York than in California (fig. 5). A scant 2.5 percent of California inmates with a "high need" for drug treatment received professionally run treatment (as opposed to being in inmate self-help groups), far below the national average (without California) of 9 percent. This percentage reflects the number of prisoners who report "ever" participating in a program while they were in prison, and it says nothing about the quality or intensity of the program they participated in. The lack of rehabilitative programs coupled with high recidivism rates in California has led to demands for change and a renewed focus on providing prison programs.

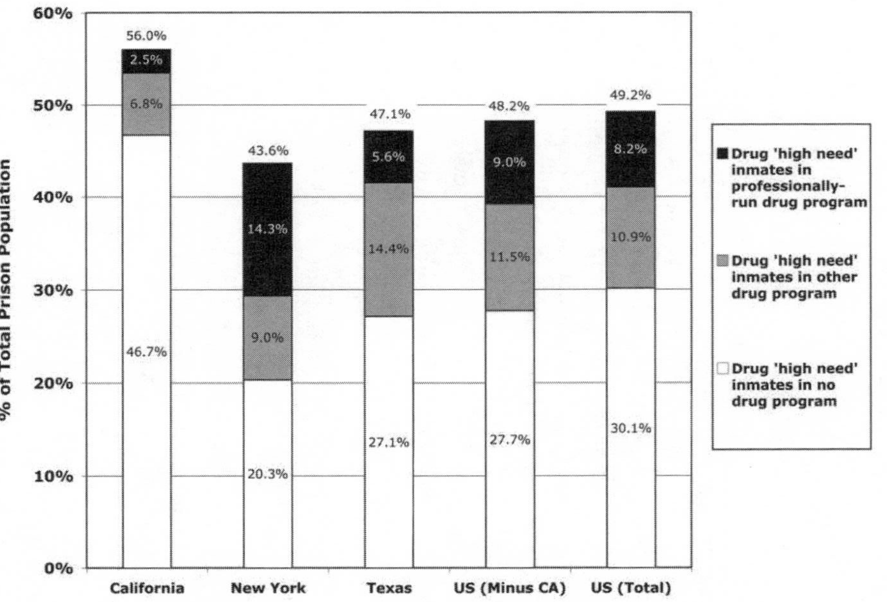

FIG. 5.—Inmate need for drug treatment and treatment received, California versus nation, 1997. "Any" treatment includes residential facilities/units, counseling by professionals, detoxification units, self-help groups, peer counseling, education programs, or other alcohol abuse programs. "Professionally-run" treatment includes residential facilities/units, counseling by professionals, and detoxification units. Source: Reanalysis by University of California, Irvine, students of the 1997 *Survey of Inmates in State and Federal Correctional Facilities*, Bureau of Justice Statistics, U.S. Department of Justice.

Similar shortcomings are evident concerning alcohol counseling. While 42 percent of the state's prisoners report having a high need for alcohol treatment—meaning that they reported being an alcoholic and admitted that their alcohol problem contributed to their criminality and social functioning—just 7.5 percent reported receiving any alcohol treatment (including self-help groups), and only 1 percent reported participating in programs run by professional staff. These numbers are considerably lower than national averages, which show roughly the same percentage of inmates reporting a high need for treatment (43 percent) but with 17.7 percent participating and nearly 7 percent participating in professionally run programs.

When it comes to educational and vocational skills, the needs of California's prisoners are no more acute than the rest of the nation, but California does not address those needs as effectively as some other states do. Like comparable states, roughly 15 percent of California's inmates have a high need for educational or vocational training—meaning they had been unemployed frequently, had few job skills, and had below eighth grade education levels. If these same high-need inmates were incarcerated in New York or Texas, they would be more likely to receive that training. California prisoners with a high need for education or job training report participating in such programs half as often as their New York counterparts. This is true even though participation in a program is defined liberally, so that participation in a program even for one day would count, regardless of the program's quality.

That California's numbers are so poor thus suggests that the vast majority of inmates who could benefit from education programs or vocational training are not getting even the most rudimentary and minimal forms of assistance. Of course, it is possible that education and job training programs have expanded in California's prisons since 1997, when these data were collected, but budget cuts for rehabilitation services and programs since then suggest that the situation may have gotten worse. California prisoners are effectively incapacitated but get little help in preparing to reenter society.

V. Demographics and Criminal Records

More than 171,000 people were in California prisons in 2007. Who are they, and what dangers do they pose to the public at large? Some suggest prisoners are mostly first-time and nonviolent offenders, whereas other analysts have reached markedly different conclusions, arguing that the vast majority of those in prison and being released are dangerous career criminals. The debate is not simply academic. If the public perceives returning prisoners as having many needs and posing little risk, they are more likely to be sympathetic and willing to invest in rehabilitation and work programs. But if the public believes most returning inmates are dangerous career criminals, resources are more likely to be invested in law enforcement and surveillance. In one scenario, the state will prioritize the delivery of services to offenders, while in the other it will prioritize public safety.

Because of the political overtones, accurately answering the question "Who is in California prisons?" has important policy significance. It is surprising, therefore, how little is known about the demographic characteristics, conviction crimes, and criminal records of those in prisons. Even the recidivism potential of California prisoners is unavailable because there are no detailed longitudinal follow-up studies of what happens after they are released. Some very basic demographic information about the inmate population and its criminal history is available over time.

A. Age, Gender, and Race

California prisoners resemble prisoners nationwide. They are mostly young, minority, and male. But California's inmates are older than the national average, older than past inmates, and more likely to grow old behind bars than in the past. The number of female inmates, though still far lower than the number of male inmates, is steadily increasing, and the percentages of members of racial minorities behind bars continue to increase, with the most significant increases in the Latino population.

1. *Age.* The average age of California's adult prisoners has been steadily increasing. The average male prisoner was 36 years old in 2007 and the average female prisoner was 37. In 1984, the averages for both men and women were 6 years younger (30 years for men, 31 for women). California's three strikes law and "truth-in-sentencing" policies—requiring inmates to serve 85 percent of the prison term imposed—mean that a greater percentage of prisoners spend more time behind bars today than in past years, and the average ages are increasing as a result.

Not only are there more older inmates, but more inmates are growing old behind bars. Since 1984, the percentage of inmates older than 45 has been increasing steadily. In 1984, 6.8 percent of the prison population was 45 or older. By 2004, approximately 33,000 (20 percent) of California inmates were 45 or older (Vitiello and Kelso 2005). There were also 8,510 "elderly" inmates (over 55). The California Legislative Analyst's Office (2005*a*) predicts that this number will increase to 30,200 by 2022 and will constitute 16 percent of the prison population.

In a prison setting, 55 is considered elderly because prisoners' risky lifestyles, poor access to health care, and substance-abuse histories take heavy tolls. Medically speaking, the average prisoner appears to be about 10 years older than a nonincarcerated individual of the same age. On average, the cost of incarcerating offenders older than age 55 is $69,000 per year, or three times the roughly $22,000 national average cost to keep younger, healthier offenders in prison (Aday 2003).

Most additional costs are related to health care. Under the 1976 Supreme Court decision *Estelle v. Gamble* (429 US 97 [1976]), prison administrators must provide free health care to all inmates, making prisoners the only U.S. residents who have a constitutionally recognized right to health care. Failure to provide such care, the court said, would constitute "deliberate indifference to [inmates'] serious health care needs" in violation of the Eighth Amendment. Despite this court-imposed guarantee, prisons are seldom equipped to take care of elderly prisoners. Rarely are there specially trained nurses, and California has no institutions dedicated exclusively to the care of elderly inmates. Most anecdotal evidence reveals that elderly prisoners are left to fend for themselves (California Legislative Analyst's Office 2005*a*).

As the average age of the inmate population continues to creep upward, these costs will move upward as well. By 2022, according to the California Legislative Analyst's Office, care for California's elderly inmates will cost the state $1 billion per year (California Legislative Analyst's Office 2005*a*). As is true nationally, 65 percent of elderly California prisoners are incarcerated for violent offenses. But 35 percent of California's 8,510 elderly prisoners were sentenced for nonviolent crimes (Vitiello and Kelso 2005). These numbers, along with the skyrocketing costs of providing medical care and older inmates' lower recidivism rates, mean the public safety benefits of imprisonment decline as the cost of incarceration increases. Keeping older inmates behind bars may be an effective way to punish particularly heinous offenses or to send a deterrent message to criminals, but the incapacitation benefits are negligible—another example of excess leading to deprivation. California imprisons elderly inmates at high costs, contributing to overcrowding, which in turn creates pressure to release other inmates early or divert sometimes more dangerous inmates to alternatives.

2. *Gender.* Prisoners are mostly male and always have been. By the end of 2006, however, women accounted for 6.6 percent of California prisoners, up from 3 percent in 1964 and 1974 and 6 percent in 1984 and 1994. This increase mirrors a national trend: women accounted for 7 percent of all prisoners in 2004 (Harrison and Beck 2006). Texas, the federal system, and California between them house more than a third of all female inmates. The overall number of California prisoners has grown by 727 percent since 1964. The number of female prisoners grew by 1,618 percent.

Harsher punishment of drug crimes has contributed to women's increased incarceration, as figure 6 illustrates. Of the state's female inmates, 29 percent are serving time for drug-related offenses (see fig. 11). The growth in the percentage of women is often attributed to the war on drugs. During the decade after passage of mandatory drug laws in 1986, the number of women incarcerated for drug crimes rose precipitously. Mandatory sentencing laws required judges to sentence men and women to the same punishment if they committed the same offense. Extenuating circumstances often cannot be fully considered. California's Determinate Sentencing Law, for example, does not allow judges to take into account women's role in caring for children, the subordinate roles women play in many crimes, or women's lower recidivism rates after release.[22]

California has also seen increases in the number of women convicted of crimes against persons and property. In 2004, 29 percent of female prisoners had been convicted of crimes against persons, 36 percent of property crimes, and 5 percent of other offenses (e.g., public order offenses such as prostitution). Thus the increase in women inmates cannot be attributed solely to drug crimes.

Regardless of the crime of which they were convicted, female in-

[22] Bureau of Justice Statistics' researchers Langan and Levin (2002) report that men released from prison were more likely than women to be rearrested (68 percent vs. 58 percent), reconvicted (48 percent vs. 40 percent), and resentenced to prison for a new crime (26 percent vs. 17 percent) within 3 years of release.

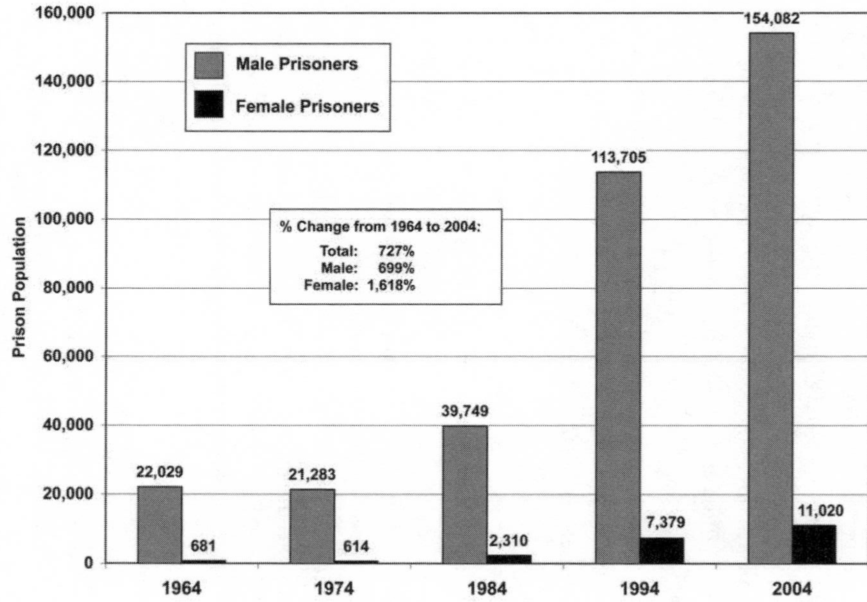

FIG. 6.—Male and female prisoners in California, 1964–2004. Source: *California Prisoners and Parolees*, California Department of Corrections and Rehabilitation, various years.

mates have different needs than males. A prison system primarily designed for men typically does a poor job of responding to those needs. For example, 64 percent of women imprisoned in California are mothers, nearly a third have children under the age of 6, and half were living with their children in the month prior to their arrest (Little Hoover Commission 2004). Most of these women expect to be reunited with their children after release, and yet prisons often make it very difficult for mothers and children to maintain meaningful connections during the mother's period of incarceration.

Women behind bars typically fit a personal profile that cries out for effective psychological counseling: 40 percent of women in state prisons nationally report physical or sexual abuse as minors (Bloom, Owen, and Covington 2003). More than half of the women in California's prisons do not have a GED or high school diploma, and most have never earned more than $6.50 an hour in legitimate employment (Little Hoover Commission 2004). Despite these distinctive needs, and the direct influence female prisoners have on their children's development (Murray and Farrington, in this volume), few prison or parole programs respond adequately to women's situation.

3. *Race and Ethnicity.* The prison population overrepresents racial minorities relative to their presence in the state's resident population (fig. 7). Racial and ethnic minorities are 53 percent of the California population but 72 percent of its prison population. In this regard California mirrors the nation, which overincarcerates minorities relative to their percentages in the general population (Bonczar 2003).

Lin and Jannetta (2006) calculated California's "correctional control rate" by race and ethnicity using the data previously shown in figure 2. At year-end 2004, 3 percent of all black adults living in California were in prison, almost 2 percent were on parole, and 1 percent were in jail. Roughly 6 percent of black adult Californians were thus incarcerated or on parole. In comparison, only 1.7 percent of Latino adults and 0.8 percent of white adults were then incarcerated or on parole. These differences between black and white rates are slightly greater than the national rates. The differences between Latino and white rates were slightly less pronounced than in the national data (Harrison and Beck 2005).

The overrepresentation of ethnic minorities is troubling, and it is worsening. Since 1964, the percentage of the California prison population that is black, Latino, or "other" has increased significantly.

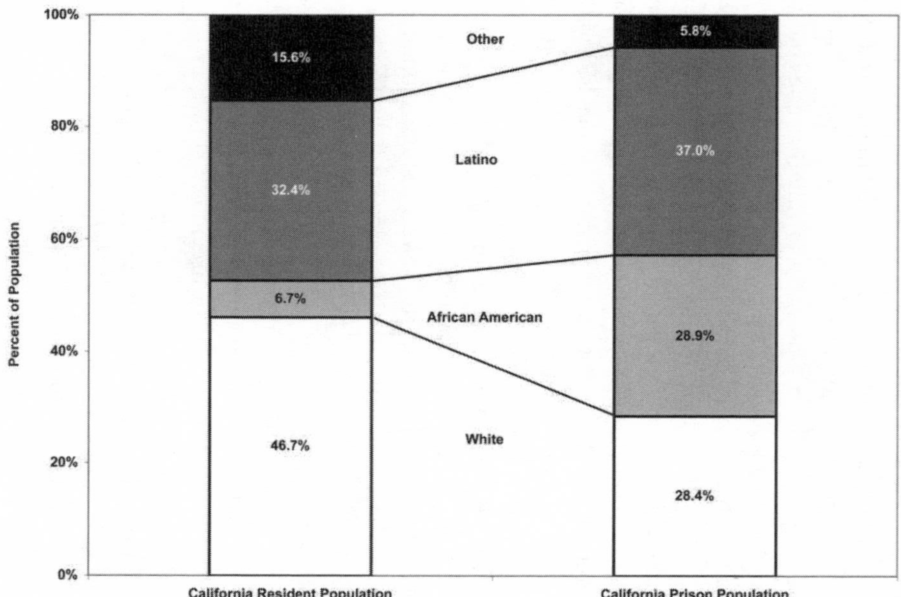

FIG. 7.—California resident versus prison populations by race and ethnicity, 2004. Sources: California resident population from http://www.census.gov/statab/www/states. California prison population from *California Prisoners and Parolees 2004*, California Department of Corrections and Rehabilitation, 2005, http://www.cdcr.ca.gov/ReportsResearch/OffenderInfoServices/Annual/CalPris/CA:PRISd2004.pdf, table 11, p. 35 of 112.

Whites greatly outnumbered minorities in prison 40 years ago, but between 1964 and 1984 blacks and Latinos were incarcerated in higher numbers while the number of white inmates increased only somewhat. As the state prison population grew dramatically from the 1980s through today, minorities have come to outnumber whites behind bars (see fig. 8).

Figures 9 and 10 show racial or ethnic group trends in the prison population since 1964. Latino males and females have increased substantially as a proportion of the overall prison population. The percentages of white males and females have declined. The percentages of African American males and females have remained relatively stable.

Part of the explanation for the dramatic increases in Latinos may have to do with a tendency, over time, to make more accurate assessments of inmate ethnicity. Some Latinos formerly were categorized as white but more recently are likely to be accurately categorized during intake. Corrections system experts say the increase in Latino inmates is real, not simply an artifact of how demographic data are collected.

Neither can the increase in Latino inmates be attributed simply to the growth of the Latino population in California. In 1970, Latinos were 12 percent of the California general population. In 2005, they were 32 percent (U.S. Census Bureau 2006). But population does not account for the prison increase, as figure 9 shows. It compares percentage changes in prison populations with percentage changes in California's population for various groups. Latino male and female imprisonment rate increases are out of proportion to their growth in the resident population. If population increase alone were at work, the incarceration of Latino men and women would have risen at the same rate. Women's numbers increased far more dramatically.

Between 1964 and 2004, the state's Latino population (both male and female) increased fivefold. During that same period, the prison population of Latino males went up 16 times and of Latino females more than 81 times. The "other" category also showed dramatic increases, with the male prison population classified as "other" increasing 25 times, and the female prison population increasing 32 times. In the state's general population, however, individuals classified as ethnically "other" increased only sevenfold during this period.

The explanation for these extraordinary increases is not clear. They are not simply a function of the way the population data are calculated, and they are not caused by the growth of the state's population more

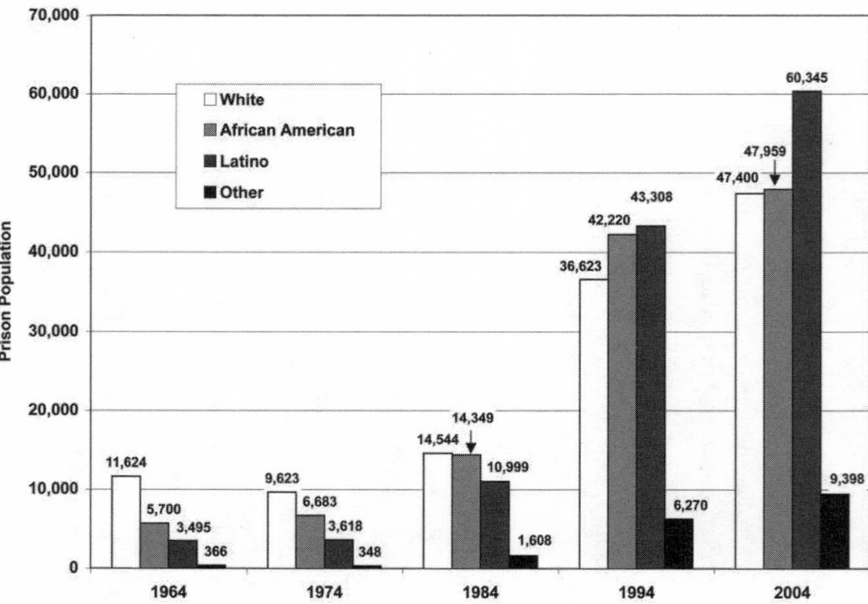

FIG. 8.—Total California prison population by race and ethnicity, 1964–2004. Source: *California Prisoners and Parolees*, California Department of Corrections and Rehabilitation, various years.

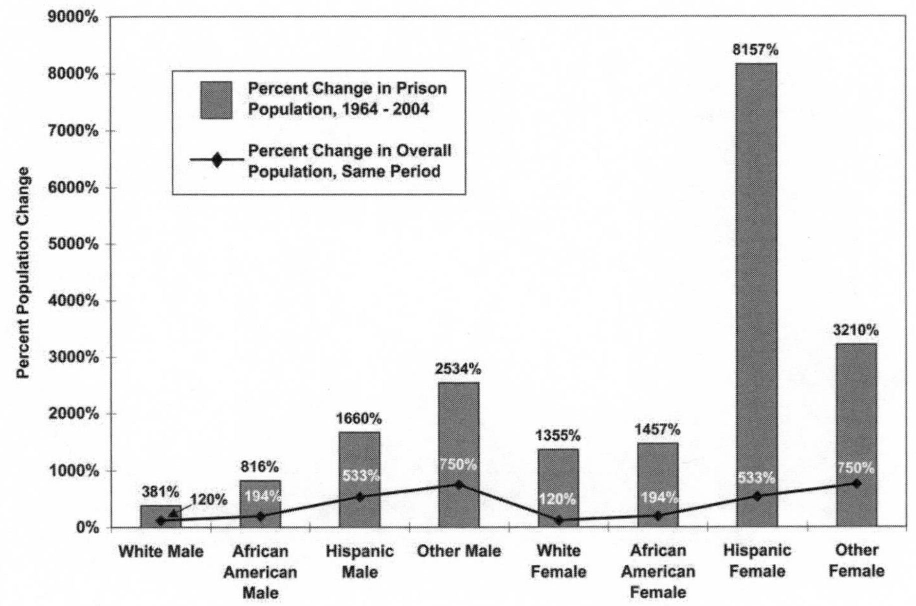

FIG. 9.—California prison and resident populations by race and gender, 1964–2004. Sources: U.S. Census Bureau, State and County Quick Facts (http://quickfacts.census.gov/qfd/states/06000.html); and California Department of Finance (http://www.dof.ca.gov/HTML/DEMOGRAP/Eth70–90.htm).

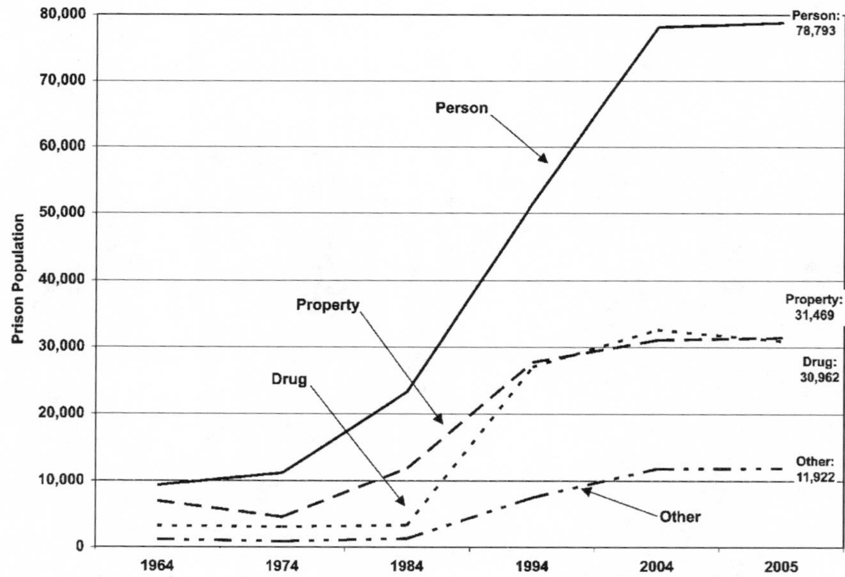

FIG. 10.—Most serious conviction crime for California male felons, 1964–2005. Source: *California Prisoners and Parolees*, California Department of Corrections and Rehabilitation, calculated from the in-prison population on December 31, various years.

generally, but it is difficult to say with any certainty what is behind the changes. Criminologists have spent considerable time exploring the explanations for racial disparities in incarceration, but the analysis has rarely looked at Latinos or "others" as a separate group simply because they are not a particularly large category in available national data sets. Much analysis has been focused on disparities between black and white incarceration rates, with researchers concluding that higher rates of offending among blacks are the primary explanation for their disproportionately high levels of incarceration (Blumstein 1993). A recent meta-analysis of race and sentencing, however, suggests that African Americans are generally sentenced more harshly than whites (particularly for drug crimes), although the magnitude of this race effect is small and highly variable (Mitchell 2005). In the case of Latinos, it is difficult to say whether discrimination, high rates of offending, or some other cause is behind the growing ethnic disparities.

B. *Conviction Crimes*

It is at least partly true that the increase in California's prison population has been caused by the war on drugs, which has sent drug offenders to prison more frequently than in the past. As figures 10 and 11 demonstrate, drug convictions among California's male felons increased significantly beginning in the 1980s. Among female felons, the numbers jumped even more dramatically.

Nonetheless, the rapid increase in California's prison population has not been caused primarily by increases in drug offenders but by increases in individuals convicted of violent crimes, particularly for males. Combining males and females, 67 percent of the overall increase in the growth of the California prison population since 1994 has been caused by crimes against persons, whereas only 10.4 percent is attributable to drug crimes.[23] The analysis looks somewhat different when the prison population is broken down by gender. The increase in the female prison population over the last decade has been the result of convictions for personal, property, and drug crimes, suggesting that the war on drugs has had a more dramatic effect on incarceration rates

[23] National analyses by Blumstein and Beck (1999) reached similar conclusions. Between 1995 and 2001, violent offenders accounted for 63 percent of the growth of the U.S. state prison population; 15 percent was attributable to drug offenders.

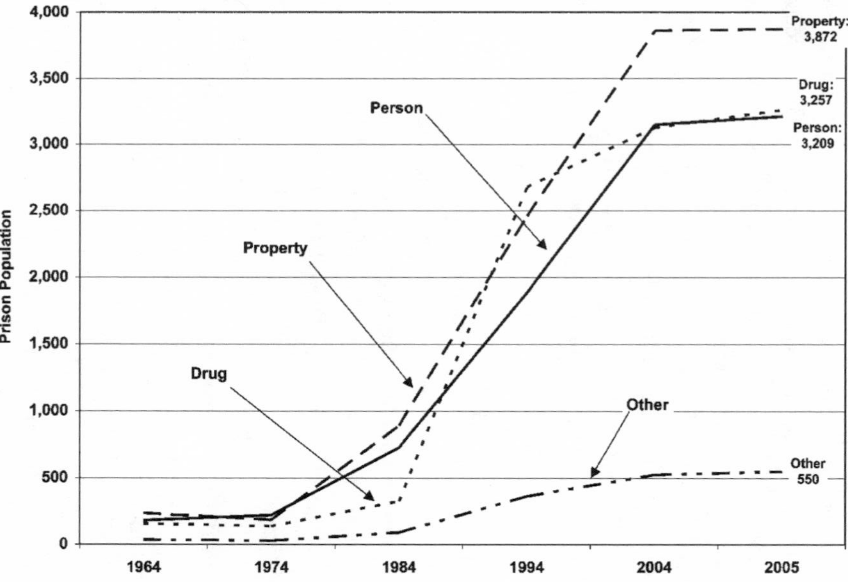

FIG. 11.—Most serious conviction crime for California female inmates, 1964–2005. Source: *California Prisoners and Parolees*, calculated from the in-prison population on December 31, various years, California Department of Corrections and Rehabilitation.

for women than for men.[24] Among women, 38 percent of prisoner population growth since 1994 is the result of crimes against persons. Among men, 70 percent of the growth is the result of crimes against persons. This should not be a surprise, since violent criminals stay in prison much longer and, over time, contribute disproportionately to increases in the overall size of the prison population.[25]

C. Prior Criminal Record and Status at Arrest

The Bureau of Justice Statistics (BJS) periodically conducts the *Survey of Inmates in State and Federal Correctional Facilities*, which is a nationally representative sample of state and federal inmates. The BJS permitted UCI researchers access to the latest survey so that California inmates could be compared with all state prisoners in terms of prior record, status at arrest, and current crime (see table 2).

Among California prisoners, 20 percent are "first-termers" who had not been sentenced previously to probation, jail, or prison as a juvenile or adult. This is slightly lower than the 24 percent national average. Twelve percent of first-termers were committed for a violent crime. Forty-seven percent of California prisoners are currently, or previously have been, sentenced to prison for a violent crime—and 14 percent have at least two prison commitments for violent crimes. These figures are similar to national averages. At the other end of the "seriousness" continuum, 33 percent of all California prisoners are "nonviolent" recidivists—with no prior sentences (jail, prison, probation) for any violent crime.

Table 2 also shows that a larger percentage of California prisoners

[24] Crimes against persons include homicide, robbery, assault and battery, sex offenses, and kidnapping. Property crimes include burglary, theft, vehicle theft, forgery, and fraud. Drug crimes include possession, possession for sale, sale, and manufacturing. Other crimes include escape, driving under the influence, arson, possession of weapon, and other offenses.

[25] It is important to distinguish the "in-prison" population from the "incoming" or "exiting" prison population. On average, people committed to prison for violent crimes serve longer prison terms than those committed for nonviolent or drug crimes. Violent offenders eventually get out, but not as quickly, and so their proportion in prison release cohorts is lower. Nonviolent and drug offenders receive short sentences and recycle back to the community faster than violent offenders. Hence, their proportions in prison entrance and prison release cohorts are higher. For this reason, analysts studying prisoner reentry examine prison release or parole cohorts if they wish to understand reentry but must use in-prison data to talk about the overall growth of the prison population. The difference between in-prison and prison release cohorts accounts for some of the discrepancy in figures cited by those who argue that prisoners are not a particularly serious group (they tend to use incoming or release cohorts) and those who argue that the majority of prisoners are serious or career criminals (they tend to use in-prison samples).

TABLE 2

Criminal History and Current Crime, California versus U.S. Prisoners (in Percent)

Criminal Record	California	All State Prisoners Combined
No previous prison sentence	19	24
Current violent offense	12	15
Current drug offense	3	4
Current other offense	4	5
Violent recidivists—current and prior violent prison term	47	47
Current violent prison term only	15	18
Prior violent prison term only	18	12
Nonviolent recidivists	33	29
Number of prior sentences to probation or incarceration:		
0	20	24
1	12	17
2	14	16
3–5	25	24
6–10	17	12
11 or more	12	6
Criminal justice status at time of arrest:		
None	41	52
Probation	20	22
Parole	38	24
Escape	.4	.7

SOURCE.—Reanalysis of the 1997 *Survey of Inmates in State and Federal Correctional Facilities*, Bureau of Justice Statistics.

NOTE.—Percentages may not total 100 percent because of rounding and a small percentage of cases with missing data (~1.0 percent). The table does not include federal prisoners. Prior record includes both juvenile and adult sentences.

has served six or more prior criminal sentences than the national average (29 percent of California inmates versus 18 percent of those in other states). This is clearly related to figures showing that 58 percent of California prisoners (compared to 46 percent nationally) were on probation or parole when they were arrested for their current crime. No matter what measure is used, California prisoners have a greater number of prior criminal sentences than inmates in other states, but there is no evidence to suggest that they engage in more violence.

California is sending individuals in and out of prison in a way that does not correspond to the risks they pose. A large percentage of Californians who are nonviolent criminals are accumulating very extensive criminal records as a result of the catch-and-release system. Despite their records, they may not be any more dangerous than offenders in other states who are left "on the street" and successfully handled through an array of community-based intermediate sanctions. However, California's sentencing system also releases violent offenders who amass lengthy criminal records—individuals who, in a system more carefully tailored to protect public safety, probably should not have been released in the first place.

VI. Prison Release and Parole Supervision

Each year about 120,000 prisoners return home from California prisons. On one level, this is not particularly noteworthy. Prisoners have always faced the challenge of moving from confinement in correctional institutions to liberty on the street. Yet, from a number of policy perspectives, prisoner reentry has critical importance in California. The fourfold increase in incarceration rates strained the capacity of the prison system. Overcrowding forced the closure of many rehabilitation and work programs. Most prisoners do not get the help they need. Nonetheless, most eventually are released at a predetermined date under the state's Determinate Sentencing Law. Virtually all are assigned to postprison parole supervision in which services are limited. The outcome is predictable: two-thirds of parolees return to prison within 3 years—nearly twice the national average. California plays a continuous game of "catch and release." Inmates cycle in and out of prison with significant consequences for offender rehabilitation, costs, and public safety.

A. Determinate Sentencing and Its Unanticipated Consequences

Why can't California prisons hold onto inmates who pose a high public safety risk if released? The answer is that California's 1976 Determinate Sentencing Law makes it extremely difficult for corrections officials to keep inmates in prison, regardless of their future dangerousness. Determinate sentencing eliminated discretionary parole release. The judge imposes a prison term expressed as a number of years of imprisonment, often referred to as a "fixed" term of imprisonment. The judge selects one of three specific terms for a particular crime, with the lower term reserved for cases with mitigating circumstances and the higher term for cases where there were aggravating circumstances. If neither mitigating nor aggravating factors exist, the middle term is presumptively appropriate. For over 3 decades, state judges have been required to impose fairly rigid sentences regardless of individual offenders' backgrounds and proclivities.

California prisoners serve a statutorily specified portion of the term the judge ordered and are automatically released when that period elapses. This term generally can be reduced only through sentence reduction credits (such as "good time" or "earned time"). Without sentence reduction credits, offenders must serve a statutorily defined percentage of the term imposed by the court. The "determinacy" refers to the effort to ensure that time served by offenders is determined primarily by the length of the sentence imposed by the judge rather than by discretionary release decisions.

Only inmates convicted of heinous crimes (such as murder or kidnap for ransom) and those convicted of a third strike receive an indeterminate sentence and an opportunity to appear before the Board of Parole Hearings to seek parole. As of June 2005, 12.3 percent of all adult prisoners were serving life with the possibility of parole, 4.7 percent were third-strike inmates, and 0.4 percent had death sentences. That combined 17.4 percent of the prison population was serving an indeterminate sentence that, at least in theory, could be terminated through discretionary parole release. Even for these individuals, though, parole is more an abstract possibility than a day-to-day reality. California governors generally veto any recommended grant of parole for serious offenders. The remaining 82.6 percent of California's inmates—136,125 men and women—were serving determinate sentences. The only way for them to get out of prison is to serve the statutorily mandated percentage of the sentence a judge gave them, with some reductions allowed for good-time and earned-time credits. Once that time is up, however, they are automatically released, whether they are rehabilitated or incorrigible, and no matter how likely they may to be to reoffend.

Sentencing in California was not always handled this way. Before 1976, nearly all inmates received indeterminate sentences. A judge would specify a minimum and a maximum length of incarceration, and inmates were released by a parole board, which attempted to evaluate each individual's degree of rehabilitation. California was a leader in developing parole risk prediction instruments that were a model for instruments adopted by parole boards across the country. Indeterminate sentencing coupled with discretionary parole release was well entrenched throughout the United States, and for most of the twentieth century was considered to be a routine and good correctional practice. Offenders were viewed as individuals who needed "treatment," and the length of the treatment depended on how well the patient responded. At least in theory, punishments were to fit the criminal rather than the crime. California became the second state after Maine to abolish indeterminate sentencing and discretionary parole release for inmates not sentenced to life terms.

The significance of California's adoption of determinate sentencing cannot be overstated. Determination of how long an inmate would serve in prison was taken out of the hands of parole boards and placed in the hands of the legislature—a change that might sound fine in theory but which turned sentencing into one more way for elected representatives to score points with their constituents. From 1984 to 1991, the legislature passed over 1,000 crime bills, with almost none of them reducing sentences and many imposing sentence enhancements (Simpson 1991). Media-driven add-ons and enhancements to California's sentencing laws ratcheted up penalties, and therefore the size of the prison population, but also greatly complicated sentencing decision making, a development that reduced its transparency and deterrent value.

The elimination of discretionary parole release undercut incentives for inmates to rehabilitate themselves while incarcerated. Some inmates may recognize the intrinsic value of improving themselves, but many others will participate if they believe it reduces their prison stay. Inmates, however, who know they will be released whether or not they participate in programs are effectively discouraged from participation. Eliminating the incentive to engage in rehabilitation programs was unfortunate, because benefits accrue to inmates who participate in drug treatment programs—regardless of their initial motivation for doing so (Anglin and Hser 1990). Removing the possibility of discretionary release undercut one of the most effective mechanisms for encouraging rehabilitation.

Most importantly, the elimination of discretionary release undercut public safety by lessening the ability of state officials to keep violent and dangerous prisoners behind bars. A horrible example is Richard Allen Davis, the parolee who murdered Polly Klaas. While in prison under indeterminate sentencing, Davis was denied parole six times. But after California moved to determinate sentencing and abolished discretionary parole, Davis had to be released automatically because he had served the amount of prison time the new law demanded. He walked out of prison, a free man. Less than 4 months later, he kidnapped and murdered Klaas. Abolishing discretionary parole release, in Davis's case, undermined the system's ability to keep an obviously dangerous offender off the street. Davis is hardly unusual in this respect. It is now common for serious criminals who have completed their sentences to be released directly to the community from California's Secure Housing Unit facilities—a shift from 23 hours a day in windowless, "supermax" solitary confinement to the unstructured and complicated realities of life outside the prison walls.

No one would argue for a return to the unfettered discretion that parole boards exercised in the 1960s. The old system led to unwarranted disparities that often reflected the personal philosophies and prejudices of parole board members rather than the risks posed by offenders. But California effectively threw the baby out with the bath water when it abandoned indeterminate sentencing and discretionary parole release, eliminating not just the weaknesses of the old system but also its most critical strengths.

B. Parole Supervision

The shift from indeterminate sentencing spelled the end of discretionary parole release, but left in place postprison parole supervision for all offenders, establishing an unusual hybrid system whose policy ramifications appear not to have been recognized. A policy history of the passage of the determinate sentencing law reveals almost no discussion of parole supervision (Messinger and Johnson 1978), and interviews with those central to the law's passage indicated that parole supervision did not arise in the debates over sentencing reform (Parnas and Salerno 1978). Everyone assumed that the previous postprison supervision system would remain intact. On the surface, that may have appeared to make sense. Over the long term, however, that decision has contributed significantly to California's unusually high recommitment rate.

Nearly all California prisoners serve a period of parole upon release. Technically, the Board of Parole Hearings can waive parole, but waivers are rare (Fama 2004). In the overwhelming majority of cases, an inmate is simply released to parole supervision on expiration of his or her prison term, with the parole term functioning not as a reward for good behavior (as it would in an indeterminate system) but as a period of extended surveillance and services.

While on parole, a prisoner remains in the custody of the Department of Corrections and Rehabilitation. The parolee is supervised by a parole agent and must comply with parole conditions. If a parolee violates the conditions, the agent can refer the case to the Board of Parole Hearings, which can revoke parole and order a return to custody for up to 1 year. Prisoners who are considered sexually violent predators or mentally disordered offenders may be referred to civil commitment proceedings and committed to a state hospital instead of being released.

The lengths of parole periods are determined by statute. Most prisoners—those serving determinate terms for crimes occurring on or after January 1, 1979—are subject to a 3-year minimum parole period, with a maximum of 4 years. However, the lengths of parole terms have been extended in recent years for certain offenders. Californians recently passed Proposition 83 (Jessica's Law), which requires sex offenders released on parole to be subject to Global Positioning System (GPS) tracking for life.[26]

California's nearly universal parole supervision stands in sharp contrast to most states' approach. Some states supervise only certain high-risk prisoners after release. A few states, including Maine and Virginia, abolished parole supervision altogether. Michigan supervises parolees for only 2 years, compared to California's longer supervision periods. Some states, including New York and Texas, release fewer inmates through a nondiscretionary process but subject all inmates to supervision upon release. Still others, including Florida, release all inmates through a nondiscretionary process but subject fewer than half to supervision. Only one other state—Illinois—follows the California approach, combining determinate sentencing with near universal parole supervision. Figure 12 illustrates how unusual the hybrid approach is.

Because of how California's parole supervision system works, parole officers supervise some individuals who pose far more serious threats to society than does the typical parolee in a state with discretionary release. California parole officers often claim that their high revocation

[26] See Office of the Attorney General, State of California, for details on The Sexual Predator Punishment and Control Act: Jessica's Law, at http://ag.ca.gov/, accessed May 21, 2007.

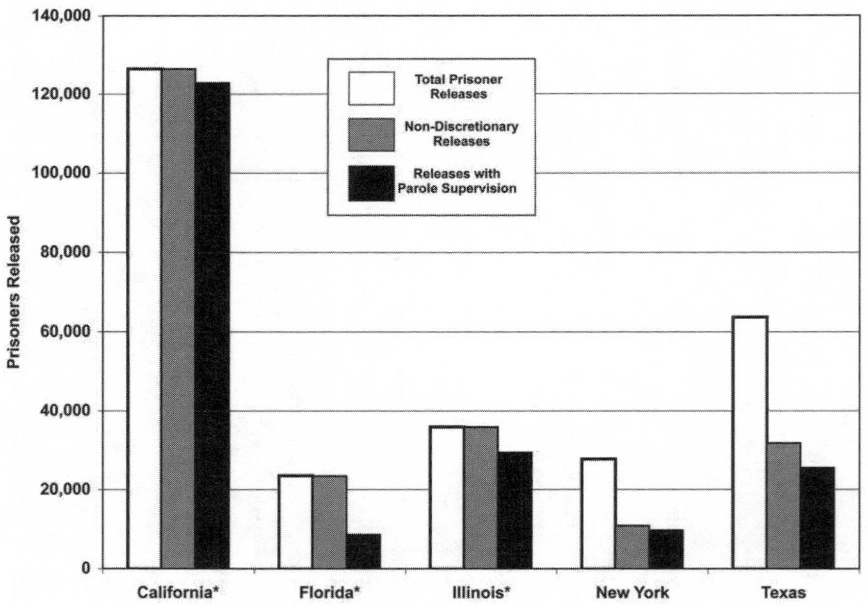

FIG. 12.—Prisoners released without parole board review (nondiscretionarily) and with parole supervision, by state, 2004. * indicates determinate sentencing states. Source: Data compiled from *Directory 2005*, American Correctional Association, 2005.

rates are a by-product of release of parolees who were almost certain to reoffend and should not have been released in the first place.

California's system undercuts public safety and inflates recidivism figures. Inmates "churn" in and out of the correctional system in a nonstop game of catch and release. The imposition of short, determinate sentences for parole violations ensures that offenders are re-released whether or not they are rehabilitated, and the heavy use of parole supervision ensures that two-thirds are quickly thrown back into custody. The combination system maximizes both risks to the community and state expense. It is no accident that California is virtually alone in its use of this dysfunctional hybrid.

C. Caseloads and Supervision Levels

When California inmates are released, they are given any money they have in their prison trust account and $200 in "gate money." Those who have served fewer than six consecutive months are given even less money, calculated at a rate of $1.10 per day up to a maximum $200. As inadequate as this may seem, California's gate money is among the highest in the nation. One-third of states provide no gate money at all (Petersilia 2003).

Before release, parolees are assigned a parole agent in the parolee's community. A released prisoner is usually paroled to the county of his or her legal residence prior to incarceration. Generally parolees must make face-to-face contact with their parole officer by the first working day following release, and the agent typically has them sign a written description of their conditions of supervision. Parole conditions are similar in most California jurisdictions and include not carrying weapons, reporting changes of address and employment, and submitting to searches. Special conditions can be imposed. Sex offenders may be required to participate in therapy, register as sex offenders, and refrain from entering child safety zones. Most parolees have drug-testing conditions that allow them to be randomly tested. Parolees with histories of gang-related violence may be required to stay away from gang members.

Parolees are assigned to one of seven supervision levels, with the level determining the frequency and level of oversight. The classifications are high control, high service, control service, second striker, high-risk sex offender, minimum service, and other. Table 3 describes

TABLE 3

California Parole Population Caseloads and Supervision Requirements, 2005

California Parolee Classification	Active Parolees	Selected Parole Contact and Testing Requirements
High Control Parolees who were convicted of violent felonies in Penal Code 667.5(c), must register as sex offenders, are validated gang members, or are high-notoriety cases.	15,077 (11.3%)	■ 2 face-to-face contacts per month (one must be at residence) ■ First home visit within 6 days of release ■ 1 drug test per month, if required ■ 2 collaterals per quarter
High Service Parolees who have special service needs (severe addiction problems) or behavioral patterns (severe mental illness).	1,597 (1.2%)	■ 2 face-to-face contacts per month (one must be at residence) ■ 1 drug test per month, if required (civil addicts may have weekly testing) ■ 2 collaterals per quarter
Control Service (CS) Parolees who require active supervision. Refers to parolees who do not meet the criteria for High Control or High Services.	58,125 (43.6%)	■ 1 face-to-face in residence every other month ■ 2 drug tests per quarter ■ 1 collateral every 90 days ■ Most CS cases drop to MS automatically at 180 days
Second Striker Parolees with at least two prior convictions for serious or violent offenses. Ideal ratio of 40:1.	10,266 (7.7%)	■ 2 face-to-face per month; 4 per quarter in home ■ 1 drug test per month ■ 2 collaterals per month
High Risk Sex Offender (HRSO) Defined by the California Department of Justice, using criteria set forth under PC 290(n)(1), PC 667.5 and 667.6. Ideal ratio of 40:1.	2,321 (1.7%)	■ 2 face-to-face per month; 4 per quarter in home ■ 1 drug test per month ■ 2 collaterals per month ■ Quarterly meeting with person who knows parolee well

Minimum Service (MS) Parolees who are on monthly mail-in, and these are counted as "contacts." These individuals need to make only two to three face-to-face or collateral contacts with their parole officer each year.	28,003 (21.0%)	■ 1 home visit within 30 days of being assigned to MS ■ 1 face-to-face or collateral every 4 months ■ 1 monthly report turned in by fifth of every month ■ Face-to-face contact 30 days prior to discharge ■ Drug testing waived
Other Includes deportees or pending deportation (13,508). Also includes enhanced outpatient, mentally disordered, and missing classification.	17,411 (13.1%)	
Total California parolees supervised	133,198	
Parolees At Large Parolees who are being supervised by a California parole agent and abscond supervision. A warrant is issued, parole is suspended, and location is unknown.	19,446 (14.6%)	
Civil Addicts The Narcotic Addict Evaluation Authority determines suitability for release of individuals committed into the "civil addict" program—a civil commitment to the California Rehabilitation Center for adult offenders who the court believes would be best served through this alternative to prison.	1,821 (1.4%)	
Direct Court Releases Parolees who report to parole after being directly released from court (not prison).	151 (.1%)	

SOURCE.—Data provided by Division of Parole Operations, California Department of Corrections and Rehabilitation.

what the designations mean, the percentage of active parolees in each classification level at year-end 2005, and the relevant contact levels.

These categories document a form of supervision that is unlikely to provide the extensive service and surveillance activities needed for the highest-risk offenders. Twenty-three percent of California's parolees fall into the "minimum service" category, meaning that they will see a parole officer only twice a year. This costs money to provide and takes parole officers' time but cannot possibly provide meaningful oversight. Another 43 percent of parolees fall into the "control service" classification, meaning that they will see a parole officer twice every 3 months. This level of supervision is more than minimum supervision but is unlikely to give a strong sense that the state is paying much attention to a parolee's actions.

These two classifications account for 65 percent of parolees. Given that offenders are placed in low-risk categories because they are not expected to be recidivists, it is hard not to wonder whether cursory oversight is an effective use of resources.

This issue is particularly pressing because California loses track of many parolees. Nearly 15 percent—more than 19,000 people—are "parolees-at-large," meaning that they have absconded and their whereabouts are unknown. This is the highest absconding rate in the nation and is far above the 7 percent national average (Glaze and Palla 2005).

Here again, California has failed rationally to sort inmates into meaningful supervision categories—placing all inmates on parole, regardless of risk and needs, resulting in caseloads so large that the truly dangerous cannot be supervised and those needing services cannot be helped.

VII. Understanding California's Recidivism

California is dubiously distinguished with the nation's highest recidivism rate. Of approximately 120,000 inmates released each year, 66 percent are back behind bars within 36 months—compared to a 40 percent national average (Langan and Levin 2002). But recidivism can be defined in different ways. Some states define recidivism as a new arrest of an ex-prisoner, some as a new conviction, and some as a return to prison or jail. It is these different responses that must be compared, and not the generic label of "recidivism," to get a meaningful comparative sense of how the states are performing. Another complicating factor is that some categories of ex-inmates have a much higher likelihood of re-offending than others. A state that is home to a disproportionately high share of such likely re-offenders may have a higher recidivism rate even though it operates relatively successful programs for former inmates. Saying that California is "the worst" when it comes to recidivism, then, amounts to applying a label that does not describe the correctional system very clearly and fails to compare it carefully to other state systems.

A. State Variation in Prisoner Recidivism

Fischer (2005) undertook a more nuanced comparison of California's recidivism rate using the Bureau of Justice Statistics national database on prisoners released in 1994 (Langan and Levin 2002). Fisher found that California's 3-year recidivism rate could plausibly be set anywhere between 27 percent and 70 percent based on counting as recidivists, respectively, only those resentenced to prison or only those rearrested (see table 4). At the end of the 3-year follow-up period, 66 percent of all California parolees had been returned to prison, 27 percent for a new criminal conviction and 39 percent for a so-called technical violation.

Fischer sought to understand how that 66 percent figure compared to the numbers from Illinois, Texas, North Carolina, New York, and Florida during the same period, when similarly serious offenders were compared. California's high recidivism rate might be influenced by the nature of its offender population. Ex-prisoners who are young, male, involved with a gang, and have extensive prior criminal records are more prone to commit new crimes than are ex-offenders with fewer such characteristics. If these factors are not accounted for, or "statistically controlled," cross-state comparisons are misleading. The BJS database allowed Fischer to control for gender, race, prior arrests, prior prison sentences, original conviction offense, and age at release.

Fischer concluded that California ex-offenders fared moderately better than similar individuals in some states and moderately worse than those in others. The likelihood of rearrest was 12 percent higher in Illinois and 34 percent higher in Florida than in California, controlling for available demographics and criminal history. However, prisoners released in North Carolina had a 40 percent lower likelihood of rearrest when compared to California prisoners, inmates in Texas had a 38

TABLE 4

Percentage of California Parolees Recidivating within 3 Years of Release

			Returned to Jail or Prison			Returned to Prison		
Conviction Offense	Rearrested	Reconvicted	New Crime	Technical Violation	Total	New Crime	Technical Violation	Total
Violent	63	40	29	35	64	20	42	62
Property	77	56	42	32	74	33	38	71
Drugs	71	51	39	27	66	27	35	62
Public order	63	41	32	34	66	22	41	63
Other	68	44	32	41	73	22	48	70
Total	70	49	37	32	69	27	39	66

SOURCE.—Fischer (2005).

percent lower probability, and inmates in New York had a 25 percent lower probability over the 3-year follow-up period, even after controlling for relevant risk indicators. California's statistics are dramatically different from those in much of the rest of the nation only when considering technical violations.

B. No Mere Technicality

To understand technical violations in California, one must first realize that California uses parole supervision and revocation as crime policy tools far more than does any other state. Almost all California prisoners are released to parole supervision. When parolees fail to comply with parole conditions, as the majority apparently do, parole officers are responsible for reacting to their misbehavior. Diverting a parolee to a halfway house or seeking rearrest and prosecution could be appropriate in some cases but, as shown in figure 13, a large number are returned to prison for "administrative, parole" violations. The number of parole returns to prison in 2004 was about 77,000 per year, down from 90,000 in 2000. As figure 13 makes clear, the number of parolees returned to prison for new criminal convictions has remained fairly constant for a decade. The greatest increase since 1990 has been for administrative or technical violations.

It would be easy—and wrong—to conclude that California could reduce recidivism by eliminating enforcement of these "technicalities."

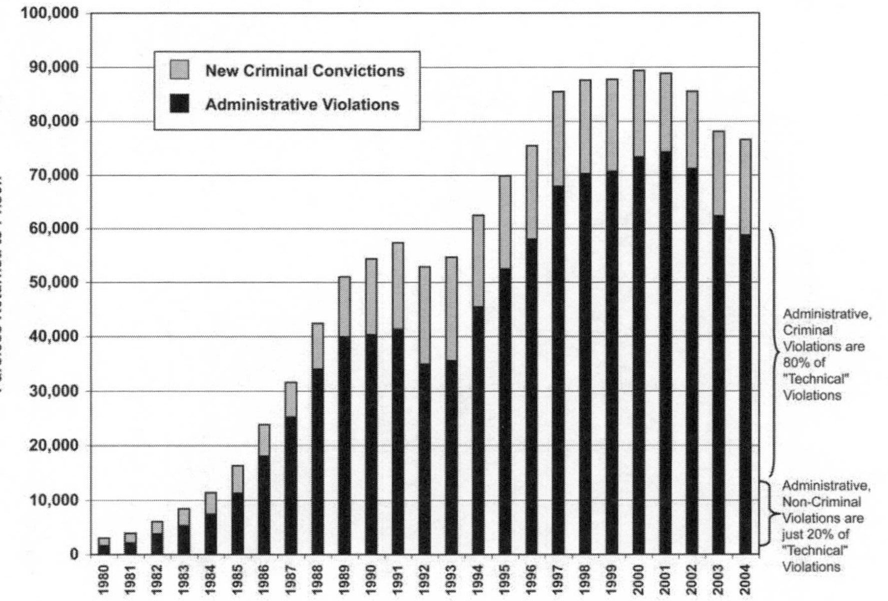

FIG. 13.—California parolees returned to prison administrative violations versus new criminal convictions, 1980–2004. The analysis of the percentage of administrative violations that are criminal violations versus noncriminal violations comes from 2001, the last year California collected the data permitting such a calculation. Source: Data provided by the Division of Adult Parole Operations, California Department of Corrections and Rehabilitation, various years.

Although the label "administrative violation" to describe a technical violation makes the process sound almost like a clerical error, California uses technical violations to respond to a wide range of serious criminal behavior that other jurisdictions would handle through rearrest and prosecution. In other states, technical violations usually involve failures to take drug tests or report to a parole officer. In California, these may include allegations of rape, robbery, and even murder.

California's technical violations—"administrative returns"—include "administrative criminal returns" and "administrative non-criminal returns." As figure 13 shows, 80 percent of administrative or technical returns are considered criminal, meaning that they are associated with new criminal activity. Unlike a return based on a new criminal conviction, where the alleged crime must be proved beyond a reasonable doubt at trial, an administrative return takes place after a hearing by the Board of Parole Hearings. The standard of proof is civil rather than criminal, so allegations need only be proved by a preponderance of the evidence rather than beyond a reasonable doubt.

Just 20 percent of parole violators returned to prison in 2004 are purely technical violators of the sort seen in other states. The rest of the "technical or administrative" violations involved allegations of new criminal activity. Jeremy Travis (2003) looked in detail at crimes handled through the administrative, criminal violation route using data supplied by the California Department of Corrections. He found that 47,161 parole violators were returned in 2000 due to administrative criminal returns. Of these 7,573 (16 percent) were classified as Type II crimes, which are serious and violent felonies. Seventy-eight parolees returned to prison for parole violations were suspected of committing murder, 384 of rape, 3,681 of felony assault battery and assault, and 524 of robbery.

Travis found very little difference (less than 1 month) between the prison terms served by those returned to prison for criminal or non-criminal reasons. The slight difference is striking when comparing the most severe with the least severe categories. Parolees returned to prison for homicides served on average 9.9 months; those returned for "pure technicals" served on average 4.2 months (Travis 2003). Travis finds the practice "troubling on several levels. First, it can be viewed as constituting an end-run on the traditional pathway of prosecution and conviction for criminal acts, avoiding the safeguards of the adversarial system and the transparency of court proceedings. Second, the penalties available for this misconduct are grossly disproportionate to the offense. Under the parole violation statutes, a person can be incarcerated for up to a year for a technical violation. Convictions for the offenses underlying these violations—murder, rape and robbery—could have brought much longer prison sentences" (Travis and Christiansen 2006, p. 5).

The use of administrative returns to respond to serious crimes has been challenged for denying the accused the significant legal protections of a complete trial. Travis questions whether California's procedures amount to a parallel system of criminal adjudication, with lower burdens of proof and a less adversarial process. Dealing with serious crimes in this way, in his view, gives short shrift to defendants' basic legal rights and curtails the state's ability to impose appropriate sentences for serious offenses.

Blumstein and Beck (2005) examined the postrelease activity of prisoners who had served comparable sentences in New York, Florida, Illinois, and California and tracked them for 7 years after leaving prison. Nearly 10 percent of California prisoners cycled in and out of prison six or more times over the 7-year period. They remained in their home communities for less than half the time of parolees in other states (9.3 months compared to 20 months), and spent less time in prison than their counterparts who were reincarcerated. The California subjects were given sentences averaging just 7.9 months and typically served less than half that time. The authors used "churning" to describe this constant, restless cycling between home and prison and found that fewer than 0.1 percent of prisoners from other states churned in the way that was common in California.

California is much more likely to use incarceration as a casual, short-term response to criminal behavior, while other states employ incarceration as a decisive and dramatic break with day-to-day life. Where California employs a catch-and-release policy that churns inmates back and forth between prison and community, other states "catch" fewer individuals in prison and keep those people behind bars for some time. This is a critical distinction between California and other large states.

This unusual approach is the source of many problems. Short prison terms mean that criminals are quickly put back on the street to commit new crimes, harming public safety. Rapid churning in and out of prison wastes the resources of parole commissioners and parole officers, who must reprocess the same individuals over and over. Churning disrupts the continuity of prison life, making it difficult or pointless for inmates, who know they will be back on the streets in a few months, to participate in educational, vocational, or substance-abuse programs. And churning encourages the spread of prison gang culture into communities where inmates are discharged, while undercutting the deterrent effect of serving prison time.

VIII. Conclusions and Recommendations

This examination of the causes and consequences of California's rapid prison expansion reveals a system collapsing of its own weight, despite staggering costs, now at more than $43,000 per year per inmate. Ten percent of the state's 2007–8 general fund is allocated to state corrections. Based on current spending trends, California's prison budget will overtake spending on the state's universities in 5 years (Sterngold 2007). No other large state spends close to as much on its prisons compared with its universities. There appears no end in sight, as the inmate population is projected to increase to 179,558 by June 30, 2008, about a 4 percent annual growth rate.[27] On May 3, 2007, Governor Schwarzenegger signed legislation providing $7.7 billion to add 53,000 prison and jail beds—the largest prison construction expansion in the nation's history.[28] But California cannot build its way out of its overcrowding crisis. It must fundamentally alter its sentencing structure, expand evidence-based rehabilitation programs, implement intermediate sanctions for diverting some parole violators, and invest in community partnerships focused on reentry success.

A. A Permanent, Independent, and Nonpartisan Sentencing Commission

California's most urgent need is to repair its broken sentencing system. The Determinate Sentencing Law shifted the purpose of imprisonment from rehabilitation to punishment. An explosion of "tough-on-

[27] California Legislative Analyst's Office, Analysis of the 2007–2008 Budget Bill: Judicial and Criminal Justice, http://ww.lao.ca.gov/analysis_2007/crim_justice/cj_05_anl07.aspx #AdultCorrections, accessed May 9, 2007. Over the past 20 years, the state inmate population has grown at an average annual rate of 5 percent, increasing from 59,000 inmates in 1986 to 171,800 inmates in 2007.

[28] Assembly Bill 900, also known as the Public Safety and Offender Rehabilitation Services Act of 2007, ties construction funding to benchmarks on delivering rehabilitation programs and improving overall CDCR management. See http://www.leginfo.ca.gov/pub/07−08/bill/asm/ab_0851−0900/ab_900_bill_20070503_chaptered.pdf, accessed May 9, 2007.

crime" legislation followed, creating a complex, bureaucratic, expensive, and irrational sentencing system that is largely responsible for the current overcrowding crisis. A recent review revealed 80 substantive increases in sentence length for specific crimes since the enactment of determinate sentencing.[29] In addition, the legislature increased sentences in other ways and limited the discretion of sentencing judges to make determinations with respect to the imposition, aggravation, or enhancement of sentences. Legal scholars have dubbed the incremental changes "drive-by" sentencing laws, because they are often enacted as knee-jerk responses to horrific, high-profile, and frequently isolated crimes (Zimring, Hawkins, and Kamin 2001). As the Little Hoover Commission (2007, p. 35) noted, "The result is a chaotic labyrinth of laws with no cohesive philosophy or strategy." The system is so complex that judges and lawyers need special software to apply the rules. Moreover, piecemeal alterations to the rules have led to irrational outcomes. For example, kidnapping for purposes of robbery carries a life sentence, but kidnapping for purposes of rape does not (Geissler 2005). California urgently needs to find a way to promote rational sentencing policy that is at least somewhat insulated from political pressure. It also needs to find a way to link sentencing policy with correctional resources (both short-term crowding issues and long-term budgetary issues).

Confronted with similar policy challenges, nearly two dozen other states have established sentencing commissions to enact or recommend sentencing laws and guidelines, and California should do the same. Commissions can provide political cover to elected officials, who may have a difficult time justifying to their constituents why they voted for a sentencing policy that appears to make them "soft on crime." The American Law Institute (2007, p. 7) recently recommended that state legislatures establish "permanent sentencing commission(s) with the authority to promulgate sentencing guidelines." California's Little Hoover Commission (2007), a bipartisan, independent state oversight agency, recently urged creation of a sentencing commission, noting that "time is running out" and that the need is urgent.

There is now widespread agreement that California needs a sen-

[29] See "Increases in California Sentencing since the Enactment of Determinate Sentencing Act," by Stanford Criminal Justice Center and included as app. F in Little Hoover Commission (2007). See Dansky (2006), available at http://www.law.stanford.edu/program/centers/scjc/#sentencing_and_corrections_policy_project.

tencing commission. Without it, California will have no way to control who goes to prison and who does not and no way to tie those decisions to budget allocations. As a result, the soon-to-be-built cells will quickly be filled and California's prisons will remain overcrowded.

B. Evidence-Based Rehabilitation Programs in Prison and Parole

There is a compelling need to establish rehabilitation programs that prepare offenders for law-abiding lives. We must reinvest in prison work, education, and substance abuse programs. We cannot reduce recidivism unless programs are funded that open up opportunities for ex-convicts to create alternatives to a criminal lifestyle. Ironically, just as evidence was building that certain rehabilitation programs do reduce recidivism, California was dismantling those very programs. Few inmates leaving California prisons today have participated in education, substance abuse, or vocational training, almost guaranteeing their failure after release. Those failures put pressure on California to build more prisons, which in turn takes money away from rehabilitation programs that might have helped offenders in the first place.

Several effective correctional interventions can reduce recidivism, if the programs are well designed, well implemented, and targeted appropriately. The devil is not in the principle but in the details. It is realistic to expect about a 10 percent reduction in recidivism overall, although different programs have different expected recidivism reduction outcomes (see Wilson, Gallagher, and MacKenzie 2000; Lochner and Moretti 2004; Aos, Miller, and Drake 2006; MacKenzie 2006; Lipsey and Cullen 2007; National Research Council 2007).

The Washington State Institute for Public Policy reviewed 571 rigorous evaluations of adult and juvenile corrections programs and found several programs that reduce recidivism between 5 percent and 17 percent. Programs such as in-prison "therapeutic communities" with strong postrelease reentry services have been shown to be effective for drug-involved offenders. Vocational education in prison and for parolees has yielded good results when combined with aftercare. Cognitive behavioral treatment in prison and in the community has been shown to be successful. Intensive community supervision programs that emphasize the delivery of treatment services, not just surveillance, yield impressive results in reducing future criminal behaviors by released offenders. Gender-responsive programs have demonstrated good outcomes for women offenders. These programs can reduce the need for future prison construction and are cost effective (Aos, Miller, and Drake 2006).

But implementing evidence-based programs alone will not reduce recidivism. Unless California reduces its prison population, it will have neither sufficient space nor the proper environment to deliver effective programming. It must also train its employees to ensure that they are qualified to deliver and support adult offender programming and trained to identify and manage prisoners and parolees based on assessments of risks and needs, rather than on the security-level classification system that currently drives prison placement. Most current correctional staff were hired and trained under a "custody" model of corrections, rather than a "rehabilitation" model. Education and training will be required to engage staff in the shift from an emphasis solely on custody to an emphasis on rehabilitation and reentry. Without staff buy-in, the culture of CDCR will not change and the best evidence-based programs will not be implemented appropriately.

C. Intermediate Sanctions and Parole Violation Guidelines

California must employ parole supervision more selectively, reserving scarce resources for higher-risk offenders. Using a normed and validated instrument assessing risks of recidivism, California should release low-risk, nonviolent, non–sex registrants without placing them on parole supervision. Recall from table 3 that 23 percent of California's parolees see their parole officer only twice a year. These people probably could have been released from prison without parole supervision, saving resources and not jeopardizing public safety.

Second, nonviolent, nongang, and non–sex registrant parolees should be automatically discharged after 12 months on parole if they have incurred no new arrests or serious parole violations. The public has little to lose. Every moderate-risk parolee does at least 12 months on parole. Recidivism studies consistently show that inmates who are going to return to crime do so quickly (Langan and Levin 2002; National Research Council 2007). Parolees who wish to remain criminally active are under parole supervision when they most need to be. If prisoners can remain completely arrest-free for a year, they have low probabilities of recidivism thereafter. Recidivism rates are further reduced when a parolee participates in work, education, and substance abuse programs. Parolees self-select into low-risk-of-recidivism groups, so the public safety implications of an "earned discharge" system are minimal, and the cost efficiencies will increase because parolees who do not need supervision will be removed from crowded caseloads (Petersilia 2007).

California should develop parole violation decision-making guidelines for determining sanctions for parole violations. In 2005, 62,000 parolees were returned to prison for parole violations and served, on average, a 4-month prison term. Although parole violators cycle through the system quickly, they burden an already stressed intake system and add to prison overcrowding. Using parole violation guidelines will allow responses to violations to be fairer and more consistent, based on guidelines that are appropriate to offender risk level and the seriousness of the violation. Similar decisions made for similar situations also increases compliance of parolees, whereas dramatically different responses undermine trust and the legitimacy of the system. The guidelines system must be accompanied by an expanded and credible array of intermediate sanctions programs.

D. Community Partnerships for Reentry Planning and Service Delivery

Criminal justice agencies cannot improve reentry success alone. Researchers have documented the importance of informal social controls, or "stakes-in-conformity," for reducing recidivism (Laub, Sampson, and Allen 2001). Ultimately, formal social control mechanisms (e.g., police, parole officers) must give way to informal social controls (e.g., neighbors, family, churches, employers) for long-term reintegration success. Some parole supervision requirements, such as finding a job, serve as important pressures toward legitimate activities and greater ties with law-abiding citizens, but ultimately those who succeed are usually connected to informal social controls. A number of community partnership initiatives have emerged around reentry, including a U.S. Department of Justice initiative (Young, Taxman, and Byrne 2002). Results show that community assets can be leveraged around prisoner reentry, but that requires concerted efforts to educate and engage businesses, families, and social service agencies. Community reentry partnerships hold great promise for increasing parolee success, since communities come to learn that they have a vested interest in offenders' reentry success and offenders come to understand, in many cases for the first time, that they have a place in the community.

It has long been said that "as goes California, so goes the nation." In the case of corrections, let us hope this is untrue. There is excess at every level in California: budgets increasing by $1 billion each year, guard salaries out of step with national norms and other public service employees, parole caseloads so high as to be meaningless, and a prison population that continues to grow each year. Yet the excess produces few tangible results. California's violent crime rate is increasing (up 3 percent in 2006 after a several year decline),[30] gangs are gaining strongholds in prisons and communities, nearly one out of seven parolees absconds with little consequence, and very few offenders get the help they desperately need. California leaders must debate whether further investments in the state's prison system are warranted. If they continue down the current path, the damaging consequences of California's mass incarceration experiment will be felt for generations to come.

REFERENCES

Aday, R. H. 2003. *Aging Prisoners: Crisis in American Corrections*. New York: Praeger.

American Correctional Association. 2005. *Directory*. Lanham, MD: American Correctional Association.

American Law Institute. 2007. *Model Penal Code: Sentencing*. Tentative draft. Philadelphia.

Anglin, M. D., and Y. I. Hser. 1990. "Treatment of Drug Abuse." In *Drugs and Crime*, edited by M. Tonry and J. Q. Wilson. Vol. 13 of *Crime and Justice: A Review of Research*, edited by Michael Tonry. Chicago: University of Chicago Press.

Aos, S., M. Miller, and E. Drake. 2006. *Evidence-Based Adult Corrections Programs: What Works and What Does Not*. Olympia: Washington State Institute for Public Policy.

Austin, J. 2003. *Findings in Prison Classification and Risk Assessment*. Washington, DC: Federal Bureau of Prisons.

Beck, A. J., and P. M. Harrison. 2006. *Sexual Violence Reported by Correctional Authorities*. Washington, DC: Bureau of Justice Statistics.

Berk, R. A., and J. de Leeuw. 1999. "An Evaluation of California's Inmate Classification System Using a Generalized Regression Discontinuity Design" (electronic version). *UCLA Reprints* from http://preprints.stat.ucla.edu/218/218.pdf.

[30] From January through September 2006, the number of reported violent crimes increased 3.4 percent when compared to the same period in 2005. The increase in this category can be attributed to increases in homicide (up 3.4 percent), forcible rape (up 2.6 percent), and robbery (up 15.3 percent). Aggravated assault offenses decreased by 3.2 percent during this period. See http://ag.ca.gov/cjsc/, accessed May 18, 2007.

Bloom, B., B. Owen, and S. Covington. 2003. *Gender-Responsive Strategies: Research, Practice, and Guiding Principles for Women Offenders*. Washington, DC: National Institute of Corrections.

Blumstein, A. 1993. "Racial Disproportionality of U.S. Prison Populations Revisited." *University of Colorado Law Review* 64:743–60.

Blumstein, A., and A. J. Beck. 1999. "Population Growth in U.S. Prisons: 1980–1996." In *Prisons*, edited by M. Tonry and J. Petersilia. Vol. 26 of *Crime and Justice: A Review of Research*, edited by M. Tonry. Chicago: University of Chicago Press.

———. 2005. "Reentry as a Transient State between Liberty and Recommitment." In *Prisoner Reentry and Crime in America*, edited by J. Travis and C. Visher. Cambridge: Cambridge University Press.

Blumstein, A., and J. Wallman. 2000. *The Crime Drop in America*. New York: Cambridge University Press.

Bobbitt, M., and M. Nelson. 2004. *The Front Line: Building Programs that Recognize Families' Role in Reentry*. New York: Vera Institute of Justice.

Bonczar, T. 2003. *Prevalence of Imprisonment in the U.S. Population, 1974–2001*. Washington, DC: U.S. Department of Justice.

Braman, D. 2004. *Doing Time on the Outside: Incarceration and Family Life in Urban America*. Ann Arbor: University of Michigan Press.

Bureau of Justice Statistics. 2000. *Census of State and Federal Correctional Facilities*. Washington, DC: U.S. Department of Justice.

———. 2003. *Census of State and Federal Correctional Facilities*. Washington, DC: U.S. Department of Justice.

California Department of Corrections and Rehabilitation. 2006*a*. *Adult Population Projections 2007–2012*. Sacramento: California Department of Corrections and Rehabilitation.

———. 2006*b*. "Facts and Figures." Retrieved January 9, from http://www.cdcr.ca.gov.

———. 2007. *Weekly Report of Population*. Sacramento: California Department of Corrections and Rehabilitation.

California Department of Finance. 2007. *California Budget 2007–2008*. Sacramento: California Department of Finance.

California Expert Panel on Adult Offender Recidivism Reduction Programming. 2007. *A Roadmap for Effective Offender Programming in California: Report to the California State Legislature*. Sacramento: California Department of Corrections and Rehabilitation.

California Legislative Analyst's Office. 2005*a*. *Analysis of the 2003–2004 Budget Bill*. Sacramento: California Legislative Analyst's Office.

———. 2005*b*. *Analysis of 2005–2006 Budget Bill, Judiciary and Criminal Justice*. Sacramento: California Legislative Analyst's Office.

———. 2007. *California's Criminal Justice System: A Primer*. Sacramento: California Legislative Analyst's Office.

California Office of the Attorney General. 2006. *Crime in California 2005*. Sacramento: Department of Justice.

Carlson, P. M. 2001. "Prison Interventions: Evolving Strategies to Control Security Threat Groups." *Corrections Management Quarterly* 5(1):10–22.

Chen, K., and J. M. Shapiro. 2004. "Does Prison Harden Inmates? A Discontinuity-Based Approach." Social Science Research Network. http://papers.ssrn.com/sol3/papers.cfm?abstract_id=470301.

Clear, T. R. 2007. *Imprisoning Communities: How Mass Incarceration Makes Disadvantaged Neighborhoods Worse*. New York: Oxford University Press.

Clear, T., G. Cole, and M. Reisig. 2006. *American Corrections*. 7th ed. Belmont, CA: Thomson Wadsworth.

Clear, T., D. Rose, E. Waring, and K. Scully. 2003. "Coercive Mobility and Crime: A Preliminary Examination of Concentrated Incarceration and Social Disorganization." *Justice Quarterly* 20(1):33–64.

Culp, R. 2005. "Frequency and Characteristics of Prison Escapes in the United States: An Analysis of National Data." *Prison Journal* 85(3):270–91.

Dansky, K. 2006. *Contemporary Sentencing Reform in California: A Report to the Little Hoover Commission*. Palo Alto, CA: Stanford Criminal Justice Center.

Enthoven, A., and R. Kronick. 1989. "A Consumer Choice Health Plan for the 1990s: Universal Health Insurance in a System Designed to Promote Quality and Economy." *New England Journal of Medicine* 320:29–37.

Fabelo, A. 2007. *Justice Reinvestment: A Framework to Improve Effectiveness of Justice Policies in Texas*. New York: Council of State Governments.

Fama, S. 2004. *The California State Prisoners Handbook: A Comprehensive Practical Guide to Prison and Parole Law*. San Quentin, CA: The Prison Law Office.

Federal Bureau of Investigation. 2006. *Crime in the United States*. Washington, DC: U.S. Department of Justice.

Fischer, R. 2005. *Are California's Recidivism Rates Really the Highest in the Nation?* Irvine, CA: Center for Evidence-Based Corrections.

Fleisher, M. S., and R. H. Rison. 2000. "Gang Management in Corrections." *Prison and Jail Administration* 1:7–18.

Florida Department of Corrections. 2005. "Inmate Escapes: Fiscal Year 2004–2005." Retrieved April 2006, from http://www.dc.state.fl.us/pub/escape/fy/0405/04−05EscapeReport.pdf.

Furillo, A. 2007. "Prisons' Legal Strain: State's Costs Skyrocket as Correctional System Struggles to Comply with Court Orders in Eight Inmate Rights Cases." *Sacramento Bee*, February 4, p. A1.

Gaes, G. 2001. *The Influence of Prison Gang Affiliation on Violence and Other Prison Misconduct*. Washington, DC: Bureau of Prisons.

Garland, D. 2001. *The Culture of Control: Crime and Social Order in Contemporary Society*. Chicago: University of Chicago Press.

Geissler, L. E. 2005. "Creating and Passing a Successful Sentencing Commission in California: An Examination of Failed Attempts in California and Successful Sentencing Commissions across the Country." Unpublished manuscript. Palo Alto, CA: Stanford Law School.

Gendreau, P., T. Little, and C. Goggin. 1996. "A Meta-analysis of Adult Offender Recidivism: What Works?" *Criminology* 34(4):575–607.

Gibbons, J. J., and N. Katzenbach. 2006. *Confronting Confinement: A Report of the Commission on Safety and Abuse in America's Prisons*. Washington, DC: Commission on Safety and Abuse in America's Prisons.

Glaser, D. 1995. *Preparing Convicts for Law-Abiding Lives: The Pioneering Penology of Richard A. McGee*. Albany: State University of New York Press.

Glaze, L., and S. Palla. 2005. *Probation and Parole in the United States, 2004*. Washington, DC: Bureau of Justice Statistics.

Haney, C. 2006. *Reforming Punishment: Psychological Limits to the Pains of Imprisonment*. Washington, DC: American Psychological Association.

Harrison, P. M., and A. J. Beck. 2005. *Prisoners in 2004*. Washington, DC: Bureau of Justice Statistics.

———. 2006. *Prisoners in 2006*. Washington, DC: Bureau of Justice Statistics.

Hartney, C. 2006. *US Rates of Incarceration: A Global Perspective*. San Francisco: National Council on Crime and Delinquency.

Institute of Governmental Studies. 2005. *California Correctional Peace Officers Association*. Berkeley: University of California.

Jenness, V., C. Maxson, K. Matsuda, and J. Sumner. 2007. *Violence in California Facilities: An Empirical Examination of Sexual Assault*. Irvine, CA: Center for Evidence-Based Corrections.

Langan, P., and D. Levin. 2002. *Recidivism of Prisoners Released in 1994*. Washington, DC: Bureau of Justice Statistics.

Laub, J., R. Sampson, and L. Allen. 2001. "Explaining Crime over the Life Course: Toward a Theory of Age-Graded Informal Social Control." In *Explaining Criminals and Crime: Essays in Contemporary Criminological Theory*, edited by R. Paternoster and R. Bachman. New York: Oxford University Press.

Levitt, S. D. 2004. "Understanding Why Crime Fell in the 1990s: Four Factors That Explain the Decline and Six That Do Not." *Journal of Economic Perspectives* 18(1):163–90.

Lin, J., and J. Jannetta. 2006. *The Scope of Correctional Control in California*. Irvine, CA: Center for Evidence-Based Corrections.

Lipsey, M. W., and F. T. Cullen. 2007. "The Effectiveness of Correctional Rehabilitation: A Review of Systematic Reviews." *Annual Review of Law and Social Science* 3 (December). http://www.annualreviews.org.

Little Hoover Commission. 2004. *Breaking the Barriers for Women on Parole*. Sacramento: Little Hoover Commission.

———. 2007. *Solving California's Corrections Crisis: Time Is Running Out*. Sacramento: Little Hoover Commission.

Lochner, L., and E. Moretti. 2004. "The Effect of Education on Crime: Evidence from Prison Inmates, Arrests, and Self Reports." *American Economic Review* 94:155–89.

Lynch, J. P., and W. J. Sabol. 2001. *Prisoner Reentry in Perspective*. Washington, DC: Urban Institute.

Macallair, D. 2002. *California Correctional Facility Growth*. San Francisco: Center on Juvenile and Criminal Justice.

MacKenzie, D. L. 2006. *What Works in Corrections: Reducing the Criminal Activities of Offenders and Delinquents*. New York: Cambridge University Press.

Mauer, M., and M. Chesney-Lind, eds. 2002. *Invisible Punishment: The Collateral Consequences of Mass Imprisonment*. Washington, DC: New Press.

Messinger, S. L., and P. E. Johnson. 1978. "California's Determinate Sentencing Statute: History and Issues." In *Determinate Sentencing: Reform or Regression*. Washington, DC: National Institute of Law Enforcement and Criminal Justice.

Mitchell, O. 2005. "A Meta-analysis of Race and Sentencing Research: Explaining the Inconsistencies." *Journal of Quantitative Criminology* 21(4): 439–66.

Morain, D. 2006. "OT Pushes Guards' Pay Past $100,000; as Crowding at State Prisons Boosts Overtime, 6,000 Earn Six Figures." *Los Angeles Times*, December 23, p. A1.

Mumola, C. 2005. *Suicide and Homicide in State Prisons and Local Jails*. Washington, DC: Bureau of Justice Statistics.

Murray, J., and D. P. Farrington. In this volume. "Effects of Parental Imprisonment on Children."

National Research Council. 2007. *Parole, Desistance from Crime, and Community Integration*. Washington, DC: National Academy of Sciences.

Parnas, R., and M. B. Salerno. 1978. "The Influence behind, Substance and Impact of the New Determinate Sentencing Law in California." *U.C. Davis Law Review* 11:29–40.

Pattillo, M., D. Weiman, and B. Western, eds. 2004. *Imprisoning America: The Social Effects of Mass Incarceration*. New York: Russell Sage.

Petersilia, J. 1999. "Parole and Prisoner Reentry in the United States." In *Prisons*, edited by M. Tonry and J. Petersilia. Vol. 26 of *Crime and Justice: A Review of Research*, edited by M. Tonry. Chicago: University of Chicago Press.

———. 2003. *When Prisoners Come Home: Parole and Prisoner Reentry*. New York: Oxford University Press.

———. 2006. *Understanding California Corrections*. Berkeley: California Policy Research Center.

———. 2007. "Employ Behavioral Contracting for 'Earned Discharge' Parole." *Criminology and Public Policy* 6(4):1501–9.

Pomfret, J. 2006. "California's Crisis in Prison System a Threat to Public." *Washington Post*, June 11, p. A03.

Ruth, H., and K. R. Reitz. 2003. *The Challenge of Crime: Rethinking Our Response*. Cambridge, MA: Harvard University Press.

Schwarzenegger, Arnold. 2007. *State of the State Address*. Sacramento: State of California.

Scudder, K. 1952. *Prisoners Are People*. Garden City, NY: Doubleday.

Simpson, R. 1991. *Jailhouse Blues: Hard Times for County Tax Payers: A Study of Rising Costs of Incarceration in California*. Sacramento: California Counties Foundation.

Spelman, W. 2000. "What Recent Studies Do (and Don't) Tell Us about Imprisonment and Crime." In *Crime and Justice: A Review of Research*, vol. 27, edited by Michael Tonry. Chicago: University of Chicago Press.

Steman, D. 2007. *Reconsidering Incarceration: New Directions for Reducing Crime*. New York: Vera Institute of Justice.

Sterngold, J. 2007. "Prisons' Budget to Trump Colleges': No Other Big State Spends as Much to Incarcerate Compared with Higher Education Funding." *San Francisco Chronicle*, May 21, p. A1.

Sumner, J., and K. Matsuda. 2006. *Shining Light in Dark Corners: An Overview of Prison Rape Elimination Legislation and Introduction to Current Research*. Irvine: University of California.

Tonry, M. 2004. *Thinking about Crime: Sense and Sensibility in American Penal Culture*. New York: Oxford University Press.

Travis, J. 2003. *Parole in California, 1980–2000: Implications for Reform*: Washington, DC: Urban Institute.

———. 2005. *But They All Come Back: Facing the Challenges of Prisoner Reentry*. Washington, DC: Urban Institute.

Travis, J., and K. Christiansen. 2006. "Failed Reentry: The Unique Challenges of Back-End Sentencing." Paper presented at the Back End Sentencing and Technical Parole Violations conference, Stanford Law School, November 4.

University of California. 2006. "Professor Series, Regular Salary Academic Series." Retrieved July 25, from http://www.ap.uci.edu/salary/CurrentScales/prof-FY.pdf.

U.S. Census Bureau. 2006. United States Population (electronic version) from http://quickfacts.census.gov/qfd/states/06000.html.

Vitiello, M., and C. Kelso. 2005. "A Proposal for a Wholesale Reform of California's Sentencing Practice and Policy." *Loyola of Los Angeles Law Review* 38:101–64.

Walmsley, R. 2007. *World Prison Population List*. 7th ed. London: International Centre for Prison Studies.

Werth, R., and J. Sumner. 2006. *Inside California's Prisons and Beyond: A Snapshot of In-Prison and Re-entry Programs*. Irvine: University of California.

Wilson, D. B., C. A. Gallagher, and D. L. MacKenzie. 2000. "A Meta-analysis of Corrections-Based Education, Vocation, and Work Programs for Adult Offenders." *Journal of Research in Crime and Delinquency* 37(4):347–68.

Young, D., F. S. Taxman, and J. M. Byrne. 2002. *Engaging the Community in Offender Reentry*. College Park: University of Maryland.

Zimring, F. E., G. Hawkins, and S. Kamin. 2003. *Punishment and Democracy: Three Strikes and You're Out in California*. New York: Oxford University Press.

Michael Tonry

Learning from the Limitations of Deterrence Research

ABSTRACT

Public policy and scientific knowledge concerning deterrence have long been marching in different directions. Despite the proliferation of three-strikes, mandatory minimum, and concealed weapons laws and retention of capital punishment in 37 states, there is little credible evidence that changes in sanctions affect crime rates, and there is no credible evidence that capital punishment deters better than life sentences or that allowing citizens to carry concealed weapons deters at all. There is evidence that changes in enforcement and sanctions can affect some kinds of behavior—for example, tax compliance, speeding, illegal parking—and there are plausible grounds for believing that other deterrable behaviors can be identified. Doing so will require fine-grained studies that take account of offender characteristics and perceptions, offending situations, and whether and how new enforcement strategies and sanctions systems are implemented.

The state of the art of policy-relevant knowledge about the deterrent effects of the criminal justice system is little different in 2008 than it was 30 years ago when the National Academy of Sciences (NAS) panel on deterrence and incapacitation reported that the existence of a criminal justice system has overall deterrent effects, there is a widely shared intuition that penalty increases have marginal deterrent effects but the available evidence is highly ambiguous and contested, and there is no credible evidence that capital punishment deters homicide any more

Michael Tonry is Sonosky Professor of Law and Public Policy and director, Institute on Crime and Public Policy, University of Minnesota, and senior fellow, Netherlands Institute for the Study of Crime and Law Enforcement, Leiden. He is grateful to Anthony N. Doob, Daniel Nagin, and Alex Piquero for reading and commenting helpfully on earlier drafts.

0192-3234/2008/0037-0007$10.00

effectively than penalties that would otherwise be imposed (Blumstein, Cohen, and Nagin 1978). There is some evidence, as Beccaria and Bentham believed, that certainty and promptness of punishment are more important than severity. Because there are differences in order of magnitude in the abilities of police and courts to alter the promptness of their behavior or affect would-be offenders' perceptions of risk, changes in police practices are more likely to achieve deterrent effects than are changes in sentencing policies and practices. The capacity of the police, however, to achieve long-term crime-reductive effects—as opposed to short-term effects from well-publicized crackdowns (Sherman 1990)—is limited by practical constraints on availability of police resources. Finally, there is considerable evidence that police, prosecutors, judges, and juries often alter their behavior to offset the effects of punishment policy changes with which they disagree, thereby undermining the likelihood of achieving marginal deterrent effects.

There is little point in continuing to investigate these subjects in the same old ways for another 30 years. There are, however, some other lessons about future research agendas to be derived from current knowledge. First, macro-level modeling of deterrent effects of changes in sanctions policies by economists and econometricians has reached a dead end, as Ronald Coase in 1978 predicted would happen concerning subjects on which the economist's advantage was primarily one of technique.[1] Results are inevitably fragile and highly sensitive to minor specification changes. Such research is incapable of taking into account whether and to what extent purported policy changes are implemented, whether and to what extent their adoption or implementation is perceived by would-be offenders, and whether and to what extent offenders are susceptible to influence by perceived changes in legal threats. At the very least, macro-level research on deterrent effects should test the null hypothesis of no effect rather than the price theory assumption that offenders' behavior will change in response to changes in legal threats.

Second, useful research on deterrence will have to become much more nuanced than it has mostly been so far. Whether changes in legal threats are implemented in practice and whether would-be offenders

[1] "Once some of these practitioners [social scientists other than economists] have acquired the simple, but valuable, truths which economics has to offer, and this is the natural competitive response, economists who try to work in the other social sciences will have lost their main advantage and will face competitors who know more about the subject matter than they do" (Coase 1978, p. 210).

perceive those changes are important questions, of course, but so are differences in individuals' susceptibility to changes in legal threats. To many, probably most, people, perceived changes will have no effects on behavior either because their personal values and circumstances remove them altogether from the class of would-be offenders or, conversely, because their values and circumstances make them more or less immune from changes in legal threats. Wikström (2007, ms. 28), for example, argues that "inclusion of subjects who would never be motivated to or consider committing the crime/crimes in question" is a major shortcoming of many micro-level deterrence studies.[2]

Third, however, studies of the implementation of penalty changes may, turned around, provide important insights into prevailing norms concerning the seriousness of crimes and acceptable severities of punishment. It is at least as important to study why penalty changes have little or no effect on crime rates as to study whether they have effects. Penalty laws that are seldom applied, such as most habitual offender and three-strikes laws, or that are routinely circumvented by officials, such as many mandatory minimum sentence laws, are patently out of step with prevailing norms; otherwise they would be applied or enforced. Their non- or partial application or enforcement is likely to be among the reasons why such laws have little discernible effect. The correct conclusion to be drawn from studies that show that penalty laws are routinely circumvented is not that officials are misbehaving but that laws are out of step with prevailing norms and should be altered or repealed.

Although readers of this essay are unlikely to be laypeople, it may be useful to say a couple of things that would be said in a talk to laypeople on this subject. The first is that it is natural to suppose that changes in disincentives to crime will change peoples' behavior. Often they do. Human beings are influenced by incentives and disincentives, and offenders are human beings. For relatively minor forms of prohibited behavior such as illegal parking, fast driving, or littering, significant increases in the perceived likelihood of apprehension or severity of penalties influence behavior. When the threat of having an illegally parked car towed goes up, people become more careful parkers. When speeding drivers see marked police cars stopped by the side

[2] Others have made the same argument (e.g., Pogarsky 2002) and tried to take account of it in their research designs (e.g., Bachman, Ward, and Paternoster 1992; Piquero and Tibbetts 1996).

of a highway, they slow down. Similarly, for calculated instrumental crimes such as tax evasion (e.g., Klepper and Nagin 1989), increases in perceived risks of apprehension appear to deter prospective wrongdoers significantly (though much of this literature is based on laboratory research and responses to hypothetical what-if questions, which raises significant external validity issues).

The debates about whether penalties deter at all, or whether increases in penalties produce marginal increases in deterrence, are not mostly about those kinds of behavior. They are about the mass of ordinary property, "morals" (drugs, prostitution, gambling, etc.), and violent crimes. Typically, these crimes are not committed in public, like driving, parking, and littering offenses, and often they are not highly calculated. Most, however, are unambiguously wrongful, which means that many people will not commit them under any but exceptional circumstances. Many of these crimes are impulsive or are committed under the influence of drugs, alcohol, peer influences, powerful emotions, or situational pressures. Many are committed by people who are deeply socialized into deviant values and lifestyles. These characteristics of many would-be offenders do not mean that it is a priori impossible to affect would-be offenders' criminal choices by means of legal threats. They do mean that doing so is far from being a matter merely of enacting harsher laws, imposing harsher penalties, or adopting more aggressive policing strategies.

Another thing to be said to a lay audience is that thinking and knowledge about deterrence are important. Policy makers would like to believe that penalties and penalty increases deter because those beliefs provide a basis for trying to do something about troubling social problems. The difficulty is that mistaken beliefs in deterrence may lead to adoption of seriously mistaken policies.

Three times in the last 30 years, American state and federal policy makers have adopted major policy changes on the basis of deterrence research findings that were subsequently repudiated.[3] These were the enactment of capital punishment statutes (and the U.S. Supreme Court's upholding of them) in the context of Isaac Ehrlich's claim that every execution saves the lives of eight would-have-been victims (Ehr-

[3] Findings on the alleged deterrent effects of capital punishment or "shall-issue" concealed weapons laws were in both cases invoked by proponents of such laws, but support for them was so ideological and the political impetus behind them so strong that it is not unlikely that most would have been enacted when they were irrespective of research results (see, e.g., Tonry and Green 2003).

lich 1975);[4] the enactment in a majority of American states of mandatory arrest policies in misdemeanor domestic violence cases on the basis of Sherman and Berk's finding that arrests deterred future violence against the original victims (Sherman and Berk 1984; later repudiated by Sherman himself [Sherman, Schmidt, and Rogan 1992]); and the enactment in many states in the last decade of "shall-issue" laws mandating issuance to most adults of licenses to carry concealed firearms in public on the basis of Lott's finding that carrying concealed weapons reduces violent crime rates because would-be assailants are deterred by the knowledge that a potential victim may be carrying a gun (Lott 1998).[5] All three findings have since been shown to be incorrect or not generalizable, but most of the capital punishment, mandatory arrest, and concealed weapons laws whose enactment they influenced (or seemed to justify) remain in effect. The implication is that policy makers should set very high evidentiary standards when considering evidence about the deterrent effectiveness of penalties before adopting policies predicated on deterrence rationales.

Although in the last 30 years there has not been a huge amount of research on deterrence, several small literatures have accumulated. First, since the mid-1990s, a handful of American economists have attempted to model the deterrent effects of capital punishment on homicide and concluded that each execution saves, for example, 18 lives (Dezhbakhsh, Rubin, and Shepherd 2003). The theory is that would-be offenders' knowledge that capital punishment is authorized or that some murderers have been executed will make them less likely to kill people. This work has been discredited by other economists (e.g., Donohue and Wolfers 2005) and by noneconomists (e.g., Fagan, Zimring, and Geller 2006). The only credible conclusions that can be drawn are either that capital punishment has no deterrent effects on homicide or that there is no credible evidence that it does. This conclusion accords with a recent review of this literature by Levitt and Miles (2007, pp. 474–76). Some analyses suggest that executions lead to increases in homicide, possibly through a brutalization effect (e.g., Katz, Levitt, and Shustorovich 2003).

Second, since the late 1980s, a small number of economists have

[4] Solicitor general Robert Bork cited Ehrlich's work in arguing before the U.S. Supreme Court in *Gregg v. Georgia*, 428 U.S. 153 (1976), a decision upholding the constitutionality of existing capital punishment laws in the United States.

[5] In 1994, 1995, and 1996, 13 American states adopted shall-issue laws (Lott 2000, p. 169, n. 7).

attempted to model the crime-preventive effects of letting most ordinary citizens (usually except children, some former felons, and the mentally ill) carry concealed weapons in public places (e.g., Lott and Mustard 1997; Lott 1998, 2000). The hypothesis is that would-be offenders will be deterred by the knowledge that prospective victims may be armed and able to use firearms to defend themselves. Although Lott and his colleagues have concluded that allowing citizens to carry concealed weapons has substantial crime prevention effects, his results have been discredited by other economists on both technical (e.g., Ayres and Donohue 2003*b*; Cook and Ludwig 2003) and ethical (Ayres and Donohue 2003*a*; Donohue 2004)[6] grounds and by noneconomists (e.g., Black and Nagin 1998). A recent U.S. NAS review of that research concludes that there is no credible evidence that enactment of shall-issue laws has measurable deterrent effects: "The committee concludes that with the current evidence it is not possible to determine that there is a causal link between the passage of right-to-carry laws and crime rates. It is also the committee's view that additional analysis along the lines of the current literature is unlikely to yield results that will persuasively demonstrate a causal link between right-to-carry laws and crime rates" (Wellford, Pepper, and Petrie 2005, pp. 150–51).

Third, since the 1980s, a small number of researchers have attempted to demonstrate that private possession of firearms reduces criminal victimization and more than offsets harmful consequences of private ownership of firearms including accidental injuries and deaths and suicides (e.g., Kleck and Kates 2001). The hypotheses are that would-be offenders are deterred by knowledge that prospective victims have guns and that offenders desist from initiated crimes when they learn victims are armed. The most authoritative reviews of this literature conclude that the claims are unconvincing (e.g., Cook 1991; Ludwig 2000). The recent NAS panel was agnostic: "Ultimately, researchers may conclude that it is impossible to effectively measure many aspects of defensive gun use" (Wellford, Pepper, and Petrie 2005, p. 108; also see pp. 110–11, 117).

Fourth, from the mid-1970s through the late 1980s, evaluators investigated the effects of new laws expressly aimed at reducing crime rates through the deterrent effects of increased penalties. Mostly these

[6] Research ethics, that is. Serious questions have been raised about repeated systematic errors in Lott's data and about other matters. Details and references to a supporting literature can be found in Ayres and Donohue (2003*a*) and Donohue (2004).

laws prescribed mandatory minimum sentences for offenders convicted of particular crimes. The hypothesis is that knowing that use of a gun in a robbery will result in a minimum 5-year sentence, or an extra 2 years on top of the otherwise appropriate sentence, for two examples, makes would-be offenders less likely to carry or use a gun. The evaluations concluded either that there were no measurable deterrent effects or that there were short-term effects that quickly wasted away (Tonry 1996, chap. 5). There were two primary reasons: there was little evidence that offenders were aware of the harsher potential penalties; more important, most evaluations showed that the increased penalties were seldom imposed. In some cases, the prescribed "harsher" punishments were less severe than offenders would otherwise have received. In others, judges and lawyers altered their charging, plea negotiation, and fact-finding practices to nullify the law's effects. There has been little recent research on implementation of harsh mandatory punishments, but the two latest major studies produced the same pattern of findings as earlier studies (McCoy and McManimon 2004; Merritt, Fain, and Turner 2006).

Fifth, during the 1990s, American policy makers implemented a number of tough-on-crime initiatives, most notably zero-tolerance policing in New York City and a broadly framed "three-strikes-and-you're-out" law in California, and claimed dramatic crime reductions through deterrence. Rudolph Giuliani, the New York mayor; William Bratton, his police chief at the time; and their representatives claimed credit for the happy correlation, as did governor Pete Wilson of California. However, no sophisticated study has shown that the policy changes substantially affected the crime rate changes. American crime rates peaked in 1990–91 in the United States, three to four years before zero-tolerance policing was put into place and California's three-strikes law was enacted, both in 2004. Preexisting downward trends in homicide and robbery rates continued after the initiatives were announced, but neither the timing of the downturns nor the pitches of the slopes were significantly different in California and New York than in other populous states or large cities, respectively. The most exhaustive examinations of the evidence conclude that there is no credible basis for believing that the policy changes substantially influenced declines in crime rates (Harcourt 2001 [New York City]; Zimring, Hawkins, and Kamin 2001 [California]; Tonry 2004, chap. 5 [both]; Harcourt and Ludwig 2006 [New York City]; Taylor 2006 [New York City]).

Sixth, since the early 1980s researchers have been investigating threat communications and perceptions. A sizable literature demonstrates that ordinary citizens are largely uninformed about the operation of the justice system, the content of the criminal law, and the severity of punishments (Roberts et al. 2002). For a hypothesis that a change in practice or policy will affect behavior to be plausible, there must be some basis for believing that the people whose behavior is being targeted will know about the change.[7] A small but growing literature examines whether and how experience with the criminal justice system, or peers' experiences of the justice system, affect perceptions of risk and how those perceptions affect behavior (e.g., Pogarsky, Piquero, and Paternoster 2004; Matsueda, Kreager, and Huizinga 2006; Lochner 2007). A largely psychological literature has investigated what people know and provided additional knowledge and then tried to determine how that knowledge might affect behavior. This literature is afflicted by two common problems of laboratory research: its subjects are usually college students (rather than offenders), and its outcome measure is how subjects say their behavior would be affected rather than how their behavior changes. A related subliterature asks offenders whether in retrospect they would have behaved differently had they known what the penalties would be or if they had known that the penalties would be even greater. Both the main and the narrower literature report that people say they would have altered their behavior (the major works are cited in Pratt et al. [2006]).

Those literatures are not all examined in detail here. There is little point in reprising discussion of the literatures on deterrent effects of mandatory minimum sentence laws, major broad-based policy changes (e.g., zero-tolerance policing, three strikes), possession of weapons for self-defense, or threat perception. These have been exhaustively reviewed before, and no important original research findings have recently been published. Section III briefly discusses the less often reviewed research on capital punishment and concealed weapons. Before that, perhaps surprisingly, Section I discusses Robert Ellickson's *Order without Law* (1991), an examination of the influence of civil law,

[7] And, separately, that they will be influenced by that knowledge. There are two other important issues: whether the change is implemented as announced and whether changes in practice are sustained.

and knowledge about it, on cattlemen's behavior. Ellickson is a law and economics specialist, and his work raises fundamental issues germane to thinking about deterrence and offers arguments that may explain why econometric research based on aggregate data is seldom instructive concerning deterrence. Section II is an overview of the major reviews and meta-analyses of deterrence research. Section IV sets out conclusions and a short agenda for research that might sharpen understanding of the deterrent effects of penalties.

Alex Piquero, who read an earlier draft of this essay, asked why another review of the literatures on deterrence is needed, given that relatively little, if anything, has been learned about deterrent effects since Daniel Nagin reviewed the literature for *Crime and Justice* in 1998. There are three answers. First, the economics literatures on concealed weapons and capital punishment largely postdate Nagin's essay. Second, those literatures make it clear that such studies of sanction effects—aggregate, macro-level studies relying on official crime data—are unlikely ever to yield credible results. Third, however, more promisingly, since 1998, micro-level studies have begun to emerge on how offenders' (and their acquaintances') criminal justice system experiences affect their perceptions of legal threats and their behavior.

It is important to stress, however, that I believe it is a Good Thing that work by economists on the criminal justice system has increased greatly in the past 10 years (see, e.g., Bushway and Reuter, in this volume), even if I'm exceedingly skeptical about the likely value of additional econometric studies of deterrence. Economists' distinctive disciplinary frame and analytical techniques are likely to yield important new insights into a wide range of subjects (e.g., the effects of imprisonment on labor force participation [Bushway, Stoll, and Weiman 2007] and the costs and consequences of imprisonment [Raphael and Stoll, forthcoming]).

I. Order without Law

Ellickson's *Order without Law* (1991) examines compliance with civil laws affecting cattle farmers in rural Shasta County, California. This may not appear to be an obvious place to begin an examination of research on the deterrent effects of criminal penalties. It is a useful place to start, however, for two reasons. First, both Ellickson's discussions of how cattle farmers deal with recurring potential civil law problems and a five-level model he develops for understanding what kinds of knowledge and other considerations influence their behavior are apposite to thinking about how criminal laws and punishments influence behavior. Second, the book is in some ways a report on an economist's (more specifically, a law and economics specialist's) gradual realization that economic models sometimes grossly oversimplify how humans make choices. This may be part of the explanation for why some of the economists whose work is discussed in Section III (capital punishment and concealed weapons) so often get things so badly wrong.

A. How Cattle Farmers Deal with Legal Problems

Ellickson's discovery was that cattle farmers in Shasta County had little knowledge of the law, confidently believed things to be true about the law that were false, and resolved almost all their conflicts without consulting the law or lawyers. In addition, local officials, police, and insurance adjustors also often were unaware of relevant laws and shared the farmers' views on dispute settlement. This surprised Ellickson as a scholar of law and economics because that school of thought presupposes that people order their affairs on the basis of calculations of self-interest in relation to the strengths of their legal positions.

Shasta County is a rural area in Northern California that, important for Ellickson's interests, had "open" and "closed ranges" in the early 1980s when he carried out his field work. In open ranges, usually on land owned by the American federal government or timber companies and leased to the cattlemen, cattle are allowed to wander at will. In closed ranges, cattle must be confined within fences. What happens when cattle damage another farmer's crops illustrates the difference. In open range, the crop grower must bear the loss unless his crops were fenced in. In closed range, the cattle farmer is liable. Put differently, in open range, a grower must build fences to keep the cattle out. In closed range, a cattle farmer must build fences to keep his cattle in.

Ellickson examined three kinds of disputes: damage to crops by wandering cattle; obligations to repair, or contribute to repair, fences along joint boundary lines; and auto accidents involving cattle. An old and elaborate body of California law governs damages by different kinds of animals under different kinds of circumstances (negligently roaming versus purposely roaming animals; cattle and horses versus goats and swine; circumstances in which owners are liable without fault versus circumstances in which they are liable only if negligent or reckless), but farmers never resorted to legal proceedings or invoked legal remedies to sort out these cases. Instead they resolved things by agreement, by self-help, and by threatening or seeking informal community disapproval of the cattle's owner. Often, though, they did nothing at all, knowing that other minor disputes and differences would inevitably later arise and that both parties would realize that the responsible party had some reciprocating to do. The farmers believed, and acted on the belief, that their obligations for damage by animals depended in large part on whether they were kept in open or closed range. Sometimes as a strictly legal matter they were right about that and sometimes they were wrong, but that did not make any difference to how the disputes were resolved.

California statutes provided detailed and precise rules on responsibility for fence building and maintenance. Shasta County farmers were mostly unaware of these laws but instead observed well-established conventions that largely but not entirely paralleled the statutory provisions. They were mostly based on "community welfare" norms rather than stakeholders' immediate self-interest. This apparently surprised Ellickson, as a law and economics scholar, since individuals operating outside systems of legal control are expected primarily to engage in self-interested competition.

Automobile accidents raised more complicated issues. Cattle farmers believed that the farmer should and would win in collisions with cattle in open range, but that the driver should and would win in collisions in closed range. Because of this, many open-range farmers did not insure themselves adequately or at all for liability for accidents in which their cattle were involved. California law made no such distinction. As a legal matter, the question in either kind of case was who if anyone is negligent, and how much of the responsibility for the accident is attributable to that negligence?[8] In practice, Shasta County farmers and residents dealt with accidents informally, between themselves, usually observing the (legally nonexistent) open- and closed-range distinction. They never resorted to courts or lawyers. The only court cases involved plaintiffs who were not locals.

What Ellickson learned was that the farmers often did not know or

[8] California is a "comparative negligence state," which means that responsibility for the loss and for making it good is apportioned on the basis of relative fault. In other U.S. states, "contributory negligence" by a plaintiff bars any recovery.

much care what the law was concerning matters of interest to themselves, preferred to and tended to resolve disputes informally, and observed social norms that could be described as based on community welfare premises.

B. How Economists Understand Legal Problems

As his work progressed, Ellickson felt obliged to read works by law and society specialists, who attempt to understand legal problems in their social contexts and who explore implications of social structures, functions, and norms for understanding institutions and practices. In the end, he concluded that "I must confess my suspicion that law-and-society scholars, because they better understand the importance of informal social controls, would better be able than the law-and-economics scholars to predict the essentials of what was found in Shasta County" (Ellickson 1991, p. 8).

Ellickson explains that most law and economics scholars adopt a view of Ronald Coase (1960), one of the movement's founders, that "the state functions as the sole creator of operative rules of entitlement" (p. 4) and that many economists "rarely shrink from applying in every context the model of rational, self-interested, human behavior that they borrow from economics proper" (p. 7). Elsewhere, concerning deterrent effects, Coase wrote, "Punishment, for example, can be regarded as the price of crime. *An economist will not debate whether increased punishment will reduce crime;* he will merely try to answer the question, by how much?" (1978, p. 210; emphasis added). This may explain why economists, especially politically conservative ones, tend to conclude that increased penalties must in the nature of things have marginal deterrent effects and that capital punishment must deter homicide better than other penalties do.

John Donohue, one of the handful of widely respected senior American economists specializing in studies of the criminal justice system, observes that deterrence studies may implicitly challenge fundamental economic presuppositions. In responding to an article by Gary Becker, the "founder" of modern economic studies of the criminal law and punishment (Becker 1968), and judge Richard Posner, law and economics' most famous expositor, Donohue observes that Becker analogizes punishment analyses to price theory: "Becker suggests that price theory can fill in where empirical evidence is lacking: capital punishment is akin to a rise in the price of murder and hence might be expected to lessen the number of murders" (2006, p. 4). He asks whether many economists' vigorous defense of traditional economic models of choice in relation to criminals' behavioral choices is in effect a defense of price theory itself.

C. Conceptual Models of Punishment Effects

Ellickson described a world that is more complicated than many economists assume it to be, one in which community welfare norms sometimes trump self-interest, and in which legal threats only occasionally influence behavior. He developed a five-level model of social control (Ellickson 1991, p. 131):

1. First party controls (self-control)
2. Second party controls (other persons in direct contractual relations)
3. Social controls (informal social controls through norms)
4. Organizational controls (enforcement of organizational rules)
5. Governmental (legal) controls (state enforcement through law).

This model is important for law and economics specialists because it makes clear that the fifth level, usually their focus, is but a small part of the story.[9] That would surprise few social scientists. Durkheim ([1893] 1933), for example, argued that the criminal law's direct effects (levels 4 and 5) through deterrence are modest at best and not especially important; their indirect effects through their interactions with social norms (level 3) and social norms' effects on private behavior (levels 1 and 2) are what matters.

Ellickson's model is also relevant, in a loose way, for thinking about deterrence of criminal behavior by means of legal threats. Whether individuals do or do not engage in criminal behavior is determined by a mixture of personal, situational, social, and organizational factors in addition to the criminal law's legal threats.

Many sociological and psychological models of criminality resemble Ellickson's but are considerably more complex as they attempt to iden-

[9] The fourth level, organizational behavior and controls, which economists studying punishment generally ignore, is where laws are and are not applied. Typical studies of deterrent effects of increased penalties nearly always treat statutory changes as the indicators of changes in sanction threats, without attending to the questions whether officials have the capacity or the will to implement the increased threats. As the literature on mandatory minimum sentence laws demonstrates (Tonry 1996, chap. 5), one or both are typically lacking.

tify and measure the myriad personal, social, situational, and environmental factors associated with criminal behavior. A recent meta-analysis by Pratt et al. (2006) attempts to measure the much more nuanced deterrence effects that such research investigates.

Wikström's (2007) theoretical overview of deterrence tries to explore interactions between moral socialization and legal threats. He concludes that

> law abidance is largely a question of an individual's *moral education* (of which their deterrence experiences are a part) through which they have developed moral rules and moral habits that preclude them from engaging in crime. I have also argued that individuals breach the law either out of *habit*, or by making a *deliberate choice*, and that only in the latter case is there a question of whether or not *deterrence* may influence their choice to abide by or breach the law. I have also maintained that *rationality* and an individual's *capability to exercise self-control* come into play as factors only when an individual deliberates over action alternatives . . . . Crime is fundamentally a question of morality and moral habits. (2007, ms. p. 37; emphasis. in original)

Ellickson's book, though it is not about criminal law, punishment, or deterrence, nonetheless provides a platform for considering those subjects. Shasta County farmers have little knowledge of the law relevant to the disputes they most commonly encounter. Their disputes are resolved primarily through interactions in Ellickson's first three levels (personal morality, contractual relationships, and local social norms). There is little reason to suppose that most would-be offenders most of the time operate in Ellickson's fifth level.

II. Reviews of Deterrence Research

Knowledge of the deterrent effects of criminal punishments is little different in 2007 than it was in 1978 when the U.S. National Academy of Sciences Panel on Deterrence and Incapacitation issued its report (Blumstein, Cohen, and Nagin 1978). A substantial body of work has since accumulated, some of it on new subjects, but the main substantive conclusions to be drawn have changed little.

The panel was convened to evaluate the evidence underlying Isaac Ehrlich's claim that each execution in the United States prevented eight murders through its deterrent effects (Ehrlich 1975). More generally, it assessed research on deterrence and incapacitation that had accumulated in the aftermath of publication of Gary Becker's influential early article "Crime and Punishment: An Economic Approach" (Becker 1968). There were three principal conclusions on deterrence:

1. Taken as a whole, the criminal justice system has a general deterrent effect.
2. No conclusions can be reached on whether capital punishment deters homicides.
3. Though the evidence is unclear, it is likely that marginal changes in punishments have marginal deterrent effects.

Were a similar panel convened today, it would discuss additional subjects, notably research on threat perception, natural experiments, and the deterrent effects of concealed weapons laws. It would, however, affirm two of the 1978 conclusions: the overall system deters and no evidence-based conclusions can be reached about capital punishment. On the third question—marginal deterrence—it would discuss stronger support for the existence of marginal deterrent effects for some crimes under some circumstances but conclude, as a practical matter, that few policy changes can reasonably be expected to achieve those effects. On the fourth substantive question—whether allowing private citizens to carry concealed firearms in public places reduces crime—the panel would decide that no conclusion can be reached (as an NAS panel convened partly to address that question did conclude [Wellford, Pepper, and Petrie 2005]).

The critical question for policy makers is whether marginal increases in penalties can reasonably be expected to reduce the incidence of crime. Outside the United States, for example, in other English-speaking countries or in most European countries, the other three questions have little policy relevance. Death penalty statutes and laws allowing citizens to carry concealed firearms in public are not in the offing. No one seriously doubts that the system as a whole has some deterrent effects, compared with a hypothetical situation in which there were no criminal penalties; but in any case, no real-world policy makers would consider doing away with criminal penalties.

A considerable number of exhaustive reviews of deterrence research have been commissioned and published since the NAS panel issued its report in 1978. Most have reached pretty much the same conclusions. The Home Office of England and Wales commissioned a multiyear review of the evidence (von Hirsch et al. 1999). Three widely cited and influential reviews have been published in *Crime and Justice* (Cook 1980; Nagin 1998; Doob and Webster 2003), and other reviews have been published elsewhere (e.g., Pratt et al. 2006) or soon will be (e.g., Bushway, forthcoming). Three reviews by economists (Lewis 1986; Levitt 2002; Levitt and Miles 2007), to the contrary, concluded that increased penalties produce lower crime rates through deterrence; these reviews draw almost entirely on analyses by economists, and neither cite nor discuss the larger deterrence literature produced by noneconomists.[10] The most recent major review, a meta-analysis by Pratt et al. (2006), examines a wide range of multivariate studies in sociology, psychology, and criminology that test deterrence effects (broadly defined, to include certainty and severity of punishments, effects of different kinds of punishments, and effects of nonlegal social and shaming consequences of crime).

As a practical matter of criminal justice policy, the critical question is whether marginal changes in sanctions have measurable deterrent effects. The major broad-based reviews reach similar conclusions that no credible evidence demonstrates that increasing penalties reliably achieves marginal deterrent effects.

In 1980, Cook concluded that existing studies showed that "there exist feasible actions on the part of the criminal justice system that may be effective in deterring [certain] crimes . . . . [But the] studies do *not* demonstrate that all types of crimes are potentially deterrable, and certainly they provide little help in predicting the effects of any specific governmental action" (1980, p. 215; emphasis in original).

In 1998, Nagin observed that he "was convinced that a number of studies have credibly demonstrated marginal deterrent effects," but concluded that it was "difficult to generalize from the findings of a specific study because knowledge about the factors that affect the efficacy of policy is so limited" (1998, p. 4). He highlighted four major factors: the relation between short- and long-term effects, the relation between risk perceptions and sanctions policies, the methods of implementation, and the extent of implementation.

Von Hirsch et al. conclude that "there is as yet no firm evidence regarding the extent to which raising the severity of punishment would enhance deterrence of crime" (1999, p. 52).

[10] The reviews by social scientists, to the contrary, almost always discuss the economics literature. I comment on this curious pattern in the conclusion.

Doob and Webster, adopting the null hypothesis approach, noted in 2003 some inconclusive or weak evidence of marginal deterrence but concluded that "there is no plausible body of evidence that supports policies based on this premise [that increased penalties reduce crime]. On the contrary, standard social scientific norms governing the acceptance of the null hypothesis justify the present (always rebuttable) conclusion that sentence severity does not affect levels of crime" (2003, p. 146).

The three works by economists, summarizing work principally by economists, find that increases in punishment achieve marginal deterrent effects. Lewis describes "a substantial body of evidence which is largely consistent with the existence of a deterrent effect from longer sentences" (1986, p. 60). Levitt, relying principally on data from two of his own analyses, describes them as evidence "for a deterrent effect of increases in expected punishment" (2002, p. 445). Levitt and Miles conclude that "the new empirical evidence [produced by economists] generally supports the deterrence model. . . . Evidence of the crime-reducing effects of the scale of policing and incarceration is consistent across different methodological approaches" (2007, p. 456).

The Levitt and Miles (2007) review is the most recent. In discussion of research on shall-issue laws and deterrent effects of capital punishment above, I have, using quotations from this article, indicated the authors' skepticism about deterrent claims based on those literatures. In addition, they discuss evidence on the effects of increasing police numbers; they conclude that increased numbers are associated with declines in crime rates but are unable to conclude whether this is for deterrent (more visible policing provides disincentives to offending) or incapacitative reasons (more high-rate offenders are apprehended and incarcerated (pp. 468–70).

Relatively little attention is paid to the marginal deterrence hypothesis. Most of the discussion of sanctions other than the death penalty (pp. 470–74) considers whether increases in the scale of imprisonment have reduced crime rates and, concluding that it has, to what degree that effect has been achieved through deterrence and to what degree through incapacitation. Levitt (1996) himself conducted one such study in which, using aggregate state-level police arrest data, he attempted to learn whether states in which courts ordered prisons to reduce their populations experienced higher crime rate increases than states that were not subject to such orders (he concluded that each released prisoner produces an additional 15 crimes annually). Marvell and Moody (1994) looked at the effects of increased imprisonment rates on crime rates and concluded that increased imprisonment yielded lower crime rates though the estimates were considerably lower than Levitt's. A major difficulty with aggregate research of this kind is that it does not address the marginal deterrence hypothesis, and thus provides no guidance to policy makers wondering whether increased incarceration of bicycle thieves or street robbers will reduce bicycle theft or robbery. A second difficulty is that it provides no insight into whether asserted crime rate reduction effects result from incapacitation or deterrence.

One article by Kessler and Levitt (1999) gets closer to testing the marginal deterrence hypothesis. It attempts to identify reductions in crime rates resulting from the passage in 1982 of California's Proposition 8 (which provided sentence enhancements for designated crimes) and, concluding that there was a crime reduction effect, to disentangle its deterrent and incapacitative elements. However, as Webster, Doob, and Zimring (2006) demonstrate, Kessler and Levitt fell prey to a classic mistake: by examining data at 2-year intervals, the analysis missed a longer-term downward trend in crime rates for all five crimes examined (homicide, rape, robbery, aggravated assault with a firearm, and residential burglary), which adequately explained the reduction in crime rates. For four of the five offenses, crime rates peaked 2 years before passage of the referendum and continued afterward, making the continuing decline as likely to be the continuation of preexisting trends as the result of the policy change.[11]

The meta-analysis by Pratt et al., by contrast citing no economists, produced a main finding, one "noted by previous narrative reviews of the deterrence literature," that "the effects of severity estimates and deterrence/sanctions composites, even when statistically significant, are too weak to be of substantive significance (consistently below −.1)" (2006, p. 379).

[11] This is a common pattern. California crime rates began to fall 3 years before its three-strikes law was enacted, providing a rich opportunity to politicians to compare rates the year before the new law was enacted with rates afterward and to claim that the law caused the decline (Zimring, Hawkins, and Kamin 2001). In the 1970s, the initial evaluations of California's Uniform Determinate Sentencing Law (1976) concluded that compared with the year before enactment the law produced higher prison commitment rates and reduced sentence lengths. Subsequent evaluations that looked at longer time series showed that both patterns began several years before the law was enacted, making the subsequent patterns merely the continuation of preexisting trends (Blumstein et al. 1983, chap. 4).

That article, however, potentially illuminates a useful role deterrence theory might play in understanding individual, social, and structural influences on behavior. That would be to integrate deterrence ideas and theories into much more nuanced accounts of human behavior that allow for the contingent influences on behavior of individual, social, and structural conditions; variations in threat perceptions; and variations in the nature and degree of implementation of crime prevention strategies. They note, for example, four major theoretical developments that have influenced much recent research on deterrence by social scientists. First, routine activities theories and their policy progeny, situational crime prevention programs, assume predisposed offenders and seek to prevent crime through manipulation of material opportunity structures. Second, a considerable body of research in the past 15 years has emphasized the importance of risk perceptions of the social costs (e.g., shame, loss of others' respect) associated with punishment. Third, a variety of efforts have been made to embed deterrence analyses in other theoretical frames such as self-control and experiential learning (through one's own and others' experiences) theories. Fourth, punishment interaction theories stress the important influences on individuals' threat perceptions of their own experiences with the justice system (that experience might enhance or reduce the effects of perceived legal threats). Analyses of these kinds are much more in keeping with the analyses by Ellickson (1991) and Wikström (2007) that were discussed above than they are with traditional analyses by economists that attempt to relate changes in behavior directly to changes in sanctions while ignoring all the intervening stages and processes. Levitt and Miles acknowledge, by contrast, that "the economic model of crime differs from the major branches of criminology in that it abstracts from the social processes and psychological aspects of offending and emphasizes individual choices. A cost of the economic approach is thus a loss of the social context of offending" (2007, p. 462).

I mention these developments because they point to the need for much more precise delineation of deterrence questions than to ask globally whether changes in sanctions lead to changes in criminal behavior. Whether people engage in particular actions in particular places at particular times depends on their circumstances, characteristics, and predispositions; the criminal opportunities and precipitants they face; and the perceived consequences to themselves and others. The emerging literature that focuses on and attempts to measure the effects of events (e.g., arrests) that might alter perceptions is illustrative (Matsueda, Kreager, and Huizinga 2006; Lochner 2007).

III. Economists on Concealed Weapons and Capital Punishment

Two new deterrence literatures emerged in economics beginning in the mid-1990s. One, associated with economist John Lott, examined the effects of states' enactment of shall-issue laws that required state officials to issue permits allowing citizens to carry concealed firearms in public. Although state laws varied in detail, the only circumstances in which permits could generally be denied involved criminal convictions for designated crimes and certain diagnosed mental conditions. The other literature investigated the effects on homicide rates of states' enactment of death penalty laws in the aftermath of the U.S. Supreme Court's decision in *Gregg v. Georgia*, 428 U.S. 153 (1976), upholding capital punishment laws meeting specified conditions.

Both literatures followed trajectories resembling that of Ehrlich's (1975) finding that each execution would prevent eight murders. Each attracted substantial attention, influenced policy making in important ways, or was invoked by policy makers to justify their support for new penalty laws, and was subsequently shown by other scholars to be unsound. In Lott's case the repudiation included allegations of "manufacturing data" (Donohue 2004, p. 623).[12]

Both literatures are based on econometric models using Uniform Crime Reports data on state and county arrest rates for serious offenses. They typically use time-series data to compare arrest rate trends for states enacting the laws hypothesized to have deterrent effects before and after the legal change and to compare arrest rate trends in those states with trends in states not enacting such laws. Both literatures are confounded by America's declining crime rates for 20 of the 25 years between 1981 and 2005 (declines in every year except the period 1986–91). In principle that should have been relatively easily soluble, but in practice it was not. The models in both literatures were highly sensitive to specification problems, with effects disappearing or

[12] The editor of *Science* (Kennedy 2003) suggested that a committee of scholars be appointed to investigate Lott's behavior.

signs reversing with inclusion or exclusion of particular states and years.

A. Concealed Weapons

Lott and Mustard's (1997) original analysis used annual cross-sectional time-series county-level arrest data for all 3,054 counties in the United States for the years 1977–92.[13] Concealed weapons laws were in effect in eight states in 1977, and 10 other states enacted them between 1977 and 1992.

The findings were strong:

1. "When state concealed handgun laws went into effect in a county, murders fell by 7.65 percent, and rapes and aggravated assaults by 5 and 7 percent" (Lott and Mustard 1997, p. 19).
2. "If the rest of the country had adopted right-to-carry concealed handgun provisions in 1992, at least 1,414 murders and over 4,177 rapes would have been avoided" (Lott and Mustard 1997, p. 64).
3. "The annual declines in crime from right-to-carry laws are greater for murder (2.2 percent), rape (3.9 percent), and robbery rates (4.9 percent), while the impact on aggravated assaults (0.8 percent) and the property crime rates (0.9 percent) is smaller" (Lott 2000, p. 172).
4. "For each additional year that the laws are in effect, murders fell by an additional 1.5 percent, while rape, robbery, and aggravated assaults all fell by about 3 percent each year" (Lott 2000, p. 170).

The most exhaustive surveys by economists of research on the deterrent effects of enactment of concealed weapons laws conclude that Lott's analyses are unpersuasive (Ayres and Donohue 2003*a*, 2003*b*; Cook and Ludwig 2003; Donohue 2004). Cook and Ludwig conclude that "the best empirical evidence does not support" Lott's conclusions (2003, p. 595). Ayres and Donohue, having tested more than 700 alternate regressions, concluded that there is "no credible statistical evidence that the adoption of concealed-carry (or 'shall issue') laws reduced crime" (2003*a*, p. 1372). The leading reanalysis of Lott's data by quantitatively sophisticated noneconomists reached the same conclusion (Black and Nagin 1998).

[13] The first edition of Lott (1998) updated the data through 1994; the second (2000), through 1996.

Levitt and Miles (2007) review the literature on shall-issue laws and express skepticism. They note that other analyses, including one that Levitt coauthored (Donohue and Levitt 2001), identify a long series of problems that "raised questions" about the validity of the concealed-weapons hypothesis.[14]

B. Capital Punishment

The disjuncture between conservative economists and everyone else concerning the deterrent effects of capital punishment parallels that concerning carrying concealed firearms. The most cited recent econometric 50-state analysis (partly using Lott's data) concluded that each execution saves 18 lives (Dezhbakhsh, Rubin, and Shepherd 2003). The most exhaustive critique of this literature by economists, which tested the robustness of existing studies to alternative sample periods, comparison groups, control variables, functional forms, and estimators, concluded that "our key insight is that the death penalty—at least as it has been implemented in the United States since *Gregg* ended the moratorium on executions—is applied so rarely that the number of homicides it can plausibly have caused or deterred cannot be reliably disentangled from the large year-to-year changes in the homicide rate caused by other factors" (Donohue and Wolfers 2005, p. 794). An exhaustive critique of the recent economic literature by quantitatively sophisticated noneconomists reached the same conclusion (Fagin, Zimring, and Geller 2006). Levitt and Miles concurred. After discussing a long list of critiques of recent death penalty research, they observed that "a large deterrent effect is surprising given the relatively abstemious application of the death penalty. . . . Individuals who regularly participate in criminal activities with such hazards [high death rates among street gang members and narcotics traffickers] are unlikely to be influenced by the relatively low risk of capital punishment" (2007, p. 476).

[14] These concluded that estimates "lack statistical significance when the assumption of the statistical independence of counties within the same state is relaxed"; that "passage of a concealed weapons law did not correlate with a proxy for the rate of gun ownership"; and that "after controlling for abortion rates, the laws did not correlate with crime rates." They also observed that "further tests of the behavioural implications of the concealed-weapons hypothesis have also raised questions about its validity" (Levitt and Miles 2007, p. 477).

IV. Whither Deterrence Research?

Three overriding themes emerge. First, economic and econometric studies of deterrence effects using aggregate data are unlikely to shed useful insights into the deterrent effects of punishment. They are conducted at the wrong level of analysis and are incapable of taking into account vagaries in implementation of sentencing laws, situational and circumstantial influences on offender decision making, or offenders' perceptions of risk. Second, advances in understanding of offender decision making are likely instead to emerge from work that takes account of offender characteristics (e.g., values, self-control), offender interactions with other people, and informal social control in organizational and legal contexts. Third, closer and richer studies of implementation of sentencing laws and punishment practices may increase understanding of cultural acceptance of punishment options and hence of socially optimal levels and kinds of punishment.

A recent publication of the National Bureau of Economic Research provides another reason to be skeptical of the findings of the economics and econometrics literatures on deterrence. It is understandably difficult for scholars to know much about legal systems other than their own. American economists generally analyze only American data and only data for recent decades. As Dills, Miron, and Summers (2008) demonstrate, when analyses are extended to incorporate data from other countries or are extended within the United States to cover longer periods, few of the findings of recent economic research on crime and punishment appear to be substantiated.

Only nuanced behavioral and social science analyses of the types exemplified by Ellickson (1991) and Wikström (2007) and included in the meta-analysis of Pratt et al. (2006) are likely to add significantly to current understanding of the influence of changes in law enforcement practices and sentencing policies on criminal behavior. The policy implications of such knowledge as emerges will lie primarily at the lowest three levels (self-control, second-party influences, and social control) of Ellickson's five-level model. The implications of new knowledge are unlikely to have much relevance to development of policy at governmental (legal) or criminal justice operational (organizational) levels. New knowledge may have implications at organizational levels for non–criminal justice agencies involved in formulation and implementation of public health, educational, and social welfare policies.

It is unclear to me which is more surprising: that so little credible evidence exists that criminal behavior is much affected by changes in punishment policies or that policy makers continue to believe that policy changes significantly affect behavior and that research continues to test for their crime-preventive effects. Although I have observed in this essay that understanding of deterrent effects has changed little over the past 30 years, it can also be said that understanding has changed little over the past two centuries.

Two images from eighteenth-century England when the number of offenses punishable by death greatly increased make the point: pickpockets actively at work among the crowds assembled for the executions of pickpockets (Teeters 1967); and English juries regularly nullifying the criminal law by refusing to convict obviously guilty defendants of crimes punishable by death (Hay et al. 1975). The literature on mandatory penalties mentioned in the introduction reaches similar findings: prospective penalties are seldom determinative of what would-be offenders do, and officials regularly alter their practices in order to circumvent application of penalties they consider too severe (e.g., Tonry [1996, chap. 5] presents lots of examples).

There are good reasons why little research focused primarily on the deterrent effects of changes in laws setting or changing authorized or mandated criminal punishments has recently been carried out. The research findings are so robust and so long-standing that most specialists believe we now know most of what we are likely ever to know about the deterrent effects of sanction changes. Implementation effects may be another matter. Research on local legal cultures and courtroom workgroups as organizations may shed more nuanced insights into how practitioners adjust their operations and policies to react to new or altered sanctioning policies.

Only economists seem to conclude regularly that research will demonstrate that penalty changes in general significantly affect crime patterns and rates or that capital punishment in particular is a more effective deterrent than other punishments that might be imposed. For example, Joanna Shepherd, an author of several studies finding a deterrent effect, in 2004 testified before the U.S. Congress that there was a "strong consensus among economists that capital punishment deters crime" and that "the studies are unanimous" (U.S. House 2004, pp. 10–11). Setting aside the problem that it is true neither that the studies are unanimous nor that there is a consensus among economists, why might Shepherd believe her statements to be true? There are a number of possible explanations.

Economists writing about deterrence do not seem much to read work by noneconomists on the same subject. The surveys by economists of knowledge about deterrence seldom discuss work by noneconomists (Lewis 1986; Levitt 2002; Levitt and Miles 2007). This might be seen as the result of disciplinary insularity or of disciplinary hubris; but whatever the explanation, among the consequences are apparent lack of understanding of fundamental problems with the sources of aggregate national data that are analyzed and lack of knowledge of processes of implementation and of offender ratiocination and motivation.

As works cited above by Gary Becker (1968), Ronald Coase (1978), and Isaac Ehrlich (1996), all quoted earlier in this essay, make clear, many economists assume something to be true that social scientists regard as merely a hypothesis: that offenders' choices to commit particular crimes are the products of rational calculation of the likely economic gains of particular crimes offset by the likely risks of punishment compared with likely net economic gains of available lawful employment. Other social scientists' models of offender (and nonoffender) decision making are considerably more complex and contingent.

Ronald Coase, in an essay discussing economists' incursions into substantive realms more commonly inhabited by other kinds of social scientists, and their retreats, may have explained why many economists' work on deterrence at macro levels has the characteristics it has. He makes two relevant arguments. The first is that economists' contributions will depend on whether their comparative advantage is in technique, theory, or substance. Theory he sees as derivative primarily from substance, and technique is not enough: "to the extent that [economists'] movement [into a substantive area] is based on technique or approach, we can expect a gradual displacement of economists from their newly-won ground" (Coase 1978, p. 205).[15]

The second is that "the great advantage that economics has possessed is that economists are able to use the 'measuring rod of money,'" which gives precision to their analyses (Coase 1978, p. 209). Since money is an important determinant of human economic behavior, the resulting analyses have plausible explanatory power. "It by no means

[15] See the quotation from this article in n. 1.

follows [however] that an approach developed to explain behaviour in the economic system will be equally successful in the other social sciences. In these different fields, the purposes which men seek to achieve will not be the same, the degree of consistency of behaviour need not be the same and, in particular, the institutional framework within which the choices are made are quite different. . . . [Understanding all this] will require specialized knowledge not likely to be acquired by those who work in some other discipline" (p. 208).

Coase's two points may explain why, after the flurry of work by economists on capital punishment in the 1970s, little was published until the 1990s. Ehrlich's work could not withstand close scrutiny by people possessed of comparable technical skills but vastly greater substantive knowledge (Blumstein, Cohen, and Nagin 1978). The work by economists since the mid-1990s on capital punishment and shall-issue laws has also followed the trajectory Coase predicted.

Finally, some or much of the work on deterrence by economists may be conscious or unconscious products of ideological, as opposed to merely disciplinary, ways of thinking. Dan M. Kahan (1999) offered an informative analysis of deterrence arguments in which he suggests that they are generally normative arguments in disguise. Americans hold widely divergent intuitions about the purposes of punishment, including whether for moral reasons killers should be killed. Disagreements based on deeply held moral intuition are seldom resolvable by resort to argument. Kahan suggests that seemingly technical and empirical arguments about deterrence are really camouflaged normative arguments: "The rhetoric of deterrence displaces an alternative expressive idiom . . . . Ultimately the deterrence idiom takes the political charge out of contentious issues and deflects expressive contention away from the criminal law" (1999, pp. 416–17). Put differently, many people who believe that capital punishment is morally permissible and in some cases is morally required—who believe that the state should kill people—are often uncomfortable saying that explicitly. Invocation of empirical evidence that capital punishment deters homicides provides a more comfortable rationale for laws they support for other reasons. The same analysis applies to shall-issue laws. Many of their proponents are Second Amendment ideologues. Lott's research provides an empirical fig leaf to cover what is often an ideological commitment.

Many of the economists who have written on the deterrent effects of punishments are well-known political conservatives—Gary Becker,

Richard Posner, Isaac Ehrlich, John Lott—and others such as Joanna Shepherd are less well-known conservatives. It is merely human to be deeply attached to one's intuitions. Robert Nozick (1981, pp. 2–3), writing of philosophers, observed, "When a philosopher sees that premisses he accepts logically imply a conclusion he has rejected until now, he has a choice: he may accept this conclusion or reject one of the previously accepted premisses . . . . His choice will depend upon which is greater, the degree of his commitment to the various premisses, or the degree of his commitment to denying the conclusion. It is implausible that these are independent of how strongly he wants certain things to be true." So it may be with economists. John Donohue (2006) argued that his fellow economists are committed to price theory and a model of rational self-interested behavior, and this may make it exceedingly difficult to accept that price theory is less apposite to many forms of offending than it is to some other forms of human behavior.

This review of the deterrence literature supports three main conclusions concerning future research. First, good research designs for measuring the marginal deterrent effects of sanctioning changes on would-be offenders' behavior must be much more fine-grained in the questions they attempt to answer and in the ways they try to answer them. Models or designs aimed at investigating effects of changes in laws and policies or organizational practices (Ellickson's top two levels), but that do not take account of social norms, personal obligations, social contexts, and offenders' characteristics (his bottom three levels), will not teach us very much.

There are some realms in which enforcement strategies and sanctioning changes affect behavior and in which research on the effects of legal threats may usefully influence policy. Examples include tax compliance and evasion, illegal parking, and speeding. No doubt there are others. In the Netherlands, for example, where there are more bicycles than people, policy makers may need to develop effective ways to respond to increases in bicycle theft. Or in any country, increased levels of theft or robbery of new electronic gadgets create policy needs for new preventive approaches. Often the best responses will be technological and situational, as, for example, when development of thief-resistant automobile locks led to reduced auto theft rates in many countries, but sometimes they may include changes in police practice or sanctions policies. Well-designed micro-level studies that take account of implementation patterns, offense circumstances, and offenders' perceptions may well be able to provide important policy guidance (Tonry 2008).

Second, following Doob and Webster (2003), research on the deterrent effects of sanctions and sanctions changes, especially by economists, should test the null hypothesis that sanctions changes have no effects on offenders' behavior. Isaac Ehrlich, by contrast, has observed that the

> "market model" . . . builds on the assumption that offenders, as members of the human race, respond to incentives. . . . This has been the justification for applying economic analysis to all illegal activities, from speeding and tax evasion to murder. Indeed, the distinguishing feature of the major contributions by economists has been the attempt to explain the various aspects of crime through the tools of organization and equilibrium analysis, rather than by reliance on deterministic social and environmental factors that are independent of the human will. *At least in the economic literature*, there has been little controversy concerning this approach. (1996, pp. 43–44; emphasis added)

There has, however, been substantial controversy among noneconomists about that approach. No one argues that (sane) offenders lack rationality, but many people do argue that credible research must take account of offenders' personal values and norms, of their knowledge of sanctions and sanctions changes, of the considerations and circumstances that shape offenders' choices, and of the nature and extent of implementation of legal or policy changes. So far none of the major economic literatures on the effects of sanctioning changes has withstood scrutiny by social scientists or by other economists.

Third, considerably more money and energy should be invested in studies of the implementation of legal changes intended to alter patterns of criminal punishment. A research finding that a change in sanctions policies had no significant effects on offending should come as no surprise if an implementation study showed that the change had no effects on sanctions imposed. Put another way, implementation studies examine a new policy's effects on officials' behavior. Sometimes new policies have little effect because they overload organizational systems or have resource implications that cannot be managed. Other times they have little effect because they call for dispositions that officials believe to be unjust or inappropriate and as a result do not impose.

Not so long ago, researchers developing decision tools for judges and parole boards viewed official noncompliance with punishment guidelines as indication that the guidelines were out of step with prevailing notions of justice, and thus as a sign that the guidelines themselves needed changing (Gottfredson, Wilkins, and Hoffman 1978). So it may be with many of the punishment innovations of the past 30 years. We may learn more from studies on the effects of changes in punishment laws and practices if we more often investigate why they do not operate as intended rather than whether they do.

REFERENCES

Ayres, Ian, and John J. Donohue. 2003*a*. "The Latest Misfires in Support of the 'More Guns, Less Crime' Hypothesis." *Stanford Law Review* 55:1371–98.

———. 2003*b*. "Shooting Down the 'More Guns, Less Crime' Hypothesis." *Stanford Law Review* 55:1193–1312.

Bachman, Ronet, Sally Ward, and Raymond Paternoster. 1992. "The Rationality of Sexual Offending: Testing a Deterrence/Rational Choice Conception of Sexual Assault." *Law and Society Review* 26:343–72.

Becker, Gary. 1968. "Crime and Punishment: An Economic Approach." *Journal of Political Economy* 76:169–217.

Black, D. A., and D. Nagin. 1998. "Do Right-to-Carry Laws Deter Violent Crime?" *Journal of Legal Studies* 27:209–19.

Blumstein, Alfred, Jacqueline Cohen, Susan Martin, and Michael Tonry, eds. 1983. *Sentencing Research: The Search for Reform*. Washington, DC: National Academy Press.

Blumstein, Alfred, Jacqueline Cohen, and Daniel Nagin, eds. 1978. *Deterrence and Incapacitation: Estimating the Effects of Criminal Sanctions on Crime Rates.* Washington, DC: National Academy of Sciences.

Bushway, Shawn. Forthcoming. "They All Come Back: Do They Commit More Crime than If They Never Left?" In *The Costs and Consequences of U.S. Incarceration Policy*, edited by Steven Raphael and Michael Stoll. New York: Russell Sage Foundation.

Bushway, Shawn, and Peter Reuter. In this volume. "Economists' Contribution to the Study of Crime and the Criminal Justice System."

Bushway, Shawn, Michael Stoll, and David Weiman, eds. 2007. *Barriers to Reentry? The Labor Market for Released Prisoners in Post-industrial America.* New York: Russell Sage Foundation.

Coase, Ronald. 1960. "The Problem of Social Cost." *Journal of Law and Economics* 3:1–44.

———. 1978. "Economics and Contiguous Disciplines." *Journal of Legal Studies* 7:201–11.

Cook, Philip J. 1980. "Research in Criminal Deterrence: Laying the Groundwork for the Second Decade." In *Crime and Justice: An Annual Review of Research*, vol. 2, edited by Norval Morris and Michael Tonry. Chicago: University of Chicago Press.

———. 1991. "The Technology of Personal Violence." In *Crime and Justice: A Review of Research*, vol. 14, edited by Michael Tonry. Chicago: University of Chicago Press.

Cook, Philip J., and Jens Ludwig. 2003. "Principles for Effective Gun Policy." *Fordham Law Review* 73:589–613.

Dezhbakhsh, Hashem, Paul H. Rubin, and Joanna M. Shepherd. 2003. "Does Capital Punishment Have a Deterrent Effect? New Evidence from Postmoratorium Panel Data." *American Law and Economics Review* 5:344–76.

Dills, Angela K., Jeffrey A. Miron, and Garrett Summers. 2008. "What Do Economists Know about Crime?" Working Paper no. 13759. Cambridge, MA: National Bureau of Economic Research.

Donohue, John J. 2004. "Guns, Crime, and the Impact of State Right-to-Carry Laws." *Fordham Law Review* 73:623–40.

———. 2006. "The Death Penalty: No Evidence for Deterrence." *Economists' Voice* (April): 1–6.

Donohue, John J., and Steven D. Levitt. 2001. "The Impact of Legalized Abortion on Crime." *Quarterly Journal of Economics* 116:379–420.

Donohue, John J., and Justin Wolfers. 2005. "Uses and Abuses of Empirical Evidence in the Death Penalty Debate." *Stanford Law Review* 58:791–846.

Doob, Anthony, and Cheryl Webster. 2003. "Sentence Severity and Crime: Accepting the Null Hypothesis." In *Crime and Justice: A Review of Research*, vol. 30, edited by Michael Tonry. Chicago: University of Chicago Press.

Durkheim, Émile. 1933. *The Division of Labour in Society*. Trans. George Simpson. New York: Free Press. (Originally published 1893.)

Ehrlich, Isaac. 1975. "The Deterrent Effect of Capital Punishment: A Question of Life and Death." *American Economic Review* 65:397–417.

———. 1996. "Crime, Punishment, and the Market for Offenses." *Journal of Economic Perspectives* 10(1):43–67.

Ellickson, Robert C. 1991. *Order without Law*. Cambridge, MA: Harvard University Press.

Fagan, Jeffrey, Franklin E. Zimring, and Amanda Geller. 2006. "Capital Punishment and Capital Murder: Market Share and the Deterrent Effects of the Death Penalty." *Texas Law Review* 84:1803–67.

Gottfredson, Don M., Leslie Wilkins, and Peter Hoffman. 1978. *Guidelines for Parole and Sentencing*. Lexington, MA: Lexington Books.

Harcourt, Bernard. 2001. *Illusion of Order: The False Promise of Broken Windows Policing*. Cambridge, MA: Harvard University Press.

Harcourt, Bernard, and Jens Ludwig. 2006. "Broken Windows: New Evidence from New York City and a Five-City Social Experiment." *University of Chicago Law Review* 73:271–320.

Hay, Douglas, Peter Linebaugh, John G. Rule, E. P. Thompson, and Cal

Winslow. 1975. *Albion's Fatal Tree: Crime and Society in Eighteenth-Century England*. New York: Pantheon.

Kahan, Dan M. 1999. "The Secret Ambition of Deterrence." *Harvard Law Review* 113:413–500.

Katz, Lawrence, Steven Levitt, and Ellen Shustorovich. 2003. "Prison Conditions, Capital Punishment, and Deterrence." *American Law and Economics Review* 5:318–43.

Kennedy, Donald. 2003. "Research Fraud and Public Policy." *Science* 300:393.

Kessler, Daniel P., and Steven D. Levitt. 1999. "Using Sentence Enhancements to Distinguish between Deterrence and Incapacitation." *Journal of Law and Economics* 42:343–63.

Kleck, Gary, and Don B. Kates. 2001. *Armed: New Perspectives on Gun Control*. New York: Prometheus.

Klepper, Steven, and Daniel Nagin. 1989. "Tax Compliance and Perceptions of the Risks of Detection and Criminal Prosecution." *Law and Society Review* 23:209–40.

Levitt, Steven D. 1996. "The Effect of Prison Population Size in Crime Rates." *Quarterly Journal of Economics* 111:319–25.

———. 2002. "Deterrence." In *Crime: Public Policies for Crime Control*, edited by James Q. Wilson and Joan Petersilia. Oakland, CA: Institute for Contemporary Studies Press.

Levitt, Steven D., and George Miles. 2007. "Empirical Study of Criminal Punishment." In *Handbook of Law and Economics*, vol. 1, edited by A. Mitchell Polinsky and Steven Shavell. Amsterdam: Elsevier.

Lewis, Donald E. 1986. "The General Deterrent Effect of Longer Sentences." *British Journal of Criminology* 26:47–62.

Lochner, Lance. 2007. "Individual Perceptions of the Criminal Justice System." *American Economic Review* 97:444–60.

Lott, John R., Jr. 1998. *More Guns, Less Crime: Understanding Crime and Gun Control Laws*. Chicago: University of Chicago Press. (2nd ed. 2000.)

Lott, John R., Jr., and David B. Mustard. 1997. "Crime, Deterrence, and Right-to-Carry Concealed Handguns." *Journal of Legal Studies* 26:1–68.

Ludwig, Jens. 2000. "Gun Self-Defense and Deterrence." In *Crime and Justice: A Review of Research*, vol. 27, edited by Michael Tonry. Chicago: University of Chicago Press.

Marvell, Thomas B., and Carlisle E. Moody. 1994. "Prison Population Growth and Crime Reduction." *Journal of Quantitative Criminology* 10:109–40.

Matsueda, Ross L., Derek A. Kreager, and David Huizinga. 2006. "Deterring Delinquents: A Rational Choice Model of Theft and Violence." *American Sociological Review* 71:95–122.

McCoy, Candace, and Patrick McManimon. 2004. "New Jersey's 'No Early Release Act': Its Impact on Prosecution, Sentencing, Corrections, and Victim Satisfaction." Unpublished final report. Washington, DC: National Institute of Justice.

Merritt, Nancy, Terry Fain, and Susan Turner. 2006. "Oregon's Get Tough

Sentencing Reform: A Lesson in Justice System Adaptation." *Criminology and Public Policy* 5(1):5–36.

Nagin, Daniel S. 1998. "Criminal Deterrence Research at the Outset of the Twenty-first Century." In *Crime and Justice: A Review of Research*, vol. 23, edited by Michael Tonry. Chicago: University of Chicago Press.

Nozick, Robert. 1981. *Philosophical Explanations*. Cambridge, MA: Harvard University Press.

Piquero, Alex R., and Stephen Tibbetts. 1996. "Specifying the Direct and Indirect Effects of Low Self-Control and Situational Factors in Offenders' Decision Making: Toward a More Complete Model of Rational Offending." *Justice Quarterly* 13:481–510.

Pogarsky, Greg. 2002. "Identifying 'Deterrable' Offenders: Implications for Research on Deterrence." *Justice Quarterly* 19:423–52.

Pogarsky, Greg, Alex R. Piquero, and Ray Paternoster. 2004. "Modeling Change in Perceptions about Sanction Threats: The Neglected Linkage in Deterrence Theory." *Journal of Quantitative Criminology* 20(4):343–69.

Pratt, Travis C., Francis T. Cullen, Kristie R. Blevins, Leah H. Daigle, and Tamara D. Madensen. 2006. "The Empirical Status of Deterrence Theory: A Meta-Analysis." In *Taking Stock: The Status of Criminological Theory*, edited by Francis T. Cullen, John Paul Wright, and Kristie R. Blevins. New Brunswick, NJ: Transaction.

Raphael, Steven, and Michael Stoll. Forthcoming. *The Costs and Consequences of U.S. Incarceration Policy*. New York: Russell Sage Foundation.

Roberts, Julian, Loretta J. Stalans, David Indermaur, and Mike Hough. 2002. *Penal Populism and Public Opinion*. New York: Oxford University Press.

Sherman, Lawrence W. 1990. "Police Crackdowns: Initial and Residual Deterrence." In *Crime and Justice: A Review of Research*, vol. 12, edited by Michael Tonry. Chicago: University of Chicago Press.

Sherman, Lawrence W., and Richard A. Berk. 1984. "The Specific Deterrent Effects of Arrest for Domestic Assault." *American Sociological Review* 49: 261–72.

Sherman, Lawrence W., Janelle D. Schmidt, and Dennis P. Rogan. 1992. *Policing Domestic Violence: Experiments and Dilemmas*. New York: Free Press.

Taylor, Ralph B. 2006. "Incivilities Reduction Policing, Zero Tolerance, and the Retreat from Co-production: Weak Foundations and Strong Pressures." In *Police Innovation: Contrasting Perspectives*, edited by David Weisburd and Anthony Braga. Cambridge: Cambridge University Press.

Teeters, Negley K. 1967. *Hang by the Neck: The Legal Use of Scaffold and Noose, Gibbet, Stake, and Firing Squad from Colonial Times to the Present*. With Jack H. Hedblom. Springfield, IL: Charles C. Thomas.

Tonry, Michael. 1996. *Sentencing Matters*. New York: Oxford University Press.

———. 2004. *Thinking about Crime: Sense and Sensibility in American Penal Culture*. New York: Oxford University Press.

———. 2008. "Onderzoek naar afschrikking; de noodzaak om klein te denken als we iets nieuws willen leren." *Justitiele Verkenningen* 34(2):98–117.

Tonry, Michael, and David Green. 2003. "Criminology and Public Policy in the US and the UK." In *The Criminological Foundations of Penal Policy*, edited by Andrew Ashworth and Lucia Zedner. Oxford: Oxford University Press.

U.S. House. Committee on the Judiciary. 2004. *Terrorist Penalties Enhancement Act of 2003: Hearing on H.R. 2934*. 108th Cong., 2nd sess., April 21. http://judiciary.house.gov/media/pdfs/printers/108th/93224.pdf.

von Hirsch, Andrew, Anthony E. Bottoms, Elizabeth Burney, and Per-Olof H. Wikström. 1999. *Criminal Deterrence and Sentence Severity: An Analysis of Recent Research*. Oxford: Hart.

Webster, Cheryl Marie, Anthony N. Doob, and Franklin E. Zimring. 2006. "Proposition 8 and Crime Rates in California: The Case for the Disappearing Deterrent." *Criminology and Public Policy* 5:417–48.

Wellford, Charles F., John Pepper, and Carol Petrie, eds. 2005. *Firearms and Violence: A Critical Review*. Washington, DC: National Academy Press.

Wikström, Per-Olof. 2007. "Deterrence and Deterrence Experiences—Preventing Crime through the Threat of Punishment." In *The International Handbook of Penology and Criminal Justice*, edited by S. G. Shoham. Oxford: Taylor & Francis.

Zimring, Franklin E., Gordon Hawkins, and Sam Kamin. 2001. *Punishment and Democracy: Three Strikes and You're Out in California*. New York: Oxford University Press.

Tapio Lappi-Seppälä

Trust, Welfare, and Political Culture: Explaining Differences in National Penal Policies

ABSTRACT

Countries vary enormously in their punishment policies and practices. A nascent literature has begun to explain these differences. There are no simple explanations. Neither high or rising crime rates nor heightened public anxiety or severity explains why policies become tougher or are tougher in some places than in others. The most powerful predictors of moderation in policy and practices are high levels of confidence in fellow citizens and in government, strong welfare states, and consensus compared with conflict political systems. Other important factors include insulation of the legal system from politics, the way in which justice system personnel are trained, and the nature of the mass media.

Unprecedented expansions of penal control have occurred in recent decades in different parts of the world. American imprisonment rates have increased nearly fivefold and Dutch rates sixfold since the early 1970s. Substantial changes of differing magnitudes may be observed in many countries. This increase in states' willingness to use penal power has provoked criminological and sociological explanations, most from writers in North America and English-speaking countries. An unspoken assumption that developments in the United States and England and Wales (hereafter, England) occurred elsewhere has influenced efforts to formulate general explanations of changes taking place under general conditions of late modern society. However, things have not

Tapio Lappi-Seppälä is director of the National Research Institute of Legal Policy, Helsinki.

0192-3234/2008/0037-0008$10.00

happened the same way everywhere. Alongside general growth in cultures of control, there are divergent trends and country-specific deviations. The Scandinavian countries with their more restrained penal policies serve as one important counterexample, but there are others. Overlooking these differences risks overgeneralized and simplified pictures of the dynamics of penal change.

This essay explores explanations for differences in penal severity in industrialized countries. The focus is not restricted to the Anglophonic world, but encompasses also the Scandinavian countries, western and eastern continental Europe, and the Baltic countries. The analysis includes cross-sectional and trend analyses taking account of a large number of factors related to crime: social, economic, and political factors and survey data on sentiments, fears, and public beliefs. This essay much more fully develops analyses begun in Lappi-Seppälä (2007) using quantitative data and a broader comparative perspective.

Differences in imprisonment rates cannot be explained by differences in crime. Penal severity instead is closely associated with public sentiments (fears, levels of trust, and punitiveness), the extent of welfare provision, differences in income equality, political structures, and legal cultures. The Scandinavian penal model, for example, has its roots in a consensus and corporatist political culture, high levels of social trust and political legitimacy, and a strong welfare state. The welfare state has made it possible to develop workable alternatives to imprisonment. Welfare and social equality have promoted trust and legitimacy, which facilitate compliance with norms based on legitimacy and acceptance (instead of sentence severity). These characteristics reduce political pressures to resort to symbolic penal gestures. Low imprisonment rates are by-products of consensual, corporatist, and negotiative political cultures. These political cultures are more "welfare friendly" than more majoritarian democracies. Consensus politics also lessen controversies, produce less crisis talk, inhibit dramatic policy shifts, and sustain consistent long-term policies.

Structures of the political economy and their effects and interactions with public sentiment are of fundamental importance in shaping penal policies, but other factors need to be taken into consideration. These include differences in media culture and in the responsiveness of the political system to the media. Demographic homogeneity may facilitate liberal penal policies (but is no guarantee for success; nor does multiculturalism necessarily lead to harsher regimes). Judicial structures and legal cultures play an important part, especially in explaining differences between continental and common-law countries. The power of professional elites (closely associated with political structures), small groups, and even individuals may be of great importance, depending on which countries are included in the analyses. Room must also be left for "country-specific exceptionalism." While differences in penal practices can be partly explained by reference to social, political, economic, and cultural factors, their effects are difficult to condense in terms of simple statistical models. These factors occur in different combinations in different places and at different times. Associations are neither atomistic nor mechanical. Effects are context related, and countries may experience unique changes. Explaining differences between Scandinavia and the United States, for example, involves different analyses than explaining differences among the Scandinavian countries.

Much of the analysis in this essay is based on quantitative data from international surveys, three in particular. The Council of Europe *Sourcebook of Crime and Criminal Justice Statistics* (Aebi et al. 2006) provides the basis for reported crime and prison statistics, complemented by national statistics from different countries. Survey data for crime and social sentiments (fears, punitivity, and trust) come from the International Crime Victimization Surveys (ICVS; e.g., van Kesteren, Mayhew, and Nieuwbeerta 2000), European Social Surveys (ESS; http://www.europeansocialsurvey.org), and World Values Surveys (WVS; http://worldvaluessurvey.org). Data for social, economic, and political indicators come mainly from the Organization for Economic Cooperation and Development (OECD), Eurostat, and the United Nations and from the European Union System of Social Indicators.

Here is how this essay is organized. Section I gives basic information on international trends in imprisonment rates. Section II discusses problems with imprisonment rates as policy indicators. Section III examines associations between crime and imprisonment rates cross-sectionally and over time. Sections IV–VIII examine economic, demographic, social, cultural, and political factors. Section IX explores statistical correlations and interactions between the key variables. Section X offers tentative explanations for the detected associations. Conclusions follow in Section XI.

I. Trends and National Differences in Imprisonment Rates

Recent decades have witnessed unprecedented expansion in penal control in some parts of the world. Since the early 1970s, imprisonment rates in the United States have increased nearly five times from around 160 per 100,000 to above 750. The United States seems to have strongly influenced the English-speaking world. Similar, albeit smaller, changes took place in Australia, New Zealand, and the United Kingdom. Canada is the exception. During the last 15–20 years, rates there have been broadly stable.

Trends in continental Europe are diverse. Some western European countries have fairly stable rates of 80–100 per 100,000 (France, Belgium, Germany, and Switzerland). However, there are notable exceptions. Between 1973 and 2005, the Netherlands imprisonment rate grew sixfold from 19 per 100,000 to 123. Spain more than tripled its rate in two decades from 40 per 100,000 to 140 in 2005.

The Scandinavian countries stand out in terms of stability and moderation. For almost half a century the rates in Denmark, Norway, and Sweden fluctuated within the narrow range of 40–60 prisoners per 100,000 population.

Finland followed a separate path. In the early 1950s, the rate was four times higher than in the other Nordic countries. Finland then had 200 prisoners per 100,000 inhabitants, whereas Sweden and Norway had around 50 and Denmark around 80. During the 1970s, Finland's rate continued to be among the highest in western Europe. However, a long-term decrease that started soon after the Second World War continued, and during the 1970s and 1980s, when most European countries experienced rising prison populations, the Finnish rates kept falling. By the beginning of the 1990s, Finland had reached the Nordic level of around 60 prisoners (Lappi-Seppälä 2001).

During most of the past 30 years, eastern European rates were more than double those in western Europe. In the Baltic countries, they were even higher.

Divergent trends in the United States and the Scandinavian countries are shown in figure 1. During the past 60 years things have gone fundamentally differently in Finland and in the United States. Whatever caused U.S. imprisonment trends apparently did not influence Finland. Among the western and northern European countries, three main trends stand out. There have been fairly stable but more recently

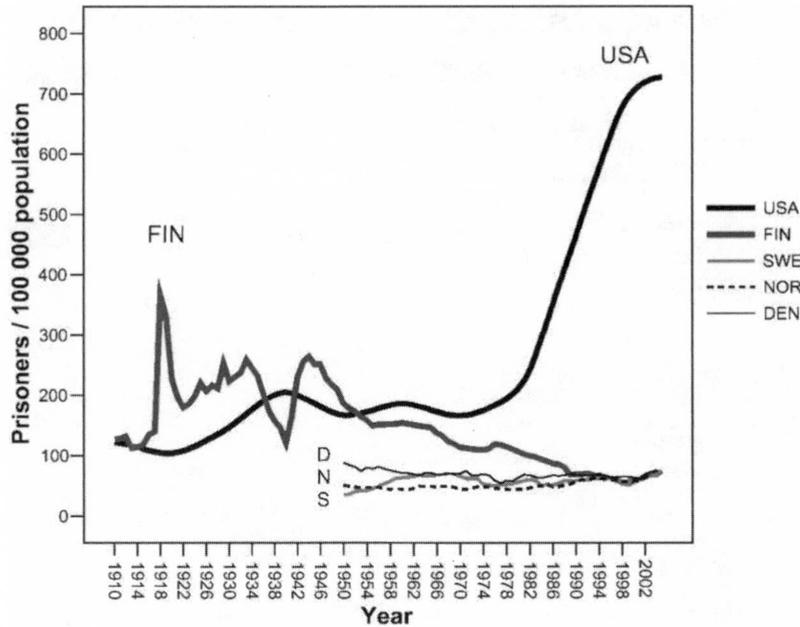

FIG. 1.—Long-term imprisonment rates in Scandinavia and the United States (source: national statistics).

rising imprisonment rates in continental Europe and Scandinavia, with the difference that the Scandinavian rates are 20–25 percent below those elsewhere, and rapidly rising imprisonment rates in England, Spain, and the Netherlands, with rates almost double those in Scandinavia.

Scandinavia as a region has among the lowest levels of prisoners, around 70–75 per 100,000 population in 2005. The corresponding figures for other western European countries were around 110, for eastern Europe around 200, for the Baltic countries around 300, for Russia 550, and for the United States 750. Imprisonment rates by regions in 2004/5 are represented in figure 2.

A number of questions call out for answers. What is behind the steep increase in imprisonment in many Anglo-Saxon and some European countries? What accounts for the moderation and stability of Scandinavian practices? What explains the huge differences to be found around the world and within regions?

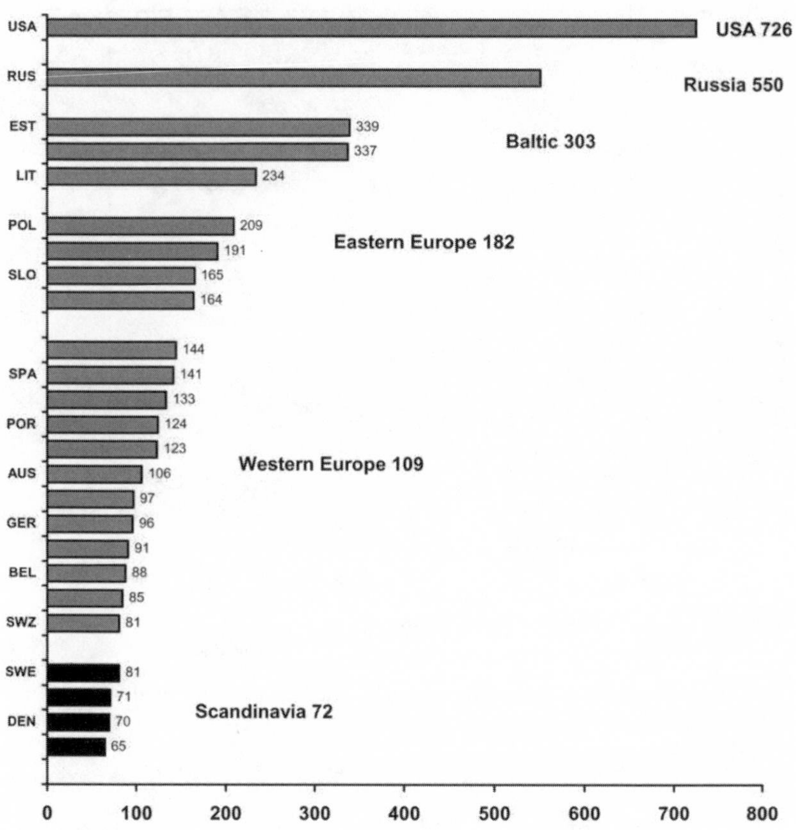

FIG. 2.—Imprisonment rates in 2004/5 (source: ICPS, http://www.prisonstudies.org/).

In what follows, possible explanations for differences are investigated with data from two samples. The first, which I call the basic sample, includes 25 industrialized countries and covers the period 1980–2005. The other, which I call the global sample, includes 99 countries for the year 2005. The basic sample of 25 industrialized countries focuses on advanced Western democracies along with some eastern European and Baltic countries for which enough data are available. The countries include 16 in western Europe, three in eastern Europe (Czech Republic, Hungary, and Poland), two Baltic countries (Estonia and Lithuania), and four Anglo-Saxon countries (United States, Canada, New

Zealand, and Australia). The cross-sectional sample covers 99 countries ranked according to the UN Human Poverty Index.

The dependent variable to be explained is the imprisonment rate per 100,000 population. Information on imprisonment rates comes from the King's College London International Centre for Prison Studies (ICPS; http://www.prisonstudies.org); Council of Europe Prison Information Bulletins; European Sourcebooks 1995, 2003, and 2006 (e.g., Aebi et al. 2006); SPACE I (Aebi and Stadnic 2007); national statistics; and various research reports. Most analyses on imprisonment rates are based on annual averages obtained from the Sourcebook 2006 and SPACE I, complemented with data from Prison Information Bulletins and national prison statistics.[1]

Factors explaining imprisonment rates fall into seven main categories:

1. *Crime.* Recorded crime data come mainly from the Council of Europe Sourcebooks (European Sourcebook 2003; Aebi et al. 2006), national statistics, and separate research reports (for Scandinavia, Falck, von Hofer, and Storgaard [2003] and for non-European countries, Farrington, Langan, and Tonry [2004]).[2] Information on victimization comes from survey data from the ICVS (van Kesteren, Mayhew, and Nieuwbeerta 2000), the EU International Crime Survey (EU ICS; van Dijk et al. 2007), and the ESS (http://www.europeansocialsurvey.org/).
2. *Fears and punitiveness.* Measurements on fears and punitiveness are based on survey data from the ICVS, the EU ICS, and the ESS (see point 1 above).
3. *Trust.* Data on trust and related social sentiments (attitudes toward immigrants) are taken from the ESS and the WVS (http://www.worldvaluessurvey.org/).
4. *Social indicators.* Social indicators include information on income distribution and public investments on social welfare. The major source for income statistics is the Luxembourg Income Study (LIS). The basic source for social expenditures is provided by OECD statistics for social indicators, the European System of Social Indicators (EUSI), and Eurostat. Data for global social and

[1] In this case the source is marked as "Sourcebook 2006 complemented."

[2] Crime and correctional data for the United States also come from http://www.albany.edu/sourcebook/, for New Zealand from http://www.stats.govt.nz/tables/ltds/ltds-social-indicators.htm, and for Canada from http://www.statcan.ca/english/.

economic comparisons come from the UN Human Development Reports and the International Monetary Fund (IMF).[3]

5. *Demographic factors.* Demographic factors include measurements on multiculturalism, the share of immigrants, and the size of foreign populations. The data come from LIS, Eurostat, and specific studies.
6. *Economic factors.* Economic factors relate to unemployment, gross domestic product (GDP), and poverty indicators. The data come from LIS and Eurostat, and for global comparisons from the UN and the IMF.
7. *Political factors.* Measurements related to political culture, the degrees on corporatism, and political behavior come from LIS and a number of specific studies.

The analyses do not aim to produce "the final causal model" explaining differences in penal severity with the help of one or two overriding factors. Individual variations between countries make such efforts futile. The aim is less ambitious and more realistic: to examine how differences in penal severity relate to differences in a number of social, economic, and political factors. The analyses proceed in several phases. First, major theoretical hypotheses concerning penal variations are tested cross-sectionally to identify factors that appear to conduce to different countries' adoption of more or less punitive policies ("risk factors" and "protective factors"; see Tonry 2007*b*). From there analyses extend to changes over time, to intercorrelations between different factors, and to regional patterns.

II. Measuring Punitiveness

My aim is to explain differences in punitiveness and penal severity. Efforts to define these phenomena—severity, punitiveness, repression—lead quickly to difficulties. Typical definitions use some of these words to define others. Definitions of punishment in criminal law jurisprudence include such elements as "pain or other consequences normally considered unpleasant," "hard treatment," "expressions of soci-

[3] For corresponding Web sites, see LIS (http://www.lisproject.org/), OECD (http://www.oecd.org/document/ and http://www.oecd.org/statsportal/), EUSI (http://www.gesis.org/en/social_monitoring/social_indicators/), Eurostat (http://epp.eurostat.ec.europa.eu/portal), UN (http://hdr.undp.org/reports/global/), and IMF (http://www.imf.org/external/data.htm).

ety's disapproval," "censure," and "infringements of the rights and interests of the defendant, in the name of justice and the protection of important social interests" (see, e.g., Hart 1968; Ross 1975; von Hirsch and Ashworth 2005). In more sociological terms, the subject is a "mix of attitudes, enactments, motivations, policies, practices, and ways of thinking that taken together express greater intolerance of deviance and deviants, and greater support for harsher policies and severe punishments" (Tonry 2007*b*, p. 5).

In these characterizations the "punitiveness dimension" is related to the value and importance of infringed interests. In legal theory, the severity of sanctions is determined by the value of the rights and interests deprived by criminal sanction. How these interests are valued in general and by each individual is far from clear (see, e.g., discussions in von Hirsch and Ashworth [2005, pp. 147–48]).

However, basic graduations are fairly unproblematic. Life has the highest absolute value. Consequently, if one wishes to measure global differences in penal severity, capital punishment should not be overlooked.[4] After life, health, physical well-being, and bodily integrity also have high priority (even when cultural differences are taken into account). Corporal punishment mostly disappeared from Western criminal justice systems in the nineteenth century but remains in use in many other parts of the world. Global comparative analyses of penal severity should thus pay attention not only to the death penalty but also to corporal punishments. Comparisons confined to democratic countries, however, avoid most of these problems. All countries included in the basic sample long ago abolished capital and corporal punishments except the United States, which retains the death penalty.[5]

Imprisonment has uncontested prominence as the principal and most severe sanction in European and industrialized Western countries (with the unfortunate exception of the United States). Consequently, most measurements of penal severity use prison as the starting point. Differences in imprisonment numbers, however, hardly tell the whole story.

[4] Amnesty International reported that by 2005, 128 countries had abolished the death penalty, either in law or in practice (http://web.amnesty.org/report2006/key_issue-5-eng). Abolitionists for all crimes included 89 states, ordinary crimes only 10 states, and abolitionism in practice 29 countries. Retentionists included 69 countries.

[5] However, several countries in the global sample have retained the death penalty as part of their sanctions system.

A. Imprisonment Rates as a Policy Indicator

Imprisonment rates per 100,000 population indicate how many of its residents the state imprisons on any given day. As an indicator of penal severity, imprisonment rates must (like any indicator) meet the basic requirements of reliability and validity.

Are imprisonment rates a reliable measure? Can they be trusted, and do they produce comparable figures between two or more countries? To answer this we must know how imprisonment rates are constructed.

The problem of validity is more substantial. Do imprisonment rates tell us what we assume they do? Are they the best indicator of punitiveness, penal severity, and the level of social control? Instead of imprisonment rates, one can identify a long list of possible alternatives. We can easily imagine several rivals, including (see in more detail Blumstein, Tonry, and van Ness [2005]) the number of people entering prison per 100,000 population; the average duration of prison terms; the probability of imprisonment, as percentages of all imposed sanctions or relative to crimes committed, recorded, prosecuted, or sentenced; the average lengths of all prison sentences and disaggregated by types of crime; the total volume of annually imposed or served prison years relative to population and to crimes committed, recorded, prosecuted, or sentenced; and the quality and conditions of prison regimes.

Prison is not the only punishment. At one end of the penalty scale, capital (and also corporal) punishments demand attention; at the other end, community sanctions and monetary penalties. Other (qualitative) dimensions of social control could be included, such as differences in police powers and practices, human rights instruments and procedural guarantees, the quality of prison regimes, and the powers and practices of other agencies besides criminal justice agencies (such as social and health authorities). A study using imprisonment rates as a key policy indicator clearly needs to justify itself. I do this in subsections 2–5 below. First, though, in subsection 1, I discuss whether and why imprisonment rates are a reliable measure of a country's penal policies for comparative purposes.

1. *Can Imprisonment Rates Be Compared?* Imprisonment rates may represent different things in different countries. The figures may—or may not—include juveniles detained in juvenile institutions, persons in drug treatment or mental health facilities, immigrants and foreigners detained on the basis of immigration laws, and new emerging sanctions

close to imprisonment, such as electronic monitoring and house arrest. Meaningful comparisons require comparable figures.

a. Juveniles. There are differences in how prison statistics deal with young offenders. Some countries include juveniles placed in juvenile institutions in their imprisonment rates and others do not. Consequently, the share of juveniles in prison varies greatly in different countries (Aebi and Stadnic 2007).

The Polish prison statistics in 2005 included almost no juveniles; in the Netherlands prisoners under age 18 made up 13 percent of the imprisonment rate. A plausible argument can be made that comparisons that aim to measure penal severity (intrusiveness of criminal sanctions) should include juvenile interventions that consist mainly of deprivation of liberty, whereas interventions guided by general principles of child welfare and the best interests of the child should be omitted. The Netherlands' (and evidently also Portugal's) rates are artificially high in standard prison population comparisons. Conversely, countries with high imprisonment rates such as Poland that exclude juveniles effectively understate their penal severity.[6]

b. Mental Patients and Foreign Administrative Prisoners. A recent Council of Europe report on imprisonment rates (Aebi and Stadnic 2007) reveals several other differences. Two major groups that are not consistently counted are offenders in mental hospitals and foreign administrative prisoners.

Most countries exclude both groups from official imprisonment rates, but with some exceptions (Aebi and Stadnic 2007). The Dutch figures contain both substantial numbers (8 percent) of mental health patients and even higher numbers (10 percent) of foreign administrative prisoners detained on the basis of aliens legislation. Mental health patients also affect the Austrian, Hungarian, and Portuguese rates. Swiss figures are increased by foreign administrative prisoners (6 percent). The reliability of these figures is uncertain, so one should be careful in drawing conclusions.[7] However, some adjustments downward in imprisonment rates would seem justified at least for Holland.

[6] Low figures in the Scandinavian countries raise similar questions. Closed juvenile treatment in Sweden and closed child welfare placements in Finland would raise the share of institutionalized juveniles in Sweden and Finland closer to the average mean of 2–3 percent. However, similar "close to prison" dispositions can probably also be found in countries that include juvenile prisoners around the average 2–3 percent.

[7] The Finnish information needed to be corrected. Some foreigners waiting for transportation have presumably also been caught in criminal activities (and not only for purely administrative reasons); total exclusion of this group would probably be incorrect.

c. Remand and Foreign Prisoners. Country profiles also differ significantly with respect to the use of remand and the relative numbers of foreign prisoners (Aebi and Stadnic 2007). Finland has the lowest (12 percent) percentage of remand prisoners and Switzerland the highest (39 percent). Even greater variations can be found concerning foreigners: 70 percent of prisoners in Switzerland are foreigners, whereas in Poland and Scotland foreigners constitute around 1 percent. Swiss prison figures are dominated by foreigners and remand prisoners.

Should these differences be taken into account in making comparisons? An affirmative answer implies that remand does not reflect the "true" use of punishment and therefore that remand prisoners should be excluded. Similarly, countries with large foreign populations "suffer" from this condition and, for that reason, have high rates in the prison statistics.

Examination of the use of remand and the number of foreigners in relation to the total number of prisoners, however, indicates that they are negatively associated with imprisonment rates. To illustrate this, imprisonment rates and the shares of remand prisoners and foreigners in prison have been plotted against each other in figure 3. Regression lines show the direction of the detected association, and the R^2 value gives information on the explanatory power of each model.

Countries with high shares of foreign prisoners tend to have lower total imprisonment rates. Countries with more remand prisoners have slightly lower rates. Foreigners and remand prisoners do not function as a general factor increasing rates and for this reason should be taken into account. As to remand prisoners, there are no substantial reasons why they should be excluded. Remand is deprivation of liberty as such and one indicator of society's willingness to use incarceration. Time spent in remand in most countries operates as a credit toward the final sentence and thus "turns" afterward into ordinary prison time.

2. *How Well Do Imprisonment Rates Measure the Intensity of Prison Use?* Imprisonment rates are not the only measure of the use of imprisonment. Instead of asking how many people are locked up at any given moment, we could ask how many people are sent each year to prison or how long they stay there. Reliable comparative court-based data on the lengths of imposed sentences are hard to find. However, the average duration of prison terms can be calculated once we know the annual average number of prisoners (*A*) and the number of admissions (*B*). The duration of prison term in months equals $(A/B) \times 12$.

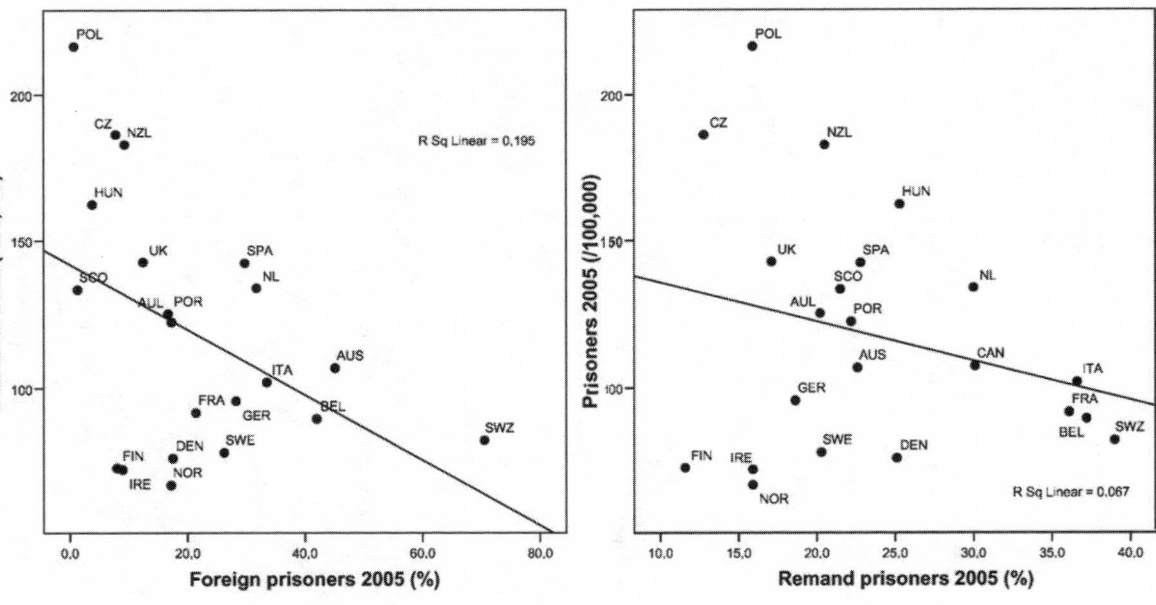

FIG. 3.—Remand and foreign prisoners, 2005, in relation to imprisonment rate (source: Aebi and Stadnic 2007)

TABLE 1

Prisoners, Admissions, and Durations, 2003/4

	Prisoners/ 100,000		Admissions/ 100,000		Average Duration (Months)
Top 5:					
Norway	68	Portugal	54	Switzerland	1.3
Finland	75	Spain	98	Scotland	2.2
Denmark	77	Finland	126	Denmark	3.0
Ireland	78	France	135	Norway	3.4
Sweden	78	Hungary	141	Sweden	3.8
Bottom 5:					
Czech Republic	184	Denmark	301	Poland	11.1
Poland	228	Lithuania	347	Czech Republic	12.4
Lithuania	235	Estonia	388	Hungary	13.8
Estonia	333	Scotland	764	Spain	17.4
United States	738	Switzerland	768	Portugal	27.1
Mean	156		260		8.6

SOURCE.—Calculated from Aebi and Stadnic (2007).

NOTE.—Canada, Ireland, New Zealand, United States, and Australia are missing from admissions and duration calculations.

Countries that send more people to prison tend also to use shorter sentences (see table 1). Switzerland and Scotland have by far the largest number of annual admissions (768 and 764 per 100,000) and the shortest average prison terms (1.3 and 2.2 months). Spain and Portugal have low numbers of admissions (98 and 54) but the longest sentences (17 and 27 months) and above-average imprisonment rates (145 and 121 per 100,000).

If admissions were used as an indicator of punitiveness, Switzerland, Scotland, and Denmark would be ranked much higher and Portugal and Spain much lower. If sentence length were used, Portugal and Spain would receive top rankings. The essential question is, however, why we should use one of these two alternatives when the imprisonment rate takes both into account. It is a function of the number of entries and the duration of the prison term. It combines these two alternatives and tells more than either does alone.

But even if the number of admissions and the lengths of average prison term do not improve the analyses, they point out two things. First, even frequent use of imprisonment may not lead to high incarceration rates if prison terms are short. Switzerland and Scandinavia demonstrate this. Second, long prison terms, even when imprisonment

TABLE 2

Imprisonment Rates Relative to Recorded Crime and Victimization

	Prisoners (Base 2005) (1)	Prisoners/ Recorded Crime (2)	Prisoners/ Victimization (3)
Ireland	72	27.3	3.3
Finland	73	10.4	5.7
Denmark	76	8.4	3.9
Sweden	78	6.4	4.8
Belgium	90	9.2	5.1
France	92	13.9	7.7
Germany	96	12.0	7.3
Italy	102	24.1	8.1
Austria	107	13.6	8.8
Portugal	122	30.6	11.7
Netherlands	134	15.7	6.8
Spain	142	59.7	15.8
United Kingdom	143	12.7	6.8
Hungary	162	39.4	16.2
Poland	217	57.1	14.5
Estonia	327	106.6	16.0
Correlation with col. 1		.91	.77

SOURCES.—Sourcebook 2006 complemented, EU ICS.

is used seldom, may lift incarceration rates above western European levels, as in Spain and Portugal. The highest rates occur, of course, when long prison terms are combined with frequent use of imprisonment (as in Estonia).

3. *Prisoner Rates Relative to Population or Relative to Crime?* The imprisonment rate is a sensible way to measure the use of imprisonment. But should we not, instead of counting prisoners relative to population, count the number of prisoners relative to crimes committed? Shouldn't the level of severity be counted relative to the offenses these sanctions are imposed for? In addition to recorded crime (with all the difficulties involved), imprisonment rates could be calculated relative to victimization data. One could construct a combination index that relates imprisonment rates to both recorded crime and victimization experiences (see table 2).

When prisoners are related to crime (cols. 2 and 3), England, the Netherlands, and Sweden appear less punitive and Ireland, Spain, and Italy appear more. Overall, however, basic imprisonment rates and imprisonment rates relative to crime are fairly strongly correlated (between .77 and .91), indicating that the results would follow similar lines irrespective of which measure is used.

4. *How Well Do Imprisonment Rates Measure Sentence Severity and the Intensity of Social Control?* Imprisonment rates are fairly comparable. Comparisons are largely unaffected by whether rates are counted relative to population or to crime. But prison is still only one part of a state's penal machinery. Social control and penal practices take many other forms. Should not an index of punishment severity take into account all other court-imposed sanctions? And if we wish to measure the use of imprisonment, should we not also include the frequency or proportion of imposed prison sentences and the lengths of court-imposed prison terms?[8] Differences in sentence length have been discussed already. However, the relation between imprisonment rates and the intensity of social control needs further comments.

Table 3 introduces four new penalty indicators: the number of criminal convictions per 100,000 population (col. 2), the number of convictions relative to crime (combination of recorded crime and victimization rates; col. 3), the number of court-imposed unsuspended sentences relative to population (col. 4), and the number of court-imposed unsuspended sentences relative to crime (combination of recorded crime and victimization rates; col. 5).

The association between imprisonment rates and other control indicators is either negative or nonexistent. In conviction statistics, low-imprisonment countries such as Finland and Denmark receive the highest rankings and high-imprisonment countries in eastern Europe and the Baltic countries receive the lowest. The picture looks pretty much the same when control is measured in terms of unsuspended prison sentences or crime indicators. (Detailed statistical analyses are reported in Lappi-Seppälä [2008].)

Owing to the reliability problems with the crime data, conclusions should rest mainly on conviction data. Here the message is clear: Imprisonment rates and convictions are inversely related. Countries with a high number of convictions (both total and unsuspended sentences) have low imprisonment rates.

How this finding should be taken into account depends on how broadly we wish to define the task. In the following analysis, impris-

[8] In addition, severity is affected by enforcement practices, which determine the duration of prison served term. Tonry (2007*b*, p. 14) provides a list of further candidates in measuring punitiveness.

TABLE 3

Criminal Convictions and Unsuspended Prison Sentences Relative to Prison Population and Crime, 2000–2005

	Prisoners 2005 (1)	Convictions 2003 (2)	Convictions/ Combined Crime (3)	Unsuspended Prisoners 2003 (4)	Unsuspended/ Combined Crime (5)
Norway	67	973	NA	208	NA
Ireland	72	971	45.7	NA	NA
Finland	73	1,487	44.5	155	34.2
Denmark	76	1,683	36.1	157	25.6
Sweden	78	974	20.0	144	20.6
Switzerland	82	682	NA	148	NA
Belgium	90	365	7.8	108	17.1
France	92	517	16.4	164	38.5
Germany	96	784	21.8	69	13.9
Italy	102	379	15.0	327	103.1
Austria	107	511	14.9	104	21.7
Portugal	122	344	15.3	48	16.7
Scotland	133	1,321	NA	237	NA
Netherlands	134	612	13.4	173	29.0
United Kingdom	143	1,364	25.1	200	27.3
Hungary	162	864	38.3	118	40.5
Czech Republic	186	578	NA	149	NA
Poland	217	713	28.3	68	22.4
Lithuania	233	485	NA	NA	NA
Estonia	327	725	30.7	NA	NA
Correlation with col. 1		−.24	.07	−.21	−.05

SOURCES.—Aebi and Stadnic (2007), Sourcebook 2006 complemented.

onment is used as a basic measure of penal severity. Omitting the use of other penalties could cause problems in countries in which the extensive use of fines and community sanctions (mainly in the Scandinavian countries) counterbalances the restrictive use of imprisonment in a way that would distort the prison-based severity rankings between countries. This may remain a topic for some dispute, depending on whether we are more interested in constructing a general measure for intensity of penal control, or in the use of the most severe sanction and the related social consequences. Regarding the first point, we do not have a clear answer to the question which of the two countries A and B has more penal control: A with a high number of convictions and community sanctions but a low imprisonment rate, or B with a high imprisonment rate but a low number of convictions and community sanctions.[9] Still, there are good reasons to argue that A has been more successful in minimizing the human, material, and social costs involved in the deprivation of liberty (and B has wasted much of the possible social and rehabilitative potentials involved in community sanctions). From this point of view, alternatives to imprisonment look more like a resource than a risk. As table 3 suggests, extensive use of prison (measured by imprisonment rates) coincides often with less frequent use of other sanctions. Put differently, overall use of imprisonment is negatively associated with the total number of criminal convictions and (on a smaller scale) with the total number of unsuspended court dispositions. The basic message is that the use of incarceration may be moderated by the use of other sanctions, and long prison sentences can be moderated by a larger number of shorter prison sentences.

B. Conclusions about Penal Severity Measures

Sentence severity and intensity of social control cannot be fully captured in a simple quantitative indicator. Still, prison is the most severe punishment used in European and industrialized Western countries. Imprisonment rates per capita are also the most convenient way to measure simultaneously the number of people sent to prison and the durations of their sentences. Punitiveness rankings of countries are fairly stable whether prisoners are counted relative to crimes committed or relative to national populations. Countries with high imprisonment rates cannot explain their policies by reference to high numbers of foreigners (or extensive use of remand) since the number of foreigners (and remand prisoners) is negatively associated with imprisonment rates. There is no serious alternative to using imprisonment rates. They remain "an excellent proxy for many other measures of societies' responses to acts defined as crimes" (Wilkins 1991, p. 13). However, two reservations need to be added.

The noncomparability of some countries' prison statistics needs to be addressed. Differing approaches to certain groups, such as juveniles, mental health patients, and foreigners detained under aliens legislation, exaggerate differences between countries. Some countries underesti-

[9] Taking into account the formal nature of monetary penalties and the supportive and social elements involved in the Scandinavian community sanctions (see Lappi-Seppälä 2007), one may doubt whether higher conviction rates would alter the basic positions. Many of the countries with low conviction rates in table 3, in turn, deal with minor offenses in administrative proceedings, which also complicates the comparisons.

TABLE 4

Alternative Measures of Punitiveness

	Prisoners I Base 2005	Prisoners II Modified 2005	Prisoners III Prisoners/Crime
Finland	73	73	16.1
Denmark	76	76	12.4
Sweden	78	78	11.2
Belgium	90	90	14.3
France	92	91	21.6
Germany	96	86	19.4
Italy	102	100	32.2
Austria	107	99	22.3
Portugal	122	118	42.4
Netherlands	134	95	22.5
United Kingdom	143	143	19.5
Hungary	162	148	55.6
Poland	217	226	71.6
Correlation with Prisoners I		.96	.88

SOURCE.—Aebi and Stadnic (2007).

NOTE.—Prisoners I shows imprisonment rates per 100,000 in 2005 (Aebi and Stadnic 2007). Prisoners II shows rates adjusted to exclude mental health patients, foreign administrative prisoners, prisoners in special drug treatment institutions, and people on electronic monitoring. Some juvenile offenders are excluded from the Dutch and Portuguese data and added to the Polish. Prisoners III shows rates relative to combined national crime and victimization rates.

mate rates by excluding juveniles detained in prison-like institutions. Variations in the extent of crime also should be taken into account. For these reasons, two additional indicators for penal severity were constructed (see table 4).

Prisoners II excludes mental health patients, foreign administrative prisoners, offenders undergoing drug treatment in special institutions, and people subject to electronic monitoring. The measure also artificially limits the number of juveniles in two countries (Netherlands and Portugal) and increases it in one (Poland) to the average of 3 percent. Another index (Prisoners III) counts imprisonment rates relative to crime (combined reported and victimization). The complementary indicators were used to check the main findings. As can be seen in table 4, both modified indicators correlate strongly ($R = .96$ and .88).

The second reservation concerns the death penalty. It is practiced in almost one-quarter of countries. This cannot be neglected in global comparisons of penal severity (or in trend analyses of even narrower scope). Measuring only prisoners would lead to mistaken results if the

TABLE 5

Imprisonment Rates and Capital Punishment in 99 Countries, 2005 (Sample 99)

Use of Death Penalty	Prisoners 2005 (/100,000)	Number
Abolitionists:		
Total	150	55
Ordinary	180	9
Practice	251	9
Retentionists	252	26
Total	189	99

SOURCES.—Death penalty: Amnesty; imprisonment rates: ICPS.

restrictive use of imprisonment is explainable in part by the use of corporal punishments and the death penalty.

However, both indicators point in the same direction. Use of the death penalty is positively associated with imprisonment rates. In the global sample of 99 countries, countries that abolished the death penalty have lower rates (150 per 100,000) and countries retaining the death penalty have higher rates (252 per 100,000). Between these two groups are countries that abolished the death penalty for ordinary crimes (180 per 100,000) and that retained the death penalty in their criminal codes but have not enforced it during the last 10 years (see table 5).

All main results point in the same direction. Factors associated with the use of imprisonment are associated with the use of the death penalty (with weaker correlations). Including the death penalty in the analyses would not have significantly altered patterns shown in the basic imprisonment rate findings. It should be no surprise that the same structural, political, and social factors that explain differences in the use of imprisonment also explain the use of the death penalty (see esp. Garland 2007, pp. 145, 151–52).

III. Crime Rates Explaining Imprisonment Rates?

It is natural to assume that the differences in imprisonment rates reflect differences in crime rates. Might Scandinavian leniency, for example, be a product of lower levels of crime? Are rising imprisonment rates a reflection of rising crime rates? Analyses are conducted separately for recorded crime and victimization data.

Since results may depend on the countries involved in comparisons, the basic sample of 25 countries has been divided into six subsamples:

I. Eur 16	Austria, Belgium, Denmark, Finland, France, Germany, Ireland, Italy, Netherlands, Norway, Portugal, Scotland, Spain, Sweden, Switzerland, and United Kingdom
II. Eur 19	= Eur16 + Czech Republic, Hungary, and Poland
III. Eur16 + Ang3	= Eur16 + Australia, Canada, and New Zealand
IV. Eur16 + Ang3 + U.S.	= Eur16 + Australia, Canada, New Zealand, and United States
V. Eur19 + Ang3	= Eur19 + Australia, Canada, and New Zealand
VI. Eur19 + Ang3 + U.S.	= Eur19 + Australia, Canada, New Zealand, and United States
VII. All	= Eur19 + Australia, Canada, New Zealand, United States, Estonia, and Lithuania

Results are given for all combinations. Imprisonment rates are usually counted for 3 years (average 2001–3), unless there is a particular need to use either earlier or more subsequent series.[10]

A. Recorded Crime

Comparing reported criminal offenses in 2003 (excluding minor traffic offenses; Aebi et al. 2006) and imprisonment rates for 2001–3 gives the results shown in part A of table 6.[11] More reported crimes are associated with fewer prisoners. To minimize the effects of recording

[10] Because of its extraordinarily high imprisonment rates, the United States is excluded from all graphical illustrations.

[11] The levels of significance in the tables are marked with asterisks: ** for significance at the .01 level and * for significance at the .05 level. All correlations are Pearson correlations. If there is missing information, the cells in the tables have been left empty. Eur16 forms the basic subsample for which all correlations have been counted. Correlations for other subsamples have been counted in each case in which there is at least one additional observation (country) in that subsample (as compared to Eur16). If not, the cell for that subsample has been left empty in the tables.

TABLE 6

Imprisonment Rates, Recorded Crime, and Victimization (Prisoners 2001–3)

Measure	Eur16	Eur19	Eur16 +Ang3	Eur16 +Ang3 +U.S.	Eur19 +Ang3	Eur19 +Ang3 +U.S.	All
			A. Reported Crime				
Reported crime 2003 (per 100,000)[a]	−.049	−.367	.092		−.271		−.454*
Reported homicides 2003 (per 100,000)	.261	.320	.289	.892**	.319	.881**	.678**
Reported assaults 2003 (per 100,000)	.465	−.086	.469		−.029		−.265
			B. Victimization				
Victim (%; ESS)	−.044	.002	−.044		.002		.002
Victimization:							
ICVS 2000, four crimes (%)	−.135	−.144	−.003	.178	−.060	.164	.164
ICVS prevalence 2000, 11 crimes (%)	.133	.169	.420	.009	.323	.012	.012
EU ICS prevalence 2005, 10 crimes (%)	−.251	−.269	−.251		−.269		.123

SOURCES.—Sourcebook 2006 complemented, ESS, ICVS, and EU ICS.
[a] Minor traffic violations are excluded.
* Significant at the .01 level.
** Significant at the .05 level.

practices, results are reported for completed homicide and, for comparison, for assaults.

For homicides the direction of the correlation changed. However, the results are heavily affected by two powerful observations from the Baltic countries. In addition, homicide is a rare event, and it has a small effect on overall imprisonment rates. Recorded assault and imprisonment rates have varying correlations in different samples. The positive correlation in Eur16 results from high reported crime rates in England and Scotland. Leaving these two countries out changes the direction of the association ($R = -.12$), and so does including the eastern countries (Eur19 $R = -.09$). The overall result in the total sample ($R =$

TABLE 7

Victimization in the Year Preceding the Survey (Percentage: Victim Once or More)

	11 Crimes (1)	4 Crimes[a] (2)	Prisoners 2000 /100,000 (3)	Prison	
				11 Crimes (4)	4 Crimes[a] (5)
Scandinavia 4	20.8	6.8	59	2.8	8.7
Western Europe 12	21.8	6.9	105	4.8	15.1
Anglo 3[b]	27.7	12.2	123	4.4	10.1
United States	21.1	6.3	700	33.2	111.1

SOURCES.—Compiled from European Sourcebook 2003 and van Kesteren, Mayhew, and Nieuwbeerta (2000), app. 4, table 1.

[a] Car theft, burglary, robbery, and assault and threat.

[b] Australia, Canada, and New Zealand.

−.27) indicates that the larger the number of reported assaults, the smaller the number of prisoners.

B. Survey Data

Results from victimization studies compare imprisonment rates with the 2000 ICVS, the ESS first round, and the 2005 EU ICS.[12] For the 2000 ICVS, a separate analysis was conducted with the four most serious crimes in the surveys.[13] All associations are weak, and all are statistically nonsignificant (see part B of table 6).

Table 7 presents a summary comparison between different regions from four sweeps of the ICVS from 1989 to 2000. Column 1 describes aggregate victimization rates for 11 offenses. Column 2 includes the same data for four serious offenses. Imprisonment rates per 100,000 are shown in column 3. Figures in columns 4 and 5 express the number of prisoners per victimization rate.

The overall victimization rate in Scandinavia is about the same as in western Europe, but the imprisonment rate is only half. The higher number of prisoners in the three Anglo-Saxon countries might be

[12] Descriptions for the ICVS measurements are to be found in van Kesteren, Mayhew, and Nieuwbeerta (2000) and for the EU ICS in van Dijk et al. (2007). The ESS survey, in turn, is designed to chart and explain the interaction between Europe's changing institutions and the attitudes, beliefs, and behavior patterns of its diverse populations. Unless otherwise stated, the results are based on the first round of the ESS (conducted in 2002; see http://www.europeansocialsurvey.org/ for details).

[13] The reason is that victimization surveys deal mainly with minor crimes, which, in most western countries, have a limited effect on imprisonment rates.

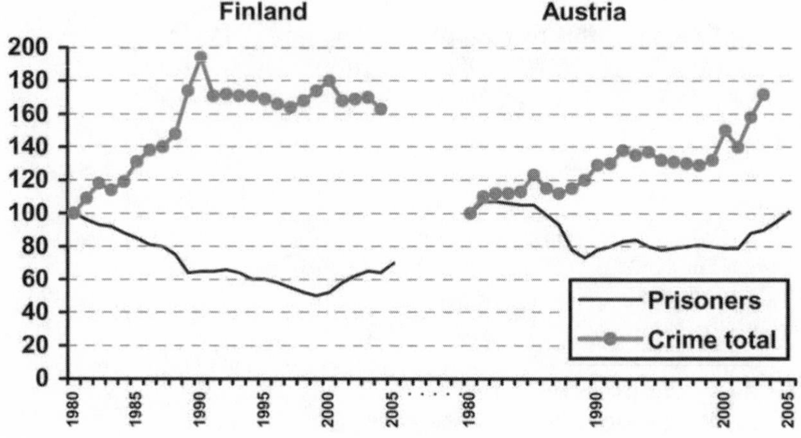

FIG. 4.—Prisoners and reported crime in Finland and Austria per 100,000 population (1980 = 100) (source: Sourcebook 2006 complemented).

partly explainable by higher victimization rates. However, the difference in American imprisonment rates, compared with those of the Scandinavian countries, cannot be explained by differences in crime since victimization rates are practically identical.

C. *Imprisonment Rates and Reported Crime, 1980–2005*

Trends for the period 1980–2005 are shown in figures 4–9. Figure 4 compares Finland and Austria. Both countries had a long-term increase in crime and falling imprisonment rates. However, the changes in Finland were more radical.

Denmark, Germany, and France have had stable imprisonment rates and (fairly) stable crime rates (fig. 5). Denmark experienced an increase in crime in the second half of the 1980s and Germany in the first half of the 1990s. During the latter half of the 1990s, crime decreased in both countries, but the imprisonment rates remained stable. In France, imprisonment rates and crime rates criss-crossed throughout the whole period, both, however, staying roughly on the same level.

Norway and England both experienced increasing crime rates and increasing imprisonment rates (fig. 6). Reported crime doubled in both countries during the 1980s. While the Norwegian crime figures continued to rise in the 1990s, crime in England fell during the first half of the 1990s. Imprisonment rates have different timing. In Norway the

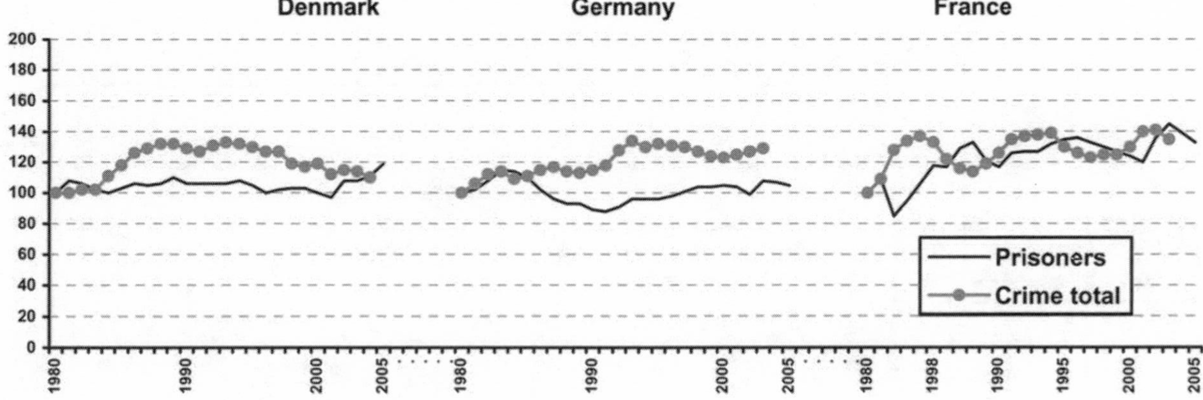

FIG. 5.—Prisoners and reported crime in Denmark, Germany, and France per 100,000 population (1980 = 100) (source: Sourcebook 2006 complemented).

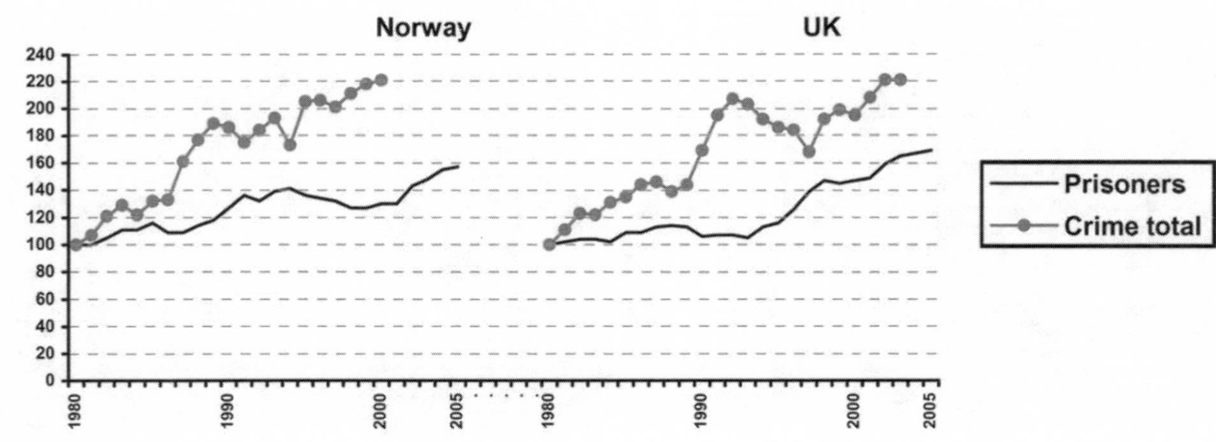

FIG. 6.—Prisoners and reported crime in Norway and the United Kingdom per 100,000 population (1980 = 100) (source: Sourcebook 2006 complemented).

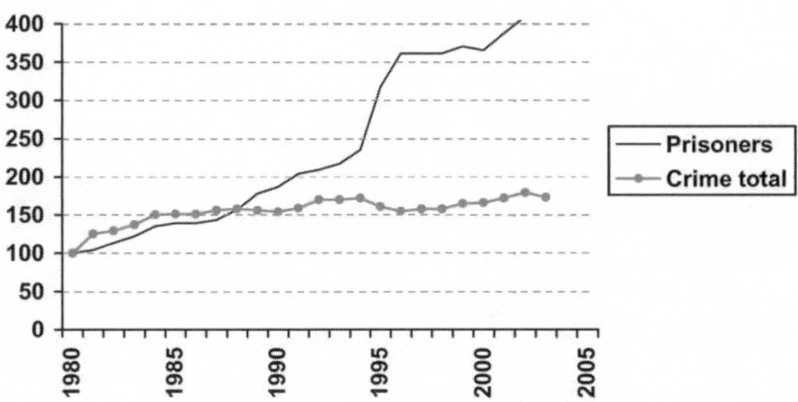

FIG. 7.—Prisoners and reported crime in the Netherlands per 100,000 population (1980 = 100) (source: Sourcebook 2006 complemented).

rise in imprisonment rates took place during the latter half of the 1980s together with an increase in reported crime. In England, the imprisonment rates started to climb after the surge in crime in the 1990s and during a time when crime rates were falling.

Between 1980 and 2005, the Dutch imprisonment rate quadrupled, during a period when crime was fairly stable. Reported crime increased only during the first half of the 1980s but has thereafter remained more or less stable (see fig. 7).

Two non-European countries, Japan and New Zealand, have quite different profiles (see fig. 8). In Japan the imprisonment rate was stable or declining (from a low level of 40 to 50 prisoners per 100,000), but began to increase during the first half of the 1990s. A few years later, reported crime took a similar turn. In New Zealand, crime was in a stable increase between 1980 and 1990 but decreased after the mid-1990s. Imprisonment rates have increased continually since 1985.

The other two non-European countries provide an example of similar crime rates and totally divergent imprisonment rates. Canada's imprisonment rates have been stable, whereas crime has been declining (after a short increase) since the 1990s. The United States has an almost identical declining crime profile and a sharply increasing prisoner

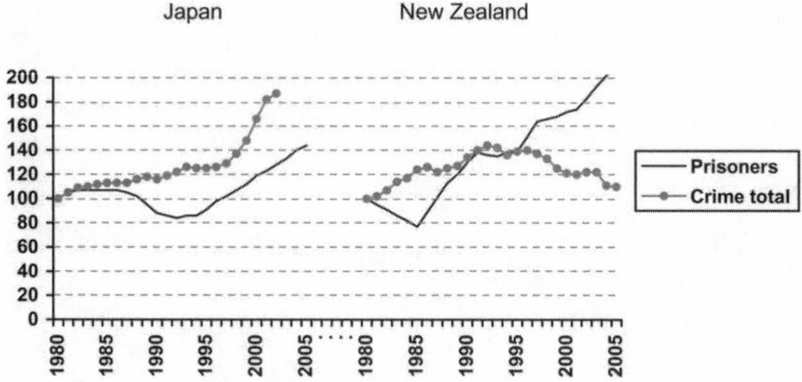

FIG. 8.—Prisoners and reported crime in Japan and New Zealand per 100,000 population (1980 = 100) (source: national statistics).

profile. Adding Finland to the picture gives an example of a pattern diametrically opposite that of the United States (see fig. 9).[14]

It is possible to reduce the number of prisoners during times when crime rates are increasing (Finland 1980–90 and Austria 1985–90). It is also possible to increase the imprisonment rates during times when crime rates are stable (Netherlands 1985–2000) and to maintain both of them stable (Denmark 1985–95, France 1985–2005). And it has been possible to increase imprisonment rates while crime rates were falling (England during most of the 1990s, New Zealand 1995–2005, and the United States 1990–2005).

D. *Changes in Imprisonment Rates after Changes in Reported Crime, 1980–2005*

A third way to establish associations between crime and imprisonment rates is to examine whether changes in crime rates correlate with subsequent changes in imprisonment rates. In figure 10, a lag effect of 1 year is assumed (crimes detected today have their main effect on

[14] At first glance the figures from the United States and Finland suggest another conclusion: Even if crime does not explain imprisonment rates, it looks as if imprisonment rates may explain crime (as imprisonment rates decreased in Finland in 1960–90 when crime increased; in the United States the opposite took place during the 1990s). However, this conclusion is premature (Lappi-Seppälä 2007). Crime rates in Finland followed the general Scandinavian pattern and remained quite similar in all Scandinavian countries between 1950 and 2005, despite radical differences in imprisonment trends.

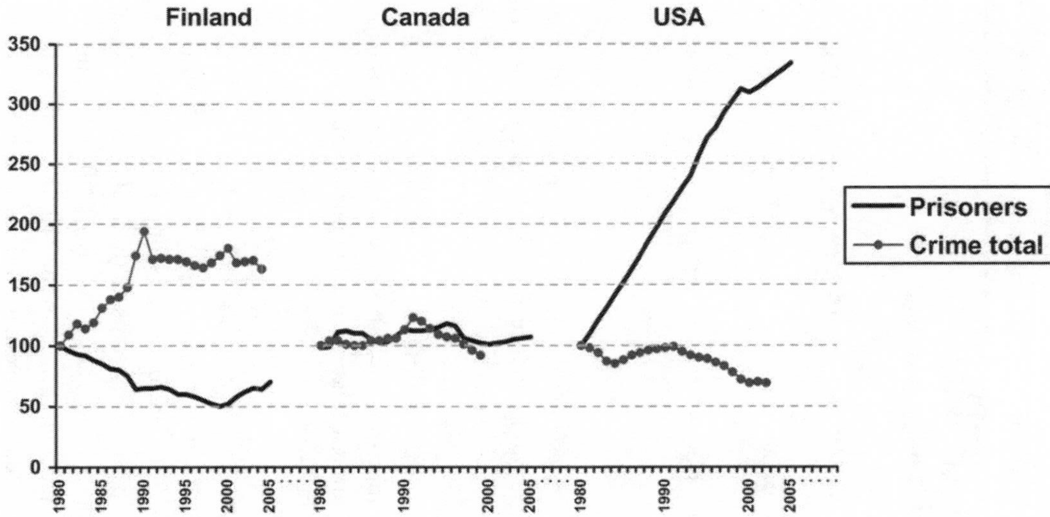

FIG. 9.—Prisoners and reported crime in Finland, Canada, and the United States per 100,000 population (1980 = 100) (source: national statistics)

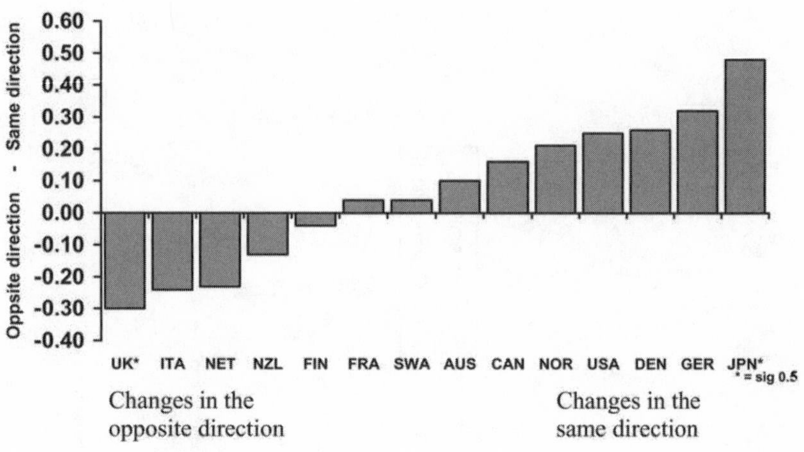

FIG. 10.—Associations between reported crime and imprisonment rates, 1980–2005 (Pearson's *r*) (source: Sourcebook 2006 complemented).

imprisonment rates next year). Since both variables show a constant increasing trend (and produce thus easily spurious correlations), correlations are based on differentiated series (differences between two years).

Associations differ in different countries. In England, Italy, and the Netherlands, imprisonment rates moved in the opposite direction from crime. In Japan, Germany, and Denmark, imprisonment rates and crime moved in the same direction.[15]

E. Conclusion about Crime and Imprisonment Rate Interactions

Imprisonment rates are unrelated to victimization rates or to reported crime. The development of imprisonment rates in 1980–2005 showed no consistent patterns with total recorded crime. Different countries exhibited different patterns in different times. These results fit well with the conclusion from the prior literature that imprisonment is largely unaffected by levels and trends in criminality (see Greenberg 1999; von Hofer 2003; Sutton 2004; Ruddell 2005). Crime is not the explanation for differences or for trends.

[15] When comparing these findings with those in Sec. IV.*B*, one must note that this analysis covers the whole period 1980–2005.

IV. Economic and Demographic Factors

Economic and demographic factors are among the classical and most often proposed explanations for major changes in criminal punishments. This section examines associations between imprisonment rates and unemployment, economic prosperity, and demographic composition.

A. Unemployment

Classical economic explanations of imprisonment patterns borrow from Marxist traditions and place labor power in a central role. Rusche and Kirchheimer (1939) argued that punishments are determined by economic rationality and are used to control the lower classes and exploit their labor power. Executions are common when there is surplus manpower, and imprisonment and forced labor are used when labor is scarce. This looked quite sensible in explorations of the birth of the predecessors of modern prisons in the sixteenth century. Today the associations between imprisonment, labor power, and unemployment are much more complicated, even from a theoretical point of view.[16] Recent attempts to explore interactions between prison use and unemployment often start from the assumption that high unemployment (and not scarcity of labor) produces higher incarceration rates because the state may elect to remove disturbing and futile populations from the streets. A hypothesis that aims to use both labor surplus and labor scarcity as explanatory factors is problematic. When examined, associations between unemployment and imprisonment rates look very different in different samples.

Results differ depending on whether analyses include eastern European (positive correlation) or Anglo-Saxon (negative correlation) countries. Unemployment hardly serves as an important general factor in either direction (see analyses in Lappi-Seppälä [2008]).

B. Gross Domestic Product

Sutton (2004) refines Rusche and Kirchheimer (1939) by including two other economic variables, GDP and inflation, in the analyses. The hypothesized mechanism between these three variables and imprison-

[16] For a fuller discussion on the relation between labor surplus and punishment, see Chiricos and Delone (1992). On the basis of results from 44 studies covering different periods, mainly between 1930 and 1985, the authors detect a positive association between labor surplus (usually measured by unemployment rates) and penal severity.

ment rates remains, however, slightly obscure. Economic prosperity as such may contribute to penal practices in several ways. Having more money makes it possible to build more prisons. But rich countries could, if they chose, build well-functioning community alternatives to imprisonment or invest in social welfare and thereby reduce the strains for the use of penal measures.

The global sample of 99 countries allowed a further examination of this association. The direction of correlation was dependent on the general level of economic prosperity (see analyses in Lappi-Seppälä [2008]).

In poorer countries with GDP below $15,000 the association is positive (more money means more prisoners), whereas in rich democracies the correlation changes direction. Building prisons is expensive, and having a positive correlation makes sense from this point of view. At some point, however, the accumulation of economic wealth becomes negatively associated with penal severity. In general, wealthy nations seem to be less punitive, with one obvious outlier—the United States.

It is not only the amount of money, but how money is spent. This brings in social and political dimensions, but first demographics need to be considered.

C. Demographics, Minorities, and Immigrants

Demographic heterogeneity is among classic candidates for differences in penal severity. According to the "minority-threat hypothesis," increases in population heterogeneity result in a greater use of formal social control and imprisonment.[17] The Scandinavian countries are demographically fairly homogeneous. There are no large ethnic minorities. Consequently, the low imprisonment rates in Scandinavia, and especially in Finland, have been explained by reference to population homogeneity (von Hofer 2003; Ruddell 2005).

1. *Multiculturalism and Immigrants.* Demographic homogeneity is usually measured by the immigration rate and the population share of nonnational populations. One may also use multiculturalism indexes, which summarize elements of ethnic, religious, and cultural differentiation. Ruddell (2005) found a positive association between the level

[17] See, e.g., Ruddell (2005). One may, e.g., assume that population homogeneity prevents conflicts and that conflict in turn increases fears and tensions, which may give rise to extremist movements and demands for tougher sentences.

of multiculturalism measured by the Stark multiculturalism index[18] and incarceration in a sample of 100 countries. Table 8 compares imprisonment rates with the share of nonnational population, the immigrant rate, and multiculturalism.

The immigrant rate, the share of nonnational populations, and asylum seekers correlate inversely: The more immigrants, the fewer prisoners. The Stark multiculturalism index had varying associations with imprisonment rates in different samples. The only significant positive association was influenced by the U.S. figures (Eur16 + Ang3 + U.S.).[19]

2. *Attitudes, Beliefs, Anxieties.* If they exist at all, associations between demographic composition and the use of penal power are subtle. Another explanation for these findings may be that the indicators are unable to capture dimensions of anxieties, fear of strangers, tensions, and feelings of insecurity. The minority threat hypothesis may, however, be tested more directly with survey data concerning attitudes and beliefs. Table 9 summarizes results from the first round of the ESS. The measurements deal with people's views on three topics: How welcome new immigrants are, what effects they have on the country's economic and cultural life (positive or negative), and whether the country should take more or fewer refugees.

Positive (but nonsignificant) correlations between imprisonment rates and the first question (are immigrants welcome?) indicate that the number of prisoners increases as attitudes become less friendly. A negative association in the second question indicates that the more positive the effects immigrants are thought to have on the society, the lower the imprisonment rates. The same structure repeats itself in the last question: The more people agreed with the statement that the "country

[18] The index defines the odds from one to 100 that any two persons will differ in their race, ethnicity, tribal affiliation, religion, or language group (Stark 2004; Ruddell 2005, p. 16).

[19] However, Ruddell (2005) reports a fairly strong positive association between these two: imprisonment increased with population heterogeneity in a sample of 100 nations (also after controlling for crime and a number of other variables). To test Ruddell's results, a separate sample with 36 democracies was formed. Associations between multiculturalism and imprisonment rates remained fairly low, and they were clearly outweighed by factors related to political structure.

The index itself raises some problems. It places Finland—the most homogeneous country in Scandinavia—at the same level of multiculturalism as France and countries such as Germany, Sweden, and Denmark. This odd (and incorrect) result arises because Finland has a 5 percent Swedish-speaking minority (which is a cultural enrichment, and not a threat to anyone). At least in this case (and presumably in others too), the index fails to function as an indicator of fears and anxieties associated with population heterogeneity.

TABLE 8

Immigrants, Nonnationals, Asylum Seekers, and Multiculturalism (Prisoners 2001–3)

Measure	Eur16	Eur19	Eur16 + Ang3	Eur16 + Ang3 + U.S.	Eur19 + Ang3	Eur19 + Ang3 + U.S.	All	Global 99
Nonnational 1998 (%; EUSI)	−.096	−.223	−.096	.227	−.223	.191		
Immigrant rate 1998 (EUSI)	−.138	−.560*	−.138	−.272	−.560*	−.298		
Asylum seekers 2002 (Eurostat)	−.391	−.439	−.391				−464*	
Multiculturalism (Stark)	.202	−.167	.294	.544*	−.076	.365		.175

SOURCES.—Sourcebook 2006 complemented, EUSI, Eurostat, and Stark (2004).
* Significant at the .01 level.
** Significant at the .05 level.

TABLE 9

Attitudes and Beliefs (ESS) (Prisoners 2001–3)

Question	Eur16	Eur19
How welcome are new immigrants? (1 = yes, 4 = no)	.48	.36
Do immigrants have positive or negative effects? (0 [negative] to 10 points)	−.68**	−.78**
Should more immigrants be admitted? (1 agree, 4 disagree)	−.51	−.24

SOURCES.—Sourcebook 2006 complemented and ESS.
* Significant at the .01 level.
** Significant at the .05 level.

had more than its share of refugees," the higher the imprisonment rates.

Table 10 establishes the associations between attitudes, multiculturalism (Stark 2004), and immigration rates. Correlations were partly unexpected. The higher the immigration rates and the share of nonnationals, the more positive the attitudes.

Demographic factors cannot be used as straightforward explanations for the levels of repression. The associations between imprisonment rates, beliefs, and attitudes are stronger and more systematic than actual demographic patterns. Associations between attitudes and the size of nonnational populations, in turn, were also unexpected. They suggest that the size of minority groups may be less important than the contents of (immigration) policies.

TABLE 10

Attitudes, Multiculturalism, and Immigration Rates

Measure	Immigration Rate	Nonnationals
Multiculturalism (Stark)	.37	.72**
How welcome are new immigrants? (1 = yes, 4 = no)	−.40	−.21
Do immigrants have positive or negative effects? (0 [negative] to 10 points)	.39	.21
Should more immigrants be admitted? (1 agree, 4 disagree)	−.18	−.02

SOURCES.—Sourcebook 2006 complemented and ESS.
* Significant at the .01 level.
** Significant at the .05 level.

V. Fears and Punitiveness

Even if the level of crime is unrelated to the use of imprisonment, crime may still importantly explain imprisonment rates through the public's perceptions and reactions and through media representations. The hypothesized association is fairly straightforward. Public perceptions and concern about crime shape how people treat crime and criminals. Fears and public sentiments may form an essential part of those explanations that combine penal changes, the rise of a "culture of fear," and "postmodern angst." Few of these assumptions have been empirically tested.

A. Fear of Crime

Associations between fear of crime and imprisonment rates can be examined with the help of victimization studies. Table 11 compares fear of crime and imprisonment rates from the ESS survey (first round) and the ICVS 2000 sweep.[20] When reading the results, one must note that different surveys include different countries. The ESS confines itself to Europe. The ICVS includes the United States, Canada, Australia, and New Zealand, and the latest EU ICS (unfortunately) confines itself to the member states of the European Union.

All surveys except in the United States produce similar results: The higher the fear of crime, the higher the number of prisoners.

B. Punitiveness

The ICVS and the EU ICS measure penal attitudes and public punitiveness by asking respondents to suggest the proper penalty for a young recidivist burglar for stealing a television set. (The ESS did not measure punitiveness.) If prison was considered an appropriate alternative, respondents were asked to indicate the preferred length of prison term. This offers three possibilities for measuring punitiveness: the share of prison sentences as a percentage of proposed penalties, the length of a proposed prison sentence (in months), and a combination of these two expressed as a "punitiveness score" (percent × length) (see table 12).

[20] Descriptions for the ICVS measurements are to be found in van Kesteren, Mayhew, and Nieuwbeerta (2000). The other survey widely used in this study is the ESS. This survey is designed to chart and explain the interaction between Europe's changing institutions and the attitudes, beliefs, and behavior patterns of its diverse populations. In its second round, the survey covers over 20 nations (see http://www.europeansocialsurvey.org/).

TABLE 11

Imprisonment Rates and Fear of Crime (Prisoners 2001–3)

Measure	Eur16	Eur19	Eur16 + Ang3	Eur16 + Ang3 + U.S.	Eur19 + Ang3	Eur19 + Ang3 + U.S.	All 25
Fear of crime (ESS)	.697**	.747**	.762**		.747**		
Feeling unsafe while walking out:							
ICVS 2000 (%)	.728*	.812**	.662**	−.251	.713**	−.157	
EU ICS 2005 (%)	.828**	.815**	.844**		.815**		.545*

SOURCES.—Sourcebook 2006 complemented, ESS, and ICVS.

* Significant at the .01 level.

** Significant at the .05 level.

TABLE 12

Imprisonment Rates and Punitiveness (Prisoners 2001–3)

Measure	Eur16	Eur19	Eur16 + Ang3	Eur16 + Ang3 + U.S.	Eur19 + Ang3	Eur19 + Ang3 + U.S.	All
Prison for burglars (ICVS 2000)	.456	.322	.426	.588*	.276	.572**	
Sentence length (ICVS 2000)	.770**	.799**	.709**	.531*	.788**	.530*	
Punitiveness scores ICVS 2000 (% × months)	.630*	.673**	.667**	.795**	.633**	.773**	
Prison for burglars (EU ICS 2005)	.279	.374	.279		.374		.278
Length of prison (EU ICS 2005)	.641*	.798**	.641*		.798**		.769**
Punitiveness scores EU ICS 2005 (% × months)	.129	.654**	.469		.654**		.586*

SOURCES.—Sourcebook 2006 complemented, ICVS, and EU ICS.

* Significant at the .01 level.

** Significant at the .05 level.

All punitiveness variables correlate positively with imprisonment rates. In general, the Scandinavian countries, Germany, France, and Austria are at the low end of the punitiveness scale (see Lappi-Seppälä 2008).

VI. Welfare and Social Equality

There is a connection between a country's welfare orientation and its penal culture. From a welfarist point of view, crime is a social problem with social causes and should be dealt with by means of social techniques and social work professions. A simple way to define the relationship between welfare and incarceration is to draw a straight line between them: "locking people up or giving them money might be considered alternative ways of handling marginal, poor populations—repressive in one case, generous in the other" (Greenberg 2001, p. 70). A war on poverty leads to different penal policies than a war on crime. The association between the emergence of punitive policies and the scaling down of the welfare state in the United States and in the United Kingdom has been noted by several commentators (e.g., Garland 2001; Cavadino and Dignan 2006). The connection between the level of repression and welfare receives support also from the Finnish story, since the period on penal liberalization in Finland started when Finland joined the Nordic welfare family. Penal reform in Finland was a part of a larger reform of social policy (Lappi-Seppälä 2007).

Factors such as high levels of social and economic security, equality in welfare resources, and generous welfare provision should contribute to lower levels of punitiveness and repression. This association has been demonstrated in several studies, most recently for the United States by Beckett and Western (2001) and cross-nationally by Downes and Hansen (2006). Associations between sentence severity and income equality have been explored by Killias (1986), Pease (1991), Greenberg (1999), and Tham (2001, 2005).

A. Income Inequality

One measure of social equality is how evenly income is distributed in society. The "fairness" of income distribution is, in turn, usually measured with the Gini index. The index expresses to what extent the real income distribution differs from the "ideal" and fair distribution of complete equality (0 = total fairness, 1 = total unfairness).

TABLE 13

Imprisonment Rates and Income Inequality (Prisoners 2001–3)

Measure	Eur16	Eur19	Eur16 + Ang3	Eur16 + Ang3 + U.S.	Eur19 + Ang3	Eur19 + Ang3 + U.S.	All 25	Global 99
Gini 2000 (LIS)	.767**	.356	.839**	.531*	.430	.494*	.561**	.139

SOURCES.—Sourcebook 2006 complemented and LIS.
* Significant at the .01 level.
** Significant at the .05 level.

It is not altogether clear, however, what income inequality indicates. Martin Killias in 1986 interpreted income equality in political terms as an indicator of power concentration. Since power is associated with economic resources, unequal income distribution might signify unequal distribution of power and relative distance between the rulers and the ruled. But income inequality can also be interpreted in terms of social equality, equality in social resources, full citizenship, society's concerns for the well-being of the poor, and underlying feelings of social solidarity. Discussions below address social dimensions. Power concentration and legitimacy are discussed in Section VII.

1. *Income Inequality in a Cross-Sectional Analysis.* Table 13 summarizes the correlations in different samples. Figure 11 plots the Gini index and prison populations in the global samples.

Looked at globally, increased income inequality seems to produce more prisoners. The association, however, is fairly weak. Some regions and areas fit this model better, especially Scandinavia and western Europe. A closer look at different subsamples produces sronger correlations and reveals different patterns (fig. 12).

There is a strong positive correlation between income distribution and imprisonment rates among the western European countries (left half of fig. 12). Including the eastern countries weakens the association significantly. However, among the eastern countries by themselves, this association remains strong (the right half of fig. 12 adds eastern countries). The small number of eastern countries prevents general conclusions. The Baltic countries generally seem to follow a pattern different from that of the former socialist countries.

2. *Changes over Time.* Changes occur over time. There may be changes in variables explaining penal severity (in this case income in-

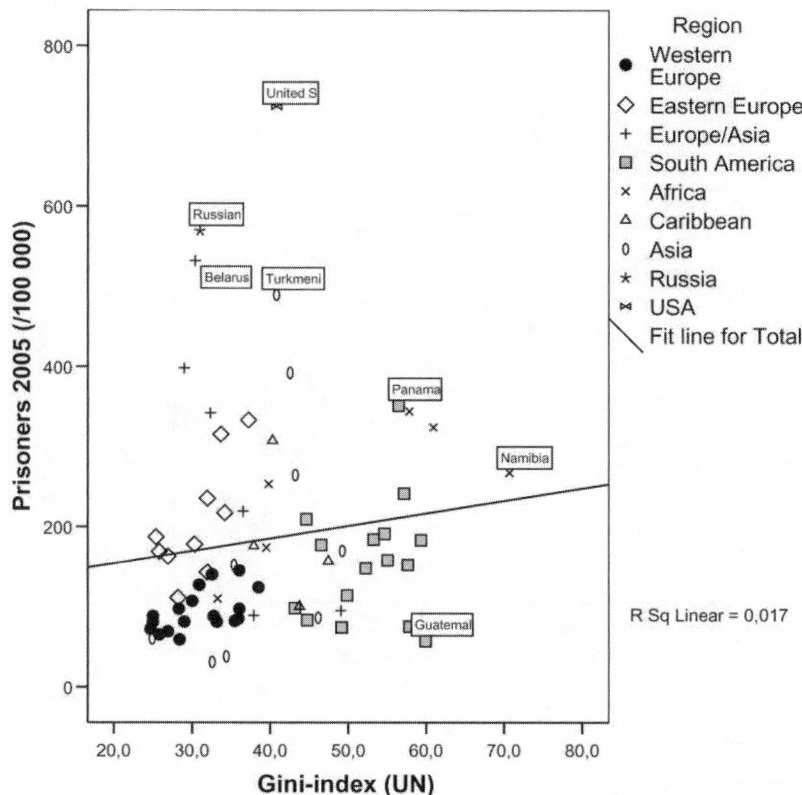

FIG. 11.—Income inequality and imprisonment rates (global sample) (sources: ICPS and UN).

equality). Associations between factors may change to one direction or another. Multiple changes may also occur (in either the same or different directions: e.g., decreasing income differences but stronger associations of these differences with punitiveness). A comparison of 15 countries for the years 1987–2000 suggests that associations between income inequality and imprisonment rates have become stronger over time. In 1987 the correlation was close to zero, but it has grown stronger each year since.

However, looking at individual countries reveals diverse trends. Countries running against the hypothesis in the 1980s were Finland, Austria, and Sweden, with growing income differences and decreasing

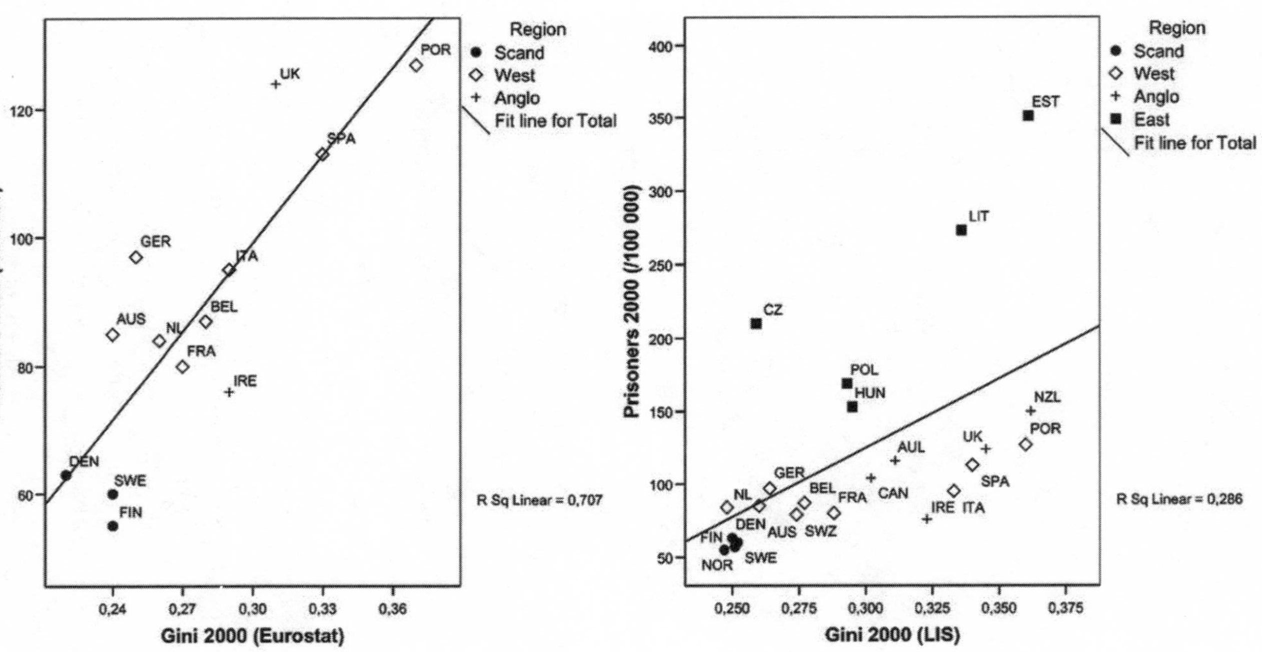

FIG. 12.—Gini index and imprisonment rates, 2000 (source: Sourcebook 2006 complemented)

or stable imprisonment rates; and Switzerland, Ireland, and Netherlands, with stable or decreasing income differences but increasing imprisonment rates. These countries may also explain the weak associations in the late 1980s. The four countries supporting most strongly the hypothesis are Belgium, England, New Zealand, and the United States. During the most recent years, developments in Sweden and Finland support the model, as income differences have increased together at the same time as imprisonment rates have increased (see Lappi-Seppälä [2008] for a detailed analysis).

Social inequality is evidently a substantial risk factor, but changes in socioeconomic factors do not have straightforward mechanical effects on imprisonment rates.[21] Country-specific deviations and developments also argue against such straightforward generalizations.

B. Social Expenditures

Another measure of social equality is the extent of state support of its poorest populations via social welfare. The public social expenditure share of GDP is the standard measure used in welfare comparisons. With OECD data from 1987–98, Downes and Hansen (2006) documented an inverse relation between welfare expenditure and the scale of imprisonment. Beckett and Western (2001) report similar findings in comparing U.S. states.

However, welfare spending may not be the ideal indicator of the "welfare state." All spending does not count equally, as pointed out by Esping-Andersen (1990, pp. 19–20). Some welfare states allocate large sums to payment of privileged civil servants; some spend enormous sums on tax subsidies for private insurance, some on means-tested social assistance; and in some countries high welfare spending may result from high unemployment. None of these has much to do with what would normally be considered a commitment to social citizenship and solidarity. To overcome these difficulties, measurements of social spending have been augmented with additional measurements. In his classical *Three Worlds of Welfare Capitalism*, Esping-Andersen formulated a general decommodification index that gives a fuller picture of how social welfare services are taken care of by the state rather than left to market forces.

[21] One may also ask how adequate a measure the Gini index is for this purpose. For example, in Finland recent growth in the Gini index mainly reflects exclusively the accumulation of sales profits for the richest 2 percent, not changes, e.g., in factory income.

1. *Welfare Provision and Decommodification in Cross-Sectional Analyses.* Table 14 compares Eurostat social expenditure statistics expressed in euros as a percentage of GDP and relative to population, and a decommodification index developed by Esping-Andersen. The analysis uses a revised and updated version of the index by Bambra (2006).

There is an inverse relation between commitment to welfare (the generosity of welfare provision) and the scale of imprisonment. Social expenditures in real terms (euros) and the decommodification index (referring to activities and efforts by the government that reduce citizens' reliance on the market) give strongest results among the western countries.

Basic associations are illustrated in figure 13. The first indicator (fig. 13, left panel) measures welfare expenditure as a proportion of GDP. In the lower right corner are countries led by Sweden and Denmark with a high proportion of GDP spent on welfare and low imprisonment rates. In the upper left corner are England, Portugal, and Spain (Canada and New Zealand).

However, relative measurements are vulnerable to changes in general economic growth. A growing economy may decrease welfare ratings whereas a recession may lead to increased (relative) spending. To overcome this problem, changes per capita in real social expenditures were counted (right panel). The association grew stronger. Ireland, with almost two decades of economic growth averaging 4.3 percent per year, changed its position toward the average.

The associations remain the same (in fact, become stronger) if basic imprisonment rates are replaced by rates relative to crime. See Lappi-Seppälä (2008) for fuller analyses.

2. *Changes in Associations over Time.* Downes and Hansen indicated that the relationship persisted over time (1987–98) and that countries that increased the share of GDP spent on welfare saw relative declines in their prison populations. The association between imprisonment rates and spending became greater over time, indicating that a "country that increases the amount of its GDP spent on welfare sees a greater decline in its imprisonment rate than in the past" (2006, p. 152). These findings are supported by my analysis covering the years 1980–2000 (see Lappi-Seppälä 2008).

Countries that decreased their (relative) social spending had the steepest increases in imprisonment rates. The results are influenced especially by developments in Ireland and the Netherlands. The in-

TABLE 14

Imprisonment Rates and Social Welfare Provision (Prisoners 2001–3)

Measure	Eur16	Eur19	Eur16 + Ang3	Eur16 + Ang3 + U.S.	Eur19 + Ang3	Eur19 + Ang3 + U.S.	All
Social expenditure 2003:							
% of GDP (Eurostat)	−.435	−.605**	−.395				−.800**
€/population (Eurostat)	−.837**	−.867**	−.741**				−.815**
Decommodification 1999	−.458	−.770**	−.859**	−.529*		−.530*	

SOURCES.—Sourcebook 2006 complemented, Eurostat, and Bambra (2006).
* Significant at the .01 level.
** Significant at the .05 level.

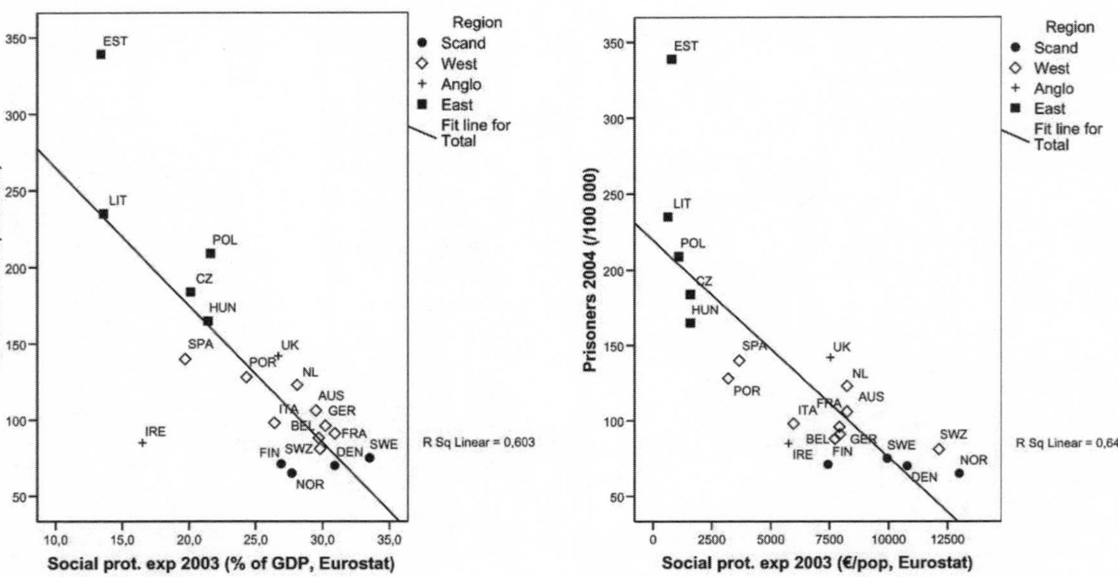

FIG. 13.—Social expenditures (2003) and imprisonment rates (sources: Sourcebook 2006 complemented and Eurostat)

crease in social expenditure investments in the Netherlands has been the lowest, in relative terms (as a percentage of GDP), and in real terms per capita.

C. Regional Patterns and Penal Regimes?

Esping-Andersen (1990) detected a pattern among western (capitalist) welfare states. Countries in Esping-Andersen's study clustered in three welfare regimes concerning the extent and structure of welfare provision, and values and principles aimed and expressed in welfare policies: social-democratic (Scandinavian) regimes, Christian democratic (conservative/European) regimes, and liberal (Anglo-Saxon) regimes. These regimes bunch particular values with particular programs and policies. Different regimes pursue different policies, and for different reasons. Esping-Andersen's findings have not been contested, although his original classification has been refined by introducing a separate southern cluster.[22] Including the former socialist countries in the analysis would require additional revisions.[23] All would rank low in terms of welfare provision, but income equality differences would emerge. Although many formerly socialist countries have maintained fairly even income distributions, the Baltic countries are approaching western neoliberal states in their income distributions and economic policies.

The relevance of welfare classifications for this analysis is simple. Should welfare matter for penal policies (as it seems to), differences between welfare regimes should be reflected in differences in penal policies. To test the hypothesis, countries have been clustered into five regions. The clustering follows Esping-Andersen's modified classification but adds clusters from the traditional former socialist countries

[22] Vogel (1997) distinguishes the northern European cluster (Scandinavia), which exhibits high levels of social expenditure and labor market participation and weak family ties, relatively low levels of class and income inequality, low poverty rates, and high levels of inequality between younger and older generations. Countries in the southern European cluster (Greece, Italy, Portugal, and Spain) have much lower welfare state provision, lower rates of employment, strong family ties, higher levels of class and income equality and poverty, but low levels of intergenerational inequality. The countries in the western European cluster (Austria, Belgium, France, Germany, Ireland, Luxembourg, the Netherlands, and the United Kingdom) occupy the middle position. However, the United Kingdom borders on the southern cluster in terms of income equality, poverty, and class inequality (see Vogel 1997; Falck, von Hofer, and Storgaard 2003). Castles (2004) uses a similar classification but treats Switzerland as a special case.

[23] So far comparative welfare theory has concentrated mainly on western countries, leaving out both former socialist countries and most of Asia (see Goodin et al. 1999).

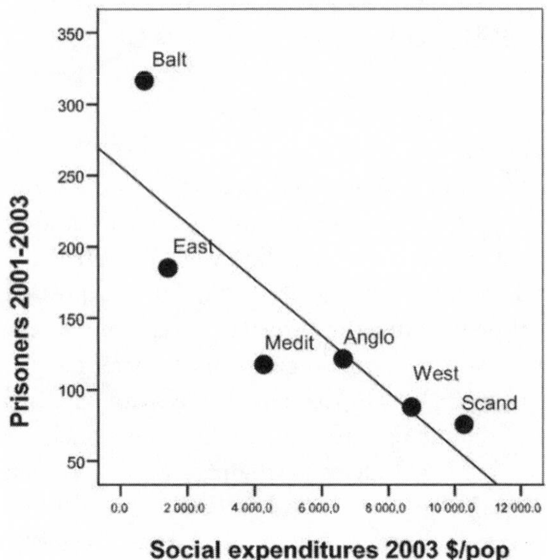

FIG. 14.—Welfare expenditures and imprisonment rates by regions (sources: Sourcebook 2006 complemented and Eurostat).

and the Baltic countries. This gives six regions (excluding the United States): Scandinavia (Finland, Denmark, Sweden, and Norway), western Europe (Austria, Belgium, France, Germany, Netherlands, and Switzerland), Mediterranean Europe (Spain, Italy, and Portugal), Anglo-Saxon countries (United Kingdom, Ireland, Australia, Canada, and New Zealand), eastern Europe (Poland, Hungary, and the Czech Republic), and the Baltic countries (Estonia and Lithuania). Figure 14 illustrates the association between imprisonment rates and welfare provision in these five regions.

The relative positions of different regimes mirror the general pattern that emerges from welfare analyses. Different welfare regimes differ in penal policies and in the use of penal power.

Figure 15 compares income inequality and imprisonment rates by regions. Results are less consistent, compared to welfare provision. The Scandinavian countries still place lowest in terms of income differences and imprisonment rates (and highest in welfare provision). Western Europe and eastern Europe are close to each other in terms of income inequality, but with clear differences in penal severity.

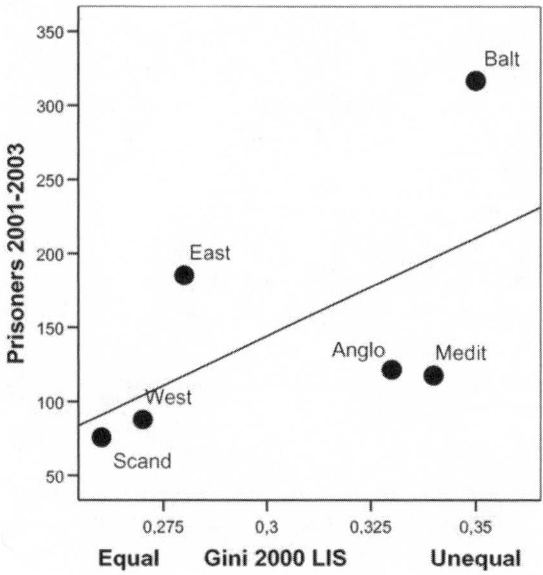

FIG. 15.—Income inequality and imprisonment rates by regions (sources: Sourcebook 2006 complemented and LIS).

VII. Trust and Legitimacy

Alongside the Durkheimian tradition, which links levels of repression to feelings of social solidarity, a Weberian tradition explains levels of penal repression in terms of power concentration and the need to defend political authority (see Killias 1986). The rise of harsh and expressive policies in the United States and in the United Kingdom has been attributed to a loss of public confidence, a legitimacy crisis, and the state's need to use expressive punishments as a demonstration of sovereignty. David Garland has referred to the state's inability to handle the crime problem and resulting "denial and acting out." Unable to admit that the situation has escaped from the government's control and to show that "something" is being done about crime, governments resort to expressive gestures and punitive responses (Garland 2001, p. 103). In the United States since the 1960s, the scope of federal government activity and responsibility expanded into fields such as health care, education, consumer protection, and discrimination, leading to a spiral of political failures. This in turn led to a collapse of confidence in government's capacity to address basic social problems. The subsequent expressive actions against crime were, in part, meant to save the government's credibility (Caplow and Simon 1999; Tonry 2004, pp. 41–44; Simon 2007). A loss of public confidence in the political system has been characterized as a major cause of the rise of punitive populism and the ascendancy of penal severity in New Zealand (Pratt and Clark 2005).

In the following analyses, political legitimacy is measured with social survey data on citizens' confidence and trust in political institutions. The analyses extend from political legitimacy to social trust (and social capital), as the surveys cover both dimensions. The ESS contains several questions measuring trust in people (horizontal, generalized, or social trust) and trust in different social institutions (vertical or institutional trust).[24] The WVS, conducted in a larger number of countries, contains similar questions measuring citizens' confidence in each other and in social and political institutions (http://www.worldvalues survey.org). Cross-sectional observations are based on the first round of the ESS (http://www.europeansocialsurvey.org). Trend analyses are based on WVS started in 1981.

A. Trust and Penal Severity in Cross-Sectional Analyses

There is a strong inverse association between the levels of repression, legitimacy, and social trust. Correlations are high, systematic, and significant in all samples. Different aspects of trust and confidence are closely associated with imprisonment rates: The higher the trust, the lower the level of repression. Figure 16 illustrates the results.

The legitimacy of social and political institutions is highest in Scandinavia and Switzerland. These countries also tend to have the lowest imprisonment rates. Close to these rankings in trust come Austria and the Netherlands. In the opposite corner are the eastern European countries and the United Kingdom. Figure 17 summarizes regional patterns between imprisonment rates and trust according to the welfare classifications explained above.

Regional patterns keep repeating themselves. The Scandinavians have higher social trust and also high levels of trust in their political

[24] Trust in people ("generalized trust") was measured with the following question: "Would you say that most people can be trusted, or that you can't be too careful in dealing with people?" (0: you can't be too careful; 10: most people can be trusted). Trust in institutions was asked in the following way: "Please tell me on a score of 0–10 how much you trust each of these institutions: country's parliament, the legal system, the police, politicians?" (0: no trust at all; 10: complete trust).

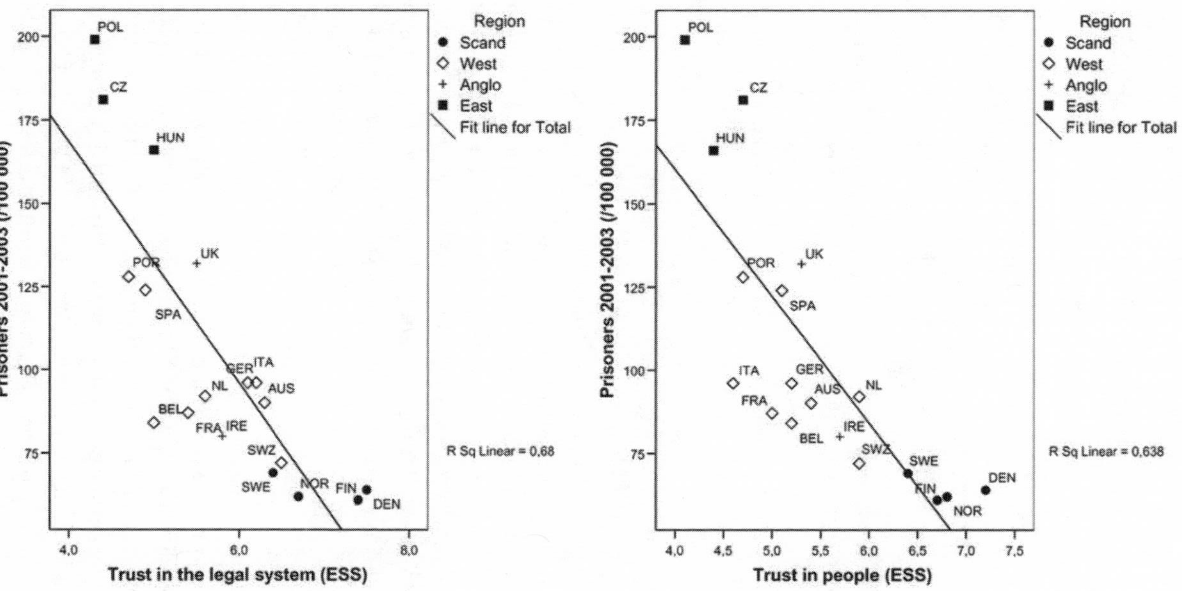

FIG. 16.—Trust in the legal system and in people (sources: Sourcebook 2006 complemented and ESS)

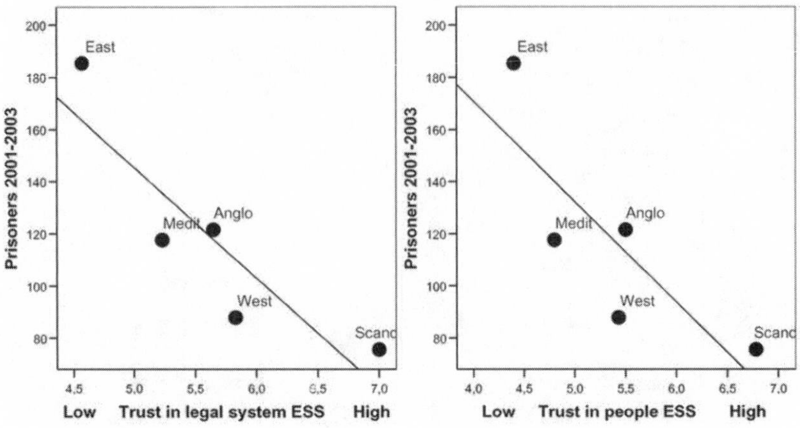

FIG. 17.—Trust and imprisonment rates by regions (sources: Sourcebook 2006 complemented and ESS).

and legal institutions. The eastern European cluster occupies the opposite position in both measurements. Continental western countries are the closest to Scandinavia in political trust but are at the same level as the Anglo-Saxon countries in social trust.

On a closer examination, levels of trust are inversely associated also with fear, punitiveness, and income inequality. They all increase as the degree of trust decreases. High levels of trust seem associated with more generous welfare provision. These associations retain their strength and direction (but not their level of significance) when other variables (fear, punitiveness, and social-economic variables) are controlled for.[25]

B. Changes over Time

Changes over time are examined in Lappi-Seppälä (2008). The results follow identical patterns. The association between trust and imprisonment rates has become stronger, in terms of both social trust and trust in the legal system. There are countries with divergent trends, such as Finland during the 1980s and early 1990s, when trust in the legal system and imprisonment rates were both decreasing. However, the general picture gives strong support to the hypothesis that social

[25] Intercorrelations and associations between the key variables are discussed separately in Sec. IX.

and political trust and penal severity are closely interrelated, and that declining trust associates with increasing imprisonment rates.

VIII. Political Cultures—Consensus or Conflict?

Socioeconomic factors, public sentiments, and feelings of trust do not by themselves turn into penal practices. In the end imprisonment rates (and social policy) result from policy choices and political actions, in the context of a given political culture. The penal policy changes in the United States, for example, have been attributed in part to the bipolar structure of the political system and the struggle for swing voters (see Caplow and Simon 1999; Tonry 2004, p. 38; Simon 2007). Scandinavian moderation has been explained by reference to corporatist and consensus models of political decision making (Kyvsgaard 2001; Bondeson 2005; Cavadino and Dignan 2006). The exceptionally mild, 30-years-long, postwar period in Dutch criminal justice policy has been attributed to the "Dutch politics of accommodation" (see Downes and Swaaningen 2007).

A. Modeling Political Economies

All these terms—political culture, political economy, (neo-)corporatism—raise definitional problems. This section explores the roles of political institutions, political environments, and economic systems, and the relations among the state, interest groups, and wage coordination mechanisms, in shaping penal policies. This can be done with an emphasis on either political or economic structures.

1. *Consensual Democracies and Majoritarian Democracies.* Democratic political systems have been characterized as "consensus" and "majoritarian" democracies (Lijphart 1999). The terms themselves express the main differences.[26] In relation to the "basic democratic principle," majoritarian democracy stresses the majority principle: The will of the majority dictates choices between alternatives. Consensus democracy emphasizes political participation over mere majorities. The majority principle means that the winner takes all; consensus means that as many views as possible are taken into account. Majority-driven politics are usually based on two-party competition and confrontation; consensus-driven policy seeks compromises. Instead of concentrating power

[26] Lijphart (1998) reports several difficulties in developing suitable and nonconfusing concepts.

in the hands of the majority, the consensus model tries to share, disperse, and restrain power in various ways, for example, by allowing all or most important parties to share executive power in broad coalitions and by allowing widespread interest group participation (Lijphart 1999, p. 34).

Several institutional arrangements separate these two systems. Consensus democracies typically have larger numbers of political parties, proportional electoral systems, and either minority governments or broad-based coalition governments. Political decision-making processes are characterized by consensus-seeking negotiations with well-coordinated and centralized interest groups actively cooperating.

2. *Corporatism and Neocorporatism.* Bringing interest group participation into the analyses encompasses broader political processes and relations among the state, corporations, workers, employers, and trade unions. The concept of (neo)corporatism captures essential features. In contemporary political science and sociology, the term refers to tripartite processes of bargaining among labor unions, private-sector organizations, and government in small and open economies.[27] Such bargaining is oriented toward dividing the productivity gains created in the economy fairly among social partners and achieving wage restraint in recessionary or inflationary periods. Neocorporatist arrangements require highly organized and centralized labor unions that bargain on behalf of all workers. Examples include the collective agreement arrangements of the Scandinavian countries, the Dutch Poldermodel system of consensus, and the Republic of Ireland's system of social partnership.[28]

There is an obvious link: consensus democracies and corporatism usually go hand in hand.[29] Scandinavian countries are typical examples

[27] The historical roots of corporatism go back to the old guild system and the early twentieth-century Italian trade unions, many organized to counter the influences of socialist ideology. The concept was revised by the late twentieth-century theory of political economy. Like its successor, neocorporatism emphasizes the role of corporate bodies in influencing government decision making but has lost the negative associations (some originating from the period of Italian fascism).

[28] Corporatism (or neocorporatism) may be given different definitions. Sutton's definition stresses the labor market dimension: Corporatism is a "set of structural arrangements through which workers, employers, and the state are jointly engaged in forging economic policies that are applied in a coordinated way across the entire economy" (2004, p. 176).

[29] However, not always. Ireland is an example of a two-party system with strong corporatist elements. More generally, the classifications in the text are ideal types. Real-world democracies fall onto a scale, in terms of both corporatism and consensualism.

TABLE 15

Imprisonment Rates per 100,000 Population in Consensus and Majoritarian Democracies, 1980–2004

	1980	1990	2000	2004	Increase 1980–2004
Consensus 11	66	67	76	88	32%
Majoritarian 5	68	92	114	129	89%
United States	221	461	684	724	228%

SOURCE.—Sourcebook 2006 complemented.

NOTE.—Consensus 11 includes Austria, Belgium, Denmark, Finland, France, Germany, Italy, Netherlands, Norway, Sweden, and Switzerland. Majoritarian 5 includes Australia, Canada, Ireland, New Zealand, and the United Kingdom.

of consensual—or corporatist—(social) democracies. Switzerland is another paradigmatic example. To this group belong also Austria, Belgium, France, Germany, Italy, and the Netherlands. Majoritarian (and usually also less corporatist) democracies include Australia, Canada, Ireland, New Zealand, the United Kingdom, and the United States.[30]

3. *The Relevance of Political Economy.* In Lijphart's analyses, consensus democracies outperform majoritarian democracies with regard to the quality of democracy and democratic representation and the "kindness and gentleness of their public policy orientation" (1999, p. 301). Consensus democracies are also characterized by better political and economic equality and enhanced electoral participation. Moreover, Lijphart found in his analyses covering the years 1992 and 1995 that consensus democracies put fewer people in prison and held much more restrictive views on the use of the death penalty (pp. 286, 297–98).

Consensus democracies are associated with more restrained penal policies (see table 15). In 1980 the imprisonment rates in the 11 consensus democracies and five majoritarian democracies (the United States is omitted) were about even. Since then, the majoritarian democracies increased their imprisonment rates by 89 percent and the consensus democracies by 32 percent. If the United States had been included, these differences would have been much greater.

[30] As Pratt and Clark (2005) report, in 1999, New Zealand moved in the corporatist direction by adopting a proportional electoral system (however, with considerable difficulties).

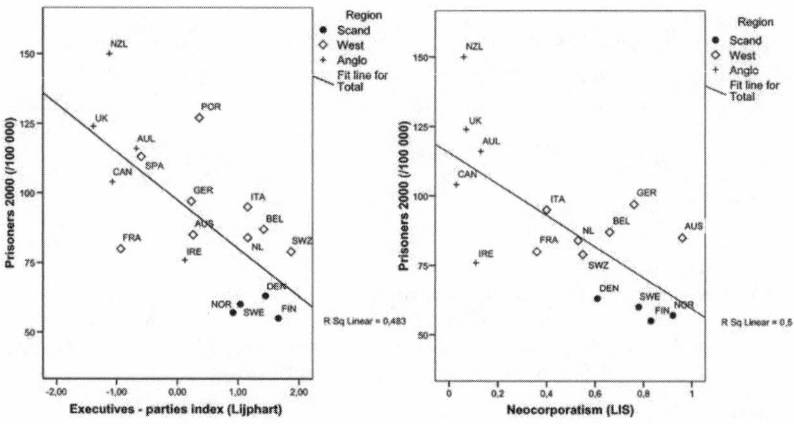

FIG. 18.–Political culture and imprisonment rates (sources: Sourcebook 2006 complemented, Lijphart [1999], and LIS).

B. Measuring Political Economy

Lijphart measured the "consensus-majoritarian quality" of democracies with indices concerning things such as the extent of interest group participation and centralization, the number of political parties, the balance of power between executives and parliaments, and the type of electoral system. Lijphart's summary index "executives-parties" (or "joint-power") and its subindices[31] allow analyses of quantitative differences in imprisonment rates by type of democracy and degrees of corporatism. The other major indicator available comes from the Luxembourg income study (Brady, Beckfield, and Stephens 2004). This 11-component neocorporatism index measures wage bargaining processes, the role of the unions, and the degree of centralization in interest group participation. Results are shown in figure 18.

Consensus democracies and neocorporatism are associated with more restrained penal policies. Among the western European countries, about half of imprisonment rate variation is explained by type of

[31] They include the concentration of executive power in single-party majority cabinets vs. executive power sharing in broad multiparty coalitions, executive-legislative relationships in which the executive is dominant vs. a wide distribution of power, two-party vs. multiparty systems, majoritarian and disproportional electoral systems vs. proportional representation, and pluralist interest group systems with free-for-all competition among groups vs. coordinated and "corporatist" interest group systems aimed at compromise and concentration (Lijphart 1999).

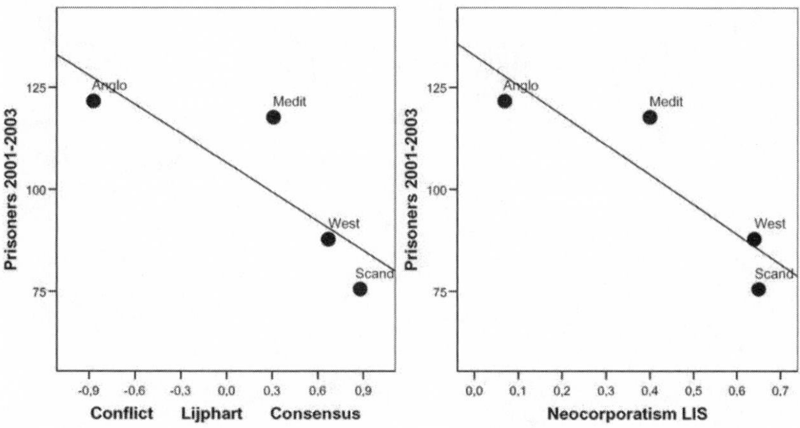

FIG. 19.—Political culture and imprisonment rates by regions (sources: Sourcebook 2006 complemented, Lijphart [1999], and LIS).

democracy and degree of corporatism. Figure 19 summarizes the associations by regions for western countries. The associations between the extent of consensualism, neocorporatism, and penal severity and imprisonment rates hold at the regional level.

IX. Intercorrelations and Penal Regimes

Differences in the strength of the welfare state, in political cultures, and in social and political trust explain differences in penal policies. Two patterns emerge. First, countries cluster in regions, closely related to classifications developed in comparative welfare theory. Second, the rank ordering of countries remains fairly similar in all measurements. This indicates strong internal associations between key variables. This section looks closely at this interdependency at country and regional levels. Basic correlations are shown in table 16.

A. Fears, Punitiveness, and Trust

Public sentiments and trust are strongly interrcorrelated. Fears are associated with punitive demands (.77**) and vary inversely with trust (−.80**). Punitiveness increases when trust decreases (−.50*).

A society with high levels of trust is a society of low fears and low punitiveness. A society of low fears and high trust is a society of low

TABLE 16

Intercorrelations (Prisoners 2001–3)

	Fear (ESS)	Punitiveness	Trust	Gini	Social Exp. %	Social Exp. €	Neocorporatism
Punitiveness (ICVS)	.766**						
Trust in people (ESS)	−.800**	−.497*					
Gini 2000 (LIS)	.615**	.580**	−.565*				
Social exp. 2003 % (Eurostat)	−.595**	−.626**	.473*	−.633**			
Social exp. 2003 € (Eurostat)	−.776**	−.592**	.803**	−.599**	.813**		
Neocorporatism (LIS)	−.762**	−.782**	.414	−.841**	.668**	.484	
Democracy index (Lijphart)	−.604*	−.545*	.501	−.627**	.453	.443	.704**

SOURCES.—Sourcebook 2006 complemented, ICVS, ESS, LIS, Eurostat, and Lijphart (1999).

NOTE.—"Social exp." means "social protection expenditure."

* Significant at the .05 level (two-tailed).

** Significant at the .01 level (two-tailed).

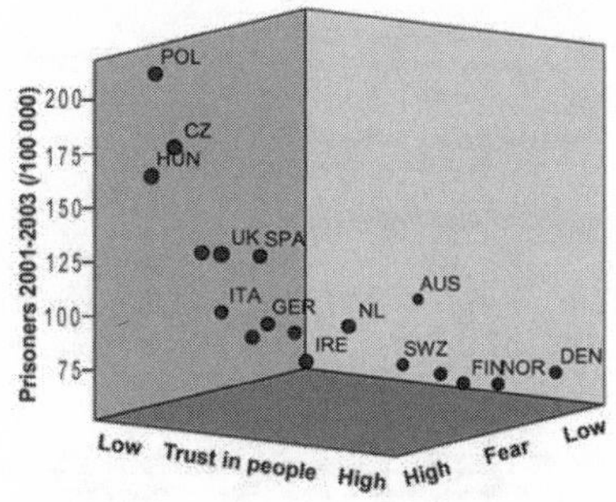

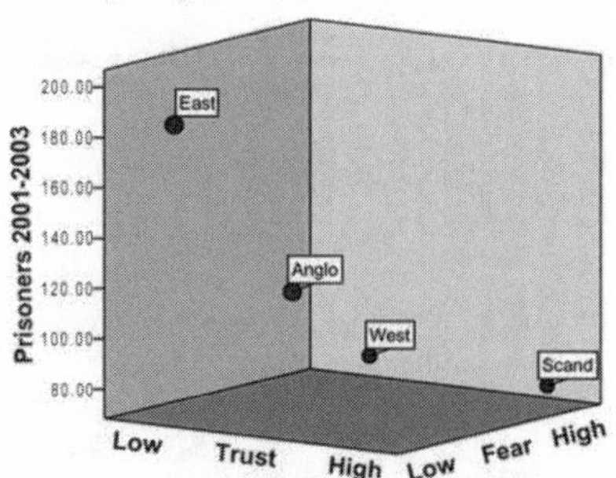

Fig. 20.—Public sentiments and imprisonment rates by regions in three-dimensional scaling (sources: Sourcebook 2006 complemented, ESS, and ICVS).

penal severity. The associations between fears, trust, and imprisonment rates are illustrated in figure 20 in a three-dimensional scaling.

The Scandinavian countries rank high in legitimacy scales and low in fear of crime and imprisonment rates. The Anglo-Saxon, former socialist, and Mediterranean countries rank high on fear, low on trust, and high on prison. The western European countries fall between Scandinavia and the Anglo-Saxon countries in most comparisons.

B. Public Sentiments and Welfare

Trust, fears, and welfare are also intercorrelated (see table 16). Strong welfare states are associated with high trust (social exp. %/trust .80** and Gini/trust −.57*) and lesser fears (social exp. %/fears −.77** and Gini/fears .62**). Consequently, countries of high trust and strong welfare (Scandinavia and Switzerland) produce fewer prisoners and lower severity, as contrasted with countries of low trust and weaker welfare states (eastern Europe) (see fig. 21).

C. Welfare, Trust, and Political Culture

Social inequality and income differences are smaller in consensus democracies (Gini/type of democracy −.63**) and in corporatist settings (Gini/neocorporatism −.84**, social exp. %/neocorporatism .67**). Strong welfare states coexist, most often in consensus and corporatist political environment. Consensus democracies, in turn, are associated with higher trust (trust/type of democracy .50). All in all, con-

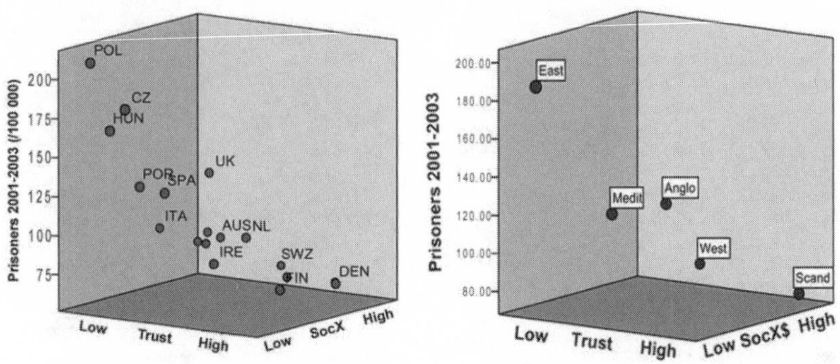

FIG. 21.—Trust in people, welfare expenditures, and imprisonment rates by regions in three-dimensional scaling (sources: Sourcebook 2006 complemented, ESS, and Eurostat).

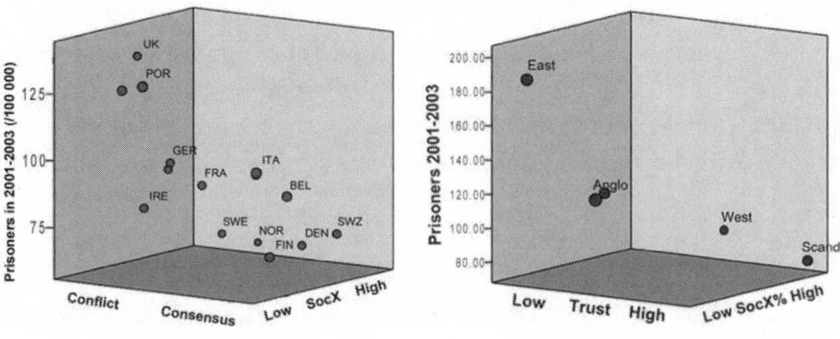

FIG. 22.—Social expenditures, political culture, and imprisonment rates by regions in three-dimensional scaling (sources: Sourcebook 2006 complemented, Lijphart [1999], Eurostat, and ESS).

sensus democracies and strong welfare states are associated with low imprisonment rates (fig. 22).

Scandinavian countries have the most centralized and organized interest group participation in policy processes, a more consensual political culture, and the lowest numbers of prisoners. The Anglo-Saxon countries are the diametrical opposite, with highly pluralistic and decentralized interest group participation, a majoritarian political culture, and high imprisonment rates. The other two regions fall in between, with the western European countries closer to Scandinavia and the Mediterranean region closer to the Anglo-Saxon region.

D. *Further Statistical Modeling?*

Statistical methods would provide opportunities for further modeling. However, both the available data and the subject limit efforts to explain trends and differences in penal policy in terms of simple statistical models. The associations are neither atomistic nor mechanical. The relevant social, political, economic, and cultural factors occur in different combinations in different places and in different times. Their effects are context related, and countries may experience unique changes that cannot be captured in abstract statistical analyses. Some factors are "unquantifiable" and have not (so far) been included in the models.[32] Therefore, instead of searching for the "final" statistical model, I concentrate on substantial explanations: why factors such as social welfare, trust, and political culture conduce to differences in penal policy and what the dynamics are of the interrelations between the key factors.[33]

X. Explaining the Explanations

Why do trust, social expenditures, income inequality, fears, and political culture affect penal severity? Subsections *A–C* explore direct links between penal severity and the variables already examined. Subsections *D* and *E* discuss internal associations and indirect effects.

A. *Welfare, Equality, and Punitiveness*

The connection between social welfare and imprisonment rates is explicit in the old slogan "Good social policy is the best criminal justice policy." This was a way of saying that society will do better investing

[32] The outcomes in statistical modeling are determined by the countries in the sample and the indicators in the model. Small samples prevent statistical conclusions. Increasing the number of countries reduces the list of explanatory factors to a bare minimum. Including countries with very different economic, political, and social characteristics makes comparisons difficult, and the message in the indicators may change. Income differences are hard to measure if salaries are paid as moonlight salaries. High support for prison may not indicate punitiveness if the only sanction available is prison. Similar dilemmas concern the time span. Shorter periods allow focused analysis but may miss important long-term structural changes. The best result is achieved, of course, by using different samples, by combining a qualitative approach with quantitative data, and by using both cross-sectional and time-series material (and from different periods).

[33] A fuller, but less structured, account is given in Lappi-Seppälä (2007).

in schools, social work, and families than in prisons. Welfarist penal policy, almost by definition, is less repressive. No wonder that the general scaling down of welfare states especially in the Anglo-Saxon countries during recent decades coincided with simultaneous growth in state control (Garland 2001). But this does not explain the association. Why does welfare affect penal severity?

1. *Solidarity.* The Durkheimian tradition emphasizes feelings of social solidarity. In David Greenberg's words, comparative penal restraint and low degrees of economic inequality may be "manifestations of a high degree of empathic identification and concern for the well-being of others" (1999, p. 297).

Solidarity with offenders explains penal moderation, but why should feelings of solidarity not have the opposite effect through empathic identification with the victim? Why feelings of solidarity in welfare society tend to ease the burden on the offender, but are not used as arguments for tougher actions in the name of the victim, needs further explanation.

2. *Shared Responsibility versus Individualism.* Penal policies in welfare societies are shaped not only by feelings of solidarity but also by broad concepts of social and collective responsibility. What matters is the society's views on the sources of risk and allocation of blame: whether risks originate from individuals who are to be blamed or whether the sources of social problems are given a wider social interpretation.

Cultural and anthropological studies suggest that risk posing in individualistic cultures is attributed to specific individuals and that the weak are blamed for the ills that befall them (Hudson 2003, pp. 51–52). Not only social sentiments of solidarity but also prevailing views of the origins and causes of social risks are important. From this perspective, rehabilitative penal policies express themselves as procedures of risk balancing among the offender, the victim, and society. Institutions such as parole, probation, and juvenile justice initially reflected a societal willingness to take risks on offenders and reduce the risk that adult imprisonment would do them more harm (Simon 2007, p. 23).[34] In more general terms, the sharing of social and economic risks via high

[34] This balancing of risks was manifestly expressed in the general policy aim of "fair distribution of harms caused by crime and crime control" in Finnish criminological theory in the 1970s (see Lappi-Seppälä 2001).

taxation and extensive social security systems has been and is the central feature of the Nordic Welfare State.[35]

Penal cultures in late modern risk society, however, are marked by atomistic and aggressive individualism. The balancing of rights of different parties has largely disappeared, and the only rights that matter for most are the safety rights of individuals ("there is only one human right—the right not to be victimized"). So the sense of shared risk and shared responsibility is weakened, as we now cope with risks by constantly scanning everyone we encounter to see whether they pose a threat (Hudson 2003, p. 74).

3. *Material Prosperity and Security.* Behind less repressive social policies are feelings of solidarity and a broad, less individualistic understanding of the origins of social risks. But a welfare society that organizes its social life around these starting points triggers other mechanisms that may contribute to less repressive policies. The material resources and economic security of an affluent welfare state may make it easier for citizens to express tolerance and empathy, when their own positions are secure. One can "afford" to be tolerant. Empathy and feelings of togetherness are easier to achieve among equals. Conversely, growing social divisions breed suspicions, fears, and feelings of otherness.

4. *Policy Alternatives.* Strong welfare states contribute to lower levels of repression by providing safeguards against social marginalization. In a generous welfare state, other and better alternatives to imprisonment are usually at hand (a functional community corrections system demands resources and proper infrastructure).

B. Trust, Fears, and Social Control

Trust and repression are interconnected. For Fukuyama, high imprisonment rates constitute "a direct tax imposed by the breakdown of trust in society" (1995, p. 11). Trust as a "reciprocal concept referring to mutual expectations of honest and co-operative behavior" (p. 26) may exist between individuals but may also concern institutions. Trust

[35] As the recent evaluation from the Research Institute of the Finnish Economy points out, the security offered by collective mechanisms for sharing risks has been instrumental in enhancing a favorable attitude to globalization and competition. The authors believe that it is essential to preserve this as one central feature of the Nordic Model in the future: Collective risk sharing should continue to offer a safety net that helps workers and their families cope with risks and adapt to new requirements in times of change (Nordic Model 2007).

in institutions (vertical, institutional trust) is one element of the legitimacy of rules or authority. Measuring trust is one way to measure legitimacy (Tyler 2003, p. 310). Trust in people (horizontal, personalized trust) is an element of social cohesion, solidarity, and human capital. Both forms of trust are essential for the functioning of social institutions. They are essential also for social control and norm compliance, and for political responses to lawbreaking.

1. *Political Legitimacy.* Declining legitimacy may call for tough measures for political reasons (in order to defend positions of power). Trust and legitimacy were central elements in Garland's analysis as in a system with high levels of confidence and trust there is less need for political posturing and expressive gestures: "punitive outbursts and demonizing rhetoric have featured much more prominently in weak political regimes than in strong ones" (1996, p. 462).

2. *Social Trust and Togetherness.* Trust is also relevant for social cohesion. Personalized trust and trust in people are indicators of social bonds and social solidarity. Decreasing trust indicates weakening solidarity and declining togetherness. And declining solidarity implies readiness for tougher actions.

3. *Social Trust and Social Control.* Trust is also relevant for social control. Communities equipped with trust are better protected against disruptive social behavior. They are "collectively more effective" in their efforts to exercise social control.[36] There is a link from trust, solidarity, and social cohesion to effective informal social control.[37]

4. *Legitimacy and Norm Compliance.* Finally, trust in institutions and legitimacy are conductive to norm compliance. Both theories of procedural justice (Tyler 2003) and traditional Scandinavian theories on the moral norm creating and enforcing effects of criminal law (Andenaes 1974; Lappi-Seppälä 1995) stress that norm compliance in a well-ordered society is based on internalized (normative) motives, not on fear (see also Bottoms 2001). The crucial condition for this to happen

[36] This ability may also be gathered under the broad label "social capital," including the existence of social networks and shared values that inhibit lawbreaking and support norm compliance. Social capital is "the pattern and intensity of networks among people and the shared values which arise from those networks." While definitions of social capital vary, the main aspects are citizenship, neighborliness, trust, shared values, community involvement, volunteering, social networks, and civic participation (http://www.statistics.gov.uk/socialcapital/). See also Kubrin and Weizer (2003) for an almost synonymous use of the terms social control and social capital.

[37] Gatti, Tremblay, and Larocque (2003) describe how social solidarity and trust enhanced social integration of children and reduced criminal behavior.

is that people perceive the system as fair and legitimate. A system that seeks to uphold norm compliance through trust and legitimacy, rather than through fear and deterrence, should be able to manage with less severe sanctions.

The associations between trust and levels of penal repression are functions of several coexisting relations. The lack of institutional trust creates political pressures toward more repressive means to maintain political authority. The lack of personal trust associated with fears results in ascending punitive demands and increases these pressures. Increased personal trust, community cohesion, and social capital strengthen informal social control. This, associated with institutional trust and norm compliance based on legitimacy, decreases the need to resort to formal social control and to the penal system.

C. *Political Culture: Consensus or Conflict?*

Political culture has direct and indirect relevance for penal policy. The direct links flow from the basic characteristics of political discourse; indirect links are discussed below. Consensus brings stability and deliberation. Political changes are gradual, not total as in majoritarian systems in which the whole crew changes at one time. In consensus democracy, new governments rarely need to raise their profiles by making spectacular policy changes. Consensus criminal justice policy places value in long-term consistency and in incremental change.[38]

While the consensus model is based on bargaining and compromise, majoritarian democracies are based on competition and confrontation that sharpen distinctions, heighten controversies, and encourage conflicts. This affects the stability and content of policies and the legitimacy of the political system as a whole.

In short, consensus politics lessen controversies, produce less crisis talk, inhibit dramatic turnovers, and sustain long-term consistent policies. Consensus democracies are less susceptible to political populism.

D. *Associations and Interactions between Different Factors*

In addition to their direct effects on penal practices, these factors are interrelated. They may reinforce, sustain, or weaken each other.

1. *Welfare–Trust.* There is a direct link from social policy and the welfare state to social and political trust. The social and economic

[38] Green (2007) offers an interesting comparison between Norway and England.

security granted by the welfare state sustains social and political trust. In this respect, different welfare systems may produce different outcomes. In general, needs-based social policy concerns "other people," those who are marginalized and culpable for their own position. Those in need are different. This feeds suspicion and distrust. Universalistic social policy that assigns benefits to everyone, grants social equality, and makes no distinctions between people has a different moral logic. Social policy concerns us all. Debates on social policy are efforts to solve common problems (Rothstein 1998). This gives strong support for social trust. The social and economic security granted by the welfare state and the feelings of social trust it promotes sustain tolerance and produce lower levels of fears, resulting in less punitive policies.

2. *Welfare–Trust–Fears and Punitiveness.* Trust, fears, and punitive demands are interrelated. Social trust (promoted by the welfare state) sustains tolerance and produces lower levels of fear, resulting in less punitive policies. The decline in trust reported in many western countries since the 1960s has been associated with the weakening of community ties, the rise of individualism, and the growth of the "culture of fear." Weakening solidarity and feelings of insecurity caused by new risks beyond individual control provide fertile ground for fear of crime. Crime is a concrete and apt object of fears and actions for anyone surrounded by growing anxieties and abstract threats of late modern society. Crime and punishment are tangible and comprehensive targets. We know what causes crime and we know how to deal with it (especially when the media and the politicians do such a good job of teaching us). Declining trust and increased fears and punitivity go a long way together.

3. *Political Culture–Welfare.* But what explains and sustains the welfare state? Part of the answer lies in political culture. Clearly, welfare states survive better in consensual and corporatist political surroundings. Consensus democracies are more egalitarian and more "welfare friendly." Generous welfare provision and smaller income differences are, to a large extent, direct consequences of large-based interest group participation and centralized wage coordination. Flexible negotiation procedures enable different kinds of trade-offs. In consensus structures in which everyone is involved, the chances that everyone (or at least most) will get (at least) something are better. Thus, there is a link from consensus politics to welfare—and from there to trust.

4. *Political Culture–Trust.* A direct link between political culture

and trust emerges. The political rhetoric of conflict democracy, constant crisis talk, and political posturing about crime have adverse effects on trust, fears, and feelings of security. In majoritarian democracies the basic role of the opposition is to demonstrate societal crises to prove the need to remove the governing party from power. Ongoing crises and constant attacks against governmental policies affect how people think about political institutions in general.

In a consensus democracy one needs to maintain good relations with one's opponents. They will be needed in future coalitions. There is less to win and more to lose in criticizing previous governments. In turn, corporatist structures, negotiations, consensual wage coordination, and cooperation between the state and market forces sustain political and social trust.

E. *Introducing Further Elements: Media, Judicial Cultures, and Legal Professions*

While consensus politics reinforce social trust, conflict democracy feeds (political) distrust but, at the same time, tries to win the confidence of a fearful and distrustful public with expressive gestures and quick fixes. This interplay is powerful enough to explain most parts of the detected differences. However, further elements need to be added.

1. *Media, Public Opinion, and Politics.* There exists a fairly extensive literature on changes in how the media deal with crime and on its role in shaping penal policies (see Jewkes [2004] and, for a comparison between England and Norway, Green [2007, p. 610]). Increased crime reporting with emphasis on violent crime and dramatized episodes in reality TV have but one effect on public perceptions and sentiment. Still, the media may adopt different policies and play different roles in different cultures. There are differences in how policy makers react to public demands and in the ways these sentiments are conveyed to policy makers.

Public opinion and sentiments are shaped in a reciprocal interaction with political decision makers, special interest groups, and the news media (see Roberts et al. 2003, pp. 86–87). Public opinion is affected by both media representations and political decisions. Sensationalist media feed public fears and distrust. They reinforce pressures from the punitive public. At the same time the media express preferences to the political system. If the political system is responsive and adaptive, the media may shape and influence policy outcomes directly and indirectly.

Finland and the United Kingdom, to take an example, occupy opposite positions among the western European countries as regards fears, punitiveness, and imprisonment rates—and the media culture. The United Kingdom has high levels of fear and large numbers of prisoners; in Finland, the situation is reversed. Comparing British and Finnish newspapers is like comparing two different worlds. Crime also has a completely different role in TV broadcasts in the United Kingdom. These differences in media culture may have both technical and deeper structural explanations. Differences may be associated with national variations in public financing and in the regulation of the media. Strong public networks assure more substantive content, more educational-cultural content, higher quality, and less low-level populism. An example of a technical explanation would be that Finnish newspapers are typically sold by subscription and not as single copies. Therefore, the papers need not sell themselves each day on newsstands. In the United Kingdom, home delivery of newspapers is relatively uncommon. Most papers are bought from a news agent, which means that papers' covers often shout for attention. More generally, conflict democracies are often burdened by aggressive media. Evidently conflict creates better (or more salable) news.

But it is not only the habits of the media. If media are more interested in crime in the United Kingdom, the political and judicial systems of the United Kingdom are more interested in media and in the media-influenced public opinion (see Roberts et al. 2003, pp. 85–86; Roberts 2004, p. 134). In Finland, tabloids do not direct governmental policies, and public opinion is not a valid argument in legal discourse. There is a marked difference in how the political and judicial systems in the United Kingdom and Finland react to media and public opinion.

2. *Judicial Cultures and Legal Professions.* Judicial cultures and legal professions are further elements. There are deep-rooted differences in judicial culture regarding the balance of powers and the extent to which judicial processes are affected by political pressures. The ideas of the Enlightenment and divisions of state powers have shielded most continental and Scandinavian courts from political intrusions. Some common-law jurisdictions, however, share features that make them more vulnerable to populist and political pressures. The U.S. legal system with politically elected criminal justice officials (prosecutors, judges,

sheriffs, and governors) is much more vulnerable to short-term populist influences on everyday sentencing practices and local policy choices than most countries' legal systems are. The need to be re-elected assures that the judiciary is much more closely attuned to public opinion and organized interest groups than in civil-law systems (see Tonry 2004, p. 206; Garland 2005, p. 363).[39] These differences are reinforced by different techniques in structuring sentencing discretion. In Scandinavian and continental sentencing structures, the legislation specifies only broad limits on punishment, and the rest is at the discretion of independent judges. This is less vulnerable to short-sighted and ill-founded political interventions than is a system in which elected bodies have the power to give detailed instructions on sentencing (see Lappi-Seppälä 2001).

Numerous details in criminal justice proceedings may affect sentencing policies. Widespread victim impact statements, unknown in Scandinavian legal systems, may affect sentencing. The Scandinavian criminal justice process represents a different view on issues surrounding the rights of the victim. Compensatory claims are always dealt with in the same process as the criminal case. They are processed by the prosecutor on behalf of the victim. Thus, the victim's rights are associated not with the right to exercise a personal vendetta in the court but with getting his or her damages and losses compensated.[40]

Legal training, judicial expertise, and professional skills matter. Judges and prosecutors may differ in their criminological knowledge, both individually and in different jurisdictions.[41] Countries with trained professional judges and in which criminology is included in the curricula of law faculties may expect to have judges and prosecutors who have broader and deeper understanding of crime and criminal justice

[39] Explaining the specific features of American penal policy falls beyond the aims of this essay. In explaining the United States, one should probably include also the constitutional heritage that has kept the nation-state weak and unable to pacify the population and to develop effective social institutions or forms of social solidarity, incomplete integration of different ethnic groups, and long-term commitments to market individualism and minimal welfare (see Garland 2007, p. 151; Tonry 2007*b*).

[40] And if not by the offender, from state funds (see Lappi-Seppälä 1996). No doubt that compensation is always ordered together with the punishment gives the public a more realistic view of the overall consequences of the crime (as contrasted to systems that hide compensation in another process, which the victims must initiate and accomplish by themselves).

[41] Dutch moderation in the 1960s and the 1970s has, e.g., been attributed in part to judges' training in criminology and their awareness of the antiprison criminological literature of that time (Downes 1982, p. 345).

policy. This expertise may be enhanced by professional training programs and by seminars and meetings for judges. The receptiveness of the judiciary to this kind of activity and exchange of information varies between jurisdictions. Effective networking between researchers and judges is essential if one wishes to increase the impact of criminological knowledge in sentencing and penal practices.

Individuals and elites matter. Penal policies may occasionally be heavily influenced by individual experts, opinion leaders, or politicians. This kind of personal and professional influence by individuals may be easier to achieve in a small country.[42]

XI. Final Observations

Probably the strongest conclusion to emerge from this essay is that penal policies and practices are inexorably related to other social policies and practices and to deep cultural characteristics such as citizens' trust in one another and the state, and citizens' perceptions of the legitimacy of state institutions.

In some ways this should be obvious and should always have been obvious. For a long time, however, it was not. As penal policies in some countries became harsher and prison populations in some countries increased rapidly in the late twentieth century, other explanations were offered. Some dealt with rising crime rates, harshening public opinion, political opportunism, and ethnic or racial conflict (see, e.g., the survey in Tonry [2004, chap. 2]). Others dealt with more general social and economic changes related to "late modernity" (Garland 2001).

An accumulating series of case studies including those published in volume 36 of *Crime and Justice* reveals, however, that these earlier accounts were simultaneously partly too simple and partly too general (see also Tonry 2007*a*). They were too simple because they attributed too great influence to individual factors—for example, crime rates or

[42] Finnish prison administration was led by Valentin Soine and K. J. Lång, two liberally minded reformists, for half a century (1945–95), providing exceptionally favorable circumstances for policy consistency. Finnish criminal justice policy was influenced for a lengthy period by a group of like-minded experts who held the key positions in the law-drafting offices, the judiciary, prison administration, and universities. This group produced four ministers of justice, one president of the Supreme Court, the Lord Chancellor, and several leading civil servants. This created conditions for ideological consistency and consensus that may have been hard to establish elsewhere. (But not impossible. The postwar welfare period in England and Wales, as described by Ryan [2003], shares a number of similarities with the Finnish situation.)

ethnic tensions—that palpably did not demonstrate the same or remotely comparable influence even in seemingly similar countries. They were too general because they overlooked country-specific characteristics and implied that transcendent global developments everywhere created similar pressures and produced similar results.

The case study literature has shown that what happens in particular countries turns on distinctive social, cultural, and political features and how they relate to particular forces and developments. The analyses reported in this essay, however, show that we can generalize about some of these features in ways that help explain why groups of countries—and not just individual ones—develop the policies and practices that they do.

REFERENCES

Aebi, Marcelo F., Kauko Aromaa, Bruno Aubusson de Cavarlay, Gordon Barclay, Beata Gruszczyñska, Hanns von Hofer, Vasilika Hysi, Jörg-Martin Jehle, Martin Killias, Paul Smit, and Cynthia Tavares. 2006. *The European Sourcebook of Crime and Criminal Justice Statistics—2006*. The Hague: Boom Juridische uitgevers.

Aebi, Marcelo, and Natalia Stadnic. 2007. *Council of Europe SPACE 1: 2005 Survey on Prison Populations*. Document PC-CP (2007) 2. Strasbourg: Council of Europe.

Andenaes, Johs. 1974. *Punishment and Deterrence*. Ann Arbor: University of Michigan Press.

Bambra, Clare. 2006. "Decommodification and the Worlds of Welfare Revisited." *Journal of European Social Policy* 16(1):73–80.

Beckett, Katherine, and Bruce Western. 2001. "Governing Social Marginality: Welfare, Incarceration, and the Transformation of State Policy." In *Mass Imprisonment: Social Causes and Consequences*, edited by David Garland. Thousand Oaks, CA: Sage.

Blumstein, Alfred, Michael Tonry, and Ashley van Ness. 2005. "Cross-National Measures of Punitiveness." In *Crime and Punishment in Western Countries, 1980–1999*, edited by Michael Tonry and David P. Farrington. Vol. 33 of *Crime and Justice: A Review of Research*, edited by Michael Tonry. Chicago: University of Chicago Press.

Bondeson, Ulla. 2005. "Levels of Punitiveness in Scandinavia: Description and Explanations." In *The New Punitiveness: Trends, Theories, Perspectives*, edited by John Pratt, David Brown, Mark Brown, Simon Hallsworth, and Wayne Morrison. Cullompton, Devon, UK: Willan.

Bottoms, Anthony. 2001. "Compliance and Community Penalties." In *Com-*

munity Penalties: Change and Challenges, edited by Anthony Bottoms, Loraine Gelsthorpe, and Sue Rex. Cullompton, Devon, UK: Willan.

Brady, David, Jason Beckfield, and John Stephens. 2004. *Comparative Welfare States Data Set*. Assembled by Evelyne Huber, Charles Ragin, and John D. Stephens (December 1997). Updated by Brady, Beckfield, and Stephens (April 2004). http://www.lisproject.org/publications/welfaredata/welfare access.htm.

Caplow, Theodore, and Jonathan Simon. 1999. "Understanding Prison Policy and Population Trends." In *Prisons*, edited by Michael Tonry. Vol. 26 of *Crime and Justice: A Review of Research*, edited by Michael Tonry. Chicago: University of Chicago Press.

Castles, Francis. 2004. *The Future of the Welfare State: Crisis Myths and Crisis Realities*. Oxford: Oxford University Press.

Cavadino, Michael, and James Dignan. 2006. *Penal Systems: A Comparative Approach*. London: Sage.

Chiricos, Theodore, and Miriam Delone. 1992. "Labor Surplus and Punishment: A Review and Assessment of Theory and Evidence." *Social Problems* 39(4):421–46.

Downes, David. 1982. "The Origins and Consequences of Dutch Penal Policy since 1945." *British Journal of Criminology* 22(4):325–62.

Downes, David, and Kristine Hansen. 2006. "Welfare and Punishment in Comparative Perspective." In *Perspectives on Punishment: The Contours of Control*, edited by Sarah Armstrong and Lesley McAra. Oxford: Oxford University Press.

Downes, David, and René van Swaaningen. 2007. "The Road to Dystopia? Changes in the Penal Climate of the Netherlands." In *Crime and Justice in the Netherlands*, edited by Michael Tonry and Catrien Bijleveld. Vol. 35 of *Crime and Justice: A Review of Research*, edited by Michael Tonry. Chicago: University of Chicago Press.

Esping-Andersen, G. 1990. *The Three Worlds of Welfare Capitalism*. Cambridge: Polity Press.

European Sourcebook of Crime and Criminal Justice Statistics. Various years. The Hague: Boom Juridische uitgevers.

Falck, Sturla, Hanns von Hofer, and Annette Storgaard. 2003. *Nordic Criminal Statistics, 1950–2000*. Report 2003:3. Stockholm: Stockholm University, Department of Criminology.

Farrington, David, Patrick Langan, and Michael Tonry, eds. 2004. *Cross-National Studies in Crime and Justice*. Washington, DC: U.S. Department of Justice, Bureau of Justice Statistics.

Fukuyama, Francis. 1995. *Trust: The Social Virtues and the Creation of Prosperity*. New York: Free Press.

Garland, David. 1996. "The Limits of the Sovereign State: Strategies of Crime Control in Contemporary Society." *British Journal of Criminology* 36(4): 445–71.

———. 2001. *The Culture of Control: Crime and Social Order in Contemporary Society*. Chicago: University of Chicago Press.

———. 2005. "Capital Punishment and American Culture." *Punishment and Society: The International Journal of Penology* 7(4):347–76.

———. 2007. "Death, Denial, Discourse: On the Forms and Functions of American Capital Punishment." In *Crime, Social Control and Human Rights: From Moral Panics to States of Denial: Essays in Honour of Stanley Cohen*, edited by David Downes, Paul Rock, Christine Chinkin, and Conor Gearlty. Cullompton, Devon, UK: Willan.

Gatti, Umberto, Richard Tremblay, and Dennis Larocque. 2003. "Civic Community and Juvenile Delinquency." *British Journal of Criminology* 43:22–40.

Goodin, Robert, Bruce Headey, Ruud Muffels, and Henk-Jan Dirven. 1999. *The Real Worlds of Welfare Capitalism*. Cambridge: Cambridge University Press.

Green, David A. 2007. "Comparing Penal Cultures: Child-on-Child Homicide in England and Norway." In *Crime, Punishment, and Politics in Comparative Perspective*, edited by Michael Tonry. Vol. 36 of *Crime and Justice: A Review of Research*, edited by Michael Tonry. Chicago: University of Chicago Press.

Greenberg, David F. 1999. "Punishment, Division of Labor, and Social Solidarity." In *The Criminology of Criminal Law*. Vol. 8 of *Advances in Criminological Theory*, edited by William S. Laufer and Freda Adler. New Brunswick, NJ: Transaction Publishers.

———. 2001. "Novos Ordo Saeclorum? A Commentary on Downes, and on Beckett and Western." In *Mass Imprisonment: Social Causes and Consequences*, edited by David Garland. Thousand Oaks, CA: Sage.

Hart, H. L. A. 1968. *Punishment and Responsibility*. Oxford: Clarendon.

Hudson, Barbara. 2003. *Justice in the Risk Society*. Thousand Oaks, CA: Sage.

Jewkes, Yvonne. 2004. *Media and Crime*. London: Sage.

Killias, Martin. 1986. "Power Concentration, Legitimation Crisis, and Penal Severity: A Comparative Perspective." *International Annals of Criminology* 24: 181–211.

Kubrin, Charise, and Ronald Weizer. 2003. "New Directions in Social Disorganization Theory." *Journal of Research in Crime and Delinquency* 40(4): 347–402.

Kyvsgaard, Britta. 2001. "Penal Sanctions and the Use of Imprisonment in Denmark." In *Penal Reform in Overcrowded Times*, edited by Michael Tonry. New York: Oxford University Press.

Lappi-Seppälä, Tapio. 1995. "General Prevention: Hypotheses and Empirical Evidence." In *Ideologi og empiri i kriminologien*, edited by Hildigunnur Ølafsdøttir. Reykjavik: Scandinavian Research Council for Criminology.

———. 1996. "Reparation in Criminal Law: Finnish National Report." In *Wiedergutmachung im Strafrecht*, edited by Albin Eser and Susanne Walther. Freiburg: Max-Planck-Institut.

———. 2001. "Sentencing and Punishment in Finland: The Decline of the Repressive Ideal." In *Punishment and Penal Systems in Western Countries*, edited by Michael Tonry and Richard Frase. New York: Oxford University Press.

———. 2007. "Penal Policy in Scandinavia." In *Crime, Punishment, and Politics in Comparative Perspective*, edited by Michael Tonry. Vol. 36 of *Crime and Justice: A Review of Research*, edited by Michael Tonry. Chicago: University of Chicago Press.

———. 2008. *Cross-Comparative Perspectives on Penal Severity: Explaining the Differences in the Use of Imprisonment*. Helsinki: National Research Institute of Legal Policy, forthcoming.

Lijphart, Arend. 1998. "Consensus and Consensus Democracy: Cultural, Structural, Functional, and Rational-Choice Explanations." *Scandinavian Political Studies* 21(2):99–108.

———. 1999. *Patterns of Democracy: Government Forms and Performance in Thirty-six Countries*. New Haven, CT: Yale University Press.

Nordic Model. 2007. *The Nordic Model—Embracing Globalization and Sharing Risks*. Helsinki: Research Institute of the Finnish Economy.

Pease, Ken. 1991. "Punishment Demand and Punishment Numbers." In *Policy and Theory in Criminal Justice*, edited by D. M. Gottfredson and R. V. Clarke. Aldershot, UK: Gower.

Pratt, John, and Marie Clark. 2005. "Penal Populism in New Zealand." *Punishment and Society: The International Journal of Penology* 7(3):303–22.

Roberts, Julian V. 2004. *The Virtual Prison: Community Custody and the Evolution of Imprisonment*. Cambridge Studies in Criminology. Cambridge: Cambridge University Press.

Roberts, Julian V., Loretta J. Stalans, David Indermaur, and Mike Hough. 2003. *Penal Populism and Public Opinion: Lessons from Five Countries*. Oxford: Oxford University Press.

Ross, Alf. 1975. *On Guilt, Responsibility and Punishment*. Berkeley: University of California Press.

Rothstein, Bo. 1998. *Just Institutions Matter*. Cambridge: Cambridge University Press.

Ruddell, Rick. 2005. "Social Disruption, State Priorities, and Minority Threat: A Cross-National Study of Imprisonment." *Punishment and Society: The International Journal of Penology* 7(1):7–28.

Rusche, Georg, and Otto Kirchheimer. 1968. *Punishment and Social Structure*. New York: Russel and Russel. (Originally published 1939.)

Ryan, Mick. 2003. *Penal Policy and Political Culture in England and Wales: Four Essays on Policy and Process*. Winchester, UK: Waterside.

Simon, Jonathan. 2007. *Governing through Crime: How the War on Crime Transformed American Democracy and Created a Culture of Fear*. New York: Oxford University Press.

Stark, Rodney. 2004. *Doing Sociology: A Global Perspective*. Belmont, TN: Wadsworth.

Sutton, John. 2004. "The Political Economy of Imprisonment in Affluent Western Democracies, 1960–1990." *American Sociological Review* 69:170–89.

Tham, Henrik. 2001. "Law and Order as a Leftist Project?" *Punishment and Society: The International Journal of Penology* 3(3):409–26.

———. 2005. "Imprisonment and Inequality." Paper prepared for the fifth annual conference of the European Society of Criminology, August 31–September 3, Kraków.

Tonry, Michael. 2004. *Thinking about Crime: Sense and Sensibilities in American Penal Culture*. Oxford: Oxford University Press.

———, ed. 2007*a*. *Crime, Punishment, and Politics in Comparative Perspective*. Vol. 36 of *Crime and Justice: A Review of Research*, edited by Michael Tonry. Chicago: University of Chicago Press.

———. 2007*b*. "Determinants of Penal Policies." In *Crime, Punishment, and Politics in Comparative Perspective*, edited by Michael Tonry. Vol. 36 of *Crime and Justice: A Review of Research*, edited by Michael Tonry. Chicago: University of Chicago Press.

Tyler, Tom. 2003. "Procedural Justice, Legitimacy, and the Effective Rule of Law." In *Crime and Justice: A Review of Research*, vol. 30, edited by Michael Tonry. Chicago: University of Chicago Press.

van Dijk, Jan, Robert Manchin, John van Kesteren, and Gegerly Hideg. 2007. *The Burden of Crime in the EU*. Tilburg, Netherlands: Tilburg University, INTERVICT.

van Kesteren, John, Pat Mayhew, and Paul Nieuwbeerta. 2000. *Criminal Victimization in Seventeen Industrialised Countries: Key Findings from the 2000 International Crime Victims Survey*. The Hague: Netherlands Ministry of Justice.

Vogel, Joachim. 1997. "Living Conditions and Inequality in the European Union 1997." Eurostat Working Papers, Population and Social Conditions, E/1997-3. Luxembourg: Eurostat.

von Hirsch, Andrew, and Andrew Ashworth. 2005. *Proportionate Sentencing*. Oxford: Oxford University Press.

von Hofer, Hanns. 2003. "Prison Populations as Political Constructs: The Case of Finland, Holland, and Sweden." *Journal of Scandinavian Studies in Criminology and Crime Prevention* 4:21–38.

Wilkins, Leslie T. 1991. *Punishment, Crime and Market Forces*. Dartmouth, UK: Aldershot.

Shawn Bushway and Peter Reuter

Economists' Contribution to the Study of Crime and the Criminal Justice System

ABSTRACT

Economists' contributions to criminal justice research can be divided into three main areas of theory, technique, and substantive expertise. Economists' work on perceptual deterrence, with its emphasis on the centrality of time discounting, has already been incorporated into criminological research. There has been a much more mixed record in taking up economic approaches to criminal justice theory: early work on prosecutors has been neglected, whereas the newer area of outcome analysis, based on maximizing behavior by criminal justice actors, has influenced criminological work on discrimination. There is a mixed record with respect to technique. Econometrics methods, particularly James Heckman's approaches to selection problems, have been influential but are often mishandled. Cost-benefit analysis, though much sought after by policy makers, has not entered mainstream criminology. One substantive area in which economists have substantive expertise concerns illegal markets, especially drug markets. The research by economists has produced important findings on intervention outcomes such as price and quantity. Criminology can benefit from collaboration with economists but need not worry that the economists will soon take over.

The study of crime has always been multidisciplinary. Apart from criminologists, sociologists are perhaps the dominant group, but psychologists and political scientists have long been prominent. Economists are among the most recent entrants, with Gary Becker's 1968 "Crime and Punishment: An Economic Approach" serving as the starting point

Shawn Bushway is associate professor at the School of Criminal Justice, University of New York at Albany. Peter Reuter is professor at the School of Public Policy and Department of Criminology, University of Maryland.

0192-3234/2008/0037-0005$10.00

for modern economists' work on crime.[1] After an initial flurry of research in the 1970s, only a few economists, most prominently Philip J. Cook and Peter Reuter, stayed involved with criminology, with intermittent work by labor economists such as Richard Freeman. In the mid to late 1990s, a flurry of new work by younger economists including Steven Levitt, Jens Ludwig, Anne Piehl, and Steven Raphael began to appear. This has generated a growing flow of articles on crime in major economics journals. This, however, has occurred largely outside the view of criminologists, and in our view, there has not been a corresponding increase in appreciation of economists or economics in criminology and criminal justice. For example, we are aware of no courses on economics and crime in graduate criminology programs, and there are very few trained economists on the faculties of major criminology departments. Conversely, economists seldom talk to, cite, or interact with other social scientists who study crime.

One possible reason for this lack of engagement is the imperialistic attitude of some economists toward other social scientists. Becker, who wrote the seminal paper on the economics of crime, more than anyone else is also responsible for attempts in recent decades to broaden economics beyond the study of economic institutions to encompass human choices under scarcity, including fertility, discrimination, and suicide (Becker 2000). Under this conception of the scope of economics, the study of crime and the criminal justice system falls well within the boundaries of economics.

Economists' study of human choice has a particular ideological slant. Economists have developed price theory, which implies that consumption of any good will decline when the price increases.[2] With admirable conceptual clarity, economists can identify the costs or prices of any given choice, including the decision to commit a crime, and identify the expected relationship between punishment and crime. The unique approach of economists means that economists and criminologists have actively butted heads over the topic of deterrence almost since economists began studying the topic.[3]

[1] Becker's article has 1,368 citations in the Social Science Citation Index as of December 2006.

[2] The famous textbook exception of a "Giffen good" (a single inferior good for which there is no good substitute and that constitutes such a large share of total expenditures that an increase in its price generates higher consumption) remains just that—a textbook exception. It is possible that for some drug addicts the condition might apply to their preferred drug, but that has never been demonstrated.

[3] A skeptic might call desire to find the relevance of price theory in a vast array of

Becker wrote his article, which describes punishment as a cost (or price) of crime, at around the same time that labeling theory, which allowed for the possibility that punishment might be criminogenic, became a major theoretical framework for criminologists and sociologists. These opposing views generated ongoing conflict between the two fields, continuing in the recent popular book *Freakonomics* in which Steve Levitt repeated the inflammatory charge by John DiIulio Jr. that "it takes a Ph.D. in criminology to doubt that keeping dangerous criminals incarcerated cuts crime" (Levitt and Dubner 2005, p. 123). A recent *Crime and Justice* essay by Doob and Webster (2003) provides a criminological critique of the willingness of economists to conclude that increased sentence lengths cause declines in crime (see also Webster, Doob, and Zimring 2006).

The two fields have clashed heatedly over empirical research on the death penalty since the 1970s, perhaps for the same reason. Despite decades of research by criminologists showing no deterrent effects of the death penalty (e.g., Sellin 1959), economist Isaac Erhlich's (1975) paper, subsequently largely discredited, showing a strong relationship between the death penalty and murder, was cited in briefs in *Gregg v. Georgia*, 428 U.S. 153 (1976), the Supreme Court decision reinstating the death penalty. After two decades of silence, some economists have published new research showing the expected or even preordained deterrent relationship between the death penalty and crime, only to have other economists demonstrate the fragility of their findings (Donohue and Wolfers 2005). The Donohue and Wolfers critique has much in common with earlier critiques of capital punishment research by criminologist Thorsten Sellin.

Thus we have two fields with ideological stances: one convinced, as a matter of belief, that punishment will reduce crime, and the other regarding this as an empirical issue but with a wealth of arguments as to why the deterrent effect might be negligible or even, in some cases, perverse. In this essay, we propose a détente. We both have economics backgrounds but have spent the bulk of our careers in and around criminology departments. We see many opportunities for cross-fertilization that are unrelated to the ideological conflict.

A good example of the potential benefits of cross-fertilization can

---

contexts to be an example of economic positivism on a par with sociological positivism in criminology.

be seen in two papers written in 1985 on the relationship between business cycles and crime at the national level using nearly identical data. One was written by two economists, Cook and Zarkin (1985), and the other by two sociologists, Cantor and Land (1985). They asked similar questions but used different techniques and different ways of measuring the business cycle. Given their simultaneity, it is not surprising that they did not cite one another. What is striking is that the Social Science Citation Index shows that only 10 of the 138 papers that cite Cantor and Land also cite Cook and Zarkin.[4] Moreover, seven of the 10 citations occurred in 1996 or later, as researchers began to propose alternative ways of measuring cyclical macroeconomic change. This delayed cross-fertilization has led directly to a richer understanding of the relationship between unemployment and crime at the national level.

Because of our belief in the benefits of cross-fertilization between economics and the other social sciences, we created a program at the University of Maryland's Population Research Center that has as its primary mission sponsorship of annual workshops that bring together criminologists, sociologists, and economists working on related crime topics.[5] It was initially depressingly easy to find scholars from different fields working on nearly identical topics who were essentially unaware of one another's work. But participants have reacted very positively to the opportunity to interact with and learn from one another, and interdisciplinary awareness was noticeably higher in the most recent workshop. This positive reaction has pushed us to think more specifically about the relative contributions of the two fields.

It is relatively easy to identify substantive expertise as criminologists' main contribution. Criminologists study crime and the criminal justice system. They know how the system works and understand data issues concerning the measurement and study of crime. Criminologists and sociologists together have developed a rich theoretical tradition that identifies potential causal mechanisms for the actions of offenders and the criminal justice system. Efforts to study crime and the criminal justice system that do not take account of research and theory by criminologists and sociologists are at best inefficient and at worst foolish.

[4] In contrast, 10 out of the 23 articles that cite Cook and Zarkin also cite Cantor and Land.

[5] Conference agendas, abstracts, and presentations for the first three workshops can be found at http://www.popcenter.umd.edu/criminologyandeconomics/home.shtml.

It is slightly more difficult to categorize the contribution of economists. Becker's original contribution was theoretical, but much recent research has been empirical and atheoretical. We decided to use the work of Nobel Prize winner Ronald Coase to guide our exploration of the potential contributions of economics to the study of crime.[6] Coase offers a framework for the examination of the contribution of economics to other fields in his essay "Economics and Contiguous Disciplines" (1978), which examined competition among disciplines.[7] Coase suggests that any discipline can be defined by three basic characteristics: a common theory or approach, common techniques of analysis, and a common subject matter. The contribution of discipline *X* to discipline *Y* will depend on the extent to which its techniques, approach, or subject matter is relevant to and different from those of discipline *Y*.

Coase argues that the lasting ability of economics to establish itself in new domains will depend on the extent to which the contribution is based on subject matter expertise. Mainstream economists study the economic system, defined by George Stigler as "the operation of economic organizations, and economic organizations are social (and rarely individual) arrangements to deal with the production of economic goods and services" (1952, p. 1). According to Coase's argument, the techniques and theoretical approach of economists that can shed light on the study of crime can quickly be appropriated by criminologists and become part of criminology. However, contributions that are based on the subject matter expertise of economics are likely to substantiate a subfield of economics and crime.

In this essay, we follow Coase's threefold classification of technique, approach, and subject matter to examine the role of economics in the study of crime. We start in Section I by discussing the basic approach of economists. That approach begins with assumptions about the behavior of individual actors that can be expressed in simplified mathematical form, generating falsifiable predictions. Actors, whether offenders or criminal justice officials, are assumed to be rational in the sense that they systematically pursue their self-interests. Actors differ in the nature of those interests, as expressed in their "objective functions." Objective functions are formalized expressions of an individual's preferences. Offenders may be characterized by unusual objective func-

[6] The field of law and economics, which taxonomically includes the study of crime, can be traced back directly to the work of Coase (1960) and Becker (1968).

[7] We thank Michael Tonry for bringing this essay to our attention.

tions. The other general insight is that maximization takes place in the context of interactions, so that empirical predictions must take into account the actions of the other affected parties. This focus on individual maximizations and on interactions constitutes an approach very different from that of criminologists.

Section II then considers three major substantive areas of criminology in which economists have made, or have the potential to make, significant contributions. In the study of deterrence, work by economists in the 1970s has been incorporated into the criminological literature on how experiences with the criminal justice system affect individual behavior through their influence on perceived risks and rewards of crime. In contrast, pioneering work by economists on understanding the decisions of prosecutors has disappeared essentially without a trace, even though it potentially had important implications for criminological research on the performance of the criminal justice system. More recently there has emerged a new economics-based approach to decision making by criminal justice officials, outcome analysis, that has provided potentially useful tests of the existence of discrimination in the system.

In Section III we turn to the use of economic technique. Econometrics, the area of statistics developed by economists, has produced many new methods of data analysis that are helpful for criminologists, particularly focused on problems of sample selection and endogeneity. Criminologists are increasingly acquiring command of these methods. The other technique, cost-benefit analysis, remains solidly in the hands of economists, who have made what modest progress has occurred in estimating the costs of crime and the returns from specific interventions.

Section IV discusses drug markets, a topic that has largely been neglected by criminologists, though it is of considerable importance to an understanding of crime in contemporary America. The study of markets is central to economics, and the basic tools of supply and demand have been used fruitfully by a few economists to understand the consequences of criminal justice interventions on outcomes of interest, such as price, consumption, and related crime. This is an area in which criminologists have much to learn from economists.

We conclude in Section V with our own judgment of the relevance of the work of economists and economics for criminology. Economists studying crime need to draw more extensively on the research of criminologists if they are to make real progress and not just reinvent the wheel. Criminology will become a stronger field if it finds a way to incorporate economic theory, technique, and substantive expertise.

I. Thinking like an Economist

Economists bring a fundamentally different approach to the study of individual and system decision making. In this section we describe two principal features of that approach. The first is the emphasis on rationality, defined not as conformity to others' values but as the realization of one's own self-interests. The second is the focus on interactions among parties with different self-interests, which has effects particularly at the aggregate level.

A. Rational Decision Making

Becker's main insight was that crime, and the control of crime, were choices that can be modeled in the standard labor economics model of individual decision making about the allocation of time. Crime is simply another choice, like the decision to work or to invest in education.[8] Such choice to an economist has a clear conceptual structure. Individuals face an array of options (goods or activities) that are linked to outcomes. In the simplest model, assuming perfect information, all choices are known and the probabilities of the associated outcomes are known. These assumptions can be, and are, relaxed, but in all cases there is an array of choices linked to outcomes. Individuals weigh these outcomes with the help of an "objective function," which is a statement of goals. This objective function evaluates the various outcomes in terms of how well they help the individual achieve his or her goals. In the simplest consumer choice model, the individual allocates a fixed amount of money between two or more goods. The individual's objective function describes what outcome will make him the happiest or most satisfied, given his income constraint.

This framework points to "opportunity cost," a central concept of economics. The cost of choice *A* is not the money price of that choice, but the cost of not choosing *B*, the next-best option. This conceptualization is crucial to understanding the cost of crime to the potential offender because the true cost of an incarceration sentence is the op-

[8] Individuals can still differ in their willingness to break the law. Becker does not assume that all individuals have the same preferences.

portunity cost of spending time in prison (Becker 1968). The subjective opportunity cost may vary among individuals, even though the actual sentence will be the same for all.

One hallmark of the economist's approach is a willingness to write the theory down in mathematical form, which includes the mathematical specification of the preference or objective function of individuals. Many well-known utility functions are described in graduate-level microeconomics textbooks such as Hal Varian's (2002), which appear to capture at least some known aspects of human behavior. These utility functions include parameters that weigh the trade-offs between returns now and in the future (time discounting) and parameters that describe the value of an additional unit given current levels of consumption. For example, economists assume diminishing marginal returns, that is, that the benefit of the next unit of a given good is smaller than the benefit of the last unit consumed. Because these objective functions must be written down mathematically, they are necessarily highly simplified descriptions of human behavior. Nonetheless, they include explicit assumptions about human behavior, and, more important, they generate clear and testable predictions.

Historically there was controversy in economics over whether evaluations of the value of a model should lie in the accuracy of its assumptions or the accuracy of its predictions (Friedman 1953). The consensus for the last half century has been that the focus should not be on modeling the exact nature of human decision making, but on creating the simplest possible formal model that generates clear and testable predictions. If these predictions are falsified, then something in the assumptions is incorrect and needs to be changed. A bedrock assumption, not subject to testing, is the fundamental belief that individuals respond to incentives. If individuals do not respond to incentives shaped by their objective functions, then the basic economic approach fails.

A fundamental misconception among criminologists is that the term "rational," when used in reference to the economic model, refers to the character of the objective function of the offender (Clarke and Felson 1993). Becker in his initial model specified a very simple static model that assumed that all individuals had the same objective function in a world of perfect information. Criminologists have rightly concluded that this model cannot explain criminal behavior; crime is driven in large part by individual differences, which economists sometimes refer to as population heterogeneity. But some criminologists go one step further and also conclude that because a rational person, that is, the average person with the "typical" objective function, would simply not behave in this manner, the economic model is invalid and should be abandoned (Clarke and Felson 1993).

Economists, however, use the word rational to refer not to the nature of the objective function but to the process by which a person makes choices relative to his or her objective function. There is considerable empirical evidence that prices affect consumption not only of idealized, perfectly rational actors, but also of patients in psychiatric institutions, animals (Kagel et al. 1981), and users of the two licit addictive substances, cigarettes and alcohol (see Manning et al. 1991). As Philip Cook elegantly argues in his 1980 defense of the economic approach to the study of crime and deterrence, the finding that criminals do not appear to behave in accord with the simple model developed by Becker does not fundamentally undercut the economic exercise, but rather suggests that the economic model needs to be further developed to predict behavior more accurately. Cook points to the need to allow the objective function (the way people weight outcomes) to vary across the population and to deal with imperfect information (that people do not always know the punishment associated with a particular crime and that punishments in the criminal justice system are uncertain) as main areas to be addressed in further developing the economic model of crime.

The process proposed by Cook is formal theory development, economics style. In economics, the basic model of any problem is written down and then extended and developed over time to reflect reality more accurately. The theory is specified with a precise formula that can be written down in testable form and then built on and tested by anyone provided that they make their assumptions clear. Becker's 1968 article on criminal behavior and Landes's 1971 article on the criminal justice system are examples of foundational papers in economics in which a basic formal economic model was written down and later extended by other researchers.

The idea that theoretical ideas need to be specified in a formula is not limited to economics. The hard sciences follow this form, and theorists in sociology have also advocated it. For example, Gibbs (1972, p. 133) suggested that empirical tests of theory virtually require formulas: "The stipulation of formulas and requisite data is a distinct step in theory construction. Neither stipulation is realized by a definition of a concept, and the theorist should not presume that a definition will somehow suggest the same formula and procedure to all investigators."

Sociologist Robert O'Brien (2001), when commenting on a theoretical debate between Britt (1997) and Greenberg (2001) regarding tests of Greenberg's theory of juvenile delinquency, describes the lack of a referential formula by theorists as a major problem in criminology.

> He [Greenberg] could help by outlining the conditions necessary for an adequate test, including the time period, level of analysis, measures of "crime" to be used, and so on. This task is not an easy one or one typically performed by criminologists. Performing this task is especially important in cases where an empirical test does not accompany a theory. Without such an empirical test accompanying a theory, it is more difficult to know how one should test a theory.
>
> In my view theorists have the right to criticize those who test their theories in an unreasonable manner, but the range of reasonableness is certainly extended when theorists do not provide clear instructions for appropriate tests. Many theories in the social sciences are discursive. Such discursive theories may be valuable in terms of the thinking of those in and out of a field, but they are difficult to test. Those who formulate their theories in a discursive manner will view a requirement that theorists explain how to test their theories as too strong a requirement. Formal theorists will view a requirement that refers only to "clear instructions for appropriate tests" as not strong enough. (O'Brien 2001, p. 373)

Formal theories, which can be written down and then modified when falsified, lead to clearer testing and clearer thinking.

The problem is that as the model becomes more complicated, it becomes harder to test. Theoretical economists have steadily and busily worked on extending the basic model to generate predictions that appear to be more consistent with observed behavior. Theoretical economists have demonstrated time and again that the economic modeling framework is flexible enough to accommodate a wide range of possible complications, such as imperfect information by potential offenders about the probability of apprehension or variation in attitudes toward risk (Garoupa 1997).

But as early as 1978, economist Charles Manski concluded that existing economic theory was "too idealized and abstract from too much of the criminal decision problem to serve as useful bases of empirical work" (1978, p. 90). Clarke and Cornish had much the same complaint when they discussed the economic model of decision making for a *Crime and Justice* essay in 1985. Almost 30 years after Manski, judge (and economist) Richard Posner's review of Steven Shavell's theoretical book *Foundations of Economic Analysis of Law* (2004) makes much the same point. The models, while rich, are abstract, do not deal with specific situations, and are therefore too hard to test (Posner 2006).[9]

Another strain or version of economics does not require the researcher to test the exact formal theory, but rather to test broad implications of the theory in a manner similar to what criminologists typically call theory testing. This is the basic approach that motivates the wildly popular book *Freakonomics* by Levitt and Dubner (2005), which is based on a series of studies by Levitt and various coauthors. Levitt examines a series of situations in which individuals have clear incentives, generates predictions of specific outcomes, and then analyzes data to compare actual outcomes with his predictions. The economic model predicts, for example, that real estate agents have lower incentives to wait for a better price than homeowners do, since the agent gets only a small share of the increment from waiting for a better offer. Levitt does not actually estimate his model, but he examines data on transactions in which real estate agents sell their own home, and he compares their selling behavior when they are agents with their behavior when they are sellers. If Levitt is right, one would expect selling realtors-owners to sell for higher prices, and have longer waiting periods, than when realtors sell another person's house. These empirical tests are not structural, which means that Levitt is not trying to estimate the key parameters of the preference function. But the apparent evidence is at least consistent with the claim of mismatched incentives. In nearly every example, Levitt develops predictions based on a simple economic model and then compares the evidence with that prediction. Colloquially, this process of generating a prediction based on the idea that incentives matter for choices is what some people mean when they say someone is "thinking like an economist." It is

[9] This mathematically rigorous kind of theory falls into a kind of parallel universe, often devoted to making economists feel better about the scientific rigor of the economic enterprise; we do not pretend to cover this other kind of theorizing in this essay. The Nobel Prize is frequently awarded to economists who do this kind of work. For example, Gerard Debreu received the prize in 1983 for showing that it was possible for markets to come to equilibrium even with very weak assumptions about the shape of individual utility functions and production functions (Debreu 1959). It involves use of sophisticated mathematics.

analogous to how thinking like a sociologist involves paying particular attention to social context. While neither approach will capture all the important variation in crime by itself, they are both valid and useful approaches to the study of behavior. At other times, thinking like an economist simply means thinking carefully or creatively about the effects of a policy change. The idea that abortion can account for part of the crime drop (Donohue and Levitt 2001) is an example of this type of creative thinking often associated with economists that could easily also be done by noneconomists.

B. Aggregate or Market Forces

It would be a mistake to focus too much on the individual and the implications of rational behavior in a discussion of the economic approach. Economics is largely the study of the supply of and the demand for goods, in which there are two sets of actors, producers and consumers, trying to maximize their objective functions (profits for producers, utility or well-being for consumers). The key claim of microeconomics is that producers and consumers can interact to reach an equilibrium price and quantity without any explicit intervention by governments or anyone else. This focus on two competing forces interacting to reach equilibrium is an explicit part of economists' thinking. Coase (1978, p. 209) suggested that this tendency by economists to think about the economic system as a unified interdependent system means that they are "more likely to uncover the basic interrelationships within a social system than is someone less accustomed to looking at the working of a system as a whole." This system focus was explicit in Becker's original approach. Becker states that "the amount of crime is determined not only by the rationality and preferences of would-be criminals but also by the economic and social environment created by public policies, including expenditures on police, punishments for different crimes and opportunities for employment, schooling, and training programs" (1993, p. 390).

In Becker's view, the social system that generates crime is not limited to potential offenders and the criminal justice system, but includes any part of the social and economic environment that changes incentives to commit crime. This fundamental realization that the total amount of crime is determined as an outcome of the interactions among all members of the system is not uniquely economic, but it is not surprising that economists have focused on this insight from the beginning of their study of crime.

In an economic market, that the quantity sold is a function of the interaction between supply and demand is recognized by the specification of two simultaneous equations, one for supply and one for demand. Producers will produce a certain amount of the good conditional on a variety of factors, including price. Consumers will agree to purchase a certain amount of the good conditional on a number of factors, including price. In equilibrium, the quantity produced is equal to the quantity demanded. Price is the mechanism by which the market reaches its equilibrium. For example, suppose that initially producers produced more than the market demanded. The only option is for producers to lower the price, at which point more will be sold. Price thus depends on quantity demanded and supplied, and vice versa. In economic language, price is *endogenous*, determined by the system of equations. Other factors are *exogenous*, meaning that they exist outside of the system and do not depend on what happens as the system arrives at equilibrium. A drought that affects the production of corn is an example of an exogenous shock to the market.

Any attempt to estimate the impact of price on the quantity demanded (or supplied) must somehow break the endogeneity of the system through the introduction of a source of exogenous variation. The most obvious would be some kind of experiment in which people would be randomly assigned different prices, but economists have developed other methods that we address in Section III. The point of this section is to suggest that in thinking about systems, economists naturally think about the extent to which any variable is endogenous or dependent on the system. This way of thinking has been essential to how economists approach the study of crime, and we believe that it forms one of the major contributions of the economic approach to the study of crime.

The key variables in the crime system are not quantity and price but crime and the crime prevention measures taken by the criminal justice system and by potential victims. Crime is dependent on, among other factors, the crime prevention measures taken in the social system. These measures are in turn dependent, however, on the amount of crime in the system, among other things. That means that crime prevention is endogenous; that is, crime and crime prevention are simultaneously determined. This may be the biggest hurdle to models that attempt to study the deterrent effects of prison and police. Places that have a lot of crime are also likely to have a lot of crime prevention. This induces a positive correlation between crime and crime prevention policies such as the number of police, when theoretically one might expect crime prevention to have a negative relationship with crime. This fundamental insight forms a key part of Nagin's 1978 article on deterrence and is a major hurdle to any empirical estimation of deterrence. At the close of the 1970s, Cook (1980) wrote an influential review essay for the second volume of *Crime and Justice* suggesting a new way forward for economic research on deterrence. This new approach largely deemphasized direct tests of the economic model and urged empirical tests of policy interventions with special attention to the problem of endogeneity between actors in what some might consider the market for crime (Cook 1986).[10]

This analogy of a market for crime, which has never become embedded in criminological thought, has value in its identification of interacting parties (most prominently, potential offenders, and the criminal justice system and potential victims) who simultaneously affect each other's behavior. Estimates of the impact of policies that fail to take into account the endogeneity of these policies and the responses of potential offenders (i.e., displacement) to these policies are fundamentally flawed. But this endogeneity is not just a statistical problem: it is a substantive problem that fundamentally frames the economists' approach to the study of crime since the criminal justice system, potential victims, and offenders all react to each other's actions. A standard critique from other economists of an analyst's policy recommendation is that the author has failed to take into account the feedback loop between the actions of the system and would-be offenders. For example, consider the potential tension between reintegration for ex-offenders and deterrence. A policy that encourages reintegration may reduce barriers to reentry but also simultaneously may lower the punishment cost of an arrest and conviction.

Cook's (1986) examination of opportunity theory from an economic point of view is an excellent example of the added value that comes from applying the economic perspective to an area often studied in criminology. Social learning theory (Cloward and Ohlin 1960) focuses on the role of opportunity to provide the social context in which in-

[10] In this notional market, the "demand for crime" is the inverse of the "demand for safety"; as the price of safety rises, the demand for crime will increase.

dividuals learn delinquent values and subcultures. Basic criminological theories of victimization tended to focus only on the lifestyle that leads to differential exposure to social contexts in the environment of potential victims. Criminal opportunity theory, as developed by both economists and criminologists (see Clarke 1983), builds on this history but adds a particular emphasis on the feedback loop between the threat of crime and the crime prevention steps of potential victims. According to Cook, a "complete theory of the volume and distribution of crime requires a complete characterization of both potential criminals and potential victims" (1986, p. 27). Situational crime prevention as a theory suggests that victimization can be affected by steps the potential victim can take to avoid victimization (Clarke 1983). This affects the targets available to potential offenders who have to establish the relative risks and rewards of any particular crime. This interaction then affects the final distributions of crime that we observe.

Cook offers this theory as a way to help explain the apparent mismatch between victimization rates and fear of crime. Women are particularly vulnerable to threats of force and present attractive targets to potential robbers, who are primarily male. And women are more frightened of robbery than men are. Men, however, were 2.7 times more likely to be victims of robbery in 2005 than women (U.S Department of Justice 2006). From a criminal opportunity theory perspective, the reason is not that men are inherently more attractive targets than women, but that women, on average, take steps to prevent robbery that men do not take. As a result, men are more attractive targets on average. From this perspective, researchers must remember that what one observes is the result of actions taken by both potential criminals and potential victims.

That individuals can take steps to prevent crime over and above those of the criminal justice system also means that researchers are likely consistently to underestimate the effects of any effective crime prevention strategy on the part of the government. Suppose that the government institutes a program that reduced the number of burglars by 20 percent in a business district in the short run. Businesses perceiving a reduced threat may become more likely to hold cash and spend less money on crime prevention. This will increase the potential returns from theft and induce additional individuals to offend. Whatever the exact interaction, criminal opportunity theory predicts a less than 20 percent reduction in crime in the long run. This is relevant not only from a policy perspective but for a research strategy. Any research effort to measure the effects of the original treatment must take into account subsequent behavioral adaptations that may lessen the initial effect.

The consequence of this analysis at the system level means that most research on the endogeneity of crime prevention and crime is done at the aggregate level (for a review of economic crime prevention studies, see Levitt and Miles [2007]). But recent work on incapacitation (Bhati 2007; Nieuwbeerta and Blokland 2007; Owens 2007; Sweeten and Apel 2007) and deterrence (Loeffler 2006; Helland and Tabarrok 2007; Kuziemko 2007) has extended these analyses to the individual level.

II. Illustrative Topics in the Economics of Crime

In this section we examine three topics that illustrate ways in which economic analysis has been used to illuminate major issues of interest to criminologists. The first, perceptual deterrence theory, is at the core of theoretical and empirical economics. Early insights from economic papers on time discounting have been incorporated into mainstream criminological research and have led to stronger empirical research on the connection between the experience of arrest and perceptions of criminal justice risks. In contrast, the second field, the behavior of sentencing agents in the courts, illustrates how the insights of economics can be lost. Early promising empirical research by economists on the behavior of prosecutors produced interesting findings that have not entered into criminological research. However, the same interest in maximization decisions by criminal justice officials, in this case police, has generated a new approach (outcome analysis), which is influencing study of disparate outcomes and the extent to which they can be interpreted as evidence of discrimination.

A. Perceptual Deterrence Theory

Coase argues that, to the extent that the theoretical approach of economics is useful for the study in another discipline, members of that discipline will acquire these insights and incorporate them into their discipline. The study of individual deterrence by criminologists has incorporated many lessons from economics and developed an interesting and important literature in criminology. Good reviews of this literature are offered elsewhere (Paternoster 1987; Nagin 1998). We highlight key articles to show how insights from economics have been incorporated into criminological research.

One lesson from the initial flurry of research on deterrence by economists was that the connection between punishment and behavior was not as strong as might have been expected (Nagin 1978). One possible explanation was that individuals did not make "good decisions," where good is defined as choices that would lead to better outcomes for the decision maker according to "typical" objective functions. One reason for these poor choices may be that severe sentences (i.e., which extend far into the future) are heavily discounted by offenders. The future is usually discounted in decision making: a dollar now is always better than a dollar in the future. But the rate of this discounting is subject to debate and may vary between individuals. An individual with a "normal" discount rate may be willing to trade 90 cents today for one dollar next year. A person with a high discount rate might be willing to trade 50 cents or less today for a dollar next year. Wilson and Herrnstein (1985) identified high time discounting as a potentially valuable explanation of criminal behavior given the time delay of imprisonment. Economists have typically considered the time discount factor when discussing the potential effects of policies that increase sentence severity (Kessler and Levitt 1999).

Research by Nagin and Pogarsky (2001, 2003) more explicitly builds on work by economists, using scenario data on college students and panel data from the National Longitudinal Study of Adolescent Health (Nagin and Pogarsky 2004) to document that individuals who discount the future more heavily are less likely to be deterred by a given punishment. They differentiate the concept of time discounting from impulsivity, which is more similar to the mainstream criminological concept of self-control. Impulsive people do not consider the consequences of their actions, whereas high time discounters do consider the consequences, but heavily discount future consequences. Cauffman and Steinberg (2000) refer to the ability to consider the larger consequences of a decision as perspective and the ability to control one's impulses as temperance. They refer to a final nontraditional feature of choice that might explain poor choices to commit crime as judgment. Judgment is the ability to avoid allowing outside immediate influences such as peers and physiological arousal to have an undue influence on behavior. Loewenstein (1996) posits that visceral factors such as anger and sexual arousal can narrow the range of consequences considered by decision makers. Nagin (2007) used his Edwin H. Sutherland Award acceptance speech to the American Society of Criminology to argue for more research into these components of choice (judgment, temperance, and perspective) that might explain why individuals, particularly young adults, are not deterred from crime despite the presence of steep penalties.

Another reason individuals might not be deterred is that they are largely unaware of the true probability and severity of sanctions. In economic terms, there may be imperfect information or even optimism bias about sanctions. Paternoster (1987) details a large body of work mostly by criminologists trying to link perceptions of risk to behavior. He also points to the need for researchers to consider how these perceptions are developed through individual experience. Stafford and Warr (1993) redefined the criminological idea of specific deterrence as information updating and identified mechanisms based on one's own and peers' experiences by which individuals could update their perceptions of punishment. The idea that the experience of peers might influence the perceptions of punishment was raised initially by Cook (1980).

A variety of empirical tests have studied the ways in which perceptions are updated using both real and vignette data (Paternoster and Piquero 1995; Piquero and Paternoster 1998; Piquero and Pogarsky 2002; Pogarsky, Piquero, and Paternoster 2004). This work has been brought together with work on how perceptions affect behavior in a recent article in the *American Sociological Review* by sociologist Ross Matsueda and colleagues (Matsueda, Kreager, and Huizinga 2006) using panel data on high-risk youths in Denver that were collected to answer these kinds of questions. This article, like others in this literature, explicitly uses concepts such as expected utility from economics to set up its analysis. It also uses formal equations to specify its models. The article finds fairly strong evidence that the individual experience of arrest leads to updating of the perceived probability of arrest. Moreover, it finds that these individual experiences, rather than the neighborhood environment, drive the formation of these expectations. Finally, the article shows that increases in the perceived probability of arrest lead to meaningful declines in offending.

A very similar article was written almost simultaneously by economist Lance Lochner (2007). It also looked at the link between personal experience and perceptions, and then at perceptions and behavior, using a different panel data set. The results of the two papers are eerily similar—both find that a 10-percentage-point increase in the probability of arrest will lead to a 3 percent decrease in theft—although the methods used are different, underscoring differences in technique between the two fields.[11] Notwithstanding the differences in technique, the similarity between the two papers underscores Coase's point that other fields can take advantage of key insights from economics, without the necessary involvement of economists.

B. Economics of Sentencing

Not all areas of criminology and criminal justice research present equally cheery stories about learning from the economic approach. A fair assessment would conclude that the economic approach has not greatly informed the current state of the art, in part because economists have not remained committed to research in the area over extended periods. In this subsection we review early work by economists and discuss ways in which the results might be relevant for current research.

Economist William Landes (1971) followed Becker with an important, if less often cited, article entitled "An Economic Analysis of the Courts." He provided a mathematical model of court behavior, which he then tested with empirical data. The criminal justice system on its face is probably more amenable to the economic approach than crime itself. The actors in the criminal justice system are known and are more likely to behave rationally, in the economic sense of consistently following their objective functions. These functions are likely to be "reasonable," in the sense of striving to achieve intuitively appealing goals. Data on the behavior of court actors are available for every case, which means that the models are likely to be easier to test.

Landes's model is very simple, and like any good economic modeler, he makes his assumptions very clear. He assumes that there is a limited number of defendants and that prosecutors and defendants each have their own perceived probabilities of conviction in a case, which is a function of the prosecutor's and defendant's resources and all other

[11] Matsueda, Kreager, and Huizinga (2006) use random-effect analysis, and Lochner (2007) uses fixed-effect methods. Matsueda, Kreager, and Huizinga use a Tobit model for the perception model and a negative binomial model in the crime equation to model more precisely the nonnormal distribution of the dependent variables. Lochner used ordinary least squares (OLS) as the primary estimator for both models. Finally, Lochner made an attempt to use an instrumental variable estimator in the crime equation. These differences are emblematic of standard approaches by the two disciplines.

information, common to both actors, that might contribute to a conviction. He assumes that the sentence to be awarded after a trial is known to both the defendant and the prosecutor and that it is independent of resources. Finally, he assumes that there are no monetary or nonmonetary costs to a trial. The prosecutor's objective function is such that he attempts to maximize the expected number of convictions weighted by the expected sentence given at trial, subject to a budget constraint on his resources. This maximization exercise produces what economists call the first-order conditions—the things that must be true if the prosecutor maximized his objective function under these assumptions. These first-order conditions create implications or predictions, which can then be tested. For example, his model predicts that pretrial detention (meaning that someone was not released on bail) would lead to higher opportunity costs for the defendant than if he were released on bail. These higher costs would lead to acceptance of longer sentences in plea bargains for those held in jail before trial relative to those who are released on bail. If making bail is a function of wealth, this model suggests that the current bail system will lead to discriminatory sentencing outcomes for those with less wealth. In particular, lower-income participants who do not make bail will be more likely to plead guilty and to receive harsher plea sentences.

Despite the highly simplified assumptions, the empirical results in Landes (1971) largely support the model's predictions particularly for bail (see also Landes 1973, 1974). William Rhodes and Brian Forst followed with models that attempted to make Landes's model more realistic. For example, Forst and Brosi (1977) extended Landes's single-period model to multiple periods in an attempt to examine the relative trade-off between case quality and criminal history as predictors of prosecutor effort. Rhodes (1976) added additional courtroom work group actors to the model. However, very little has been done to extend or test these models since the 1970s. Perhaps this lack of activity by economists accounts for why this body of work is largely unknown in the criminology literature.[12]

Economists were also heavily involved in the writing of the National Academy of Sciences volumes on sentencing in 1983 (Blumstein et al.

[12] For an exception, see a recent paper by the young economists David Abrams and Chris Rolphs (2007), which makes use of data from the classic Philadelphia Bail Experiment to estimate the optimal bail amount and the "cost of freedom" for an individual arrested for a crime.

1983). The articles in these volumes aimed to evaluate the current literature and lay out effective strategies for additional research on sentencing. Klepper, Nagin, and Tierney (1983) examine research that looks at discrimination in sentencing. They offer two particularly broad critiques of that literature. First, they note the absence of formal models of processing decisions in the criminal justice system. Without theory, empirical models may be misspecified, and inferences about social class and race at each stage may be extremely misleading. Garber, Klepper, and Nagin (1983) lay out a structural model that follows from their formal model of the criminal justice system. Klepper, Nagin, and Tierney (1983) strongly advocate against including pled cases and tried cases in the same analysis given that they follow different processes. Second, the literature did not pay attention to sample selection biases resulting from screening and processing decisions. These two concerns are obviously related, because a formal model of the courts could help estimate selection processes. A related article by Berk (1983) concerning selection problems also brought the issue of selection to the attention of sentencing researchers.

Research by criminologists in the immediate aftermath of the National Academy of Sciences report appeared to take these warnings to heart. Zatz and Hagan (1985) demonstrate how controlling for selection can dramatically alter inferences about key predictors of sentencing. Smith (1985) applied the logic of Landes's model to the plea bargain decision to show that the trial penalties in his data set were on average consistent with a model in which pleas are discounted by the probability of conviction.

But, over time, Landes (1971) and Klepper, Nagin, and Tierney (1983) have not had a lasting impact on research on the criminal justice system. Plea bargains and trial cases are almost always analyzed together, for example. Bushway, Johnson, and Slocum (2007) detail the somewhat dismal history of controls for selection in sentencing research. The principal statistical technique advocated by Berk (1983) and Klepper, Nagin, and Tierney (1983) is the Heckman two-step technique. This estimator explicitly models selection from a larger sample into a nonrandom subsample using a probit equation in the first stage and an OLS model for the subsample in the second stage. The hazard for selection into the second stage, estimated in the first probit equation, is included as a regressor in the second equation. This approach has typically been implemented in a mechanistic (and often incorrect) way to deal with the acknowledged selection problems. In general, there have been few attempts to model the selection process.

There has also been little independent progress in the development of criminal justice theory (Hagan 1989; Duffee and Allan 2007). Those theories that do exist, while often quite rich, are discursive and informal. An example is focal concerns theory, the currently dominant theory in sentencing (Steffensmeier, Kramer, and Streifel 1993; Steffensmeier, Kramer, and Ulmer 1998). It posits that courtroom actors' sentencing decisions reflect three primary "focal concerns": (1) the blameworthiness or culpability of the offender, (2) the desire to protect the community by incapacitating current offenders or deterring potential offenders, and (3) the resource constraints of the courts. The argument is that because actors do not have enough information to determine accurately an offender's culpability or dangerousness, they develop a shorthand based on stereotypes and attributions linked to such offender characteristics as race, sex, and age. "Race, age, and sex will interact to influence sentencing because of images or attributions relating these statuses to membership in social groups thought to be dangerous and crime prone" (Steffensmeier, Kramer, and Ulmer 1998, p. 768). The theory is not tested directly—key concepts such as perceived dangerousness or culpability are never operationalized—but the theory is used to interpret the finding that age, race, and sex are correlated with some sentencing outcomes. Of course, other theories also predict that age, race, and sex are correlated with sentencing outcomes.

Direct tests of focal concerns are complicated by the lack of a formal model. Some parts of the theory are consistent with Landes's model; for example, the existence of a budget constraint is common between the two models. But, essentially, focal concerns theory argues that actors such as prosecutors have a more complex objective function than the one specified by Landes and that actors cannot maximize effectively. While these assertions are clearly possible and even plausible, they are not tested in the current literature.

Ulmer and Bradley (2006), for example, attempt to use focal concerns theory to explain the size of the trial penalty—the difference between sentences following plea bargains and those following trials—with particular attention to the potential for racial discrimination by prosecutors. This is very similar to the problem modeled by Landes (1971). But Ulmer and Bradley do not include measures of the probability of conviction, the existence of pretrial detention, or considerations of attitudes toward risk, three major factors that explain plea bargaining in the Landes model. At the very least, the simple Landes model presents an important alternative explanation or competing theory that could serve as a useful stalking horse or straw man that criminologists could use to show the need for more complicated theories. Moreover, the absence of key variables predicted by Landes to be major factors underscores Klepper, Nagin, and Tierney's (1983) concerns about misspecification in the absence of formal models. Ulmer and Bradley found mixed support for focal concerns theory, but the direction for future research is unclear given the absence of a precise model describing how plea decisions are made.

Economic thinking about plea decisions provides direction for research that may cast doubt on the current consensus in the criminology literature regarding the role of race in sentencing. The literature has repeatedly shown that race appears to be correlated with incarceration risk but not with sentence length when studied using conviction data (Spohn 2000). Researchers are generally unwilling to refer to this effect as racial discrimination by judges because of the possibility of omitted variable bias—other unobserved factors such as wealth, family support, and demeanor that are correlated with race could drive the race effect—but most researchers are willing to say that this racial disparity is created at the sentencing stage. Consequently, policy reforms, such as sentencing guidelines that reduce judicial discretion, are said to be needed at the sentencing stage.

But the economic model raises some doubt about this conclusion. The model predicts that people who do not make bail are more likely both to be convicted and to receive harsher sentences. This means that a conviction sample will contain a disproportionate number of people who both are lower-class and did not make bail. The finding that race predicts incarceration but not sentence length could be the result of selection bias at the conviction stage.

Demuth (2003) convincingly shows that blacks and Hispanics are indeed more likely to be detained before trial, all else equal. Several studies have found that being held prior to adjudication is associated with an increased probability of receiving a sentence of incarceration (Rankin 1964; Farrell and Swigert 1978; Nobling, Spohn, and DeLone 1998). A master's thesis by Hart (2006), using the same data as Demuth, showed that race effects of incarceration at conviction were eliminated in an indictment sample once controls for pretrial incarceration were included. While not convincing proof, this is at least suggestive that the warnings of Klepper, Nagin, and Tierney (1983) are well taken. Models that fail to control for how people move through the criminal justice system may misallocate discretion to the wrong stage. Modeling the decision-making process carefully may lead to new empirical findings that challenge conventional wisdom and lead to both new theories and new recommendations for policy reform.

Very recent work by a new wave of economists has raised the possibility that economists can, after a long absence, once again contribute to the sentencing literature, particularly when it comes to modeling selection and discretion. Some of these contributions are very similar to criminology papers, although they usually contain some modeling twists that mark the authors as economists. For example, Mustard (2001) studied racial disparity in the federal guideline data in a manner very similar to Steffensmeier and Demuth (2000) but used dummy variables for each cell in the federal guidelines to control for the recommendations of the guidelines rather than use the linear scores for criminal history and crime severity that define the grid. The two papers reach substantively similar findings of racial disparity. Schanzenbach and Yaeger (2006) use the federal data first to replicate the basic criminological finding of racial disparity in incarceration for white-collar criminals, but then showed that accounting for the payment of fines, which is driven by an omitted variable (income), can substantially reduce these estimates.

David Bjerk (2005) studied how prosecutors use their discretion to avoid three-strikes laws in California. His work is consistent with the criminology literature on mandatory minimums, which essentially shows that prosecutors often subvert mandatory minimums imposed by legislators (e.g., Tonry 1992; Farrell 2003). He takes this insight one step further by showing that failure to take this into account can lead to an overstatement of the impact of three-strikes laws on sentencing outcomes in conviction data sets. Helland and Tabarrok (2007) use the prosecutors' discretion described by Bjerk to provide a rare economic estimate of general deterrence at the individual level. They compare the postsentencing criminal activity of criminals convicted of a strikable offense with those who were tried for a strikable offense but convicted of a nonstrikable offense. The threat of the third strike reduces arrest rates by about 15 percent. Other young economists have also started using the discretion of individual actors to identify the causal impact of deterrence and incapacitation at the individual level. For example, Ilyana Kuziemko (2007) looks at discretion at the parole level to study the specific deterrent (or rehabilitative) impact of longer sentences on imprisoned offenders in Georgia. Emily Owens (2007) uses a change in how sentencing guidelines handle juvenile records in Maryland to generate unique individual-level estimates of incapacitation. We expect that papers along these lines will be appearing in economic journals with increasing frequency.

On the theoretical front, Bjerk (forthcoming) has developed formal models of plea bargaining that attempt to make the Landes model more realistic by studying how different attitudes toward risk can induce plea bargains that include higher than expected trial penalties even in the simple frictionless system envisioned by Landes. A second theoretical paper (Bjerk 2007*a*) looks at the role of plea bargains when there is uncertainty about defendant guilt. Economists have also done some work on prosecutors that explicitly looks at the nature of their objective functions. One criticism of economic models is that economists have simplistic assumptions about what prosecutors attempt to maximize. But Glaeser, Kessler, and Piehl (2000) suggest that federal prosecutors maximize a number of dimensions, including the public profile of a case, when selecting cases to try. They argue that this selection mechanism can lead to nonrandom sampling of cases into federal court, which might complicate inference drawing on studies of federal conviction data. Schanzenbach and Tiller (2007) do not model this selection, but used the federal sentencing data to write a paper with formal theory and empirical analysis to study the effects of judge characteristics on sentencing outcomes. This paper is similar in spirit to work by criminologists studying judge effects (e.g., Johnson 2006), although again the methods and models are quite different. There is at present very little cross-fertilization in these literatures, but we have little doubt that work by both economists and criminologists studying sentencing could be improved by collaboration and cross-citation. The community of sentencing scholars in criminology is relatively small, and it is therefore an area into which a cadre of economists could quickly become integrated into (and integral to) the field.

C. *Outcome Analysis*

Recent developments in the study of racial profiling by police suggest that noneconomists are also beginning to see the potential usefulness of the economic approach for the study of discrimination. Lawsuits accusing police of racial profiling typically involve statistical evidence that search and stop rates per capita vary among different groups in the population. If blacks and whites were otherwise identical, then we could test for the presence of racial discrimination simply by comparing the fraction of blacks searched to the fraction of whites searched. Under the null hypothesis of no discrimination, whites and blacks should be searched at the same rate. However, this approach has a well-known problem: there is no particular reason to believe that all other things are equal. Socioeconomic characteristics vary considerably between blacks and whites, including characteristics (e.g., income, wages, neighborhood residence) thought to be related to crime. Since these characteristics are related both to race and to crime, rational police seeking to maximize hit rates would take them into account in deciding whom to search. For this reason, not all differentiation is equally inappropriate or illegal.

The traditional solution to this problem is to add control variables in a model that tries to predict search on the basis of race. This approach mimics the standard sentencing analysis of discrimination in which an outcome such as incarceration is regressed on all legally relevant variables plus race. The fundamental limitation of this approach is that it is unlikely that researchers observe all the potentially relevant variables that the decision maker—here, the state trooper—does. Thus there remains the substantial possibility of omitted variables bias (Engel 2008). Several courts hearing selective enforcement claims have ruled that stop and search rates are not meaningful or are insufficient for determinations of discriminatory purpose or effect.

Economists have proposed a solution to this problem known as an "outcome test." The basic intuition dates at least to Becker (1957), in his classic treatise on discrimination, and has also been used several times by Ayres (2001). The model was applied to police profiling by Knowles, Persico, and Todd (2001). It is a formal mathematical model of police behavior based on the key assumption that police are trying to maximize hits (the number of productive searches) when they conduct searches. Knowles, Persico, and Todd then build from this model to show that, under certain assumptions, the stable equilibrium will occur when all observable groups have the same hit rate at the margin. That is, police officers will make use of all available information in observable correlates such as race and behavior in their attempt to maximize hits. Intuitively, this means that if searches of one group have a lower hit rate than searches of another group, then rational, unbiased police officers would reallocate searches away from the low-hit group and toward the high-hit group; once they did that, the overall hit rate would increase. Thus, if officers actually behaved in this manner, evidence that the marginal success rate differs by race would be strong evidence of discrimination. And evidence that the marginal success rate is equal across races would then be compelling evidence of the absence of taste-based discrimination.

This test is interesting for several reasons. First, it is based explicitly on a formal economic model[13] of an actor in the criminal justice system and the response by potential offenders to that actor. Second, outcome analysis requires a very simple empirical test with no complicated econometrics. In a very short time, outcome analysis has been used by numerous economists and criminologists and has become the standard for legal tests of discrimination in racial profiling lawsuits. Third, the test has spawned a number of worthwhile discussions about the model. Criminologist Robin Engel (2008) argues that the assumptions of the model do not apply to the standard police search. This is an interesting challenge because it is made on substantive grounds, and it involves a detailed investigation of how police make decisions. Economists have challenged some key assumptions, which has led to an interesting dialogue and a number of alternative tests (Dharmapala and Ross 2004; Anwar and Fang 2006).

Perhaps the most interesting challenge is made in recent work by law professor and political scientist Bernard Harcourt (2004, 2007) arguing against using race in police decisions. His challenge is noteworthy because it assumes that the economic model is correct and poses a theoretical challenge from within the model. He notes that the policy of racial profiling may not lead to the desired effect of decreasing crime if blacks and whites are not equally deterred by police pressure. Specifically, the policy of discriminating on the basis of race could lead to increased crime and decreased fairness if blacks are less responsive to police pressure than whites are. See a related argument by Persico (2002) and Bjerk (2007*b*). This challenge puts the pressure directly on

[13] "Economic" does not refer to any money value but simply to the notion that the actors attempt to maximize their objective functions, in this case perhaps the rewards provided by their employer. This objective function can be anything deemed realistic by the modeler and does not have to be crime control.

empirical estimates of key parameters from the model. Economist Paul Heaton (2007) made a creative attempt to estimate the elasticity of response to the police by blacks using the change in police behavior in New Jersey after the state police were accused of racial profiling. His point estimates were similar to other estimates for whites (around 0.8), but his data and measures were so imprecise as to leave very wide confidence intervals around the point estimate, meaning that he cannot reject the null hypothesis that blacks have substantially lower elasticities than whites. Other data may have to be found to answer this question, but we believe that Harcourt's critique demonstrates how outcome analysis can lead to interesting theoretical and empirical discussions across disciplines.

There may be other criminal justice problems concerning which the logic of outcome analysis can be applied constructively. For example, Ayres and Waldfogel (1994) studied bail setting using outcome tests, and Bushway and Gelbach (2006) developed a formal model of bail decision making that tries to incorporate more realistic assumptions about bail setting. This type of formal modeling offers a potentially interesting path forward that will require the involvement of both criminologists and economists to make serious headway. Economists are probably required for the formal modeling, and criminologists are required for the institutional knowledge that will allow for realistic model building.

III. Specialized Economic Techniques

Coase observes that every field develops techniques and methods to address problems that arise in the study of a particular subject. This section considers the application of two core economic techniques to crime and the criminal justice system. Econometrics involves the application of specialized statistical methods and has already influenced the empirical analyses of criminologists. Cost-benefit analysis as a technique is much more rooted in economic reasoning. Economists are responsible for most of the modest advances in the application of cost-benefit analysis to criminal justice topics.

A. Econometrics

Econometrics is a substantial subfield of economics that deals primarily with the statistical analysis of observational data. Some economists who study crime are essentially applied econometricians, and their main competitive advantage is their use of these statistical tools rather than the application of the economic model. These tools can be (and have been) learned by criminologists. The result has been empirical studies that can make stronger claims about the identification of causal relationships.

Panel data models are one set of tools developed primarily by economists that have been often used by economists in the study of crime. Panel data provide multiple observations over time for individual units of observation. Almost all the aggregate studies of deterrence, which focus on the effects of the criminal justice system on crime, use panel data (see Levitt and Miles [2007] for a review).

Criminology (and sociology) has tended to use random-effect models for the estimation of panel data (Hierarchical Linear Modeling is a random-effect model), whereas economics has a clear preference for fixed-effect models. Both assume that there is an individual-specific component to the error term that is unobserved and constant over time. The difference between the models is driven by the assumptions they make about this component of the error terms. The random-effect models assume that this individual-specific component is distributed in a particular parametric form, usually the normal distribution. This means that only the parameters of that distribution need be estimated, which makes the estimator very efficient. However, the estimator generates unbiased estimates only under fairly strict assumptions about the relationship between the included variables and the error term. Fixed-effect models, by contrast, do not make any assumptions about the distribution of this unobserved part of the error term, but rather estimate it directly, usually with an individual-specific dummy variable. This is much less efficient, but requires fewer assumptions, and will lead to unbiased coefficient estimates relative to the random-effect model. This basic advantage of fixed-effect models has not been well understood in sociology (and criminology), although recent work by sociologist Charles Halaby (2004) attempts to correct this problem. In his review, he takes sociologists to task for failing to heed lessons from the econometric literature.

One substantive area in which these panel data methods are particularly relevant is the study of state dependence. The idea that offending can dynamically cause future offending is known to economists as state dependence. Labeling is one example of a state-dependent process in criminology theory. Nagin and Paternoster (1991) were the first to apply this concept from economics to criminology. The key to generating good estimates of state dependence is controlling for individual heterogeneity. Bushway, Brame, and Paternoster (1999) and Brame, Bushway, and Paternoster (1999) apply a variety of techniques from economics to study the question in criminology. Perhaps more important, state dependence is now used as a concept in criminology to describe different types of dynamic change (e.g., Laub and Sampson 2003). The initial work on state dependence led directly to work by Nagin and Land (1993), which became the semiparametric trajectory method for studying offending over the life course. This is an example in which a technique initially borrowed from economics has been further developed by noneconomists for application to a particular criminological problem (see Nagin [2005] for more details).

Another distinct empirical contribution of economics to the study of crime involves the use of explicitly causal models such as instrumental variables.[14] Instrumental variables are linked to the dependent variable exclusively through their relationship with the independent variable of interest. Or to put it another way, instrumental variables create exogenous variation in the independent variable, which can then be studied to look at the causal link between the independent and the dependent variable. Experimental random assignment is the classic instrumental variable. Random assignment creates exogenous (meaning outside the system) variation in the independent variable *X*. This variation is uncorrelated with any omitted variable and is not influenced by any simultaneous (endogenous) relationship between the independent and dependent variables. As a result of this induced variation, we should be able to generate a better estimate of the true effect of *X* on *Y*.

Most of Steve Levitt's original contributions to the study of crime have been based on the identification of interesting instrumental variables that could potentially solve the endogeneity problem identified by Nagin (1978) and Cook (1980) in their initial reviews of the deterrence literature. For example, Levitt used legally mandated reductions in prison capacity to estimate the effect of incarceration on crime (Lev-

[14] A full treatment of instrumental variables is beyond the scope of this article, and an interested reader should read assessable treatments of the topic by Angrist and Krueger (2001) and Angrist (2006). Economists are also responsible for importing other causal techniques for the study of crime such as Granger causality testing (Marvell and Moody 1994, 1996).

itt 1998). His claim was that the court decisions that reduced incarceration were not caused by crime, but were caused by larger societal forces that had nothing to do with the crime generation process. As a result, this variation is essentially random, and he can use this random variation in incarceration to study the effect of incarceration on crime at the state level.[15] Other interesting (and high-profile) papers on crime-related topics that make use of the instrumental variable technique include a paper by Jacob and Lefgren (2003), which uses teacher conference days to estimate the effects of mandatory school attendance on the crime distribution in the larger community; a paper by Kling (2006), which uses random assignment of cases to judges as instrumental variables to study the effects of sentence length on employment outcomes; a paper by McCrary (2007), which uses court-ordered hiring of police officers to study the effects of affirmative action on police hiring (and crime); and a paper by Evans and Owens (2007), which uses federal spending on Community-Oriented Policing Services as an instrument to generate additional estimates of the effects of policing on crime. In these papers, the instrumental variable methods lead to estimates that are fundamentally different from those found with traditional OLS analysis.

While this technique has been used almost exclusively by economists, there is no reason criminologists cannot use the instrumental variable technique. It is a straightforward method that is based largely on substantive expertise to identify mechanisms of exogenous change. Given this focus on substantive expertise, criminologists who can "think like economists" econometrically should have a decided advantage over the economist who knows the technique but does not know the criminal justice system or the literature in criminology. Opportunities for collaboration also clearly exist to generate new estimates in a variety of important criminological domains.

[15] This is not the same thing as saying that the court decisions are uncorrelated with crime. We have encountered noneconomists who assert that the instrumental variable, in this case the court decision, must be uncorrelated with crime. An instrument that is uncorrelated with the dependent variable is a useless instrumental variable, and Levitt shows clearly that court decisions are in fact correlated with crime rates. The key assumption of instrumental variables is that the the instrumental variable is correlated with the dependent variable only through the independent variable (in this case, incarceration rates). In arguing for the validity of his instrument, Levitt needed to argue that the only reason that court decisions are correlated with crime is that the court decision affects incarceration rates, which then affect crime.

B. Cost-Benefit Analysis

Cost-benefit analysis is a natural extension of the economist's normative framework, focused on maximizing society's welfare. In practice, it is a method that can help policy makers rationally choose between policies since it is an application of the rational choice model to the macro level of a policy maker choosing between different crime control strategies. Cost-benefit analysis starts with an assessment of whether any given program or treatment works to prevent crime and then estimates the relative costs and benefits of such a policy.

There is a large and growing demand for such analyses, part of the general movement toward greater accountability in public-sector decision making in the Western world. In the United Kingdom the Home Office has published a number of specific programmatic cost-benefit evaluations (e.g., Bowles and Pradiptyo 2004). In the United States, state government has been the principal source of such analyses. In particular the Washington State legislature established the Washington State Institute for Public Policy to evaluate policy options, and it has produced a stream of cost-benefit analyses of criminal justice interventions (e.g., Aos et al. 2001; Aos, Miller, and Drake 2006). These studies are done primarily by economists (in the United Kingdom) and by business analysts (in Washington State); criminologists are marginal to both enterprises.

In its initial formulations, cost-benefit analysis in criminal justice was limited to an assessment of crime prevention and further limited to a discussion of the costs borne by the victim and the costs saved by the criminal justice system. Various attempts have been made to arrive at valid estimates of the former category, including the creative use of contingent valuation surveys[16] and jury awards for pain and suffering; for a comprehensive review, see Cohen (2005). Mark Cohen has often been the lone economist pushing cost-benefit analysis forward as a technique for criminal justice, and his estimates of the cost of crime have been used often by both economists and criminologists seeking to evaluate the costs and benefits of various policies (e.g., Greenwood et al. 1994; Levitt 1996). It is now almost standard practice for economists estimating the effect of any given policy to conduct at least a

[16] A contingent valuation survey asks respondents to estimate how much they are willing to pay for a specific benefit, such as breathing clean air, or to avoid a specific harm, such as being mugged. These surveys are widely used in environmental policy evaluations (Arrow et al. 1993).

rudimentary cost-benefit analysis, but even sophisticated economists tend to tack this on in a rather mechanical fashion (see Levitt 1996).

Criminologists have published a number of cost-benefit analyses. Welsh, Farrington, and Sherman (2000) summarize the state of the art at the beginning of this decade. These analyses use accounting rather than economic costs. In particular, they do not consider opportunity costs where resources are not well valued by the market. Nor do they follow one of the basic rules of cost-benefit analysis, which is that alternatives have to be considered simultaneously, using a consistent set of criteria (Stokey and Zeckhauser 1978).

Donohue and Siegelman (1998), both economists, show the broader reach of cost-benefit analysis by comparing the costs and benefits of social policies versus prison. This analysis moves one step beyond criminological efforts to summarize the crime prevention power of any given policies by not only identifying policies with positive effect sizes (Sherman et al. 1997), but then evaluating the relative costs and benefits of a number of policies. Given the notorious difficulty of estimating costs and benefits, the relative comparison of programs is perhaps a more defensible approach than a one-at-a-time evaluation of the marginal benefits and costs of any given policy.

In recent years, the economic approach to cost-benefit analysis of criminal justice interventions has been extended to consider a broader set of costs and benefits. Instead of focusing only on the victim and offender, this new approach considers the actions and reactions of a broad set of individuals who might be affected by any given policy. For example, Cavanagh and Kleiman (1990) consider both the costs of operating a prison and the costs of welfare payments made to an offender's family while the offender is in prison. More broadly, Cook and Ludwig (2000) reconsider the costs of gun violence to include not just the cost to the victims, but also the costs incurred by the rest of society as they respond, a priori, to the threat of increased violence. For example, not only do victims of crime appear to respond by moving out of neighborhoods (Dugan 1999), it also appears that nonvictimized individuals move from cities in response to increased violence (Cullen and Levitt 1999), housing prices decline (Tita, Petras, and Greenbaum 2006), and business activity declines after violence surges (Greenbaum and Tita 2004).

These types of macro-level effects suggest that costs associated with suburban sprawl are at least partly attributable to crime. The recent focus on the costs of incarceration on families and communities, often the product of interdisciplinary collaboration between economists, sociologists, and criminologists, is also part of this larger awareness about the societal effects of crime and crime control efforts (e.g., Patillo, Weiman, and Western 2004).

This interest in the broader social costs of crime has led economists to search for surrogate markets that might provide measures of the willingness to pay for less crime. In a pioneering paper, Thaler (1978) took advantage of differences in crime rates across areas within a city to estimate the capitalized value of a reduction in crime rates through an analysis of housing prices. If reducing the expected number of property crimes experienced by the average household in the neighborhood by one crime raises the value of each house by, say, $10,000, then it is possible to infer that at the margin, a property crime is worth $500 (using a 5 percent rate of return). A more recent study by two economists (Linden and Rockoff 2006) showed that the requirement that a convicted sex offender's address be provided to the public had large effects on housing prices; the authors use this to estimate willingness to pay to avoid crime.

A subtler demonstration of this broader consideration of the unintended consequences of policies involves Ayres and Levitt's (1998) analysis of LoJack, an electronic device developed by a private company designed not to deter crime, but to recover a car after a theft has occurred. The device is activated after a theft (it silently transmits a signal to a police station), and police can track the automobile using equipment provided by the company. But Ayres and Levitt noticed that, besides increasing the probability of recovering a stolen car, LoJack has the potential to create a general deterrent effect given that people are not allowed, by contract with the company, to identify their car as having LoJack. Car thieves become uncertain about which car has this new technology and may decide to avoid stealing any car that has the potential of having LoJack.

A conservative estimate was that each additional 1 percentage point of LoJack market share leads to a 7 percent decline in auto theft, which makes LoJack one of the most effective crime prevention programs ever studied. The tragedy of the commons, an economic concept that deals with private underinvestment in public goods, is then applied to the cost-benefit analysis to demonstrate that investment in LoJack appears to be suboptimal. The person who installs LoJack captures only

10 percent of the social benefit it generates. This economically derived analysis then predicts that insurance companies, the main beneficiary of recovery and theft prevention, will subsidize LoJack adoption. Indeed, in some parts of South America, insurance companies install LoJack for free. Ayres and Levitt (1998) conclude that this subsidy is still less than the socially optimal level, but neither the car owner nor the insurance company will recover these benefits. Perhaps one role for government would be to encourage higher LoJack adoptions. Indeed, seven states have passed statutes requiring a subsidy for its installation.

The differentiation between public and private costs and benefits is also a major feature of cost-benefit analysis of crime prevention strategies. The economic model clearly suggests that employment and school-related activities that are not directly related to crime may affect crime. For example, Lochner and Moretti (2004) suggest that about 10–15 percent of the social benefit from increased schooling comes from crime reduction. The possibility that other social policies have crime prevention benefits is a provocative counterpoint to the insight that prison may have negative effects on individuals and communities, and not just the individual offender.

IV. Markets

The final type of contribution of economics and economists to criminology, according to Coase's three-part scheme, comes from cases in which the study of crime intersects with the economic area of expertise. Markets are at the heart of economics. After a brief discussion of labor markets and crime, we turn to an examination of a major criminal phenomenon, markets for illicit drugs. Economists have shown that the basic concepts of demand and supply and some elements of industrial organization theory can illuminate the effects of enforcement on outcomes of interest, such as the price and availability of drugs. Other economic tools have also proved useful; for example, the notion of a "tournament" may help explain the peculiar feature of contemporary drug markets in which so many participants earn low returns. Given the centrality of drug markets to crime in the United States and the extent to which criminologists have researched the consequences of drug use itself, it is striking that they have contributed so little to the study of the markets themselves.

A. Work and Crime

The most obvious example of the intersection of markets and crime involves the study of the relationship between work and crime and the criminal justice system. The two main topics are the trade-off between illegal work (crime) and legal work, and the effects of criminal history records on employment. Economists have a natural contribution to make in studies of this kind given their substantive expertise, and research in both areas contains a nice mix of research by both economists and noneconomists.[17] The contributions of both groups to the study of crime and the labor market are detailed in an exhaustive article by Jeff Fagan and Richard Freeman (1999). The coauthors are, fittingly enough, a criminologist and an economist. Perhaps not surprisingly, this is the one area in crime research in which economists and non-economists seem the most aware of the other's work, with increasingly frequent cross-citations. Indeed, recent research by criminologists, sociologists, and economists often uses many of the same techniques and data sets.[18]

B. Drug Markets

A lesser-studied area that has been dominated by economists is the study of illegal markets. In what follows we provide a review of the largest illegal market, that for drugs, which is particularly relevant for the study of crime.

The markets for illegal drugs constitute an important criminal phenomenon, particularly in the United States. Collectively they were estimated to generate $60 billion in retail sales in 2000 (and twice that in 1990) (ONDCP 2001). They matter both because they generate large criminal earnings and harms as a consequence of their operation

[17] For example, consider two articles on the macro-level relationship between the business cycle and crime on the U.S. time series that we already have referred to in the introduction. One is a high-profile article by sociologists Cantor and Land (1985) and the other a lesser-known article by economists Cook and Zarkin (1985). The main difference between the two articles lies in how they measure the concept of an economic business cycle. Paternoster and Bushway (2001) assert that Cook and Zarkin's approach is more faithful to the long-run description of change implied by the concept of a business cycle and argue that the large body of work inspired by Cantor and Land's article could have been profitably augmented by familiarity with the work of Cook and Zarkin.

[18] See, e.g., a recent edited book on the labor market effects of incarceration by Bushway, Stoll, and Weiman (2007). It has an interdisciplinary mix of authors, but the techniques and data sets are very similar across disciplines. See also Western (2002), a paper by a sociologist using the 1979 National Longitudinal Study of Youth, a classic "economics" database, to answer a question about employment and the criminal justice system.

(e.g., diverting youths from education, creating disorder and crime around marketplaces) and also because they provide dangerous substances whose use generates violent crime, at least when the drug is a stimulant. According to surveys of arrestees, about half of all arrestees have recently used narcotics (National Institute of Justice 2003). In other historical periods, illegal gambling and bootlegging of prohibited alcohol have been large and troubling markets in the United States.

Governments make a large investment of money and authority in suppressing drug markets. Drug control is probably a $40 billion annual effort in the United States (Walsh 2004). On any given day in 2005, approximately 500,000 persons were incarcerated in jails and prisons in the United States because of violations of drug prohibitions, mostly drug selling (Caulkins and Chandler 2006). Beyond being important in its own right, this effort competes with more traditional crime-fighting efforts for criminal justice resources (Rasmussen and Benson 1994; Kuziemko and Levitt 2004).

The price and conditions under which drugs are sold have important criminal consequences. If heroin were to cost $1 a dose rather than $25, the consequences for society would be very different because there would be many more users and much less crime (MacCoun and Reuter 2001). Not only would the lower prices reduce the needs of dependent users to commit crimes to fund their purchases, but they would also reduce the incentives of sellers to compete violently or to resolve conflicts about transactions through violence. The illegal price appears to be many times higher than the price would be in legal markets (Moore 1990). This is not simply a function of illegality; for example, illegal bookmakers charge roughly the same for their services that their legal counterparts do (Strumpf 2003). What explains the high prices of cocaine and heroin?

Similarly, it is important to understand the distribution of earnings in the drug trades. Drug markets would generate much smaller problems if the unskilled manager of a heroin distribution gang earned what the manager of a McDonald's earns. Instead, many senior drug dealers earn as much as a successful lawyer, without the necessity of law school; some, mostly in producer and transshipment countries, earn large fortunes. What might explain the very uneven distribution of earnings in the trade?

Finally, it is important to understand how drug markets respond to various kinds of interventions. For example, how will an increased risk of incarceration or more restrictive access to specific inputs (e.g., precursor chemicals for drugs such as methamphetamines) affect prices, the size of the market, and the distribution of returns across groups of participants?

Criminologists have done little research on drug markets, though a great deal has been done on related phenomena such as the role of drug use in crime at individual and population levels (MacCoun, Kilmer, and Reuter 2003). There is a large ethnographic literature on drug markets (e.g., Bourgois 1996; Jacobs 1999; Hoffer 2006), but minimal theorizing has been offered about the determinants of prices or of the distribution of profits among the different participants. The ethnographic literature emphasizes the relationship between involvement in the illegal market (particularly selling drugs or prostitution) and other criminal activities. The more conceptually oriented studies (e.g., Haller 1990; Morselli 2005) focus on the nature of the enterprises that populate the markets and how they relate to organized crime. The criminological literature assessing the effects of enforcement, such as the "war on drugs" (e.g., Blumstein 1993; Tonry 1995), makes references to prices but offers no specific criminological theory on how enforcement affects the working of the market.

Yet market analysis is essential to understanding the effects of the tough enforcement that has characterized U.S. drug policy for so long. In considering the effects of longer sentences on other crimes, there is no mediating factor to complicate analysis of the effect of making the activity riskier. However, the effect of increased incarceration of drug sellers and users is mediated through prices. If a small rise in prices induces many new individuals to enter the market as sellers, then toughness may have little effect.

Thus the territory is ceded to economists and their fellow travelers.[19] Markets are at the very heart of economics, both as a topic and as a method; no social science diagram is better known than the classic demand and supply intersection, showing the determinants of price and quantity in a market. Intellectually, drug markets are of interest to economists because they operate not merely without the protections provided by the government but in the face of (more or less) active

[19] Two frequently cited scholars in this section are Jonathan Caulkins and Mark Kleiman. Neither has an economics degree: Caulkins' PhD is in operations research and Kleiman's is in public policy. Both make extensive use of economic reasoning and market models.

hostility from the government. The government aims to promote competition and to smooth market operation in legal markets, even while regulating against negative external consequences (e.g., through rules on emissions controls) and perhaps influencing the distribution of revenues within enterprises (e.g., through minimum wage laws). In contrast, the state aims to eliminate, or at least reduce the extent of, illegal markets. This can lead to perverse incentives for governments. For example, in legal markets there is a well-established doctrine that monopoly control or any suppression of competition hurts society, so that the Antitrust Division of the Department of Justice and the Federal Trade Commission are empowered to detect and sanction any such anticompetitive efforts. However, the state may actually find itself allied with cartel organizers in illegal markets, if that will result in higher prices and thus reduce the production of "bads" (Buchanan 1973; Schelling 1984). Illegal markets may enable economists to learn more about the influence of purely abstract forces of competition by contrasting legal and illegal markets for similar goods.

1. *Demand and Supply.* Application of the standard competitive model to markets for illegal drugs is now regularly featured in introductory economics texts (e.g., Frank and Bernanke 2004). The most basic concepts for economists are those of demand and supply. A demand curve maps the relationship between price and the quantity consumers are willing to purchase. The supply curve maps the relationship between price and the quantity that producers (distributors) are willing to produce (provide). The market clears at the price at which the quantity demanded by consumers equals the quantity that distributors are willing to supply. Any intervention will be thought of in terms of how it affects the supply curve or the demand curve and the resulting equilibrium price and quantity.

Consider, for instance, the effect of a policy that restricts supply by incarcerating a higher fraction of drug dealers. The standard analysis is that, because drug sellers will now engage in the activity only in return for more money, the supply curve will shift up and to the left (i.e., at any given price less is supplied), increasing the market price and reducing the quantity of drugs sold in the market (see fig. 1, first graph). In the textbook analysis, the magnitude of the reduction in equilibrium quantity is shown to depend on the elasticity of demand, as is the effect on dealers' revenues. The second graph of figure 1 shows the same change but with a much less elastic demand curve.

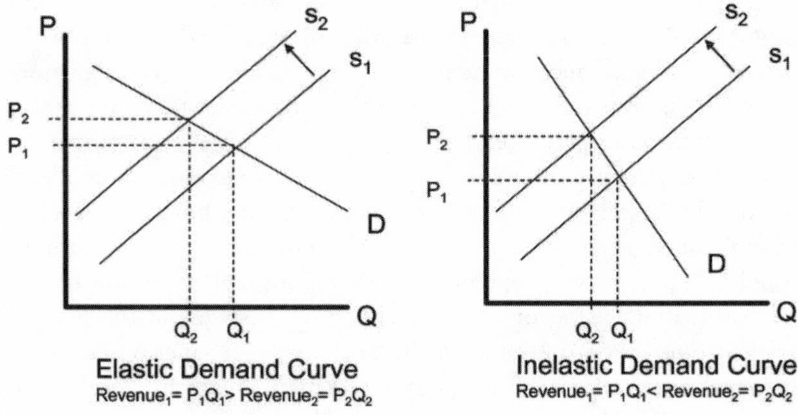

FIG. 1.—Illegal drug markets

Economists have done extensive work on estimating the price elasticity of demand for various drugs, particularly cocaine and marijuana, including the cross-elasticity between illegal drugs and cigarettes or alcohol (e.g., Cameron and Williams 2001).[20] The topic is of interest because it bears on the importance of shifting the supply curve through enforcement or legal changes and thus determining the change in prevalence and intensity of drug use. If the demand is completely inelastic (i.e., the quantity sought by customers is fixed and unaffected by price), then shifting the supply curve will simply raise the price of the drug and total expenditures. If it is very elastic (i.e., even a small increase in price will have large effects on consumption), then enforcement that raises prices a small amount may have large effects on the total consumed.

Estimating the price elasticity of the demand for drugs has been facilitated by the availability of prevalence data from population surveys (such as Monitoring the Future and the National Survey on Drug Use

[20] The price elasticity of demand is the percentage reduction in demand caused by a 1 percent increase in price; except under exceptional conditions, it is negative. There is a similar price elasticity of supply, usually positive. The cross-elasticity of marijuana and alcohol is the percentage change in the demand for marijuana caused by a 1 percent increase in the price of alcohol; the cross-elasticity will be positive if the marijuana and alcohol are substitutes and negative if they are complements. Demand is labeled "inelastic" if the absolute value of the elasticity is smaller than one, since it means that a rise in price will lead to a rise in total revenues.

and Health) and price data from the DEA (STRIDE[21]), permitting the use of sophisticated econometric techniques. Becker's work on rational addiction theory has been a major influence here (Becker and Murphy 1988).

Manski, Pepper, and Petrie (2001), in a major National Research Council report on drug policy research, report an uncomfortably wide range of estimates of price elasticities. For example, estimates for the price elasticity of the demand for cocaine vary between −0.6 and −2.5. To suggest how much this affects policy analysis, consider the effect of a policy that raises the price of cocaine by 25 percent; if the elasticity is −0.6, then consumption will fall by 15 percent, whereas it will fall by over 60 percent if the elasticity is −2.5.

Manski, Pepper, and Petrie (2001) note that among the many factors leading to differences across estimates, one major problem is that price is so heterogeneous. The models assume that there is a price index that captures variation faced by consumers over time or space. The price of milk might differ across communities within a metropolitan area (assuming that is the unit of geographic analysis), but it is meaningful to report the average price for each metropolitan area in a national sample and use that to estimate how much consumption varies as a function of price. For illegal drugs, it is known that there is substantial variation within and across metropolitan areas (ONDCP 2004), but there are no data on the share of transactions that take place at each price. The simple arithmetic average that is used for construction of prices is merely an uninformed guess as to how the large variation in prices should be averaged. The estimates thus have a very noisy independent variable.[22]

The standard economic model also predicts, slightly less intuitively, that the arrest of users (e.g., through "sell and bust" operations) will shift the demand curve downward (less is demanded at any given price). The reason is that the risk of arrest and accompanying sanctions is part of the cost of drugs. These interventions will reduce the market price

[21] STRIDE is the System to Retrieve Information from Drug Evidence. It consists of price and purity data from all undercover purchases processed in DEA labs and purity for all seizures processed in those labs. Data and publications from Monitoring the Future can be found at http://www.monitoringthe future.org/. The site for the National Survey on Drug Use and Health is http://www.oas.samsha.gov/nhsda.htm.

[22] More sophisticated price series have been developed that take account of purity variations unknown to the buyer: the "expected purity" model first developed by Caulkins (1994). However, the adjusted observations are still simply averaged to form the index for the specific city/year.

but also the total quantity sold. This will therefore decrease total revenue to the drug sellers and make it less attractive to sellers. In contrast, shifting the supply curve upward will increase the price and, in case of a price elasticity less than one in absolute value, increase the total amount of revenue for the sellers.

Over 30 years ago Mark Moore (1973) suggested that a useful way of augmenting the conventional economists' framework was to think of the "effective price" of a drug as being the sum of the money price and the other costs that the buyer incurs, including the inconvenience of finding a seller when the state prevents open advertising and the risks incurred of being sanctioned by the criminal justice system. This insight has considerable potential. For example, Moore's model suggests that enforcement against buyers may reduce demand among highly educated groups more than among the less educated because the stigma and potential earnings losses associated with arrest may be higher. Eatherly (1974) provided an early analysis; three studies have incorporated crude measures of user legal risk into demand equations. Only Caulkins has provided a recent quantitative analysis of the effects of search time, suggesting that current levels constitute a fairly minor component of total purchase cost.

Economists have done almost no research on the supply side.[23] There are, for example, no estimates of the price elasticity of the supply of cocaine. Instead, economists assume that the supply curve is flat, that is, that consumers can purchase any quantity they wish at the prevailing price established by the level of enforcement. For example, Becker, Murphy, and Grossman (2006) explicitly assume that the mar-

[23] Miron (1999, 2003) is one of the few exceptions. He has attacked the claim that illegality raises price much above the level that would prevail in a legal market. He argues that the ratio of retail price of cocaine to the farm gate price is not much higher than for other semiprocessed goods such as coffee. Thus the price of cocaine would not fall much if it were legally available. Miron's analysis is problematic. For example, he assumes that illegality does not elevate the raw materials price or the importation costs. Opium farmers in Colombia and Mexico face risks from the government in the form of eradication. They are, in fact, much higher-cost producers than farmers in either Afghanistan or Burma for precisely that reason, since governments in those countries do not pose significant threats to their opium growers. Yet the United States imports its heroin from these high-cost countries because, as a result of dense traffic and commerce generally, Colombia and Mexico are relatively safe from interdiction and thus serve as low-cost transportation sources for the United States. That is to say, the markup between export and import prices from the Latin American sources is only about 1,500 percent, as compared to 2,500 percent from Asia. This compares with import-export price differentials typically of approximately 12 percent in the market for legal goods (Reuter and Greenfield 2001).

ket for drugs is competitive and subject to constant returns to scale, so that any amount of drugs can be supplied at the minimum production cost, which is determined inter alia by the monetary equivalent of criminal justice penalties and seizures of drugs and assets.

2. *Price Determination.* The analysis above deals with the effect of marginal changes but not the most basic determinants of equilibrium. Why are cocaine and even marijuana so expensive? These are plant products subject to very modest processing, yet cocaine costs 10 times more than gold. Reuter and Kleiman (1986) offered an account of the interaction between enforcement and price in drug markets that attempts to explain this. Material, transportation, and packaging and promotion costs are negligible for illicit drugs such as cocaine and heroin; the costs of producing and refining the drug constitute less than 1 percent of the final retail price. Other nonlabor costs are similarly modest. For example, Caulkins et al. (1999) report that interviews with retail drug dealers show that they spent little money on packaging and so forth. The dominant cost of supply is labor, and the price of labor is principally determined by risks faced by participants in the trade. Risks came from two sources. The government threatens to arrest and incarcerate dealers and to seize their assets and drugs. Other participants in the trade pose threats of stealing drugs and inflicting injury. To persuade individuals to incur these risks requires compensation, just as risks in other lines of dangerous work (e.g., coal mining) also require compensation in the form of higher wages (Viscusi 1992). In this model it is the combination of illegality and tough enforcement that makes the drugs expensive. That drug-dealing organizations do not have to pay taxes, meet regulatory requirements with respect to workplace safety, and so forth turns out to have a much smaller cost-reducing impact.

This model of price formation has been used in numerous simulation studies (e.g., Reuter, Crawford, and Cave 1988; Rydell and Everingham 1994) but has not been tested in empirical studies. Reuter, MacCoun, and Murphy (1990) found that retail drug prices in Washington, DC, in 1988 could be accounted for by risk compensation and labor time, but the available measures are so crude that this constitutes a weak test.[24]

[24] For example, Reuter, MacCoun, and Murphy (1990) assumed that a value of a lost life for the affected population was $500,000. This number is an important component of the cost calculation since the estimated annual probability of being killed in the trade

Drug markets have some distinctive features that distinguish them from legal markets and other illegal markets that are important for policy purposes. For example, a substantial fraction of sellers are heavy consumers[25] and account for a large share of total consumption. Coffee retailers may like coffee a great deal more than the average purchaser, but they do not consume a noticeable fraction of the total coffee sold. However, those who sell heroin may be responsible for a third of total heroin consumed, since many sellers are opportunistic participants in that activity. Separating demand and supply effects becomes more complicated as a consequence. Treatment, a demand-side intervention, may have large supply-side effects because many of those in treatment are also sellers. Similarly, incarcerating drug sellers, the classic supply-side intervention, has the effect of locking up a substantial share of demand.[26]

3. *Earnings and Profits.* Apart from Reuter, MacCoun, and Murphy (1990), there is only one empirical study that has taken an economic approach to earnings in drug markets. Levitt and Venkatesh (2000) analyzed data from the accounts of a drug-selling gang[27] to show that most of those selling crack in this mid-1990s Chicago gang were earning roughly the legal minimum wage.[28] Only the leaders made large incomes. The conceptual innovation of the study was to introduce the notion of drug dealing as a "tournament" (e.g., Lazear and Rosen 1981). Most participants in such an activity might have low earnings, but each believes that he has an opportunity to win the "prize," namely, the large incomes associated with one of the top positions in a hierarchy. The commitment of so many college students to the rigors of playing competitive football, given the low probability of a well-paid professional career, may be partly explained that way. Levitt and Ven-

at that time in Washington was about one in 70. Though $500,000 is a plausible number, given the observable characteristics of arrested drug dealers and other studies of the value of a statistical life (e.g., Viscusi and Aldy 2003), it is highly speculative.

[25] The reason is that selling is a part-time and opportunistic activity.

[26] This has been modeled in Caulkins et al. (1997).

[27] Venkatesh, a sociologist with an ethnographic bent, has provided these accounts from subjects of his long-term study of life in Chicago housing projects.

[28] Some aspects of the Levitt and Venkatesh data set are anomalous when compared with other data on drug selling. For example, they estimate a 4-year cumulative death risk for gang members of over 25 percent, far higher than found by Reuter, MacCoun, and Murphy (1990); nor are their data consistent with other measures of drug-related mortality and the scale of cocaine markets. Similarly, the total sales volumes per participant are far lower than reported in a variety of other studies. We use the study for its analytic insights rather than its specific quantitative findings.

katesh hypothesize that it is the high earnings of a few leaders that induce many young males to continue to sell drugs even when their current returns are low.

Levitt and Venkatesh also assessed the strategies of the gang and its rivals in economic terms. For example, the value of expanding the geographic domain of the gang is increased by the limited mobility of its many customers without cars. They suggest that some sales during gang warfare periods were below the marginal cost of such sales but represented strategic decisions to build market share during a period of expansion in the demand for an addictive drug. They also suggested that the levels of violence may have been higher than optimal for the gang as a drug-selling organization because members had incentives to use violence to establish personal reputations for toughness and thus move up in the organization.

Economic analysis can also help with important claims about "monopoly control" in illegal markets. For example, it used to be asserted that the Medellin cartel had monopoly control in the U.S. cocaine market. However, that claim could be challenged by simple analysis of the price of cocaine at different stages of the distribution system and consideration of the elasticity of demand. Monopoly power is defined by the ability to limit production, whether through a cartel arrangement, use of force, or other means. A monopolist will never choose to set prices so as to face inelastic demand, that is, where an increase of 1 percent in price will reduce consumption by less than 1 percent. In that circumstance, the monopolist can always increase his profit by reducing output and thus raising prices; that will raise total revenues and lower total costs (since he produces less). Since the demand for cocaine was believed by all observers to be inelastic, monopoly was unlikely to characterize the market.[29]

Relevant here is a small literature by economists on organized crime. Schelling (1984) conceptualized the Mafia's role in illegal markets as that of a collector for centralized corrupt police agencies. Schelling offered the example of the Miami bookmaking market, at a time when neither state nor federal agencies were actively involved in gambling enforcement. The Miami Police Department (offered merely as an example, but one that had then been in the news for its corruption)

[29] More sophisticated models of price formation by monopoly suppliers under special circumstances can generate more complex findings. However, the special circumstances required for those models do not seem to apply to the wholesale cocaine market.

maximized its own potential returns by maximizing the profits of the industry, which it could, in effect, tax. The Mafia was then the cartel organizer; it extorted money from operators on behalf of the police, while retaining money for itself for providing that service. Behind the Mafia's threat of force was the implicit power of the police to act against those who were not willing to collaborate with the collector.

Both Buchanan (1973) and Schelling (1984) suggested that the government has incentives to encourage monopolies in illegal markets so as to reduce the production of undesired goods. However, that is a very incomplete analysis of the consequences of criminal monopoly. Such monopoly provides the resources for criminals to challenge the power of the state, as revealed in the systemic and high-level urban corruption long associated with the Mafia throughout much of the twentieth century. Similarly, if monopoly power increases the earnings of the most highly paid offenders, it may increase the incentive to enter these activities, as in the Levitt and Venkatesh (2000) model. Nonetheless, this market approach provides insights into the effects of policies such as the creation of overlapping police jurisdictions. If local police agencies no longer have the ability to protect illegal operators fully, as a result of extending the jurisdiction of state and federal agencies, the local police cannot safely license privileged offender groups, since one way in which a drug dealer can get a reduction in the severe federal prison sentences is to provide information about corrupt police officers. This may be an important factor in explaining the relative lack of systemic corruption in contemporary U.S. drug markets.

4. *The Path Forward.* It is hard to imagine the study of drug markets, and illegal markets generally, without the inclusion of economists and economic insights. However, it is also true that, as discussed above, there are unusual features to illegal markets that present major challenges to conventional market models: these include extreme price dispersion, the use of physical coercion, selection into the occupation by risk taking of a particular kind, and ties to other kinds of crime, for which criminologists bring specific expertise. A recent collaboration among two economists, an ethnographer, and a criminologist (Cook et al. 2005), examining the market for illicit guns in Chicago, is indicative of the path forward. Cook and his colleagues show that the very thin nature of the market (in which transactions occur at a rate two or three orders of magnitude less frequently than in drug markets) makes it very inefficient. Information is scarce and transaction costs are high.

The result is that guns are expensive and time-consuming to acquire for many prohibited purchasers such as gang members. The concepts of market analysis have been combined well with the understanding of criminality of a criminologist and the data collection skills of an ethnographer.

V. Conclusion

We have attempted to provide an overview of contributions by economists to the study of crime, using a conceptual framework from economist Ronald Coase's discourse on the nature of invasions by economics into contiguous social sciences. We have not attempted to provide a comprehensive survey of all the crime-related topics that economists have tackled. Long termed the "dismal science," economics has become quite playful. Economics journals are full of articles (many by Steve Levitt and a growing cast of collaborators) that are justified by their clever ways of finding insights into human behavior rather than advancing understanding of economic phenomena. For example, Duggan and Levitt (2002) analyzed cheating by sumo wrestlers, showing that one could use data on patterns of past results to predict when one participant was likely to have incentives to throw the contest to his rival. Donohue and Levitt (1998) developed an interesting theoretical model of the circumstances under which the availability of guns would decrease the use of criminal violence, focusing on the increased uncertainty about the outcome of conflict that they induce. Edward Glaeser, an urban economist, has produced an array of interesting models to explain, for example, the concentration of crime within cities (Glaeser, Sacerdote, and Scheinkman 1996; Glaeser and Sacerdote 1999). The study of corruption has produced a large and rich literature, particularly in the context of its effects on economic development (Rose-Ackerman 1999). Crime of all sorts is an attractive topic for such insightful exercises, and economics journals now bristle with articles potentially of some interest to at least some criminologists.

This rapid growth of articles has been motivated in part by a redefinition of economics as the study of human choice under scarcity, a definition that opens a wide array of social phenomena to study by economists. Coase was more pessimistic about the staying power of these invasions than most economists at the time his article was written. He based his skepticism on a tripartite view of the contributions that economics brings to the study of new subjects: approach/theory, techniques, and substantive expertise. He predicted that true subfields, such as the economics of crime or law and economics, would sustain themselves only to the extent to which they intersected in meaningful ways with the study of the economic system, the main area of economic expertise.

Nearly 30 years after Coase wrote, he appears remarkably prophetic. Consider the field of law and economics, which focuses mostly on civil and regulatory law. These laws regulate the economic system, and the laws are mediated through financial means (fines and lawsuits) as in markets. Because of this obvious intersection with the economic system, the field of law and economics has grown into a mature discipline. It has its own journals and professional association, and there are numerous faculty positions for economists in major law schools; for example, there are eight PhD-trained economists on the faculty of Boalt Hall Law School at Berkeley. There is even a newly created PhD program in law and economics at Vanderbilt University.

In contrast, the field of economics and crime is barely recognizable as a subfield.[30] There is no annual conference on economics and crime for economists, and most economists who study crime as their main pursuit do so in public policy schools, usually as the sole scholar interested in the topic. Many economists who have studied crime tend to exploit a particular technique such as instrumental variables models or illustrate a particular insight from public finance, and then move on to other more mainstream topics in economics. Those mainstream economists who have studied crime over a long period, such as Richard Freeman, Jeff Grogger, and Harry Holzer, have been involved with the study of the labor market and crime, a natural point of intersection between the substantive expertise of the two fields. Another group, led by Gary Becker, Steven Levitt, and their students, focuses on deterrence as an outgrowth of price theory, but there are still few examples of economists in mainstream economics departments with a primary interest in the study of deterrence. The growing interest in reentry and the effects of mass incarceration on other domains of life, such as education and employment, forms a potential new point of overlap that

[30] Only in 2007 did the National Bureau of Economic Research (NBER), a central institution in the development of economics for the last quarter century, hold its first 1-day Work Group on the Economics of Crime. Official recognition by the NBER is important for the viability of a subfield, particularly for young economists.

could sustain a field of crime and economics. And there are institutional movements, perhaps spurred on by the prominence of the work of Steven Levitt, that could lead to the final emergence of crime and economics as a subfield.

The existence or absence of a subfield of crime and economics is perhaps of only marginal importance for criminologists. To the extent to which the question is interesting, we can apply Coase's argument in the opposite direction equally well. Suppose that one examines economics of crime as an independent subfield of economics. According to Coase, criminology can contribute to this field to the extent to which the techniques, approaches, and subject matter expertise are relevant to this new field. Techniques, such as measuring self-reported crime or approaches that focus on the life course and social context, can be adopted and adapted by economists willing to take the time to learn these techniques and approaches from criminologists. But criminology can and should make a large impact on this new field of economics of crime simply because its subject matter expertise falls squarely within the confines of this new field. The field of economics of crime will do little more than reinvent the wheel if it does not explicitly recognize and exploit the subject matter expertise of criminology and criminologists. Economists intent on establishing the study of economics of crime as a separate subfield of economics would do well to concentrate on understanding and explaining why their work improves and builds on what is known in criminology.

One potential model for this evolution would be that economists could develop a relationship to criminology very similar to that of sociologists who study crime. Such sociologists often work in sociology departments and maintain their professional identity as sociologists, with the American Sociological Association as their principal affiliation. Yet, while their work appears in sociology journals, they also publish regularly in mainstream criminology journals, and they regularly attend and are recognized at the American Society of Criminology meetings. Regardless of where they appear, the articles by sociologists are cited in the mainstream criminology literature. While there are some obvious language and professional barriers for economists, we see no reason why economists who study crime while working outside of criminology departments cannot become an integral part of the interdisciplinary field of criminology.

Of course, whether this outcome is desirable to criminologists depends in part on what almost 40 years of research by economists on crime has to offer criminology. We think that criminologists who work at the intersection of crime, the criminal justice system, and the economic system are already fairly aware of and make use of the work of economists. One very productive example of this type of work exists in the work of rational choice theorists in criminology, particularly those who have been studying perceptual deterrence. These scholars have done an excellent job of building on and developing economic insight in a particularly criminological way. We find the similarity of the recent articles by Matsueda, Kreager, and Huizinga (2006) and Lochner (2007) to be testimony to the ability of criminologists and sociologists to learn from and then build on the work of economists. Matsueda, Kreager, and Huizinga's article is unique in that they also looked at the impact of perceptions of punishment and perceptions of other potential rewards (and costs) of crime besides arrest and incarceration. Thus they take the rational choice model out of a narrow focus on deterrence and make an argument for rational choice as a viable theoretical framework for the study of crime more broadly. This type of extension can be done best by criminologists who are familiar with the larger theoretical landscape about the sources of crime.

A related area that might benefit from some more cross-fertilization between economists and criminologists involves the growing area of studies that look at the interaction between dynamic factors and self-control or impulsivity. Ousey and Wilcox (2007) review this literature (see also Hay and Forrest 2006) and suggest that there is some theoretical and empirical confusion in the development of the literature. They list a number of theoretical models that predict an interaction between dynamic variables such as employment and marriage and time-stable propensity to offend. They include the criminology version of a rational choice model, via Nagin and Paternoster (1994). But they suggest that individual preferences should moderate the effects of social bonds rather than interact with time-varying characteristics. The economic model, though, is very clear that the preference function will condition the impact of the time-varying covariates that affect the decision to commit crime. If a person heavily discounts the future, large increases in the severity of future punishment will have a minimal effect on the costs of crime and therefore will not affect the decision to commit crime. This point is made formally and empirically in a recent working paper by economists Lee and McCrary (2006) on the effect of punishment on adolescent offending. Lee and McCrary have not distinguished between impulsivity and time discounting, but both groups are arriving at the same basic conclusion, at about the same time. We predict that progress in this topic will be both faster and more productive if useful insights and techniques from economics are at least considered in the discussion.

Other areas in criminology that might profit from a great willingness to engage with the work of economists include the study of illegal markets, especially drug markets. Courses in criminology programs on drugs and crime or illegal markets that do not at least discuss the economic study of markets are hard to justify. And while we understand why Gary Becker's work is not standard reading in criminology, we have a harder time understanding the lack of familiarity of criminology students with the work of economists such as Philip Cook, who has written several accessible articles in criminology outlets integrating economic and criminological thought.

Perhaps the most promising area for interaction with economists involves application of formal economic theory to the study of the criminal justice system, attempted by Landes (1971) and more recently by Knowles, Persico, and Todd (2001) and Bjerk (forthcoming). Although criminal justice theory is much less developed than criminological theory, the actors in the criminal justice system seem to be better targets for the formal, but rather simple, models of economics. Predictions from the simple models can be compared with reality and then developed into richer models that can be used to predict and explain behavior.

Economics does not appear poised to take over criminology any time soon. But, economics is a large and rich field, and some of its approaches and techniques can profitably be used by criminologists to understand the study of crime better. We have identified some of the most appropriate techniques and approaches and have identified important areas of criminological work that might benefit from more formal engagement with economics and economists. We predict that 20 years from now, economics and economists will be much more important to the study of crime than they are today.

REFERENCES

Abrams, David, and Christopher Andrew Rolphs. 2007. "Optimal Bail and the Value of Freedom: Evidence from the Philadelphia Bail Experiment." Olin Working Paper no. 343, University of Chicago Law and Economics Workshop. http://ssrn.com/abstract=995323.

Angrist, Joshua. 2006. "Instrumental Variables Methods in Experimental Criminological Research: What, Why and How." *Journal of Experimental Criminology* 2(1):23–44.

Angrist, Joshua, and Alan Krueger. 2001. "Instrumental Variables and the Search for Identification: From Supply and Demand to Natural Experiments." *Journal of Economic Perspectives* 15(1):69–85.

Anwar, Shamena, and Hanming Fang. 2006. "An Alternative Test of Racial Profiling in Motor Vehicle Searches: Theory and Evidence." *American Economic Review* 96(1):127–51.

Aos, Steven, Marna Miller, and Elizabeth Drake. 2006. *Evidence-Based Public Policy Options to Reduce Future Prison Construction, Criminal Justice Costs, and Crime Rates.* Olympia: Washington State Institute for Public Policy.

Aos, Steve, Polly Phipps, Robert Barnoski, and Roxanne Lieb. 2001. *The Comparative Costs and Benefits of Programs to Reduce Crime Version 4.0.* Olympia: Washington State Institute for Public Policy.

Arrow, Kenneth, Robert Solow, Paul Portney, Edward Leamer, Roy Radner, and Howard Schuman. 1993. "Report of the NOAA Panel on Contingent Valuation." *Federal Register* 56:4601–14.

Ayres, Ian. 2001. *Pervasive Prejudice? Unconventional Evidence of Race and Gender Discrimination.* Chicago: University of Chicago Press.

Ayres, Ian, and Steven Levitt. 1998. "Measuring Positive Externalities from Unobservable Victim Precaution: An Empirical Analysis of Lojack." *Quarterly Journal of Economics* 113(1): 43–77.

Ayres, Ian, and Joel Waldfogel. 1994. "A Market Test for Race Discrimination in Bail Setting." *Stanford Law Review* 46(5): 987–1047.

Becker, Gary. 1957. *The Economics of Discrimination.* Chicago: University of Chicago Press.

———. 1968. "Crime and Punishment: An Economic Approach." *Journal of Political Economy* 76(2): 169–217.

———. 1993. "Nobel Lecture: The Economic Way of Looking at Behavior." *Journal of Political Economy* 101(3):385–409.

———. 2000. *A Treatise on the Family.* Expanded ed. Cambridge, MA: Harvard University Press.

Becker, Gary, and Kevin Murphy. 1988. "A Theory of Rational Addiction." *Journal of Political Economy* 96:675–700.

Becker, Gary, Kevin Murphy, and Michael Grossman. 2006. "The Market for Illegal Goods: The Case of Drugs." *Journal of Political Economy* 114(1):38–60.

Berk, Richard. 1983. "An Introduction to Sample Selection Bias in Sociological Data." *American Sociological Review* 48:386–98.

Bhati, Avinash. 2007. "Estimating the Number of Crimes Averted by Incapacitation: An Information Theoretic Approach." *Journal of Quantitative Criminology* 23(4):355–75.

Bjerk, David. 2005. "Making the Crime Fit the Penalty: The Role of Prosecutorial Discretion under Mandatory Minimum Sentencing." *Journal of Law and Economics* 48(2):591–627.

———. 2007*a*. "Guilt Shall Not Escape or Innocence Suffer: The Limits of Plea Bargaining When Defendant Guilt Is Uncertain." *American Law and Economics Review* 9(2):305–29.

———. 2007*b*. "Racial Profiling, Statistical Discrimination, and the Effect of a Colorblind Policy on the Crime Rate." *Journal of Public Economic Theory* 9(3):543–67.

———. Forthcoming. "On the Role of Plea Bargaining and the Distribution of Sentences in the Absence of Judicial System Frictions." *International Review of Law and Economics.*

Blumstein, Alfred. 1993. "Racial Disproportionality of U.S. Prison Populations Revisited." *University of Colorado Law Review* 64:743–60.

Blumstein, Alfred, Jacqueline Cohen, Susan E. Martin, and Michael Tonry, eds. 1983. *Research on Sentencing: The Search for Reform.* 2 vols. Washington, DC: National Academy Press.

Bourgois, Phillippe. 1996. *In Search of Respect: Selling Crack in El Barrio.* New York: Cambridge University Press.

Bowles, Roger, and Rimawan Pradiptyo. 2004. *Reducing Burglary Initiative: An Analysis of Costs, Benefits and Cost Effectiveness.* Home Office Research Study. London: H.M. Stationery Office.

Brame, Robert, Shawn Bushway, and Raymond Paternoster. 1999. "On the Use of Panel Research Designs and Random Effects Models to Investigate Static and Dynamic Theories of Criminal Offending." *Criminology* 37:599–641.

Britt, Chester. 1997. "Reconsidering the Unemployment and Crime Relationship: Variations by Age Group and Historical Period." *Journal of Quantitative Criminology* 13:405–17.

Buchanan, James. 1973. "A Defense of Organized Crime?" In *The Economics of Crime and Punishment*, edited by Simon Rottenberg. Washington, DC: American Enterprise Institute.

Bushway, Shawn, Robert Brame, and Raymond Paternoster. 1999. "Assessing Stability and Change in Criminal Offending: A Comparison of Random Effects, Semi-parametric, and Fixed Effect Modeling Strategies." *Journal of Quantitative Criminology* 15:23–61.

Bushway, Shawn, and Jonah Gelbach. 2006. "Are Bail Amounts Racially Discriminatory? Evidence Using Outcome Analysis." Working paper. College Park: University of Maryland.

Bushway, Shawn, Brian Johnson, and Lee Ann Slocum. 2007. "Is the Magic Still There? The Relevance of the Heckman Two-Step Correction for Selection Bias in Criminology." *Journal of Quantitative Criminology* 23:151–78.

Bushway, Shawn, Michael Stoll, and David Weiman, eds. 2007. *Barriers to Reentry? The Labor Market for Released Prisoners in Post-industrial America.* New York: Russell Sage Foundation.

Cameron, Lisa, and Jenny Williams. 2001. "Cannabis, Alcohol and Cigarettes: Substitutes or Complements?" *Economic Record* 77(236):19–34.

Cantor, David, and Kenneth Land. 1985. "Unemployment and Crime Rates in the Post–World War II United States: A Theoretical and Empirical Analysis." *American Sociological Review* 50:317–32.

Cauffman, Elizabeth, and Laurence Steinberg. 2000. "Researching Adolescents' Judgement and Culpability." In *Youth on Trial: A Developmental Perspective on Juvenile Justice*, edited by Thomas Grisso and Robert G. Schwartz. Chicago: University of Chicago Press.

Caulkins, Jonathan P. 1994. *Developing Price Series for Cocaine*. MR-317-DPRC. Santa Monica, CA: Rand.

Caulkins, Jonathan P., and Sara Chandler. 2006. "Long-Run Trends in Incarceration of Drug Offenders in the US." *Crime and Delinquency* 52(4):619–41.

Caulkins, Jonathan P., Bruce Johnson, Angela Taylor, and Lowell Taylor. 1999. "What Drug Dealers Tell Us about Their Costs of Doing Business." *Journal of Drug Issues* 29(2):323–340.

Caulkins, Jonathan P., C. Peter Rydell, William Schwabe, and James Chiesa. 1997. *Mandatory Minimum Drug Sentences: Throwing Away the Key or the Taxpayers' Money?* MR-827-DPRC. Santa Monica, CA: Rand.

Cavanagh, David, and Mark Kleiman. 1990. *Cost Benefit Analysis of Prison Cell Construction and Alternative Sanctions*. NCJ 204751. Washington, DC: U.S. Government Printing Office.

Clarke, Ronald. 1983. "Situational Crime Prevention: Its Theoretical Basis and Practical Scope." In *Crime and Justice: An Annual Review of Research*, vol. 4, edited by Michael Tonry and Norval Morris. Chicago: University of Chicago Press.

Clarke, Ronald, and Derek Cornish. 1985. "Modeling Offenders' Decisions: A Framework for Research and Policy." In *Crime and Justice: An Annual Review of Research*, vol. 6, edited by Michael Tonry and Norval Morris. Chicago: University of Chicago Press.

Clarke, Ronald, and Marcus Felson. 1993. "Introduction: Criminology, Routine Activity and Rational Choice." In *Routine Activity and Rational Choice*, edited by Ronald V. Clarke and Marcus Felson. Advances in Criminological Theory, vol. 5. New Brunswick, NJ: Transaction.

Cloward, Richard, and Lloyd Ohlin. 1960. *Delinquency and Opportunity*. New York: Free Press.

Coase, Ronald. 1960. "The Problem of Social Cost." *Journal of Law and Economics* 3:1–44.

———. 1978. "Economics and Contiguous Disciplines." *Journal of Legal Studies* 7:201–11.

Cohen, Mark. 2005. *The Costs of Crime and Justice*. New York: Routledge.

Cook, Philip. 1980. "Research in Criminal Deterrence: Laying the Groundwork for the Second Decade." In *Crime and Justice: An Annual Review of Research*, vol. 2, edited by Norval Morris and Michael Tonry. Chicago: University of Chicago Press.

———. 1986. "The Demand and Supply of Criminal Opportunities." In *Crime and Justice: An Annual Review of Research*, vol. 7, edited by Michael Tonry and Norval Morris. Chicago: University of Chicago Press.

Cook, Philip, and Jens Ludwig. 2000. *Gun Violence: The Real Costs*. New York: Oxford University Press.

Cook, Philip, Jens Ludwig, Sudhir Venkatesh, and Anthony Braga. 2005. "Underground Gun Markets." Working Paper no. 11737. Cambridge, MA: NBER.

Cook, Philip, and Gary Zarkin. 1985. "Crime and the Business Cycle." *Journal of Legal Studies* 14:115–28.

Cullen, Julie, and Steven Levitt. 1999. "Crime, Urban Flight, and the Consequences for Cities." *Review of Economics and Statistics* 81(2):159–69.

Debreu, Gerard. 1959. *Theory of Value: An Axiomatic Analysis of Economic Equilibrium*. New Haven, CT: Yale University Press.

Demuth, Stephen. 2003. "Racial and Ethnic Differences in Pretrial Release Decisions and Outcomes: A Comparison of Hispanic, Black, and White Felony Arrestees." *Criminology* 41:873–908.

Dharmapala, Dhammika, and Stephen Ross. 2004. "Racial Bias in Motor Vehicle Searches: Additional Theory and Evidence." *Contributions to Economic Analysis and Policy* 3(1):art. 12. http://www.bepress.com/bejeap/contributions.

Donohue, John, and Steven Levitt. 2001. "The Impact of Legalized Abortion on Crime." *Quarterly Journal of Economics* 116(2):379–420.

———. 1998. "Guns, Violence and the Efficiency of Illegal Markets." *American Economic Review* 88(2):463–67.

Donohue, John, and Peter Siegelman. 1998. "Allocating Resources among Prisons and Social Programs in the Battle against Crime." *Journal of Legal Studies* 27(1):1–43.

Donohue, John, and Justin Wolfers. 2005. "Uses and Abuses of Statistical Evidence in the Death Penalty Debate." *Stanford Law Review* 58:791–846.

Doob, Anthony, and Cheryl Webster. 2003. "Sentence Severity and Crime: Accepting the Null Hypothesis." In *Crime and Justice: A Review of Research*, vol. 30, edited by Michael Tonry. Chicago: University of Chicago Press.

Duffee, David, and Edward Allan. 2007. "Criminal Justice, Criminology, and Criminal Justice Theory." In *Criminal Justice Theory: Explaining the Nature and Behavior of Criminal Justice*, edited by David Duffee and Edward Maquire. New York: Routledge.

Dugan, Laura. 1999. "The Effect of Criminal Victimization on a Household's Moving Decision." *Criminology* 37(4):901–29.

Duggan, Mark, and Steven Levitt. 2002. "Winning Isn't Everything: Corruption in Sumo Wrestling." *American Economic Review* 92(5):1594–1605.

Eatherly, Billy. 1974. "Drug Law Enforcement: Should We Arrest Pushers or Users?" *Journal of Political Economy* 82:210–14.

Ehrlich, Isaac. 1975. "The Deterrent Effect of Capital Punishment: A Question of Life and Death." *American Economic Review* 65:397–417.

Engel, Robin. 2008. "A Critique of the Outcome Test in Racial Profiling Research." *Justice Quarterly* 25:1–36.

Evans, William, and Emily Owens. 2007. "COPS and Crime." *Journal of Public Economics* 91(1–2):181–201.

Fagan, Jeffrey, and Richard Freeman. 1999. "Crime and Work" In *Crime and Justice: A Review of Research*, vol. 25, edited by Michael Tonry. Chicago: University of Chicago Press.

Farrell, Jill. 2003. "Mandatory Minimum Firearm Penalties: A Source of Sentencing Disparity." *Justice Research and Policy* 5(1):95–115.

Farrell, Ronald, and Victoria Swigert. 1978. "Prior Offense Record as a Self-Fulfilling Prophecy." *Law and Society Review* 12(3):437–53.

Forst, Brian, and Kathleen Brosi. 1977. "A Theoretical and Empirical Analysis of the Prosecutor." *Journal of Legal Studies* 6(1):177–91.

Frank, Robert, and Ben Bernanke. 2004. *Principles of Microeconomics*. 2nd ed. New York: McGraw-Hill.

Friedman, Milton. 1953. "The Methodology of Positive Economics." In *Essays in Positive Economics*, edited by Milton Friedman. Chicago: University of Chicago Press.

Garber, Steven, Steven Klepper, and Daniel Nagin. 1983. "The Role of Extralegal Factors in Determining Criminal Case Disposition." In *Research on Sentencing: The Search for Reform*, vol. 2, edited by Alfred Blumstein. Washington, DC: National Academy Press.

Garoupa, Nuno. 1997. "The Theory of Optimal Law Enforcement." *Journal of Economic Surveys* 11(3):267–95.

Gibbs, Jack. 1972. *Sociological Theory Construction*. Hinsdale, IL: Dryden.

Glaeser, Edward, Daniel Kessler, and Anne Piehl. 2000. "What Do Prosecutors Maximize? An Analysis of the Federalization of Drug Crimes." *American Law and Economics Review* 2(2):259–90.

Glaeser, Edward, and Bruce Sacerdote. 1999. "Why Is There More Crime in Cities?" *Journal of Political Economy* 107(6; suppl.):S225–S229.

Glaeser, Edward, Bruce Sacerdote, and Jose Scheinkman. 1996. "Crime and Social Interactions." *Quarterly Journal of Economics* 111(2):507–48.

Greenbaum, Robert, and George Tita. 2004. "The Impact of Violence Surges on Neighborhood Business Activity." *Urban Studies* 41(13):2495–2514.

Greenberg, David. 2001. "Time Series Analyses of Crime Rates." *Journal of Quantitative Criminology* 17:291–327.

Greenwood, Peter, C. Peter Rydell, Allan Abrahamse, Jonathan Caulkins, James Chiesa, Karyn Model, and Stephen Klein. 1994. *Three Strikes and You're Out: Estimated Benefits and Costs of California's New Mandatory-Sentencing Law*. Santa Monica, CA: Rand.

Hagan, John. 1989. "Why Is There So Little Criminal Justice Theory? Neglected Macro- and Micro-Level Links between Organization and Power." *Journal of Research in Crime and Delinquency* 26(2):116–35.

Halaby, Charles. 2004. "Panel Models in Sociological Research: Theory into Practice." *Annual Review of Sociology* 30:507–44.

Haller, Mark. 1990. "Illegal Enterprise: A Theoretical and Historical Interpretation." *Criminology* 28:207–35.

Harcourt, Bernard. 2004. "Rethinking Racial Profiling: A Critique of the Economics, Civil Liberties, and Constitutional Literature, and of Criminal Profiling More Generally." *University of Chicago Law Review* 71:1275–1381.

———. 2007. *Against Prediction: Profiling, Policing, and Punishing in an Actuarial Age*. Chicago: University of Chicago Press.

Hart, Michelle. 2006. "Race, Sentencing, and the Pretrial Process." MA thesis, University of Maryland.

Hay, Carter, and Walter Forrest. 2006. "Self-Control and Social Context: Toward a More Conditional View of the Relationship between Self-Control and Crime." Presented at the annual meeting of the American Society of Criminology, Los Angeles, November.

Heaton, Paul. 2007. "Understanding the Effects of Anti-profiling Policies." Working paper. Chicago: University of Chicago.

Helland, Eric, and Alexander Tabarrok. 2007. "Does Three Strikes Deter? A Nonparametric Estimation." *Journal of Human Resources* 42(2):309–30.

Hoffer, Lee. 2006. *Junkie Business: The Evolution and Operation of a Heroin Dealing Network*. Belmont, CA: Wadsworth.

Jacob, Brian, and Lars Lefgren. 2003. "Are Idle Hands the Devil's Workshop? Incapacitation, Concentration and Juvenile Crime." *American Economic Review* 93(5):1560–77.

Jacobs, Bruce. 1999. *Dealing Crack: The Social World of Street Corner Selling*. Boston: Northeastern University Press.

Johnson, Brian. 2006. "The Multilevel Context of Criminal Sentencing: Integrating Judge and County Level Influences in the Study of Courtroom Decision Making." *Criminology* 44(2):259–98.

Kagel, John, Raymond Battalio, Howard Rachlin, and Leonard Green. 1981. "Demand Curves for Animal Consumers." *Quarterly Journal of Economics* 96: 1–15.

Kessler, Daniel, and Steven Levitt. 1999. "Using Sentence Enhancements to Distinguish between Deterrence and Incapacitation." *Journal of Law and Economics* 42:343–63.

Klepper, Steven, Daniel Nagin, and Luke-John Tierney. 1983. "Discrimination in the Criminal Justice System: A Critical Appraisal of the Literature." In *Research on Sentencing: The Search for Reform*, vol. 2, edited by Alfred Blumstein. Washington, DC: National Academy Press.

Kling, Jeffrey. 2006. "Incarceration Length, Employment, and Earnings." *American Economic Review* 96:863–76.

Knowles, John, Nicola Persico, and Petra Todd. 2001. "Racial Bias in Motor Vehicle Searches: Theory and Evidence." *Journal of Political Economy* 109(1): 203–29.

Kuziemko, Ilyana. 2007. "Going off Parole: How the Elimination of Discretionary Prison Release Affects the Social Cost of Crime." Working paper. Cambridge, MA: Harvard University.

Kuziemko, Ilyana, and Steven Levitt. 2004. "An Empirical Analysis of Imprisoning Drug Offenders." *Journal of Public Economics* 88(9–10):2043–66.

Landes, William. 1971. "An Economic Analysis of the Courts." *Journal of Labor Economics* 14(1):61–107.

———. 1973. "The Bail System: An Economic Approach." *Journal of Legal Studies* 2:79–105.

———. 1974. "Legality and Reality: Some Evidence on Criminal Procedure." *Journal of Legal Studies* 3:287–337.

Laub, John, and Robert Sampson. 2003. *Shared Beginnings, Divergent Lives: Delinquent Boys to Age 70*. Cambridge, MA: Harvard University Press.

Lazear, Edward, and Sherwin Rosen. 1981. "Rank Order Tournaments as Optimum Labor Contracts." *Journal of Political Economy* 89:841–64.

Lee, David, and Justin McCrary. 2006. "Crime, Punishment and Myopia." Working Paper no. 11491. Cambridge, MA: NBER.

Levitt, Steven. 1996. "The Effect of Prison Population Size on Crime Rates: Evidence from Prison Overcrowding Litigation." *Quarterly Journal of Economics* 111(2):319–51.

———. 1998. "Juvenile Crime and Punishment." *Journal of Political Economy* 106:1156–85.

Levitt, Steven, and Stephen Dubner. 2005. *Freakonomics: A Rogue Economist Explores the Hidden Side of Everything*. New York: Morrow.

Levitt, Steven, and Thomas Miles. 2007. "Empirical Study of Criminal Punishment." In *The Handbook of Law and Economics*, edited by A. Mitchell Polinsky and Steven Shavell. Amsterdam: North-Holland.

Levitt, Steven, and Sudhir Venkatesh. 2000. "An Economic Analysis of a Drug-Selling Gang's Finances." *Quarterly Journal of Economics* 115(3):755–89.

Linden, Leigh, and Jonah Rockoff. 2006. "There Goes the Neighborhood? Estimates of Crime Risk on Property Values from Megan's Law." Working Paper no. 12253. Cambridge, MA: NBER.

Lochner, Lance. 2007. "Individual Perceptions of the Criminal Justice System." *American Economic Review* 97(1):444–60.

Lochner, Lance, and Enrico Moretti. 2004. "The Effect of Education on Crime: Evidence from Prison Inmates, Arrests, and Self-Reports." *American Economic Review* 94(1):155–89.

Loeffler, Charles. 2006. "Using Inter-judge Sentencing Disparity to Estimate the Effect of Imprisonment on Criminal Recidivism." Working paper. Cambridge, MA: Harvard University.

Loewenstein, George. 1996. "Out of Control: Visceral Influences on Behavior." *Organizational Behavior and Human Decision Processes* 65:272–92.

MacCoun, Robert, Beau Kilmer, and Peter Reuter. 2003. "Research on Crime-Drugs Linkage: The Next Generation of Research." In *Toward a Drugs and Crime Research Agenda for the 21st Century*, edited by Henry Brounstein and Christine Crossland. Washington, DC: National Institute of Justice.

MacCoun, Robert, and Peter Reuter. 2001. *Drug War Heresies: Learning from Other Vices, Times and Places*. Cambridge: Cambridge University Press.

Manning, Willard, Emmett Keeler, Joseph Newhouse, Elizabeth Sloss, and Jeffrey Wassermann. 1991. *The Costs of Poor Health Habits*. Cambridge, MA: Harvard University Press.

Manski, Charles. 1978. "Prospects for Inference on Criminal Behavior." In *Deterrence and Incapacitation: Estimating the Effects of Criminal Sanctions on*

Crime Rates, edited by Alfred Blumstein, Jacqueline Cohen, and Daniel Nagin. Washington, DC: National Academy Press.

Manski, Charles, John Pepper, and Carol Petrie. 2001. *Informing America's Policy on Illegal Drugs: What We Don't Know Keeps Hurting Us*. Washington, DC: National Academy Press.

Marvell, Thomas, and Carl Moody. 1994. "Prison Population Growth and Crime Reduction." *Journal of Quantitative Criminology* 10:109–40.

———. 1996. "Police Levels, Crime Rates, and Specification Problems." *Criminology* 24:606–46.

Matsueda, Ross, Derek Kreager, and David Huizinga. 2006. "Deterring Delinquents: A Rational Choice Model of Theft and Violence." *American Sociological Review* 71(1):95–122.

McCrary, Justin. 2007. "The Effect of Court-Ordered Hiring Quotas on the Composition and Quality of Police." *American Economic Review* 97:318–53.

Miron, Jeffrey. 1999. "Violence and the U.S. Prohibitions of Drugs and Alcohol." *American Law and Economics Review* 1:78–114.

———. 2003. "The Effect of Drug Prohibition on Drug Prices: Evidence from the Markets for Cocaine and Heroin." *Review of Economics and Statistics* 85(3): 522–30.

Moore, Mark. 1973. "Achieving Effective Discrimination in the Price of Heroin." *American Economic Review* 63(2):270–77.

———. 1990. "Supply Control and Drug Law Enforcement." In *Drugs and Crime*, edited by Michael Tonry and James Q. Wilson. Vol. 13 of *Crime and Justice: A Review of Research*, edited by Michael Tonry and Norval Morris. Chicago: University of Chicago Press.

Morselli, Carlo. 2005. *Contacts, Opportunities and Criminal Enterprise*. Toronto: University of Toronto Press.

Mustard, David. 2001. "Racial, Ethnic, and Gender Disparities in Sentencing: Evidence from the U.S. Federal Courts." *Journal of Law and Economics* 44: 285–314.

Nagin, Daniel. 1978. "General Deterrence: A Review of the Empirical Evidence." In *Deterrence and Incapacitation: Estimating the Effects of Criminal Sanctions on Crime Rates*, edited by Alfred Blumstein, Jacqueline Cohen, and Daniel Nagin. Washington, DC: National Academy Press.

———. 1998. "Criminal Deterrence Research at the Outset of the Twenty-first Century." In *Crime and Justice: A Review of Research*, vol. 23, edited by Michael Tonry. Chicago: University of Chicago Press.

———. 2005. *Group-Based Modeling of Development over the Life Course*. Cambridge, MA: Harvard University Press.

———. 2007. "Moving Choice to Center Stage in Criminological Research and Theory: The American Society of Criminology 2006 Sutherland Address." *Criminology* 45:259–72.

Nagin, Daniel, and Kenneth C. Land. 1993. "Age, Criminal Careers, and Population Heterogeneity: Specific Estimation of a Nonparametric, Mixed Poisson Model." *Criminology* 31:327–62.

Nagin, Daniel, and Raymond Paternoster. 1991. "On the Relationship between Past and Future Criminality." *Criminology* 29:163–89.

———. 1994. "Personal Capital and Social Control: The Deterrence Implications of a Theory of Individual Differences in Offending." *Criminology* 32: 581–606.

Nagin, Daniel, and Greg Pogarsky. 2001. "Integrating Celerity, Impulsivity, and Extralegal Sanction Threats into a Model of General Deterrence: Theory and Evidence." *Criminology* 39:404–30.

———. 2003. "An Experimental Investigation of Deterrence: Cheating, Self-Serving Bias, and Impulsivity." *Criminology* 41:501–27.

———. 2004. "Time and Punishment: Delayed Consequences and Criminal Behavior." *Journal of Quantitative Criminology* 20:295–317.

National Institute of Justice. 2003. *2000 Arrest Drug Abuse Monitoring: Annual Report*. Washington, DC: U.S. Government Printing Office.

Nieuwbeerta, Paul, and Arjan Blokland. 2007. "Selectively Incapacitating Frequent Offenders: Costs and Benefits of Various Penal Scenarios." *Journal of Quantitative Criminology* 23(4):327–53.

Nobling, Tracy, Cassia Spohn, and Miriam DeLone. 1998. "A Tale of Two Counties: Unemployment and Sentence Severity." *Justice Quarterly* 15(3): 459–85.

O'Brien, Robert. 2001. "Theory, Operationalization, Identification, and the Interpretation of Different Differences in Time Series Models." *Journal of Quantitative Criminology* 17:359–75.

ONDCP (Office of National Drug Control Policy). 2001. *What America's Users Spend on Illicit Drugs, 1988–2000*. Washington, DC: ONDCP.

———. 2004. *The Price and Purity of Illicit Drugs: 1981 through the Second Quarter of 2003*. Washington, DC: ONDCP.

Ousey, Graham, and Pamela Wilcox. 2007. "The Interaction of Antisocial Propensity and Lifecourse Varying Predictors of Delinquent Behavior: Differences by Method of Estimation and Implications for Theory." *Criminology* 45:313–54.

Owens, Emily. 2007. "More Time, Less Crime? The Incapacitative Effect of Sentence Enhancements." Working paper. College Park: University of Maryland.

Paternoster, Raymond. 1987. "The Deterrent Effect of the Perceived Certainty and Severity of Punishment: A Review of the Evidence and Issues." *Justice Quarterly* 4:173–218.

Paternoster, Raymond, and Shawn Bushway. 2001. "Theoretical and Empirical Work on the Relationship between Unemployment and Crime." *Journal of Quantitative Criminology* 17:391–408.

Paternoster, Raymond, and Alex Piquero. 1995. "Reconceptualizing Deterrence: An Empirical Test of Personal and Vicarious Experiences." *Journal of Research in Crime and Delinquency* 32:251–86.

Patillo, Mary, David Weiman, and Bruce Western. 2004. *Imprisoning America: The Social Effects of Mass Incarceration*. New York: Russell Sage Foundation.

Persico, Nicola. 2002. "Racial Profiling, Fairness, and Effectiveness of Policing." *American Economic Review* 92:1472–97.

Piquero, Alex, and Raymond Paternoster. 1998. "An Application of Stafford and Warr's Reconceptualization of Deterrence to Drinking and Driving." *Journal of Research in Crime and Delinquency* 35:5–41.

Piquero, Alex, and Greg Pogarsky. 2002. "Beyond Stafford and Warr's Reconceptualization of Deterrence: Personal and Vicarious Experiences, Impulsivity, and Offending Behavior." *Journal of Research in Crime and Delinquency* 39:153–86.

Pogarsky, Greg, Alex Piquero, and Raymond Paternoster. 2004. "Modeling Change in Perceptions about Sanction Threats: The Neglected Linkage in Deterrence Theory." *Journal of Quantitative Criminology* 20:343–69.

Posner, Richard. 2006. "A Review of Steven Shavell's *Foundations of Economic Analysis of Law*." *Journal of Economic Literature* 33:405–14.

Rankin, Anne. 1964. "The Effect of Pretrial Detention." *New York University Law Review* 39:641–56.

Rasmussen, David, and Bruce Benson. 1994. *The Economic Anatomy of a Drug War: Criminal Justice in the Commons*. Lanham, MD: Rowman and Littlefield.

Reuter, Peter, Gordon Crawford, and Jonathan Cave. 1988. *Sealing the Borders: Effects of Increased Military Efforts in Drug Interdiction*. Santa Monica, CA: RAND.

Reuter, Peter, and Victoria Greenfield. 2001. "Measuring Global Drug Markets: How Good Are the Numbers and Why Should We Care about Them?" *World Economics* 2(4):155–73.

Reuter, Peter, and Mark Kleiman. 1986. "Risks and Prices: An Economic Analysis of Drug Enforcement." In *Crime and Justice: An Annual Review of Research*, vol. 7, edited by Michael Tonry and Norval Morris. Chicago: University of Chicago Press.

Reuter, Peter, Robert MacCoun, and Peter Murphy. 1990. *Money from Crime: A Study of the Economics of Drug Dealing in Washington, D.C.* Santa Monica, CA: RAND.

Rhodes, William. 1976. "The Economics of Criminal Courts: A Theoretical and Empirical Investigation." *Journal of Legal Studies* 5:311–40.

Rose-Ackerman, Susan. 1999. *Corruption and Government: Causes, Consequences and Reform*. New York: Cambridge University Press.

Rydell, C. Peter, and Susan Everingham. 1994. *Controlling Cocaine: Supply versus Demand Programs*. Santa Monica, CA: RAND.

Schanzenbach, Max, and Emerson Tiller. 2007. "Strategic Judging under the United States Sentencing Guidelines: Positive Political Theory and Evidence." *Journal of Law, Economics and Organization* 23:24–56.

Schanzenbach, Max, and Michael Yaeger. 2006. "Prison Time and Fines: Explaining Racial Disparities in Sentencing for White-Collar Criminals." *Journal of Criminal Law and Criminology* 56:757–93.

Schelling, Thomas. 1984. *Choice and Consequence*. Cambridge, MA: Harvard University Press.

Sellin, Thorsten. 1959. *The Death Penalty*. Beverly Hills, CA: Sage.

Shavell, Steven. 2004. *Foundations of Economic Analysis of Law*. Cambridge, MA: Harvard University Press.

Sherman, Lawrence , Denise Gottfredson, Doris MacKenzie, John Eck, Peter Reuter, and Shawn Bushway. 1997. *Preventing Crime: What Works, What Doesn't, What's Promising. A Report to U.S. Congress*. College Park: University of Maryland, Department of Criminology and Criminal Justice. http://www.ncjrs.org/work.

Smith, Douglas A. 1985. "The Plea Bargaining Controversy." *Journal of Criminal Law and Criminology* 77:949–68.

Spohn, Cassia. 2000. "Thirty Years of Sentencing Reform: The Quest for a Racially Neutral Sentencing Process." In *National Institute of Justice: Criminal Justice 2000*. Washington, DC: National Institute of Justice.

Stafford, Mark, and E. Mark Warr. 1993. "A Reconceptualization of General and Specific Deterrence." *Journal of Research in Crime and Delinquency* 30: 123–35.

Steffensmeier, Darrell, and Stephen Demuth. 2000. "Ethnicity and Sentencing Outcomes in U.S. Federal Courts: Who Is Punished More Harshly?" *American Sociological Review* 65:705–29.

Steffensmeier, Darrell, John Kramer, and Cathy Streifel. 1993. "Gender and Imprisonment Decisions." *Criminology* 31:411–46.

Steffensmeier, Darrell, John Kramer, and Jeffrey Ulmer. 1998. "The Interaction of Race, Gender, and Age in Criminal Sentencing: The Punishment Cost of Being Young, Black, and Male." *Criminology* 36(4):763–98.

Stigler, George. 1952. *The Theory of Price*. Rev. ed. New York: Macmillan.

Stokey, Nancy, and Richard Zeckhauser. 1978. *A Primer for Policy Analysis*. New York: Norton.

Strumpf, Koleman. 2003. "Illegal Sport Bookmakers." Working paper. Chapel Hill: University of North Carolina.

Sweeten, Gary, and Robert Apel. 2007. "Incapacitation: Revisiting an Old Question with a New Method and New Data." *Journal of Quantitative Criminology* 23(4):303–26.

Thaler, Richard. 1978. "A Note on the Value of Crime Control: Evidence from the Property Market." *Journal of Urban Economics* 5(1):137–45.

Tita, George, Tricia Petras, and Robert Greenbaum. 2006. "Crime and Residential Choice: A Neighborhood Level Analysis of the Impact of Crime on Housing Prices." *Journal of Quantitative Criminology* 22(4):299–317.

Tonry, Michael. 1992. "Mandatory Penalties." In *Crime and Justice: A Review of Research*, vol. 16, edited by Michael Tonry. Chicago: University of Chicago Press.

———. 1995. *Malign Neglect: Race, Crime and Punishment in America*. New York: Oxford University Press.

Ulmer, Jeffrey, and Mindy Bradley. 2006. "Variation in Trial Penalties among Serious Violent Offenses." *Criminology* 44:631–70.

U.S. Department of Justice. Bureau of Justice Statistics. 2006. *A National Crime Victimization Survey 2005: Statistical Tables*. NCJ 215244. Washington, DC: U.S. Department of Justice.

Varian, Hal. 2002. *Intermediate Microeconomics*. 6th ed. Berkeley: University of California Press.

Viscusi, W. Kip. 1992. *Fatal Tradeoffs: Public and Private Responsibilities for Risk*. Oxford: Oxford University Press.

Viscusi, W. Kip, and Joseph Aldy. 2003. "The Value of a Statistical Life: A Critical Review of Market Estimates throughout the World." *Journal of Risk and Uncertainty* 27(1):5–76.

Walsh, John. 2004. "Fuzzy Math: Why the White House Drug Control Budget Doesn't Add Up." *Drug Policy Analysis Bulletin*, no. 10. http://fas.org/drugs.

Webster, Cheryl, Anthony Doob, and Franklin Zimring. 2006. "Proposition 8 and Crime Rates in California: The Case of the Disappearing Deterrent." *Criminology and Public Policy* 5(3):417–48.

Welsh, Brandon, David Farrington, and Lawrence Sherman, eds. 2000. *Costs and Benefits of Preventing Crime*. Boulder, CO: Westview.

Western, Bruce. 2002. "The Impact of Incarceration on Wage Mobility and Inequality." *American Sociological Review* 67(4):526–46.

Wilson, James Q., and Richard Herrnstein. 1985. *Crime and Human Nature: The Definitive Study of the Causes of Crime*. New York: Simon and Schuster.

Zatz, Marjorie, and John Hagan. 1985. "Crime, Time, and Punishment: An Exploration of Selection Bias in Sentencing Research." *Journal of Quantitative Criminology* 1:103–26.

David Weisburd and Alex R. Piquero

How Well Do Criminologists Explain Crime? Statistical Modeling in Published Studies

ABSTRACT

Understanding of the phenomenon of crime lies at the heart of criminology. A century and a half of theory and research has accumulated, but there does not yet exist an evaluation of how much explanatory power (summarized as the amount of variance explained) there is in criminological research. Examination of empirical tests of criminological theory in *Criminology* between 1968 and 2005 yields three key findings. The overall level of variance explained is often very low with 80 or 90 percent unexplained. There has been no improvement over time. Individual-based models provide relatively weak explanatory power, but models that took a more crime-specific focus indicated some strength. Criminologists will need to pay much more attention to "what is not explained" in criminological modeling if they are to make significant advances in understanding crime.

Description and understanding of the phenomenon of crime lie at the heart of criminology (Sutherland 1937). A century and a half of research has accumulated, much of it since 1970 (Wolfgang, Figlio, and Thornberry 1978; Bernard 1990), but quantitative summary statements

David Weisburd is Walter E. Meyer Professor of Law and Criminal Justice at the Hebrew University of Jerusalem and Distinguished Professorof Administration of Justice at George Mason University. Alex R. Piquero is professor, Department of Criminology and Criminal Justice, University of Maryland, College Park. We are grateful to David Bierie, Joshua Hinkle, Chien-Min Lin (University of Maryland), and Andrea Schoepfer (University of Florida) for their remarkable efforts in identifying and coding articles for this study. We thank our colleagues Howard Bloom, Chester Britt, Ronald Clarke, Francis Cullen, John Eck, Marcus Felson, Michael Maltz, Joe Naus, P. O. Wikström, David Wilson, and Sue-Ming Yang for their thoughtful comments on the manuscript.

0192-3234/2008/0037-0006$10.00

of criminology's ability to predict the phenomena that are its primary concerns do not yet exist.[1] How much explanatory power there is in traditional criminological research and whether explanations are consistent with theoretical expectations are important questions that deserve investigation (Bernard 1990). After all, if there is a model or theory about crime, it is reasonable to ask how well the data fit it (e.g., Lieberson 1985, p. 90).

The issue of explanatory power (typically summarized as the amount of variance explained, or R^2) is crucial for advancing theories about crime and criminality. How well a statistical model predicts crime can be an important measure of the comprehensiveness of a theory or of the extent to which a theoretical perspective provides only a partial explanation of variability. Estimates of explanatory power are useful with respect to searches for prediction, causation, and explanation (Wikström 2007), as they can provide some information with respect to the causal mechanisms and processes.[2] In turn, if traditional theories lead to statistical models with low variance explained, this would suggest falsifying theories, revising existing theories, or staking out new

[1] While we could not identify a prior study that provided an overall quantitative assessment of how well criminologists explain crime, Bernard (1990) did provide a narrative assessment of "what have we learned and why in twenty years of testing theory." As we discuss later, Bernard's concern that theory had not advanced in the 20 years prior to his paper appears to be confirmed in our analyses as well. Another more recent paper published in this series by Pratt and Cullen (2005) used a quantitative meta-analytic approach to examine the comparative effect sizes of specific predictors across models. While this work provides a quantitative analysis of the salience of specific explanatory factors, it did not examine the overall explanatory power of models employed.

[2] It is important at the outset to note that our essay examines a very specific question in regard to explanation. Variance explained is a statistical construct (described in more detail in Sec. II) that tells us how much of the statistical variation in a model is accounted for by a set of predictors (whether predicting levels of crime in geographical areas or individuals' criminal involvement). Explanation, in contrast, is often seen to be about specifying why and how some putative factors cause a particular effect. It is, in this sense, about specifying the mechanisms (or processes) that bring about a certain effect. It is about answering "why" questions with "because" answers. To explain something in this context is not only to demonstrate how much of an effect's variation is accounted for by a set of predictors but to (analytically) specify how a predictor (or set of predictors) produces the effect in question (see Wikström 2007). Moreover, correlation (prediction) is not the same as causation, for even if a model "explains" 100 percent of the variance, it does not necessarily demonstrate causation as we note below. While causation requires correlation, correlation is not proof of causation. Our focus in this essay on the total amount of variance explained (and by extension using this particular measure to provide some sort of summary statement with respect to the adequacy of specific theories) is not meant to give the impression that we believe that including an array of variables in a multivariate model and hoping for something reasonable to emerge establishes causality. For an excellent overview of the issues surrounding prediction, explanation, and causation in criminology, readers should consult Wikström (2007).

theories or approaches. Of course, a focus on assessing whether relationships follow theoretical prescriptions is equally important (see Pratt and Cullen 2005); that is, are coefficients doing what theoretically they are supposed to be doing?

The link between variance explained and policy is direct. If criminological models do very poorly in explaining crime outcomes, why should policy makers pay attention to criminology in developing prevention practices? Why should a policy maker take a specific criminological recommendation for crime prevention into account if the theory underlying it poorly predicts crime outcomes? And if most of the variability in crime cannot be accounted for by that prescription and theory, it is natural to ask whether other approaches might yield greater benefit. Conversely, if much of the variability was accounted for, the position of criminologists in advising policy makers and practitioners would be on much more solid ground. It is easier to justify policy prescriptions if our understanding of crime relates better to the real world.

While variance explained thus provides an important indicator of the state of the science of criminology, and its relevance for public policy, it also has implications for our ability to have faith in the effects of variables and the theories that they represent. As we explain later, a variable that is excluded from a statistical model of outcomes, because it is not known or not measured, can affect variables that are included. This "omitted variable bias" is an often neglected limitation of multivariate statistical models, but one that is strongly related to how well we explain the phenomenon under study. If models have relatively low explanatory power, it is reasonable to assume that important factors have been missed. Their exclusion in turn may lead to under- or overestimates of the importance of the factors measured and included in models.

Thus, variance explained provides one way to assess the state of the science of criminology and its relevance for public policy, and how that science has changed over time.[3] It is pertinent to ask how well criminologists are doing in developing multivariate models. Has there been steady improvement over time in our ability to explain outcomes?

[3] We are not suggesting that this is the only method for taking stock of theoretical advancement. More traditional narrative reviews (Bernard 1990) or meta-analyses of effects of specific variables across studies (Pratt and Cullen 2005) provide examples of other approaches that criminologists have used to examine related questions.

Which theoretical approaches appear to lead to the most complete explanations and which to the least? At what units of analysis is explanation greatest? Are certain crime types better explained than others? Are criminologists better at explaining macro or micro patterns of crime?

These are critical questions, though they have not been the subject of empirical study to date. In this essay, we review research studies in *Criminology*, the journal most criminologists would consider the most important in criminological science.[4] We examined all articles published from 1968 through 2005 that used multivariate modeling to test criminological theories. Our analyses aimed to provide an important first step in describing the state of theoretically based quantitative modeling in criminology. We hope that by asking the question "how well are we doing in predicting crime?" we will provide impetus for continued and more advanced work.

We begin in Section I by describing multivariate modeling in criminology and its importance as a tool in the development of criminology as a science. Multivariate modeling attempts to gain knowledge about the causes of crime by identifying a broad array of factors that influence a phenomenon and allows for the comparison of the effects of the factors studied. We then review variance explained, describe its relevance for evaluating multivariate modeling, identify the limitations of drawing conclusions from models that have low explained variance, and raise cautions about the use of explained variance as a measure of how well multivariate models explain crime. In Section II, we explain our choice of *Criminology*, outline the inclusion criteria for the studies in our sample, and discuss our coding mechanism. Section III describes the studies, and Section IV presents the main findings.

We address seven questions. Has there been change over time in the number of studies that report variance explained measures? What is the average R^2 across all models and all studies of interest? How have R^2 values changed over the period 1968–2005? What is the average amount of variance explained across the theoretical areas under study? What is the average R^2 across units of analysis and across sample size? What is the average R^2 by the type of data (longitudinal, cross-sectional, etc.) collected? What is the average R^2 by type of dependent variable (i.e., crime type)?

[4] We describe in more detail later in the essay our decision to draw a sample from *Criminology*.

Our review of variance explained in articles in *Criminology* leads to a number of important findings and suggests the salience of further research in this area. Although quantitative tests of criminological theory have been an important part of the work published in *Criminology*, a majority of articles published have not presented quantitative multivariate empirical tests of theory. In turn, reporting of explained variance measures began to increase in the 1980s and, with a few exceptions, continued at about the same rate until the end of the 1990s. Between 10 and 25 percent of *Criminology* articles each year include multivariate models explaining crime and reporting variance explained statistics. Our examination of these studies highlights a lack of basic, descriptive statistical information that can be used to understand the data and where the data come from. We are not the first to identify this problem of "descriptive validity" in criminological study (see Farrington 2003*b*; Lösel and Beelmann 2003); our work reinforces the importance of correcting this problem.

Overall, there is a great deal of unexplained variance in crime. Studies in our sample had an average explained variance statistic of .389, with a quarter at less than 20 percent. Modeling over time does not seem to have improved. There do not appear to be strong differences in variance explained by theoretical area, though there are important differences by both level of analysis and crime type with higher units of aggregation and more serious (officially based) and more tightly focused crime types evincing higher levels of variance explained.

In discussing implications of these findings, we focus on three aspects of our work: low variance explained observed across studies, lack of evidence of improvement in criminological explanation over time, and weakness of explanations in individual-based models and the apparently greater strength of models that take a more crime-specific focus. Our findings offer an empirical backdrop to Bernard's (1990) observation that criminology has not made sufficient progress in falsifying some theories and accumulating verified knowledge in the context of others. Of course, this must be tempered by the possibility that much variance in crime is stochastic, that measures of key independent and dependent variables are far from perfect, and that limitations of models reflect real limitations in explaining crime more generally. We offer several recommendations that might lead to improved levels of explained variance and better understanding of its meaning. One possible explanation for our findings is that criminology is not focused enough on advancing and building on prior knowledge and approaches, and is not paying sufficient attention to theoretical processes underlying crime.

In concluding, we argue that criminologists concerned with policy questions should look more often toward experimental methods. A more general understanding of crime is not necessary to develop unbiased estimates of particular prevention practices or policy prescriptions in randomized experiments. Moreover, such knowledge is critical to the identification of specific variable effects in multivariate modeling (e.g., Wikström 2007, p. 120). In turn, more attention needs to be paid to development of theory. Theoretical advances should be subjected to sophisticated empirical tests so that theories can be refined or changed as knowledge accumulates (Wikström 2007, pp. 119, 132). Criminologists need to pay much greater attention to what they do not explain and focus more clearly on unexplained variance and its implications. Are low levels of explained variance due to inadequate theory or poor data and measurement, or is there some more general principle operating that limits our ability to explain crime and criminals? To what extent can we assume that unexplained variance is stochastic, and to what extent must we accept that systematic biases enter into the quantitative models we develop? Criminologists cannot continue to be satisfied with achieving a certain threshold of explained variance without confronting these larger questions that challenge the value of quantitative models for advancing theory and policy.

I. The Importance of Variance Explained

Though oftentimes misused or misapplied (Maltz 1994), multivariate modeling has been a critical tool in the development of criminology (Weisburd 2001). Multivariate modeling is a statistical approach to understanding crime that tries to identify the broad array of factors that influence crime outcomes and allows for the comparison of the specific effects of the factors that are studied. For example, criminologists have long been interested in understanding why juveniles initially become involved in crime, and why some persist and others desist (Shaw and McKay 1932; Wolfgang, Figlio, and Sellin 1972; Blumstein et al. 1986; Piquero, Farrington, and Blumstein 2003). A researcher using multivariate modeling typically begins by identifying factors believed to influence involvement in crime among juveniles and collects information on those factors (i.e., the independent variables, or X_i) and criminal involvement (i.e., the dependent variable, or Y). Typically the researcher fits a linear model that includes a constant (B_0):

$$Y = B_0 + B_1X_1 + \cdots + B_iX_i.$$

Such models assume a causal relationship between the independent and dependent variables, though in practice researchers often use cross-sectional data in which such an assumption is made but cannot be proved. Importantly, this model, which may include a large number of independent variables, is seen as providing a description of the broad array of factors that influence juvenile involvement in crime.

In trying to advance theory, multivariate models are the predominant tools employed by criminologists, economists, and sociologists. By contrast, theory testing in psychology is generally experimental and relies on isolating specific variables, using random allocations of subjects to treatment and control conditions—an approach that is much rarer (though growing) in criminology (Sherman and Berk 1984; Sherman 2005; Weisburd 2005; Farrington and Welsh 2006*a*, 2006*b*). Multivariate modeling has important advantages. As Heckman and Smith (1995) observed, modeling approaches allow the scientist to examine not only a factor in isolation (as is typical in the experimental sciences) but the natural variation and interaction of factors across a wide array of variables.

Multivariate modeling provides a framework for examining complex relationships among a series of independent variables and a dependent variable. It also allows for measurement of how well such models explain the phenomena under study. In the colloquial sense, multivariate modeling not only provides information regarding the influences of specific factors, but also provides a means for showing how well criminologists do in explaining crime overall. The reason is that statistical modeling generally allows assessment not only of how each factor influences the phenomenon of interest, but also of how the accumulation of factors improves predictions. In most cases, this is expressed as the "percentage of variance explained" (R^2).

Percentage of variance explained takes into account two main sources of variation. One is the total variability in the sample examined, or the "total sum of squares": $\sum (Y_i - \bar{Y})^2$. That variation is measured in terms of the difference between the observed values of Y and the mean of Y (the best estimate of Y in the absence of the regression model). The second source of variation in R^2 is the "explained sum of squares": $\sum (\hat{Y}_i - \bar{Y})^2$. This represents the predictive improvement that is gained from estimating the regression model. Percentage of variance explained in a simple linear regression model is gained by estimating the proportion of the total sum of squares that is accounted for by the explained sum of squares:

$$R^2 = \frac{\sum (\hat{Y}_i - \bar{Y})^2}{\sum (Y_i - \bar{Y})^2}.$$

This ratio allows estimates of how much the regression model improves ability to predict the outcomes observed. If the percentage of variance explained is very high, it suggests that the goodness of fit of the model to the data is very good. A low R^2 implies that the model does not add much to what is already known from calculating the mean for the dependent variable. Variance explained provides a direct assessment of how well a model, and by implication theories,[5] explain the phenomenon being examined. If systematic factors influence the occurrence of crime and criminological theory successfully identifies such factors, the percentage of variance explained should, on average, be very high.

The approach described so far applies to linear models relying on an ordinary least squares regression framework. Other multivariate methods such as two-stage least squares, Tobit regression, or count models (Poisson or negative binomial) also use a direct application of the variance explained approach. However, for specific types of nonlinear regression, the development of measures of explained variance is less clear. For example, while there is no direct R^2 measure for logistic regression, a number of "pseudo-R^2" measures have been proposed. In these cases statisticians have tried to develop measures that are comparable to the variance explained coefficient in the linear model.

[5] To be sure, a low R^2 does not mean that the theory is problematic. For example, the empirical test may be poorly specified, the test may include poor measures of the key theoretical constructs, or researchers may have assessed only part of the theory (and some results may yield support for that part of the theory). A more detailed discussion of these issues appears later.

A. Correct Model Specification

It is intuitively obvious why a large amount of explained variance in a regression model is a good result, since it represents the ability of the theory as represented by a model to explain the phenomenon under study. But a high or low R^2 can also be used as an indicator of the success of a model in meeting one of the central assumptions in multiple regression: "correct model specification." Its principal component is that all "independent" or predictor variables that affect the outcome of interest (the dependent variable) must be included in the statistical models that are estimated (Weisburd and Britt 2007).[6] When this assumption is violated, it is difficult to have confidence in the predictions developed from a regression model or in the regression coefficients gained for specific independent variables.

If the model estimated has a variance explained of 10 or 20 percent, it is difficult to argue that all systematic causes of *Y* have been included. While it is possible that the vast majority of the "unexplained variance" is not systematic and that important variables have not been omitted, such an assumption becomes tenuous when R^2 is very low. Pedhauzer (1982, p. 36) argues that this assumption may be "highly questionable" when the independent variables explain "a relatively small proportion of the variance in *Y*." Even if a regression model meets a much higher standard of explained variance, such as 40 or 50 percent, it may still be unreasonable to assume that all of the unexplained variance is random and not the product in part of omitted systematic factors.

The assumption that important independent variables have not been excluded has important implications for confidence in the predictions provided by a model or in the effects of specific variables. A variable that was an important predictive factor but was not included in the regression model estimated (because it is unmeasured or unknown) would lead the regression model to provide inaccurate predictions of *Y*. Regression models cannot take into account measures that are not accounted for or measured incorrectly and adjust outcomes for them. If one purpose of multivariate modeling is to inform public policies, a model that omits relevant factors will lead to inappropriate policy recommendations.

The problem of model misspecification has a second and equally important implication. If an omitted variable is related to a factor in-

[6] It also assumes that the variables included are measured correctly and included in their correct form.

cluded in the model, the estimate of the coefficient for the included factor will be biased.[7] An example is a model in which a prison term is used to predict recidivism. It is well known that the likelihood of receiving a prison term is related to the seriousness of an offender's prior record, and that the seriousness of a prior record is strongly related to the probability of future recidivism (Blumstein et al. 1983). The estimation of a regression model including imprisonment but excluding prior record would result in a biased estimate of the regression coefficient for imprisonment because the effect of imprisonment is confounded with that of prior record.[8] A finding that prison increased recidivism might arise because those receiving prison sentences had more serious prior records and were more likely to recidivate in the first place. If prior record is omitted, the regression will mistakenly attribute a causal effect to imprisonment that is due instead to the confounding of imprisonment and prior record. Multivariate modeling provides a statistical tool for correcting this problem. However, when a relevant predictor of the dependent variable is unmeasured or unknown and that predictor is related to a variable included in the model, the regression estimate for the included variable will be over- or underestimated.

Incorrect model specification can thus have important consequences for defining valid results in multiple regressions. It is one of the primary problems and central dilemmas of multivariate modeling (Mustard 2003), the other being sample selection bias, such as that caused by the continual analysis of conviction databases to make inferences about discretion in the system as a whole, including decisions made by police and prosecutors (personal communication from Shawn Bushway, February 15, 2007). Most statistical manipulation is an attempt to do something about this problem. Because researchers recognize that they

[7] The traditional regression assumption may be expressed by noting that the error term and the included independent or predictor variables are independent. When a relevant predictor is excluded that is related to an included independent variable, its effect is found in the error term, which thus becomes correlated with the independent variable of interest. For a discussion of this assumption in regression, see Pedhauser (1982, chap. 2) and Weisburd and Britt (2007, chap. 16).

[8] This is illustrated in the equation for a simple regression with two independent variables. When the correlations between X_1 and X_2, and X_2 and Y, are greater or less than zero, the coefficient b will be affected:

$$b_{x_1} = \left(\frac{r_{y,x_1} - (r_{y,x_2} r_{x_1,x_2})}{1 - r^2_{x_1,x_2}}\right)\left(\frac{s_y}{s_{x_1}}\right).$$

cannot correctly predict outcomes or correctly identify the influence of specific variables on an outcome without taking a series of relevant independent variables into account, they use multivariate methods. Nonetheless, the assumption of correct model specification may challenge the validity of the conclusions reached.

B. *The Limitations of R^2*

A number of scholars have warned against overreliance on R^2 in assessing the strength of theoretical models (e.g., Duncan 1975; Lieberson 1985; Cramer 1987; Moksony 1990). Some cautions should be kept in mind.

There is much debate regarding the development of appropriate measures of variance explained for nonlinear models (e.g., see Kvalseth 1985; Anderson-Sprecher 1994), particularly when the outcome measures deal with problems that are not based on interval-level distributions and thus have no real measure of variance. The difficulty of making comparisons between such measures and a linear model R^2 is reflected in the alternative pseudo-R^2 measures for logistic regression (e.g., Cox and Snell's [1989] R^2 or Nagelkerke's R^2) that often give variant estimates of variance explained. The difficulties of comparison are discussed below. Nonetheless, a broad statement across models is necessary, and this limitation does not outweigh the potential for gaining a more complete understanding of theoretical explanation over time and across different types of studies.

A second statistical problem in using R^2 as a measure for how well multivariate models explain crime was raised by James Barrett (1974). He noted that two models that fit the data with approximately the same accuracy can provide different outcomes for R^2. The reason is that the value of R^2 is influenced not only by the fit of the model to the data, but also by the "steepness of the regression surface." Barrett notes that "in analyzing two or more sets of data, predictions for a regression equation based on a steep regression surface with a larger R^2 might not be more precise (and could be less precise) than the predictions based on an equation with a surface not so steep with a smaller R^2" (1974, p. 19). In practice this may not be a serious limitation for our purposes since it suggests that a model in which the measures more strongly affect the outcome will have a larger R^2 than one in which the measures together have less predictive strength. The R^2 measure takes into account both the strength of the model in predicting the data and the extent to which the predictions fit the observed distribution of the data.[9]

The nature of the distribution of the dependent variable can affect estimates of R^2 (Blalock 1964; Weisberg 1985).[10] Ranney and Thigpen (1981) show that when the values of the dependent variable are spread more widely, R^2 values will increase even when the basic relationships in the data are similar. They also note that as sample size increases, R^2, all else being equal, will decrease, in part because a larger sample size naturally leads to greater variability. This is not likely to have a large influence on R^2 values, though an increase in the range of values can have much larger effects, especially in models that already have a very high R^2. There is no reason to believe that the range of values varies systematically in studies of crime, and R^2 values in criminology are seldom high (e.g., above .70).

Finally, a low R^2 does not necessarily mean that findings are unimportant; in some cases "less could be better" (Lieberson 1985, p. 94). Nor does a large R^2 necessarily justify a conclusion that the theory tested has strong explanatory power. In some cases, small effects may have considerable substantive importance. As Abelson (1985, p. 129) notes, percentage of variance explained is sometimes a misleading index of influence when tiny influences produce meaningful outcomes. However, when a model overall has a relatively small R^2, it naturally leads to the question of whether a researcher left out important sources of explanation.

A large R^2, in turn, can sometimes be as much a statistical manipulation as an indication of model strength (King 1986; Moksony 1990). For example, the use of prior delinquency to predict current delinquency does not get at the underlying causes of delinquency per se but merely reflects the consistent pattern that prior behavior is a good predictor of present behavior. The addition of variables measuring prior crime or delinquency in the absence of the original causes of such behavior, however, will result in high R^2 values. This approach is particularly common in models using time-related data, where measures of the outcome in prior time periods are naturally included as

[9] Anscombe (1973) makes a similar point but does so visually and quantitatively—with an R^2 of .667 no less.

[10] Duncan (1975, pp. 55–66) has observed that the variance and range of both the dependent and independent variables, which likely vary from setting to setting (and data set to data set), will affect the relative importance attributed to each independent variable (see also Lieberson 1985, p. 117).

part of the statistical model estimates. However, where a model is not correctly specified, such measures will likely include significant bias, meaning that estimates of the independent effect of prior crime or delinquency will be highly questionable.[11]

II. The Study

Variance explained provides a quantitative method for assessing the development of science in criminology. The reason is that R^2 examines how well the models estimated predict sample data in each study and examines the amount and extent of explanatory power in statistical models of crime. It provides a measure of how well criminologists are doing in practice and whether some areas are more promising than others.[12]

Our first task in applying this approach was to develop a data set that would identify representative studies in criminology. We rejected drawing a sample from all "crime studies" as too cumbersome. We would have had to scan a very large group of journals, and there would have been disagreement as to which studies fall within "criminology" and which journals to include. We decided to focus on a single journal. The obvious choice was *Criminology*, the official journal of the American Society of Criminology (ASC). The ASC is the main professional organization for American criminologists (with strong participation from around the world), and its flagship journal represents professional criminological research over the last four decades.

Criminology's citation and impact scores are high and rival those of leading journals in other fields. The most recent journal rankings from the Institute for Scientific Information (ISI) identify *Criminology* as the leading professional journal in criminology, sixth of 96 in sociology, and twenty-ninth of 101 in law. *Criminology*'s impact score in 2005 was 2.013, second only to *Crime and Justice* at 2.588. The ISI's 2006 impact factors and rankings indicate that *Criminology*'s impact factor rose from 2.013 to 2.060, and its ranking increased from 2 of 27 to 1 of 27 in

[11] The likelihood of bias in the estimate of the measure of prior crime is very high because it is likely to be related to unmeasured causes of crime in the model.

[12] It is also important to note that our approach does not assume that the R^2 values in the studies examined represent population estimates. Such an assumption would be problematic, in part, because of the use of sample variances in developing variance explained measures. Our analysis examines how well the models estimated predict sample data in each study. In this sense, we are assessing how well criminologists are doing in practice and not the actual explanatory power of the theories examined.

Criminology & Penology. Data from SCI-Bites rank *Criminology* as the leading criminology/penology journal with respect to impact factor between 1981 and 2004 in criminology/penology (http://www.in-cites.com/research/2005/july_4_2005-2.html; Web site visited February 15, 2007). Finally, *Criminology* is consistently used in publication and citation count studies and is regarded qualitatively as the leading journal in criminology (Sorenson and Pilgrim 2002; Rice, Cohn, and Farrington 2005; Steiner and Schwartz 2006; Cohn and Farrington 2007).[13]

Identifying and Coding Studies. We developed a protocol for inclusion of studies. Development of criteria and coding practices took account of various assumptions and constraints. These included legacy issues, transparency, and inclusiveness.

1. *Legacy issues.* To get a general sense of criminology over the past half century, we created a database that would provide an overview of the current state of the field. The criteria and coding system developed were designed to be dynamic so that data from new studies can be added.
2. *Transparency.* The criteria and coding system were designed to be transparent. We outline and justify our coding decisions below.
3. *Inclusiveness.* It is extremely unlikely that our criteria will satisfy the conditions of all studies given varying definitions of crime methodology. For studies we adjudged ineligible, we kept detailed records as to why they were excluded.

To be included, a study must have been published in *Criminology* and used multivariate statistical modeling to explain crime, delinquency, and other deviant behaviors within some theoretical context. The study first must use statistical modeling in capturing the targeting phenomenon;[14] second, must focus on one of the following units of analysis: individual, groups of individuals, organizations, or geographic area (i.e.,

[13] We recognize that our findings are necessarily limited by our selection of *Criminology*. As such, we encourage other scholars to expand the range of our database to include other criminological/criminal justice journals, including journals that regularly publish empirical research such as *Journal of Research in Crime and Delinquency* and *Journal of Quantitative Criminology*. We should also note that we did not identify *Justice Quarterly*, the official journal of the Academy of Criminal Justice Sciences, for our analysis because it has focused much more directly on criminal justice system studies.

[14] As noted at the outset, our interest is in studies using nonexperimental data and statistical modeling to understand the causes of crime. In this context, we exclude from our analyses experimental studies that use random allocation as a method for isolating specific variable effects. In our discussion, we return to the issue of experimental studies and their utility for developing science in criminology.

public funding or sentence length is not eligible); and third, must report statistics that are more sophisticated than simple correlations or cross-tabulations.

The database includes a number of fields that contain in-depth information regarding the empirical study and, oftentimes, specific coding fields meant to capture slightly different ways researchers presented information (some of these made coding of certain empirical models difficult). Besides descriptive aspects of the database and the specific study (title, authors, year, volume, issue, etc.), the key fields included the theory used/tested;[15] who collected the data (i.e., researcher, census); sample size; unit of analysis (i.e., individual, neighborhood, state, country); type of data (i.e., longitudinal, cross-sectional); methodology (i.e., least-squares regression, logistic regression); dependent variable (i.e., robbery, homicide, delinquency); number of covariates; whether variables from competing theories were controlled; whether the study reported R^2; value of R^2; type of R^2; inclusion of other fit statistics (e.g., log likelihood, root mean square error of approximation, Bayesian information criterion); whether the article discussed possible effects of excluded variables; and any concluding remarks or comments deemed relevant. The Appendix contains the master coding document.

The four coders were advanced graduate students who had completed their training in criminological theory, methods, and statistics. Each independently coded the studies. The coders were extensively trained, and when questions were raised by one or more coders, they were dealt with in an open forum with the other coders and the authors of this essay. In questionable cases, the team came to a shared resolution. Such resolutions sometimes involved requests for further information from authors.

We examined intercoder reliability for two issues of the journal (vol. 37, no. 1, and vol. 38, no. 2).[16] Each coder independently coded the articles, deemed them eligible or ineligible for inclusion, and, if eligible, coded all relevant information. The coders were in near-perfect agreement on eligibility of studies to be included; the type of theory

[15] It was the case that some of the articles did not expressly state that they were testing a particular theory, but instead that they were testing issues that could be considered a theory or major aspects of theories. In these situations, the empirical article was coded as "combined" and not being representative of testing a specific criminological theory.

[16] For the issue in vol. 38, all coders identified and coded all relevant studies. For the issue in vol. 37, the two coders responsible for the bulk of the coding effort overall identified and coded all relevant studies.

being assessed; the sample size and number of predictors in the model; the type of data collection; the type of dependent variable; and whether an R^2 was reported and, if so, its value.[17] Frequent spot-checks failed to identify significant errors. There was overall very high agreement among coders.

III. Description of Studies

Criminology has been published since 1963, but in the early years it was more a newsletter than a peer-reviewed journal. It contained information on criminology or criminal justice programs, reports from annual meetings, letters to the editor, and lists of books received. Between 1963 and 1967, no article satisfied the criteria for inclusion in this analysis.

During the period 1968–2005, *Criminology* published 1,306 articles. Of these, 259 included some quantitative test of criminological theory. Two hundred and seven included multivariate modeling with some statistic of goodness of fit or variance explained. Most of the remaining 52 studies did not use multivariate modeling. However, these also included some articles in which authors did not report explained variance indicators even though such statistics could have been calculated. Of the 207 included studies, 38 included goodness of fit measures that could not be converted or compared to R^2. Chi-square statistics, or log likelihood measures, were common in this category, as were fit statistics for multilevel models. The final sample thus included 169 unique articles, or 81 percent of the 207 qualifying studies.

In analyzing sample attrition, we found some tendency for more recent articles not to report R^2 or an equivalent variance explained measure ($r = .266$, $p < .05$). This is not surprising since nonlinear models for which variance explained measures are not available or easily calculated became more common only recently. It is difficult to assess the extent to which the loss of some articles and resultant R^2 values biases our analyses and conclusions. We did not detect any discernible pattern of missing R^2 values for individual studies on yearly average R^2 over time.

[17] The only meaningful difference that was found was in the number of models coded for a specific article. Importantly, this would be expected to have little impact on our analyses since we generally rely on the model with the highest variance explained reported. And in that regard there was perfect agreement among the coders.

We noted earlier potential limitations of comparing pseudo-R^2 or R^2 measures developed for nonlinear models with linear R^2 coefficients. The majority of the 169 articles reported R^2 for linear models; only a handful (10) reported pseudo-R^2 values. A difference-of-means analysis of the maximum R^2 values across models reporting pseudo versus simple linear model R^2 indicated that the former evinced a somewhat lower explained variance (mean of .32) than the latter (mean of .479); however, this comparison must be viewed with caution because of the small number of articles that reported pseudo-R^2 estimates.

Many studies included more than one multivariate model. We erred on the side of inclusion and coded all "full" models, resulting in 961 models for the 169 articles. We coded only one model when different dimensions were added step by step to a full model.

We considered including multiple models from single articles in the analyses, since authors often developed alternative models for explaining outcomes examined, or examined different outcomes, and sometimes used a different constellation of predictors (in stepwise fashion) to examine differences on the same outcomes. We decided, however, that problems of dependency of these models would lead to significant analytical problems and possible biases in our description of the studies. Accordingly, the analyses below are generally based on only one model from each study. We chose the model with the highest variance explained, under the assumption that this represented the researchers' best explanatory effort. This means that our estimates will have an "upward" bias. In specific cases, for example, analysis across specific crime types, we included more than one model per study. This is reasonable since the models may be considered independent estimates for each separate dimension (crime type outcome).[18]

The explained variance for each model includes all variables in the model (including control variables such as age, sex, and race) and not just the theoretical variables. We did not partial out the variance explained only by the theoretical variables. This may result in overstating the effects of the theoretical variables, given that in most models some variation is explained by covariates that have little to do with theoretical models tested (e.g., gender and age).

[18] Of course, our use of the term "independent" above does not exclude the fact that the same investigators are involved and the same cases are used. Any estimates shown in the same paper are associated simply by virtue of authorship.

IV. Results

Findings are presented in relation to the following seven questions: Has there been a change in the number of studies that report variance explained measures over time? What is the average R^2 across all models and all studies of interest? What has been the change in R^2 values over the period covered? What is the average amount of variance explained across the various theoretical areas under study? What is the average R^2 across units of analysis and across sample size? What is the average R^2 by the type of data (longitudinal, cross-sectional, etc.) collected? What is the average R^2 by type of dependent variable (i.e., crime type)?

A. Has There Been a Change in the Number of Studies That Report Variance Explained Measures over Time?

Of the articles in *Criminology* during the period examined, 207 or 15.8 percent included multivariate modeling testing some aspect of criminological theory and reported some measure of goodness of fit or variance explained. Quantitative tests of criminological theory were included in 259 (19.8 percent) of the *Criminology* articles. These data certainly suggest that quantitative tests have been important in criminology. However, some observers might be surprised at the large number of *Criminology* articles that do not include multivariate empirical theory tests. Whatever the contribution of such quantitative methods to criminological science, significant attention has been given to other methods and concerns, notwithstanding that *Criminology* also publishes many theoretically oriented (nonempirical) articles, analyses of criminal justice system issues (police, courts, corrections), and qualitative studies.

The distribution of reporting of multivariate models with variance explained statistics is important because it provides a descriptive portrait of our data over time (see fig. 1*A*). In figure 1*B*, the same data are reported as a proportion of articles published in *Criminology* each year. Reporting of R^2 measures began to increase in the 1980s and, with the exception of 1986 and 1990, continued at about the same level until the end of the 1990s. When these two exceptional years are excluded, between 10 and 25 percent of *Criminology* articles from 1981 through 1998 include multivariate models with variance explained statistics. In 1986, 40 percent of articles fit these criteria, and in 1990 there were no articles of this type. There was a spike in the absolute number of studies around the turn of the century and in the proportion

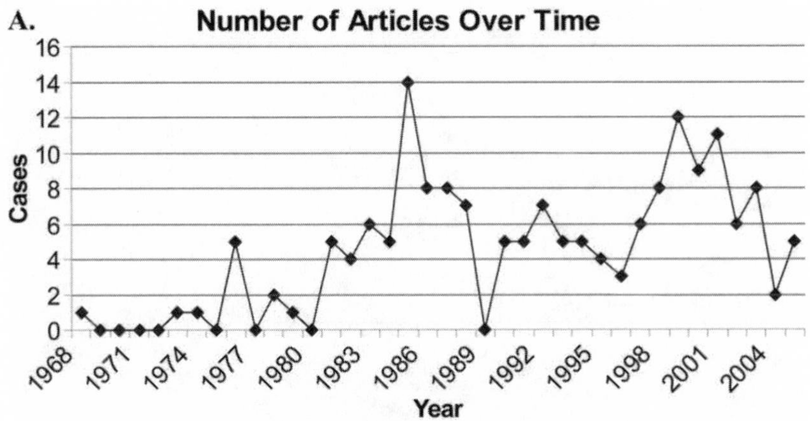

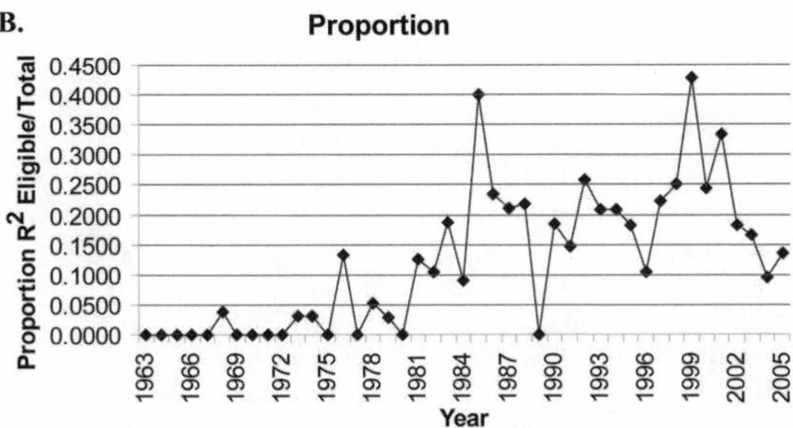

FIG. 1.—*A*, Number of unique articles that were coded meeting eligibility criteria (N = 169). *B*, Proportion of unique articles that were coded meeting eligibility criteria (N = 169) of total *Criminology* articles.

of studies (over 40 percent in 1999). There appear to be declines in the number and proportion of studies after 2002.[19]

[19] We also looked at the same statistics including all 207 studies that included either a variance explained or a noncomparable fit statistic. The overall distributions are very similar. However, following our earlier observation of a positive correlation between attrition and time, the proportion of articles is somewhat more likely to be underreported in later years. Even here, however, the overall relationship follows closely those we report in fig. 1.

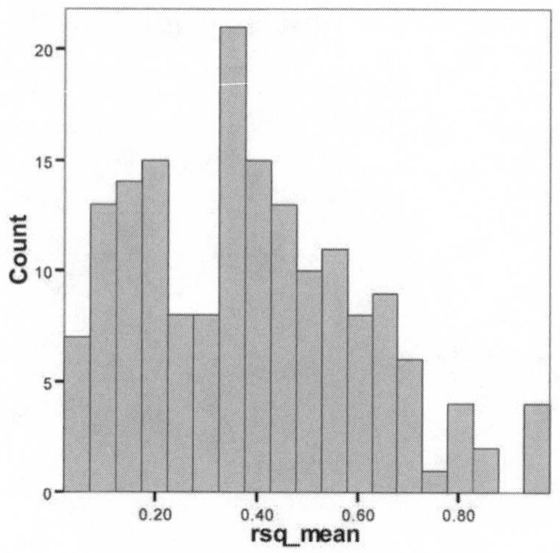

FIG. 2.—Histogram of R^2 values (N = 169 unique articles)

B. What Is the Average R^2 across All Models?

Of articles that reported an R^2 value, the average R^2 was .389 (standard deviation of .220), with a minimum of .001 and a maximum of .984. The former study (Longshore, Turner, and Stein 1996) examined self-reported crimes of force among drug offenders. The latter (O'Brien 1991) used census and Uniform Crime Reports data to assess the relationship between sex ratios and rape rates.[20]

The median R^2 value was .365. A histogram of the average R^2 values displayed in figure 2 shows a clustering in the lower third, with rapidly decreasing numbers as average R^2 increases. In a large number of articles, R^2 values are extremely small. Some 25 percent of the 169 articles exhibit R^2 values below .20, and over 70 percent have an R^2 under .50. About one-tenth report R^2 values below .10. This means that most crime studies explain less than 50 percent of the variance beyond the threshold criterion (the mean of Y for linear models), and many models

[20] The rather high R^2 value in the O'Brien (1991) study may be due to overspecification. The sample size of 42 (rape arrest rate for six time periods by seven age groups) included dummy codes for the time periods and age groups (plus sex ratio and a constant, yielding 13 coefficients in the model). The model had only three degrees of freedom for each regression coefficient. Coupled with the fact that the dependent variable had limited variability, it is not surprising that the model explained 98 percent of the variance. Thirteen random independent variables may have done almost as well (see Cohen and Cohen 1983).

leave 80–90 percent of variance unaccounted for.[21] This occurs despite our having biased our results upward by selecting the highest R^2 value reported in each article.

C. What Is the Change over Time?

Tracking change over time provides an important measure of the development of criminology as a science. It is understandable for models of theory to be weaker earlier in the development of a science. But as science develops, the level of explanation should improve. That would happen, in part, because theories become rarified over time; because scientists build on the work of earlier scientists; and because, all else being equal, the addition of better measures and additional explanatory variables should lead to better explanation.[22]

Has the value of R^2 changed over time? Have criminologists become better at explaining the variance in crime? Figure 3 presents the results. A few things are worth pointing out. First, there are some erratic spikes at the beginning of the time series, with some rather large and some rather small R^2 values. Not much should be made of this because of the very small number of studies (as shown in fig. 1*A*). Second, and more important, beginning in the mid-1980s when the number of cases began to increase significantly, and continuing throughout the remainder of the time series, R^2 values are concentrated in a tight range between .20 and .40, without clear indications of improvement over time.

Analysis of whether average R^2 values (aggregated by article) are correlated with publication year yields a slight negative correlation ($r = -.068$, $p = .721$). This is likely influenced by the small number of cases prior to 1980. When we removed 1980 and earlier cases and reestimated the correlation, we obtained an even stronger negative correlation ($r = -.296$, $p = .160$). These correlations are not statistically significant, in part because of the small number of units of analysis (i.e., the year, $n = 30$ unique years).

[21] If we use the total number of models ($N = 961$), our findings of low variance explained are reinforced. For example, across the 961 model estimations, 25 percent yield R^2 estimates under .137, 50 percent yield R^2's under .30, and three-fourths (75 percent) have R^2's under .50.

[22] As we noted earlier, a number of issues may influence estimates of variance explained. The totality of these is such that we see only what emerges as a measure of R^2, not always what goes into the model specification across studies, over time, etc. Of course, if science improves, we would expect—all things being equal—R^2 to improve. As we do not know whether all else is (always) equal, caution should be used in drawing strong inferences from an improving (or decreasing) R^2. Still, we think that a descriptive account of how R^2 varies over time provides an important and interesting piece of information.

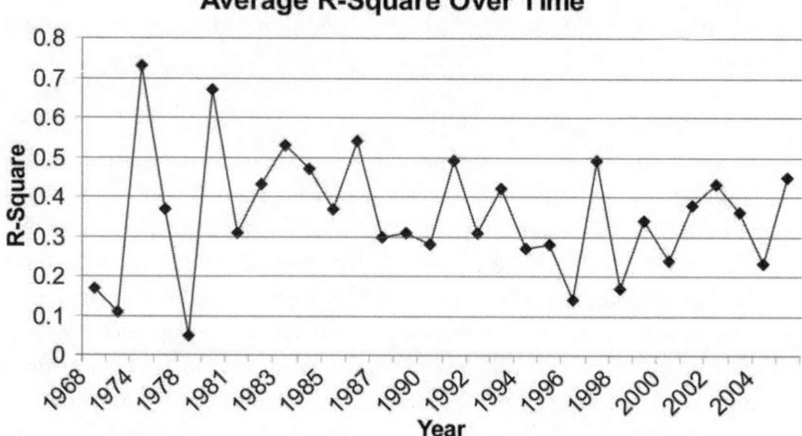

FIG. 3.—Aggregate R^2 value over time (N = 169 articles). Years with zero observations are removed for ease of presentation.

There appears to be little improvement and possibly to have been a decline in average R^2 values over time. A scientific model would predict improvement in R^2 over time, but we find a negative correlation.[23] This relationship raises serious questions. Criminology does not appear to be evolving along a science-like track over time, one centered on improvement. Why not? Are researchers not building on prior knowledge? Are data problems and measurement limitations plaguing efforts to understand crime?

D. *What Is the Average R^2 across Areas of Study?*

Maltz (2006) observed that competing criminological theories abound and that all seem to be supported by statistically significant findings. Can they all be true? This raises the question whether average R^2 varies across areas of study. Do some theoretical models explain more of the variance in crime than others? Such a question strikes at the heart of criminological theory, as some theories make bolder claims

[23] This brings up a larger issue about how far we have come as a science with respect to building theoretical models that explain crime and justice (see Wellford 1989, 2007; Bernard 1990). Is it the case that new theories are simply "old wine in new bottles" and that the reason our explanatory power has not saliently increased over time is that we do not have many new ideas about the causes of crime? This is a provocative statement, one that we return to later in the discussion section.

TABLE 1

Average R^2 According to Theoretical Area (Sorted by Highest Average R^2) (N = 169 Articles)

Theoretical Area	Number of Articles	Average R^2	Standard Deviation
Rational choice	2	.782	.261
Absolute deprivation/conflict	2	.550	.019
Relative deprivation/inequality	9	.499	.196
Routine activity	5	.464	.262
Social disorganization	14	.444	.205
Differential association	7	.428	.104
Social control	9	.379	.164
Deterrence	6	.378	.255
Subculture/code of the street	3	.364	.169
Theory competition	3	.362	.246
Integrated	10	.349	.187
Anomie/strain	9	.341	.194
Shame/reintegration	2	.312	.024
Self-control	8	.275	.178
Developmental	1	.255	NA
Combined	79	.373	.242
Total/average	169	.389	.220

about being able to explain variance (see Akers et al. 1979), whereas others are more minimalist.

The larger debate about general theories of crime, their scope (Walker and Cohen 1985), and the extent to which they explain all crime at all times (Gottfredson and Hirschi 1990) continue to be a source of controversy. Braithwaite (1989, p. 3) has argued that "general theory is not required to explain all of the variance for all types of cases, but some of the variance for all types of cases." So, perhaps a modest amount of variance explained should not be viewed fatally after all.[24]

Table 1 presents the average largest R^2 value by theoretical area,[25]

[24] We do not want to give readers the impression that we are holding criminological explanations up to a standard that they account for as close to 100 percent of the variance as possible. After all, aside from issues of measurement error, sampling, and other problems, as we note later, it may not be reasonable to expect a perfectly complete theory to account for 100 percent of the variance in crime (e.g., Lieberson 1985, p. 93).

[25] A few points about our classification system with respect to the theoretical labels in table 1 are in order. Our theoretical classification system was designed to be an initial, descriptive first step. For example, some readers may note that including Thornberry, Moffitt, and Patterson and others into a hybrid "developmental theory" classification muddies the waters; but at the same time, many scholars consider these specific theoretical

ranked from highest to lowest on the basis of the 169 unique articles. We do not differentiate across theoretical areas by whether the models employ data at the individual level or at the macro level, though theories differ in whether they focus on macro- or micro-level factors.[26] A large number of cases fall under the "combined" category. The reason is that many empirical tests did not indicate the criminological theory being tested, included combinations of theories (e.g., developmental and neuropsychological), or focused on feminist, power control, institutional anomie, and related theories that do not fall under the more general categories employed.

Rational choice theories exhibit the highest average R^2 (.782). This finding should be viewed with some caution, however, because very few articles fell into this category, and they tended to be earlier efforts that considered rational choice at the macro level. Deterrence theory, which can be considered a micro-level counterpart of rational choice theory, was more prevalent in the number of articles and had an average R^2 of .378.

For most areas of study, R^2 values fall within a fairly restricted range. When rational choice theory is excluded, all but two areas fall between .30 and .55. The exceptions are self-control and developmental theories,[27] which have values of .275 and .255, respectively. Generally speaking, the averages across theoretical areas in table 1 suggest that the more macro-oriented theories yielded higher average R^2 values. For example, social disorganization theories generated an average R^2 value of .444, and relative deprivation and routine activities theories yielded average R^2 values of .499 and .464. More micro- or individual-based theories of crime had somewhat lower average R^2 values (e.g., self-control theories). Newer theories such as shame/reintegration (average R^2 of .312), which have not been subject to intense empirical scrutiny, appear to have lower R^2 values.

One limitation of our analyses is that the models we assess include "control variables" such as sex, age, and race/ethnicity. Of course, such

---

models as falling under the purview of a larger, more general class of developmental/life course theories (Farrington 2003*a*). Certainly, different researchers may create different classification systems, and we encourage such refined and continued development.

[26] It should be noted that the theoretical areas differ in typical unit of analysis (which may have an effect on explained variance) as well as the number and nature of the nontheoretical constructs included in the models.

[27] It is important to note that many tests of developmental theory employ methodologies that do not necessarily lend themselves easily to goodness of fit statistics, such as R^2.

variables also indicate "theories" about crime, but often are not central to the theoretical perspectives identified. The inclusion of such factors follows the regression assumption of correct model specification. Wikström and Butterworth (2006) noted that the predictive power of sex and ethnicity is much less than is often perceived: "an individual's sex generally only explains 1 percent or 2 percent of the variance in crime involvement; hence knowing that a person is male or female does not help us very much in knowing whether or not they are likely to commit a crime" (Wikström 2007, p. 133, n. 21). Still, separating the effects of the theoretically relevant variables from the effects of "control" variables would be useful in future research since models that include these variables may have different R^2 values than models that exclude them.

The averages reported suggest that some theoretical domains are doing better than others, though the absolute differences are not very large. Some models explain much more variance because they include factors that artificially inflate R^2 values. For example, several use past-year delinquency to predict present delinquency.[28] However, a good deal of variability in delinquency or crime can be identified by including criminal behavior from prior years. While inclusion of prior delinquency or crime has important theoretical implications (Nagin and Paternoster 1991; Paternoster et al. 1997), it does not generally bring us much further toward understanding delinquency or crime.[29]

Some scholars advocate theoretical competition, which would include variables from rival theories in a model, all of which would contribute in some way to increases in R^2. Other scholars prefer that theories be assessed on their own merits without any sort of competition (Hirschi 1979; Bernard 1990).[30] Among the articles we analyzed, the

[28] For example, in our database, studies that use forms of crime/deviance to predict crime/deviance evince a higher R^2 value when compared to studies that do not use forms of crime/deviance to predict crime/deviance (average R^2's equal .447 and .384, respectively).

[29] On this point, Wikström (2007, p. 133) has recently argued that "while past behavior may be a very useful predictor for assessing future risk of offending, it should not be part of a causal model to explain crime involvement."

[30] It is also useful to bear in mind Lieberson's (1985, p. 106) point that while empirical data can be used to determine (under certain conditions) whether a theory is useful, empirical data should not be the sole criterion in assessing whether one theory is more important than another theory. As he notes, "One can always say whether, in a given empirical context, a given variable or theory accounts for more variation than another. But it is almost certain that the variation observed is not universal over time and place. Hence the use of such a criterion first requires a conclusion about the variation over time and place in the dependent variable. If such an analysis is not forthcoming, the

average R^2 value for models that control for competing theories is somewhat lower compared with the average R^2 value for studies that do not control for competing theories (R^2 = .374 and .396, respectively; $t = -0.665$, $p = .508$). The number of covariates in the model is significantly and inversely correlated with the average R^2 ($r = -.214$, $p = .006$).[31]

While the average R^2 values would likely change to the extent that we recategorize the domains (e.g., adding rational choice and routine activities together, etc.), the differences we observe raise interesting questions. Do macro-level theories provide greater opportunities for advancing explanation in criminological theory? Conversely, do the very low values of commonly used explanatory paradigms such as self-control theory suggest that they deserve less attention than they have recently received?

Our analyses raise intriguing issues, but our findings should not be overinterpreted. Macro- and micro-level theories are often investigated at different levels of analysis (and studies conducted at higher levels of aggregation generally have higher R^2's than those conducted using individual-level data). A fair conclusion is that major theories, especially at the micro level, seem to perform about the same in average R^2 outcomes. Most criminological theories have some (but limited) relevance to explaining crime.[32]

E. What Is the Average R^2 across Unit of Analysis or across Sample Size?

Another interesting and related question concerns whether the average largest R^2 varies according to the unit of analysis. To examine this, we tabulated the average R^2 by the various units of analysis in the 169 articles. The results are shown in table 2.

---

theoretical conclusion is undermined by the absence of information. The evaluation of one variable vs. another is possibly justified, but only if it is clear that the comparison is meant to hold only within the context of the observed variation."

[31] This finding is contrary to the statistical expectation that, all else being equal, an increase in the number of measures in a model will lead to an increase in the R^2 value (Freedman 1983, p. 152). We suspect (though this is not reliably recorded across the studies) that the explanation for this finding is that authors report adjusted R^2 statistics that take into account the inflation caused by adding additional variables.

[32] This raises the intriguing question that, if all theories explain a modest amount of variation, what might be said about their cumulative effect in explaining crime? It appears, one might argue, that theorists have each identified a set of factors or processes that explain variation in offending. Taken together, then, they may offer a more comprehensive idea of what is involved in crime.

TABLE 2

Average R^2 According to Unit of Analysis (N = 169 Articles).

Unit of Analysis	Number of Articles	Average R^2	Standard Deviation
Neighborhood or census tract	15	.621	.189
Country	11	.568	.232
State	5	.566	.292
SMSA	7	.495	.156
Group of individuals	6	.494	.333
Others	6	.429	.360
City/county	23	.414	.153
Individual	94	.302	.168
Micro place (address or street segment)	1	.295	NA
Incident	1	.124	NA
Total/average	169	.389	.220

Higher units of aggregation generally yield a higher average R^2.[33] At the top are studies employing neighborhoods or census tracts as units of analysis (average R^2 = .621), followed by countries (average R^2 = .568) and states (average R^2 = .566). The lowest values are for incidents (R^2 = .295) or micro places (R^2 = .124), though each unit is represented by only one study. Studies of individuals anchor the low part of the distribution with an average R^2 of .302. The correlation between R^2 and unit of analysis is .293 ($p < .001$) using τb as a measure

[33] We are certainly not the first to observe that correlations (or explained variance) across aggregate entities are typically much higher than correlations (or explained variance) across individuals. Blalock (1961, pp. 113–14; emphasis in original) has noted that "We must recognize that in shifting units of analysis we are likely also to affect the degree to which other uncontrolled factors may vary. Notions of how important a variable is usually involve the *amount* of variation in that variable, as well as the nature of any relationships it may have with other variables. Therefore, *in shifting units we may also vary the degree to which any particular variable is considered 'important.'* Variables that are important for one set of units may not be important for another . . . . Finally, it should be pointed out that in many instances where groupings have been made according to geographical or physical criteria (e.g., by states, communities, societies, neighborhoods), we might generally expect to find at least some correlations that are considerably larger than those found using persons as units. Not all correlations using groups as units will be large, of course. *But finding a high correlation does not demonstrate the superiority of sociological or ecological variables over others. It may merely mean that, as a result of the grouping operation, we have controlled out the effects of other variables.* If this is realized, we may take advantage of these grouping effects to help us better understand the nature of the relationships among factors that remain as real variables. But we should avoid jurisdictional disputes about which variables are 'really' most important." In general, "the larger the units, the less the variation" (p. 180).

TABLE 3

Average R^2 According to Type of Data Collected (N = 169 Articles)

Type of Data	Number of Articles	Average R^2	Standard Deviation
Interrupted time series	6	.578	.164
Other	7	.425	.283
Cross-sectional	113	.384	.212
Longitudinal data	36	.380	.243
Panel data	7	.301	.156
Total/average	169	.389	.220

of association and the 169 unique articles. The correlation is similar (τb = .256, $p < .001$) using the more inclusive model database of 961.

Some part of the relationship may be due to the correlation between unit of analysis and sample size. Studies with higher units of aggregation tend on average in our review to have smaller sample sizes. In turn, larger analyzed samples tend to evince somewhat lower R^2's ($r = -.211$, $p = .017$) in our analyses. However, this does not appear to explain the relationship between unit of analysis and R^2. Using the 169 unique articles, when we control for sample size, there remains a moderate and statistically significant correlation between unit of analysis and R^2 ($r = .384$, $p < .001$).

It is striking, given the relatively lower R^2 values of individual-based studies, that these are the majority we identified. Of the studies in our sample, 56 percent use individuals as the primary unit of analysis.

F. What is the Average R^2 by Type of Data (Longitudinal, Cross-Sectional, etc.) Collected?

Average R^2 may vary according to the type of data collected. Cross-sectional studies may generate a higher R^2 than longitudinal studies, because of the difficulty of finding strong and significant relationships over time (i.e., the "longitudinal law"; see Moffitt 1993). Table 3 reports this analysis.

The most striking finding relates not to R^2 but to the distribution of studies. More than three-quarters use cross-sectional data. Longitudinal studies are one in five. Given the difficulty of establishing causality in cross-sectional studies, this finding is particularly important.

Interrupted time-series analyses yield higher average R^2 values (.578) than cross-sectional studies (.384), suggesting that the longitudinal law

TABLE 4

Average R^2 According to Crime Type (N = 169 Articles, but 270 Models)

Crime Type	Number of Models	Average R^2	Standard Deviation
Rape/forcible rape	4	.564	.286
Robbery	20	.550	.206
Burglary	19	.517	.222
Homicide/murder rate	33	.498	.210
Overall violent crime/delinquent rate	29	.447	.256
Overall property crime/delinquent rate	16	.445	.248
Drug/substance abuse	16	.349	.185
Overall crime/delinquent rate	56	.336	.194
Other	61	.318	.188
Theft/larceny	10	.291	.231
All index offenses	1	.283	NA
Deviant behavior (running away, truancy, antisocial behavior)	5	.228	.076
Total/average	270	.399	.224

NOTE.—Although 169 articles formed the basis of the database, this table includes multiple statistical models from unique articles if they contributed more than one dependent variable crime type.

is not empirically supported by our data. One explanation may relate to the unit of analysis. Interrupted time-series analysis typically employs macro-level data, whereas cross-sectional studies usually involve individuals as the unit of analysis. Time-series analyses generally include lagged variables that relate strongly to the outcome variable, such as the inclusion of some sort of autoregressive parameter among the independent variables. Because of the small numbers, however, it is premature to draw any firm conclusions about the longitudinal law among the individual-based longitudinal studies in our analysis.

G. What Is the Average R^2 by Dependent Variable?

Another important question concerns the relationship between the dependent or outcome variable (i.e., crime type) and the average R^2. Are criminologists better at explaining some forms of crime than others?

As table 4 shows, the average R^2 value does vary by crime type. At the high end, R^2 values are highest for rape/forcible rape (.564) and robbery (.550), and are smallest for such deviant behaviors as running away and truancy (.228). It is encouraging that explanatory models are stronger for the most serious criminal behaviors, suggesting that criminologists do better on subjects concerning which policy prescriptions are most important.

Our analyses provide general support for a more focused and specific approach to modeling crime outcomes. The models that focus on very specific types of crime explain more variance than those that try to explain broad types of crime. This is consistent with the argument of some criminologists for a crime-specific approach to crime prevention (see Cornish and Clarke 1986; Felson 1998). The highest values of R^2 (between .50 and .56) are found for studies that explain rape, robbery, burglary, and homicide. The lowest are for broad offense categories such as index offenses (one study, R^2 = .283) and deviant behavior (R^2 = .228). The average R^2 for overall violent crime or overall property crime is not much different from that of the highest-rate offenses (R^2 = .45).[34]

V. Discussion

We focus here on three aspects of our findings and their implications. The first concerns the low R^2 observed across studies, the second with the lack of evidence of improvement in criminological explanation over time, and the third with the weakness of explanations in individual-based models and the comparative strength of models taking a more crime-specific approach.

Most models explain less than half of the variance in the dependent variable, and a quarter explain less than 20 percent. This estimate is likely to be inflated, since our analyses are based on the highest R^2 value reported in each article. This finding is not out of line with the experience of quantitative researchers who are often pleased with an

[34] It is the case that most of the studies found near the top of table 4 (with the highest R^2 values) are macro-level studies, and most macro-level studies assess more macro-oriented theories of crime, in particular social disorganization. So, in some sense there is an interaction between crime type (and theoretical classification) and unit of analysis with respect to explained variance estimates. Some readers may also interpret the results found in table 4 not so much as due to crime type, but instead as related to the seriousness of offending. Most individual-level studies—especially those using self-report data—employ measures that mainly capture nonserious to modestly serious offending (the base rate for serious offending in most self-report study samples is low). It may be that explaining variation is "easier" when differentiating between those who will or will not commit serious offenses (i.e., individual differences will matter more in this domain of offending).

R^2 above .30. But it does raise significant policy issues that are often ignored.

How much confidence should be placed in models that explain so little variance? What level is "good enough" for developing policy prescriptions? The gap between criminologists and policy makers is well illustrated by *McCleskey v. Kemp*, 481 U.S. 279 (1987), in which use of multivariate methods was prominent. Justice Powell, who delivered the opinion of the court, accepted that quantitative models could be used to support inferences regarding core legal issues even if the court was less interested in statistical conclusions than in findings regarding the individual case. However, he noted that the multivariate statistical model developed by Baldus, Woodworth, and Pulaski (1990) did not explain enough of the variance for judges to have confidence in the outcome. He accepted, in this regard, the discussion of the case in a lower court:

> The District Court noted the inability of any of the models to predict the outcome of actual cases. As the court explained, statisticians use a measure called an "r^2" to measure what portion of the variance in the dependent variable (death sentencing rate, in this case) is accounted for by the independent variables of the model. A perfectly predictive model would have an r^2 value of 1.0. A model with no predictive power would have an r^2 value of 0. The r^2 value of Baldus' most complex model, the 230-variable model, was between .46 and .48. Thus, as the court explained, "the 230-variable model does not predict the outcome in half of the cases." (481 U.S. 279 at 361).

Justice Powell placed the R^2 reported by Baldus and his colleagues in the context of a finding of no variance explained and one of perfect variance explained, assuming that something in the middle was just not good enough.

Of course, a low R^2 does not mean that the individual variable effects are not important. Studies in medicine sometimes explain very small variance, but have significant implications for public health. Rosenthal (1990) showed that aspirin cut the risk of a heart attack approximately in half but explained only 0.0011 of the variance (0.11 percent). Jacob Cohen, who developed the standardized mean difference measure, "Cohen's *d*" (Cohen 1988), argues that a large effect size is equivalent to a *d* of .8. The R^2 equivalent for this value for a model including a single independent variable is only .138.

Nor can one assume that a theory is inadequate simply because of a low R^2. There are many ways to evaluate a theory, and sometimes variance explained is not ideal or even adequate. As Lieberson notes, the finding that variance explained is not very high "is not necessarily due to the operation of other forces or problems with the data":

> It is certainly possible that the theory is wrong or incomplete or the data inadequate, but it is also necessary to consider whether the criterion for the maximum proportion is in error. Obviously, the amount of variation that a theory expects to explain cannot be a figure that is arrived at by a subjective or post hoc statement conveniently made equal to the actual proportion accounted for. Appropriately rigorous criteria must be used. One must keep in mind, however, that in many cases an analysis of the variance explained, goodness-of-fit, or other statistical procedure used to account for variability, is not at all an appropriate step for evaluating the theory. (Lieberson 1985, p. 117)

But even if a study with a low R^2 can have important implications for theory and policy, the troubling problem remains of omitted variable bias and its impact on predictions of outcomes and the validity of specific effects of variables included in a regression model. And although we have no direct estimate of how well models predict outcomes for cases that did not report R^2 or related measures of variance explained, it is likely that the predictive power of those models is not greatly dissimilar from those included in our analyses.

Thus, two questions naturally arise. How much faith should be placed in predictions of crime outcomes that are drawn from multivariate models? How trustworthy are estimates of variable outcomes? There is no way to answer these questions short of knowing the correct or true model for every crime outcome. Much of the unexplained variance may be random and thus affect neither the validity of predictions nor estimates of specific parameters. Causes of individual criminality, for example, may be so individualistic and varied, and found in such different places over the life course, that it is very difficult for scholars to identify them or for public policy makers to use them to develop crime prevention policies (Weisburd and Waring 2001). The causes of criminality may be similar to the causes of changes in weather or other phenomena for which long-range forecasts are difficult. The chain of causal events involves many factors that can have varied effects and thus make long-term prediction difficult (Laub and Sampson 2003).[35] If we could explain *only* 20 percent of the variance in human decision making and a statistical study using some constellation of variables had an R^2 of .19, we would have an almost perfectly fitting theoretical model as applied to the data.[36]

Low explained variance, in turn, may be more a function of poor methodology or measurement than a limitation in the state of criminological theory. This does not add confidence to the believability of statistical models, but suggests that the problem lies not in theories but in data and measurement. Most "tests" of theories are limited. This is especially true when secondary data are used and key theoretical constructs are measured with two or three items. Very rarely do scholars undertake primary data collection in which studies attempt to measure all aspects of a theory.[37] Theories are seldom measured completely or with fully defensible measures. As a result, their capacity to explain variation is hampered. Maltz (in a personal communication dated April 24, 2007) argues that people are so inherently different that we should expect them to behave differently in the same circumstances. Thus, by taking the average value of their varying characteristics to develop theories (about what the average offender looks like), we risk conflating individuals who are deviant (well off the mean) but are usually deviant in different ways (Maltz 1994). Accordingly, the problem with low variance explained may be less with criminologists' theories than with capacities to measure and assess them.[38]

[35] In this context it may be that, in certain instances, observing the variables in a weather map is more informative than being given the probability of rain; as such, moving from model development to methods that portray variables in maps or graphs (exploratory data analysis) may generate important (and new) hypotheses (personal communication from Michael Maltz, April 24, 2007).

[36] Because in practice there is generally no way of knowing the percent of variance that can be explained with systematic factors, we generally have little to gauge such estimates against.

[37] As a rare exception, Akers et al. (1979) measured 15 dimensions of social learning theory and generated explained variance estimates of over 50 percent.

[38] Some may also observe that no one "model"—or study—can incorporate detailed measures of all dimensions of all major theories. As a result, no one model can ever truly indicate what the true capacity of our theoretical models—when taken together—is to explain crime. This may be why some scholars prefer meta-analysis, which can tell us across all studies what the effect size of each dimension of each theory is. When such effect sizes are lined up as a roster of predictors, one can get a sense of what our theories can tell us empirically. More generally, as some scholars have observed, the challenge with explaining and predicting crime is that, in all likelihood, Gottfredson and Hirschi (1990) not withstanding, it has a number of (causal) influences at various levels of analysis (biological, psychological, family, community, situational, economic, etc.). When this is

More generally, our findings speak to the heart of the criminological paradigm. If there is something different about offenders compared with nonoffenders and these differences are important, our models' explanatory power should be large if we identified and measured those factors. Examples of this thinking include personality-type theories, psychopathy explanations, and self-control theory (e.g., Wilson and Herrnstein 1985; Gottfredson and Hirschi 1990). If there is no fundamental difference between offenders and nonoffenders and offenders are defined almost exclusively by situations so that individuals with varying backgrounds tend to act similarly in the same situation (Cornish and Clarke 1986),[39] then we would expect low explanatory power. And if people come into situations bringing with them their background, not necessarily limited to inherent differences but also including differences in behavioral patterns, habits, socialization, values, and beliefs that have been acquired by experiences in previous situations, and then come into contact with situational choices (Nagin and Paternoster 1993; Piquero and Tibbetts 1996; Horney 2006), the expected explanatory power will likely vary somewhere between the two previous explanations. We did not set out to conduct a stringent test of these basic assumptions, but the results do raise questions about basic underlying assumptions and perhaps point to a perspective that seeks to understand behavioral variability across individuals and situations.[40]

Scholars in criminology have spent too little time considering "variance unexplained." Do our models reflect a young science that has yet to develop strong enough theory? Is it a problem of data limitations and available measures? Are we doing about as well as can be expected given the stochastic nature of individual behavior and the more general

---

compounded with our inability to accurately measure the dependent variable, some may view a median R^2 of .37 as quite impressive.

[39] Readers will recall the classic Chicago school notion that crime/deviance was not the "response of abnormal people to normal conditions" (i.e., directed at the early criminologists who were searching for fundamental biological, psychological, or constitutional attributes that more or less permanently distinguished offenders and nonoffenders), but primarily the "response of normal people to abnormal conditions" (i.e., thereby pointing to the importance of studying differences in the social structure—social disorganization, anomie, inequality, etc. across groups that were criminogenic and produced higher probabilities of crime regardless of who was exposed to those conditions) (Short 1976).

[40] It is important to point out that most theories systematically ignore the role of situational factors in crime. We believe that this is unfortunate since crimes are likely the result of the interaction between an individual's disposition and the situational factors he or she encounters.

problem of crime? Or are we simply not devoting enough time to theorizing and making more precise statements about how a theory may be falsified (e.g., Moffitt 1993)?

We have no basis for making strong statements regarding these questions because criminologists have for the most part not asked them. Opening such a dialogue is important for criminology to develop as a science that can inform public policy (Sherman 2005; Greenberg 2006).

It is unreasonable in our view to assume that models that leave 80 or 90 percent of variance unexplained have identified the major causes of outcomes of interest. If such unknown or unmeasured causes of *Y* are related to an independent variable of interest, estimates of that independent variable will be biased. As Pedhauzer (1982, p. 36) remarks, "Assume, for example, that the proportion of variance due to a regression is .10, that is, that 10 percent of the variance is accounted for. Such a finding would be considered by most researchers in the social sciences as meaningful and being of medium magnitude . . . . But since 90 percent of the variance is unaccounted for, it is very questionable that of all of the variables 'responsible' for this percentage of the variance none is related to *X* [the included independent variable]."

Criminologists need to begin more systematic discussions among themselves and with policy makers concerning how much confidence can be put in findings from multivariate models. It is reasonable to be cautious about models that explain only 10 or 20 percent of variance, but what about models that explain 30–50 percent? There can be no blanket rule since the validity of such models is dependent on how much unexplained variance is due to random error. Criminology is a long way from more established fields such as economics in which scholars have made very strong claims regarding the validity of multivariate methods for policy science (e.g., see Heckman and Smith 1995). But we need to address this issue directly if we are to avoid conclusions like those reached by Justice Powell in *McCleskey v. Kemp* (1987).

Low variance explained in multivariate models suggests that criminologists concerned with policy should look more often to experimental methods (Sherman 2005). Criminology has not traditionally been an experimental science, though there has been growth in experimental studies in recent decades (Farrington 2003*b*; Weisburd and Petrosino 2005; Farrington and Welsh 2006*a*, 2006*b*; Boruch 2007). Experimental methods provide a statistical solution to at least one of the limitations of multivariate models. Randomized experiments do not provide better predictions of outcomes than multivariate models, but when implemented properly, they can provide unbiased estimates of the effects of specific variables of interest.[41] Given that criminological models often explain so little variance, experimental methods should be used much more often than they are, especially when significant policy questions are being examined (see also Committee on Improving Evaluation of Anti-crime Programs 2005; Lipsey et al. 2006).[42]

While the low variance explained in articles in *Criminology* is troubling, it is more troubling that there has been little improvement in explanatory models over time. Our data suggest a negative correlation between R^2 and time, implying that criminologists reporting their work in *Criminology* are doing somewhat worse as the discipline matures.

There may be many other potential explanations for our findings. Criminologists may have begun to ask more difficult questions that are less amenable to explanation. Models may have evolved, and R^2 values today may not be directly comparable to those of 10 or 20 years ago. This is certainly the case more recently, when models are more likely to include nonlinear dependent variables employing pseudo-R^2 measures or employ methodologies that do not allow for direct measurement of variance explained. Or criminologists may not be devoting enough attention to building a knowledge base of accumulated factors (Braithwaite 1989; Bernard 1990) and to providing careful descriptions of crime and criminal activity (Piquero, Farrington, and Blumstein 2007; Wellford 2007).[43]

But this finding raises important concerns irrespective of changes in measures and focus. Even if changes in the models used have affected R^2 values to some extent, it does not explain lack of improvement over time. Moreover, our findings are consistent with an earlier narrative

[41] The statistical reason for this develops from the randomization of units to treatment and control conditions. As noted earlier, the bias caused by omitted variables develops from the correlations between those variables and both the dependent variable and the independent variables. In a randomized experiment, random allocation of the variable of interest means that it can be assumed to be unrelated to any other independent variable examined. In this case, the estimate of the variable of interest can be assumed to be unbiased.

[42] Of course, randomized experiments are one potential avenue for advancing theory, but there are others. For example, data visualization (Maltz 1998; Maltz and Mullany 2000) and data mining (Berk 2005) techniques may provide useful insights.

[43] Like Lieberson (1985, p. 115), we believe that "it is premature to think about variability in an event before knowledge is developed about the fundamental cause of the event itself."

review of advances in criminological theory by Bernard (1990, p. 329), who concluded that "criminology has failed to make scientific progress in the past twenty years in the sense of falsifying some theories and accumulating verified knowledge in the context of other theories."

One potential explanation is that criminology is not sufficiently focused on advancing and building on prior knowledge and approaches. We found little evidence of replication of models over time. Perhaps this is a matter of scale. A more exhaustive survey of articles in criminology would be warranted before drawing strong conclusions. But it is reasonable to say that criminology appears to be searching for paradigms (see Laub [2004] for a view of turning points in the field of criminology), very rarely falsifying theories, and even more sparingly specifying the conditions under which precise hypotheses and theoretical statements are evaluated (see also Bernard 1990). This may mean that there is a lack of evidence of significant advance because criminologists have not settled clearly enough on specific areas of inquiry and have not come to agreement about interpretation of the basic facts of crime (e.g., Braithwaite 1989; Felson 1998).

At the same time, if our findings were replicated in 10 or 20 years, it would suggest strongly that multivariate modeling of crime outcomes has reached a ceiling threshold that is unlikely to be breached without a major breakthrough in criminological science. Another possible conclusion is that much variance is stochastic, and the limitations of our models reflect real limitations in potential to explain crime more generally.

One element of our findings arguing against such a ceiling, or at least a relatively low one, is the substantive difference in R^2 values across units of analysis and types of dependent variables (i.e., crime types). Studies using individuals as units of analysis exhibited much lower variance explained than those that examined larger aggregates of places or persons. Studies that examined specific crimes had much more success than those that examined more general types of crime.

The finding regarding individuals is interesting, because criminologists testing theory have placed the greatest emphasis on understanding individual offending (Nagin 2005). The majority of studies in our sample use individuals as the unit of analysis, and this is consistent with the more general focus of criminology on understanding why individuals become involved in crime. While individual deviance and criminality is a critical area, other levels of analysis may provide important opportunities for advancing theory and practice. Criminologists need to consider whether the focus on offenders should be less dominant. Recent research suggests, for example, the salience of trying to understand the development of crime at specific places (e.g., Weisburd et al. 2004).

A focus on more specific types of crime is likely to lead to better explanations (Felson 1998).[44] There is a long-running argument in criminology concerning the salience of crime-specific versus general explanations (e.g., Cornish and Clarke 1986; Gottfredson and Hirschi 1990). We found that analyses of more specific crimes produce larger average R^2 values. Does that mean that specific theories have greater success in predicting specific types of crime? We cannot draw this conclusion because the number of cases left for each comparison would be very small. Nonetheless, models explaining specific types of crime have greater overall explanatory power. We do not know whether this is a statistical artifact of the limited variability of specific crime studies.

VI. Conclusions

We began with an interest in how well criminologists explain crime. We sought a global picture of the state of criminological theory. We recognize the limitations of variance explained as a measure and of our focus on *Criminology*, but we believe nonetheless that our analyses provide an important first step in describing the state of theoretically based modeling in our discipline. Multivariate testing of criminological theory has been an important part of criminology since the 1980s, though it is perhaps less dominant in *Criminology* than many observers might have presumed.

There is much work to be done. Most of the variance in dependent measures of studies we examined remains unexplained, and this has implications for both theory and policy.[45] That criminology is not de-

[44] Marcus Felson (in a personal communication dated June 19, 2007) notes that specific hypotheses that link clear and tangible phenomena will lead us to real results (i.e., falsification or acceptance). For example, the hypothesis that "largely abandoned settings are difficult to supervise and easily taken over for crime purposes" allows us to study how much is abandoned, when it is abandoned, and what that does to crime opportunity.

[45] We recognize that one's interpretation of how well criminological models do with respect to explaining and predicting crime is subjective. One could peruse the leading journals of other social science disciplines such as psychology and sociology to examine how their macro- and micro-level studies fare with respect to explained variance in an effort to determine whether criminology is on par with its close disciplinary connections. And, such a perusal might lead to a slightly different view than the one expressed here-

veloping models of crime with more explanatory power over time is troubling. Maltz (1994, p. 457) has suggested that much more can be done to improve research in criminology and criminal justice, particularly concerning data collection, analysis, and presentation.

There is also considerable room for theoretical progress (Bernard 1990; Wellford 2007), beginning with accurate depictions and definitions of crime (Wikström 2007). Criminologists should invest greater effort in consistent development of modeling for the testing of theory. Elliott, Huizinga, and Ageton (1985, p. 125) noted that since any one theory explains only between 10 and 20 percent of the variance, integrated theories are needed: "Stated simply, the level of explained variance attributable to separate theories is embarrassingly low, and, if sociological explanations for crime and delinquency are to have any significant impact upon future planning and policy, they must be able

---

in. Some may believe that, within the limits of measurement challenges and error, we are developing theories that explain a modest amount of variation independent of one another and can identify likely risk factors for intervention. In this sense, cumulatively, the insights into crime they provide may not be too bad. It is possible that our perspective of the data on explained variation is more of a function of methodological limitations (we cannot measure all theories completely and in a single model) than it is of an immature science in need of some sort of midcourse correction. For example, some may note that the median R^2 value obtained in our analysis (.37) is impressive. For some, the real issue may not be the proportion of total variance explained but the proportion of explainable variance explained (a point alluded to above). Consider the amount of error in measures of crime. One common measure of crime at the individual level is arrest; however, the construct of interest is engagement in criminal behavior. As a measure of criminal behavior, arrest has rather poor reliability and validity. Much criminal behavior is not detected by arrest, and even if we view it as merely an indicator of degree of criminality, the concordance between the amount of criminal activity and arrest/no arrest will be substantially less than one (Brame et al. 2004). For example, if we measure criminal behavior for two adjacent 1-month periods, the "test-retest" correlation will be low, even if the criminal activity of the individuals was relatively constant across the 2-month period. Computing a correlation coefficient (ϕ) on the concordant validity data for delinquency using the Farrington et al. (1996) data produces a validity coefficient of .20 (row 6, table 3). Regression models at the individual level are thus seriously constrained in how much variance they can explain. At the macro level, the measurement of the dependent variable is better and may explain the higher R^2 for such studies. From a modeling perspective, the issue is not so much the difference between the actual level of crime and the measured level of crime but the relative rankings of the areas (cities, countries, etc.). That is, if we conceptualize the dependent variable as an index of relative levels of crime and not absolute levels of crime, the reliability and validity in the ranking of areas are likely to be higher than the reliability of arrest at the individual level (ranking of individuals into high and low levels of criminal activity). High-crime areas are more likely to show higher levels of arrest than low-crime areas even if both represent undercounts. All of this, of course, makes it very difficult to determine whether a given model is correctly specified. Only by adding to the descriptive knowledge base we have initiated here will we be in a better position to assess these issues. We would like to thank Francis Cullen and David Wilson for their comments with respect to these issues.

to demonstrate greater predictive power." Criminologists would do well to approach the study of crime within a theory-research-theory interchange in which they constantly and consistently move back and forth. Such an approach is the essence of scientific creativity (Maltz 2006).

Our findings point to the importance of focusing on specific crime problems (and situations) and suggest the difficulty of predicting individual criminality. We do not want criminologists to abandon individual-based theories and the prediction of individual crime patterns. Developmental and life course theories (Farrington 2003*a*) that are receiving a significant amount of attention today[46] are identifying new and emerging areas of inquiry as theorists continue "borrowing" from other disciplines (Osgood 1998). Others are developing contingency-based hypotheses that build on classic theories of crime (such as deterrence and labeling) and attempt to understand better the conditions under which they may relate to crime or desistance from crime, and whether such relationships vary across crime type. Sherman's (1993) defiance theory and Tittle's (1995) control balance theory are examples, but both are too new and understudied to gauge their explanatory usefulness.

Our overall conclusion is that there is a lack of "descriptive validity" in criminology (Farrington 2003*b*; Lösel and Beelmann 2003). A number of studies could not be included in our analysis because they failed to provide basic (and potentially available) statistical information. Criminology journals should require researchers to present such basic information as sample size, R^2, and so forth. Criminologists can follow the lead of psychology, where, for example, *Law and Human Behavior* requires that all tables include the sample size and effect sizes.

This analysis provides useful insights into the state of criminology, but more work is warranted. Future research should expand and replicate our efforts and answer a group of questions beyond the scope of this work. Similar analyses of other samples of criminological studies from other journals—including those that specialize in empirical investigation of crime issues (i.e., *Journal of Quantitative Criminology*,

[46] An important question, of course, with respect to developmental/life course theories is the extent to which their explanatory power is any better than that of other nondevelopmental/life course theories. As we noted earlier, however, many empirical tests of developmental theory do not provide any sort of R^2 measure.

Journal of Research in Crime and Delinquency)—should demonstrate whether our findings hold up in replications.[47]

Some might argue that focusing on explained variation is not the best way to demarcate which explanatory factors identified by theories are most relevant. For example, despite its own methodological issues and shortcomings, some criminologists prefer using meta-analysis to measure the "effect size" of theoretical constructs, which may provide a good sense of the relative importance of the constructs of interest. If such constructs are treated as risk factors, they can then be used as targets for intervention. And if they are targeted for change and then produce reductions in crime, that is evidence that they may be causally related to crime. Such studies are, in effect, "tests" of criminological theories. To the extent that they target theoretical constructs for change, they provide a test of the theory's ability to explain the reduction in crime (e.g., Cullen et al. 2003). Randomized experiments provide a particularly salient opportunity for developing this method for advancing criminological theory. Randomized experiments, however, are not prone to the omitted variable biases that seriously challenge multivariate modeling.

It is important to compare how criminology stands in relation to other social sciences, such as sociology, psychology, or economics. We could not identify similar studies in these areas, but such studies do exist in environmental sciences, where examinations of variance explained exist in ecological and evolutionary studies (Møller and Jennions 2002; Peek et al. 2003).

Perhaps most important, criminologists need to pay much greater attention to what they do not explain. Are low R^2 values due to inadequate theory or poor data, or is there some more general principle operating that limits ability to explain crime and criminals?[48] To what extent can we assume that unexplained variance is stochastic, and to what extent must we accept that systematic biases enter into the quantitative models we develop?

Criminologists cannot continue to accept current thresholds of ex-

[47] Of course, it is also possible that criminologists are publishing empirical studies with higher variance explained in outlets outside of *Criminology* (the journal) and criminology more generally, such that our estimates may be influenced by such exclusion.

[48] Relatedly, it may be of interest to predict R^2 itself in a multivariate model, where variance explained is predicted by issues such as aggregation level, type of dependent variable, year, etc. Such an analysis may provide insight into what part of the R^2 can be explained by the combined study characteristics.

plained variance without confronting these larger questions. As Wikström (2007, p. 136) notes, a sizable knowledge gap remains with respect to a deeper understanding of what processes cause people to commit crime and why certain areas experience more crime than others. A two-pronged approach of better theory and better and more sophisticated theory testing will provide a much stronger foundation for the development of effective crime control policies.

APPENDIX

Database Structure

The following outline represents the total structure of the database.

1. Coder
2. Case ID
3. Author(s) of article
4. Full reference
5. Date of publication
6. Issue and volume in *Criminology*
7. Theory used to model the phenomenon:

    1.00 Deterrence
    2.00 Rational choice
    3.00 Social disorganization
    4.00 Routine activity
    5.00 Social control
    6.00 Labeling
    7.00 Biological theory
    8.00 Self-control
    9.00 Developmental theory (Moffitt, Patterson, Thornberry, etc.)
    10.00 Differential association
    11.00 Anomie/strain theory
    12.00 Subculture/code of the street
    13.00 Integrated theory
    14.00 Theory competition
    15.00 Shame and reintegration
    16.00 Absolute deprivation/conflict
    17.00 Relative deprivation/inequality
    18.00 Social support/altruism
    19.00 Macro-level predictors
    20.00 Others (please specify)
    21.00 This study is not eligible

Methodological Qualifications

1. Year of data collection (for DV)
2. Who collected the data? (1) self-collection (2) others (secondary data analysis)
3. Describe the data set if it's secondary data (e.g., NYS, UCR, or NCVRS)
4. Sample size (count the valid sample size for the corresponding model)
5. Unit of analysis:

    1.00 Individual
    2.00 Group of individuals
    3.00 Micro place (address or street segment)
    4.00 Neighborhood or census tract
    5.00 City or county
    6.00 Country
    7.00 Incident
    8.00 Multilevel
    9.00 Other

6. Type of data, longitudinal or not, etc.:

    1.00 Cross-sectional
    2.00 Panel data
    3.00 Longitudinal data
    4.00 Interrupted time-series analysis
    5.00 Other

7. If longitudinal, record the length (number of months)
8. Methodology used to analyze data:

    1.00 Correlation
    2.00 Least-squares regression
    3.00 Logistic regression
    4.00 SEM (log likelihood, AIC, RMSEA, etc.)
    5.00 Chi-square
    6.00 Multinomial logistic regression
    7.00 Binomial logistic regression
    8.00 Others (BIC etc.)
    9.00 Randomized experiment (should be excluded)
    10.00 Quasi experiment
    11.00 Relative risk
    12.00 ARIMA
    13.00 Hierachical linear model
    14.00 Tobit model

9. Dependent variable:

   1.00 Overall crime/delinquent rate
   2.00 Overall violent crime/delinquent rate
   3.00 Overall property crime/delinquent rate
   4.00 Robbery
   5.00 Burglary
   6.00 Homicide/murder rate
   7.00 Rape/forcible rape
   8.00 All index offenses
   9.00 Theft/larceny
   10.00 Drug/substance abuse
   11.00 Deviant behavior (including running away, truancy, antisocial behavior etc.)
   12.00 Other (specify)

10. Number of the covariates used in the model
11. Are the variables of competing theories controlled? (1) yes (2) no
12. Type of outcome statistics:

   1.00 Chi-square statistic (with one degree of freedom, i.e., from a 2×2 table):
   Chi-square value
   Exact two-tailed p-value (if reported)
   Nominal significance level (two-tailed) (circle below):
   $p < .05$: yes no; $p < .01$: yes no
   2.00 t-statistic for difference between means:
   t-value
   Degrees of freedom
   or sample size for each condition
   Treatment group/postcomparison n
   Comparison group/precondition n
   3.00 Analysis of variance (ANOVA):
   F-statistic
   Degrees of freedom for the numerator
   Degrees of freedom for the denominator
   η/η^2
   Sum of squares in the numerator
   Sum of squares in the denominator
   Number of cases in each condition
   Treatment group/postcomparison n
   Comparison group/precondition n
   Exact two-tailed p-value (if reported)
   Nominal significance level (circle below):
   $p < .05$: yes no; $p < .01$: yes no
   4.00 Other statistical test:
   Name of test

Exact p-level:
Nominal significance level (circle below)
$p < .05$: yes no; $p < .01$: yes no

13. Concluding remarks used: Write the exact concluding remarks used in reference to the finding in terms of the performance of the model. Put page number next to the quotations.

REFERENCES

Abelson, Robert P. 1985. "A Variance Explanation Paradox: When a Little Is a Lot." *Psychological Bulletin* 97:129–33.

Akers, Ronald L., Marvin D. Krohn, Lonn Lanza-Kaduce, and Marcia Radosevich. 1979. "Social Learning and Deviant Behavior: A Specific Test of a General Theory." *American Sociological Review* 44:636–55.

Anderson-Sprecher, Richard. 1994. "Model Comparisons and R^2." *American Statistician* 48:113–17.

Anscombe, F. J. 1973. "Graphs in Statistical Analysis." *American Statistician* 27: 17–21.

Baldus, David C., George Woodworth, and Charles A. Pulaski Jr. 1990. *Equal Justice and the Death Penalty*. Boston: Northeastern University Press.

Barrett, James. 1974. "The Coefficient of Determination—Some Limitations." *American Statistician* 28:19–20.

Berk, Richard A. 2005. "Data Mining within a Regression Framework." In *Data Mining and Knowledge Discovery Handbook*, edited by Oded Maimon and Lior Rokach. New York: Springer.

Bernard, Thomas J. 1990. "Twenty Years of Testing Theories: What Have We Learned and Why?" *Journal of Research in Crime and Delinquency* 27:325–47.

Blalock, Hubert M., Jr. 1961. *Causal Inferences in Nonexperimental Research*. Chapel Hill: University of North Carolina Press.

———. 1964. *Causal Inferences in Non-experimental Research*. Chapel Hill: University of North Carolina Press.

Blumstein, Alfred, Jacqueline Cohen, Susan E. Martin, and Michael Tonry, eds. 1983. *Research on Sentencing: The Search for Reform*. Vol. 1. Washington, DC: National Academies Press.

Blumstein, Alfred, Jacqueline Cohen, Jeffrey A. Roth, and Christy A. Visher, eds. 1986. *Criminal Careers and "Career Criminals."* Washington, DC: National Academies Press.

Boruch, Robert. 2007. "The Null Hypothesis Is Not Called That for Nothing: Statistical Tests in Randomized Trials." *Journal of Experimental Criminology* 3:1–20.

Braithwaite, John. 1989. *Crime, Shame, and Reintegration*. New York: Cambridge University Press.

Brame, Robert, Jeff Fagan, Alex R. Piquero, Carol Schubert, and Laurence Steinberg. 2004. "Criminal Careers of Serious Delinquents in Two Cities." *Youth Violence and Juvenile Justice* 2:256–72.

Cohen, Jacob. 1988. *Statistical Power Analysis for the Behavioral Sciences*. 2nd ed. Hillsdale, NJ: Erlbaum.

Cohen, Jacob, and Patricia Cohen. 1983. *Applied Multiple Regression/Correlation Analysis for the Behavioral Sciences*. 2nd ed. Hillsdale, NJ: Erlbaum.

Cohn, Ellen, and David P. Farrington. 2007. "Changes in Scholarly Influence in Major American Criminology and Criminal Justice Journals between 1986 and 2000." *Journal of Criminal Justice Education* 18:6–34.

Committee on Improving Evaluation of Anti-crime Programs. 2005. *Improving Evaluation of Anti-crime Programs*. Washington, DC: National Research Council.

Cornish, Derek, and Ronald V. Clarke. 1986. *The Reasoning Criminal: Rational Choice Perspectives on Offending*. New York: Springer-Verlag.

Cox, David R., and E. Joyce Snell. 1989. *The Analysis of Binary Data*. 2nd ed. London: Chapman and Hall.

Cramer, Jan Solomon. 1987. "Mean and Variance of R^2 in Small and Moderate Samples." *Journal of Econometrics* 35:253–66.

Cullen, Francis T., John Paul Wright, Paul Gendreau, and D. A. Andrews. 2003. "What Correctional Treatment Can Tell Us about Criminological Theory: Implications for Social Learning Theory." In *Social Learning Theory and the Explanation of Crime: A Guide for the New Century*, edited by Ronald L. Akers and Gary F. Jensen. Advances in Criminological Theory, vol. 11. New Brunswick, NJ: Transaction Publishers.

Duncan, Otis Dudley. 1975. *Introduction to Structural Equation Models*. New York: Academic Press.

Elliott, Delbert S., David Huizinga, and Suzanne S. Ageton. 1985. *Explaining Delinquency and Drug Use*. Beverly Hills, CA: Sage.

Farrington, David P. 2003*a*. "Developmental and Life-Course Criminology: Key Theoretical and Empirical Issues—the 2002 Sutherland Award Address." *Criminology* 41:221–55.

———. 2003*b*. "Methodological Quality Standards for Evaluation Research." *Annals of the American Academy of Political and Social Science* 587:49–68.

Farrington, David P., Rolf Loeber, Magda Stouthamer-Loeber, Welmoet B. Van-Kammen, and Laura Schmidt. 1996. "Self-Reported Delinquency and a Combined Delinquency Seriousness Scale Based on Boys, Mothers, and Teachers: Concurrent and Predictive Validity for African-Americans and Caucasians." *Criminology* 34:493–518.

Farrington, David P., and Brandon Welsh. 2006*a*. "A Half Century of Randomized Experiments on Crime and Justice." In *Crime and Justice: A Review of Research*, vol. 34, edited by Michael Tonry. Chicago: University of Chicago Press.

———. 2006*b*. *Preventing Crime: What Works for Offenders*. New York: Springer.

Felson, Marcus. 1998. *Crime and Everyday Life*. Newbury Park, CA: Sage.

Freedman, David A. 1983. "A Note on Screening Regression Equations." *American Statistician* 37:152–55.

Gottfredson, Michael R., and Travis Hirschi. 1990. *A General Theory of Crime*. Stanford, CA: Stanford University Press.

Greenberg, David. 2006. "Criminological Research and Crime Control Policy: Not a Marriage Made in Heaven." *Criminology and Public Policy* 5:203–12.

Heckman, James J., and Jeffrey A. Smith. 1995. "Assessing the Case for Social Experiments." *Journal of Economic Perspectives* 9:85–110.

Hirschi, Travis. 1979. "Separate and Unequal Is Better." *Journal of Research in Crime and Delinquency* 16:34–38.

Horney, Julie. 2006. "An Alternative Psychology of Criminal Behavior." *Criminology* 44:1–16.

King, Gary. 1986. "How Not to Lie with Statistics: Avoiding Common Mistakes in Quantitative Political Science." *American Journal of Political Science* 30:666–87.

Kvalseth, Tarald O. 1985. "Cautionary Note about R^2." *American Statistician* 39:279–85.

Laub, John H. 2004. "The Life Course of Criminology in the United States." *Criminology* 42:1–26.

Laub, John H., and Robert J. Sampson. 2003. *Shared Beginnings, Divergent Lives*. Cambridge, MA: Harvard University Press.

Lieberson, Stanley. 1985. *Making It Count: The Improvement of Social Research and Theory*. Berkeley: University of California Press.

Lipsey, Mark W., Carol Petrie, David Weisburd, and Denise Gottfredson. 2006. "Improving the Evaluation of Anti-crime Programs: Summary of a National Research Council Report." *Journal of Experimental Criminology* 2: 271–307.

Longshore, Douglas, Susan Turner, and Judith A. Stein. 1996. "Self-Control in a Criminal Sample: An Examination of Construct Validity." *Criminology* 34:209–28.

Lösel, Friedrich, and Andreas Beelmann. 2003. "Effects of Child Skills Training in Preventing Antisocial Behavior: A Systematic Review of Randomized Evaluations." *Annals of the American Academy of Political and Social Science* 587:84–109.

Maltz, Michael D. 1994. "Deviating from the Mean: The Declining Significance of Significance." *Journal of Research in Crime and Delinquency* 31: 434–63.

———. 1998. "Visualizing Homicide: A Research Note." *Journal of Quantitative Criminology* 14:391–410.

———. 2006. "Some *p*-Baked Thoughts ($p > 0.05$) on Experiments and Statistical Significance." *Journal of Experimental Criminology* 2:211–26.

Maltz, Michael D., and Jacqueline M. Mullany. 2000. "Visualizing Lives: New

Pathways for Analyzing Life Course Trajectories." *Journal of Quantitative Criminology* 16:255–81.

Moffitt, Terrie E. 1993. "Adolescence-Limited and Life-Course-Persistent Antisocial Behavior: A Developmental Taxonomy." *Psychological Review* 100: 674–701.

Moksony, Ferenc. 1990. "Small Is Beautiful: The Use and Interpretation of R^2 in Social Research." *Szociologiai Szemle* (special issue):130–38.

Møller, Anders P., and Michael D. Jennions. 2002. "How Much Variance Can Be Explained by Ecologists and Evolutionary Biologists?" *Oecologia* 132: 492–500.

Mustard, David B. 2003. "Reexamining Criminal Behavior: The Importance of Omitted Variable Bias." *Review of Economics and Statistics* 85:205–11.

Nagin, Daniel S. 2005. *Group-Based Modeling of Development*. Cambridge, MA: Harvard University Press.

Nagin, Daniel S., and Raymond Paternoster. 1991. "On the Relationship of Past to Future Participation in Delinquency." *Criminology* 29:163–89.

———. 1993. "Enduring Individual Differences and Rational Choice Theories of Crime." *Law and Society Review* 27:467–96.

O'Brien, Robert M. 1991. "Sex Ratios and Rape Rates: A Power-Control Theory." *Criminology* 29:99–114.

Osgood, D. Wayne. 1998. "Interdisciplinary Integration: Building Criminology by Stealing from Our Friends." *Criminologist* 23(1):3–5, 41.

Paternoster, Raymond, Charles W. Dean, Alex Piquero, Paul Mazerolle, and Robert W. Brame. 1997. "Generality, Continuity, and Change in Offending." *Journal of Quantitative Criminology* 13:231–66.

Pedhauzer, Elazar J. 1982. *Multiple Regression in Behavioral Research: Explanation and Prediction*. 2nd ed. New York: Holt, Rinehart, and Winston.

Peek, Michael S., A. Joshua Leffler, Stephan D. Flint, and Ronald J. Ryel. 2003. "How Much Variance Is Explained by Ecologists? Additional Perspectives." *Oecologia* 137:161–70.

Piquero, Alex R., David P. Farrington, and Alfred Blumstein. 2003. "The Criminal Career Paradigm." In *Crime and Justice: A Review of Research*, vol. 30, edited by Michael Tonry. Chicago: University of Chicago Press.

———. 2007. *Key Issues in Criminal Career Research: New Analyses from the Cambridge Study in Delinquent Development*. New York: Cambridge University Press.

Piquero, Alex R., and Stephen G. Tibbetts. 1996. "Specifying the Direct and Indirect Effects of Low Self-Control and Situational Factors in Offenders' Decision Making: Toward a More Complete Model of Rational Offending." *Justice Quarterly* 31:601–31.

Pratt, Travis C., and Frances T. Cullen. 2005. "Assessing Macro-Level Predictors and Theories of Crime: A Meta-Analysis." In *Crime and Justice: A Review of Research*, vol. 32, edited by Michael Tonry. Chicago: University of Chicago Press.

Ranney, Gipsie B., and Charles C. Thigpen. 1981. "The Sample Coefficient of Determination in Simple Linear Regression." *American Statistician* 35: 152–53.

Rice, Steven, Ellen G. Cohn, and David P. Farrington. 2005. "Where Are They Now? Trajectories of Publication 'Stars' from American Criminology and Criminal Justice Programs." *Journal of Criminal Justice Education* 16: 244–64.

Rosenthal, Robert. 1990. "How Are We Doing in Soft Psychology?" *American Psychologist* 45(June):775–77.

Shaw, Clifford, and Henry McKay. 1932. *Juvenile Delinquency and Urban Areas*. Chicago: University of Chicago Press.

Sherman, Lawrence W. 1993. "Defiance, Deterrence, and Irrelevance: A Theory of the Criminal Sanction." *Journal of Research in Crime and Delinquency* 30:445–73.

———. 2005. "The Use and Usefulness of Criminology, 1751–2005: Enlightened Justice and Its Failures." *Annals of the American Academy of Political and Social Science* 600:115–35.

Sherman, Lawrence W., and Richard A. Berk. 1984. "The Specific Deterrent Effects of Arrest for Domestic Assault." *American Sociological Review* 49: 261–72.

Short, James F. 1976. *Delinquency, Crime, and Society*. Chicago: University of Chicago Press.

Sorenson, Jon R., and Rocky Pilgrim. 2002. "The Institutional Affiliations of Authors in Leading Criminology and Criminal Justice Journals." *Journal of Criminal Justice* 30:175–82.

Steiner, Benjamin, and John Schwartz. 2006. "The Scholarly Productivity of Institutions and Their Faculty in Leading Criminology and Criminal Justice Journals." *Journal of Criminal Justice* 34:393–400.

Sutherland, Edwin. 1937. *Principles of Criminology*. Philadelphia: Lippincott.

Tittle, Charles R. 1995. *Control Balance: Toward a General Theory of Deviance*. Boulder, CO: Westview.

Walker, Henry A., and Bernard P. Cohen. 1985. "Scope Statements: Imperatives for Evaluating Theory." *American Sociological Review* 50:288–301.

Weisberg, Sanford. 1985. *Applied Linear Modeling*. New York: Wiley.

Weisburd, David. 2001. "Magic and Science in Multivariate Sentencing Models: Reflections on the Limits of Statistical Methods." *Israel Law Review* 35: 225–48.

———. 2005. "Editor's Introduction." *Journal of Experimental Criminology* 1: 1–8.

Weisburd, David, and Chester Britt. 2007. *Statistics in Criminal Justice*. 3rd ed. New York: Springer.

Weisburd, David, Shawn Bushway, Cynthia Lum, and Sue-Ming Yang. 2004. "Trajectories of Crime at Places: A Longitudinal Study of Street Segments in the City of Seattle." *Criminology* 42:283–322.

Weisburd, David, and Anthony Petrosino. 2005. "Experiments, Criminology." In *The Encyclopedia of Social Measurement*, edited by Kimberly Kempf-Leonard. New York: Elsevier.

Weisburd, David, and Elin Waring. 2001. *White-Collar Crime and Criminal Careers*. New York: Cambridge University Press.

Wellford, Charles F. 1989. "Toward an Integrated Theory of Criminal Behavior." In *Theoretical Integration in the Study of Deviance and Crime: Problems and Prospects*, edited by Steven F. Messner, Marvin D. Krohn, and Allen E. Liska. Albany: SUNY Press.

———. 2007. "Forward." In *Key Issues in Criminal Career Research: New Analyses of the Cambridge Study in Delinquent Development*, by Alex R. Piquero, David P. Farrington, and Alfred Blumstein. New York: Cambridge University Press.

Wikström, Per-Olof H. 2007. "In Search of Causes and Explanations of Crime." In *Doing Research on Crime and Justice*, 2nd ed., edited by Roy D. King and Emma Wincup. Oxford: Oxford University Press.

Wikström, Per-Olof H., and David A. Butterworth. 2006. *Adolescent Crime: Individual Differences and Lifestyles*. Cullompton, Devon, UK: Willan.

Wilson, James Q., and Richard J. Herrnstein. 1985. *Crime and Human Nature*. New York: Simon & Schuster.

Wolfgang, Marvin E., Robert M. Figlio, and Thorsten Sellin. 1972. *Delinquency in a Birth Cohort*. Chicago: University of Chicago Press.

Wolfgang, Marvin E., Robert M. Figlio, and Terence P. Thornberry. 1978. *Evaluating Criminology*. New York: Elsevier.